The World Economy, Population Growth, and the Global Ecosystem

The World Economy, Population Growth, and the Global Ecosystem

A Unified Theoretical Model of Interdependent Dynamic Systems

Harland Wm. Whitmore, Jr.

palgrave
macmillan

First published in 2007 by
PALGRAVE MACMILLAN™
Houndmills, Basingstoke, Hampshire RG21 6XS and
175 Fifth Avenue, New York, N.Y. 10010
Companies and representatives throughout the world

PALGRAVE MACMILLAN is the global academic imprint of the Palgrave Macmillan division of St. Martin's Press, LLC and of Palgrave Macmillan Ltd. Macmillan® is a registered trademark in the United States, United Kingdom and other countries. Palgrave is a registered trademark in the European Union and other countries.

ISBN-13: 978–1–4039–8424–1
ISBN-10: 1–4039–8424–7

Library of Congress Cataloging-in-Publication Data

Whitmore, Harland Wm., 1939–
The world economy, population growth, and the global ecosystem : a unified theoretical model of interdependent dynamic systems / Harland Wm. Whitmore, Jr.
p. cm.
Includes bibliographical references and index.
ISBN 1–4039–8424–7 (alk. paper)
1. International economic relations—Environmental aspects. 2. Population—Environmental aspects. 3. Environmental economics. I. Title.

HF1359.W494 2007
337.01—dc22 2007002100

A catalogue record for this book is available from the British Library.

Design by Newgen Imaging Systems (P) Ltd., Chennai, India.

First edition: September 2007

10 9 8 7 6 5 4 3 2 1

Printed in the United States of America.

To my supportive wife, Jan, my best friend

Contents

List of Figures

List of Tables

Acknowledgments

Chris Chappell and his assistant Julia Cohen were my initial contacts at Palgrave Macmillan. I am especially grateful to Chris for taking an interest in my manuscript. Editor Aaron Javsicas was very helpful in the acquisitions stage of the process. Manager Erin Ivy capably supervised the production stage. She and the team at Newgen Imaging Systems Limited did a terrific job reading and editing not only the text but also the many equations and symbols contained in the book. Katherine Ankofski, Aaron's very able assistant, deserves special thanks for guiding me every step along the way. I am truly grateful for her expertise and encouragement. Everyone at Palgrave Macmillan made the publishing experience as pleasurable as possible. A warm thank you to each of you.

1

Introduction

The earth's human populations function as a world economy operating within a global ecosystem. The objective of this study is to develop a unified theoretical model that explains the basic dynamic interdependencies among these systems. Economic activity affects human health, human mortality, and population growth as well as the health of the global ecosystem. The ability of natural resources to provide life-sustaining services, in turn, impact important economic choices with respect to population growth, spending, and production. Policy actions taken by governments and/or central banks may improve or impair the vitality of the world ecology-economy. Government sectors decide acceptable pollution levels as well as the appropriate scales of their infrastructures. These decisions affect not only the ability of renewable resources to grow but also the productive efficiency of their industries. Central banks engage in financial transactions that affect the levels and relative magnitudes of world interest rates and exchange rates. These variables affect the levels and composition of spending around the world and consequently affect the end-of-period stocks of the various manufactured goods and natural resources, which in turn affect future production, employment, prices, and wages.

The Global Ecosystem

The earth's biosphere encompasses the atmosphere, hydrosphere, and a small portion of the lithosphere. It contains all of the planet's various ecosystems. These self-supporting systems contain myriad plants, animals, and other organisms that interact with each other and with the nonliving parts of the environment. For the purpose of this study, the biosphere is viewed as comprising a single aggregate ecosystem. The total mass (weight and mass are equal at sea level) of the global ecosystem is divided among the following:

- A basic fungible and slowly renewable resource, **B**, for example, clean air and clean (ocean) water. The basic renewable resource is freely shared by all countries.
- Three country-specific renewable resources (soils, crops, and animals), **R1**, **R2**, and **R3**. **R1** grows in Country One; **R2** grows in Country Two; and **R3** grows in Country Three. By assumption, these resources are not traded among the three countries. The renewable resources appear in their natural state as well as in a processed/marketable state.
- Three human populations, **H1**, **H2**, and **H3**. **H1** resides in Country One; **H2** inhabits Country Two; and **H3** lives in Country Three. By assumption, humans do not migrate across countries. H1, H2, and H3 refer to the human populations measured in terms of mass. The total mass of each human population corresponds to the number of inhabitants in each country (N1, N2, and N3) multiplied by the average mass per person in that country.
- A nonrenewable resource, **NR**, consisting of various fossil fuels and minerals, is mined or extracted only in Country One. The **NR** industry exports the resource to the government sectors in all three countries for the purpose of adding to their infrastructures. The capital goods industry in Country Two also imports the nonrenewable resource in order to build capital goods; the consumption goods industry in Country Three imports the nonrenewable resource as an input into its production as well. The nonrenewable resource exists both in a natural state as well as in a processed/marketable state.
- Physical capital, **K**, is produced only in Country Two. This good is used by the mining industry in Country One, by the capital goods industry in Country Two, and by the consumer goods industry in Country Three. The government sectors in all three countries also purchase capital goods to aid in the production of the public services that they provide their constituencies.
- Consumption goods, **C**, produced only in Country Three. These goods are purchased by the household sectors in all three countries.
- Treated and stored waste, **S**, and untreated waste (pollution), **P***.

A flow of waste, **W***, is generated during the period by production in the NR, K, and C industries by human consumption of the renewable resources and consumption goods in the three countries and by the deaths of humans. Some existing waste is naturally assimilated by the basic renewable resource, with **A** representing this amount; some waste is recycled by the NR industry as a recovered portion of the nonrenewable resource (minerals only). Some waste is also recycled by the government sectors as a renewable resource (drinking water) in their country. Of course, the waste assimilated or recycled during the period is no longer categorized as waste at the end of the period; recycled waste becomes an addition to the stocks of the various natural resources. The waste that is neither assimilated nor recycled during the period is either treated and stored or emerges as pollution. The waste treated and stored, **S**, remains inert for a significant period of time. The addition to **S** and any addition to untreated waste (pollution) during the period represent an increase in entropy. Entropy is a necessary result of economic activity.

The World Economy

The three-country model developed in this study consists of a total of 18 sectors. Each country contains

- a household sector (consisting of all single adults and all family units);
- an agricultural (nontradable renewable resource) sector;
- an industrial sector (mining/extraction in the case of Country One, capital goods manufacture in the case of Country Two, and consumption goods production in Country Three);
- a private banking sector;
- a central bank;
- a government sector.

By international treaty, each government sector issues a given number of tradable pollution allowances to its nonfinancial business sector.

Together the nonfinancial business sectors make international markets for the goods **NR**, **K**, and **C**. In addition, the private banks and the central banks make international markets for the interest-earning assets issued within each country. The three government sectors and the world's industrial sectors combine to make an international market in pollution allowances. The governmental, agricultural, industrial, and household sectors in each country together make a market for labor in that country. The households and the renewable resource industries in each country make a national market for **R1**, **R2**, and **R3**. Taken together these markets simultaneously represent markets for the noninterest-bearing deposits and currencies issued in each country. The resulting international transactions in real and financial assets also establish the exchange rates among the three countries' units of account.

Steps in the Decision-Making Process

1. Given the size of B and the level of P*at the beginning of the period and given their estimate of the nutrients the three country-specific renewable resources will extract from B during the period, the government sectors together ascertain the ability of the biosphere to assimilate waste emissions during the current period and announce the number of pollution allowances that will be issued at the beginning of the current period.

2. The government sector in each country estimates the amount of organic and inorganic waste that its household sector will generate during the current

period. Organic waste arises from human mortality and from the household sector's consumption of the country-specific renewable resource. The household sectors generate inorganic waste as they consume C (inorganic goods and services). Each government estimates the cost of recycling or treating and storing the waste that it estimates will be generated by its household sector during the period. Each government then sets the fee (tax) it will charge its household sector that period for these sanitation services.

In addition, the government sector in each country decides the amount of labor services to combine with the stock of physical capital it holds at the beginning of the current period to provide the predetermined current level of general public services (other than sanitation services) to its households.

The government sector in each country also provides its household sector with a menu of alternative amounts of general public services—immunizations, justice systems, public safety, schools, and so on—that could be in place by the beginning of next period together with the corresponding levels of next-period taxes it expects will be necessary to finance each of the alternative projects.

Besides the above mentioned services, each government sector provides an infrastructure (roads, power plants, airports, and seaports) that directly benefits the business sectors in its country. The augmentation to the infrastructure during the period is chosen exogenously by the government sector in this model (presumably—but not explicitly modeled here—with input from the business sectors). The government chooses the minimum cost combination of inputs required to add to the infrastructure (a process that requires nonrenewable resources and the transformation services provided by current labor services). Additions to the infrastructure during the current period will not benefit the business sectors until next period. Each government collects a tax from its nonfinancial business sectors to pay for the cost of augmenting the country's infrastructure.

Finally, because the level of general public services (parks and other environmental amenities) is also enhanced by the stock of the country-specific renewable resources, R1, R2, and R3, each government subsidizes its own renewable resource industry for maintaining the stock of its resource at a minimum level, determined by that country's government. Of course, for the subsidy to be effective, at the minimum inventory, the subsidy must exceed the net profit the renewable resource industry could earn if it instead harvested the resource and sold it rather than keeping it in its inventory during the period and collecting the subsidy.

3. The household sector in each country then selects the amount of general public services it is willing to pay for next period.

4. The R1, R2, R3, NR, K, and C industries then set product prices and decide upon the levels of current production and current labor hours in light of genuine pervasive uncertainty (limited, asymmetric, partial knowledge of the market demands for their products, and the values of current period interest rates and exchange rates). The NR, K, and C industries also set the wage rates that they anticipate will provide them with the number of employees they seek by the beginning of next period in their respective industries. (Labor is immobile across countries.) During this phase, the worldwide market demand for pollution allowances is also

determined, and the price of pollution allowances is set at the market-clearing price.

5. Given current production levels, incomes, wage rates, and product prices, the financial markets then determine interest rates in each country and the exchange rates among the countries' units of account. While total spending on all goods and services was established in the production-decision phase, the composition of spending is determined in this stage together with interest rates and exchange rates. Some spending occurs as unanticipated changes in inventories, which is financed by (applied to) additional borrowing (debt retirement) in the bond markets. Under flexible exchange rates and variable interest rates, the three markets for money can be solved for the interest rates that clear the respective bond markets. Then two of the bond market equations can be solved to obtain the relative values of the units of account among the three countries. (Five of the six excess demands for money and bonds are independent; the three money markets are functions of the three interest rates alone; the three bond market excess demands are functions of the three interest rates and the two (independent) exchange rates. Given the three excess demands for money, two of these bond excess demands are independent. The remaining bond excess demand is implied by the excess demands in the other five markets.) With the completion of this step, as interest rates and the exchange rates become known, the end-of-period human populations, numbers of employees, and stocks of all physical and financial assets and waste are also determined along with spending, saving, and investment in each country and industry. Involuntary unemployment, unintended investment, or unintended saving may prevail in at least one country. The end-of-period stocks provide the starting point for a new round of decision making in the following period.

Other Features of the Model

1. *Materials balance holds at every stage of mass transfer (production and consumption).* The mass associated with a produced good necessarily equals the mass of the raw materials and intermediate goods used as inputs in its production minus the waste generated in its production. The production functions used in this study reflect this irrefutable fact. Furthermore, the mass of each organism (human and nonhuman) changes during the period by the amount of mass it consumes minus the waste it generates during the period. In addition, as it moves through the various organisms and production processes, the total mass (organic and inorganic) contained in the global ecosystem must remain constant.

2. *Conventional versus green accounting highlighted.* The conventional concept of value added refers to value added in terms of market transactions. It is defined as the value of current production minus purchases of intermediate goods and services (including interest paid to other firms and business taxes paid to the government) from other sectors. The green concept of net value added in terms of market transactions deducts the value of the waste generated in production (which includes depreciation

of physical capital) from the conventional concept of value added in terms of market transactions and adds the value of the waste either recycled or treated and stored. In this study, net value added in terms of market transactions also corresponds to the conventional value added in terms of market transactions minus the value of pollution allowances purchased.

The green concept of imputed net value added in terms of nonmarket activities refers to the imputed value of nonmarket production minus imputed value of nonmarket consumption. Green net value added is the sum of net value added in terms of market transactions and the imputed net value added in terms of nonmarket activities. Consequently, net value added is equal to the value added in terms of market transactions, minus the value of the net waste generated (found by subtracting from the total amount of wasted generated the amount of waste recycled or treated and stored), plus the imputed value of nonmarket production, and minus the imputed value of nonmarket consumption.

The conventional measure of national income pertains exclusively to market transactions. In particular, conventional national income is defined as the total (market) income currently earned by the factors of production (equal to the sum of the market values added). In this study, the green concept of net national income corresponds to the net income associated with market transactions (the value of current production minus purchases of intermediate goods from other sectors minus the net waste generated) plus the imputed net income from nonmarket activities (the imputed value of nonmarket saving). Green net national income consists of the sum of dividends, wages, interest paid to households, taxes, net business saving, and the imputed net income associated with nonmarket activities. The imputed net income associated with nonmarket activities is equal to the imputed value of nonmarket production minus imputed value of nonmarket consumption—the imputed value of nonmarket saving.

Aggregating the net values added across all sectors within a country yields the green measure of net national product. Aggregating these values across countries, in terms of one country's unit of account, yields a measure of net world product and income in terms of that country's unit of account.

3. *Cash flow constraints, explicit bond markets, and interdependent financial markets.* At every stage in the decision-making process, with all variables valued in terms of a consistent set of (current-period) prices, every sector faces an explicit ex ante cash flow (budget) constraint stipulating that the level of net wealth in the balance sheet it plans for the close of the current period must exceed the level of net wealth in its beginning-of- period balance sheet by the same amount as the sector's planned saving for the current period. The decisions of every sector in every market—including the bond markets—are specified explicitly. At the sectoral level, the budget constraints impose restrictions upon the responses of a given sector to a change in any particular parameter it faces. Summing across the ex ante cash flow restrictions of the various sectors, nationwide or worldwide, yields a set of one or more conditions with respect to the market excess demands in the various financial markets. The resulting set depends upon which exchange rates (if any) are allowed to float and upon whether a given central bank manages its monetary base or its interest rate.

4. *The decision making of every government and every private economic sector is based upon first principles.* Every one of these sectors attempts either to minimize cost (as in the case of the government sectors) or to maximize present utility or to maximize the present value of the anticipated stream of dividends to its owners. The activities of the central banks, on the other hand, may be designed to peg interest rates or exchange rates at arbitrary levels, or to produce autonomously determined changes in the monetary base.

5. *Because wages and prices are set at the beginning of the period on a take-it-or-leave-it basis before the actual market demand and supply functions are known, involuntary unemployment, unintended investment, and unintended saving may occur.* Firms operating under conditions of imperfect competition may not be able to hire everyone they would like to hire. Households may find that not everyone who would like to be employed by the end of the period has been employed in the next period. Firms may not sell as many goods as they planned during the period. Households may not be able to buy as many goods as they desired to. To the extent that firms engage in unintended investment, they borrow in the bond market. To the extent that they engage in unintended disinvestment, they lend in the bond market. To the extent that households cannot buy as many goods as they would like, they also lend their excess funds in the bond market.

6. *Contributions of the government sectors specified explicitly.* Unlike most macroeconomic models, the contributions of the government sectors to economic welfare are specified explicitly in the present model. Furthermore, the contribution of government is not limited to a public service that merely increases household utility. One role of the government sectors is to promote sustainability of the human populations by undertaking policies aimed at protecting and preserving the global ecosystem. The government sectors do so by issuing a restricted number of pollution allowances, by subsidizing the renewable resource industries for the purpose of maintaining minimum stocks of these resources over time, and by recycling or treating and storing human waste. In addition, governments exist to add to their country's infrastructure and to provide the levels of general public services chosen by their households.

7. *The interest rates and exchange rates relevant to macroeconomic (national income) analysis refer to their values during the period, not to their values at a point in time.* The standard approach used in macroeconomic analysis implicitly (sometimes explicitly) imposes a wealth constraint upon the private sector, which requires that the sum of the market demand for money and the market demand for bonds equal the sum of the initial stocks of money and bonds. Because the bond market is viewed as the mirror image of the money market in this case, an increase in real income, which all textbooks agree causes the demand for money to rise, must, to be consistent, imply that the market demand for bonds is negatively related to current income—an implausible assumption.

Unfortunately conventional macroeconomic analysis separates financial market decisions from the decisions to save and invest, even though the linkage between saving and investment, on the one hand, and the financial markets, on the other, is central to intertemporal decision making. The act of saving involves the transfer of purchasing power from the present to the future. The act of real investment involves the purchase or building of physical capital in the present that will not become productive until the future—capital accumulation requires waiting time. Both saving and investment are flows; they are income account items, occurring during the current period as opposed to a particular moment in time. Saving cannot take place in a vacuum; typically, it requires the accumulation of financial assets during the period. Real investment usually requires external financing during the current period. The conventional microfoundations of the saving and investment decisions rely upon budget constraints that link each sector's decisions on the income and product accounts not only to their initial balance sheet (which each sector takes as given) but also to their planned balance sheet for the close of the period. According to these first principles, the household and nonfinancial business (and even the government) sectors take their initial balance sheets as given but formulate plans for an end-of-period balance sheet consistent with their initial net wealth and their plans on the income and/or product accounts. Their planned balance sheets for the end of the period contain their end-of-period demands for money and physical capital and their end-of-period demands for or supplies of bonds. The relevant price at which each item is valued in the income and product accounts as well as in each sector's initial and planned end-of-period balance sheet is that price at which the item will trade during the period, not at a particular moment in time. This is true for financial assets as well as for goods. Therefore, just as the exchange rate relevant for the decision to buy foreign or domestic goods during the period is the exchange rate that prevails during the period, the interest rate relevant to these financial decisions is the interest rate that prevails during the current period, not the one associated with a particular moment in time. The bond market is specified explicitly in the present model.

To be consistent with the microfoundations of these nonbank sectors, the banking sectors must also take their initial balance sheets as given but plan a new balance sheet for the end of the period consistent with their initial net wealth and their planned saving on the income account. This means, for instance, that a new definition of the money supply emerges in which the money supply refers not to the given amount of money in circulation at the beginning of the period but rather to the amount of money that would be in circulation by the end of the period consistent with the intertemporal plans of the banking sectors.

8. *Consistency between the household sector's labor supply function and the assumption that the sector takes its current disposable income as given in deciding how much to consume or save during the period.* The standard treatment views the household sector as taking its current real disposable income as given at least in so far as it decides current consumption and personal saving. However, the households are also viewed as simultaneously deciding how much labor to supply to the labor market. Clearly their labor supply cannot pertain to the current period, for if their current real disposable income will remain unchanged regardless of how much they decide to work this period, the households would have no incentive to work at all during the current period. In the present treatment, the households take their current real disposable incomes as given—including their current wage incomes. Their relevant labor market decisions pertain to how much labor they want to supply next period.

Waste is generated by industries in the production of goods and by households in the consumption of those goods. Waste may be recycled, treated and stored, or it may be released as pollution. Pollution reduces the abilities of the various organisms to grow. Although a portion of pollution may be assimilated by the basic (fungible) renewable resource (clean air and water) and although the international agreement may limit the amount of pollution released to the amount the ecosystem is capable of assimilating, over time, the entropy of the global ecosystem increases, if only because the treated and stored waste remains inert for an extended period.

In this study, human births depend upon the marginal utility from additional children and the opportunity cost of having more children. Human deaths depend upon average weight, pollution, and public services. The implications of various public policies upon the operation of the complete system are also explored. Alternative policies of the various central banks (managed interest rates versus managed monetary base, managed versus floating exchange rates); governments (tariffs versus free trade); and the international agreement (change in number of pollution credits) are examined to discern potential differential effects upon the world economy and the global ecosystem. Although the effects of alternative uses of development aid are not examined here, the implications of technological change occurring in each industry with respect to both mass per unit of product and mass wasted per unit of product are considered. Also, the implications of an increase in infrastructure or an increase in other public services that reduce human mortality in a given country are considered. For the purpose of this study, the world economy consists of three open economies.

Chapter 2 contains a specification of the equations of motion for the various physical items found in the global ecosystem. The overall conservation of mass is also stated for this ecosystem. In general, economic activity causes entropy. Except for the amount that is recycled and for an indeterminate amount of mass that is assimilated over time back into the fungible basic resource, economic activity removes mass from this resource as well as from the nonrenewable and country-specific renewable resources and deposits that mass as pollution or stored and treated waste.

Chapter 3 presents the initial decisions facing the three government sectors with respect to their current employment of labor hours, the menus they present to their household sectors for possible levels of general public services offered for next period, and their decisions to enhance their infrastructures during the period. Chapter 4 contains an analysis of the household sectors' decisions with respect to the number of their childbirths during the period and with respect to their selections of general public services and corresponding taxes for next period.

In chapter 5, the analysis of the current pricing, employment, and production decisions of the nonrenewable resource industry is presented. Similar analyses are undertaken in chapters 6 and 7 for the capital goods and consumption goods industries, respectively. An analysis of the current pricing, employment, and production decisions of the three country-specific renewable resource industries is given in chapter 8. The conservation of mass holds for all producers, including the government sectors, in all countries. Specifically, the mass emerging from a production process cannot exceed the mass entering that production process, no matter how much labor or capital is used to transform that mass.

The decisions of the private banking and central banking sectors in all three countries are analyzed in chapter 9. Chapter 10 contains a summary of the world's production, pricing, wage-setting, and employment decisions for the current period. Conventional versus green measures of national and world incomes and products are discussed in chapter 11. In chapter 12, the nonbank sectors are revisited now that they have learned their current incomes, wages, and prices. In this chapter, each nonbank sector's end-of-period demands and/or supplies of the various financial assets are specified as functions of the previously established production, product prices, wages, and employment levels as well as functions of current interest rates and exchange rates.

In chapter 13, the financial market decisions of all sectors in all countries are combined to form markets for money and bonds in each country under the assumption of variable interest rates and flexible exchange rates. Chapter 14 contains a derivation of the various forms of Walras's Law relevant to flexible versus fixed exchange rate regimes. These derivations are obtained summing across the budget (cash flow) constraints facing the various sectors and then rearranging terms. In chapter 15, it is shown that the end-of-period stocks of resources, manufactured goods, and human populations depend upon their initial stocks, current production, and current interest rates and exchange rates. Current production determines current total actual spending, but current interest rates and exchange rates determine the composition of actual spending in terms of planned versus unplanned spending. Therefore, current interest rates and exchange rates influence the level of unplanned investment by the various industries.

Chapter 16 contains an analysis of central bank policies under fixed versus floating exchange rates and under managed versus variable interest rates. It is found that in general the results of central bank policy associated with simpler models of a large open economy do not carry over to the more complete model specified in this book. In virtually all cases, no definitive qualitative results hold for the effects of central bank policies upon world interest rates and exchange rates in the larger model.

In chapter 17, the effects of the various types of technical change are discussed along with the effects of several public policies. Chapter 18 contains a summary and conclusion.

2

The Global Ecosystem

Ecosystem Dynamics, Mass Balance, and Entropy

The earth's biosphere, encompassing its atmosphere (gaseous mass surrounding the earth and held in place by the earth's gravitational force), hydrosphere (water upon the earth's surface), and a small portion of its lithosphere (upper part of the earth consisting of its crust and upper mantle), contains the planet's various ecosystems. These self-supporting systems contain myriad plants, animals, and other organisms that interact with each other and with the nonliving parts of the environment. For the purpose of this study the biosphere is viewed as encompassing a single global ecosystem. The total mass of the global ecosystem is divided into 11 major categories:

1. a fungible slowly renewable basic resource (clean air and ocean water), B;
2. three country-specific natural renewable resources (consisting of different combinations of fresh water, soils, plants, and animals), R1, R2, and R3;
3. three country-specific processed/transformed marketable renewable resources (harvested, frozen, canned, smoked, purified, pasteurized, transported, and various other forms of the natural renewable resources), $R1^T$, $R2^T$, and $R3^T$;
4. three human populations, N1, N2, and N3 measured in terms of people; in terms of mass these populations are represented by $H1 = \omega_1 \cdot N1$, $H2 = \omega_2 \cdot N2$, and $H3 = \omega_3 \cdot N_3$, where $\omega_i (i = 1, 2, 3)$ denotes average weight of humans in country i.
5. a nonrenewable unextracted/unmined resource (fossil fuels and minerals), NR;
6. a mined/extracted/transported marketable resource, NR^T;
7. capital goods, $\kappa \cdot K$ (the symbol κ represents average mass per unit of capital goods, K);
8. consumption goods, $\gamma \cdot C$ (the symbol γ represents mass per unit of consumption goods, C);

9. public infrastructure (roads, bridges, airports, seaports, power plants) in each country, I1, I2, and I3,
10. treated and stored waste, S;
11. untreated waste (pollution), P*.

Inorganic waste is generated by the NR, K, and C industries during their production processes as well as by the households in each country as they use and dispose of the inorganic consumption goods (goods made from the nonrenewable resources) they buy during the period. The NR industry is assumed to recycle a portion of the waste it generates, while the K and C industries are assumed to treat and store a portion of their wastes. The government sectors are assumed to treat and store all inorganic waste generated by their respective household sectors.

Organic waste is generated by the households in each country as humans die and as they consume the renewable resource marketed in their country. This organic waste generated within a country is assumed to be either recycled or treated and stored by that country's government sector. The amount of organic waste recycled by a government sector is assumed to be less than the organic waste generated by its household sector due to the consumption of the country's renewable resource.

If the untreated inorganic waste generated during a period exceeds the amount of waste that the basic fungible resource is capable of assimilating during the period, the level of pollution increases. Entropy increases by the amount of inorganic waste generated (but not recycled) during the period in excess of assimilation, regardless of whether the waste is treated and stored.

Assume that the ability of the basic resource to assimilate pollution during a period, $A(\bullet)$, is an increasing function not only of the amount of the basic resource at the beginning of the period, B_t, but also of the amounts of each of the country-specific renewable resources, $R1_t$, $R2_t$, and $R3_t$ at the beginning of period. In addition, the ability of the basic resource to assimilate pollution is taken as a decreasing function of the amount of pollution in existence at the beginning of the period, P^*_t. Let $g_1(\bullet)$, $g_2(\bullet)$, and $g_3(\bullet)$ denote the amounts of natural growth in R1, R2, and R3, respectively, during the period. Assume that the amount of growth in each country-specific renewable resource is positively related to the corresponding amount of the renewable resource at the beginning of the period as well as to the initial stock of the basic resource but negatively related to the stock of pollution at the beginning of the period. Ceteris paribus, the higher the growth rates of R1, R2, and R3, the smaller the growth rate of B. Therefore, the stock of the basic resource at the end of the period may be given by

$$B_{t+1} = B_t + A\left(B_t, R1_t, R2_t, P^*_t\right) - g_1\left(R1_t, B_t, P^*_t\right) - g_2\left(R2_t, B_t, P^*_t\right) - g_3\left(R3_t, B_t, P^*_t\right) \quad (2.1)$$

where it is assumed for the purpose of this analysis that a larger initial stock of R1, R2, and/or R3 increases the ability of the basic resource to assimilate pollutants by a greater amount than the corresponding increase in the growth of the renewable resource(s) decreases the amount of the basic resource available at the end of the period, so that the net effect upon B_{t+1} due to an increase in any one of $R1_t$, $R2_t$, or $R3_t$ is positive.

Equation (2.1) is intended to characterize in very general and elementary terms the basic carbon, water, and nitrogen cycles through which these elements and their compounds move through air, oceans, soil, and living organisms and to highlight the damage to these natural cycles caused by pollution. For instance, plants take CO_2 from the air and produce sugars and O_2 through photosynthesis. Animals and humans eat the plants and inhale O_2 to produce energy. Plants, animals, and humans release CO_2 back into the atmosphere through respiration. When organisms die, decomposers in the soil and water put CO_2 back into the atmosphere. A portion of the CO_2 falls to earth and dissolves in water. Water falls to earth through precipitation and is absorbed by plants and animals. Their transpiration and wastes go to the oceans where water evaporates back into the atmosphere. Nitrogen-fixing bacteria in the soil transform nitrogen they remove from the air. Plants obtain nitrogen from the soil, and animals obtain nitrogen from plants. Decomposers and other bacteria break down animal wastes and return the nitrogen to the soil and to the atmosphere. Therefore, the ability of the atmosphere and oceans to absorb pollution is positively related to the amounts of the country-specific renewable resources, but the larger the stocks of these resources, the greater their natural growth and the more elements and compounds they remove from the atmosphere and oceans. Water pollution kills plants and animals in the water. Hydrocarbons and other compounds released into the air by economic activity also harm plants, animals, and humans and retard the natural cycles referred to above.

The amounts of the three country-specific renewable resources at the end of the period are assumed to equal their respective amounts at the beginning of the period plus their natural growths, referred to above, minus the amounts of the resources harvested, respectively, by the R1, R2, and R3 industries (denoted by $R1^T$, $R2^T$, and $R3^T$, respectively), but plus the amount of the organic waste recycled by the corresponding government sector:

$$R1_{t+1} = R1_t + g_1\left(R1_t, B_t, P_t^*\right) - R1^T + \alpha_1 \cdot OW^*H1 \tag{2.2}$$

$$R2_{t+1} = R2_t + g_2\left(R2_t, B_t, P_t^*\right) - R2^T + \alpha_2 \cdot OW^*H2 \tag{2.3}$$

$$R3_{t+1} = R3_t + g_3\left(R3_t, B_t, P_t^*\right) - R3^T + \alpha_3 \cdot OW^*H3 \tag{2.4}$$

where OW^*H1 represents the total household organic waste recycled or treated and stored by the G1 sector and where α_1 represents the fraction of total household organic waste recycled as R1 by the G1 sector. The fraction of total organic waste treated and stored by the G1 sector, $(1 - \alpha_1) \cdot OW^*H1$, includes all organic waste associated with human deaths in Country One. Analogously, OW^*H2 and OW^*H3 represent the total household organic waste recycled or treated and stored by the G2 and G3 sectors, respectively, with α_2 representing the fraction of their waste that is recycled as R2 by the G2 sector and α_3 representing the fraction of their waste that is recycled as R3 by the G3 sector.

The amounts of the three country-specific processed/marketable renewable resources at the end of the period (respectively $R1_{t+1}^{T^*}$, $R2_{t+1}^{T^*}$, and $R3_{t+1}^{T^*}$) are assumed to equal their respective amounts at the beginning of the period ($R1_t^{T^*}$, $R2_t^{T^*}$, and

$R3_t^{T^*}$) plus the respective amounts of the natural resources transformed during the period minus the amount of the resource sold to the household sectors in the respective countries during the period ($R1H1_t$, $R2H2_t$, and $R3H3_t$):

$$R1_{t+1}^{T^*} = R1_t^{T^*} + R1^T - R1H1_t \geq 0 \tag{2.5}$$

$$R2_{t+1}^{T^*} = R2_t^{T^*} + R2^T - R2H2_t \geq 0 \tag{2.6}$$

$$R3_{t+1}^{T^*} = R3_t^{T^*} + R3^T - R3H3_t \geq 0 \tag{2.7}$$

It is assumed that $R1H1 > \alpha_1 \cdot OW^*H1$, $R2H2 > \alpha_2 \cdot OW^*H2$, and $R3H3 > \alpha_3 \cdot OW^*H3$.

The total mass of each of the human populations at the end of the period ($H1_{t+1}, H2_{t+1}$, and $H3_{t+1}$) is equal to the population's mass at the beginning of the period ($H1_t$, $H2_t$, and $H3_t$, respectively) plus the amount of the renewable resource the corresponding household sector consumes during the period minus the total organic waste generated by these households (including that resulting from death), OW^*H1, OW^*H2, and OW^*H3:

$$H1_{t+1} = H1_t + R1H1 - OW^*H1 \tag{2.8}$$

$$H2_{t+1} = H2_t + R2H2 - OW^*H2 \tag{2.9}$$

$$H3_{t+1} = H3_t + R3H3 - OW^*H3 \tag{2.10}$$

The total mass of the unextracted/unprocessed nonrenewable resource at the end of the period, NR_{t+1}, is equal to its mass at the beginning of the period, NR_t, minus the amount of the nonrenewable resource extracted/processed/transported during the period, NR^T, minus the waste generated by the NR industry in extracting and converting NR into a marketable product, W*NR, but plus the amount of NR recycled by the NR industry during the period, RW*NR. (For simplicity, it is assumed that neither the capital goods nor the consumption goods industry recycles its waste into NR.)

$$NR_{t+1} = NR_t - NR^T - W^*NR + RW^*NR \tag{2.11}$$

The total mass of the extracted/processed/transported nonrenewable resource at the end of the period, $NR_{t+1}^{T^*}$, is equal to its mass at the beginning of the period, $NR_t^{T^*}$, plus the amount of the natural nonrenewable resource transformed during the period, NR^T, minus the amount of the processed NR purchased by the capital goods industry, NRK^T, the consumption goods industry, NRC^T, and the three government sectors, $NRG1^T$, $NRG2^T$, and $NRG3^T$:

$$\begin{aligned} NR_{t+1}^{T^*} = NR_t^{T^*} + NR^T - NRK^T - NRC^T - NRG1^T \\ - NRG2^T - NRG3^T \geq 0 \end{aligned} \tag{2.12}$$

For simplicity, it is assumed that neither the capital goods nor the consumption goods industry recycles inorganic waste into NR.

The total mass of privately produced physical capital at the end of the period, $\kappa \cdot K_{t+1}$, is equal to its mass at the beginning of the period, $\kappa \cdot K_t$ (held either by the capital goods industry itself or by a government sector, the nonrenewable resource sector or the consumption goods sector), plus the amount of the capital good produced during the period from the nonrenewable resource (measured in units of mass), NRK^T, minus the waste generated by the K industry (other than physical depreciation of capital) during the period, W^*K, and minus the physical depreciation of capital held by the three government sectors and the nonrenewable resource, capital goods and consumption goods industries:

$$\kappa \cdot K_{t+1} = \kappa \cdot K_t + NRK^T - W^*K - \delta \cdot \kappa \cdot (K_{NRt} + K_{Kt} + K_{Ct} + K_{G1t} + K_{G2t} + K_{G3t}) \quad (2.13)$$

where δ denotes the rate at which capital depreciates.

The total mass of inorganic consumption goods at the end of the period, $\gamma \cdot C_{t+1}$ (held by the consumption goods industry as inventory), is equal to its mass at the beginning of the period, $\gamma \cdot C_t$ (held by the consumer goods industry), plus the amount of the consumer good produced during the period from the nonrenewable resource (measured in units of mass), NRC^T, minus the waste generated by the C industry during the period, W^*C, and minus the consumer goods purchased by the three household sectors during the period:

$$\gamma \cdot C_{t+1} = \gamma \cdot C_t + NRC^T - W^*C - \gamma \cdot CH1 - \gamma \cdot CH2 - \gamma \cdot CH3 \quad (2.14)$$

The stocks of the public infrastructures (in terms of units in the three countries at the end of the period, $I1_{t+1}$, $I2_{t+1}$, and $I3_{t+1}$, respectively), equal their stocks at the beginning of the period, $I1_t$, $I2_t$, and $I3_t$, plus the amounts that the respective government sectors add to their infrastructures during the period. Let ι denote the mass per unit of infrastructure in each country. Then the respective stocks of infrastructure in each country in terms of mass are given by

$$\iota \cdot I1_{t+1} = \iota \cdot I1t + NRG1^T \quad (2.15)$$

$$\iota \cdot I2_{t+1} = \iota \cdot I2_t + NRG2^T \quad (2.16)$$

$$\iota \cdot I3_{t+1} = \iota \cdot I3_t + NRG3^T \quad (2.17)$$

The stock of treated and stored waste at the end of the period, S_{t+1}, is equal to the stock of stored waste at the beginning of the period, S_t, plus the waste treated and stored by the three government sectors, $(1 - \alpha_1) \cdot OW^*H1 + \gamma \cdot CH1 + \delta \cdot \kappa \cdot K_{G1t}$, $(1 - \alpha_2) \cdot OW^*H2 + \gamma \cdot CH2 + \delta \cdot \kappa \cdot K_{G2t}$, and $(1 - \alpha_3) \cdot OW^*H3 + \gamma \cdot CH3 + \delta \cdot \kappa \cdot K_{G3t}$; by the capital goods industry, SW^*K; and by the consumption goods industry, SW^*C, during the period. Then the stock of stored waste at the close of the current period is given by

$$\begin{aligned} S_{t+1} = S_t &+ (1 - \alpha_1) \cdot OW^*H1 + (1 - \alpha_2) \cdot OW^*H2 \\ &+ (1 - \alpha_3) \cdot OW^*H3 + \gamma \cdot (CH1 + CH2 + CH3) \\ &+ \delta \cdot \kappa \cdot (K_{G1t} + K_{G2t} + K_{G3t}) + SW^*K + SW^*C \end{aligned} \quad (2.18)$$

The amount of pollution (untreated waste) at the end of the period, P^*_{t+1}, is equal to the amount of pollution at the beginning of the period, P^*_t, plus the waste generated by the NR, K, and C sectors and by the H1, H2, and H3 sectors, minus the waste recycled by the NR industry, RW*NR, the waste treated and stored by the K industry, SW*K, the waste treated and stored by the C industry, SW*C ,the waste either recycled or treated and stored by the G1, G2, and G3 sectors, and the waste assimilated by the basic fungible renewable resource, $A(\bullet)$:

$$\begin{aligned} P^*_{t+1} = P^*_t &+ (W^*NR + \delta \cdot \kappa \cdot K_{NRt} - RW^*NR) \\ &+ (W^*K + \delta \cdot \kappa \cdot K_{Kt} - SW^*K) + (W^*C + \delta \cdot \kappa \cdot K_{Ct} - SW^*C) \\ &- A\left(B_t, R1_t, R2_t, R3_t, P^*_t\right) \end{aligned} \tag{2.19}$$

where $(W^*NR + \delta \cdot \kappa \cdot K_{NR_t} - RW^*NR)$ represents the pollution generated by the NR industry, $(W^*K + \delta \cdot \kappa \cdot K_{Kt} - SW^*K)$ represents the pollution generated by the K industry, and $(W^*C + \delta \cdot \kappa \cdot K_{Ct} - SW^*C)$ represents the pollution generated by the C industry. Because the government sectors either recycle or treat and store all waste generated by themselves and by their respective households in this model, neither government nor household activity results directly in a net increase in the level of pollution.

Summing across equations (2.1)–(2.19) yields global materials balance; the total mass in existence within the global ecosystem at the end of the period is equal to the total mass in existence within the global ecosystem at the beginning of the period:

$$\begin{aligned} &B_{t+1} + R1_{t+1} + R2_{t+1} + R3_t + R1^{T^*}_{t+1} + R2^{T^*}_{t+1} + R3^{T^*}_{t+1} + H1_{t+1} + H2_{t+1} \\ &\quad + H3_{t+1} + NR_{t+1} + NR^{T^*}_{t+1} + \kappa \cdot K_{t+1} + \gamma \cdot C_{t+1} + S_{t+1} + P^*_{t+1} \\ &\quad + \iota \cdot I1_{t+1} + \iota \cdot I2_{t+1} + \iota \cdot I3_{t+1} \\ &= B_t + R1_t + R2_t + R3_t + R1^{T^*}_t + R2^{T^*}_t + R3^{T^*}_t + H1_t + H2_t \\ &\quad + H3_t + NR_t + NR^{T^*}_t + \kappa \cdot K_t + \gamma \cdot C_t + S_t + P^*_t \\ &\quad + \iota \cdot (I1_t + I2_t + I3_t) \end{aligned} \tag{2.20}$$

Equation (2.20) represents one implication of materials balance. Materials balance restrictions also hold within each of the world economy's production functions and among transfers of goods within markets.

Human Population Dynamics

The human population in each country at the end of the period exceeds its population at the beginning of the period by the excess of births over deaths. Let $\eta_{1t}(\bullet)$, for instance, represent the endogenously determined number of births in Country One. The births in each country will be derived as functions of the marginal utility of having more children and the opportunity cost of more children. Let $\mu^*_{N1}(\bullet)$, for instance, denote the endogenous mortality rate in Country One. As shown below, the mortality rates are assumed to be increasing functions of the level of pollution at the beginning of the period, P^*_t, and the square of the deviation of the average weight per person from their "ideal" weight. These mortality rates are also assumed to be decreasing functions of the public health and human services the corresponding government provides during the current period. Let g_{H1t}, for instance, represent the level of general public services provided by the government sector in Country One. Then the following equations represent the dynamics of the respective human populations:

$$N1_{t+1} = N1_t + \eta_{1t}(\bullet) - \mu^*N1\left[P^*_t, g_{H1t}, (\omega_{1t} - \omega_{I1t})^2\right] \cdot N1_t \qquad (2.21)$$

$$N2_{t+1} = N2_t + \eta_{2t}(\bullet) - \mu^*N2\left[P^*_t, g_{H2t}, (\omega_{2t} - \omega_{I2t})^2\right] \cdot N2_t \qquad (2.22)$$

$$N3_{t+1} = N3_t + \eta_{3t}(\bullet) - \mu^*N3\left[P^*_t, g_{H3t}, (\omega_{3t} - \omega_{I3t})^2\right] \cdot N3_t \qquad (2.23)$$

where, for instance, $\omega_{1t}(= H1_t/N1_t)$ represents the average weight per person in Country One at beginning of the current period and where ω_{I1t} denotes the "ideal" weight per person in that country. The total organic waste generated by the households during the period, OW*H1, OW*H2, and OW*H3, minus the mass of organic human waste generated by the households as humans die in Country One, Country Two, and Country Three during the period $\omega_{1t}.\mu^*_{N1}[P^*_t, g_{H1t}, (\omega_{1t} - \omega_{I1t})^2] \cdot N1_t$, $\omega_{2t}.\mu^*_{N2}[P^*_t, g_{H2t}, (\omega_{2t} - \omega_{I2t})^2] \cdot N2_t$, and $\omega_{3t}.\mu^*_{N3}[P^*_t, g_{H3t}, (\omega_{3t} - \omega_{I3t})^3] \cdot N3_t$ represents the organic waste generated by the household sectors during the period unrelated to death.

Table 2.1 summarizes the classification of waste flows within the global eco-system.

Table 2.1 Classification of Waste Flows

Organic

Total organic waste generated = OW*H1 + OW*H2 + OW*H3.
Organic waste recycled by governments = $\alpha_1 \cdot$ OW*H1 + $\alpha_2 \cdot$ OW*H2 + $\alpha_3 \cdot$ OW*H3.
Organic waste treated/stored by governments = $(1 - \alpha_1) \cdot$ OW*H1 + $(1 - \alpha_2) \cdot$ OW*H2 + $(1 - \alpha_3) \cdot$ OW*H3.
Portion of organic waste treated/stored related to human deaths =
$\omega_{1t} \cdot \mu^*_{N1}\left[P^*_t, g_{H1t}, (\omega_{1t} - \omega_{1It})^2\right] \cdot N1_t + \omega_{2t} \cdot \mu^*_{N2}\left[P^*_t g_{H2t}, (\omega_{2t} - \omega_{I2t})\right] \cdot N2_t + \omega_{3t} \cdot \mu^*_{N3}\left[P^*_t, g_{H3t}, (\omega_{3t} - \omega_{I3t})^2\right] \cdot N3_t$.

Inorganic

Total inorganic waste generated = $W^*NR + \delta \cdot \kappa \cdot K_{NRt} + W^*K + \delta \cdot \kappa \cdot K_{Kt} + W^*C + \delta \cdot \kappa \cdot K_{Ct} + \delta \cdot \kappa \cdot K_{G1t} + \delta \cdot \kappa \cdot K_{G2t} + \delta \cdot \kappa \cdot K_{G3t} + \gamma \cdot CH1 + \gamma \cdot CH2 + \gamma \cdot CH3$.
Inorganic waste recycled = RW*NR (by NR industry).
Inorganic waste treated/stored = $SW^*K + SW^*C + \delta \cdot \kappa \cdot K_{G1t} + \delta \cdot \kappa \cdot K_{G2t} + \delta \cdot \kappa \cdot K_{G3t} + \gamma \cdot CH1 + \gamma \cdot CH2 + \gamma \cdot CH3$.
Inorganic pollution generated = $(W^*NR + \delta \cdot \kappa \cdot K_{NRt} - RW^*NR) + (W^*K\delta \cdot \kappa \cdot K_{Kt} - SW^*K) + (W^*C + \delta \cdot \kappa \cdot K_{Ct} - SW^*C)$.

Pollution Allowances

Number of Pollution Allowances Issued

Assume that the growth in the slowly renewable basic fungible resource, B, during the period is positively related to the amount of pollution, P*, it is capable of assimilating during the period but negatively related to the amount of nutrients withdrawn by the three country-specific renewable resources during the period. The amount of pollution assimilated, A(•), during the period is an increasing function of the stocks of B, R1, R2, and R3 at the beginning of the period but a decreasing function of the level of pollution at the beginning of the period. From (2.1), repeated here for convenience as (2.24), the amount of nutrients withdrawn from B during the period by a country-specific renewable resource is positively related to the stock of that resource at the beginning of the period and positively related to the stock of the basic resource at the beginning of the period but negatively related to the stock of pollution at the beginning of period.

$$\begin{aligned} B_{t+1} = {} & A\left(B_t, R1_t, R2_t, R3_t, P^*_t\right) - g_1\left(R1_t, B_t, P^*_t\right) - g_2\left(R2_t, B_t, P^*_t\right) \\ & - g_3\left(R3_t, B_t, P^*_t\right) + B_t \end{aligned} \tag{2.24}$$

The government sectors issue pollution allowances during the current period. Each allowance permits the holder to emit one unit of mass in the form of pollution into the biosphere. The total number of allowances issued corresponds to the amount of pollution the government sectors deem the global basic resource can assimilate after allowing for the nutrients that they estimate will be withdrawn from that resource by the three country-specific renewable resources, so that the stock of B does not fall over time.

Note that from (2.19), the level of pollution will diminish or at least remain unchanged over time as long as

$$\begin{aligned} A(B_t, R1_t, R2_t, R3_t, P^*_t) \geq {} & (W^*NR + \delta \cdot \kappa \cdot K_{NRt} - RIW^*NR) \\ & + (W^*K + \delta \cdot \kappa \cdot K_{Kt} - SW^*K) \\ & + (W^*C + \delta \cdot \kappa \cdot K_{Ct} - SW^*C) \end{aligned} \tag{2.25}$$

Let Ω represent the number of pollution credits issued at the beginning of the current period. From (2.19), if Ω is less than $A(B_t, R1_t, R2_t, R3_t, P^*_t) - g_1(R1_t, B_t, P^*_t) - g_2(R2_t, B_t, P^*_t) - g_3(R3_t, B_t, P^*_t)$, assuming this amount is positive and assuming that (2.25) holds, not only will pollution diminish over time, but the level of the basic resource will also grow or at least not diminish over time.

We assume

$$A(B_t, R1_t, R2_t, R3_t, P_t^*) - g_1(R1_t, B_t, P_t^*) - g_2(R2_t, B_t, P_t^*) \\ - g_3(R3_t, B_t, P_t^*) \geq \Omega \geq 0 \quad (2.26)$$

The level of pollution emitted during a period consists of the sum of the unrecycled waste generated by the NR industry and the untreated waste generated by the K and C industries. We assume that each government sector either treats and stores or recycles all the organic and inorganic waste generated by its household sector. Untreated and unrecycled waste increases the level of pollution, $P_{t+1}^* - P_t^*$, during the period. Pollution reduces the ability of the basic resource to provide nutrients to the renewable resources and reduces the ability of the country-specific renewable resources to grow; it also increases human mortality.

The NR industry is capable of engaging in recycling during the period. The K and C industries are capable of storing and treating a portion of the waste generated in the production of their goods. To the extent that a sector elects to abate/recycle a unit of mass, the number of pollution allowances it would otherwise decide to buy during the period is reduced by that amount. Recycled waste becomes an addition to the stock of the nonrenewable resource. The NR industry may recycle this waste thereby adding to its inventory of NR by the end of the period. The amount of pollution/waste generated by each industry is assumed to be an increasing function of the mass contained in the total number of units produced by that industry and a decreasing function of the labor time devoted to abatement/recycling.

Market for Pollution Allowances

The government sectors issue pollution allowances at the beginning of the current period equivalent to or less than the volume of pollution they collectively decide the biosphere is capable of assimilating during the current period at the preexisting target level. In this fashion, the volume of pollution at the end of the current period will once again be no greater than the target amount. Each of the NR, K, and C industries receives some of these pollution allowances. The market price for pollution allowances is established at the point at which the sum of the (net) demands for pollution allowances by the three sectors is equal to the target volume issued by the government sectors. The demand for pollution allowances by an individual sector is equal to the amount of waste it plans to create in its mining or manufacturing operations minus the amount of pollution abatement it wishes to produce and the amount of waste it plans to recycle at the current price of pollution rights. The demand for pollution allowances by an individual country's mining or manufacturing sector may be less than its allocation, in which case that sector decides to sell some of its pollution allowances to the mining or manufacturing sector in another country.

Let

$\overline{P}$ = the target level of pollution agreed upon by the three government sectors.

$\phi \cdot \overline{P}$ = the amount of pollution the biosphere can assimilate at the target level of pollution, where $\phi \leq 1$. The government sectors issue pollution allowances during the current period no greater than $\phi \cdot \overline{P}$; therefore, $\Omega \leq \phi\overline{P}$.

$W^*NR + \delta \cdot \kappa \cdot K_{NRt}$ = the amount of waste the NR industry plans to generate during the current period.

$W^*K + \delta \cdot \kappa \cdot K_{Kt}$ = the amount of waste the K industry plans to generate during the current period.

$W^*C + \delta \cdot \kappa \cdot K_{Ct}$ = the amount of waste the C industry plans to generate during the current period.

RW^*NR = the amount of inorganic waste the NR industry plans to recycle during the current period.

SW^*K = the amount of inorganic waste the K industry plans to treat and store during the current period.

SW^*C = the amount of inorganic waste the C industry plans to treat and store during the current period.

$\overline{P}^d$ = the (net) demand for pollution allowances by the three mining and manufacturing industries.

Then the total amount of pollution the three industrial sectors plan to generate this period, and, therefore, their demand for pollution allowances during the current period is given by the sum

$$\overline{P}^d = (W^*NR + \delta \cdot \kappa \cdot K_{NRt} - RW^*NR) + (W^*K + \delta \cdot \kappa \cdot K_{Kt} - SW^*K) + (W^*C + \delta \cdot \kappa \cdot K_{Ct} - SW^*C) \quad (2.27)$$

Let

p_t^P = the current equilibrium price of pollution allowances (expressed in terms of the home country's currency).

Then, from the above discussion, the equilibrium price of pollution allowances (expressed in terms of the home country's currency), p_t^P, is the one for which

$$\Omega = (W^*NR + \delta \cdot \kappa \cdot K_{NRt} - RW^*NR) + (W^*K + \delta \cdot \kappa \cdot K_{Kt} - SW^*K) + (W^*C + \delta \cdot \kappa \cdot K_{Ct} - SW^*C) \quad (2.28)$$

Let

Ω_{NR} = the number of pollution allowances received by the NR industry.

Ω_K = the number of pollution allowances received by the K industry.

$\Omega_C = \Omega - \Omega_{NR} - \Omega_K$ = the number of pollution allowances received by the C industry.

Then, from (2.28),

$$\begin{aligned}
&[\Omega_{NR} - (W^{*}NR + \delta \cdot \kappa \cdot K_{NRt} - RW^{*}NR)] \\
&\quad + [\Omega_{K} - (W^{*}K + \delta \cdot \kappa \cdot K_{NRt} - SW^{*}K)] \\
&\quad + [\Omega_{C} - (W^{*}C + \delta \cdot \kappa \cdot K_{Ct} - SW^{*}K)] = 0 \qquad (2.29)
\end{aligned}$$

At the current equilibrium price of pollution allowances, the sum of the industrial sectors' excess supplies of pollution allowances is equal to zero.

3

The Government Sectors

Introduction

Each of the G1, G2, and G3 sectors provides three types of goods and services to their constituencies. In addition, they subsidize the renewable resource industry in their country not only for the purpose of maintaining a minimum inventory of that resource to support the basic fungible renewable resource but also for the purpose of aiding in the provision of general public services.

First, each government sector provides sanitation services by recycling or treating and storing waste generated by their household sector during the period. Since the amount of waste generated by the households during the current period is determined not only by their current mortality but also by their purchases of the country-specific renewable goods (R1, R2, or R3) and the consumption goods, C, during the period, and since their current purchases of R1, R2, R3, and C are influenced by the interest rates and exchange rates prevailing during the period, the actual level of household waste generated during the period is not determined until current interest rates and exchange rates are established. Therefore, at the beginning of the period, before interest rates and exchange rates are revealed, the government sectors must estimate the amount of waste they anticipate their respective household sectors will generate during the period and levy a tax (user fee) on their households to pay for the estimated level of sanitation services that will be required. For simplicity, the volume of waste recycled or treated and stored during the period is assumed to be jointly produced by the amount of waste currently generated by the households and by the transformation services provided by the amount of labor time the government sectors devote to sanitation during the period; the services of physical capital in the provision of sanitation services are ignored here.

Second, the government sectors provide general public services (other than the waste disposal and sanitation services mentioned above) to their households (a judicial system, police and fire protection, health care, parks, national defense, education, etc.) during the current period. The current levels of general public services were selected by the respective household sectors last period in light of the tax bill their corresponding government sectors stated last period would be necessary for them to collect this period in order to finance these current services. At the beginning of the current period, the households decide the level of general public services they desire for the next period based upon the present utility derived from these anticipated services and the taxes which their government sectors estimate will be necessary next period to finance them. Similar to the recycling and treatment and storage of household waste, these general public services promote the life expectancy of humans (i.e., reduce their mortality rate) as well as enhance household sector utility. The governments are assumed to require labor services and privately manufactured capital to provide these general public services.

Third, the government sector in each country provides an infrastructure (roads, power, airports, and seaports) that directly benefits (increases the productivity of) all the business sectors in its country. It differs from capital goods accumulation by a specific industry because the latter directly benefits only the productivity of that industry. The augmentation to the infrastructure during the period is chosen exogenously by the government sector in this model (presumably—but not explicitly modeled here—with input from the business sectors). The government chooses the minimum cost combination of inputs required to add to the infrastructure (a process that requires nonrenewable resources and the transformation services provided by current labor services). Additions to the infrastructure during the current period will not benefit the business sectors until next period.

Because the stock of the renewable resource in a country contributes to the ability of the basic fungible renewable resource, B, to assimilate pollution and to provide nutrients to the various renewable resources worldwide, each government subsidizes the renewable resource industry in their country for the purpose of maintaining the stock of its resource at or above an arbitrary minimum level. The level of general public services (parks and other environmental amenities) is also enhanced by the stock of the country-specific renewable resource. Of course, for the subsidies to be effective, they must exceed the revenues that the renewable resource industries could receive if they instead harvested and sold their minimum inventories.

As the current period opens in this model, then, each government sector faces five immediate tasks. First the government estimates the volume of waste that will be generated during the current period by its household sector and then estimates the cost of recycling or treating and storing that waste so that it can determine current fees (taxes) for sanitation services. Second, the government decides the amount of current labor services necessary to combine with the stock of physical capital it holds at the beginning of the period in order to provide the level of general public services its households decided last period that they wanted provided during the current period (and agreed to a current level of taxes for the expressed purpose of financing their provision).

Third, the government prepares a menu of alternative levels of general public services for next period accompanied by a specification of the corresponding minimum levels of personal taxes required next period to finance the provision of each alternative. (The personal taxes must cover as well the subsidy the government will pay its renewable resource industry next period.) Each government then presents the menu to its respective household sector so that it may select next period's provision of these general public services. Since the selection by the household sector occurs before current wage rates, interest rates, and exchange rates are revealed, each government sector will be free during the current period as these rates become known, to alter the combination of inputs (manufactured capital and labor) it intends to use next period to produce the level of general public services selected in this early step by the households. Therefore, it will be necessary to revisit each government sector later in the analysis in order to derive their effective end-of-period demands for physical capital and workers, which will become jointly determined with current interest rates and exchange rates.

The fourth immediate task of the government is to decide the amount to add to the country's infrastructure during the period and to announce to the business sectors the corporate taxes they will be required to pay this period to finance the addition. The additional corporate taxes will be set to cover the principal and interest on any debt the government sector may have outstanding at the beginning of the period associated with its infrastructure account. Because the selection of infrastructure augmentation occurs before exchange rates and the price of the nonrenewable resource are revealed, the government sectors may run surpluses or deficits on their infrastructure accounts during the current period.

Finally, the government sectors must decide the minimum levels of R1, R2, and R3 per capita that they will require their renewable resource industries to hold in reserve during the period as well as the subsidies the governments will pay their respective renewable resource industries for doing so.

G1 Sector's Initial Decisions

G1 Sector's Current-Period Waste Treatment and Storage

The household sector in Country One generates organic waste, OW^*H1, and inorganic waste, $\gamma \cdot CH1$, during the current period. The organic waste consists of human remains and human waste resulting from the consumption of the renewable resource. The G1 sector either recycles or treats and stores the total human waste generated during the period. Let α_1 represent the fraction of organic human waste recycled during the period and $(1 - \alpha_1)$ denote the fraction of organic human waste treated and stored during the period.

Let

$$W^*H1 = \text{total human waste generated during the current period}$$
$$= OW^*H1 + \gamma \cdot CH1.$$

The G1 sector hires labor services during the current period to recycle and to treat and store human waste. The current-period production function for these sanitation services is given by

$$W^*G1 = \min\left[W^*H1;\ y_{G1}\left(\beta_1 \cdot h_{G1t}^{W^*H1} \cdot N1_{G1t}\right)\right] \tag{3.1}$$

where

W^*G1 = the total amount of human waste recycled or treated and stored by Country One's government sector = W^*H1.

$\alpha_1 \cdot OW^*G1$ = the amount of organic human waste recycled as R1 during the period ($\alpha_1 \cdot W^*G1 < R1H1$) by G1.

$(1 - \alpha_1) \cdot OW^*G1 + \gamma \cdot CH1$ = the amount of human waste (organic and inorganic) treated and stored during the period by G1 (where it is assumed that $(1 - \alpha_1) \cdot OW^*G1 > \omega_{1t} \cdot \mu^*_{N1}\left[P^*_t, g_{H1t}, (\omega_{1t} - \omega_{I1t})^2\right] \cdot N1_t$).

$y_{G1}(\bullet)$ = sanitation services provided by labor in the G1 sector during the current period.

β_1 = the efficiency of labor in providing sanitation services. (This coefficient could be viewed as an increasing function of the general public services provided by the G1 sector last period.)

$h^{W^*H1}_{G1t}$ = the average number of hours the G1 sector's current employees are used for providing sanitation services for household waste during the current period.

$N1_{G1t}$ = the number of people in the H1 sector employed at the beginning of the current period by the G1 sector.

Assuming the G1 sector does not use more transformation services than is necessary to recycle/treat/store the anticipated waste generated by the households, the amount of labor used for waste abatement is found by setting the amount of waste mass to be abated, W^*H1, equal to the transformation services, $y_{G1}(\beta_1 \cdot h^{W^*H1}_{G1t} \cdot N1_{G1t})$, and solving for $h^{W^*H1}_{G1t} \cdot N1_{G1t}$:

$$h^{W^*H1}_{G1t} \cdot N1_{G1t} = h^{W^*H1}_{G1t} \cdot N1_{G1t}\big(\underset{+}{W^*H1}, \underset{-}{\beta_1}\big) \tag{3.2}$$

where

$$\frac{\partial\left(h^{W^*H1}_{G1t} \cdot N1_{G1t}\right)}{\partial(W^*H1)} = \frac{1}{\left\{\beta_1 \cdot \left[dy_{G1}/d\left(h^{W^*H1}_{G1t} \cdot N1_{G1t}\right)\right]\right\}} > 0$$

and

$$\frac{\partial\left(h^{W^*H1}_{G1t} \cdot N1_{G1t}\right)}{\partial\beta_1} = \frac{-h^{W^*H1}_{G1t} \cdot N1_{G1t}}{\beta_1} < 0.$$

See figure 3.1.

The amount the G1 sector spends recycling and treating and storing waste during the current period is equal to $W1_t \cdot h^{W^*H1}_{G1t} \cdot N1_{G1t}$. The government collects a waste sanitation tax (user charge), Tx_{W^*G1t}, from its household sector during the current period equal to the amount it anticipates it will spend on sanitation services during the current period:

$$Tx_{W^*G1t} = W1_t \cdot h^{W^*H1}_{G1t} \cdot N1_{G1t} \tag{3.3}$$

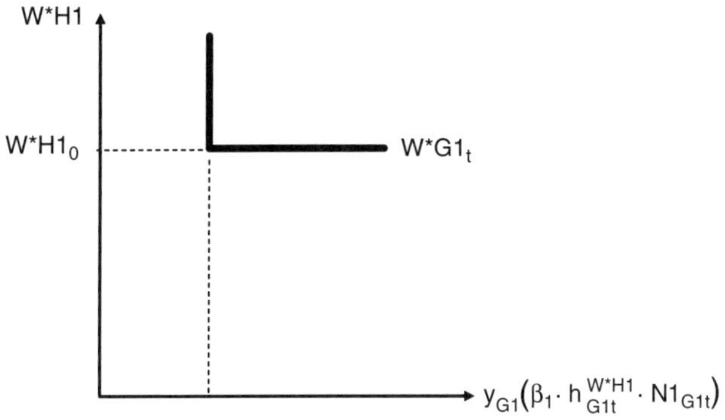

Figure 3.1 Current-Period Labor Services Used by G1 in Sanitation

This tax is in addition to the amounts discussed below. To the extent that government spending on sanitation, general public services, and infrastructure exceeds the tax revenue it collects during the period, the government borrows an amount equal to its current deficit in the country's bond market during the period.

G1 Sector's Current Production of General Public Services

The level of general public services to be provided to the household sector in Country One this period, g_{1H1t}, was decided by the H1 sector last period in light of the menu prepared for it by the G1 sector last period. The current-period production function for these services is given by (see figure 3.2):

$$g_{1H1t} = \min\left[g_{1H1}\left(h_{G1t}^{GH1} \cdot N1_{G1t}, K_{G1t}\right), \frac{\overline{R1}_t}{(\xi_{G1} \cdot N1_t)}\right] \quad (3.4)$$

where

g_{1H1t} = the level of general public services to be produced by the G1 sector during the current period.
h_{G1t}^{GH1} = the average number of hours the G1 sector decides to use its employees during the current period to provide general public services.
K_{G1t} = the (predetermined) amount of physical capital held by Country One's government sector at the beginning of the current period.
$\overline{R1}_t$ = the minimum inventory of the country-specific renewable resource that Country One's government sector requires the R1 industry to maintain during the period.
ξ_{G1} = the amount of $\overline{R1}_t$ per capita required per unit of general public services produced.

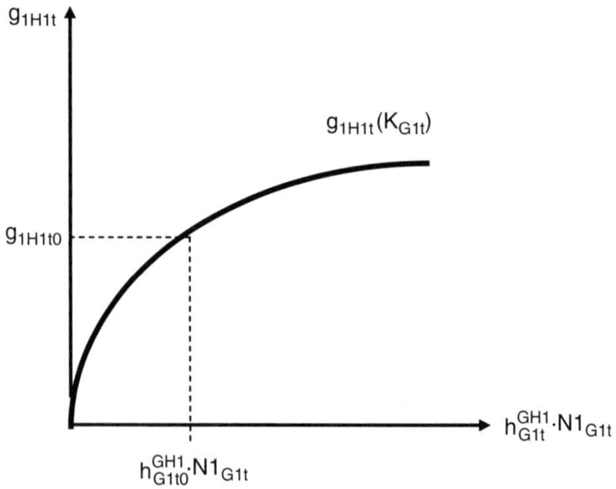

Figure 3.2 Current-Period Production of General Public Services

$\xi_{G1} \cdot N1_t$ = the amount of R1 required to provide a unit of general public services to the entire H1 sector during the current period.

$\overline{R1}_t/(\xi_{G1} \cdot N1_t)$ = the volume of general public services that $\overline{R1}_t$ can support during the period.

Therefore, the average number of hours this government requires its current employees to work in order to provide general public services is given by

$$h_{G1t}^{GH1} \cdot N1_{G1t} = h_{G1t}^{GH1} \cdot N1_{G1t}\underset{\quad\;\; + \qquad -}{\left(g_{1H1t}, K_{G1t}\right)} \tag{3.5}$$

where $\partial(h_{G1t}^{GH1} \cdot N1_{G1t})/\partial \cdot g_{1H1t} > 0$ and $\partial(h_{G1t}^{GH1} \cdot N1_{G1t})/\partial \cdot K_{G1t} < 0$. According to (3.5), the number of hours, $h_{G1t}^{GH1} \cdot N1_{G1t}$, that the G1 sector uses its current employees to produce the predetermined level of general public services, g_{1H1t}, increases with the volume of services to be provided but decreases with the amount of physical capital, K_{G1t}, the G1 sector holds at the beginning of the period.

Also, the amount of $\overline{R1}_t$ the G1 sector requires the R1 sector to maintain in inventory in order to support general public services, g_{1H1t}, is given by

$$\overline{R1}_t = g_{1H1t} \cdot N1_t \cdot \xi_{G1} \tag{3.6}$$

By assumption, the amount $\overline{R1}_t$ is also deemed sufficient to support the basic fungible renewable resource during the period.

Preparation of Next Period's Menu of General Public Services

Next period's production function of general public services is given by

$$g_{1H1t} = \min\left[g_{1H1}\left(h1 \cdot N1^{de}_{G1H1(t+1)}, K^{de}_{G1(t+1)}\right), \frac{\overline{R1}_{t+1}}{\left(\xi_{G1} \cdot N1^{e}_{t+1}\right)} \right] \tag{3.7}$$

with $g_{1H1}(\bullet)$ displaying positive, but diminishing, marginal products and zero cross-products.

$g_{1H1(t+1)}$ = the level of general public services to be produced by the G1 sector next period.
$h1$ = the "standard" average number of hours, which the government (and everyone else in Country One) expects this period that all employees will work next period.
$N1^{de}_{G1H1(t+1)}$ = the number of workers the government expects at the beginning of the current period (before it learns current product prices, wage rates, interest rates, and exchange rates) that it will employ by the beginning of next period to provide general public services. The government will be free during the current period to alter its demand for workers for next period as current product prices, wage rates, and interest rates become established.
$K^{de}_{G1(t+1)}$ = the amount of physical capital the G1 sector expects at the beginning of the current period (before it learns current product prices, wage rates, and interest rates) that it will hold by the beginning of next period to provide general public services. The G1 sector will be free during the current period to alter its demand for physical capital for next period as current product prices, wage rates, and interest rates become established.
$\xi_{G1} \cdot N1^{e}_{t+1}$ = the amount of R1 the G1 sector anticipates will be required to provide a unit of general public services to the entire H1 sector next period.

The G1 sector's current-period budget constraint for general public services is given by

$$\begin{aligned} p^{G1}_{B1} \cdot \left(B1^{se}_{G1(t+1)} - B1_{G1t}\right) = {} & W1_t \cdot h^{GH1}_{G1t} \cdot N1_{G1t} + \varepsilon^{G1} \cdot p^{G1}_{Kt} \\ & \cdot \left[K^{de}_{G1(t+1)} - (1-\delta) \cdot K_{G1t}\right] - \Pi^{CB1G1}_{t} \\ & + B1_{G1t} + p^{G1}_{xt} \cdot \overline{R1}_t - Tx_{G1H1t} \end{aligned} \tag{3.8}$$

where

p^{G1}_{B1} = the current-period price of Country One's bonds anticipated by the G1 sector at the beginning of the current period before current product prices, wages, and interest rates are established.
$B1^{se}_{G1(t+1)}$ = the number of bonds the G1 sector plans at the beginning of the current period (before current product prices, wages, and interest rates are established) to have outstanding by the end of the current period as a result of its current sanitation

and general public services activities during the current period. The government will be free during the current period to alter its end-of-period supply of G1 bonds as these prices and interest rates become known.

$B1_{G1t}$ = the (predetermined) number of bonds the G1 sector has outstanding at the beginning of the current period associated with earlier sanitation and general public services deficits.

$W1_t$ = the money wage rate announced last period by Country One's NR sector. This wage rate is paid to all workers employed during the current period in Country One.

ε^{G1} = the value of Country Two's unit of account in terms of Country One's unit of account that the G1 sector anticipates at the beginning of the current period will prevail during the period.

$\varepsilon^{G1} \cdot p_{Kt}^{G1}$ = the current-period price of capital goods (in terms of Country One's unit of account) anticipated by the G1 sector at the beginning of the current period, before the price (in terms of the second country's unit of account) is announced by the K sector and before current exchange rates are established.

Tx_{G1H1t} = the (predetermined) tax revenue the G1 sector collects during the current period associated with the general public services that the H1 sector elected last period to receive during the current period.

p_{xt}^{G1} = the current-period subsidy (expressed in terms of Country One's unit of account) for each unit of the renewable resource, R1, that the G1 sector pays the R1 industry during the period to withhold from harvest during the period.

Π_t^{CB1G1} = the revenue that the G1 sector anticipates receiving from its central bank during the current period.

δ = the rate of physical depreciation of capital.

According to (3.8), the G1 sector must plan to borrow in the first country's bond market during the current period the amount by which the sum of its current wage bill, expenditures upon physical capital during the current period, its current subsidy to the R1 industry, and its current interest expense exceeds the sum of its current tax revenue and its revenue from its central bank.

The personal tax revenue the G1 sector anticipates it will require next period to provide general public services is given by

$$Tx_{G1H1(t+1)} = W1_{t+1}^{G1} \cdot h1 \cdot N1_{G1H1(t+1)}^{de} + \left(1 + p_{B1}^{G1}\right) \cdot B1_{G1(t+1)}^{se} - (1-\delta) \cdot \varepsilon^{G1} \cdot p_{K(t+1)}^{G1} \cdot K_{G1(t+1)}^{de} - \Pi_{t+1}^{CB1G1} + p_{x(t+1)}^{G1} \cdot \overline{R1}_{t+1} \tag{3.9}$$

where

$Tx_{G1H1(t+1)}$ = the level of taxes to be collected by the G1 sector next period for general public services.

$W1_{t+1}^{G1}$ = the money wage rate the G1 sector anticipates its NR industry will announce this period. The wage rate set by that sector will be paid next period to all workers employed next period in Country One.

$\varepsilon^{G1} \cdot p^{G1}_{K(t+1)}$ = next period's price of capital goods (in terms of Country One's unit of account) anticipated by the G1 sector at the beginning of the current period.

Π^{CB1G1}_{t+1} = the revenue that the home country's government sector anticipates this period that it will receive from the home central bank next period.

$p^{G1}_{x(t+1)}$ = the per unit subsidy (expressed in terms of Country One's unit of account) that the G1 sector anticipates paying next period to the R1 industry for withholding the amount $\overline{R1}_{t+1}$ from harvest next period.

According to (3.9), the G1 sector plans during the current period that the level of taxes it collects next period will be sufficient to pay next period's anticipated wage bill, next period's subsidy to the R1 industry, and the principal and interest on any debt it plans to have outstanding by the end of the current period over and above the revenue it anticipates it will collect next period from the sale of its physical capital held at the beginning of that period net of depreciation, and net of the revenue it anticipates receiving next period from its central bank.

At this point, the objective of the G1 sector is to derive a menu for its household sector that minimizes the level of next period's taxes associated with each alternative level of general public services for next period. To derive this menu, the G1 sector minimizes (3.9) with respect to its end-of-period demand for employees, $N1^{de}_{G1H1(t+1)}$, and physical capital, $K^{de}_{G1(t+1)}$, for each alternative level of $g_{1H1(t+1)}$, subject to next period's production function for $g_{1H1(t+1)}$ and this period's budget constraint—conditions (3.7) and (3.8) respectively. Solving (3.8) for $B^{se}_{G1(t+1)}$ and substituting its expression into (3.9) reduces the minimization problem to

$$\begin{aligned} Tx_{G1H1(t+1)} &= W1^{G1}_{t+1} \cdot h1 \cdot N1^{de}_{G1H1(t+1)} + p^{G1}_{x(t+1)} \cdot \overline{R1}_{t+1} \\ &\quad - (1-\delta) \cdot \varepsilon^{G1} \cdot p^{G1}_{K(t+1)} \cdot K^{de}_{G1(t+1)} - \Pi^{CB1G1}_{t+1} \\ &\quad + \left[\frac{\left(1+p^{G1}_{b1}\right)}{p^{G1}_{b1}}\right] \cdot \Big\{W1_t \cdot h^{GH1}_{G1t} \cdot N1_{G1t} + \varepsilon^{G1} \cdot p^{G1}_{Kt} \\ &\quad \cdot \left[K^{de}_{G1(t+1)} - (1-\delta) \cdot K_{G1t}\right] - \Pi^{CB1G1}_{t} + B1_{G1t} + p^{G1}_{xt} \cdot \overline{R1}_t \\ &\quad - Tx_{G1H1t} + p^{G1}_{b1t} \cdot B1_{G1t} + W1_t \cdot h^{W^*H1}_{G1t} \cdot N1_{G1t} - Tx_{W^*G1t}\Big\} \\ &\quad + \lambda \cdot \Bigg\{g_{1H1(t+1)} - \min\Bigg[g_{1H1}\left(h1 \cdot N1^{de}_{G1H1(t+1)}, K^{de}_{G1(t+1)}\right), \\ &\quad \frac{\overline{R1}_{t+1}}{\left(\xi_{G1} \cdot N1^{e}_{t+1}\right)}\Bigg]\Bigg\} \end{aligned} \tag{3.10}$$

The first-order necessary conditions become:

$$W1^{G1}_{t+1} \cdot h1 - \lambda \cdot \left[\frac{\partial\left(g_{1H1}\right)}{\partial\left(h1 \cdot N1^{de}_{G1H1(t+1)}\right)}\right] \cdot h1 = 0 \tag{3.11}$$

$$\varepsilon^{G1} \cdot p_{Kt}^{G1} \cdot \left(r_1^{G1} + \delta - \pi_K^{G1}\right) - \lambda \cdot \left[\frac{\partial\left(g_{1H1}\right)}{\partial\left(K_{G1(t+1)}^{de}\right)}\right] = 0 \tag{3.12}$$

$$g_{1H1(t+1)} - \min\left[g_{1H1}\left(h1 \cdot N1_{G1H1(t+1)}^{de}, K_{G1(t+1)}^{de}\right), \frac{\overline{R1}_{t+1}}{\left(\xi_{G1} \cdot N1_{t+1}^{e}\right)}\right] = 0 \tag{3.13}$$

where$(1 + p_{b1}^{G1})/p_{b1}^{G1} = 1 + r_1^{G1}$ and $-(1-\delta)\cdot\varepsilon^{G1}\cdot p_{K(t+1)}^{G1} + (1+r_1)\cdot\varepsilon^{G1}\cdot p_{Kt}^{G1} = -(1-\delta)\cdot(1+\pi_K^{G1})\cdot\varepsilon^{G1}\cdot p_{Kt}^{G1} + (1+r_1)\cdot\varepsilon^{G1}\cdot p_{Kt}^{G1} \approx \varepsilon^{G1}\cdot p_{Kt}^{G1}\cdot(r_1^{G1} + \delta - \pi_K^{g1})$.

The symbol π_K^{G1} represents the G1 sector's anticipated rate of change in the price of K (in units of Country One's unit of account) between the current and next period; $\varepsilon^{G1} \cdot p_{Kt}^{G1} \cdot (r_1^{G1} + \delta - \pi_K^{G1})$ denotes the "user cost of capital." Together (3.11) and (3.12) yield the condition that the cost minimizing G1 sector combines labor and capital so that the technical rate of substitution of labor for capital (i.e., the absolute value of the amount by which physical capital may be changed [reduced]) without affecting the level of output if a unit of labor is added to production, $[\partial(g_{1H1})/\partial(h1 \cdot N1_{G1H1(t+1)}^{de})]/[\partial(g_{1H1})/\partial(K_{G1(t+1)}^{de})]$, is equal to the anticipated market rate of substitution, $W1_{t+1}^{G1}[\varepsilon^{G1} \cdot p_{Kt}^{G1} \cdot (r_1 + \delta - \pi_K^{G1})]$.

$$\frac{\left[\partial\left(g_{1H1}\right)/\partial\left(h1 \cdot N1_{G1H1(t+1)}^{de}\right)\right]}{\left[\partial\left(g_{1H1}\right)/\partial\left(K_{G1(t+1)}^{de}\right)\right]} = \frac{W1_{t+1}^{G1}}{\left[\varepsilon^{G1} \cdot p_{Kt}^{G1} \cdot \left(r_1 + \delta - \pi_K^{G1}\right)\right]} \tag{3.14}$$

Because the marginal products of both labor and capital are diminishing, an increase in $W1_{t+1}^{G1}$ causes the G1 sector to plan to use more capital and less labor than otherwise in the production of a given amount of $g_{1H1(t+1)}$; an increase in the user cost of capital elicits the opposite response. From (3.13), the G1 sector will add to both its labor and capital inputs as the level of $g_{1H1(t+1)}$ increases. Therefore the following notional (tentative) demand functions for labor and capital emerge associated with providing general public services next period:

$$N1_{G1H1(t+1)}^{de} = N1_{G1H1(t+1)}^{de} \cdot \left[\underset{+}{g_{1H1(t+1)}}, \underset{-}{W1_{t+1}^{G1}}, \underset{+}{\varepsilon^{G1} \cdot p_{Kt}^{G1} \cdot \left(r_1 + \delta - \pi_K^{G1}\right)}\right] \tag{3.15}$$

$$K1_{G1(t+1)}^{de} = K_{G1(t+1)}^{de}\left[\underset{+}{g_{1H1(t+1)}}, \underset{+}{W1_{t+1}^{G1}}, \underset{-}{\varepsilon^{G1} \cdot p_{Kt}^{G1} \cdot \left(r_1 + \delta - \pi_K^{G1}\right)}\right] \tag{3.16}$$

Substituting these demand functions back into (3.9), yields the necessary menu, expression (3.17), showing the minimum level of taxes the government anticipates it must collect next period from its household sector to provide each alternative level of

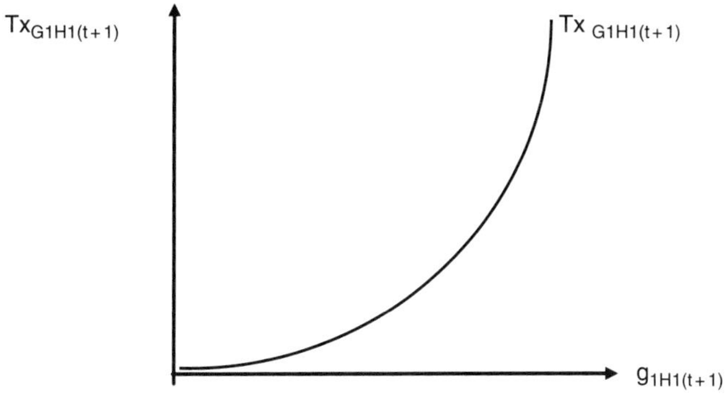

Figure 3.3 Next Period's Menu of General Public Services

general public services. See figure 3.3.

$$\begin{aligned}
Tx_{G1H1(t+1)} = {} & W1^{G1}_{t+1} \cdot h1 \cdot N1^{de}_{G1H1(t+1)} \Big[g_{1H1(t+1)}, W1^{G1}_{t+1}, \varepsilon^{G1} \cdot p^{G1}_{Kt} \\
& \cdot \left(r_1 + \delta - \pi^{G1}_K \right) \Big] + \varepsilon^{G1} \cdot p^{G1}_{Kt} \cdot \left(r_1 + \delta - \pi^{G1}_K \right) \cdot K^{de}_{G1(t+1)} \\
& \Big[g_{1H1(t+1)}, W1^{G1}_{t+1}, \varepsilon^{G1} \cdot p^{G1}_{Kt} \cdot \left(r_1 + \delta - \pi^{G1}_K \right) \Big] - \Pi^{CB1G1}_{t+1} \\
& + p^{G1}_{xt(t+1)} \cdot \overline{R1}_{t+1} + (1 + r_1) \Big[W1_t \cdot h^{GH1}_{G1t} \cdot N1_{G1t} \\
& - (1 - \delta) \cdot p^{G1}_{Kt} \cdot K_{G1t} - \Pi^{CB1G1}_{t+1} + B1_{G1t} + p^{G1}_{xt} \cdot \overline{R1}_t \\
& - Tx_{G1H1t} + p^{G1}_{b1} \cdot B1_{G1t} \Big] \qquad (3.17)
\end{aligned}$$

From (3.17), because the anticipated marginal products of both labor and capital diminish as the G1 sector contemplates adding to $g_{1H1(t+1)}$, the necessary marginal tax revenue increases with $g_{1H1(t+1)}$. The position of the tax menu rises with the anticipated wage rate, the anticipated user cost of capital, the G1 debt outstanding at the beginning of the period, and the current-period G1 deficit. The tax menu shifts vertically downward the greater the revenue it anticipates receiving next period from its own central bank net of the subsidy it plans to pay the R1 industry next period.

G1 Sector's Decision to Augment Country One's Infrastructure

As described above, the fourth immediate task of the government sector is to decide the amount to add to the country's infrastructure during the period and to announce to the business sectors the corporate taxes they will be required to pay next period to finance the addition.

Let

$I1_t$ = the infrastructure in Country One at the beginning of the current period.
$\Delta I1_t$ = the addition to the infrastructure produced by the G1 sector during the current period.
$NRG1^T$ = the amount of the processed/delivered nonrenewable natural resource the G1 sector buys during the current period.
p^{G1e}_{NRt} = the current-period price of the nonrenewable resource that the G1 sector anticipates at the beginning of the period will prevail during the current period.

The current-period production function for $\Delta I1_t$ is assumed to be given by

$$\Delta I1_t = \min\left[\frac{NRG1^T}{\iota, y^*\left(h^{\Delta I}_{G1t} \cdot N1_{G1t}\right)}\right] \tag{3.18}$$

where

ι = the amount (mass) of NR^T required to produce one unit of infrastructure during the current period.
$y^*(\bullet)$ = the services provided by labor and the existing infrastructure at the beginning of the period to transform NR^T into $\Delta I1_t$.
$h^{\Delta I}_{G1t}$ = the average number of hours the G1 sector uses its current employees to transform NR^T into a change in infrastructure during the current period.

Assuming the G1 sector wastes neither the nonrenewable resource nor labor services, the change in the infrastructure may be expressed as a function of current labor services:

$$\Delta I1_t = y^*\left(h^{\Delta I}_{G1t} \cdot N1_{G1t}\right) \tag{3.19}$$

and the amount of the nonrenewable resource the G1 sector uses in the transformation process is given by

$$NRG1^T = \iota \cdot \Delta I1_t \tag{3.20}$$

From (3.20), once the G1 sector decides $\Delta I1_t$, the necessary labor services are given by

$$h^{\Delta I}_{G1t} \cdot N1_{G1t} = h^{\Delta I}_{G1t} \cdot N1_{G1t} \cdot \underset{+}{(\Delta I1_t)} \tag{3.21}$$

where $d\left(h^{\Delta I}_{G1t} \cdot N1_{G1t}\right)/d \cdot (\Delta I1_t) = 1/\left[dy^*/d\left(h^{\Delta I}_{G1t} \cdot N1_{G1t}\right)\right] > 0$.

The current level of corporate taxes will be set to cover the principal and interest on the amount of debt the government has outstanding at the beginning of the period associated with its infrastructure operations.

Let

Tx_{G1I1t} = the level of corporate taxes the G1 sector announces at the beginning of the current period = $Tx_{R1t} + Tx_{NRt}$.

The cost minimizing G1 sector then selects the level of Tx_{G1I1} necessary to finance its employment of current labor services and the purchase of NR^T that will enable it to produce the predetermined change in infrastructure, $\Delta I1_t$:

$$Tx_{G1It} = \left(p_{B1t}^{G1} + 1\right) \cdot B1_{G1I1t} + W1_t \cdot h_{G1t}^{\Delta I} \cdot N1_{G1t}(\Delta I1_t) + p_{NRt}^{G1e} \cdot NRG1^T \tag{3.22}$$

In addition to the current wage expense and the anticipated expenditure on NR^T during the period, current corporate taxes cover any principal plus interest the G1 sector (re)pays associated with any deficit the sector incurred last period as it augmented the country's infrastructure last period. The potential for a deficit (or surplus) exists in the current period as well because the G1 sector decides upon the current amount of the NR^T input it will use this period prior to learning the actual market price for that input, which has not yet been announced by the NR sector.

G2 Sector's Initial Decisions

G2 Sector's Current-Period Waste Treatment and Storage

In a manner analogous to the corresponding derivation for the G1 sector's demand for sanitation labor services, the G2 sector's notional demand for labor services for the current period for the purpose of recycling or treating and storing waste is given by

$$h_{G2t}^{W^*H2} \cdot N2_{G2t} = h_{G2t}^{W^*H2} \cdot N2_{G2t}\left(\underset{+}{W^*H2}, \underset{-}{\beta_2}\right) \tag{3.23}$$

where

$$\frac{\partial\left(h_{G2t}^{W^*H2} \cdot N2_{G2t}\right)}{\partial\,(W^*H2)} = \frac{1}{\left\{\beta_2 \cdot \left[\dfrac{dy_{G2}}{d\left(h_{G2t}^{W^*H2} \cdot N2_{G2t}\right)}\right]\right\}} > 0$$

and

$$\frac{\partial\left(h_{G2t}^{W^*H2} \cdot N2_{G2t}\right)}{\partial\beta_2} = \frac{-h_{G2t}^{W^*H2} \cdot N2_{G2t}}{\beta_2} < 0.$$

W^*H2 = total human waste generated during the current period.

W^*G2 = the total amount of human waste recycled or treated and stored by Country Two's government sector ($= W^*H2$).

$\alpha_2 \cdot OW^*H2$ = the amount of organic human waste recycled as R2 during the period ($\alpha_2 \cdot OW^*H2 < R2H2$) by G2.

$(1-\alpha_2)\cdot OW^*H2+\gamma\cdot CH2$ = the amount of human waste (organic and inorganic) treated and stored during the period by G2 (where it is assumed that $(1-\alpha_2)\cdot OW^*H2 > \omega_{2t}\cdot \mu^*_{N2}[P^*_t, g_{H2t}, (\omega_{2t}-\omega_{I2t})^2]\cdot N2_t$).

$y_{G2}(\bullet)$ = waste abatement services provided by labor.

β_2 = the efficiency of labor in providing sanitation services. (This coefficient may be viewed as an increasing function of the general public services provided by the G2 sector last period.)

$h^{W^*H2}_{G2t}$ = the average number of hours the G2 sector's current employees are used to sanitize household waste during the current period.

$N2_{G2t}$ = the number of people in the H2 sector employed by G2 at the beginning of the period.

The amount the G2 sector spends recycling and treating and storing waste during the current period is equal to $W2_t \cdot h^{W^*H2}_{G2t} \cdot N2_{G2t}$. The government collects a waste sanitation tax (user charge) from its household sector during the current period equal to the amount it anticipates it will spend on sanitation services during the current period:

$$Tx_{W^*G2t} = W2_t \cdot h^{W^*H2}_{G2t} \cdot N2_{G2t} \tag{3.24}$$

This tax is in addition to the amounts discussed below. To the extent that government spending on sanitation, general public services, and infrastructure exceeds the tax revenue it collects during the period, the government borrows an amount equal to its current deficit in the country's bond market during the period.

G2 Sector's Current Production of General Public Services

Similar to the derivation of the G1 sector's demand for labor for providing general public services, the number of hours the G2 sector requires its current employees to work in order to provide general public services is given by

$$h^{GH2}_{G2t} \cdot N2_{G2t} = h^{GH2}_{G2t} \cdot N2_{G2t}\left(\underset{+}{g_{2H2t}}, \underset{-}{K_{G2t}}\right) \tag{3.25}$$

where

$$\frac{\partial\left(h^{GH2}_{G2t} \cdot N2_{G2t}\right)}{\partial g_{2H2t}} > 0$$

and

$$\frac{\partial\left(h^{GH2}_{G2t} \cdot N2_{G2t}\right)}{\partial K_{G2t}} < 0.$$

According to (3.25), the number of hours, $h^{GH2}_{G2t} \cdot N2_{G2t}$ that the government uses its current employees to produce the predetermined amount of general public services, g_{2H2t}, increases with the volume of services to be provided but decreases with the amount of physical capital, K_{G2t}, the sector holds at the beginning of the period.

Also, the amount of $\overline{R2}_t$ the G2 sector requires the R2 sector to maintain in inventory in order to provide general public services, g_{2H2t}, is given by

$$\overline{R2}_t = g_{2H2t} \cdot N2_t \cdot \xi_{G2} \tag{3.26}$$

where

g_{2H2t} = the level of general public services to be produced by the G2 sector during the current period.
$N2_t$ = the population of Country Two at the beginning of the current period.
K_{G2t} = the (predetermined) amount of physical capital held by Country Two's government sector at the beginning of the current period devoted to general public services.
$\overline{R2}_t$ = the minimum inventory of the country-specific renewable resource that Country Two's government sector requires the R2 industry to maintain during the period.
ξ_{G2} = the amount of $\overline{R2}_t$ per capita required per unit of general public services produced.
$\xi_{G2} \cdot N2_t$ = the amount of R2 required to provide a unit of general public services to the entire H2 sector during the current period.
$\overline{R2}_t/(\xi_{G2} \cdot N2_t)$ = the volume of other (nonsanitation) general public services that $\overline{R2}_t$ can support during the period.

G2 Sector's Preparation of Next Period's Menu of General Public Services

In accordance with the analysis provided for the corresponding menu preparation by the G1 sector, the minimum level of taxes the G2 sector anticipates it must collect next period from the household sector to provide each alternative level of general public services.

$$\begin{aligned} Tx_{G2H2(t+1)} = {} & W2^{G1}_{t+1} \cdot h2 \cdot N2^{de}_{G2H2(t+1)} \Big[g_{2H2(t+1)}, W2^{G1}_{t+1}, p^{G1}_{Kt} \\ & \cdot \left(r_2 + \delta - \pi^{G2}_K\right)\Big] + p^{G2}_{Kt} \cdot \left(r_2 + \delta - \pi^{G2}_K\right) \cdot K^{de}_{G2(t+1)} \\ & \Big[g_{2H2(t+1)}, W2^{G2}_{t+1}, p^{G2}_{Kt} \cdot \left(r_2 + \delta - \pi^{G2}_K\right)\Big] - \Pi^{CB2G2}_{t+1} \\ & + p^{G2}_{x(t+1)} \cdot \overline{R2}_{t+1} + (1 + r_2)\Big[W2_t \cdot h^{GH2}_{G2t} \cdot N1_{G2t} \end{aligned}$$

$$- (1 - \delta) \cdot p_{Kt}^{G2} \cdot K_{G2t} - \Pi_{t+1}^{CB2G2} + B2_{G2t} + p_{xt}^{G2} \cdot \overline{R2}_t$$
$$-Tx_{G2H2t} + p_{B2t}^{G2} \cdot B2_{G2t}\Big] \qquad (3.27)$$

where $(1 + p_{B2}^{G2})/p_{B2}^{G2} = 1 + r_2^{G2}$. The symbol π_K^{g2} represents the G2 sector's anticipated rate of change in the price of K (in units of Country Two's unit of account) between the current and next period; $p_{Kt}^{G2} \cdot (r_2^{G2} + \delta - \pi_K^{g2})$ denotes the corresponding "user cost of capital." The symbols found in (3.27) are defined as follows:

$g_{2H2(t+1)}$ = the level of general public services to be produced by the G2 sector next period.

h2 = the "standard" average number of hours, which the government expects this period that its employees will work next period. In fact we assume that every sector expects that all employees will work the standard number of hours next period.

$N2_{G2H2(t+1)}^{de}$ = the number of workers the government expects at the beginning of the current period (before it learns current product prices, wage rates, interest rates, and exchange rates) that it will employ by the beginning of next period to provide general public services. The government will be free during the current period to alter its demand for workers for next period as current product prices, wage rates, and interest rates become established.

$K_{G2(t+1)}^{de}$ = the amount of physical capital the G2 sector expects at the beginning of the current period (before it learns current product prices, wage rates, and interest rates) that it will hold by the beginning of next period to provide general public services. The G2 sector will be free during the current period to alter its demand for physical capital for next period as current product prices, wage rates, and interest rates become established.

$\xi_{G2} \cdot N2_{t+1}^{e}$ = the amount of R2 the G2 sector anticipates will be required to provide a unit of general public services to the entire H2 sector next period.

p_{B2}^{G2} = the current-period price of Country Two's bonds anticipated by the G2 sector at the beginning of the current period before current product prices, wages, and interest rates are established.

$B2_{G2(t+1)}^{se}$ = the number of bonds the G2 sector plans at the beginning of the current period (before current product prices, wages, and interest rates are established) to have outstanding by the end of the current period as a result of its current waste abatement and general public services activities during the current period. The government will be free during the current period to alter its end-of-period supply of G2 bonds as these prices and interest rates become known.

$B2_{G2t}$ = the (predetermined) number of bonds the G2 sector has outstanding at the beginning of the current period associated with earlier waste abatement and general public services deficits.

$W2_t$ = the money wage rate announced last period by Country Two's Q sector. This wage rate is paid during the current period to all workers employed during the current period in Country Two.

p_{Kt}^{G2} = the current-period price of capital goods (in terms of Country Two's unit of account) anticipated by the G2 sector at the beginning of the current period, before the price (in terms of the second country's unit of account) is announced by the Q sector.

Tx_{G2H2t} = the (predetermined) tax revenue the G2 sector collects during the current period associated with general public services the H2 sector elected last period to receive during the current period.

p_{xt}^{G2} = the current-period subsidy (expressed in terms of Country Two's unit of account) for each unit of the renewable resource, R2, that the G2 sector pays the R2 industry during the period to withhold from harvest during the period.

Π_t^{CB2G2} = the revenue the G2 sector anticipates receiving from its central bank during the current period.

$Tx_{G2H2(t+1)}$ = the level of taxes to be collected by the G2 sector next period for general public services

$W2_{t+1}^{G2}$ = the money wage rate the G2 sector anticipates its capital goods industry will announce this period. The wage rate set by that sector will be paid next period to all workers employed next period in Country Two.

$p_{K(t+1)}^{G2}$ = next period's price of capital goods (in terms of Country Two's unit of account) anticipated by the G2 sector at the beginning of the current period.

Π_{t+1}^{CB2G2} = the revenue that the second country's government sector anticipates this period that it will receive from its central bank next period.

$p_{x(t+1)}^{G2}$ = the per unit subsidy (expressed in terms of Country Two's unit of account) that the G2 sector anticipates paying next period to the R2 industry for withholding the amount $\overline{R}\,\overline{2}_{t+1}$ from harvest next period.

G2 Sector's Decision to Augment Country Two's Infrastructure

In a manner analogous to the analysis of the G1 sector's decision to augment its country's infrastructure, the G2 sector arbitrarily decides upon $\Delta I2_t$ as the current change in the country's infrastructure. The necessary labor services are given by

$$h_{G2t}^{\Delta I} \cdot N2_{G2t} = h_{G2t}^{\Delta I} \cdot N2_{G1t}\underset{+}{(\Delta I2_t)} \tag{3.28}$$

where

$$d\left(h_{G2t}^{\Delta I} \cdot N2_{G2t}\right)/d\left(\Delta I2_t\right) = 1/\left[dy^*/d\left(h_{G2t}^{\Delta I} \cdot N2_{G1t}\right)\right] > 0.$$

ι = the amount (mass) of NR^T required to produce one unit of infrastructure during the current period.

$y^*(\bullet)$ = the services provided by labor and the existing infrastructure at the beginning of the period to transform NR into $\Delta I2_t$.

$h_{G2t}^{\Delta I}$ = the average number of hours the G2 sector uses its current employees to transform NR into a change in infrastructure during the current period.

$\Delta I2_t$ = the addition to the infrastructure produced by the G2 sector during the current period.

$NRG2^{T}$ = the amount of the transformed nonrenewable resource the G2 sector buys during the current period.
p_{NRt}^{G2} = the current-period price of the nonrenewable resource that the G2 sector anticipates at the beginning of the period will prevail during the current period (in terms of Country One's unit of account).
$(1/\varepsilon)^{G2}$ = the value of Country One's unit of account in terms of Country Two's unit of account anticipated by the G2 sector at the beginning of the current period.

The amount of the nonrenewable resource the G2 sector uses in the transformation process is given by

$$NRG2_{t}^{Td} = \iota \cdot \Delta I2t \tag{3.29}$$

The current level of corporate taxes will be set to cover the principal and interest on the amount of debt the government has outstanding at the beginning of the period associated with its infrastructure operations.

Let

Tx_{G2I2t} = the level of corporate taxes the G2 sector announces at the beginning of the current period = $Tx_{R2t} + Tx_{Kt}$.

The cost minimizing G2 sector then selects the level of Tx_{G2I2} necessary to finance its employment of current labor services and the purchase of NR that will enable it to produce the predetermined change in infrastructure, $\Delta I2_t$:

$$\begin{aligned} Tx_{G2I2t} = {} & \left(p_{B2(t+1)}^{G2} + 1\right) \cdot B2_{G2I2t} + W2_t \cdot h_{G2t}^{\Delta I} \cdot N_{G2t}(\Delta I2_t) \\ & + \left[\frac{(p_{NRt}^{G2})}{\varepsilon^{G2}}\right] \cdot \iota \cdot \Delta I2_t \end{aligned} \tag{3.30}$$

G3 Sector's Initial Decisions

G3 Sector's Current-Period Waste Treatment and Storage

In a manner analogous to the corresponding derivation for the G1 sector's demand for sanitation labor services, the G3 sector's notional demand for labor services for the current period for the purpose of recycling or treating and storing waste is given by

$$h_{G3t}^{W^*H3} \cdot N3_{G3t} = h_{G3t}^{W^*H3} \cdot N3_{G3t}\underset{\quad +\quad\ -}{(W^*H3,\ \beta_3)} \tag{3.31}$$

where

$$\frac{\partial\left(h_{G3t}^{W^*H3}\cdot N3_{G3t}\right)}{\partial(W^*H3)}=\frac{1}{\left\{\beta_3\cdot\left[\frac{dy_{G3}}{d\left(h_{G3t}^{W^*H3}\cdot N3_{G3t}\right)}\right]\right\}}>0$$

and

$$\frac{\partial\left(h_{G3t}^{W^*H3}\cdot N3_{G3t}\right)}{\partial\beta_3}=\frac{-h_{G3t}^{W^*H3}\cdot N3_{G3t}}{\beta_3}<0.$$

And where

W^*H3 = total human waste generated during the current period.
W^*G3 = the total amount of human waste recycled or treated and stored by Country Three's government sector ($= W^*H3$).
$\alpha_3 \cdot W^*H3$ = the amount of organic human waste recycled as R3 during the period ($\alpha_3 \cdot W^*H3 < R3H3$) by G3.
$(1-\alpha_3)\cdot OW^*H3+\gamma\cdot CH3(1-\alpha_3)\cdot OW^*H3+\gamma\cdot CH3$ = the amount of human waste (organic and inorganic) treated and stored during the period by G3 (where it is assumed that $(1-\alpha_3)\cdot OW^*H3 > \omega_{3t}\cdot\mu^*_{N3}[P^*_t, g_{H3t}, (\omega_{3t}-\omega_{I3t})^2]\cdot N3_t$).
$y_{G3}(\bullet)$ = waste abatement services provided by labor.
β_3 = the efficiency of labor in providing sanitation services. (This coefficient may be viewed as an increasing function of the general public services provided by the G3 sector last period.)
$h_{G3t}^{W^*H3}$ = the average number of hours the G3 sector's current employees are used to sanitize household waste during the current period.
$N3_{G3t}$ = the number of people employed by Country Three at the beginning of the period.

The amount the G3 sector spends recycling and treating and storing waste during the current period is equal to $W3_t\cdot h_{G3t}^{W^*H3}\cdot N3_{G3t}$. The government collects a waste sanitation tax (user charge) from its household sector during the current period equal to the amount it anticipates it will spend on sanitation services during the current period:

$$Tx_{W^*G3t}=W3_t\cdot h_{G3t}^{W^*H3}\cdot N3_{G3t} \tag{3.32}$$

This tax is in addition to the amounts discussed below. To the extent that government spending on sanitation, general public services, and infrastructure exceeds the tax revenue it collects during the period, the government borrows an amount equal to its current deficit in the country's bond market during the period.

G3 Sector's Current Production of General Public Services

Similar to the derivation of the G1 sector's demand for labor for providing general public services, the average number of hours the G3 sector requires its current employees to work in order to provide general public services is given by

$$h_{G3t}^{GH3} \cdot N3_{G3t} = h_{G3t}^{GH3} \cdot N3_{G3t}\left(\underset{+}{g_{3H3t}}, \underset{-}{K_{G3t}}\right) \tag{3.33}$$

where

$$\frac{\partial\left(h_{G3t}^{GH3} \cdot N3_{G3t}\right)}{\partial\, g_{3H3t}} > 0$$

and

$$\frac{\partial\left(h_{G3t}^{GH3} \cdot N3_{G3t}\right)}{\partial K_{G3t}} < 0.$$

According to (3.33), the number of hours, $h_{G3t}^{GH3} \cdot N3_{G3t}$, that the government uses its current employees to produce the predetermined amount of general public services, g_{3H3t}, increases with the volume of services to be provided but decreases with the amount of physical capital, K_{G3t}, the sector holds at the beginning of the period.

Also, the amount of $\overline{R3}_t$ the G3 sector requires the R3 sector to maintain in inventory in order to provide general public services, g_{3H3t}, is given by

$$\overline{R3}_t = g_{3H3t} \cdot N3_t \cdot \xi_{G3} \tag{3.34}$$

where

g_{3H3t} = the level of general public services to be produced by the G3 sector during the current period.

$h_{G3t}^{GH3} \cdot N3_{G3t}$ = the number of hours the G3 sector decides to use its employees during the current period to provide general public services.

K_{G3t} = the (predetermined) amount of physical capital held by Country Three's government sector at the beginning of the current period devoted to general public services.

$\overline{R3}_t$ = the minimum inventory of the country-specific renewable resource that Country Three's government sector requires the R3 industry to maintain during the period.

ξ_{G3} = the amount of $\overline{R3}_t$ per capita required per unit of general public services produced.

$\xi_{G3} \cdot N3_t$ = the amount of R3 required to provide a unit of general public services to the entire H3 sector during the current period.

$\overline{R3}_t/(\xi_{G3} \cdot N3_t)$ = the volume of other (nonsanitation) general public services that $\overline{R3}_t$ can support during the period.

G3 Sector's Preparation of Next Period's Menu of General Public Services

In accordance with the analysis provided for the corresponding menu preparation by the G1 sector, the minimum level of taxes the G3 sector anticipates it must collect next period from the household sector to provide each alternative level of general public services.

$$
\begin{aligned}
Tx_{G3H3(t+1)} = {} & W3^{G3}_{t+1} \cdot h3 \cdot N3^{de}_{G3H3(t+1)} \Bigg\{ g_{3H3(t+1)}, W3^{G3}_{t+1}, \\
& \left[p^{G3}_{K1} \cdot \left(\frac{\varepsilon}{\tilde{\varepsilon}} \right)^{G3} \right] \cdot \left(r_3 + \delta - \pi^{G3}_{K} \right) \Bigg\} \\
& + \left[p^{G3}_{Kt} \cdot \left(\frac{\varepsilon}{\tilde{\varepsilon}} \right)^{G3} \right] \cdot \left(r_3 + \delta - \pi^{G3}_{K} \right) \cdot K^{de}_{G3(t+1)} \\
& \Bigg\{ g_{3H3(t+1)}, W3^{G3}_{t+1}, \left[p^{G3}_{Kt} \cdot \left(\frac{\varepsilon}{\tilde{\varepsilon}} \right)^{G3} \right] \cdot \left(r_3 + \delta - \pi^{G3}_{K} \right) \Bigg\} \\
& - \Pi^{CB3G3}_{t+1} + p^{G3}_{x(t+1)} \cdot \overline{R3}_{t+1} + (1 + r_3) \Big\{ W3_t \cdot h^{GH3}_{G3t} \cdot N3_{G3t} \\
& - (1 - \delta) \cdot \left[p^{G3}_{Kt} \cdot \left(\frac{\varepsilon}{\varepsilon^*} \right)^{G3} \right] \cdot K_{G3t} - \Pi^{CB3G3}_{t} \\
& + B3_{G3t} + p^{G3}_{xt} \cdot \overline{R3}_t - Tx_{G3H3t} + p^{G3}_{B3} \cdot B3_{G3t} \Big\} \qquad (3.35)
\end{aligned}
$$

where

$g_{3H3(t+1)}$ = the level of general public services to be produced by the G3 sector next period.

$h3$ = the "standard" average number of hours, which the government expects this period that its employees will work next period. In fact we assume that every sector expects that all employees will work the standard number of hours next period.

$N3^{de}_{G3H3(t+1)}$ = the number of workers the government expects at the beginning of the current period (before it learns current product prices, wage rates, interest rates, or exchange rates) that it will employ by the beginning of next period to provide general public services. The government will be free during the current period to alter its demand for workers for next period as current product prices, wage rates, and interest rates become established.

$K^{de}_{G3(t+1)}$ = the amount of physical capital the G3 sector expects at the beginning of the current period (before it learns current product prices, wage rates, and interest rates) that it will hold by the beginning of next period to provide general public services. The G3 sector will be free during the current period to alter its demand for physical capital for next period as current product prices, wage rates, and interest rates become established.

$\xi_{G3} \cdot N3^{e}_{t+1}$ = the amount of R3 the G3 sector anticipates will be required to provide a unit of general public services to the entire H3 sector next period.

p^{G3}_{B3} = the current-period price of Country Three's bonds anticipated by the G3 sector at the beginning of the current period before current product prices, wages, and interest rates are established.

$B3^{se}_{G3(t+1)}$ = the number of bonds the G3 sector plans at the beginning of the current period (before current product prices, wages, and interest rates are established) to have outstanding by the end of the current period as a result of its current waste abatement and general public services activities during the current period. The government will be free during the current period to alter its end-of-period supply of G3 bonds as these prices and interest rates become known.

$B3_{G3t}$ = the (predetermined) number of bonds the G3 sector has outstanding at the beginning of the current period associated with earlier waste abatement and general public services deficits.

$W3_t$ = the money wage rate announced last period by Country Three's C sector. This wage rate is paid during the current period to all workers employed during the current period in Country Three.

p^{G3}_{Kt} = the current-period price of capital goods (in terms of Country Two's unit of account) anticipated by the G3 sector at the beginning of the current period, before the price (in terms of the second country's unit of account) is announced by the K sector.

$(\varepsilon/\tilde{\varepsilon})^{G3}$ = the G3 sector's anticipated value of Country Two's unit of account in terms of Country Three's unit of account, where ε denotes the value of Country Two's unit of account in terms of Country One's unit of account and ε^* represents the value of Country Three's unit of account in terms of Country One's unit of account.

Tx_{G3H3t} = the (predetermined) tax revenue the G3 sector collects during the current period associated with general public services the H3 sector elected last period to receive during the current period.

p^{G3}_{xt} = the current-period subsidy (expressed in terms of Country Three's unit of account) for each unit of the renewable resource, R3, that the G3 sector pays the R3 industry during the period to withhold from harvest during the period.

Π^{CB3G3}_{t} = the revenue the G3 sector anticipates receiving from its central bank during the current period.

$Tx_{G3H3(t+1)}$ = the level of taxes to be collected by the G3 sector next period for general public services.

$W3^{G3}_{t+1}$ = the money wage rate the G3 sector anticipates its Q industry will announce this period. The wage rate set by that sector will be paid next period to all workers employed next period in Country Three.

$p^{G3}_{K(t+1)}$ = next period's price of capital goods (in terms of Country Two's unit of account) anticipated by the G3 sector at the beginning of the current period.

Π^{CB3G3}_{t+1} = the revenue that the second country's government sector anticipates this period that it will receive from the home central bank next period.

$p^{G3}_{x(t+1)}$ = the per unit subsidy (expressed in terms of Country Three's unit of account) that the G3 sector anticipates paying next period to the R3 industry for withholding the amount $\overline{R3}_{t+1}$ from harvest next period.

where $(1 + p^{G3}_{B3})/p^{G3}_{B3} = 1 + r^{G3}_{3}$.

The symbol π_K^{G3} represents the G3 sector's anticipated rate of change in the price of K (in units of Country Three's unit of account) between the current and next period; $[p_{xt}^{G3} \cdot (\varepsilon/\tilde{\varepsilon})^{G3}] \cdot (r3^{G3} + \delta - \pi_K^{G3})$ denotes the corresponding "user cost of capital."

G3 Sector's Decision to Augment Country Three's Infrastructure

In a manner analogous to the analysis of the G1 sector's decision to augment its country's infrastructure, the G3 sector arbitrarily decides upon $\Delta I3_t$ as current change in the country's infrastructure. The necessary labor services are given by

$$h_{G3t}^{\Delta I} \cdot N3_{G3t} = h_{G3t}^{\Delta I} \cdot N3_{G3t}\underset{+}{(\Delta I3_t)} \qquad (3.36)$$

where

$$\frac{d\left(h_{G3t}^{\Delta I} \cdot N3_{G3t}\right)}{d\left(\Delta I3_t\right)} = \frac{1}{\left[dy^*/d\left(h_{G3t}^{\Delta I} \cdot N3_{G3t}\right)\right]} > 0.$$

ι = the amount (mass) of NR^T required to produce one unit of infrastructure during the current period.

$y^*(\bullet)$ = the services provided by labor and the existing infrastructure at the beginning of the period to transform NR into $\Delta I3_t$.

$h_{G3t}^{\Delta I}$ = the average number of hours the G3 sector uses its current employees to transform NR into a change in infrastructure during the current period.

$\Delta I3_t$ = the addition to the infrastructure produced by the G3 sector during the current period.

$NRG3^T$ = the amount of the transformed nonrenewable resource the G3 sector buys during the current period.

p_{NRt}^{G3} = the current-period price of the nonrenewable resource that the G3 sector anticipates at the beginning of the period will prevail during the current period (in terms of Country One's unit of account).

$(1/\tilde{\varepsilon})^{G3}$ = the value of Country One's unit of account in terms of Country Three's unit of account anticipated by the G3 sector at the beginning of the current period.

The amount of the nonrenewable resource the G3 sector uses in the transformation process is given by

$$NRG3_t^{Td} = \iota \cdot \Delta I3_t \qquad (3.37)$$

The current level of corporate taxes will be set to cover the principal and interest on the amount of debt the government has outstanding at the beginning of the period associated with its infrastructure operations.

Let

Tx_{G3I3t} = the level of corporate taxes the G3 sector announces at the beginning of the current period = $Tx_{Ct} + Tx_{R3t}$.

The cost minimizing G3 sector then selects the level of Tx_{G3I3} necessary to finance its employment of current labor services and the purchase of NR that will enable it to produce the predetermined change in infrastructure, $\Delta I3_t$:

$$Tx_{G3I3t} = \left(p^{G3}_{B3(t+1)} + 1\right) \cdot B3_{G3I3t} + W3_t \cdot h^{\Delta I}_{G3t} \cdot N3_{G3t}\,(\Delta I3_t) + \left[\frac{\left(p^{G3}_{NRt}\right)}{(\tilde{\varepsilon})^{G3}}\right] \cdot \iota \cdot \Delta I3_t \qquad (3.38)$$

Chapter 4 contains an analysis of the household sectors' initial decisions.

4

The Household Sectors' Initial Choices

Introduction

The household sectors face a wide variety of choices in this model. They select their consumption of the nontraded renewable resource produced in their country (R1, R2, or R3), their consumption of the consumer goods, C, produced in Country Three, their supply of labor to their country's labor market, the number of childbirths in their country, the level of general (nonsanitation) public services (and the corresponding level of personal taxes) to be provided by their country's government sector next period, and their current saving. Each household sector must also decide its planned holdings of money and bonds for the end of the period. These portfolio decisions must conform to the sector's planned saving during the period. In particular, with all assets and liabilities measured in current-period prices, the net value of the planned accumulations or decumulations of money and bonds during the period must equal the sector's planned nominal saving during the period.

To simplify the analysis, each household sector's decisions are divided into two parts with the less flexible decisions being made first. The first set of decisions is made before current wages, prices, interest rates, and exchange rates are known; the second set is made once current wages and prices have been announced.

H1 Sector's Initial Set of Decisions

The first set of effective decisions facing the H1 sector at the beginning of the period encompass (1) the level of general public services the sector will instruct the G1 sector to provide next period, $g_{1H1(t+1)}$, given the associated level of taxes necessary to receive them, $Tx_{G1H1(t+1)}$; and (2) the number of births in the H1 sector during the current period, $\eta 1$. Although the H1 sector's anticipated current and future consumption of consumer goods, namely CH1, and the country-specific renewable resource, R1H1, and its anticipated supply of labor are mutually determined with the decisions to be made in the first step, these notional demands for consumption and this notional supply of labor do not necessarily reflect effective decisions. The H1 sector will be able to change its demands for current and future goods and its supply of labor once current product prices and wages are actually announced. Only after product prices and wages are announced will the H1 sector then decide its effective levels of current consumption, saving, and supply of labor. The H1 sector's effective consumption demand, ex ante saving, labor supply, and end-of-period demands for financial assets become mutually determined with current interest rates and exchange rates.

The objective of the household sector is to maximize present utility, that is, the felicity the household sector experiences at the beginning of the current period in light of its plans for (1) current and future consumption of both R1 and C; (2) current and future sanitation and general public services; (3) leisure; and (4) births, $\eta 1$ (together with the necessary time spent childrearing) during the current and next periods. For simplicity, the H1 sector's present utility is assumed to be represented by additive positive increasing functions of: the country's current and future levels of sanitation and general public services, the H1 sector's consumption per capita of R1 and C in both the current and next periods, current childbirths, and current and future leisure per capita. For simplicity, as the H1 sector makes this initial set of decisions, its planned saving during the current period is restricted to bond accumulation; we ignore the productivity of money balances (its ability to save time) and the sector's corresponding end-of-period demands for money in this step.

In this first step, the H1 sector contemplates allocating the total hours available to its adults during the current period, $h1_t^T \cdot N1_t$, to childrearing and leisure; the number of hours the households will work for their various employers during the current period will be determined by their employers as they set production and product prices. However, in this step the households do anticipate working a certain number of hours during the current period, just as they anticipate receiving a certain amount of dividends from each of the private banking and nonfinancial business sectors during the period.

Let

$N1_t$ = the adult population of Country One at the beginning of the current period.
$R1H1_t/N1_t$ = per capita consumption of R1 by H1 during the current period.
$CH1_t/N1_t$ = per capita consumption of C by H1 during the current period.
W^*H1_t = the total human waste—organic and inorganic—recycled or treated and stored by G1 during the current period.
g_{1H1t} = the general public services the H1 sector will receive from G1 during the current period.
η_{1t} = the number of childbirths within H1 during the current period.
$h1_t^T$ = the total number of "hours" during the current period.
$h1_t^T \cdot N1_t$ = the total number of hours available to the H1 sector during the current period.
τ_1 = the average number of hours required per child for childrearing.
$h1_t^W$ = the average number of hours the H1 adult population, $N1_t$, anticipates it will work for all employers during the current period.

$R1H1_{t+1}/N1_{t+1}$ = anticipated per capita consumption of R1 by H1 during next period.
$CH1_{t+1}/N1_{t+1}$ = anticipated per capita consumption of C by H1 during next period.
W^*H1_{t+1} = the anticipated human waste to be recycled or treated and stored by G1 next period.
$g_{1H1(t+1)}$ = the general public services the H1 sector will receive from G1 next period.
$h1^T_{t+1} \cdot N1_t$ = the total number of hours available to the H1 sector next period.
$h1^s_t$ = the standard number of hours employees expect to work next period.
$N1^s_{t+1}$ = the number of people in H1 that plan to work next period.

The utility function of the H1 sector associated with the initial set of decisions with respect to current-period childbirths and general public services for next period may then be represented by (4.1):

$$\begin{aligned} U1 = {} & U1_{R1t}\left(\frac{R1H1_t}{N1_t}\right) + U1_{CH1t}\left(\frac{CH1_t}{N1_t}\right) \\ & + U_{W^*G1H1t}(W^*H1_t) + U_{g1H1t}(g_{1H1t}) + U1\eta_{1t}(\eta_{1t}) \\ & + U1_{lt}\left[\left(h1^T_t \cdot N1_t - \tau \cdot \eta_{1t} - h1^W_t \cdot N1_t\right)/N1_t\right] \end{aligned}$$

Maximize

$$\begin{aligned} & + U1_{R1(t+1)}\left[\frac{R1H1_{t+1}}{N1_{t+1}}\right] + U1_{CH1(t+1)}\left(\frac{CH1_{t+1}}{N1_{t+1}}\right) \\ & + U_{W^*G1H1(t+1)}(W^*H1_{t+1}) + U_{g1H1(t+1)}(g_{1H1(t+1)}) \\ & + \frac{U1_{l(t+1)}\left[\left(h1^T_{t+1} \cdot N1_{t+1} - h1^s_t \cdot N1^s_{t+1}\right)\right]}{N1_{t+1}} \end{aligned} \tag{4.1}$$

where the population at the end of the current period is given by

$$N1_{t+1} = N1_t + \eta_{1t} - \mu^*_{N1}\left[P^*_t, g_{H1t}, (\omega_{1t} - \omega_{I1t})^2\right] \cdot N1_t \tag{4.2}$$

and where average weight at the beginning of the period is given by $\omega_{1t} = H1_t/N1_t$. The symbol g_{H1t} represents the combined level of sanitation and general public services provided by the G1 sector during the current period. The greater the value of the predetermined level of g_{H1t}, the lower the mortality rate of the H1 sector during the current period.

The household sector attempts to maximize present utility subject to its budget constraint. This constraint stipulates that total planned household spending (including taxes) on both privately produced products (C and R1), sanitation (W^*H1), and general public services each period (g_{1H1t} and $g_{1H1(t+1)}$), plus planned personal saving is equal to their current anticipated income, consisting of wage and nonwage income, minus personal saving.

The H1 sector decides the optimal levels of childbirths in the current period and the amount of general public services for next period given its current-period and next- period time constraints, its current-period and next-period budget constraints, and the menu the G1 sector has presented to the H1 sector for general public services. The menu, given in (3.17) states that next period's taxes for general public services are an increasing function of the level of those services selected by the H1 sector. The menu is written in simplified form as (4.3):

$$Tx_{G1H1(t+1)} = Tx_{G1H1(t+1)}(g_{1H1(t+1)}) \tag{4.3}$$

The H1 sector incorporates the menu into next period's budget constraint.

It is assumed that the households take their anticipated current wage and nonwage incomes as given but decide how many people they want to have employed next period under the assumption that everyone who seeks to be employed by the beginning of next period will be able to work. In terms of the abstract unit of account of Country One, the budget constraint facing the household sector during the current period is given by

$$\begin{aligned} &\Pi 1^{e}_{t} - Tx1_{t} + W1_{t} \cdot h1^{W}_{t} \cdot N1t + B1^{H1}_{t} \\ &= p^{H1}_{R1t} \cdot \left(\frac{R1H1_{t}}{N1_{t}}\right) \cdot N1_{t} + p^{H1}_{Ct} \cdot \tilde{\varepsilon}^{H1} \cdot \left(\frac{CH1_{t}}{N1_{t}}\right) \cdot N1_{t} \\ &\quad + p^{H1}_{B1} \cdot \left(B1^{d}_{H1(t+1)} - B1_{H1t}\right) \end{aligned} \tag{4.4}$$

where

$\Pi 1^{e}_{t}$ = the total dividends the H1 sector anticipates it will receive from the R1, NR, and PB1 sectors this period.

And where

$Tx1_{t} = Tx_{W*G1t} + Tx_{G1H1t}$ = current-period personal taxes for sanitation and general public services as defined in chapter 3.

$W1_{t}$ = the money wage that was announced last period by the NR sector and is paid by every employer in Country One during the current period.

$B1_{H1t}$ = the number of domestic bonds held by the H1 sector at the beginning of the current period. Each bond pays one unit of domestic money as interest during the current period. Therefore, this symbol also represents the H1 sector's interest income during the period.

p^{H1}_{R1t} = the price of R1 the H1 sector anticipates will prevail during the current period.

p^{H1}_{Ct} = the price of C the H1 sector anticipates will prevail during the current period (in units of Country Three's unit of account).

$\tilde{\varepsilon}^{H1}$ = the exchange rate the H1 sector anticipates will prevail during the current period between its country's unit of account and Country Three's unit of account (the value of Country Three's unit of account in terms of Country One's unit of account).

p^{H1}_{B1} = the price of domestic bonds anticipated by the H1 sector.

$B1^{d}_{H1(t+1)}$ = the number of domestic bonds the H1 sector plans to hold by the end of the current period before current interest rates are known.

The budget constraint the H1 sector anticipates facing next period is given by

$$\begin{aligned}&\Pi 1^{e}_{t+1} - Tx_{G1H1(t+1)}(g_{1H1(t+1)}) - Tx_{W*G1(t+1)}\\&+ W1^{H1}_{t+1} \cdot h1^{s}_{t+1} \cdot N1^{s}_{t+1} + \left(1 + p^{H1}_{B1}\right) \cdot B1^{d}_{H1(t+1)}\\&= p^{H1}_{R1(t+1)} \cdot \left(\frac{R1H1_{t+1}}{N1_{t+1}}\right) \cdot N1_{t+1} + p^{H1}_{C(t+1)} \cdot \tilde{\varepsilon}^{H1} \cdot \left(\frac{CH1_{t+1}}{N1_{t+1}}\right) \cdot N1_{t+1}\end{aligned} \tag{4.5}$$

where

$\Pi 1^{e}_{t+1}$ = the total dividends the H1 sector anticipates receiving from the R1, NR, and PB1 sectors.
$p^{H1}_{R1(t+1)}$ = the price of R1 that the H1 sector anticipates will prevail next period.
$R1H1_{t+1}$ = the number of units of R1 the H1 sector anticipates buying next period.
$p^{H1}_{G(t+1)}$ = the price of C that the H1 sector anticipates will prevail next period (in terms of Country Three's unit of account).
$CH1_{t+1}$ = the number of units of C the H1 sector anticipates buying next period.

Solving (4.5) for $B1^{d}_{H1(t+1)}$:

$$B1^{d}_{H1(t+1)} = \frac{\left[\begin{array}{l} p^{H1}_{R1(t+1)} \cdot \left(\frac{R1H1_{t+1}}{N1_{t+1}}\right) \cdot N1_{t+1} + \left(\frac{CH1_{t+1}}{N1_{t+1}}\right) \cdot N1_{t+1} \\ -\Pi 1^{e}_{t+1} + Tx_{G1H1(t+1)}(g_{1H1(t+1)}) + Tx_{W*G1(t+1)} \\ -W1^{H1}_{t+1} \cdot h1^{s}_{t+1} \cdot N1^{s}_{t+1} \end{array}\right]}{\left(1 + p^{H1}_{B1}\right)} \tag{4.6}$$

Substituting the right-hand side of (4.6) for $B1^{d}_{H1(t+1)}$ into (4.3) yields

$$\begin{aligned}&\Pi 1_{t} - Tx1_{t} + W1_{t} \cdot h1^{W}_{t} \cdot N1_{t} + \left(1 + p^{H1}_{B1}\right) \cdot B1_{H1t} + \left[\frac{1}{(1 + r_{1})}\right] \cdot \big[\Pi 1^{e}_{t+1}\\&-Tx_{g1H1(t+1)}(g_{1H1(t+1)}) - Tx_{G1W*G1(t+1)} + W1_{t+1} \cdot h1^{s}_{t+1} \cdot N1^{s}_{t+1}\big]\\&= p^{H1}_{R1t} \cdot \left(\frac{R1H1_{t}}{N1_{t}}\right) \cdot N1_{t} + p^{H1}_{Ct} \cdot \tilde{\varepsilon}^{H1} \cdot \left(\frac{C3H1_{t}}{N1_{t}}\right) \cdot N1_{t}\\&+ \left[\frac{1}{(1 + r1)}\right] \cdot \Bigg[p^{H1}_{R1(t+1)} \cdot \left(\frac{R1H1_{t+1}}{N1_{t+1}}\right) \cdot N1_{t+1}\\&+p^{H1}_{C(t+1)} \cdot \tilde{\varepsilon}^{H1} \cdot \left[\frac{C3H1_{t+1}}{N1_{t+1}}\right] \cdot N1_{t+1}\Bigg]\end{aligned} \tag{4.7}$$

where $1/(1+r_1) = p^{H1}_{B1}/(1+p^{H1}_{B1})$ since $r_1 = 1/p^{H1}_{B1}$. According to (4.7), the H1 sector's constraint states that the present value of current and future consumption must equal the present value of the sector's present and future disposable income.

At this point in the analysis, the objective of the household sector in Country One is to maximize (4.1) subject to (4.2) and (4.7). Therefore, the objective is to maximize

$$
\begin{aligned}
\mathbf{U1} = {} & U1_{R1t}\left(\frac{R1H1_t}{N1_t}\right) + U1_{CH1t}\left(\frac{CH1_t}{N1_t}\right) + U_{W^*G1H1t}(W^*G1_t) \\
& + U_{G1H1t}(g_{1H1t}) + U1_{\eta_{1t}}(\eta_{1t}) \\
& + U1_{lt}\left[\frac{(h1^T_t \cdot N1t - \tau \cdot \eta_{1t} - h1^W_t \cdot N1_t)}{N1_t}\right] \\
& + U1_{R1(t+1)}\left[\frac{R1H1_{t+1}}{\{N1_t + \eta_{1t} - \mu^*_{N1}\left[P^*_t, g_{H1t}, (\omega_{1t} - \omega_{I1t})^2\right] \cdot N1t\}}\right] \\
& + U1_{CH1(t+1)}\left(\frac{CH1_{t+1}}{\{N1_t + \eta_{1t} - \mu^*_{N1}\left[P^*_t, g_{H1t}, (\omega_{1t} - \omega_{I1t})^2\right] \cdot N1t\}}\right) \\
& + U_{W^*G1H1(t+1)}(W^*G1_{t+1}) + U_{g1H1(t+1)}(g_{1H1(t+1)}) \\
& + U1_{l(t+1)}\frac{\left[\left(\begin{array}{l} h1^T_{t+1} \cdot \{N1_t + \eta_{1t} - \mu^*_{N1}\left[P^*_t, g_{H1t}, (\omega_{1t} - \omega_{I1t})^2\right] \\ \cdot N1t\} - h1^s_t \cdot N1^s_{t+1} \end{array}\right)\right]}{\{N1_t + \eta_{1t} - \mu^*_{N1}\left[P^*_t, g_{H1t}, (\omega_{1t} - \omega_{I1t})^2\right] \cdot N1t\}} \\
& + \lambda\Bigg\{\Pi1_t - Tx1_t + W1_t \cdot h1^W_t \cdot N1_t + \left(1 + p^{H1}_{B1}\right) \cdot B1_{H1t} \\
& + \left[\frac{1}{(1+r_1)}\right] \cdot \left[\Pi1^e_{t+1} - Tx_{g1H1(t+1)}(g_{1H1(t+1)}) - Tx_{G1W^*G1(t+1)}\right. \\
& \left. + W1_{t+1} \cdot h1^s_{t+1} \cdot N1^s_{t+1}\right] - p^{H1}_{R1t} \cdot \left(\frac{R1H1_t}{N1_t}\right) \cdot N1_t \\
& - p^{H1}_{Ct} \cdot \tilde{\varepsilon}^{H1} \cdot \left(\frac{C3H1_t}{N1_t}\right) \cdot N1_t - \left[\frac{1}{(1+r_1)}\right] \cdot \left[p^{H1}_{R1(t+1)} \cdot \left(\frac{R1H1_{t+1}}{N1_{t+1}}\right)\right. \\
& \left.\left. \cdot N1_{t+1} + p^{H1}_{C(t+1)} \cdot \tilde{\varepsilon}^{H1} \cdot \left(\frac{C3H1_{t+1}}{N1_{t+1}}\right) \cdot N1_{t+1}\right]\right\} \qquad (4.8)
\end{aligned}
$$

The sum of the terms within braces and multiplied by λ is equal to zero.

In this step, the household sector attempts to maximize present utility not only with respect to current births and general public services but also with respect to its current and future consumption of both the renewable resource and the consumption good and its supply of labor next period. However, all decisions except for current births and next period's general public services are notional in the sense that they will be revised if necessary as current-period prices, wages, and interest rates become known. Therefore, at this juncture attention is focused only upon the decisions that are effective at the beginning of the period—current births and general public services selected for next period.

Maximizing (4.8) with respect to $g_{1H1(t+1)}$ and η_{1t} yields the following first-order necessary conditions for an interior solution to maximizing present utility:

$$\frac{\partial U1}{\partial g_{1H1(t+1)}} \equiv \frac{dU_{G1H1(t+1)}}{d(g_{1H1(t+1)})} - \lambda \cdot \left[\frac{1}{(1+r_1)}\right] \cdot \left[\frac{dTx_{G1H1(t+1)}}{d(g_{1H1(t+1)})}\right] = 0 \qquad (4.9)$$

$$\frac{\partial U1}{\partial(\eta_{1t})} \equiv \frac{dU1\eta_{1t}}{d(\eta_{1t})} - \left(\frac{dU1_{lt}}{dl_t}\right)\left[\frac{\tau}{N_{1t}}\right]$$
$$+ d\left(\frac{U1_{R1(t+1)}}{d\left(\dfrac{R1H1_{t+1}}{N1_{t+1}}\right)} \cdot \left[-\frac{R1H1_{t+1}}{(N1_{t+1})^2}\right]\right)$$
$$+ d\left(\frac{U1_{CH1(t+1)}}{d\left(\dfrac{CH1_{t+1}}{N1_{t+1}}\right)} \cdot \left[-\frac{CH1_{t+1}}{(N1_{t+1})^2}\right]\right) = 0 \qquad (4.10)$$

$$\frac{\partial U1}{\partial \lambda} \equiv \Pi 1_t - Tx1_t + W1_t \cdot h1_t^W \cdot N1_t + \left(1 + p_{B1}^{H1}\right) \cdot B1_t^{H1}$$
$$+ \left[\frac{1}{(1+r_1)}\right] \cdot \left[\Pi 1_{t+1}^e - Tx_{G1H1(t+1)}(g_{1H1(t+1)}) - Tx_{W*G1(t+1)}\right.$$
$$\left. + W1_{t+1} \cdot h1_{t+1}^s \cdot N1_{t+1}^s\right] - p_{R1t}^{H1} \cdot \left(\frac{R1H1_t}{N1_t}\right) \cdot N1_t - p_{Ct}^{H1} \cdot \tilde{\varepsilon}^{H1}$$
$$\cdot \left(\frac{C3H1_t}{N1_t}\right) \cdot N1_t - \left[\frac{1}{(1+r_1)}\right] \cdot \left[p_{R1(t+1)}^{H1} \cdot \left(\frac{R1H1_{t+1}}{N1_{t+1}}\right) \cdot N1_{t+1}\right.$$
$$\left. + p_{C(t+1)}^{H1} \cdot \tilde{\varepsilon}^{H1} \left(\frac{C3H1_{t+1}}{N1_{t+1}}\right) \cdot N1_{t+1}\right] = 0 \qquad (4.11)$$

H1 Sector's Demand for General Public Services Next Period

According to (4.9) the household sector will increase the amount of general public services it desires next period up to the point at which the present value of the extra taxes necessary to provide an extra unit of general public services is equal to the increase in present utility from the prospect of receiving the extra services next period. Although the demand for these services also depends at least indirectly upon the anticipated wage next period and upon the array of product prices the H1 sector anticipates will prevail during the current and next periods, if these services are viewed as "normal" goods, then, by definition, the H1 sector's demand for them will grow with their current disposable income. In particular, ceteris paribus, as their current disposable income rises the H1 sector will devote a portion of that increase to increased current saving in order to finance the sector's increased tax liability next period necessary to finance these extra services the sector demands for next period. The H1 sector will respond in the same fashion to an increase in their initial wealth. However, letting $Tx_{G1H1(t+1)}'$ represent the marginal tax rate, $dTx_{G1H1(t+1)}/d(g_{1H1(t+1)})$, in (4.12), the H1 sector will reduce the amount of general public services it demands for next period, the greater the marginal cost of (the less efficient the government becomes in) providing these services. Therefore, a very simplified demand function for general public services next period may be given by

$$g_{1H1(t+1)} = g_{1H1(t+1)}\left(\underset{+}{\overline{Y}_{H1t}},\ \underset{+}{p_{B1}^{H1} \cdot B1_{H1t}},\ \underset{-}{Tx'_{G1H1(t+1)}}\right) \tag{4.12}$$

where $\overline{Y}_{H1t}$ represents the sector's current disposable income and beginning-of-period financial wealth.

H1 Sector's Childbirths during the Current Period

According to (4.10), the households will increase the number of children born during the current period up to the point at which the net increase in present utility is equal to zero. The additional children directly increase utility (presumably at a decreasing rate), but the net increase in utility is diminished by the loss in leisure time due to the extra time spent childrearing and by the reduced present utility associated with reduced future per capita consumption of the renewable resource and the consumption good, holding the anticipated total amount of consumption of these goods constant. The H1 sector will elect to increase childbirths during the current period until the marginal utility of an extra birth is equal to the marginal cost. In this case the marginal cost is represented by the foregone leisure time associated with child care, which in turn is positively related to the number of hours necessary to parent another child. In the present model, the H1 sector takes the (at this point, anticipated) number of working hours as given, since they are established by the H1 sector's employers during the current period. Ceteris paribus, the longer people work during the period or the greater the amount of time they spend parenting another child, the greater the marginal utility of extra leisure and, therefore, the greater the marginal cost of having another child. Therefore, ignoring the indirect effects operating through other parameters the H1 sector faces at the beginning of the current period, ceteris paribus, the number of children born will decrease the greater the number of hours the existing population works during the current period and the greater the number of hours required to care for a child, τ.

$$\eta_{1t} = \eta_{1t}\left(\underset{-}{h1_t^W},\ \underset{-}{\tau}\right) \tag{4.13}$$

H2 Sector's Initial Set of Decisions

H2 Sector's Demand for General Public Services Next Period

Analogous to the H1 sector's demand for general public services, a very simplified demand function for general public services next period for the H2 sector may be given by

$$g_{2H2(t+1)} = g_{2H2(t+1)}\left(\underset{+}{\overline{Y}_{H2t}},\ \underset{+}{p_{B2}^{H2} \cdot B2_{H2t}},\ \underset{-}{Tx_{G2H2(t+1)'}}\right) \tag{4.14}$$

H2 Sector's Childbirths during the Current Period

Analogous to the H1 sector's choice of the number of childbirths, the following simplified function is assumed:

$$\eta_{2t} = \eta_{2t}\left(\underset{-}{h2_t^W},\ \underset{-}{\tau}\right) \tag{4.15}$$

H3 Sector's Initial Set of Decisions

H3 Sector's Demand for General Public Services Next Period

Analogous to the H1 sector's demand for general public services, a very simplified demand function for general public services next period for the H3 sector may be given by

$$g_{3H3(t+1)} = g_{3H3(t+1)}\left(\underset{+}{\overline{Y}_{H3t}},\ \underset{+}{p_{B3}^{H3} \cdot B3_{H3t}},\ \underset{-}{Tx'_{G3H3(t+1)}}\right) \tag{4.16}$$

H3 Sector's Childbirths during the Current Period

Analogous to the H1 sector's choice of the number of childbirths, the following simplified function is assumed:

$$\eta_{3t} = \eta_{3t}\left(\underset{-}{h3_t^W},\ \underset{-}{\tau_3}\right) \tag{4.17}$$

In chapter 5, the nonrenewable resource industry is analyzed.

5

The Nonrenewable Resource Industry

At the beginning of the current period, an initial stock of unextracted/unmined NR, NR_t, exists. Let NR^d_{t+1} represent the industry's desired stock of natural NR for the end of the current period, which is determined in accordance with its objective to maximize the present value of its operations.

The NR industry applies a variable amount of labor together with a given stock of physical capital to transform the mass of natural NR that it desires to convert into a marketable product, NR^T, possibly by changing its physical, chemical, biological, or aesthetic characteristics and/or its location. The current level of transformation services, $T_{NR}(\cdot)$, is assumed to be a positive increasing function of (variable) labor hours, $h_{NR} \cdot N1_{NRt}$, applied during the period, where $N1_{NRt}$ denotes the predetermined number of people employed in the NR industry at the start of the current period and where h_{NR} represents the (average) number of hours these employees work for the NR industry during the period transforming natural nonrenewable resources into marketable products. It is assumed that the marginal transformation of labor, T'_{NR}, is positive but diminishing.

Under these assumptions, the production function for current marketable NR, NR^T_t, is given by (5.1):

$$NR^T_t = \min\left[\frac{(NR_t - NR^d_{t+1})}{(1+\varphi)}, \tau_{NR}(I1_t) \cdot T_{NRt}(h_{NR} \cdot N1_{NRt}, K_{NRt})\right] \geq 0 \tag{5.1}$$

where $1 \geq \varphi > 0$ is the fraction of NR wasted in the process of being transformed into marketable form, K_{NRt} denotes the stock of physical capital held by the NR sector at the beginning of the current period, and $\tau_{NR}(I1_t) > 0$ with $\tau'_{NR}(\cdot) > 0$, represents the contribution of the infrastructure of Country One at the beginning of the period to the transformation services of labor and capital.

Assuming the NR industry purposefully wastes neither the transformation services nor the amount of NR available for transformation, the amount of (transformed or marketable) NR produced may be viewed as equal to $\tau_{NR}(I1_t) \cdot T_{NRt}(h_{NR} \cdot N1_{NRt}, K_{NRt})$:

$$NR_t^T = \tau_{NR}(I1_t) \cdot T_{NRt}(h_{NR} \cdot N1_{NRt}, K_{NRt}) \quad (5.2)$$

In addition, in terms of mass, the amount of natural NR transformed in the production process into marketable NR and waste may be viewed as

$$NR_t - NR_{t+1}^{dp} = (1 + \varphi) \cdot \tau_{NR}(I1_t) \cdot T_{NRt}(h_{NR} \cdot N1_{NRt}, K_{NRt}) \quad (5.3)$$

Solving (5.3) for NR_{t+1}^{dp} yields the following expression for the preliminary planned inventory of unprocessed NR for the end of the current period (before recycling):

$$NR_{t+1}^{dp} = NR_t - (1 + \varphi) \cdot \tau_{NR}(I1_t) \cdot T_{NRt}(h_{NR} \cdot N1_{NRt}, K_{NRt}) \quad (5.4)$$

The amount of transformed NR that is not sold during the current period is assumed to be added to the industry's inventory of processed NR:

$$NR_{t+1}^{T*} = NR_t^{T*} + \tau_{NR}(I1_t) \cdot T_{NRt}(h_{NR} \cdot N1_{NRt}, K_{NRt}) - NRK_t - NRC_t - NRG1_t - NRG2_t - NRG3_t \geq 0 \quad (5.5)$$

where NRK_t corresponds to the actual amount of NR purchased by the capital goods industry in Country Two during the current period, NRC_t corresponds to the actual amount of NR purchased by the consumer goods industry in Country Three during the current period, $NRG1_t$ represents the amount of transformed NR purchased by the government sector in Country One, $NRG2_t$ represents the amount of transformed NR purchased by the government sector in Country Two, $NRG3_t$ represents the amount of transformed NR purchased by the government sector in Country Three, NR_t^{T*} represents the initial inventory of transformed NR at the beginning of the period, and NR_{t+1}^{T*} denotes the inventory of transformed NR at end of current period.

During the current period, the industry generates new waste products equal to

$$W^*NR = \varphi \cdot \tau_{NR}(I1_t) \cdot T_{NRt}(h_{NR} \cdot N1_{NRt}, K_{NRt}) + \kappa \cdot \delta \cdot K_{NRt} \quad (5.6)$$

in terms of mass, where κ represents the mass per unit of K_{NRt} and δ denotes the rate of physical depreciation. A portion of the total waste generated during the current period is recycled and adds to the stock of NR by the end of the period. The sector must pay a fee, p_w, in terms of its currency, to obtain a pollution allowance for every unit of wasted mass it discharges (unrecycled) into the environment over and above the allowance it receives from its government sector. To the extent that the industry engages in recycling, it reduces (increases) the number of allowances it must buy (may sell) in the pollution allowance market.

Assume the following transformation function for recycling waste during the current period:

$$RW^*NR_t = \min\left[\varphi \cdot \tau_{NR}(Il_t) \cdot T_{NRt}(h_{NR} \cdot N1_{NRt}, K_{NRt}) + \kappa \cdot \delta \cdot K_{NRt} - \Omega_{NRt}^d, T_{NRt}^w\left(h_{NR}^w \cdot N1_{NRt}\right)\right] \geq 0 \quad (5.7)$$

where RW^*NR_t represents the amount of waste recycled during the current period, Ω^d_{NRt} represents the sector's desired holdings of pollution allowances, and $T^w_{NRt}(\cdot)$ represents the transformation function for converting waste into recycled NR. For simplicity, it is assumed that labor is the only resource necessary to provide this service.

Assuming that neither transformation services nor mass are otherwise wasted in the recycling process,

$$RW^*NR_t = T^w_{NRt}\left(h^w_{NR} \cdot N1_{NRt}\right) \tag{5.8}$$

Then the industry's current expenses associated with discharging and recycling nonrenewable resource waste during the period, $C^*_{NR,W}$, is equal to

$$C^*_{NR,W} = p_w \cdot \left[\varphi \cdot \tau_{NR}(I1_t) \cdot T_{NRt}(h_{NR} \cdot N1_{NRt}, K_{NRt}) + \kappa \cdot \delta \cdot K_{NRt} - T^w_{NRt}\left(h^w_{NR} \cdot N1_{NRt}\right) - \Omega_{NR}\right] + W1_t \cdot h^w_{NR} \cdot N1_{NRt} \tag{5.9}$$

where $W1_t$ denotes the current money wage prevailing in Country One (announced last period). Note that since Ω^d_{NRt} is equal to $\varphi \cdot \tau_{NR}(I1_t) \cdot T_{NRt}(h_{NR} \cdot N1_{NRt}, K_{NRt}) + \kappa \cdot \delta \cdot K_{NRt} - T^w_{NRt}(h^w_{NR} \cdot N1_{NRt})$, the sum in brackets on the right-hand side of (5.9) corresponds to the industry's excess demand for pollution allowances, $\Omega^d_{NRt} - \Omega_{NR}$.

Taking the current wage rate and the NR industry's forecast of the current-period demand function for NR^T_t, $NRK^{de}_t + NRC^{de}_t + NRG1^{de}_t + NRG2^{de}_t + NRG3^{de}_t$ as given, the NR industry attempts to maximize the present value of the dividends it plans paying the industry's shareholders during the current and next periods. Then the firm's desired current-period sales of NR^T_t (in terms of mass) is given by

$$NRK^{de}_t + NRC^{de}_t + NRG1^{de}_t + NRG2^{de}_t + NRG3^{de}_t = \tau_{NR}(I1_t) \cdot T_{NRt}(h_{NR} \cdot N1_{NRt}, K_{NRt}) + NR^{T^*}_t \tag{5.10}$$

where, for simplicity, it is assumed that the industry's desired inventory of processed NR for the end of the period is equal to zero.

Each period, dividends equal net income minus net business saving. Net income is equal to the value of production, $p_{NRt} \cdot \tau_{NR}(I1_t) \cdot T_{NRt}(h_{NR} \cdot N1_{NRt}, K_{NRt})$—where p_{NRt} represents the price of NR set by the NR industry—minus current expenses (in this case, wages, taxes, interest, pollution allowances purchased, and depreciation). Therefore, dividends equal the value of production minus wages, taxes, interest, pollution allowances purchased, depreciation, and net business saving. Measured in terms of current-period market prices, net business saving is necessarily equal to the sum of the sector's net increase in assets (measured in terms of current-period prices) minus the net increase in liabilities (also measured in terms of current-period prices) during the period.

With p_{NRt} representing the current market price that the NR industry sets during the current period, the industry plans to acquire—$p_{NRt} \cdot NR^{T^*}_t$ in inventories of processed NR during the current period, measured in terms of current market prices. Let $B1_{NRt}$ represent the number of NR industry bonds outstanding in Country One's bond market at the beginning of the current period. Let p^{NR}_{B1} represent the market price of bonds issued in Country One's bond market that the NR industry expects will prevail during the current period. Each bond outstanding presumably pays one unit of Country One's currency as interest income during the current period. Then the market value of the NR industry's initial debt in Country One's bond market in terms of anticipated market prices is represented by $p_{B1}^{NR} \cdot B1_{NRt}$. Let $B1_{NR(t+1)}^{se}$ denote the number of bonds the NR industry plans to have outstanding by the end of the current period as it decides current-period production and announces the current-period price of NR^T and the wage rate. Then the amount that the NR industry plans to borrow in Country One's bond market during the current period is given by $p_{B1}^{NR} \cdot (B1_{NR(t+1)}^{se} - B1_{NRt})$. The current level of planned net business saving, S_{NRt}^d, by the NR industry must be consistent with the market value of the sector's planned accumulation of inventories of processed NR plus the value of its planned accumulation of physical capital, $p_{Kt}^{NR} \cdot \varepsilon^{NR} \cdot (K_{NR(t+1)}^d - K_{NRt})$ minus its planned current-period borrowing, where p_{Kt}^{NR} denotes the NR industry's anticipated current-period price of capital goods in terms of Country Two's unit of account and where ε^{NR} represents the NR industry's anticipated value of Country Two's unit of account in terms of Country One's unit of account. Therefore, we have

$$S_{NRt}^d \equiv -p_{NRt} \cdot NR_t^{T^*} + p_{Kt}^{NR} \cdot \varepsilon^{NR} \cdot \left(K_{NR(t+1)}^d - K_{NRt}\right) - p_{B1}^{NR} \cdot \left(B1_{NR(t+1)}^{se} - B1_{NRt}\right) \quad (5.11)$$

The sector's planned level of dividends for the current period, Π_{NRt}^d, is given by

$$\begin{aligned}\Pi_{NRt}^d = {} & p_{NRt} \cdot \left\{\tau_{NR}(I1_t) \cdot T_{NRt}(h_{NR} \cdot N1_{NRt}, K_{NRt}) + NR_t^{T^*}\right\} \\ & - \delta \cdot p_{Kt}^{NR} \cdot \varepsilon^{NR} \cdot K_{NRt} - Tx_{NRG1t} \\ & - p_w \cdot \left[\varphi \cdot \tau_{NR}(I1_t) \cdot T_{NRt}(h_{NR} \cdot N1_{NRt}, K_{NRt}) - T_{NRt}^w\left(h_{NR}^w \cdot N1_{NRt}\right)\right] \\ & - W1_t \cdot \left(h_{NR} + h_{NR}^w\right) \cdot N1_{NRt} - B1_t^{NR} \\ & - p_{Kt}^{NR} \cdot \varepsilon^{NR} \cdot \left(K_{NR(t+1)}^d - K_{NRt}\right) + p_{B1}^{NR} \cdot \left(B1_{NR(t+1)}^{se} - B1_{NRt}\right)\end{aligned} \quad (5.12)$$

where the planned reduction in processed inventories is valued in terms of the current market price of NR^T and where δ represents the depreciation rate of physical capital. The symbol Tx_{NRG1t} denotes the taxes that the NR sector pays the G1 sector during the current period.

At the beginning of the period, the NR industry announces its product price, p_{NRt}. Let the following demand function represents the NR industry's forecast of the current-period demand for its product:

$$\begin{aligned}NR_t^{Tde} &= NRK_t^{Tde} + NRC_t^{Tde} + NRG1_t^{Tde} + NRG2_t^{Tde} + NRG3_t^{Tde} \\ &= NRK_t^{Tde}(p_{NRT}, \omega_{NR,K}) + NRC_t^{Tde}(p_{NRT}, \omega_{NR,C}) \\ &\quad + NRG1_t^{Tde} + NRG2_t^{Tde} + NRG3_t^{Tde}\end{aligned}$$

$$= NR_t^{Tde}\left(p_{NRT}, \omega_{NR,K}, \omega_{NR,C}, NRG1_t^{Tde} + NPG2_t^{Tde} + NPG3_t^{Tde}\right)$$
$$\qquad - \quad + \quad + \qquad\qquad + \tag{5.13}$$

where $NR_t^{Tde}(\cdot)$ denotes the NR industry's forecast at the beginning of the current period of the current real market demand for NR^T by the capital goods industry in Country Two, the consumer goods industry in Country Three, and all three government sectors. It is assumed that the derivative of $NR_t^{Tde}(\cdot)$ with respect to p_{NRt} is negative (the sign will become verified later with the specification of the economic behavior of the K and C industries); $\omega_{NR,K}$ denotes a vector of shift parameters that the NR industry forecasts affect the K sector's demand for NR^T; $\omega_{NR,C}$ denotes a vector of shift parameters that the NR industry forecasts affect the C sector's demand for NR^T. Solving the inverse function for p_{NRt} yields

$$p_{NRt} = p_{NRt}\left(NR_t^{Tde}, \omega_{NR,K}, \omega_{NR,K}, NRG1_t^{Tde} + NRG2_t^{Tde} + NRG3_t^{Tde}\right)$$
$$\qquad - \quad + \quad + \qquad\qquad + \tag{5.14}$$

where

$$\frac{\partial p_{NRt}}{\partial\left(NR_t^{Tde}\right)} \equiv \frac{1}{\left[\partial\left(NR_t^{Tde}\right)/\partial p_{NRt}\right]} < 0$$

$$\frac{\partial p_{NRt}}{\partial \omega_{NR,K}} \equiv -\frac{\left[\partial\left(NR_t^{Tde}\right)/\partial \omega_{NR,K}\right]}{\left[\partial\left(NR_t^{Tde}\right)/\partial p_{NRt}\right]} > 0$$

$$\frac{\partial p_{NRt}}{\partial \omega_{NR,C}} \equiv -\frac{\left[\partial\left(NR_t^{Tde}\right)/\partial \omega_{NR,C}\right]}{\left[\partial\left(NR_t^{Tde}\right)/\partial p_{NRt}\right]} > 0$$

and

$$\frac{\partial p_{NRt}}{\partial\left(NRG1_t^{Tde} + NRG2_t^{Tde} + NRG3_t^{Tde}\right)} \equiv -\frac{\left[\partial\left(NR_t^{Tde}\right)/\partial\left(NRG1_t^{Tde} + NRG2_t^{Tde} + NRG3_t^{Tde}\right)\right]}{\left[\partial\left(NR_t^{Tde}\right)/\partial p_{NRt}\right]} > 0 \tag{5.15}$$

An increase in $\omega_{NR,K}$, $\omega_{NR,C}$, or $NRG1_t^{Tde} + NRG2_t^{Tde} + NRG3_t^{Tde}$ represents an outward shift in the NR industry's forecast of the market demand for its product.

The price, p_{NRt}, given by (5.14) represents the maximum uniform price the NR sector expects it can value each alternative quantity of NR it transforms during the current period. Based upon this function, the sector's forecasted current total revenue, TR_t^{NRe}, function is given by

$$TR_t^{N\,Re} = p_{NRt} \cdot NR_t^{Tde}$$
$$= p_{NRt}\left(NR_t^{Tde}, \omega_{NR,K}, \omega_{NR,C}, NRG1_t^{Tde} + NRG2_t^{Tde} + NRG3_t^{Tde}\right) \cdot NR_t^{Tde}$$
$$= TR_t^{NRe}\left(NR_t^{Tde}, \omega_{NR,K}, \omega_{NR,C}, NRG1_t^{Tde} + NRG2_t^{Tde} + NRG3_t^{Tde}\right) \tag{5.16}$$

Substituting the right-hand side of (5.10) for NR_t^{Tde} in (5.16) yields

$$TR_t^{NRe} = TR_t^{NRe}\Big[\tau_{NR}(I1_t) \cdot T_{NRt}(h_{NR} \cdot N1_{NRt}, K_{NRt}) + NR_t^{T^*}, \omega_{NR,K}, \omega_{NR,C}, NRG1_t^{Tde} + NRG2_t^{Tde} + NRG3_t^{Tde}\Big] \tag{5.17}$$

Substituting the right-hand side of (5.17) for the first term, $p_{NRt} \cdot \{\tau_{NR}(I1_t) \cdot T_{NRt}(h_{NR} \cdot N1_{NRt}, K_{NRt}) + NR_t^{T^*}\}$, on the right-hand side of (5.12) yields

$$\begin{aligned}\Pi_{NRt}^{d} = {} & TR_t^{N\,Re}\Big[\tau_{NR}(I1_t) \cdot T_{NRt}(h_{NR} \cdot N1_{NRt}, K_{NRt}) \\ & + NR_t^{T^*}, \omega_{NR,K}, \omega_{NR,C}, NRG1_t^{Tde} + NRG2_t^{Tde} + NRG3_t^{Tde}\Big] \\ & - \delta \cdot p_{Kt}^{NR} \cdot \varepsilon^{NR} \cdot K_{NRt} - Tx_{NRG1t} \\ & - p_w \cdot [\varphi \cdot \tau_{NR}(I1t) \cdot T_{NRt}(h_{NR} \cdot N1_{NRt}, K_{NRt}) - T_{NRt}^{w}(h_{NR}^{w} \cdot N1_{NRt})] \\ & - W1_t \cdot \left(h_{NR} + h_{NR}^{W}\right) \cdot N1_{NRt} - B1_{NRt} \\ & - p_{Kt}^{NR} \cdot \varepsilon^{NR} \cdot \left(K_{NR(t+1)}^{d} - K_{NRt}\right) + p_{B1}^{NR} \cdot \left(B1_{NR(t+1)}^{se} - B1_{NRt}\right)\end{aligned} \tag{5.18}$$

as the expression for the amount the NR industry plans to distribute as dividends during the current period.

Assume next period's planned production of marketable NR, NR_{t+1}^{Te}, is given by

$$NR_{t+1}^{Te} = \min\left[\frac{\{NR_t - (1+\varphi) \cdot \tau_{NR}(I1_t) \cdot T_{NRt}(h_{NR} \cdot N1_{NRt}, K_{NRt}) + T_{NRt}^{W}\left(h_{NR}^{W} \cdot N1_{NRt}\right)\}}{(1+\varphi)}, \tau_{NR}(I1_t + \Delta I1_t) \cdot T_{NR(t+1)}^{Te}\left(h_{NR}^{e} \cdot N1_{NR(t+1)}^{Te}, K_{NR(t+1)}^{d}\right)\right] \tag{5.19}$$

In particular, next period's planned production of NR^T is assumed to be constrained, first, by the amount of unextracted/unmined NR the industry anticipates will be available for processing next period and, second, by the level of transformation services provided by labor, capital, and the infrastructure, $I1_t + \Delta I1_t$, next period.

From (5.19), assuming that the sector does not produce more waste than necessary, the amount of marketable NR the industry plans to produce (and sell) next period may be represented by

$$NR_{t+1}^{Te} = \frac{\left\{\begin{matrix} NR_t - (1+\varphi) \cdot \tau_{NR}(I1_t) \cdot T_{NRt} \\ (h_{NR} \cdot N1_{NRt}, K_{NRt}) + T_{NRt}^{W}(h_{NR}^{W} \cdot N1_{NRt}) \end{matrix}\right\}}{(1+\varphi)} \tag{5.20}$$

To avoid unnecessarily wasting either natural resources or transformation services, the industry combines them in the following way:

$$\tau_{NR}(I1_t + \Delta I1_t) \cdot T^{Te}_{NR(t+1)}\left(h^e_{NR} \cdot N1^{Te}_{NR(t+1)}, K^d_{NR(t+1)}\right)$$
$$= \frac{NR_t}{(1+\varphi)} - \tau_{NR}(I1_t) \cdot T_{NRt}(h_{NR} \cdot N1_{NRt}, K_{NRt})$$
$$+ \frac{T^W_{NRt}\left(h^W_{NR} \cdot N1_{NRt}\right)}{(1+\varphi)} \tag{5.21}$$

This restriction represents the combinations of NR and transformation services along the expansion path associated with the processing of NR next period. Therefore, the amount of labor the NR industry plans to use next period for the purpose of transforming NR may be expressed in terms of the stock of NR_t, the number of hours the industry plans to use its current employees for transformation and recycling services, the stock of capital the sector holds at the beginning of the period, and the stock of physical capital the sector plans to hold by the end of the current period. Totally differentiating (5.21) yields

$$\tau_{NR}(I1_t + \Delta I1_t) \cdot \left[\frac{\partial T^{Te}_{NR(t+1)}}{\partial\left(h^e_{NR} \cdot N1^{Te}_{NR(t+1)}\right)}\right] \cdot d\left(h^e_{NR} \cdot N1^{Te}_{NR(t+1)}\right)$$
$$+ \tau_{NR}(I1_t + \Delta I1_t) \cdot \left[\frac{\partial T^{Te}_{NR(t+1)}}{\partial\left(K^d_{NR(t+1)}\right)}\right] \cdot d\left(K^d_{NR(t+1)}\right)$$
$$= d\left[\frac{NR_t}{(1+\varphi)}\right] - \tau_{NR}(I1_t) \cdot \left[\frac{\partial T_{NRt}}{\partial(h_{NR} \cdot N1_{NRt})}\right] \cdot d(h_{NR} \cdot N1_{NRt})$$
$$- \tau_{NR}(I1_t) \cdot \left[\frac{\partial T_{NRt}}{\partial(K_{NRt})}\right] \cdot d(K_{NRt})$$
$$+ \left[\frac{1}{(1+\varphi)}\right] \cdot \left[\frac{dT^w_{NRt}}{d\left(h^w_{NR} \cdot N1_{NRt}\right)}\right] \cdot d\left(h^w_{NR} \cdot N1_{NRt}\right) \tag{5.22}$$

or

$$d\left(h^e_{NR} \cdot N1^{Te}_{NR(t+1)}\right)$$
$$= \left[\frac{1}{\left\{\tau_{NR}(I1_t + \Delta I1_t) \cdot \left[\partial T^{Te}_{NR(t+1)} \Big/ \partial\left(h^e_{NR} \cdot N1^{Te}_{NR(t+1)}\right)\right]\right\}}\right]$$
$$\cdot \left[d\left[\frac{NR_t}{(1+\varphi)}\right] + \left[\frac{1}{(1+\varphi)}\right] \cdot \left[\frac{dT^w_{NRt}}{d\left(h^w_{NR} \cdot N1_{NRt}\right)}\right] \cdot d\left(h^w_{NR} \cdot N1_{NRt}\right)\right.$$
$$- \tau_{NR}(I1_t) \cdot \left[\frac{\partial T_{NRt}}{\partial(h_{NR} \cdot N1_{NRt})}\right] \cdot d(h_{NR} \cdot N1_{NRt})$$

$$- \tau_{NR}(I1_t) \cdot \left[\frac{\partial T_{NRt}}{\partial(K_{NRt})}\right] \cdot d(K_{NRt})$$

$$-\tau_{NR}(I1_t + \Delta I1_t) \cdot \left[\frac{\partial T^{Te}_{NR(t+1)}}{\partial\left(K^{d}_{NR(t+1)}\right)}\right] \cdot d\left(K^{d}_{NR(t+1)}\right)\Bigg] \tag{5.23}$$

Therefore,

$$h^{e}_{NR} \cdot N1^{Te}_{NR(t+1)} = h^{e}_{NR} \cdot N1^{Te}_{NR(t+1)} \left[\underset{+}{\frac{NR_t}{(1+\varphi)}}, \underset{-}{h_{NR} \cdot N1_{NRt}}, \underset{-}{K_{NRt}}, \underset{-}{I1_t}, \underset{+}{h^{w}_{NR} \cdot N1_{NRt}}, \underset{-}{K^{d}_{NR(t+1)}}\right] \tag{5.24}$$

During next period, the industry generates new waste products, W^*NR_{t+1}:

$$W^*NR_{t+1} = \varphi \cdot \frac{\left\{\begin{array}{c} NR_t - (1+\eta) \cdot \tau_{NR}(I1_t) \cdot T_{NRt} \\ (h_{NR} \cdot N1_{NRt}, K_{NRt}) + T^{w}_{NRt}\left(h^{w}_{NR} \cdot N1_{NRt}\right) \end{array}\right\}}{(1+\varphi)} \tag{5.25}$$

in terms of mass. Again, the sector must pay a fee, p_w, in terms of its currency, to obtain a pollution allowance for every unit of wasted mass it discharges into the environment over and above the pollution allowances issued to it by its government sector, Ω_{NR}. To the extent that the industry engages in recycling or treating and storing waste, it reduces the amount it pays for pollution allowances (increases the amount it receives from selling pollution allowances) in the market. (Since the sector does not look beyond the end of next period, it does not plan to recycle any NR next period because it will not become available until after next period.) However, the sector still has an incentive to treat and store waste next period. Assume the following transformation function for treating and storing waste next period:

$$\begin{aligned} SW^*NR_{t+1} = \min \Bigg\{\Bigg[\left[\frac{\varphi}{(1+\varphi)}\right] \{NR_t - (1+\varphi) \cdot \tau_{NR}(I1_t) \\ \cdot T_{NRt}(h_{NR} \cdot N1_{NRt}, K_{NRt}) + T^{w}_{NRt}\left(h^{w}_{NR} \cdot N1_{NRt}\right)\} \\ -\Omega^{d}_{NR(t+1)}\Bigg], T^{S}_{NR(t+1)}\left(h^{e}_{NR} \cdot N1^{Se}_{NR(t+1)}\right)\Bigg\} \geq 0 \end{aligned} \tag{5.26}$$

where SW^*NR_{t+1} represents the amount of waste treated during the next period and $T^{S}_{NR(t+1)}(\cdot)$ represents the transformation function for converting waste into treated and stored material, with $N1^{Se}_{NR(t+1)}$ representing the number of employees the sector anticipates using to treat and store waste next period.

Assuming that neither transformation services nor mass are unnecessarily wasted in the treatment and storage process,

$$SW^*NR_{t+1} = T^{S}_{NR(t+1)}\left(h^{e}_{NR} \cdot N1^{Se}_{NR(t+1)}\right) \tag{5.27}$$

Then the industry's anticipated expenses associated with discharging and treating waste during next period, C^{e}_{SW*NR}, is equal to

$$C^{e}_{SW*NR} = p_{w} \cdot \left[\left[\frac{\varphi}{(1+\varphi)}\right] \cdot \{NR_{t} - (1+\eta) \cdot \tau_{NR}(I1_{t}) \cdot T_{NRt}(h_{NR} \cdot N1_{NRt}, K_{NRt}) + T^{w}_{NRt}\left(h^{w}_{NR} \cdot N1_{NRt}\right)\} - T^{S}_{NR(t+1)}\left(h^{e}_{NR} \cdot N1^{Se}_{NR(t+1)}\right) - \Omega^{e}_{NR(t+1)}\right] + W1_{t+1} \cdot h^{e}_{NR} \cdot N1^{Se}_{NR(t+1)} \quad (5.28)$$

where $\Omega^{e}_{NR(t+1)}$ represents the number of pollution allowances the NR industry expects will be allocated to it next period and where $W1_{t+1}$ represents the wage rate the NR industry announces this period that it will pay next period.

The NR industry also forecasts the net market supply function of people who will be available to work next period after subtracting its estimate of the government sector's (G1) and the R1 industry's demands for employees for next period. The forecasted net supply of labor is assumed to be positively related to the money wage, $W1_{t+1}$, that the NR industry announces this period that it is willing to pay its employees next period (presumably the government and the R1 industry will also pay this wage and their demands will be filled first with the households indifferent to their potential employer). Assume the forecasted net labor supply function is given by

$$N1^{Se}_{t+1} = N1^{se}(W1_{t+1}, \gamma_{NR}) \quad (5.29)$$

where γ_{NR} denotes a vector of parameters that the nonfinancial business sector anticipates will shift the labor supply function and where $\partial N1^{se}/\partial W1_{t+1} > 0$. Taking the inverse of this function yields an expression for the minimum wage the sector estimates it needs to announce in order to attract a given number of employees to work next period:

$$W1_{t+1} = W1(N1^{Se}_{t+1}, \gamma_{NR}) \quad (5.30)$$

where $\partial(W1)/\partial(N1^{se}_{t+1}) > 0$. From this inverse function, next period's anticipated labor cost function, $\overline{C}(\bullet) \cdot h^{e}_{NR}$, may be expressed as a function of the number of people the NR industry plans to employ by the beginning of next period, $N1^{de}_{NR(t+1)}$, where it is assumed that the sector sets the money wage so that it generates the anticipated number of applicants (of homogeneous quality) that the sector wants to hire next period:

$$\overline{C}\left(N1^{de}_{NR(t+1)}, \gamma_{NR}\right) \cdot h^{e}_{NR} = \left[W1\left(N1^{de}_{NR(t+1)}, \gamma_{NR}\right) \cdot N1^{de}_{NR(t+1)}\right] \cdot h^{e}_{NR} \quad (5.31)$$

where $\partial\overline{C}/\partial N1^{de}_{NR(t+1)} = W1_{t+1} + N1^{de}_{NR(t+1)} \cdot \left(\partial W1/\partial N1^{de}_{NR(t+1)}\right) > 0$ denotes the expected marginal factor cost of labor.

The NR industry also makes a preliminary forecast of next period's demand for its product, from which it obtains its anticipated revenue function associated with that demand:

$$\begin{aligned} TR^{NRe}_{t+1} &= p^{e}_{NR(t+1)} \cdot NR^{Tde}_{t+1} \\ &= p^{e}_{NR(t+1)}\left(NR^{Tde}_{t+1}, \omega^{e}_{NR,K}, \omega^{e}_{NR,C}, NRG1^{Tde}_{t+1}\right. \\ &\quad \left. + NRG2^{Tde}_{t+1} + NRG3^{Tde}_{t+1}\right) \cdot NR^{Tde}_{t+1} \\ &= TR^{NRe}_{t+1}\left(NR^{Tde}_{t+1}, \omega^{e}_{NR,K}, \omega^{e}_{NR,C}, NRG1^{Tde}_{t+1} + NRG2^{Tde}_{t+1} + NRG3^{Tde}_{t+1}\right) \end{aligned} \quad (5.32)$$

where NR^{Tde}_{t+1} denotes the number of units of NR the NR industry anticipates selling to the capital goods and consumer goods industries next period plus the amount it plans to sell to the three government sectors next period. Then the firm's desired next-period sales of NR^{T}_{t+1} (in terms of mass) is given by

$$NR^{de}_{t+1} = \frac{\left\{\begin{array}{c} NR_t - (1+\varphi)\cdot\tau_{NR}(I1_t)\cdot T_{NRt} \\ (h_{NR}\cdot N1_{NRt}, K_{NRt}) + T^{w}_{NRt}\left(h^{w}_{NR}\cdot N1_{NRt}\right) \end{array}\right\}}{(1+\varphi)} \quad (5.33)$$

Each period, dividends equal net income minus net business saving. Next period's anticipated net income is equal to the value of production, $p^{e}_{NR(t+1)}\cdot\{NR_t - (1+\varphi)\cdot \tau_{NR}(I1_t)\cdot T_{NRt}(h_{NR}\cdot N1_{NRt}, K_{NRt}) + T^{w}_{NRt}(h^{w}_{NR}\cdot N1_{NRt})\}/(1+\varphi)$, minus next period's expenses (wages, taxes, interest, pollution allowances, and depreciation). Therefore, dividends equal the value of production minus wages, taxes, interest, depreciation, pollution allowances, and net business saving. Measured in terms of next period's market prices, net business saving is necessarily equal to the sum of the sector's net increase in assets minus the net increase in liabilities during the period.

The industry presumably plans to acquire no inventories of processed NR during next period. For simplicity, it is assumed that the sector plans to liquidate next period the portion of physical capital that it holds at the beginning of next period that does not depreciate next period, $(1-\delta)\cdot p^{NR}_{K(t+1)}\cdot \varepsilon^{NR}\cdot K^{d}_{NR(t+1)}$, where $p^{NR}_{K(t+1)}$ is the price of capital the sector expects will prevail next period and ε^{NR} represents the anticipated exchange rate (this period and next period). Again, let $B1^{s}_{NR(t+1)}$ denote the number of bonds the NR industry plans to have outstanding by the beginning of next period. Then the amount that the NR industry plans to borrow in Country One's bond market during next period is given by $-p^{NR}_{B1}\cdot B1^{s}_{NR(t+1)}$. The planned level of net business saving next period, $S^{d}_{NR(t+1)}$, by the NR industry must be consistent with the market value of the sector's planned net accumulation of assets minus its planned borrowing. Therefore, we have

$$S^{d}_{NR(t+1)} \equiv -(1-\delta)\cdot p^{NR}_{K(t+1)}\cdot \varepsilon^{NR}\cdot K^{d}_{NR(t+1)} + p^{NR}_{B1}\cdot B1^{s}_{NR(t+1)} \quad (5.34)$$

The sector's planned dividends for the next period, $\Pi^{d}_{NR(t+1)}$, are given by

$$\Pi^{d}_{NR(t+1)} = TR^{NRe}_{t+1}\left[\frac{\left\{\begin{matrix} NR_t - (1+\varphi)\cdot \tau_{NR}(I1_t)\cdot T_{NRt} \\ (h_{NR}\cdot N1_{NRt}, K_{NRt}) + T^{w}_{NRt}\left(h^{w}_{NR}\cdot N1_{NRt}\right)\end{matrix}\right\}}{(1+\varphi)},\right.$$

$$\left.\omega^{e}_{NR,K}, \omega^{e}_{NR,C}, NRG1^{Tde}_{t+1} + NRG2^{Tde}_{t+1} + NRG3^{Tde}_{t+1}\right]$$

$$+ (1-\delta)\cdot p^{NR}_{K(t+1)}\cdot \varepsilon^{NR}\cdot K^{d}_{NR(t+1)} - Tx_{NRG1(t+1)} - \left(1+p^{NR}_{B1}\right)\cdot B1^{s}_{NR(t+1)}$$

$$- p_w\cdot\left[\left[\frac{\varphi}{(1+\varphi)}\right]\cdot\left\{NR_t - (1+\varphi)\cdot\tau_{NR}(I1_t)\cdot T_{NRt}(h_{NR}\cdot N1_{NRt}, K_{NRt})\right.\right.$$

$$\left.\left.+T^{w}_{NRt}\left(h^{w}_{NR}\cdot N1_{NRt}\right)\right\} - T^{S}_{NR(t+1)}\left(h^{e}_{NR}\cdot N1^{Se}_{NR(t+1)}\right) - \Omega^{e}_{NR(t+1)}\right]$$

$$- \overline{C}\left\{N1^{Se}_{NR(t+1)} + \left[N1^{Te}_{NR(t+1)}\left[\frac{NR_t}{(1+\varphi)}\right], h_{NR}\cdot N1_{NRt}, K_{NRt}, I1_t,\right.\right.$$

$$\left.\left.h^{w}_{NR}\cdot N1_{NRt}, K^{d}_{NR(t+1)}\right], \gamma_{NR}\right\}\cdot h^{e}_{NR} \tag{5.35}$$

Solving (5.18) for the industry's end-of-period supply of bonds, $B1^{s}_{NR(t+1)}$, yields

$$B1^{s}_{NR(t+1)} = \left(\frac{1}{p^{NR}_{B1}}\right)\cdot\left[\Pi^{NRd}_{t} - TR^{NRe}_{t}\left[\tau_{NR}(I1t)\cdot T_{NRt}(h_{NR}\cdot N1_{NRt}, K_{NRt})\right.\right.$$

$$+ NR^{T*}_{t}, \omega_{NR,K}, \omega_{NR,C}, NRG1^{de}_{t} + NRG2^{de}_{t} + NRG3^{de}_{t}$$

$$\left.+\delta\cdot p^{NR}_{Kt}\cdot\varepsilon^{NR}\cdot K_{NRt}\right]$$

$$+ p_w\cdot\left[\varphi\cdot\tau_{NR}(I1_t)\cdot T_{NRt}(h_{NR}\cdot N1_{NRt}, K_{NRt})\right.$$

$$\left.- T^{w}_{NRt}\left(h^{w}_{NR}\cdot N1_{NRt}\right)\right] + W1_t\cdot(h_{NR} + h^{w}_{NR})\cdot N1_{NRt}$$

$$\left.+ \left(1+p^{NR}_{B1}\right)\cdot B1_{NRt} + p^{NR}_{Kt}\cdot\varepsilon^{NR}\cdot\left(K^{d}_{NR(t+1)} - K_{NRt}\right)\right] \tag{5.36}$$

Substituting the right-hand side of (5.36) for $B1^{s}_{NR(t+1)}$ in (5.35) yields the following expression for the present value of the industry's anticipated stream of dividends to its owners:

$$\frac{\Pi^{d}_{NR(t+1)}}{1+r_{1t}} + \Pi^{d}_{NRt} = \left[\frac{1}{(1+r_{1t})}\right]$$

$$
\cdot \left\{ TR^{NRe}_{t+1} \left[\frac{\left\{ \begin{array}{c} NRt - (1+\varphi)\cdot \tau_{NR}(I1_t)\cdot T_{NRt} \\ (h_{NR}\cdot N1_{NRt}, K_{NRt}) + T^{w}_{NRt}(h^{w}_{NR}\cdot N1_{NRt}) \end{array} \right\}}{(1+\varphi)}, \right. \right.
$$

$$
\left. \omega^{e}_{NR,K}, \omega^{e}_{NR,C}, NRG1^{Tde}_{t+1} + NRG2^{Tde}_{t+1} + NRG3^{Tde}_{t+1} \right]
$$

$$
+ (1-\delta)\cdot p^{NR}_{K(t+1)}\cdot \varepsilon^{NR}\cdot K^{d}_{NR(t+1)} - Tx_{NRG1(t+1)}
$$

$$
- p_w \cdot \left[\left[\frac{\varphi}{(1+\varphi)}\right]\cdot \left\{NR_t - (1+\varphi)\cdot \tau_{NR}(I1_t)\cdot T_{NRt}\,(h_{NR}\cdot N1_{NRt}, K_{NRt}) \right.\right.
$$

$$
\left. \left. + T^{w}_{NRt}\left(h^{w}_{NR}\cdot N1_{NRt}\right)\right\} - T^{S}_{NR(t+1)}\left(h^{e}_{NR}\cdot N1^{Se}_{NR(t+1)}\right) - \Omega^{e}_{NR(t+1)}\right]
$$

$$
- \overline{C}\left\{N1^{Se}_{NR(t+1)} + N1^{Te}_{NR(t+1)}\left[\frac{NR_t}{(1+\varphi)}, h_{NR}\cdot N1_{NRt}, K_{NRt}, I1_t, \right.\right.
$$

$$
\left.\left.\left. h^{w}_{NR}\cdot N1_{NRt}, K^{d}_{NR(t+1)}\right], \gamma_{NR}\right\}\cdot h^{e}_{NR}\right\}
$$

$$
+ TR^{NRE}_{t}\left[\tau_{NR}(I1_t)\cdot T_{NRt}(h_{NR}\cdot N1_{NRt}, K_{NRt}) + NR^{T^*}_{t}, \right.
$$

$$
\left. \omega_{NR,K}, \omega_{NR,C}, NRG1^{Tde}_{t} + NRG2^{Tde}_{t} + NRG3^{Tde}_{t}\right]
$$

$$
- \delta\cdot p^{NR}_{Kt}\cdot \varepsilon^{NR}\cdot K_{NRt} - Tx_{NRG1t}
$$

$$
- p_w \cdot \left[\varphi\cdot \tau_{NR}(I1_t)\cdot T_{NRt}(h_{NR}\cdot N1_{NRt}, K_{NRt}) - T^{W}_{NRt}\left(h^{W}_{NR}\cdot N1_{NRt}\right)\right]
$$

$$
- W1_t\cdot \left(h_{NR} + h^{w}_{NR}\right)\cdot N1_{NRt} - \left(1 + p^{NR}_{B1}\right)\cdot B1_{NRt}
$$

$$
- p^{NR}_{Kt}\cdot \varepsilon^{NR}\cdot \left(K^{d}_{NR(t+1)} - K_{NRt}\right) \tag{5.37}
$$

where $\left(1 + p^{NR}_{B1}\right)/p^{NR}_{B1}$ becomes $(1 + r_{1t})$ where $r_{1t} = 1/p^{NR}_{B1}$.

Maximizing (5.37) with respect to h_{NR}, h^{w}_{NR}, $K^{d}_{NR(t+1)}$, and $N1^{Se}_{NR(t+1)}$ yields the first-order necessary conditions (5.38)–(5.41).

$$
\frac{\partial\left[\dfrac{\Pi^{d}_{NR(t+1)}}{(1+r_{1t})} + \Pi^{d}_{NRt}\right]}{\partial h_{NR}} \equiv \left[\frac{1}{(1+r_{1t})}\right]\cdot\left[\frac{\partial TR^{NRe}_{t+1}}{\partial T^{Te}_{NR(t+1)}}\right]
$$

$$
\cdot\left\{-(1+\varphi)\cdot \tau_{NR}(I1_t)\cdot\left[\frac{\partial T_{NRt}}{\partial(h_{NR}\cdot N1_{NRt})}\right]\right\}\cdot N1_{NRt}
$$

$$+\left[\frac{1}{(1+r_{1t})}\right]\cdot p_w\cdot\varphi\cdot\tau_{NR}(I1_t)\cdot\left[\frac{\partial T_{NRt}}{\partial(h_{NR}\cdot N1_{NRt})}\right]\cdot N1_{NRt}$$
$$-\left[\frac{1}{(1+r_{1t})}\right]\cdot\left[\frac{\partial\overline{C}}{\partial N1^{Te}_{NR(t+1)}}\right]\cdot\left[\frac{\partial N1^{Te}_{NR(t+1)}}{\partial(h_{NR}\cdot N1_{NRt})}\right]\cdot N1_{NRt}$$
$$+\left[\frac{\partial TR^{NRe}_t}{\partial T_{NRt}}\right]\cdot\tau_{NR}(I1_t)\cdot\left[\frac{\partial T_{NRt}}{\partial(h_{NR}\cdot N1_{NRt})}\right]\cdot N1_{NRt}$$
$$-p_w\cdot\varphi\cdot\tau_{NR}(I1_t)\cdot\left[\frac{\partial T_{NRt}}{\partial(h_{NR}\cdot N1_{NRt})}\right]\cdot N1_{NRt}-W1_t\cdot N1_{NRt}=0 \tag{5.38}$$

According to (5.38), the nonrenewable resource industry will plan to add labor hours for the purpose of producing marketable NR during the period up to the point at which the present value of the marginal reduction in next period's net income is equal to the marginal increase in the current period's net income associated with adding an hour of labor to NR^T production this period. According to the first term on the right-hand side of the identity symbol in (5.38), as the industry adds a unit of labor to mine/extract a unit of NR this period, it reduces next period's anticipated revenue since the industry will have less NR available to market next period. A portion of the loss in next period's revenue is due to the extra waste generated during the current period associated with the extraction/mining of the resource. The second term on the right-hand side of (5.38) takes into account the fact that by having less NR available to extract/mine next period, the sector's cost of pollution allowances will fall, which reduces the cost next period of using more labor this period and therefore increases the present value of the sector's anticipated income stream to its owners. The third term on the right-hand side of (5.38) is also positive, indicating that if the sector has less available to produce next period, it will cut back on the number of employees it requires next period to mine/extract NR, thereby conserving next period's wage expense. Assuming that the sum of the first three terms is negative, the NR industry expects that next period's net income—and therefore the present value of that income—will decrease as the sector adds more labor hours in the current period. The fourth term on the right-hand side of (5.38) represents the current-period marginal revenue product from adding an extra unit of labor to the mining/extraction of NR this period. The fifth term represents the increase in the cost of obtaining pollution allowances for the extra waste generated in the process of producing more NR this period. The last term represents the extra wage expense this period of using an extra hour of labor.

$$\frac{\partial\left[\frac{\Pi^d_{NR(t+1)}}{(1+r_{1t})}+\Pi^d_{NRt}\right]}{\partial h^w_{NR}}\equiv p_w\cdot\left[\frac{\partial T^w_{NRt}}{\partial\left(h^w_{NR}\cdot N1_{NRt}\right)}\right]\cdot N1_{NRt}-W1_t\cdot N1_{NRt}$$
$$+\left[\frac{1}{(1+r_{1t})}\right]\cdot\left(\frac{\partial TR^{NRe}_{t+1}}{\partial NR^{de}_{t+1}}\right)\cdot\left[\frac{\partial T^W_{NRt}}{\partial\left(h^w_{NR}\cdot N1_{NRt}\right)}\right]$$

$$\cdot N1_{NRt} - \left[\frac{1}{(1+r_{1t})}\right] \cdot p_w \cdot \left[\frac{\varphi}{(1+\varphi)}\right] \cdot \left[\frac{\partial T^{w}_{NRt}}{\partial\left(h^{w}_{NR} \cdot N1_{NRt}\right)}\right] \cdot N1_{NRt}$$

$$-\left[\frac{1}{(1+r_{1t})}\right] \cdot \left[\frac{\partial \overline{C}}{\partial N1^{Te}_{t+1}}\right] \cdot \left[\frac{\partial N1^{Te}_{NR(t+1)}}{\partial\left(h^{w}_{NR} \cdot N1_{NRt}\right)}\right] \cdot N1_{NRt} = 0 \quad (5.39)$$

According to condition (5.39), the nonrenewable resource industry will hire labor during the current period for the purpose of recycling the resource up to the point at which the present value of the net income to be earned from the extra available resource next period (the sum of the last three terms) equals the net reduction in current income (the sum of the first two terms) associated with hiring labor for the next period. The first term to the right of the identity symbol is positive; it represents the current saving to be realized during the current period from the reduction in pollution allowances the sector is required to purchase this period because it is using some labor to recycle some of the waste it generates this period. The negative second term represents the current wage cost of the labor used in the recycling process. The positive third term denotes the present value of the extra revenue the sector anticipates earning next period from selling the extra resource associated with its current recycling effort on the margin. The positive fourth term represents the present value of the anticipated reduction in the cost of purchasing pollution allowances next period as a result of hiring more labor for recycling this period. The fifth term indicates the present value of the anticipated marginal factor (labor) cost associated with the higher production of the renewable resource next period resulting from the marginal recycling this period.

$$\frac{\partial\left[\frac{\Pi^{d}_{NR(t+1)}}{(1+r_{1t})} + \Pi^{d}_{NRt}\right]}{\partial K^{d}_{NR(t+1)}} \equiv \left(\frac{\partial TR^{NRe}_{t+1}}{\partial T^{Te}_{NR(t+1)}}\right) \cdot \tau_{NR}(I1_t + \Delta I1_t) \cdot \left[\frac{\partial T^{Te}_{NR(t+1)}}{\partial\left(K^{d}_{NR(t+1)}\right)}\right]$$

$$= (1+r_{1t}) \cdot p^{NR}_{Kt} \cdot \varepsilon^{NR} - (1-\delta) \cdot p^{NR}_{K(t+1)} \cdot \varepsilon^{e}_{NR} \quad (5.40)$$

According to (5.40), the present value maximizing NR sector will purchase capital goods during the current period up to the point at which the anticipated marginal revenue product of physical capital held at the beginning of next period is equal to the user cost of capital, shown by the sum on the (far) right-hand side of (5.40). The potential effect of physical capital upon the marginal product of labor next period is ignored in condition (5.40).

$$\frac{\partial\left[\frac{\Pi^{d}_{NR(t+1)}}{(1+r_{1t})} + \Pi^{d}_{NRt}\right]}{\partial N1^{Se}_{NR(t+1)}} \equiv p_w \cdot \left[\frac{\partial T^{S}_{NR(t+1)}}{\partial\left(h^{e}_{NR} \cdot N1^{Se}_{NR(t+1)}\right)}\right]$$

$$\cdot h^{e}_{NR} = \left\{\frac{\partial \overline{C}}{\partial N1^{Se}_{NR(t+1)}}\right\} \quad (5.41)$$

Condition (5.41) stipulates that the NR industry add to its stock of employees for the purpose of treating and storing waste next period up to the point at which the saving due to the reduction in pollution allowance purchases is equal to the marginal labor cost of hiring an additional worker next period.

Totally differentiating these first-order conditions and then solving simultaneously for h_{NR}, h^{w}_{NR}, $K^{d}_{NR(t+1)}$, and $N1^{Se}_{NR(t+1)}$ yields the NR sector's demand for labor hours for producing marketable NR during the current period, its demand for labor hours for the purpose of recycling waste during the current period, its (notional) end-of-period demand for physical capital, and its (notional) demand for workers for treating and storing waste next period. The direct effects operating through the own first-order conditions are assumed to prevail in the following specifications.

Demand Function for h_{NR}

From (5.38), the nonrenewable industry's current-period demand for labor hours for the purpose of producing marketable NR is positively related to the interest rate the sector anticipates will prevail during the current period in Country One, since an increase in that rate reduces the present value of next period's lost income arising from the fact that the sector is mining/extracting the marginal unit of NR during the current period rather than waiting until next period to do so. However, the larger the rate of waste per unit of NR extracted/mined this period, or the higher the current wage rate the sector pays its current employees, or the higher the price of pollution allowances, the less labor the sector wants to hire during the current period. Finally, the amount of infrastructure in place in Country One at the beginning of the current period positively affects the marginal product of labor during the current period, thereby positively affecting the NR sector's demand for current labor hours. Therefore, the following demand function for h_{NR} results from condition (5.38):

$$h^{d}_{NR} = h^{d}_{NR}(\underset{+}{r_1}, \underset{-}{p_w}, \underset{-}{\varphi}, \underset{-}{W1_t}, \underset{+}{I1_t}) \tag{5.42}$$

Demand Function for h^{w}_{NR}

From (5.39), the nonrenewable industry's current-period demand for labor hours for the purpose of recycling NR is negatively related to the interest rate the sector anticipates will prevail during the current period in Country One, since an increase in that rate reduces the present value of next period's income arising from selling the currently recycled NR next period. An increase in the price of pollution allowances also causes the sector to increase its demand for labor to recycle NR this period since the higher p_w increases the return to that labor because it enables the sector to reduce its unrecycled mass for which it must pay for pollution allowances. However, the larger the rate of waste per unit of NR extracted/mined this period or the higher the current wage rate the sector pays its current employees the fewer hours it uses current labor time to recycle waste. Therefore, the following demand function for h_{NR} results from condition (5.39):

$$h^{w}_{NR} = h^{w}_{NR}\underset{-\ \ +\ \ -\ \ +}{(r_1, p_w, \varphi, W1_t)} \tag{5.43}$$

Demand Function for $K^{d}_{NR(t+1)}$

According to condition (5.40), the nonrenewable industry's end-of-period demand for physical capital is negatively related to the anticipated user cost of capital, $(1+r_{1t}) \cdot p^{NR}_{Kt} \cdot \varepsilon^{NR} - (1-\delta) \cdot p^{NR}_{K(t+1)} \cdot \varepsilon^{e}_{NR}$. Therefore, the end-of-period demand is negatively related to the current price of capital in terms of Country One's currency, $p^{NR}_{Kt} \cdot \varepsilon^{NR}$, to the anticipated current interest rate, and to the rate of physical depreciation of capital, δ. Finally, the anticipated marginal product of capital next period is positively related to the amount of infrastructure the G1 sector plans to have in place by the beginning of next period.

$$K^{d}_{NR(t+1)} = K^{d}_{NR(t+1)}\left(\underset{-}{r1}, \underset{-}{\delta}, \underset{-}{p^{NR}_{Kt} \cdot \varepsilon^{NR}}, \underset{+}{I1_t + \Delta I1_t}\right) \tag{5.44}$$

Demand Function for $N1^{Se}_{NR(t+1)}$

According to (5.41), the NR industry's demand for labor for the purpose of treating and storing waste next period is positively related to the price of pollution allowances, since an increase in that price increases the value of the marginal product of labor devoted to treating and storing waste. In addition, the greater the shift parameter, γ_{NR}, the greater the net market of labor the NR industry anticipates next period at a given money wage. Consequently a larger value of γ_{NR} lowers the marginal factor (labor) cost next period and increases the sector's demand for labor for treating and storing waste next period.

$$N1^{Se}_{NR(t+1)} = N1^{Se}_{NR(t+1)}(\underset{+}{p_w}, \underset{+}{\gamma_{NR}}) \tag{5.45}$$

From the above functions, it is possible to solve also for the remaining decision variables.

Current Production of the Marketable Nonrenewable Resource

Current-period production of the marketable nonrenewable resource is positively related to the infrastructure in place in Country One at the beginning of the current period, the stock of physical capital held by the NR industry at the beginning of the current period, and the labor hours the sector devotes to mining/extracting the resource during the current period. Therefore, from (5.42) the following supply function for the marketable nonrenewable resource emerges:

$$\begin{aligned} NR_t^{Ts} &= \tau_{NR}(I1_t) \cdot T_{NRt}\left[h_{NR}^d(r_1, p_w, \varphi, W1_t, I1_t) \cdot N1_{NRt}, K_{NRt}\right] \\ &= NR_t^{Ts}(\underset{+}{r_1}, \underset{-}{p_w}, \underset{-}{\varphi}, \underset{-}{W1_t}, \underset{+}{I1_t}, \underset{+}{K_{NRt}}) \end{aligned} \qquad (5.46)$$

Current Product Price

Substituting the NR industry's demand for labor for the purpose of mining/extracting the nonrenewable resource this period into the inverse of the sector's estimated current-period demand function for its product yields the current-period pricing function of the NR sector. As shown in (5.47) below, the NR industry announces a lower price for its product the greater the infrastructure in place in Country One at the beginning of the current period and the greater its initial inventory of marketable NR^T. On the other hand, the higher wage rate or the higher the price of pollution allowances, or the greater the amount of waste generated per unit of NR mined/extracted during the current period, the higher the product price the NR industry announces at the beginning of the current period.

$$\begin{aligned} p_{NRt} &= p_{NRt}\Big(\tau_{NR}(I1t) \cdot T_{NRt}\left[h_{NR}^d(r_1, p_w, \varphi, W_t, I1_t) \cdot N1_{NRt}, K_{NRt}\right] \\ &\quad + NR_t^{T^*}, \omega_{NR,K}, \omega_{NR,C}, NRG1_t^{Tde} + NRG2_t^{Tde} + NRG3_t^{Tde}\Big) \\ &= p_{NRt}\Big(\underset{-}{r_1}, \underset{+}{p_w}, \underset{+}{\varphi}, \underset{+}{W_t}, \underset{-}{I1_t}, \underset{-}{K_{NRt}}, \underset{-}{NR_t^{T^*}}, \underset{+}{\omega_{NR,K}}, \underset{+}{\omega_{NR,C}}, \\ &\quad \underset{+}{NRG1_t^{Tde} + NRG2_t^{Tde} + NRG3_t^{Tde}}\Big) \end{aligned} \qquad (5.47)$$

Wage-Setting Function

The wage rate the NR sector announces for next period is found by substituting the solutions given by (5.42)–(5.45) into the inverse of the NR industry's estimate of the net supply of workers to the industry next period, shown in (5.30). In light of (5.19), the signs of the variables in $h_{NR}^d(\cdot)$ and $K_{NR(t+1)}^d(\cdot)$ are reversed from those in (5.42) and (5.44) because the more labor the sector hires this period to extract/mine NR or the more physical capital it holds by the beginning of next period, the less labor it will require next period.

$$W1_{t+1} = W1 \Big\{ N1^{e}_{NR(t+1)}(p_w, \gamma_{NR}) + N1^{Te}_{NR(t+1)} \Big[\frac{NR_t}{(1+\varphi)}, h^{d}_{NR}$$

+ + +

$$(r_1, p_w, \varphi, W1_t, I1_t), K_{NRt}, h^{w}_{NR}(r_1, p_w, \varphi, W1_t),$$

− + + + − − − + − −

$$K^{d}_{NR(t+1)}\Big(r_1, \delta, p^{NR}_{Kt} \cdot \varepsilon^{NR}, I1_t + \Delta I1_t\Big)\Big], \gamma_{NR}\Big\}$$

+ + + − −

$$= W1\Big(p_w, \gamma_{NR}, \varphi, r_1, p^{NR}_{Kt} \cdot \varepsilon^{NR}, K_{NRt}, I1_t, \Delta I1_t\Big) \tag{5.48}$$

+ − ? ? + + − −

A question mark indicates that the direction of the effect of an increase in the variable above the question mark upon the dependent variable, in this case, W1, is unclear.

Waste Generation

The waste, including depreciation, generated by the nonrenewable resource industry during the current period varies directly with the amount of waste generated per unit of output, φ, and with the amount of marketable NR produced during the period, which in turn varies directly with the number of labor hours employed during the period to mine/extract NR.

$$W^{*}NR_t = \varphi \cdot \tau_{NR}(I1_t) \cdot T_{NRt}\Big[h^{d}_{NR}(r_1, p_w, \varphi, W1_t, I1_t), K_{NRt}\Big] + \kappa \cdot \delta \cdot K_{NRt}$$

+ − − − + +

$$= W^{*}NR_t(\varphi, I1_t, r_1, p_w, W1_t, K_{NRt}, \kappa, \delta) \tag{5.49}$$

+ + + − − + + +

Recycled NR

The amount of NR recycled during the current period, RW*NR, is found by substituting (5.43) into the transformation function $T^{w}_{NRt}\big(h^{w}_{NR} \cdot N1_{NRt}\big)$.

$$RW^{*}NR = T^{w}_{NRt}\big[h^{w}_{NR}(r_1, p_w, \varphi, W1_t)\big]$$

− + − −

$$= RW^{*}NR(r_1, p_w, \varphi, W1_t) \tag{5.50}$$

− + − −

Excess Demand for Pollution Allowances

The NR sector's excess demand for pollution allowances during the current period is equal to its waste generation function minus its recycled NR function minus its initial allocation of pollution allowances.

$$\Omega^d_{NR} - \Omega_{NRt} = W^*NR_t(\varphi, I1_t, r_1, p_w, W1_t, K_{NRt}) - RW^*NR(r1, p_w, \varphi, W1_t)$$

$$+ + + - - + \qquad - + - -$$

$$- \Omega_{NRt}\Omega^d_{NR} - \Omega_{NRt} = \Omega^d_{NR}(\varphi, I1_t, r_1, p_w, W1_t, K_{NRt}) - \Omega_{NRt} \quad (5.51)$$

$$+ + + - ? +$$

NR Sector's Supply of Bonds

Assuming that the nonrenewable resource industry does not plan to engage in net saving during the period (i.e., it plans to distribute all net income during the current period as dividends), then from (5.11) the sector's end-of-period supply of bonds to Country One's bond market, before it learns the demand for its product and the price of capital, is given by

$$p^{NR}_{B1} \cdot B1^s_{NR(t+1)} = p^{NR}_{B1} \cdot B1_{NRt} - p_{NRt} \cdot NR^{T^*}_t + p^{NR}_{Kt} \cdot \varepsilon^{NR} \cdot \left[K^d_{NR(t+1)}\left(r_1, \delta, p^{NR}_{Kt} \cdot \varepsilon^{NR}, I1_t + \Delta I1_t\right) - K_{NRt}\right]$$

$$= p^{NR}_{B1} \cdot B1^s_{NR(t+1)}\left(p^{NR}_{B1} \cdot B1_{NRt} - p_{NRt} \cdot NR^{T^*}_t, \right.$$

$$+1$$

$$\left. r_1, \delta, p^{NR}_{Kt} \cdot \varepsilon^{NR}, I1_t + \Delta I1_t, K_{NRt}\right) \quad (5.52)$$

$$- - \quad - \quad + \quad -$$

where it is assumed the NR sector's demand for capital is elastic with respect to its price.

Dividends Paid to Shareholders during Current Period

Given the assumption that the NR industry's planned net business saving during the current period is zero, the sector's dividend payments to its shareholders during the period are equal to the value of current production of NR minus current wages, interest, taxes, depreciation, and the sector's net purchases of pollution allowances.

$$\Pi^d_{NRt} = p_{NRt} \cdot \{\tau_{NR}(I1t) \cdot T_{NRt}(h_{NR} \cdot N1_{NRt}, K_{NRt})\} - W1_t \cdot (h_{NR} + h^w_{NR}) \cdot N1_{NRt} - B1_{NRt} - T_{xNRG1t} - \delta \cdot p^{NR}_{Kt} \cdot \varepsilon^{NR} \cdot K_{NRt} - p_w \cdot [\varphi \cdot \tau_{NR}(I1t) \cdot T_{NRt}(h_{NR} \cdot N1_{NRt}, K_{NRt}) - T^w_{NRt}(h^w_{NR} \cdot N1_{NRt})] \quad (5.53)$$

Chapter 6 contains an analysis of the capital goods industry.

6

The Capital Goods Industry

At the beginning of the current period, an initial stock of physical capital, K_{Kt}, is held by the capital goods industry. Let $K^d_{k(t+1)}$ represent the capital goods industry's desired stock of capital for the end of the current period, which is determined in accordance with its objective to maximize the present value of its operations.

The capital goods industry applies a variable amount of labor together with its given stock of physical capital to transform the mass of marketed NR that it purchases to convert into a marketable product, K. The current level of transformation services, $T_K(\bullet)$, is assumed to be a positive increasing function of (variable) labor hours, $h_K \cdot N2_{Kt}$, applied during the period, where $N2_{Kt}$ denotes the number of people employed in the capital goods industry at the start of the current period and where h_K represents the (average) number of hours these employees work for the capital goods industry during the current period transforming nonrenewable resources into physical capital. We assume that the marginal transformation of labor, T'_K, is positive but diminishing.

Under these assumptions, the production function for capital goods, K^T_t, is given by (6.1):

$$K^T_t = \min\left\{\left[\frac{NRK^d_t}{(\kappa + \varphi_K)}\right], \tau_K(I2_t) \cdot (h_k \cdot N2_{Kt}, K_{Kt})\right\} \geq 0 \tag{6.1}$$

where

NRK^d_t = the amount of NR purchased by the K industry during the current period.
κ = the amount of NR necessary to produce (embodied within) a unit of physical capital.
ϕ_K = the amount of NR necessarily wasted in the process of being transformed into a unit of physical capital.
$\tau_K(I2_t)$ with $\tau'_K(\bullet) > 0$ represents the contribution of the infrastructure in Country Two at the beginning of the period, $I2_t$, to the transformation services of labor and capital.

Assuming the capital goods industry wastes neither the transformation services nor the amount of NRK_t^d unnecessarily, the number of capital goods (in terms of units) produced is equal to $\tau_K(I2_t) \cdot T_{Kt}(h_K \cdot N2_{Kt}, K_{Kt})$:

$$K_t^T = \tau_K (I2_t) \cdot T_{Kt} (h_K \cdot N2_{Kt}, K_{Kt}) \tag{6.2}$$

In addition, in terms of mass, the amount of natural NR transformed in the production process into either physical capital or waste becomes

$$NR_t^{Kd} = (\kappa + \varphi_K) \cdot \tau_K (I2_t) \cdot T_{Kt} (h_K \cdot N2_{Kt}, K_{Kt}) \tag{6.3}$$

The amount of physical capital that is not sold during the current period and that does not physically depreciate is assumed to be added to the industry's inventory of K:

$$\begin{aligned} K_{K(t+1)} = {} & (1-\delta) \cdot K_{Kt} + \tau_K (I2_t) \cdot T_{Kt} (h_K \cdot N2_{Kt}, K_{Kt}) - KNR_t - KC_t \\ & - KG1_t - KG2_t - KG3_t \geq 0 \end{aligned} \tag{6.4}$$

where $KNR_t (= K^d_{NR(t+1)} - (1-\delta) \cdot K_{NRt})$ corresponds to the actual amount of physical capital purchased by the nonrenewable resource industry in Country One during the current period, $KC_t(= K^d_{C(t+1)} - (1-\delta) \cdot K_{Ct})$ corresponds to the actual amount of physical capital purchased by the consumer goods industry in Country Three during the current period, $KG1_t(= K^d_{G1(t+1)} - (1-\delta) \cdot K_{G1t})$ denotes the amount of physical capital purchased by the G1 sector during the current period, $KG2_t(= K^d_{G2(t+1)} - (1-\delta) \cdot K_{G2t})$ represents the amount of physical capital purchased by the G2 sector during the current period, $KG3_t(= K^d_{G3(t+1)} - (1-\delta) \cdot K_{G3t})$ represents the amount of physical capital purchased by the G3 sector during the current period, δ represents the rate of depreciation of physical capital, and $K_{K(t+1)}$ denotes the end of current-period inventory of K held by the K industry.

During the current period, the industry generates new waste products equal to W^*K in terms of mass:

$$W^*K = \varphi_K \cdot \tau_K(I2_t) \cdot T_{Kt} (h_K \cdot N2_{Kt}, K_{Kt}) + \kappa \cdot \delta \cdot K_{Kt} \tag{6.5}$$

The sector must pay a fee, p_w/ε^K , in terms of its currency, to obtain a pollution allowance for every unit (in terms of mass) of wasted mass it discharges into the environment over and above the pollution allowances, Ω_{Kt}, allocated to it in the current period, and where ε^K represents the value of Country Two's unit of account in terms of Country One's unit of account that the capital goods industry expects to prevail during the period before exchange rates are actually established. To the extent that the industry engages in treating and storing waste, it reduces the number of allowances it must buy in the market. (In fact it is possible for the K industry to treat and store enough mass during the period that it generates less untreated waste than the number of pollution allowances it receives, in which case it would earn revenue by selling its excess supply of pollution allowances during the period.)

Assume the following transformation function for treating and storing waste during the current period:

$$SW^*K_t = \min\left[\varphi_K \cdot \tau_{Kt}(I2_t) \cdot T_{Kt}(h_K \cdot N2_{Kt}, K_{Kt}) + \kappa \cdot \delta \cdot K_{Kt} - \Omega^d_{Kt}, T^S_{Kt}\left(h^S_K \cdot N2_{Kt}\right)\right] \geq 0 \quad (6.6)$$

where SW^*K_t represents the amount of waste (in terms of mass) treated and stored during the current period, Ω^d_{Kt} represents the industry's desired holdings of pollution allowances during the current period, and $T^S_{Kt}(\bullet)$ represents the transformation function for treating and storing waste during the current period.

For simplicity, we assume that labor is the only resource necessary to provide this service.

Assuming that neither transformation services nor mass are wasted in the treatment and storage process,

$$SW^*K_t = T^S_{Kt}\left(h^S_K \cdot N2_{Kt}\right) \quad (6.7)$$

Then the industry's current expenses associated with generating, treating, and storing waste during the period, $C^*_{K,W}$, is equal to

$$C^*_{K,W} = (p_w/\varepsilon^K) \cdot \left[\phi_K \cdot \tau_K(I2_t) \cdot T_{Kt}(h_K \cdot N2_{Kt}, K_{Kt}) + \kappa \cdot \delta \cdot K_{Kt} - T^S_{Kt}\left(h^S_K \cdot N2_{Kt}\right)\right] + W2_t \cdot h^S_K \cdot N2_{Kt} \quad (6.8)$$

Taking the current wage rate and the capital goods industry's forecast of the current-period demand function for K^T_t, $KNR^{de}_t + KC^{de}_t + KG1^{de}_t + KG2^{de}_t + KG3^{de}_t$ as given, the capital goods industry attempts to maximize the present value of the dividends it intends to pay to the industry's shareholders during the current and next periods. Then the industry's desired current-period sales of K^T_t (in terms of units) is given by

$$KNR^{de}_t + KC^{de}_t + KG1^{de}_t + KG2^{de}_t + KG3^{de}_t = \tau_K(I2_t) \cdot T_{Kt}(h_K \cdot N2_{Kt}, K_{Kt}) - \left[K^d_{K(t+1)} - (1-\delta) \cdot K_{Kt}\right] \quad (6.9)$$

where $[K^d_{K(t+1)} - (1-\delta) \cdot K_{Kt}]$ represents the portion of current production that is used to replace capital that depreciates during the period, $\delta \cdot K_{Kt}$, plus the sector's desired increase in its stock of physical capital by the end of the period, $K^d_{K(t+1)} - K_{Kt}$.

Each period, dividends equal net income minus net business saving. Net income is equal to the value of current production of capital goods minus current expenses (wages, interest, taxes, purchases of the nonrenewable resource, and depreciation). Therefore, current dividends equal the value of current production minus wages, interest, taxes, outlays for pollution allowances and intermediate goods (the nonrenewable resource), depreciation and net business saving. Measured in terms of current-period market prices, net business saving is necessarily equal to the sum of the sector's net increase in assets (measured in terms of current-period prices) minus the net increase in liabilities (also measured in terms of current-period prices) during the period.

Let p_{Kt} represent the market price that the K industry sets during the current period. Then, measured in terms of current market prices, the value of current production is given by $p_{Kt} \cdot \tau_K(I2_t) \cdot T_{Kt}(h_K \cdot N2_{Kt}, K_{Kt})$. The industry plans to acquire the amount $p_{Kt} \cdot (K^d_{K(t+1)} - K_{Kt})$ in physical capital during the current period. Let $B2_{Kt}$ represent the number of K industry bonds outstanding in Country Two's bond market at the beginning of the current period. Let p^K_{B2} represent the current-period market price of bonds issued in Country Two's bond market that the capital goods industry anticipates will prevail during the period before interest rates and exchange rates are established. Each bond outstanding presumably pays one unit of Country Two's currency as interest income during the current period. Then the market value of the capital goods industry's debt in Country Two's bond market is represented by $p^K_{B2} \cdot B2_{Kt}$. Let $B2^s_{K(t+1)}$ denote the number of bonds the industry plans to have outstanding by the end of the current period. Then the amount which the industry plans to borrow in Country Two's bond market during the current period is given by $p^K_{B2} \cdot (B2^s_{K(t+1)} - B2_{Kt})$. The current level of planned net business saving, S^d_{Kt}, by the capital goods industry must be consistent with the market value of the sector's planned accumulation of physical capital minus its planned current-period borrowing. Therefore, it follows that

$$S^d_{Kt} \equiv p_{Kt} \cdot \left(K^d_{K(t+1)} - K_{Kt}\right) - p^K_{B2} \cdot \left(B2^s_{K(t+1)} - B2_{Kt}\right) \tag{6.10}$$

The sector's planned dividends for the current period, Π^d_{Kt}, are given by

$$\begin{aligned}\Pi^d_{Kt} = p_{Kt} \cdot &\left\{\tau_K(I2_t) \cdot T_{Kt}(h_K \cdot N2_{Kt}, K_{Kt}) - \left[K^d_{K(t+1)} - (1-\delta) \cdot K_{Kt}\right]\right\}\\ &- \left(p^K_{NRt}/\varepsilon^K\right) \cdot (\kappa + \varphi_K) \cdot \tau(I2_t) \cdot T_{Kt}(h_K \cdot N2_{Kt}, K_{Kt}) - Tx_{KG2t}\\ &- \left(p_w/\varepsilon^K\right) \cdot \Big[\varphi_K \cdot \tau_K(I2_t) \cdot T_{Kt}(h_K \cdot N2_{Kt}, K_{Kt}) + \kappa \cdot \delta \cdot K_{Kt}\\ &- T^S_{Kt}\left(h^S_K \cdot N2_{Kt}\right)\Big] - W2_t \cdot \left(h_K + h^S_K\right) \cdot N2_{Kt}\\ &+ p^K_{B2} \cdot \left(B2^s_{K(t+1)} - B2_{Kt}\right) - B2_{Kt}\end{aligned} \tag{6.11}$$

where the planned real investment is valued in terms of the current market price of physical capital and where Tx_{KG2} denotes the business taxes that the G2 sector levies upon the capital goods industry in the current period.

At the beginning of the period, the capital goods industry announces its product price, p_{Kt}. The following demand function represents the industry's forecast of the current-period demand for its product:

$$
\begin{aligned}
K_t^{de} &= KNR_t^{de} + KC_t^{de} + KG1_t^{de} + KG2_t^{de} + KG3_t^{de} \\
&= KNR_t^{de}\left(p_{Kt}, \omega_{KNR}\right) + KC_t^{de}\left(p_{Kt}, \omega_{KC}\right) + KG1_t^{de} + KG2_t^{de} + KG3_t^{de} \\
&= K_t^{de}\Big(\underset{-}{p_{\,rmKt}}, \underset{+}{\omega KNR}, \underset{+}{\omega KC}, \underset{+}{KG1_t^{de} + KG2_t^{de} + KG3_t^{de}}\Big)
\end{aligned}
\tag{6.12}
$$

where $K_t^{de}(\bullet)$ denotes the industry's forecast, at the beginning of the current period, of the current real market demand for capital goods by the nonrenewable resource industry in Country One, by the consumer goods industry in Country Three, and by the three government sectors. Assume that the derivative of $K_t^{de}(\bullet)$ with respect to p_{Kt} is negative (the sign is verified in the specification of the economic behavior of the NR and consumer goods industries), ω_{KNR} denotes a vector of shift parameters that the capital goods industry forecasts affect the NR sector's demand for capital goods, ω_{KC} denotes a vector of shift parameters that the capital goods industry forecasts affect the consumer goods sector's demand for capital goods. Solving the inverse function for p_{Kt} yields

$$
p_{Kt} = p_{Kt}\Big(\underset{-}{K_t^{de}}, \underset{+}{\omega_{KNR}}, \underset{+}{\omega_{KC}}, \underset{+}{KG1_t^{de} + KG2_t^{de} + KG3_t^{de}}\Big) \cdot K_t^{de} \tag{6.13}
$$

where

$$
\begin{aligned}
\frac{\partial p_{Kt}}{\partial\left(K_t^{de}\right)} &\equiv \frac{1}{\left[\partial\left(K_t^{de}\right)/\partial p_{Kt}\right]} < 0 \\
\frac{\partial p_{Kt}}{\partial \omega_{KNR}} &\equiv -\frac{\left[\partial\left(K_t^{de}\right)/\partial \omega_{KNR}\right]}{\left[\partial\left(K_t^{de}\right)/\partial p_{Kt}\right]} > 0 \\
\frac{\partial p_{Kt}}{\partial \omega_{KC}} &\equiv -\frac{\left[\partial\left(K_t^{de}\right)/\partial \omega_{KC}\right]}{\left[\partial\left(K_t^{de}\right)/\partial p_{Kt}\right]} > 0
\end{aligned}
\tag{6.14}
$$

and

$$
\frac{\partial p_{Kt}}{\partial\left(KG1_t^{de}+KG2_t^{de}+KG3_t^{de}\right)} \equiv -\frac{\left[\partial\left(K_t^{de}\right)/\partial\left(KG1_t^{de} + KG2_t^{de} + KG3_t^{de}\right)\right]}{\left[\partial\left(K_t^{de}\right)/\partial p_{Kt}\right]} > 0
$$

An increase in ω_{KNR}, ω_{KC}, or $KG1_t^{de} + KG2_t^{de} + KG3_t^{de}$ represents an outward shift in the capital goods industry's forecast of the market demand curve for its product.

The price, p_{Kt}, given by (6.13) represents the maximum uniform price the capital goods sector expects it can value each unit of physical capital it makes during the period. Based upon this function, the sector's forecasted current total revenue, TR_t^{Ke}, function is given by

$$\begin{aligned} TR_t^{Ke} &= p_{Kt} \cdot K_t^{de} = p_{Kt}\left(K_t^{de}, \omega_{KNR}, \omega_{KC}, KG1_t^{de} + KG2_t^{de} + KG3_t^{de}\right) \cdot K_t^{de} \\ &= TR_t^{Ke}\left(\underset{-}{K_t^{de}}, \underset{+}{\omega_{KNR}}, \underset{+}{\omega_{KC}}, \underset{+}{KG1_t^{de} + KG2_t^{de} + KG3_t^{de}}\right) \end{aligned} \tag{6.15}$$

Substituting the right-hand side of (6.9) for K_t^{de} in (6.15) yields

$$\begin{aligned} TR_t^{Ke} = &TR_t^{Ke}\Big\{\tau_K(I2_t) \cdot T_{Kt}(h_K \cdot N2_{Kt}, K_{Kt}) - \Big[K_{K(t+1)}^d \\ &-(1-\delta) \cdot K_{Kt}\Big]\ \omega_{KNR}, \omega_{KC}, KG1_t^{de} + KG2_t^{de} + KG3_t^{de}\Big\} \end{aligned} \tag{6.16}$$

Substituting the right-hand side of (6.16) for the first term, $p_{Kt} \cdot \{\tau_K(I2_t) \cdot T_{Kt}(h_K \cdot N2_{Kt}, K_{Kt}) - [K_{K(t+1)}^d - (1-\delta) \cdot K_{Kt}]\}$, on the right-hand side of (6.11) yields

$$\begin{aligned} \Pi_{Kt}^d = &TR_t^{Ke}\Big\{\tau_K(I2_t) \cdot T_{Kt}(h_K \cdot N2_{Kt}, K_{Kt}) - \Big[K_{K(t+1)}^d - (1-\delta) \cdot K_{Kt}\Big], \\ &\omega_{KNR}, \omega_{KC}, KG1_t^{de} + KG2_t^{de} + KG3_t^{de}\Big\} - \left(p_{NRt}^K/\varepsilon^K\right) \\ &\cdot (\kappa + \varphi_K) \cdot \tau(I2_t) \cdot T_{Kt}(h_K \cdot N2_{Kt}, K_{Kt}) - Tx_{KG2t} - \left(p_w/\varepsilon^K\right) \\ &\cdot \Big[\varphi_K \cdot \tau_K(I2_t) \cdot T_{Kt}(h_K \cdot N2_{Kt}, K_{Kt}) + \kappa \cdot \delta \cdot K_{Kt} - T_{Kt}^S\left(h_K^S \cdot N2_{Kt}\right)\Big] \\ &- W2_t \cdot \left(h_k + h_K^S\right) \cdot N2_{Kt} + p_{B2}^K \cdot \left(B2_{K(t+1)}^S - B2_{Kt}\right) - B2_{Kt} \end{aligned} \tag{6.17}$$

as the expression for the amount the capital goods industry plans to distribute as dividends during the current period.

It is assumed that next period's planned production of K, K_{t+1}^{Te}, is given by

$$\begin{aligned} K_{t+1}^{Te} = \min\Big\{&\Big[NR_{t+1}^{Kd}/(\kappa + \varphi_K)\Big], \tau_K(I2_t + \Delta I2) \\ &\cdot T_{K(t+1)}^{Te}\left(h_K^e \cdot N2_{K(t+1)}^{Te}, K_{K(t+1)}^d\right)\Big\} \end{aligned} \tag{6.18}$$

In particular, next period's planned production of capital goods is assumed to be constrained, first, by the amount of NR the capital goods industry anticipates it will purchase next period, NR_{t+1}^{Kd}, and, second, by the level of transformation services provided by labor and capital next period. From (6.18), assuming that the sector does not produce more waste than necessary, the number of capital goods the industry plans to produce next period is given by

$$K_{t+1}^{Te} = \tau_K(I2_t + \Delta I2) \cdot T_{K(t+1)}^{Te}\left(h_K^e \cdot N2_{K(t+1)}^{Te}, K_{K(t+1)}^d\right) \tag{6.19}$$

where $I2_t + \Delta I2$ denotes the infrastructure that the G2 sector plans to have in place by the beginning of next period and where $\tau_K(I2_t + \Delta I2) > 1$ represents the contribution of next period's infrastructure to the ability of labor and capital to transform the nonrenewable resource into capital goods. To avoid unnecessarily wasting either natural resources or transformation services, the capital goods industry combines them in the following way:

$$NR^{Kd}_{t+1} = (\kappa + \varphi_K) \cdot \tau_K(I2_t + \Delta I2) \cdot T^{Te}_{K(t+1)} \left(h^e_K \cdot N2^{Te}_{K(t+1)}, K^d_{K(t+1)}\right) \tag{6.20}$$

This restriction represents the combinations of NR and transformation services along the expansion path associated with the production of capital goods next period.

The industry anticipates generating new waste products, W^*K_{t+1}, during next period given by (6.21):

$$W^*K_{t+1} = \varphi_K \cdot \tau_K(I2_t + \Delta I2) \cdot T^{Te}_{K(t+1)} \left(h^e_K \cdot N2^{Te}_{K(t+1)}, K^d_{K(t+1)}\right) + \kappa \cdot \delta \cdot K^d_{K(t+1)} \tag{6.21}$$

Again, the sector must pay a fee, p_w/ε^K, when measured in terms of its country's unit of account to obtain a pollution allowance for every unit of wasted mass it discharges into the environment over and above its pollution allowance allocation. Assume the following transformation function for recycling waste next period:

$$SW^*K_{t+1} = \min\left[\varphi_K \cdot \tau_K(I2_t + \Delta I2) \cdot T^{Te}_{K(t+1)} \left(h^e_K \cdot N2^{Te}_{K(t+1)}, K^d_{K(t+1)}\right) + \kappa \cdot \delta \cdot K^d_{K(t+1)} - \Omega^d_{K(t+1)}, T^S_{K(t+1)} \left(h^e_K \cdot N2^{Se}_{K(t+1)}\right)\right] \geq 0 \tag{6.22}$$

where SW^*K_{t+1} represents the amount of waste treated and stored during the next period, $\Omega^d_{K(t+1)}$ represents the sector's demand for pollution allowances for next period, and $T^S_{K(t+1)}(\bullet)$ represents the transformation function for converting untreated waste into treated and stored waste next period, with $N2^{Se}_{K(t+1)}$ representing the number of employees the sector expects to use to treat and store waste next period.

Assuming that neither transformation services nor mass are unnecessarily wasted in the treatment and storage process, the amount of treated and stored waste planned by the capital goods industry for next period is given by

$$SW^*K_{t+1} = T^S_{K(t+1)} \left(h^e_K \cdot N2^{Se}_{K(t+1)}\right) \tag{6.23}$$

Then the industry's anticipated expenses associated with discharging, treating, and storing next period, $C^e_{K,W}{}^*$, is equal to

$$C^e_{K,W^*} = \left(p_w/\varepsilon^K\right) \cdot \left\{\varphi_K \cdot \tau_K(I2_t + \Delta I2) \cdot T^{Te}_{K(t+1)} \left(h^e_K \cdot N2^{Te}_{K(t+1)}, K^d_{K(t+1)}\right) + \kappa \cdot \delta \cdot K^d_{K(t+1)} - T^S_{K(t+1)} \left(h^e_K \cdot N2^{Se}_{K(t+1)}\right)\right\} + W2_{t+1} \cdot h^e_K \cdot N2^{Se}_{K(t+1)} \tag{6.24}$$

The capital goods industry also forecasts the net market supply function of people who will be available to work next period after subtracting its estimate of its government sector's and the R2 industry's demands for employees for next period. The forecasted net supply of labor is assumed to be positively related to the money wage, $W2_{t+1}$, that the capital goods industry announces this period that it is willing to pay its employees next period (presumably the G2 sector and the R2 industry will also pay this wage and their demands will be filled first with the households indifferent as to their potential employer). Assume the forecasted net labor supply function is given by

$$N2^{se}_{t+1} = N2^{se}(W2_{t+1}, \gamma_2) \tag{6.25}$$

where γ_2 denotes a vector of parameters that the capital goods sector anticipates will shift the labor supply function and where $\partial(N2^{se}_{t+1})/\partial(W2_{t+1}) > 0$. The inverse of this function yields an expression for the minimum wage the sector estimates it needs to announce in order to attract a given number of employees for next period.

$$W2_{t+1} = W2(N2^{se}_{t+1}, \gamma_2) \tag{6.26}$$

where $\partial(W2)/\partial(N2^{se}_{t+1}) > 0$. From this inverse function, next period's anticipated labor cost function, $\overline{C}_{K(\bullet)}$, may be expressed as a function of the number of people the capital goods industry plans to employ by the beginning of next period, $N2^{Kde}_{t+1}$, where it is assumed that the sector sets the money wage so that it generates the anticipated number of applicants (of homogeneous quality) that the sector wants to hire next period:

$$\overline{C}_K = \left(N2^{Kde}_{t+1}, \gamma_2\right) = W2\left(N2^{Kde}_{t+1}, \gamma_2\right) \cdot h^e_K \cdot N2^{Kde}_{t+1} \tag{6.27}$$

where $\partial\overline{C}_K/\partial N2^{Kde}_{t+1} = h^e_K \cdot W2_{t+1} + h^e_K \cdot N2^{Kde}_{t+1} \cdot (\partial W2/\partial N2^{Kde}_{t+1}) \geq 0$ denotes next period's marginal factor cost of an extra employee.

Next period's anticipated net income is equal to the anticipated value of next period's production, $p^e_{K(t+1)} \cdot \tau_K(I2_t + \Delta I2) \cdot T^{Te}_{K(t+1)}(h^e_K \cdot N2^{Te}_{K(t+1)}, K^d_{K(t+1)})$, minus next period's expenses (wages, interest, purchases of the nonrenewable resource, and depreciation), where $p^e_{K(t+1)}$ represents the market price that the capital goods industry anticipates this period setting next period for its product. Next period's anticipated dividends equal the value of production next period minus next period's wages, interest, taxes, depreciation, and net business saving. Measured in terms of next period's market prices, net business saving is necessarily equal to the sum of the sector's net increase in assets minus the net increase in liabilities during the period.

For simplicity, we assume that at the beginning of the current period, the sector plans to hold an arbitrary amount of physical capital by the end of next period, $K^{de}_{K(t+2)}$. Let $B2^s_{K(t+1)}$ denote the number of bonds the capital goods industry plans to have outstanding by the beginning of next period. Then the amount that the industry plans to borrow in Country Two's bond market during next period is given by $-p^K_{B2} \cdot B2^s_{K(t+1)}$. The planned level of net business saving next period, $S^d_{K(t+1)}$, by the industry must be consistent with the market value of the sector's planned net accumulation of assets minus its planned borrowing. Therefore, we have

$$S^{d}_{K(t+1)} \equiv p^{e}_{K(t+1)} \cdot \left(K^{de}_{K(t+2)} - K^{de}_{K(t+1)}\right) + p^{K}_{B2} \cdot B2^{s}_{K(t+1)} \tag{6.28}$$

The sector's planned dividends for next period, $\Pi^{d}_{K(t+1)}$, are given by

$$\begin{aligned}\Pi^{d}_{K(t+1)} = p^{e}_{K(t+1)} \cdot &\Big\{\tau_K(I2_t + \Delta I2) \cdot T^{Te}_{K(t+1)}\left(h^{e}_{K} \cdot N2^{Te}_{K(t+1)}, K^{d}_{K(t+1)}\right)\\ &- \left[K^{de}_{K(t+2)} - (1-\delta) \cdot K^{de}_{K(t+1)}\right]\Big\}\\ &- \left(p_w/\varepsilon^{K}\right) \cdot \Big\{\varphi_K \cdot \tau_K(I2_t + \Delta I2) \cdot T^{Te}_{K(t+1)}\left(h^{e}_{K} \cdot N2^{Te}_{K(t+1)}, K^{d}_{K(t+1)}\right)\\ &- T^{S}_{K(t+1)}\left(h^{e}_{k} \cdot N2^{Se}_{K(t+1)}\right)\Big\}\\ &- \overline{C}_K\left(N2^{de}_{K(t+1)} + N2^{Se}_{K(t+1)}, \gamma_2\right) - Tx_{KG2(t+1)} - (1+p^{K}_{B2}) \cdot B2^{s}_{K(t+1)}\\ &- \left(p^{K}_{NR(t+1)}/\varepsilon^{K}\right) \cdot (\kappa + \varphi_K) \cdot \tau_K(I2_t + \Delta I2)\\ &\cdot T^{Te}_{K(t+1)}\left(h^{e}_{K} \cdot N2^{Te}_{K(t+1)}, K^{d}_{K(t+1)}\right)\left(h^{e}_{K} \cdot N2^{Te}_{K(t+1)}, K^{d}_{K(t+1)}\right)\end{aligned} \tag{6.29}$$

where $p^{K}_{NR(t+1)}$ represents the next period price of NR that the capital goods industry anticipates will prevail next period, $Tx_{KG2(t+1)}$ represents next period's taxes upon the capital goods industry, and where the number of units of capital goods the sector plans to sell next period is given by

$$\begin{aligned}K^{de}_{t+1} = \tau_K(I2_t + \Delta I2) \cdot T^{Te}_{K(t+1)}&\left(h^{e}_{K} \cdot N2^{Te}_{K(t+1)}, K^{d}_{K(t+1)}\right)\\ &- \left[K^{de}_{K(t+2)} - (1-\delta) \cdot K^{de}_{K(t+1)}\right]\end{aligned} \tag{6.30}$$

At the beginning of the current period, the capital goods industry plans to announce its product price for the next period, $p^{e}_{K(t+1)}$. Let the following demand function represent the capital goods industry's forecast of the demand curve for its product next period:

$$\begin{aligned}K^{de}_{t+1} &= KNR^{de}_{t+1} + KC^{de}_{t+1} + KG1^{de}_{t+1} + KG2^{de}_{t+1} + KG3^{de}_{t+1}\\ &= KNR^{de}_{t+1}\left(p^{e}_{K(t+1)}, \omega^{*}_{K,NR}\right) + KC^{de}_{t+1}\left(p^{e}_{K(t+1)}, \omega^{*}_{K,C}\right)\\ &\quad + KG1^{de}_{t+1} + KG2^{de}_{t+1} + KG3^{de}_{t+1}\\ &= K^{de}_{t+1}\left(\underset{-}{p^{e}_{K(t+1)}}, \underset{+}{\omega^{*}_{KNR}}, \underset{+}{\omega^{*}_{KC}}, \underset{+}{KG1^{de}_{t+1} + KG2^{de}_{t+1} + KG3^{de}_{t+1}}\right)\end{aligned} \tag{6.31}$$

where $K^{de}_{t+1}(\bullet)$ denotes the capital goods industry's forecast at the beginning of the current period of the real market demand for capital goods by the nonrenewable resource industry in Country One, by the consumer goods industry in Country Three, and by all three government sectors next period. It is assumed that the derivative of $K^{de}_{t+1}(\bullet)$ with respect to $p^{e}_{K(t+1)}$ is negative (the sign is verified in the specification of the economic behavior of the nonrenewable resource and consumer goods industries), ω^{*}_{KNR} denotes a vector of shift parameters that the capital goods industry forecasts affect the NR sector's next period demand for physical capital, ω^{*}_{KC3} denotes a vector of shift parameters that the capital goods industry forecasts will affect the consumer goods sector's demand for capital goods, and $KG1^{de}_{t+1} + KG2^{de}_{t+1} + KG3^{de}_{t+1}$ represents the sector's forecast of the total demand for capital goods next period by the three government sectors. Solving the inverse function for $p^{e}_{K(t+1)}$ yields

$$p^{e}_{K(t+1)} = p^{e}_{K(t+1)}\Big(\underset{-}{K^{de}_{t+1}}, \underset{+}{\omega^{*}_{KNR}}, \underset{+}{\omega^{*}_{KC}}, \underset{+}{KG1^{de}_{t+1} + KG2^{de}_{t+1} + KG3^{de}_{t+1}}\Big) \tag{6.32}$$

The product price, $p^{e}_{K(t+1)}$, given by (6.32) represents the maximum uniform price the capital goods sector expects it can value each alternative quantity of physical capital it produces during the period. Based upon this function, the sector's forecasted total revenue, TR^{Ke}_{t+1}, function for next period is given by

$$\begin{aligned} TR^{Ke}_{t+1} &= p^{e}_{K(t+1)} \cdot K^{de}_{t+1} \\ &= p^{e}_{K(t+1)}\Big(K^{de}_{t+1}, \omega^{*}_{KNR}, \omega^{*}_{KC}, KG1^{de}_{t+1} + KG2^{de}_{t+1} + KG3^{de}_{t+1}\Big) \cdot K^{de}_{t+1} \\ &= TR^{Ke}_{t+1}\Big(K^{de}_{t+1}, \underset{+}{\omega^{*}_{KNR}}, \underset{+}{\omega^{*}_{KC}}, \underset{+}{KG1^{de}_{t+1} + KG2^{de}_{t+1} + KG3^{de}_{t+1}}\Big) \end{aligned} \tag{6.33}$$

Substituting the right-hand side of (6.30) for K^{de}_{t+1} in (6.33) yields

$$\begin{aligned} TR^{Ke}_{t+1} = TR^{Ke}_{t+1}\Big\{&\tau_K(I2_t + \Delta I2) \cdot T^{Te}_{K(t+1)}\Big(h^{e}_{K} \cdot N2^{Te}_{K(t+1)}, K^{d}_{K(t+1)}\Big) \\ &- \Big[K^{de}_{K(t+2)} - (1-\delta) \cdot K^{de}_{K(t+1)}\Big], \omega^{*}_{KNR}, \omega^{*}_{KC}, KG1^{de}_{t+1} \\ &+ KG2^{de}_{t+1} + KG3^{de}_{t+1}\Big\} \end{aligned} \tag{6.34}$$

Substituting the right-hand side of (6.34) for the first term, $p^{e}_{K(t+1)} \cdot \{\bullet\}$, on the right-hand side of (6.29) yields

$$\begin{aligned} \Pi^{d}_{K(t+1)} = TR^{Ke}_{t+1}\Big\{&\tau_K(I2_t + \Delta I2) \cdot T^{Te}_{K(t+1)}\Big(h^{e}_{K} \cdot N2^{Te}_{K(t+1)}, K^{d}_{K(t+1)}\Big) \\ &- \Big[K^{de}_{K(t+2)} - (1-\delta) \cdot K^{de}_{K(t+1)}\Big], \omega^{*}_{KNR}, \omega^{*}_{KC}, KG1^{de}_{t+1} \\ &+ KG2^{de}_{t+1} + KG3^{de}_{t+1}\Big\} \end{aligned}$$

$$
\begin{aligned}
&- \left(p_w/\varepsilon^K\right)\cdot \left\{\varphi_K\cdot\tau_K\,(I2_t+\Delta I2)\cdot T^{Te}_{K(t+1)}\left(h^e_K\cdot N2^{Te}_{K(t+1)}, K^d_{K(t+1)}\right)\right.\\
&\left.-T^S_{K(t+1)}\left(h^e_K\cdot N2^{Se}_{K(t+1)}\right)\right\}\\
&-\overline{C}_K\left(N2^{Te}_{K(t+1)}+N2^{Se}_{K(t+1)},\gamma_2\right)-Tx_{KG2(t+1)}-(1+p^K_{B2})\cdot B2^s_{K(t+1)}\\
&-\left(p^K_{NR(t+1)}/\varepsilon^K\right)\cdot(\kappa+\varphi_K)\cdot\tau_K(I2_t+\Delta I2)\\
&\cdot T^{Te}_{K(t+1)}\left(h^e_K\cdot N2^{Te}_{K(t+1)}, K^d_{K(t+1)}\right) \qquad (6.35)
\end{aligned}
$$

as the expression for the amount the capital goods industry plans to distribute as dividends next period.

Solving (6.35) for the industry's end of period supply of bonds, $B2^s_{K(t+1)}$, and substituting the result into (6.17) yields the following expression for the present value of the industry's stream of dividends:

$$
\begin{aligned}
&\Pi^d_{Kt}+\Pi^d_{K(t+1)}/(1+r_2)\\
&\quad= TR^{Ke}_t\left\{\tau_K(I2_t)\cdot T_{Kt}\left(h_K\cdot N2_{K(t+1)}, K_{Kt}\right)\right.\\
&\quad-\left[K^d_{K(t+1)}-(1-\delta)\cdot K_{Kt}\right], \omega_{K,NR}, \omega_{K,C}, KG1^{de}_{t+1}+KG2^{de}_{t+1}\\
&\quad\left.+KG3^{de}_{t+1}\right\}-\left(p^K_{NRt}/\varepsilon^K\right)\cdot(\kappa+\varphi_K)\cdot\tau_K(I2_t)\cdot T_{Kt}(h_K\cdot N2_{Kt}, K_{Kt})\\
&\quad-Tx_{KG2t}-\left(p_w/\varepsilon^K\right)\cdot\left[\varphi_K\cdot\tau_K(I2_t)\cdot T_{Kt}\left(h_K\cdot N2_{Kt}, K_{Kt}\right)+\kappa\cdot\delta\cdot K_{Kt}\right.\\
&\quad\left.-T^S_{Kt}\left(h^S_K\cdot N2_{Kt}\right)\right]-W2_t\cdot\left(h_K+h^S_K\right)\cdot N2_{Kt}-\left(1+p^K_{B2}\right)\cdot B2_{Kt}\\
&\quad+[1/(1+r_2)]\cdot\left\{TR^{Ke}_{t+1}\left\{\tau_K(I2_t+I\Delta 2)\cdot T^{Te}_{K(t+1)}\left(h^e_K\cdot N2^{Te}_{Kt}, K^d_{K(t+1)}\right)\right.\right.\\
&\quad-\left[K^{de}_{K(t+2)}-(1-\delta)\cdot K^{de}_{K(t+1)}\right], \omega^*_{KNR}, \omega^*_{KC}, KG1^{de}_{t+1}+KG2^{de}_{t+1}\\
&\quad\left.+KG3^{de}_{t+1}\right\}-\left(p_w/\varepsilon^K\right)\cdot\left\{\varphi_K\cdot\tau_K\,(I2_t+I\Delta 2)\cdot T^{Te}_{K(t+1)}\right.\\
&\quad\left.\left(h^e_K\cdot N2^{Te}_{K(t+1)}, K^d_{K(t+1)}\right)-T^S_{K(t+1)}\left(h^e_K\cdot N2^{Se}_{K(t+1)}\right)\right\}\\
&\quad-\overline{C}_K\left(N2^{Te}_{K(t+1)}+N2^{Se}_{K(t+1)},\gamma_2\right)-Tx_{KG2(t+1)}-\left(p^K_{NR(t+1)}/\varepsilon^K\right)\\
&\quad\left.\cdot(\kappa+\varphi_K)\cdot\tau_K(I2_t+\Delta I2)\cdot T^{Te}_{K(t+1)}\left(h^e_K\cdot N2^{Te}_{K(t+1)}, K^d_{K(t+1)}\right)\right\} \qquad (6.36)
\end{aligned}
$$

where $1/(1+r_2) = p^K_{B2}/(1+p^K_{B2})$. The capital goods industry's objective at the beginning of the current period is to maximize the right-hand side of (6.36) with respect to h_K, h^S_K, $K^d_{K(t+1)}$, $N2^{Te}_{K(t+1)}$, and $N2^{Se}_{K(t+1)}$. Doing so yields the first-order necessary conditions (6.37)–(6.41). In this model the capital goods industry has one more degree of freedom than the nonrenewable resource industry because the latter must reckon with the fact that the more NR it mines/extracts during the current period the less NR will be available next period.

According to (6.37), the capital goods industry will employ its current employees up to the point at which the value of the marginal product of an extra hour of labor, $(\partial TR_t^{Ke}/\partial K_t^{de}) \cdot \tau_K(\text{I2tright}) \cdot [\partial T_{Kt}/\partial(h_K \cdot N2_{Kt})]$, net of the cost of the extra intermediate goods (including the wasted raw material) necessary to accompany the extra labor, $(p_{NRt}^K/\varepsilon^K) \cdot (\kappa + \varphi_K) \cdot \tau_K(I2_t) \cdot [\partial T_{Kt}/\partial(h_K \cdot N2_{Kt})]$, and net of the cost of the extra pollution allowances that the industry must purchase (holding constant its current treatment and storage of waste) in conjunction with the extra waste, $(p_w/\varepsilon^K) \cdot \varphi_K \cdot \tau_K(I2_t) \cdot [\partial T_{Kt}/\partial(h_K \cdot N2_{Kt})]$, is equal to the current wage rate in Country Two, $W2_t$:

$$\partial\left[\Pi_{Kt}^d + \Pi_{K(t+1)}^d/(1+r_2)\right]/\partial h_K$$
$$\equiv \left[\partial TR_t^{Ke}/\partial K_t^{de} - \left(p_{NRt}^K/\varepsilon^K\right) \cdot (\kappa + \varphi_K) - \left(p_w/\varepsilon^K\right) \cdot \varphi_K\right]$$
$$\cdot\, \tau_K(I2_t) \cdot \left[\partial T_{Kt}/\partial(h_K \cdot N2_{Kt})\right] \cdot N2_{Kt} - W2_t \cdot N2_{Kt} = 0 \qquad (6.37)$$

Condition (6.38) stipulates that the capital goods industry will use its current employees for the purpose of treating and storing waste up to the point at which the value of the marginal product of labor in treating and storing waste, in terms of the value of the pollution allowances this activity conserves, $[(p_w/\varepsilon^K) \cdot \varphi_K] \cdot [\partial T_{Kt}^S/\partial(h_K^S \cdot N2_{Kt})]$, is equal to the current money wage rate in Country Two, $W2_t$:

$$\partial\left[\Pi_{Kt}^d + \Pi_{K(t+1)}^d/(1+r_2)\right]/\partial h_K^S$$
$$\equiv \left[\left(p_w/\varepsilon^K\right) \cdot \varphi_K\right] \cdot \left[\partial T_{Kt}^S/\partial(h_K^S \cdot N2_{Kt})\right] \cdot N2_{Kt} - W2_t \cdot N2_{Kt} = 0 \qquad (6.38)$$

The present value of an additional unit of capital held at the end of the current period consists of the present value of the marginal product of capital held at that time, $[1/(1+r_2)] \cdot [\partial TR_{t+1}^{Ke}/\partial K_{t+1}^{de}] \cdot [\partial T_{K(t+1)}^{Te}/\partial K_{K(t+1)}^d]$, plus the present value of the revenue the industry anticipates receiving next period by selling that portion of the extra capital that has not physically deteriorated by the end of next period, $[1/(1+r_2)] \cdot [\partial TR_{t+1}^{Ke}/\partial K_{t+1}^{de}](1-\delta)$. Condition (6.39) states that the capital goods industry will demand physical capital for the end of the current period up to the point at which the present value of an additional unit of capital held at the beginning of next period is equal to the current opportunity cost in terms of the current revenue forgone because the industry elects to add to its own stock of physical capital during the period, $\partial TR_t^{Ke}/\partial K_t^{de}$, plus the present value of the extra pollution allowances the sector must buy next period in conjunction with the extra waste that will be produced during next period's production as a result of the extra unit of capital the sector adds to its stock by the end of the current period, $[1/(1+r_2)] \cdot [(p_w/\varepsilon^K) \cdot \varphi_K] \cdot \tau_K$

$(I2_t + \Delta I2) \cdot [\partial T^{Te}_{K(t+1)}/\partial K^{d}_{K(t+1)}]$, and plus the present value of the extra intermediate goods, NR^T, it must buy next period in conjunction with the extra production it will undertake next period as a result of adding to its current end-of-period stock of capital, $(p^{K}_{NR(t+1)}/\varepsilon^K) \cdot (\kappa + \phi_K) \cdot \tau_K(I2_t + \Delta I2) \cdot [\partial T^{Te}_{K(t+1)}/\partial K^{d}_{K(t+1)}]$:

$$\partial\left[\Pi^{d}_{Kt} + \Pi^{d}_{K(t+1)}/(1+r_2)\right]/\partial K^{d}_{K(t+1)}$$
$$\equiv -\left[\partial TR^{Ke}_{t}/\partial K^{de}_{t}\right] + [1/(1+r2)] \cdot \left[\left\{\left[\partial TR^{Ke}_{t+1}/\partial K^{de}_{t+1}\right]\right.\right.$$
$$\left.- \left\{\left[\left(p_w/\varepsilon^K\right) \cdot \varphi_K + \left(p^{K}_{NR(t+1)}/\varepsilon^K\right) \cdot (\kappa + \varphi_K)\right]\right\}\right\} \cdot \tau_K(I2_t + \Delta I2)$$
$$\left.\cdot\left[\partial T^{Te}_{K(t+1)}/\partial K^{d}_{K(t+1)}\right] + \left[\partial TR^{Ke}_{t+1}/\partial K^{de}_{t+1}\right](1-\delta)\right] = 0 \qquad (6.39)$$

Condition (6.40) stipulates that the capital goods industry demands workers for next period for the purpose of producing capital goods up to the point at which the marginal revenue product of the last worker, $[\partial TR^{Ke}_{t+1}/\partial T^{Te}_{K(t+1)}] \cdot \tau_K(I2_t + \Delta I2) \cdot [\partial T^{Te}_{K(t+1)}/\partial N2^{Te}_{K(t+1)}] \cdot h^{e}_{K2}$, net of the marginal cost of the extra nonrenewable resource necessary to produce an extra unit of capital (including the nonrenewable resource wasted in the production process), $[(p^{K}_{NR(t+1)}/\varepsilon^K)] \cdot (\kappa + \varphi_K) \cdot \tau_K(I2_t + \Delta I2) \cdot [\partial T^{Te}_{K(t+1)}/\partial N2^{Te}_{K(t+1)}] \cdot h^{e}_{K2}$, and net of the marginal cost of the extra pollution allowances the sector must purchase next period in conjunction with the extra waste it plans to generate, $[(p_w/\varepsilon^K) \cdot \varphi_K] \cdot \tau_K(I2_t + \Delta I2) \cdot [\partial T^{Te}_{K(t+1)}/\partial N2^{Te}_{K(t+1)}] \cdot h^{e}_{K2}$, are equal to the marginal factor (labor) cost of adding to its stock of employees by the beginning of next period, $\partial\overline{C}_K/\partial N2^{Te}_{t+1}$:

$$\partial\left[\Pi^{d}_{Kt} + \Pi^{d}_{K(t+1)}/\,(1+r2)\right]/\partial N2^{Te}_{K(t+1)}$$
$$\equiv [1/(1+r2)] \cdot \left[\left[\partial TR^{K2e}_{t+1}/\partial N2^{Te}_{K(t+1)}\right]\right.$$
$$\cdot\, \tau_K(I2_t + \Delta I2) \cdot \left[\partial T^{Te}_{K(t+1)}/\partial N2^{Te}_{K(t+1)}\right] \cdot h^{e}_{K2}$$
$$- \left[(p_w/\varepsilon^K) \cdot \varphi_K\right] \cdot \tau_K(I2_t + \Delta I2) \cdot \left[\partial T^{Te}_{K2(t+1)}/\partial N2^{Te}_{K(t+1)}\right] \cdot h^{e}_{K2}$$
$$- \left[\left(p^{K}_{NR(t+1)}/\varepsilon^K\right)\right] \cdot (\kappa + \varphi_K) \cdot \tau_K(I2_t + \Delta I2) \cdot \left[\partial T^{Te}_{K(t+1)}/\partial N2^{Te}_{K(t+1)}\right]$$
$$\left.\cdot\, h^{e}_{K2} - \left[\partial\overline{C}_K/\partial N^{Te}_{K(t+1)}\right]\right] = 0 \qquad (6.40)$$

Finally, according to (6.41), the capital goods industry will demand workers for next period for the purpose of treating and storing waste up to the point at which the value of the marginal product of that labor in terms of the value of the extra pollution allowances saved, $(p_w/\varepsilon^K) \cdot [\partial TR^S_{K(t+1)}/\partial N2^{Se}_{K(t+1)}] \cdot h^e_K$, is equal to the marginal factor cost of hiring an extra worker next period, $\partial \overline{C}_K/\partial N2^{Kde}_{t+1}$:

$$\frac{\partial \left[\Pi^d_{Kt} + \Pi^d_{K(t+1)}/(1+r_2)\right]}{\partial N2^{Se}_{K(t+1)}} \equiv \left[\frac{1}{(1+r2)}\right] \cdot \left[\left(\frac{p_w}{\varepsilon^K}\right) \cdot \left[\frac{\partial TR^S_{K(t+1)}}{\partial N2^{Se}_{K(t+1)}}\right] \cdot h^e_{K2} - \left[\frac{\partial \overline{C}_K}{\partial N2^{Kde}_{t+1}}\right]\right] = 0 \quad (6.41)$$

Totally differentiating conditions (6.37)–(6.41) and solving for the changes in $h_K, h^S_K, K^d_{K(t+1)}, N2^{Te}_{K(t+1)}$, and $N2^{Se}_{K(t+1)}$ yields the industry's demand functions for current labor hours and its end-of-period demands for physical capital and workers. To simplify the analysis only the parameters entering into the own first-order conditions are assumed to affect the industry's demands for labor and capital.

Demand Function for h_K

From (6.37), an increase in the anticipated price of the nonrenewable resource in terms of Country One's unit of account, p^K_{NRt}; an increase in the price of pollution allowances in terms of Country One's unit of account, p_w; an increase in the mass of the nonrenewable resource wasted per unit of physical capital produced, φ_K; or an increase in the mass of the nonrenewable resource contained in a unit of physical capital, κ, decreases the net value of the marginal product of an hour of labor during the current period, thereby reducing the capital goods sector's demand for current labor hours for the purpose of producing capital goods during the current period. An increase in the expected value of Country Two's unit of account in terms of Country One's unit of account, ε^K, reduces the price of both a unit of the nonrenewable resource and the price of one pollution allowance in terms of Country Two's unit of account, inducing the capital goods industry to produce more capital goods during the current period and to use more labor hours for that purpose during the current period. An increase in the current money wage rate, $W2_t$, increases the marginal cost of using employees another hour, causing the capital goods industry to reduce its demand for labor for the purpose of transforming the nonrenewable resource into physical capital during the period. Finally, the larger the infrastructure in Country Two at the beginning of the current period, the greater is the value of the net marginal product of labor in transforming the nonrenewable resource into physical capital. Consequently, the following demand function for labor hours for transforming the nonrenewable resource emerges as (6.42):

$$h_{Kt} = h_{Kt}\left(\underset{-}{p^K_{NRt}}, \underset{-}{p_w}, \underset{-}{\kappa}, \underset{-}{\varphi_K}, \underset{+}{\varepsilon^K}, \underset{-}{W2_t}, \underset{+}{I2_t}\right) \quad (6.42)$$

Demand Function for h^s_k

From (6.38), an increase in the price of pollution allowances in terms of Country One's unit of account, p_w, or an increase in the mass of the nonrenewable resource wasted per unit of physical capital produced, φ_K, increases the value of the marginal product of an hour of labor during the current period in treating and storing waste, thereby increasing the capital goods sector's demand for current labor hours for that purpose. An increase in the value of Country Two's unit of account in terms of Country One's unit of account, ε^K, produces the opposite effects. An increase in the current money wage rate, $W2_t$, increases the marginal cost of using employees another hour, causing the capital goods industry to reduce its demand for labor for the purpose of treating and storing waste during the period. Therefore, (6.38) implies the following demand function for labor hours for treating and storing waste:

$$h^S_{Kt} = h^S_{Kt}\Big(\underset{+}{p_w},\ \underset{+}{\varphi_K},\ \underset{-}{\varepsilon^K},\ \underset{-}{W2_t}\Big) \tag{6.43}$$

Demand Function for $K^d_{K(t+1)}$

According to (6.39), an increase in the rate of interest in Country Two's bond market, r_2, reduces the present value of the anticipated net revenue from an extra unit of physical capital held by the beginning of next period, thereby reducing the capital goods sector's demand for physical capital. An increase in the rate of depreciation, δ_K, reduces the sector's end-of-period demand for capital because it reduces the revenue the industry anticipates receiving next period by selling that portion of the extra capital that has not physically deteriorated by the end of next period. An increase in the price of pollution allowances, p_w, an increase in the amount of the nonrenewable resource contained in a unit of physical capital produced next period, κ, or an increase in the waste produced per unit of physical capital produced next period, φ_K, increases the sector's marginal cost of producing capital goods next period, causing the sector to reduce its demand for physical capital for the beginning of that period. An increase in the value of Country Two's unit of account in terms of Country One's unit of account, ε, produces the opposite result. Therefore, the following demand function for physical capital for the end of the current period by the capital goods industry is specified by (6.44):

$$K^d_{K(t+1)} = K^d_{K(t+1)}\Big(\underset{-}{r_2},\ \underset{-}{\delta},\ \underset{-}{p_w},\ \underset{-}{\kappa},\ \underset{-}{\varphi_K},\ \underset{+}{\varepsilon^K}\Big) \tag{6.44}$$

Demand Function for $N2^{Te}_{K(t+1)}$

From (6.40), an increase in p_w, κ, or φ_K also increases the marginal cost of adding another worker for the purpose of producing capital goods next period. An increase in ε produces the opposite result. Therefore the following demand function for workers to build capital goods next period is given by

$$N2^{Te}_{K(t+1)} = N2^{Te}_{K(t+1)}\left(\underset{-}{p_w},\ \underset{-}{\kappa},\ \underset{-}{\varphi_K},\ \underset{+}{\varepsilon^K}\right) \tag{6.45}$$

Demand Function for $N2^{Se}_{K(t+1)}$

From (6.41), an increase in p_w increases the value of the marginal revenue of adding another worker for the purpose of treating and storing waste next period. An increase in ε produces the opposite result. Therefore the following demand function for workers to treat and store waste next period is given by

$$N2^{Se}_{K(t+1)} = N2^{Se}_{K(t+1)}\left(\underset{+}{p_w},\ \underset{-}{\varepsilon^K}\right) \tag{6.46}$$

Given the solution for these functions, the current production, demand for the renewable resource, pricing, wage setting, waste generation, pollution allowance demand, bond supply, and shareholder dividends decisions emerge.

Current Production of Capital Goods, K^T_t

From (6.2), current production of physical capital is positively related to the infrastructure in place in Country Two at the beginning of the period, the stock of capital held by the capital goods industry at the beginning of the period, and the capital goods industries use of labor to transform the nonrenewable resource into physical capital during the period. From (6.42), the sector's demand for labor to transform NR into capital goods is negatively related to p^{NR}_t, p_w, κ, φ_K, and $W2_t$ but positively related to ε and $I2_t$. Therefore the current production of capital goods function is given by (6.47):

$$\begin{aligned} K^T_t &= \tau_K\,(I2_t)\cdot T_{Kt}\,(h_K \cdot N2_{Kt}, K_{Kt}) \\ &= K^T_t\left(\underset{+}{K_{Kt}},\ \underset{+}{I2_t},\ \underset{-}{p^{NR}_t},\ \underset{-}{p_w},\ \underset{-}{\kappa},\ \underset{-}{\varphi_K},\ \underset{+}{\varepsilon^K},\ \underset{-}{W2_t}\right) \end{aligned} \tag{6.47}$$

Current Demand for the Nonrenewable Resource, NRK^{Td}_t

From (6.3), the sector's use of the nonrenewable resource during the current period is proportionate to the level of its production of capital goods during the current period. Assuming that the direct effect of an increase of θ_K or η_K upon the required amount of the nonrenewable resource exceeds the indirect effect operating through the sector's demand for transformation services provided by labor during the current period, the sector's demand for the renewable resource this period is given by (6.48):

$$
\begin{aligned}
NRK_t^{Td} &= (\kappa + \varphi_K) \cdot \tau_K(I2_t) \cdot T_{Kt}(h_K \cdot N2_{Kt}, K_{Kt}) \\
&= NRK_t^{Td}\Big(\underset{+}{K_{Kt}},\ \underset{+}{I2_t},\ \underset{-}{p^K_{NRt}},\ \underset{-}{p_w},\ \underset{+}{\kappa},\ \underset{+}{\varphi_K},\ \underset{+}{\varepsilon^K},\ \underset{-}{W2_t}\Big)
\end{aligned}
\tag{6.48}
$$

Current Product Price, p_{Kt}

The sector's pricing function, developed above as (6.13), is negatively related to the number of units it desires to sell during the period but positively related to the sector's estimate of the positions of the demand curves for capital goods by the nonrenewable resource and consumer goods industries and the demands for physical capital by the three government sectors. However, from (6.9), the number of units the sector plans to sell during the period is equal to the number of units of capital it produces, K_t^T, minus its planned accumulation of physical capital during the period and the number of units of replacement investment, $K^d_{K(t+1)} - (1-\delta) \cdot K_{Kt}$. Substituting (6.47) for K_t^T and (6.44) for $K^d_{K(t+1)}$ yields an expression for the number of units of physical capital the sector plans to sell during the period. Assuming that the effects operating upon the sector's own end of period demand for capital are small relative to those operating through the industry's production decision and current depreciation the signs of the net effects are given in (6.49) below:

$$
\begin{aligned}
K_t^{de} &= K_t^T - \left[K^d_{K(t+1)} - (1-\delta) \cdot K_{Kt}\right] \\
&= K_t^T\Big(\underset{+}{K_{Kt}},\ \underset{+}{I2_t},\ \underset{-}{p^K_{NRt}},\ \underset{-}{p_w},\ \underset{-}{\kappa},\ \underset{-}{\varphi_K},\ \underset{+}{\varepsilon^K},\ \underset{-}{W2_t}\Big) \\
&\quad - K^d_{K(t+1)}\Big(\underset{-}{r_2},\ \underset{-}{\delta},\ \underset{-}{p_w},\ \underset{-}{\kappa},\ \underset{-}{\varphi_K},\ \underset{-}{\varepsilon^K}\Big) + (1-\delta) \cdot K_{Kt} \\
&= K_t^{de}\Big(\underset{+}{K_{Kt}},\ \underset{+}{I2_t},\ \underset{-}{p^K_{NRt}},\ \underset{-}{p_w},\ \underset{-}{\kappa}, \underset{-}{\varphi_K},\ \underset{+}{\varepsilon^K},\ \underset{-}{W2_t},\ \underset{+}{r_2},\ \underset{-}{\delta}\Big)
\end{aligned}
\tag{6.49}
$$

Substituting (6.49) into (6.13) yields the following pricing function for the capital goods industry:

$$
p_{Kt} = p_{Kt}\Big(\underset{-}{K_t^{de}},\ \underset{+}{\omega_{KNR}},\ \underset{+}{\omega_{KC}},\ \underset{+}{KG1_t^{de} + KG2_t^{de} + KG3_t^{de}}\Big)
$$

$$= p_{Kt} \cdot \Big(\underset{-}{K_{Kt}}, \underset{-}{I2_t}, \underset{+}{p^K_{NRt}}, \underset{+}{p_w}, \underset{+}{\kappa}, \underset{+}{\varphi_K}, \underset{-}{\varepsilon^K}, \underset{+}{W2_t}, \underset{-}{r_2}, \underset{+}{\delta}, \underset{+}{\omega_{KNR}}, \underset{+}{\omega_{KC}},$$

$$\underset{+}{KG1^{de}_t + KG2^{de}_t + KG3^{de}_t}\Big) \tag{6.50}$$

Parametric changes that increase the cost of current production, such as higher prices for the nonrenewable resource and/or pollution allowances, induce the capital goods industry to raise the price of physical capital.

Wage-Setting Function

The wage rate the capital goods sector announces for next period is found by substituting the solutions given by (6.45) and (6.46) into the inverse of the capital goods industry's estimate of the net supply of workers to the industry next period, shown in (6.26). Assuming that the parametric effects upon the sector's demand for labor for the purpose of producing capital goods exceed those operating upon its demand for labor for the purpose of treating and storing waste, the signs of the effects are given in (6.51) below:

$$W2_{t+1} = W2\left\{N2^{Te}_{K(t+1)}\left(\underset{-}{pw}, \underset{-}{\kappa}, \underset{-}{\varphi_K}, \underset{+}{\varepsilon^K}\right) + N2^{Se}_{K(t+1)}\left(\underset{+}{p_w}, \underset{-}{\varepsilon^K}\right), \gamma_2\right\}$$

$$= W2\left(\underset{-}{p_w}, \underset{-}{\kappa}, \underset{-}{\varphi_K}, \underset{+}{\varepsilon^K}, \underset{+}{\gamma^2}\right) \tag{6.51}$$

Waste Generation

The waste generated by the capital goods industry during the current period, W^*K_t, is given by (6.5). Substitute (6.42) for h_K in (6.5) to yield (6.52):

$$W^*K_t = \varphi_K \cdot \tau_K\,(I2_t) \cdot \left(h_{Kt}\left(\underset{-}{p^{NR}_t}, \underset{-}{p_w}, \underset{-}{\kappa}, \underset{-}{\varphi_K}, \underset{+}{\varepsilon^K}, \underset{-}{W2_t}, \underset{+}{I2_t}\right) \cdot N2_{Kt}, K_{Kt}\right)$$

$$+ \kappa \cdot \delta \cdot K_{Kt}$$

$$= W^*K_t\left(\underset{+}{\varphi_K}, \underset{+}{I2_t}, \underset{-}{p^K_{NRt}}, \underset{-}{p_w}, \underset{+}{\kappa}, \underset{+}{\delta}, \underset{+}{K_{Kt}}, \underset{+}{\varepsilon^K}, \underset{-}{W2_t}\right) \tag{6.52}$$

Treated and Stored Waste

The amount of waste treated and stored by the capital goods industry during the period is given by (6.6). Substitute (6.43) for h_K^S in (6.6) to obtain (6.53):

$$SW^*K_t = T_{Kt}^S \left[h_{Kt}^S \left(\underset{+}{p_w}, \underset{+}{\varphi_K}, \underset{-}{\varepsilon^K}, \underset{-}{W2_t} \right) \cdot N2_{Kt} \right]$$

$$= SW^*K \left(\underset{+}{p_w}, \underset{+}{\varphi_K}, \underset{-}{\varepsilon^K}, \underset{-}{W2_t} \right) \tag{6.53}$$

Excess Demand for Pollution Allowances

The capital goods industry's excess demand for pollution allowances during the current period is equal to its waste generation function minus its waste treatment and storage function minus its initial allocation of pollution allowances. In excess demand function (6.54) it is assumed that the parametric changes that affect waste generation dominate those that affect treatment and storage:

$$\Omega_K^d - \Omega_{Kt} = W^*K_t \left(\underset{+}{\varphi_K}, \underset{+}{I2_t}, \underset{-}{p_{NRt}^K}, \underset{-}{p_w}, \underset{+}{\kappa}, \underset{+}{\delta}, \underset{+}{K_{Kt}}, \underset{+}{\varepsilon^K}, \underset{-}{W2_t} \right)$$

$$- SW^*K \left(p_w, \varphi_K, \varepsilon^K, W2_t \right) - \Omega_{Kt}$$

$$\Omega_K^d - \Omega_{Kt} = \Omega_K^d \left(\underset{+}{\varphi_K}, \underset{+}{I2_t}, \underset{-}{p_{NRt}^K}, \underset{-}{p_w}, \underset{+}{\kappa}, \underset{+}{\delta}, \underset{+}{K_{Kt}}, \underset{+}{\varepsilon^K}, \underset{-}{W2_t} \right) - \Omega_{Kt} \tag{6.54}$$

Capital Goods Industry's Supply of Bonds

Assuming that the capital goods industry does not plan to engage in net saving during the current period (i.e., it plans to distribute all net income during the current period as dividends), then, from (6.10), the sector's end-of-period supply of bonds to Country Two's bond market is given by (6.55) where p_{Kt} is given by (6.50). The effects of parametric changes that affect the pricing decision are suppressed in (6.54), for simplicity.

$$p_{B2}^K \cdot B2_{K(t+1)}^s = p_{B2}^K \cdot B2_{Kt} + p_{Kt}(\bullet) \cdot \left(K_{K(t+1)}^d \left(\underset{-}{r_2}, \underset{-}{\delta}, \underset{-}{p_w}, \underset{-}{\kappa}, \underset{-}{\varphi_K}, \underset{+}{\varepsilon^K} \right) - K_{Kt} \right)$$

$$= p_{B2}^{K} \cdot B2_{K(t+1)}^{s}\left(\underset{-}{r_2}, \underset{-}{\delta}, \underset{-}{p_w}, \underset{-}{\kappa}, \underset{-}{\varphi_K}, \underset{+}{\varepsilon^K}, \underset{+}{B2_{Kt}}\right) \tag{6.55}$$

Dividends Paid to Shareholders during the Current Period

Given the assumption that the capital goods industry's planned net business saving during the current period is zero, the sector's dividend payments to its shareholders during the same period are equal to the value of current production of capital goods minus current wages, interest, taxes, depreciation, and the sector's net purchases of pollution allowances:

$$\begin{aligned}
\Pi_{Kt}^{d} = {} & p_{Kt} \cdot \{\tau_K(I2_t) \cdot T_{Kt}(h_K \cdot N2_{Kt}, K_{Kt}) - \delta \cdot K_{Kt}\} \\
& - (p_{NRt}^{K}/\varepsilon^{K}) \cdot (\kappa + \varphi_K) \cdot T_{Kt}(h_K \cdot N2_{Kt}, K_{Kt}) - Tx_{KG2t} \\
& - (p_w/\varepsilon^{K}) \cdot [\varphi_K \cdot \tau_K(I2_t) \cdot T_{Kt}(h_K \cdot N2_{Kt}, K_{Kt}) \\
& + \kappa \cdot \delta \cdot K_{Kt} - T_{Kt}^{S}(h_K^{S} \cdot N2_{Kt})] \\
& - W2_t \cdot (h_K + h_K^{S}) \cdot N2_{Kt} - B2_{Kt}
\end{aligned} \tag{6.56}$$

Chapter 7 contains an analysis of the consumption goods industry's decisions before current interest rates and exchange rates are determined.

7

The Consumption Goods Industry

At the beginning of the current period, the consumer goods industry holds an initial stock of physical capital, K_{Ct}. Let $K^{d}_{C(t+1)}$ represent the industry's desired stock of physical capital for the end of the current period, which is determined in accordance with its objective to maximize the present value of its operations.

The consumer goods industry applies a variable amount of labor together with its given stock of physical capital to transform the mass of marketed nonrenewable resource, NR, that it desires to convert into a marketable product, C. The current level of transformation services, $T_C(\bullet)$, is assumed to be a positive increasing function of (variable) labor hours, $h_{Ct} \cdot N3_{Ct}$, applied during the period, where $N3_{Ct}$ denotes the number of people employed in the consumer goods industry at the start of the current period and where h_{Ct} represents the (average) number of hours these employees work for the consumer goods industry during the period transforming nonrenewable resources into consumer goods. The marginal transformation of labor, T'_C, is assumed to be positive, but diminishing.

Under these assumptions, the production function for consumer goods, C^{T}_{t}, is given by (7.1):

$$C^{T}_{t} = \min\left[\frac{NR^{Cd}_{t}}{(\gamma + \varphi_C)}, \tau(I3_t) \cdot T_{Ct}(h_{Ct} \cdot N3_{Ct}, K_{Ct})\right] \geq 0 \tag{7.1}$$

where

NR^{Cd}_{t} denotes the amount of the nonrenewable resource purchased by the consumer goods industry during the current period.

γ equals the amount of the nonrenewable resource necessary to produce (embodied within) a unit of consumer goods.

φ_C denotes the amount of the nonrenewable resource unavoidably wasted in the process of being transformed into a unit of consumer goods, given current production techniques.

$\tau(I3_t)$, with $\tau'(\bullet) > 0$, represents the contribution of the infrastructure in Country Three at the beginning of the period, $I3_t$, to the transformation services of labor and physical capital.

Assuming the consumer goods industry wastes neither the transformation services nor the amount of NR_t^{Cd} unnecessarily, the number of consumer goods produced during the current period is equal to $\tau(I3_t) \cdot T_{Ct}(h_{Ct} \cdot N3_{Ct}, K_{Ct})$:

$$C_t^T = \tau(I3_t) \cdot T_{Ct}(h_{Ct} \cdot N3_{Ct}, K_{Ct}) \tag{7.2}$$

In addition, in terms of mass, the amount of the nonrenewable resource transformed in the production process into consumer goods and waste becomes

$$NR_t^{Cd} = (\gamma + \varphi_C) \cdot \tau(I3_t) \cdot T_{Ct}(h_{Ct} \cdot N3_{Ct}, K_{Ct}) \tag{7.3}$$

The number of consumer goods not sold during the current period is assumed to be added to the industry's inventory of consumer goods by the end of the period:

$$\begin{aligned} C_{C(t+1)} = {} & C_{Ct} + \tau(I3_t) \cdot T_{Ct}(h_{Ct} \cdot N3_{Ct}, K_{Ct}) \\ & - CH1_t - CH2_t - CH3_t \geq 0 \end{aligned} \tag{7.4}$$

where

C_{Ct} represents the industry's initial inventory of consumer goods.
$CH1_t$ corresponds to the actual number of consumer goods purchased by the households in Country One during the current period.
$CH2_t$ corresponds to the actual number of consumer goods purchased by the households in Country Two during the current period.
$CH3_t$ represents the actual number of consumer goods purchased by the households in Country Three during the current period.
$C_{C(t+1)}$ denotes the end of current-period inventory of consumer goods held by the consumer goods industry.

During the current period, the industry generates new waste products equal to W^*C_t in terms of mass:

$$W^*C_t = \varphi_C \cdot \tau(I3_t) \cdot T_{Ct}(h_{Ct} \cdot N3_{Ct}, K_{Ct}) + \kappa \cdot \delta \cdot K_{Ct} \tag{7.5}$$

where $\kappa \cdot \delta \cdot K_{Ct}$ represents in terms of mass the physical depreciation of the physical capital the consumer goods industry holds at the beginning of the current period. The sector must pay a fee, $p_w/\tilde{\varepsilon}^C$, in terms of its country's unit of account, to obtain a pollution allowance for every unit of wasted mass it discharges, where $\tilde{\varepsilon}^C$ denotes the value of Country Three's unit of account in terms of Country One's unit of account anticipated by the C industry at the beginning of the period. To the extent that the industry engages in treating and storing waste, it reduces the number of pollution allowances it must buy during the period. (In fact it is possible for the consumer goods industry to treat and store more waste during the current period than is necessary to meet its current allocation of pollution allowances, in which case it would receive revenue during the period by selling the pollution allowances it did not use.)

Assume the following transformation function for treating and storing waste during the current period:

$$SW^*Ct = \min\Big[\varphi_C \cdot \tau(I3_t) \cdot T_{Ct}(h_{Ct} \cdot N3_{Ct}, K_{Ct}) + \kappa \cdot \delta \cdot K_{Ct} - \Omega^d_{Ct}, T^S_{Ct}\left(h^S_{Ct} \cdot N3_{Ct}\right)\Big] \geq 0 \qquad (7.6)$$

where

SW^*C_t represents the amount of waste (in terms of mass) treated and stored during the current period.
Ω^d_{Ct} represents the consumer goods industry's desired holding of pollution allowances.
$T^S_{Ct}(\bullet)$ represents transformation function for treating and storing waste during the current period. For simplicity, we assume that labor is the only resource necessary to provide this service.

Assuming that neither transformation services nor mass are wasted in the treating and storing process, the amount of mass treated and stored may be represented as

$$SW^*Ct = T^S_{Ct}\left(h^S_{Ct} \cdot N3_{Ct}\right) \qquad (7.7)$$

The industry's current expenses associated with generating, treating, and storing waste during the period, C_{C,W^*}, is equal to

$$C_{C,W^*} = \left(\frac{P_W}{\tilde{\varepsilon}C}\right) \cdot \Big[\varphi_C \cdot \tau(I3_t) \cdot T_{Ct}(h_{Ct} \cdot N3_{Ct}, K_{Ct}) + \kappa \cdot \delta \cdot K_{Ct} - T^S_{Ct}\left(h^S_{Ct} \cdot N3_{Ct}\right)\Big] + W3_t \cdot h^S_{Ct} \cdot N3_{Ct} \qquad (7.8)$$

Taking the current wage rate and the consumer goods industry's forecast of the current-period demand function for consumer goods, $C^{de}_t = CH1^{de}_t + CH2^{de}_t + CH3^{de}_t$, as given, the consumer goods industry attempts to maximize the present value of the dividends it intends to pay to the industry's shareholders during the current and next periods. Then the industry's desired current-period sales of consumer goods (in terms of units) is given by

$$C^{de}_t = CH1^{de}_t + CH2^{de}_t + CH3^{de}_t = \tau(I3_t) \cdot T_{Ct}(h_{Ct} \cdot N3_{Ct}, K_{Ct}) + C_{Ct} \qquad (7.9)$$

Each period, dividends equal net income minus net business saving. Net income is equal to the value of production, $T_{Ct}(h_{Ct} \cdot N3_{Ct}, K_{Ct})$, minus current expenses (wages, interest, taxes, purchases of the nonrenewable resource, purchases of pollution allowances, and depreciation). Therefore, dividends equal the value of production minus wages, interest, taxes, outlays for intermediate goods and pollution allowances, depreciation and net business saving. Measured in terms of current-period market prices, net business saving is necessarily equal to the sum of the sector's net increase in assets minus the net increase in liabilities, during the current period.

Let p_{Ct} represent the current market price that the consumer goods industry sets. Then, measured in terms of current market prices, the industry plans to acquire $-p_{Ct} \cdot C_{Ct}$ in inventories of consumer goods during the current period. Furthermore, the industry plans to acquire $p^C_{Kt} \cdot (\varepsilon/\tilde{\varepsilon})^C \cdot (K^d_{C(t+1)} - K_{Ct})$ of physical capital during the current period in terms of Country Three's unit of account. Let $B3_{Ct}$ represent the number of the consumer goods industry's bonds outstanding in Country Three's bond market at the beginning of the current period. Let p_{B3} represent the current-period market price of bonds issued in Country Three's bond market. Each bond outstanding presumably pays one unit of Country Three's currency as interest income during the current period. Then the market value of the consumer goods industry's debt in Country Three's bond market is represented by $p_{B3} \cdot B3_{Ct}$. Let $B3^s_{C(t+1)}$ denote the number of bonds the consumer goods industry plans to have outstanding by the end of the current period. Then the amount that the industry plans to borrow in Country Three's bond market during the current period is given by $p_{B3} \cdot (B3^s_{C(t+1)} - B3_{Ct})$. The current level of planned net business saving, S^d_{Ct}, by the consumer goods industry must be consistent with the market value of the sector's planned accumulation of physical capital minus its planned current-period borrowing. Therefore, we have

$$S^d_{Ct} \equiv -p_{Ct} \cdot C_{Ct} + p^C_{Kt} \cdot \left(\frac{\varepsilon}{\tilde{\varepsilon}}\right)^C \cdot \left(K^d_{C(t+1)} - K_{Ct}\right) - p_{B3} \cdot \left(B3^s_{C(t+1)} - B3_{Ct}\right) \qquad (7.10)$$

The sector's planned dividends for the current period, Π^{Cd}_t, are given by

$$\begin{aligned} \Pi^d_{Ct} = {} & p_{Ct} \cdot \{\tau(I3_t) \cdot T_{Ct}(h_{Ct} \cdot N3_{Ct}, K_{Ct}) + C_{Ct}\} \\ & - p^C_{Kt} \cdot \left(\frac{\varepsilon}{\tilde{\varepsilon}}\right)^C \cdot \left[K^d_{C(t+1)} - (1-\delta) \cdot K_{Ct}\right] - Tx_{CG3t} \\ & - \left(\frac{p^C_{NRt}}{\tilde{\varepsilon}^C}\right) \cdot (\gamma + \varphi_C) \cdot \tau(I3_t) \cdot T_{Ct}(h_{Ct} \cdot N3_{Ct}, K_{Ct}) \\ & - \left(\frac{p_w}{\tilde{\varepsilon}^C}\right) \cdot \left[\varphi_C \cdot \tau(I3_t) \cdot T_{Ct}(h_{Ct} \cdot N3_{Ct}, K_{Ct}) + \kappa \cdot \delta \cdot K_{Ct} \right. \\ & \left. - T^S_{Ct}\left(h^S_{Ct} \cdot N3_{Ct}\right)\right] - W3_t \cdot \left(h_{Ct} + h^S_{Ct}\right) \cdot N3_{Ct} \\ & + p_{B3} \cdot \left(B3^s_{C(t+1)} - B3_{Ct}\right) - B3_{Ct} \end{aligned} \qquad (7.11)$$

where the planned real investment of consumer goods is valued in terms of the current market price of consumer goods and where Tx_{CG3t} denotes the business taxes that the G3 sector levies upon the consumer goods industry during the current period.

At the beginning of the period, the consumer goods industry announces its product price, p_{Ct}. Let the following demand function represent the industry's forecast of the current-period demand for its product:

$$\begin{aligned} C_t^{de} &= CH1_t^{de} + CH2_t^{de} + CH3_t^{de} \\ &= CH1_t^{de}\left(p_{Ct}, \omega_{CH1}\right) + CH2_t^{de}\left(p_{Ct}, \omega_{CH2}\right) + CH3_t^{de}\left(p_{Ct}, \omega_{CH3}\right) \\ &= C_t^{de}\left(p_{Ct}, \omega_{CH1}, \omega_{CH2}, \omega_{CH3}\right) \end{aligned} \tag{7.12}$$

where $C_t^{de}(\bullet)$ denotes the consumer goods industry's forecast at the beginning of the current period of the current real market demand for consumer goods by the households in Country One, Country Two, and Country Three. It is assumed that the derivative of $C_t^{de}(\bullet)$ with respect to p_{Ct} is negative (the sign is verified in the specification of the economic behavior of the H1, H2, and H3 households); ω_{CH1} denotes a vector of shift parameters that the industry forecasts affect the H1 sector's demand for consumer goods; ω_{CH2} denotes a vector of shift parameters that the industry forecasts affect the H2 sector's demand for consumer goods; and ω_{CH3} denotes a vector of shift parameters that the industry forecasts affect the H3 sector's demand for consumer goods. Solving the inverse function for p_{Ct} yields

$$p_{Ct} = p_{Ct}\Big(\underset{-}{C_t^{de}}, \underset{+}{\omega_{CH1}}, \underset{+}{\omega_{CH2}}, \underset{+}{\omega_{CH3}}\Big) \tag{7.13}$$

where

$$\begin{aligned} \frac{\partial p_{Ct}}{\partial\left(C_t^{de}\right)} &\equiv \frac{1}{\left[\partial\left(C_t^{de}\right)/\partial p_{Ct}\right]} < 0 \\ \frac{\partial p_{Ct}}{\partial \omega_{CH1}} &\equiv -\frac{\left[\partial\left(C_t^{de}\right)/\partial \omega_{CH1}\right]}{\left[\partial\left(C_t^{de}\right)/\partial p_{Ct}\right]} > 0 \\ \frac{\partial p_{Ct}}{\partial \omega_{CH2}} &\equiv -\frac{\left[\partial\left(C_t^{de}\right)/\partial \omega_{CH2}\right]}{\left[\partial\left(C_t^{de}\right)/\partial p_{Ct}\right]} > 0 \end{aligned} \tag{7.14}$$

and

$$\frac{\partial p_{Ct}}{\partial \omega_{CH3}} \equiv -\frac{\left[\partial\left(C_t^{de}\right)/\partial \omega_{CH3}\right]}{\left[\partial\left(C_t^{de}\right)/\partial p_{Ct}\right]} > 0$$

An increase in $\omega_{CH1}, \omega_{CH2}$, or ω_{CH3} represents an outward shift in the industry's forecast of the market demand for its product.

The price p_{Ct} given by (7.13) represents the maximum uniform price the sector expects each unit of consumer goods yields during the period. Based upon this function, the sector's forecasted current total revenue, TR_t^{Ce}, function is given by

$$\begin{aligned} TR_t^{Ce} &= p_{Ct} \cdot C_t^{de} = p_{Ct}\left(C_t^{de}, \omega_{CH1}, \omega_{CH2}, \omega_{CH3}\right) \cdot C_t^{de} \\ &= TR_t^{Ce}\left(C_t^{de}, \omega_{CH1}, \omega_{CH2}, \omega_{CH3}\right) \end{aligned} \tag{7.15}$$

Substituting the far right-hand side of (7.9) for C_t^{de} in (7.15) yields

$$TR_t^{Ce} = TR_t^{Ce}\{\tau(I3_t) \cdot T_{Ct}(h_{Ct} \cdot N3_{Ct}, K_{Ct}) + C_{Ct}, \omega_{CH1}, \omega_{CH2}, \omega_{CH3}\} \quad (7.16)$$

Substituting the right-hand side of (7.16) for the first term, $p_{Ct} \cdot \{\iota(I3_t) \cdot T_{Ct}(h_{Ct} \cdot N3_{Ct}, K_{Ct}) + C_{Ct}\}$, on the right-hand side of (7.11) yields

$$\begin{aligned}
\Pi_{Ct}^{d} &= TR_t^{Ce}\{\tau(I3_t) \cdot T_{Ct}(h_{Ct} \cdot N3_{Ct}, K_{Ct}) + C_{Ct}, \omega_{CH1}, \omega_{CH2}, \omega_{CH3}\} \\
&\quad - p_{Kt}^{C} \cdot \left(\frac{\varepsilon}{\bar{\varepsilon}}\right)^{C} \cdot \left[K_{C(t+1)}^{d} - (1-\delta_K) \cdot K_{Ct}\right] - Tx_{CG3t} \\
&\quad - \left(\frac{p_{NRt}^{C}}{\tilde{\varepsilon}^{C}}\right) \cdot (\gamma + \varphi_C) \cdot \tau(I3_t) \cdot T_{Ct}(h_{Ct} \cdot N3_{Ct}, K_{Ct}) \\
&\quad - \left(\frac{p_w}{\tilde{\varepsilon}^{C}}\right) \cdot \left[\varphi_C \cdot \tau(I3_t) \cdot T_{Ct}(h_{Ct} \cdot N3_{Ct}, K_{Ct}) + \kappa \cdot \delta \cdot K_{Ct}\right. \\
&\quad \left. - T_{Ct}^{S}\left(h_{Ct}^{S} \cdot N3_{Ct}\right)\right] - W3_t \cdot \left(h_{Ct} + h_{Ct}^{S}\right) \cdot N3_{Ct} \\
&\quad + p_{B3} \cdot \left(B3_{C(t+1)}^{s} - B3_{Ct}\right) - B3_{Ct}
\end{aligned} \quad (7.17)$$

as the expression for the amount the consumer goods industry plans to distribute as dividends during the current period.

Assume next period's planned production of consumer goods, C_{t+1}^{Te}, is given by

$$C_{t+1}^{Te} = \min\left\{\left[\frac{NR_{t+1}^{Cd}}{(\theta_C + \varphi_C)}\right], \tau_C(I3_t + \Delta I3) \cdot T_{C(t+1)}^{Te}\left(h_C^{e} \cdot N3_{C(t+1)}^{Te}, K_{C(t+1)}^{d}\right)\right\} \quad (7.18)$$

In particular, next period's planned production of consumer goods is assumed to be constrained, first, by the amount of the nonrenewable resource, NR_{t+1}^{Cd}, the consumer goods industry anticipates it will purchase next period and, second, by the level of transformation services provided by labor and capital next period, $T_{C(t+1)}^{Te}(\bullet)$. From (7.18), assuming that the sector does not produce more waste than necessary, the number of consumer goods the industry plans to produce next period is given by:

$$C_{t+1}^{Te} = \tau_C(I3_t + \Delta I3) \cdot T_{C(t+1)}^{Te}\left(h_C^{e} \cdot N3_{C(t+1)}^{Te}, K_{C(t+1)}^{d}\right) \quad (7.19)$$

where $I3_t + \Delta I3$ denotes the infrastructure that the G3 sector plans to have in place by the beginning of next period and where $\tau_C(I3_t + \Delta I3) > 1$ represents the contribution of next period's infrastructure to the ability of labor and physical capital to transform the nonrenewable resource into consumer goods. To avoid unnecessarily wasting either natural resources or transformation services, the industry combines them in the following way:

$$NR_{t+1}^{Cd} = (\gamma + \varphi_C) \cdot \tau_C(I3_t + \Delta I3) \cdot T_{C(t+1)}^{Te}\left(h_C^{e} \cdot N3_{C(t+1)}^{Te}, K_{C(t+1)}^{d}\right) \quad (7.20)$$

This restriction represents the combinations of the nonrenewable resource and transformation services along the expansion path associated with the production of consumption next period.

The industry anticipates generating new waste products, W^*C_{t+1}, during next period given by (7.21):

$$W^*C_{t+1} = \varphi_C \cdot \tau_C \left(I3_t + \Delta I3\right) \cdot T^{Te}_{C(t+1)}\left(h^e_C \cdot N3^{Te}_{C(t+1)}, K^d_{C(t+1)}\right) + \kappa \cdot \delta \cdot K^d_{C(t+1)} \qquad (7.21)$$

Again, the sector must pay a fee, p_w/ε^C, in terms of its country's unit of account, to obtain a pollution allowance for every unit of wasted mass it discharges into the environment over and above its pollution allowance allocation. Assume the following transformation function for treating and storing waste next period:

$$SW^*C_{t+1} = \min\left[\varphi_C \cdot \tau_C(I3_t + \Delta I3) \cdot T^{Te}_{C(t+1)}\left(h^e_C \cdot N3^{Te}_{C(t+1)}, K^d_{C(t+1)}\right) + \kappa \cdot \delta \cdot K^d_{C(t+1)} - \Omega^d_{C(t+1)}, T^S_{C(t+1)}\left(h^e_C \cdot N3^{Se}_{C(t+1)}\right)\right] \geq 0 \qquad (7.22)$$

where SW^*C_{t+1} represents the amount of waste treated and stored during the next period. $\Omega^d_{C(t+1)}$ represents the industry's demand for pollution allowances for next period. $T^S_{C(t+1)}(\bullet)$ represents transformation function for converting waste into treated and stored material, with $N3^{Se}_{C(t+1)}$ representing the number of employees the sector anticipates using to treat and store waste next period.

Assuming that neither transformation services nor mass are unnecessarily wasted in the treating and storing process, the amount of treated and stored waste planned for next period is given by

$$SW^*C_{t+1} = T^S_{C(t+1)}\left(h^e_C \cdot N3^{Se}_{C(t+1)}\right) \qquad (7.23)$$

Then the industry's anticipated expenses associated with discharging, treating, and storing waste during next period, $C^e_{C,W}{}^*$, is equal to

$$C^e_{C,W}{}^* = \left(\frac{p_w}{\tilde{\varepsilon}^C}\right) \cdot \left\{\varphi_C \cdot \tau_C \left(I3_t + \Delta I3\right) \cdot T^{Te}_{C(t+1)}\left(h^e_C \cdot N3^{Te}_{C(t+1)}, K^d_{C(t+1)}\right) + \kappa \cdot \delta \cdot K^d_{C(t+1)} - T^S_{C(t+1)}\left(h^e_C \cdot N3^{Se}_{C(t+1)}\right)\right\} + W3_{t+1} \cdot h^e_C \cdot N3^{Se}_{C(t+1)} \qquad (7.24)$$

The consumer goods industry also forecasts the net market supply function of people who will be available to work next period after subtracting its estimate of its government sector's and the R3 industry's demands for employees for next period. The forecasted net supply of labor is assumed to be positively related to the money wage, $W3_{t+1}$, that the consumer goods industry announces this period that it is willing to pay its employees next period (presumably the government and the R3 industry will also pay this wage and their demands will be filled first with the households indifferent as to their potential employer). Assume the forecasted net labor supply function is given by

$$N3^{Se}_{t+1} = N3^{Se}_{t+1}\left(W3_{t+1}, \gamma_3\right) \tag{7.25}$$

where γ_3 denotes a vector of parameters that the capital sector anticipates will shift the labor supply function and where $\partial(N3^{se}_{t+1})/\partial(W3_{t+1}) > 0$. The inverse of this function yields an expression for the minimum wage the sector estimates it needs to announce in order to attract a given number of employees to work next period.

$$W3_{t+1} = W3\left(N3^{Se}_{t+1}, \gamma_3\right) \tag{7.26}$$

where $\partial(W3_{t+1})/\partial(N3^{se}_{t+1}) > 0$. From this inverse function, we may express next period's anticipated labor cost function, $\overline{C}_C(\bullet)$, as a function of the number of people the consumer goods industry plans to employ by the beginning of next period, $N3^{de}_{C(t+1)}$, where we assume that the sector sets the money wage so that it generates the anticipated number of applicants (of homogeneous quality) that the sector wants to hire next period:

$$\overline{C}_C\left(N3^{de}_{C(t+1)}, \gamma_3\right) = W3\left(N3^{de}_{C(t+1)}, \gamma_3\right) \cdot h^e_{C3} \cdot N3^{de}_{C(t+1)} \tag{7.27}$$

where

$$\frac{\partial \overline{C}_C}{\partial N3^{de}_{C(t+1)}} = h^e_{C3} \cdot W3_{t+1} + h^e_{C3} \cdot N3^{de}_{C(t+1)} \cdot \left(\frac{\partial W3}{\partial N3^{de}_{C(t+1)}}\right) > 0$$

denotes next period's marginal factor cost of an extra employee.

Next period's anticipated net income is equal to the anticipated value of next period's production, $p^e_{C(t+1)} \cdot \tau_C(I3_t + \Delta I3) \cdot T^{Te}_{C(t+1)}(h^e_C \cdot N3^{Te}_{C(t+1)}, K^d_{C(t+1)})$, minus next period's expenses (wages, interest, taxes, purchases of the nonrenewable resource and pollution allowances, and depreciation), where $p^e_{C(t+1)}$ represents the market price that the consumer goods industry expects to set for its product next period. Therefore, next period's anticipated dividends equal the value of next period's production minus next period's wages, interest, taxes, purchases of nonrenewable resources and pollution allowances, depreciation and net business saving. Measured in terms of next period's market prices, net business saving is necessarily equal to the sum of the sector's net increase in assets minus the net increase in liabilities during the period.

For simplicity, it is assumed that at the beginning of the current period, the sector plans to hold an arbitrary amount of physical capital by the end of next period, $K^{de}_{C(t+2)}$. Let $B3^s_{C(t+1)}$ denote the number of bonds the consumer goods industry plans to have outstanding by the beginning of next period. Then the amount that the industry plans to borrow in Country Three's bond market during next period is given by $-p_{B3} \cdot B3^s_{C(t+1)}$ The planned level of net business saving next period, $S^d_{C(t+1)}$, by the consumer goods industry must be consistent with the market value of the sector's planned net accumulation of assets minus its planned borrowing. Therefore,

$$S^{d}_{C(t+1)} = \left[p^{C}_{K(t+1)} \cdot \left(\frac{\varepsilon}{\tilde{\varepsilon}}\right)^{C}\right] \cdot \left(K^{de}_{C(t+2)} - K^{de}_{C(t+1)}\right) + p_{B3} \cdot B3^{s}_{C(t+1)} \tag{7.28}$$

The sector's planned dividends for next period, $\Pi^{d}_{C(t+1)}$, are given by

$$\begin{aligned}
\Pi^{d}_{C(t+1)} = p^{e}_{C(t+1)} \cdot \Bigg\{ & \tau_{C}\,(I3_{t} + \Delta I3) \cdot T^{Te}_{C(t+1)}\left(h^{e}_{C} \cdot N3^{Te}_{C(t+1)}, K^{d}_{C(t+1)}\right) \\
& - \left[p^{C}_{K(t+1)} \cdot \left(\frac{\varepsilon}{\tilde{\varepsilon}}\right)^{C}\right] \cdot \left[K^{de}_{C(t+2)} - (1-\delta) \cdot K^{de}_{C(t+1)}\right]\Bigg\} \\
& - \left(\frac{p_{w}}{\tilde{\varepsilon}^{C}}\right) \cdot \Big\{\varphi_{C} \cdot \tau_{C}\,(I3_{t} + \Delta I3) \cdot T^{Te}_{C(t+1)}\left(h^{e}_{C} \cdot N3^{Te}_{C(t+1)}, K^{d}_{C(t+1)}\right) \\
& + \kappa \cdot \delta \cdot K^{d}_{C(t+1)} - T^{S}_{C(t+1)}\left(h^{e}_{C} \cdot N3^{Se}_{C(t+1)}\right)\Big\} \\
& - \overline{C}_{C3}\left(N3^{Te}_{C(t+1)} + N3^{Se}_{C(t+1)}, \gamma_{2}\right) - Tx_{CG3(t+1)} \\
& - \left(\frac{p^{C}_{NR(t+1)}}{\tilde{\varepsilon}^{C}}\right) \cdot (\gamma + \varphi_{C}) \cdot \tau_{C}\,(I3_{t} + \Delta I3) \\
& \cdot T^{Te}_{C(t+1)}\left(h^{e}_{C} \cdot N3^{Te}_{C(t+1)}, K^{d}_{C(t+1)}\right) - \left(1 + p_{B3}\right) \cdot B3^{s}_{C(t+1)}
\end{aligned} \tag{7.29}$$

where $p^{C}_{NR(t+1)}$ represents the next-period price of the nonrenewable resource that the consumer goods industry anticipates will prevail next period. At the beginning of the current period, the consumer goods industry plans next period to announce its product price, $p^{e}_{C(t+1)}$. Let the following demand function represent the industry's forecast of the demand for its product next period:

$$\begin{aligned}
C^{de}_{t+1} &= CH1^{de}_{t+1} + CH2^{de}_{t+1} + CH3^{de}_{t+1} \\
&= CH1^{de}_{t+1}\left(p^{e}_{C(t+1)}, \omega^{*}_{C3H1}\right) + CH2^{de}_{t+1}\left(p^{e}_{C(t+1)}, \omega^{*}_{C3H2}\right) \\
&\quad + CH3^{de}_{t+1}\left(p^{e}_{C(t+1)}, \omega^{*}_{C3H3}\right) \\
&= C^{de}_{t+1}\left(p^{e}_{C(t+1)}, \omega^{*}_{C3H1}, \omega^{*}_{C3H2}, \omega^{*}_{C3H3}\right)
\end{aligned} \tag{7.30}$$

where $C^{de}_{t+1}(\bullet)$ denotes the consumer goods industry's forecast at the beginning of the current period of the real market demand for consumer goods by the three household sectors next period. We assume that the derivative of $C^{de}_{t+1}(\bullet)$ with respect to $p^{e}_{C(t+1)}$ is negative (the sign is verified in the specification of the economic behavior of the H1, H2, and H3 industries); ω^{*}_{CH1} denotes a vector of shift parameters that the industry forecasts affect the H1 sector's next-period demand for consumer goods; ω^{*}_{CH2} denotes a vector of shift parameters that the industry forecasts will affect the H2 sector's demand for consumer goods next period; and ω^{*}_{CH3} denotes a vector of shift parameters that the industry forecasts will affect the H3 sector's demand for consumer goods next period. Solving the inverse function of (7.30) for $p^e_{C(t+1)}$ yields

$$p^e_{C(t+1)} = p^e_{C(t+1)}\left(\underset{-}{C^{de}_{t+1}}, \underset{+}{\omega^*_{CH1}}, \underset{+}{\omega^*_{CH2}}, \underset{+}{\omega^*_{CH3}}\right) \tag{7.31}$$

The price $p^e_{C(t+1)}$ given by (7.31) represents the maximum uniform price the consumer goods sector expects it can value each alternative quantity of goods it produces during the period. Based upon this function, the sector's forecasted total revenue, TR^{Ce}_{t+1}, function for next period is given by

$$\begin{aligned} TR^{Ce}_{t+1} &= p^e_{C(t+1)} \cdot C^{de}_{t+1} = p^e_{C(t+1)}\left(C^{de}_{t+1}, \omega^*_{CH1}, \omega^*_{CH2}, \omega^*_{CH3}\right) \cdot C^{de}_{t+1} \\ &= TR^{Ce}_{t+1}\left(C^{de}_{t+1}, \omega^*_{CH1}, \omega^*_{CH2}, \omega^*_{CH3}\right) \end{aligned} \tag{7.32}$$

Substituting the right-hand side of (7.19) for C^{de}_{t+1} in (7.32) yields

$$\begin{aligned} TR^{Ce}_{t+1} = TR^{Ce}_{t+1}\Big\{&\tau_C(I3_t + \Delta I3) \cdot T^{Te}_{C(t+1)}\left(h^e_C \cdot N3^{Te}_{C(t+1)}, K^d_{C(t+1)}\right), \\ &\omega^*_{CH1}, \omega^*_{CH2}, \omega^*_{CH3}\Big\} \end{aligned} \tag{7.33}$$

Substituting the right-hand side of (7.33) for the first term, $p^e_{C(t+1)} \cdot \{\bullet\}$, on the right-hand side of (7.29) yields

$$\begin{aligned} \Pi^d_{C(t+1)} = TR^{Ce}_{t+1}\Big\{&\tau_C\,(I3_t + \Delta I3) \cdot T^{Te}_{C(t+1)}\left(h^e_C \cdot N3^{Te}_{C(t+1)}, K^d_{C(t+1)}\right), \\ &\omega^*_{CH1}, \omega^*_{CH2}, \omega^*_{CH3}\Big\} - \left[p^C_{K(t+1)} \cdot \left(\frac{\varepsilon}{\tilde{\varepsilon}}\right)^C\right] \\ &\cdot\left[K^{de}_{C(t+2)} - (1-\delta)\cdot K^{de}_{C(t+1)}\right] - \left(\frac{P_w}{\tilde{\varepsilon}C}\right)\cdot\Big\{\varphi_C \cdot \tau_C\,(I3_t + \Delta I3) \\ &\cdot T^{Te}_{C(t+1)}\left(h^e_C \cdot N3^{Te}_{C(t+1)}, K^d_{C(t+1)}\right) + \kappa\cdot\delta\cdot K^d_{C(t+1)} \\ &- T^S_{C(t+1)}\left(h^e_C \cdot N3^{Se}_{C(t+1)}\right)\Big\} - \overline{C}_{C3}\Big(N3^{Te}_{C(t+1)} \\ &+ N3^{Se}_{C(t+1)}, \gamma_2\Big) - Tx_{CG3(t+1)} - \left(\frac{P^C_{NR(t+1)}}{\tilde{\varepsilon}C}\right)\cdot(\gamma + \varphi_C) \\ &\cdot \tau_C\,(I3_t + \Delta I3) \cdot T^{Te}_{C(t+1)}\left(h^e_C \cdot N3^{Te}_{C(t+1)}, K^d_{C(t+1)}\right) \\ &- \left(1 + p_{B3}\right)\cdot B3^s_{C(t+1)} \end{aligned} \tag{7.34}$$

as the expression for the amount the consumer goods industry plans to distribute as dividends next period. Solving (7.34) for the industry's end-of-period supply of bonds, $B3^s_{C(t+1)}$, and substituting the result into (7.17) yields the following expression for the present value of the industry's stream of dividends:

$$\Pi^{d}_{Ct} + \frac{\Pi^{d}_{C(t+1)}}{(1+r_3)} = TR^{Ce}_{t+1}\left\{\tau(I3_t)\cdot T_{Ct}(h_{Ct}\cdot N3_{Ct}, K_{Ct}) + C_{Ct}, \omega_{CH1}, \omega_{CH2}, \omega_{CH3}\right\}$$
$$- p^{C}_{Kt}\cdot\left(\frac{\varepsilon}{\tilde{\varepsilon}}\right)^{C}\cdot\left[K^{d}_{C(t+1)} - (1-\delta)\cdot K_{Ct}\right] - Tx_{CG3t}$$
$$-\left(\frac{p^{C}_{NRt}}{\tilde{\varepsilon}^{C}}\right)\cdot(\gamma+\varphi_C)\cdot\tau(I3_t)\cdot T_{Ct}(h_{Ct}\cdot N3_{Ct}, K_{Ct})$$
$$-\left(\frac{p_w}{\tilde{\varepsilon}^{C}}\right)\cdot\left[\varphi_C\cdot\tau(I3_t)\cdot T_{Ct}(h_{Ct}\cdot N3_{Ct}, K_{Ct}) + \kappa\cdot\delta\cdot K_{Ct}\right.$$
$$\left. - T^{S}_{Ct}\left(h^{S}_{Ct}\cdot N3_{Ct}\right)\right] - W3_t\cdot\left(h_{Ct}+h^{S}_{Ct}\right)\cdot N3_{Ct} - \left(1+p_{B3}\right)\cdot B3_{Ct}$$
$$+\left[\frac{1}{(1+r_3)}\right]\cdot\left[TR^{Ce}_{t+1}\left\{\tau_C(I3_t+\Delta I3)\right.\right.$$
$$\left.\cdot T^{Te}_{C(t+1)}\left(h^{e}_{C}\cdot N3^{Te}_{C(t+1)}, K^{d}_{C(t+1)}\right), \omega^{*}_{CH1}, \omega^{*}_{CH2}, \omega^{*}_{CH3}\right\}$$
$$-\left[p^{C}_{K(t+1)}\cdot\left(\frac{\varepsilon}{\tilde{\varepsilon}}\right)^{C}\right]\cdot\left[K^{de}_{C(t+2)} - (1-\delta)\cdot K^{de}_{C(t+1)}\right]$$
$$-\left(\frac{p_w}{\tilde{\varepsilon}^{C}}\right)\cdot\left\{\varphi_C\cdot\tau_C(I3_t+\Delta I3)\cdot T^{Te}_{C(t+1)}\left(h^{e}_{C}\cdot N3^{Te}_{C(t+1)}, K^{d}_{C(t+1)}\right)\right.$$
$$\left.+\kappa\cdot\delta\cdot K^{d}_{C(t+1)} - T^{S}_{C(t+1)}\left(h^{e}_{C}\cdot N3^{Se}_{C(t+1)}\right)\right\}$$
$$-\overline{C}_{C3}\left(N3^{Te}_{C(t+1)} + N3^{Se}_{C(t+1)}, \gamma_2\right) - Tx_{CG3(t+1)}$$
$$-\left(\frac{p^{C}_{NR(t+1)}}{\tilde{\varepsilon}^{C}}\right)\cdot(\gamma+\varphi_C)\cdot\tau_C(I3_t+\Delta I3)\cdot T^{Te}_{C(t+1)}$$
$$\left.\left(h^{e}_{C}\cdot N3^{Te}_{C(t+1)}, K^{d}_{C(t+1)}\right)\right] \quad (7.35)$$

where $1/(1+r_3) = p_{B3}/(1+p_{B3})$. The consumer goods industry's objective at the beginning of the current period is to maximize the right-hand side of (7.35) with respect to h_{Ct}, h^{S}_{Ct}, $K^{de}_{C(t+1)}$, $N3^{Te}_{C(t+1)}$, and $N3^{Se}_{C(t+1)}$. Doing so yields the first-order necessary conditions (7.36)–(7.40):

$$\frac{\partial\left[\Pi^{d}_{Ct}+\Pi^{d}_{C(t+1)}/(1+r_3)\right]}{\partial h_{Ct}} = \left[\frac{\partial TR^{Ce}_{t}}{\partial C^{de}_{t}} - \left(\frac{p^{C}_{NRt}}{\tilde{\varepsilon}^{C}}\right)\cdot(\gamma) - \left(\frac{p_w}{\tilde{\varepsilon}^{C}}\right)\cdot\varphi_C(I3_t)\right]$$
$$\cdot\tau(I3_t)\cdot\left[\frac{\partial T_{Ct}}{\partial(h_{Ct}\cdot N3_{Ct})}\right]\cdot N3_{Ct}$$
$$- W3_t\cdot N3_{Ct} = 0 \quad (7.36)$$

According to (7.36), the consumer goods industry will use its current employees during the current period up to the point at which the value of the marginal product of labor in producing consumer goods, net of the marginal cost of the extra renewable resource the industry must buy to produce the extra amount of the consumer goods, and net of the marginal cost of the extra pollution allowances associated with the additional waste generated in producing the extra consumer goods is equal to the additional wage expense from using its workers an extra hour for the purpose of producing consumer goods.

$$\frac{\partial\left[\Pi^{d}_{Ct} + \Pi^{d}_{C(t+1)}/\,(1+r_3)\right]}{\partial h^{S}_{Ct}} = \left(\frac{P_w}{\tilde{\varepsilon}^C}\right)\cdot\left[\frac{\partial T^{S}_{Ct}}{\partial\left(h^{S}_{Ct}\cdot N3_{Ct}\right)}\right] \cdot N3_{C3t} - W3_t \cdot N3_{Ct} = 0 \qquad (7.37)$$

Condition (7.37) stipulates that the present value maximizing consumer goods industry's use of current employees for the purpose of treating and storing waste during the current period up to the point at which the value of the marginal product of that labor in terms of the value of the pollution allowances that are conserved by this effort is equal to the current marginal cost of an extra hour of labor time.

$$\begin{aligned}\frac{\partial\left[\Pi^{d}_{Ct} + \Pi^{d}_{C(t+1)}/(1+r_3)\right]}{\partial K^{de}_{C(t+1)}} &= +\left[\frac{1}{(1+r_{3t})}\right] \\ &\cdot\left\{\left[\frac{\partial TR^{Ce}_{t+1}}{\partial C^{de}_{t+1}}\right]\cdot \tau_C(I3_t+\Delta I3)\cdot\left[\frac{\partial T^{Te}_{C(t+1)}}{\partial K^{d}_{C(t+1)}}\right]\right. \\ &+\left[p^{C}_{K(t+1)}\cdot\left(\frac{\varepsilon}{\bar{\varepsilon}}\right)^{C}\right]\cdot(1-\delta)-\left(\frac{P_w}{\tilde{\varepsilon}^C}\right) \\ &\left.\cdot\left[\varphi_C\cdot\tau_C(I3_t+\Delta I3)\cdot\left[\frac{\partial T^{Te}_{C(t+1)}}{\partial K^{d}_{C(t+1)}}\right]+\kappa\cdot\delta\right\}\right. \\ &-\left(\frac{p^{C}_{NR(t+1)}}{\tilde{\varepsilon}^C}\right)\cdot(\gamma+\varphi_C)\cdot\tau_C(I3_t+\Delta I3) \\ &\left.\left.\cdot\left[\frac{\partial T^{Te}_{C(t+1)}}{\partial K^{d}_{C(t+1)}}\right]\right]\right] - p^{C}_{Kt}\cdot\left(\frac{\varepsilon}{\bar{\varepsilon}}\right)^{C} = 0 \qquad (7.38)\end{aligned}$$

From (7.38), the consumer goods industry will continue to buy additional physical capital during the current period up to the point at which the present value of the marginal product of physical capital next period, $[1/(1+r_3)]\cdot[\partial TR^{Ce}_{t+1}/\partial C^{de}_{t+1}]\cdot \tau_C(I3_t+\Delta I3)\cdot[\partial T^{Te}_{C(t+1)}/\partial K^{d}_{C(t+1)}]$, net of the present value of the marginal cost of the extra nonrenewable resource necessary in order for the physical capital to transform it into consumer goods, $[1/(1+r_3)]\cdot(p^{C}_{NR(t+1)}/\tilde{\varepsilon}^C)\cdot(\gamma+\varphi_C)\cdot\tau_C(I3_t+\Delta I3)\cdot[\partial T^{Te}_{C(t+1)}/\partial K^{d}_{C(t+1)}]$, and net of the present value of the marginal cost of the extra waste produced next period not only in transforming the nonrenewable resource, but also in terms of physical depreciation of capital in the transformation process, $t[1/(1+r_{3t})] \cdot (p_w/\tilde{\varepsilon}^C) \cdot \{\varphi_C \cdot \tau_C(I3_t + \Delta I3) \cdot [\partial T^{Te}_{C(t+1)}/\partial K^d_{C(t+1)}] + \kappa \cdot \delta\}[1/(1 + r_3)] \cdot (p_w/\tilde{\varepsilon}^C) \cdot \{\varphi_C \cdot \tau_C(I3_t + \Delta I3) \cdot [\partial T^{Te}_{C(t+1)}/\partial K^d_{C(t+1)}] + \kappa \cdot \delta$, is equal to the user cost of capital, $p^C_{Kt} \cdot (\varepsilon/\tilde{\varepsilon})^C - \{[p^C_{K(t+1)} \cdot (\varepsilon/\tilde{\varepsilon})^C] \cdot (1 - \delta)\}/(1 + r_3)$. The user cost of capital in this case is equal to the current price of a unit of capital in terms of Country Three's unit of account minus the present value of the market value of that portion of a unit of physical capital that does not depreciate next period:

$$\frac{\partial\left[\Pi^d_{Ct} + \Pi^d_{C(t+1)}/(1 + r_3)\right]}{\partial N3^{Te}_{C(t+1)}} = \left[\frac{1}{(1 + r_3)}\right] \cdot \left[\left\{\left(\frac{\partial TR^{Ce}_{t+1}}{\partial C^{de}_{t+1}}\right) - \left(\frac{p_w}{\tilde{\varepsilon}^C}\right) \cdot \varphi_C - \left(\frac{p^C_{NR(t+1)}}{\tilde{\varepsilon}^C}\right) \cdot (\gamma + \varphi_C)\right\} \cdot \tau_C(I3_t + \Delta I3) \cdot \frac{\partial T^{Te}_{C(t+1)}}{\partial\left(h^e_C \cdot N3^{Te}_{C(t+1)}\right)} \cdot h^e_C - \left(\frac{\partial \bar{C}_{C3}}{\partial N3^{Te}_{C(t+1)}}\right)\right] = 0 \tag{7.39}$$

Condition (7.39) states that the present value maximizing consumer goods industry will continue to add employees to its workforce for next period up to the point at which the present value of next period's value of the marginal product of labor, net of the marginal cost of the extra nonrenewable resource the sector must purchase for the labor to transform it into consumer goods next period, and net of the marginal cost of the extra pollution allowances the sector must buy because of the extra waste generated next period is equal to the present value of the marginal factor (labor) cost of hiring another person to work next period.

$$\frac{\partial\left[\Pi^d_{Ct} + \Pi^d_{C(t+1)}/(1 + r_{3t})\right]}{\partial N3^{Se}_{C(t+1)}} = \left[\frac{1}{(1 + r_3)}\right] \cdot \left[\left(\frac{p_w}{\tilde{\varepsilon}^C}\right) \cdot \left(\frac{\partial T^S_{C3(t+1)}}{\partial N3^{Se}_{C(t+1)}}\right) \cdot h^e_C - \left(\frac{\partial \bar{C}_{C3}}{\partial N3^{Se}_{C(t+1)}}\right) \cdot h^e_C\right] = 0 \tag{7.40}$$

According to (7.40), the consumer goods sector will hire people to treat and store waste next period up to the point at which the present value of the pollution allowance cost saved by hiring the marginal worker is equal to the present value of the marginal factor cost of the marginal employee next period.

Totally differentiating conditions (7.36)–(7.40) and solving for the changes in h_{Ct}, h^s_{ct}, $K^{de}_{C(t+1)}$, $N3^{Te}_{C(t+1)}$, and $N3^{Se}_{C(t+1)}$ yields the industry's demand functions for current labor hours, its end-of-period demand for physical capital, and its demand for workers for next period. To simplify the analysis, only the parameters entering the own first-order conditions are assumed to affect the individual demand functions.

Demand Function for h_{Ct}

From (7.36), an increase in the price of the nonrenewable resource in terms of Country One's unit of account, p^{C}_{NRt}, an increase in the price of pollution allowances in terms of Country One's unit of account, p_w, an increase in the mass of the nonrenewable resource wasted per unit of consumer goods produced, φ_C, or an increase in the mass of the nonrenewable resource contained in a unit of consumer goods, γ, reduces the net value of the marginal product of an hour of labor for the purpose of transforming the nonrenewable resource into consumer goods during the current period, thereby reducing the consumer goods industry's demand for labor for that purpose. An increase in the value of Country Three's unit of account in terms of Country One's unit of account anticipated by the C industry, $\tilde{\varepsilon}^C$, reduces the prices of both the nonrenewable resource and pollution allowances in the current period, inducing the consumer goods industry to use more current labor for the purpose of transforming the nonrenewable resource into consumer goods. An increase in the current money wage, $W3_t$, increases the marginal cost of an additional unit of labor in the current period, thereby reducing the sector's demand for h_{Ct}. Finally, the larger the infrastructure of Country Three at the beginning of the current period, $I3_t$, the greater the value of the marginal product of labor for transforming the nonrenewable resource into consumer goods and the greater, ceteris paribus, the industry's demand for those labor services. Therefore, the following demand for labor hours by the industry for the purpose of transforming the nonrenewable resource into consumer goods results from the above analysis:

$$h_{Ct} = h_{Ct}\left(\underset{-}{p^{C}_{NRt}}, \underset{-}{p_w}, \underset{-}{\varphi_C}, \underset{-}{\gamma}, \underset{+}{\tilde{\varepsilon}^C}, \underset{-}{W3_t}, \underset{+}{I3_t}\right) \qquad (7.41)$$

Demand Function for h^{S}_{Ct}

From (7.37), an increase in the price of pollution allowances in terms of Country One's unit of account increases the value of the marginal product of a current labor hour used to treat and store waste during the current period; an increase in the value of Country Three's unit of account in terms of Country One's unit of account reduces the value of the marginal product of labor used to treat and store waste, because it reduces the price the consumer goods industry must pay in terms of its own unit of account to obtain a pollution allowance. Therefore an increase in p_w increases the industry's demand for labor in the current period for treating and storing waste, while an increase in $\tilde{\varepsilon}^C$ produces the opposite effect. The higher the current money wage, the higher the marginal cost of adding an extra hour of labor to treat and store waste, so that an increase in $W3_t$ reduces the industry's current demand for that labor. The demand function (7.42) follows from these considerations:

$$h^S_{Ct} = h^S_{Ct}\left(\underset{+}{p_w}, \underset{-}{\tilde{\varepsilon}^C}, \underset{-}{W3_t}\right) \tag{7.42}$$

Demand Function for $K^{de}_{C(t+1)}$

From (7.38), an increase in the interest rate in Country Three's bond market, r_{3t}, reduces the present value of the consumer goods industry's anticipated marginal net revenue from an extra unit of physical capital held by the beginning of next period; an increase in r_{3t} also reduces the present value of the anticipated net market value of a unit of physical capital next period, thereby raising the user cost of capital to the consumer goods industry. Consequently, an increase in r_{3t} reduces the sector's demand for physical capital for the end of the period. An increase in the anticipated price of physical capital announced by the capital goods industry in terms of Country Two's unit of account, p^C_{Kt}, increases the user cost of capital and induces the consumer goods industry to reduce its end-of-period demand for capital goods. An increase in either the price of pollution allowances or the anticipated price of the nonrenewable resource reduces the present value of the net income the consumer goods sector anticipates earning on a unit of physical capital held by the beginning of next period. Therefore, an increase in either p_w or $p^C_{NR(t+1)}$ reduces the sector's demand for capital. An increase in the value of Country Three's unit of account in terms of Country One's unit of account, $\tilde{\varepsilon}^C$, reduces the price of pollution allowances and the nonrenewable resource in terms of Country Three's unit of account; it also reduces the user cost of capital to the consumer goods industry. Therefore a rise in $\tilde{\varepsilon}^C$ causes the consumer goods sector to increase its demand for physical capital. Holding $\tilde{\varepsilon}^C$ constant, a rise in the value of Country Two's unit of account in terms of Country One's unit of account also raises the value of Country Two's unit of account in terms of Country Three's unit of account, $(\varepsilon/\tilde{\varepsilon})^C$. Therefore a rise in ε^C increases the price of physical capital in terms of Country Three's unit of account, causing the sector to reduce its demand for capital for the end of the period. An increase in any one of the amount of mass in a unit of physical capital, κ, the rate of physical depreciation of capital, δ, the amount of mass contained in a unit of consumer goods, γ, or the amount of mass wasted in producing a unit of consumer goods, φ_C, all reduce the present value of next period's value of the marginal product of physical capital for the consumer goods industry, causing the sector to reduce its demand for capital for the end of the period. Therefore, the following demand for capital by the consumer goods industry emerges:

$$K^{de}_{C(t+1)} = K^{de}_{C(t+1)}\left(\underset{-}{r_{3t}}, \underset{-}{p^C_{Kt}}, \underset{-}{p^C_{NRt}}, \underset{-}{p_w}, \underset{-}{\varphi_C}, \underset{-}{\gamma}, \underset{-}{\kappa}, \underset{-}{\delta}, \underset{-}{\varepsilon^C}, \underset{+}{\tilde{\varepsilon}^C}\right) \tag{7.43}$$

Demand Function for $N3^{Te}_{C(t+1)}$

According to (7.39), an increase in the price of pollution allowances in terms of Country One's unit of account, an increase in the amount of mass contained in a unit of consumer goods, or an increase in the amount of mass wasted in producing a unit of consumer goods all reduce the value of the net marginal revenue from an extra employee next period. An increase in the value of Country Three's unit of account in terms of Country One's unit of account reduces the price the consumer goods industry must pay for pollution credits, thereby increasing the sector's demand for employees for next period. These considerations yield the following demand function for employees for the purpose of transforming the nonrenewable resource into consumer goods next period:

$$N3^{Te}_{C(t+1)} = N3^{Te}_{C(t+1)}\left(\underset{-}{p_w}, \underset{+}{\tilde{\varepsilon}^C}, \underset{-}{\varphi_C}, \underset{-}{\gamma}\right) \tag{7.44}$$

Demand Function for $N3^{Se}_{C(t+1)}$

The consumer goods industry's demand for employees for next period for the purpose of treating and storing waste from (7.40) is positively related to the price of a pollution allowance in terms of Country Three's unit of account. This yields the following demand function:

$$N3^{Se}_{C(t+1)} = N3^{Se}_{C(t+1)}\left(\underset{+}{p_w}, \underset{-}{\tilde{\varepsilon}^C}\right) \tag{7.45}$$

From the above demand functions for labor and capital it is possible to solve for current production, the sector's nonrenewable resource demand, pricing, wage setting, and demand for pollution allowances.

Current Production of Consumer Goods

The current-period production function for consumer goods is given earlier by (7.2) as an increasing function of h_{Ct} and K_{Ct}. Substituting the right-hand side of (7.41) for h_{Ct} in (7.2) yields the consumer goods industry's production of consumer goods during the current period.

$$\begin{aligned} C^T_t &= \tau(I3_t) \cdot T_{Ct}(h_{Ct} \cdot N3_{Ct}, K_{Ct}) \\ &= C^T_t\left(\underset{-}{p^C_{NRt}}, \underset{-}{p_w}, \underset{-}{\varphi_C}, \underset{-}{\gamma}, \underset{+}{\tilde{\varepsilon}^C}, \underset{-}{W3_t}, \underset{+}{I3t}, \underset{+}{K_{Ct}}\right) \end{aligned} \tag{7.46}$$

Current Demand for the Nonrenewable Resource

The consumer goods industry's demand for the nonrenewable resource during the current period is presented in (7.3) earlier as an increasing function of h_{Ct}, K_{Ct}, $I3_t$, φ_C and γ. Substituting the right-hand side of (7.41) for h_{Ct} in (7.3) yields the consumer goods industry's demand for the nonrenewable resource during the current period. It is assumed that the direct effects of an increase in the amount of the nonrenewable resource contained in a unit of consumer goods and the amount of the nonrenewable resource wasted in the production of a unit of consumer goods dominates the negative effects of these changes upon the sector's demand for the resource operating through the sector's demand for current labor.

$$\begin{aligned} NRC_t^{Td} &= (\gamma + \varphi_C) \cdot \tau(I3_t) \cdot T_{Ct}(h_{Ct} \cdot N3_{Ct}, K_{Ct}) \\ &= NRC_t^{Td}\left(\underset{-}{p_{NRt}^{C}}, \underset{-}{p_w}, \underset{+}{\varphi_C}, \underset{+}{\gamma}, \underset{+}{\tilde{\varepsilon}^C}, \underset{-}{W3_t}, \underset{+}{I3_t}, \underset{+}{K_{Ct}}\right) \end{aligned} \tag{7.47}$$

Current Product Price of Consumer Goods

The consumer goods pricing function is shown in (7.13) as negatively related to the number of units of consumer goods the sector desires to sell during the current period but positively related to the sector's estimate of the positions of the demand curves for consumer goods by the three household sectors. However, from (7.9), the number of units of consumer goods the industry plans to sell during the current period, C_t^{de}, is equal to the number of units it decides to produce during the period, C_t^T, plus the number of consumer goods in its initial inventory, C_{Ct}. Therefore, from (7.46), the number of units of consumer goods the sector plans to sell during the current period is given by (7.48):

$$C_t^{de} = C_t^T + C_{Ct} = C_t^{de}\left(\underset{-}{p_{NRt}^{C}}, \underset{-}{p_w}, \underset{-}{\varphi_C}, \underset{-}{\gamma}, \underset{+}{\tilde{\varepsilon}^C}, \underset{-}{W3_t}, \underset{+}{I3_t}, \underset{+}{K_{Ct}}, \underset{+1}{C_{Ct}}\right) \tag{7.48}$$

Substituting the far right-hand side of (7.48) for C_t^{de} in (7.13) yields the pricing function (7.49):

$$\begin{aligned} p_{Ct} &= p_{Ct}\left(\underset{-}{C_t^{de}}, \underset{+}{\omega_{CH1}}, \underset{+}{\omega_{CH2}}, \underset{+}{\omega_{CH3}}\right) \\ &= p_{Ct}\left(\underset{+}{p_{NRt}^{C}}, \underset{+}{p_w}, \underset{+}{\varphi_C}, \underset{+}{\gamma}, \underset{-}{\tilde{\varepsilon}^C}, \underset{+}{W3_t}, \underset{-}{I3_t}, \underset{-}{K_{Ct}}, \underset{-}{C_{Ct}}, \underset{+}{\omega_{CH1}}, \underset{+}{\omega_{CH2}}, \underset{+}{\omega_{CH3}}\right) \end{aligned} \tag{7.49}$$

Parametric changes that raise the marginal cost of current production of consumer goods cause the sector to raise the price of its product; the more capital held by the industry at the beginning of the period and the larger the nation's infrastructure at the beginning of the period, the lower the price that the consumer goods industry charges.

Wage-Setting Function

The wage rate set this period by the consumer goods industry for next period is found by substituting the right-hand sides of (7.44) and (7.45) into the inverse of the consumer goods industry's estimate of the net supply of workers to the industry next period, given by (7.26). It is assumed in (7.50) that the parametric effects upon the sector's demand for workers to transform the nonrenewable resource dominate those upon the sector's demand for workers to treat and store waste next period.

$$\begin{aligned} W3_{t+1} &= W3\left(\underset{+}{N3^{Se}_{t+1}}, \underset{+}{\gamma_3}\right) \\ &= W3\left[N3^{Te}_{C(t+1)}\left(\underset{-}{p_w}, \underset{+}{\tilde{\varepsilon}^C}, \underset{-}{\varphi_C}, \underset{-}{\gamma}\right) + N3^{Se}_{C(t+1)}\left(\underset{+}{p_w}, \underset{-}{\tilde{\varepsilon}^C}\right), \gamma_3\right] \\ &= W3\left(\underset{-}{p_w}, \underset{+}{\tilde{\varepsilon}^C}, \underset{-}{\varphi_C}, \underset{-}{\gamma}, \underset{+}{\gamma_3}\right) \end{aligned} \tag{7.50}$$

Waste Generation

The waste generated by the consumer goods industry during the current period, W^*C_t, is given by (7.5). Substituting the right-hand side of (7.41) for h_{Ct} in (7.5) yields the optimal amount of waste generated by the consumer goods industry during the current period. It is assumed in (7.51) that the direct effect of an increase in the amount of waste generated per unit of consumer goods produced dominates the indirect effect operating through the industry's demand for labor for transforming the nonrenewable resource into consumer goods.

$$\begin{aligned} W^*C_t &= \varphi_C \cdot \tau(I3_t) \cdot T_{Ct}(h_{Ct} \cdot N3_{Ct}, K_{Ct}) + \kappa \cdot \delta \cdot K_{Ct} \\ &= \varphi_C \cdot \tau(I3_t) \cdot T_{Ct}\left[h_{Ct}\left(\underset{-}{p^C_{NRt}}, \underset{-}{p_w}, \underset{-}{\varphi_C}, \underset{-}{\gamma}, \underset{+}{\tilde{\varepsilon}^C}, \underset{-}{W3_t}, \underset{+}{I3_t}\right), K_{Ct}\right] + \kappa \cdot \delta \cdot K_{Ct} \\ &= W^*C_t\left(\underset{+}{\varphi_C}, \underset{+}{I3_t}, \underset{-}{p^C_{NRt}}, \underset{-}{p_w}, \underset{-}{\gamma}, \underset{+}{\tilde{\varepsilon}^C}, \underset{-}{W3_t}, \underset{+}{K_{Ct}}, \underset{+}{\kappa}, \underset{+}{\delta}\right) \end{aligned} \tag{7.51}$$

Treated and Stored Waste

The amount of waste generated by the consumer goods industry during the current period is given by (7.7). Substituting the industry's demand for labor time for the purpose of treating and storing waste during the current period, (7.42), into (7.7) yields the solution for the optimal amount of waste that the industry treats and stores during the current period as a function of the parameters facing it.

$$\begin{aligned} SW^*C_t &= T^S_{Ct}\left[h^S_{Ct}\left(p_w, \tilde{\varepsilon}^C, W3_t\right)\cdot N3_{Ct}\right] \\ &= SW^*C_t\left(\underset{-}{p_w}, \underset{+}{\tilde{\varepsilon}^C}, \underset{-}{W3_t}\right) \end{aligned} \tag{7.52}$$

Excess Demand for Pollution Allowances

The consumer goods industry's excess demand for pollution allowances during the current period is equal to its waste generation, (7.51), minus its waste treatment and storage, (7.52), and minus its initial allocation of pollution allowances, Ω_{Ct}. In (7.53), it is assumed that the parametric effects upon optimal waste generation dominate those upon optimal treatment and storage of waste.

$$\begin{aligned} \Omega^d_{Ct} - \Omega_{Ct} &= W^*C_t\left(\underset{+}{\varphi C}, \underset{+}{I3_t}, \underset{-}{p^C_{NRt}}, \underset{-}{p_w}, \underset{-}{\gamma}, \underset{+}{\tilde{\varepsilon}^C}, \underset{-}{W3_t}, \underset{+}{K_{Ct}}, \underset{+}{\kappa}, \underset{+}{\delta}\right) \\ &\quad - SW^*C_t\left(\underset{-}{p_w}, \underset{+}{\tilde{\varepsilon}^C}, \underset{-}{W3_t}\right) \\ &= \Omega^d_{Ct}\left(\underset{+}{\varphi C}, \underset{+}{I3_t}, \underset{-}{p^C_{NRt}}, \underset{-}{p_w}, \underset{-}{\gamma}, \underset{+}{\tilde{\varepsilon}^C}, \underset{-}{W3_t}, \underset{+}{K_{Ct}}, \underset{+}{\kappa}, \underset{+}{\delta}\right) - \Omega_{Ct} \end{aligned} \tag{7.53}$$

Consumer Goods Industry's Market Supply of Bonds

Assuming that the consumer goods industry does not plan to engage in net saving during the period, deciding instead to distribute to its owners as dividends all the after-tax net income it earns during the current period, then from (7.10), the sector's provisional end-of-period supply of bonds to Country Three's bond market is given by (7.54), where p_{Ct} is given by (7.49) and $K^d_{C(t+1)}$ is given by (7.43). The effects of parametric changes that affect pricing decisions are assumed to be minor relative to those that affect the sector's end-of-period demand for physical capital.

$$\begin{aligned} &p_{B3}\cdot B3^s_{C(t+1)} \\ &\quad = -p_{Ct}\left(\underset{+}{p^C_{NRt}}, \underset{+}{p_w}, \underset{+}{\varphi C}, \underset{+}{\gamma}, \underset{-}{\tilde{\varepsilon}^C}, \underset{+}{W3_t}, \underset{-}{I3_t}, \underset{-}{K_{Ct}}, \underset{-}{C_{Ct}}, \underset{+}{\omega_{CH1}}, \underset{+}{\omega_{CH2}}, \underset{+}{\omega_{CH3}}\right) \end{aligned}$$

$$\cdot C_{Ct} + p_{Kt}^{C} \cdot \left(\frac{\varepsilon}{\tilde{\varepsilon}}\right)^{C} \cdot K_{C(t+1)}^{d}\left(\underset{-}{r3_t}, \underset{-}{p_{Kt}^{C}}, \underset{-}{p_{NRt}^{C}}, \underset{-}{p_w}, \underset{-}{\varphi C}, \underset{-}{\gamma}, \underset{-}{\kappa}, \underset{-}{\delta}, \underset{-}{\varepsilon^{C}}, \underset{+}{\tilde{\varepsilon}^{C}}\right)$$

$$- p_{Kt}^{C} \cdot \left(\frac{\varepsilon}{\tilde{\varepsilon}}\right)^{C} \cdot (1-\delta) \cdot K_{CT} + p_{B3} \cdot B3_{Ct}$$

$$= p_{B3} \cdot B3_{C(t+1)}^{s}\left(\underset{-}{r_{3t}}, \underset{-}{p_{Kt}^{C}}, \underset{-}{p_{NRt}^{C}}, \underset{-}{p_w}, \underset{-}{\varphi_C}, \underset{-}{\gamma}, \underset{-}{\kappa}, \underset{-}{\delta}, \underset{-}{\varepsilon^{C}}, \underset{+}{\tilde{\varepsilon}^{C}}\right) \quad (7.54)$$

Dividends Paid to Shareholders during the Current Period

Given the assumption that the consumer goods industry does not plan to engage in net saving during the current period, the sector's dividends to its shareholders are equal to the value of current production of consumer goods minus current wages, interest, taxes, depreciation, and the sector's purchases of the nonrenewable resources and pollution allowances.

$$\Pi_{Ct}^{d} = \left[p_{Ct} \cdot \tau(I3_t) \cdot T_{Ct}(h_{Ct} \cdot N3_{Ct}, K_{Ct}) - p_{Kt}^{C} \cdot \left(\frac{\varepsilon}{\tilde{\varepsilon}}\right)^{C} \cdot \delta \cdot K_{Ct}\right] - Tx_{CG3t}$$

$$- \left(\frac{p_{NRt}^{C}}{\tilde{\varepsilon}^{C}}\right) \cdot (\gamma + \varphi_C) \cdot (I3_t) \cdot T_{Ct}(h_{Ct} \cdot N3_{Ct}, K_{Ct})$$

$$- \left(\frac{p_w}{\tilde{\varepsilon}^{C}}\right) \cdot \left[\varphi_C \cdot \tau(I3_t) \cdot T_{Ct}(h_{Ct} \cdot N3_{Ct}, K_{Ct}) + \kappa \cdot \delta \cdot K_{Ct}\right.$$

$$\left. - T_{Ct}^{S}\left(h_{Ct}^{S} \cdot N3_{Ct}\right)\right]$$

$$- W3_t \cdot \left(h_{Ct} + h_{Ct}^{S}\right) \cdot N3_{Ct} - B3_{Ct} \quad (7.55)$$

In chapter 8, the production, pricing, and employment decisions are specified for the three country-specific renewable resource industries before current interest rates and exchange rates are established.

8

The Renewable Resource Industries

Country One's Renewable Resource (R1) Industry

At the beginning of the current period, an initial stock of natural R1, $R1_t$, exists, where $R1_t \geq \overline{R1}_t$. During the current period, this stock would grow naturally by the net amount $g_{R1}(B_t, P_t^*) \cdot R1_t$, where $g_{R1}(\bullet)$ denotes the natural net growth rate of R1 and where g_{R1} is positively related to the beginning stock of the basic resource, B_t, but negatively related to the level of global pollution at the beginning of the current period, P_t^*.

Let $R1_{t+1}^d$ represent the industry's desired stock of R1 for the end of the current period, which is determined in accordance with its objective to maximize the present value of its operations. The G1 sector stipulates that the R1 industry maintain a stock of R1 by the end of the current period of $\overline{R1}_{t+1} \geq 0$. Therefore, it is assumed that $R1_{t+1}^d = \overline{R1}_{t+1} + R1_{t+1}^{d'}$, where $R1_{t+1}^{d'} \geq 0$.

The R1 industry applies a variable amount of labor to transform the mass of natural R1 that it desires to convert into a marketable product, $R1^T$, changing its physical, chemical, biological, or aesthetic characteristics and/or its location. The current level of transformation services, $T_{R1}(\bullet)$, is assumed to be a positive increasing function of (variable) labor hours, $h_{R1} \cdot N1_{R1t}$, applied during the period, where $N1_{R1t}$ denotes the number of people employed in the R1 industry at the start of the current period and where h_{R1} represents the (average) number of hours these employees work for the R1 industry during the period. Assume that the marginal transformation of labor, T'_{R1}, is positive, but diminishing. The infrastructure in place in Country One at the beginning of the period, $I1_t$, positively affects both the total and marginal products of labor.

Under these assumptions, the production function for current marketable R1, $R1_t^T$, is given by (8.1):

$$R1_t^T = \min\left[g_{R1}\left(B_t, P_t^*\right) \cdot R1_t - \left(\overline{R1}_{t+1} + R1_{t+1}^{d'} - R1_t\right),\right.$$
$$\left.\tau_{R1t}\left(h_{R1t} \cdot N1_{R1t}\right)\right] \quad (8.1)$$

where $\tau_{R1}(I1_t) > 0,\ \tau'_{R1} > 0$.

Assuming the R1 industry wastes neither the transformation services of labor nor the amount of R1 available for transformation, the amount of (transformed) R1 produced may be viewed as equal to $\tau_{R1}(I1_t) \cdot T_{R1t}(h_{R1t} \cdot N1_{R1t})$:

$$R1_t^T = \tau_{R1}\left(I1_t\right) \cdot T_{R1t}\left(h_{R1t} \cdot N1_{R1t}\right) \quad (8.2)$$

In addition, in terms of mass, the amount of R1 transformed in the production process may be viewed as

$$g_{R1}\left(Bt, P_t^*\right) \cdot R1_t - \left(\overline{R1}_{t+1} + R1_{t+1}^{d'} - R1_t\right)$$
$$= \tau_{R1}\left(I1_t\right) \cdot T_{R1t}\left(h_{R1t} \cdot N1_{R1t}\right) \quad (8.3)$$

Solving (8.3) for $R1_{t+1}^{d'}$ yields the following expression for the planned inventory of unprocessed R1 for the end of the current period over and above the required amount:

$$R1_{t+1}^{d'} = \left[1 + g_{R1}\left(B_t, P_t^*\right)\right] \cdot R1_t - \tau_{R1t}\left(I1_t\right) \cdot T_{R1t}\left(h_{R1t} \cdot N1_{R1t}\right)$$
$$- \overline{R1}_{t+1} \geq 0 \quad (8.4)$$

The amount of transformed R1 that is not sold during the current period is assumed to be added to the industry's inventory of processed R1:

$$R1_{t+1}^{T^*} = R1_t^{T^*} + \tau_{R1}\left(I1_t\right) \cdot T_{R1t}\left(h_{R1t} \cdot N1_{R1t}\right) - R1H1_t \geq 0 \quad (8.5)$$

where R1H1 corresponds to the actual amount of transformed R1 purchased by the households in Country One during the current period, $R1_t^{T^*}$ represents the initial inventory of transformed R1 at the beginning of the period, and $R1_{t+1}^{T^*}$ denotes the inventory of transformed R1 at the end of current period.

Taking the current wage rate set by the nonrenewable resource industry, $W1_t$, and the R1 industry's forecast of the current-period demand function for $R1_t^T$, $R1H1_t^{de}$, as given, the R1 industry attempts to maximize the present value of the dividends it intends to pay to the industry's shareholders during the current and next periods. Then the firm's desired current-period sales of $R1_t^T$ (in terms of mass) is given by

$$R1H1_t^{de} = \tau_{R1}\left(I1_t\right) \cdot T_{R1t}\left(h_{R1t} \cdot N1_{R1t}\right) - \left(R1_{t+1}^{T^*d} - R1_t^{T^*}\right) \quad (8.6)$$

where $R1_{t+1}^{T^*d}$ represents the industry's desired inventory of processed R1 for the end of the period.

Each period, dividends equal market-based net income minus market-based net business saving. Let p_{R1t} represent the current market price that the R1 industry sets during the current period. Market-based net income is equal to the value of production, $p_{R1t} \cdot \tau_{R1}(I1_t) \cdot T_{R1t}(h_{R1} \cdot N1_{R1t})$, minus current market expenses (in this case, wages, net taxes, and interest). Therefore, dividends equal the value of production minus wages, net taxes, and interest and minus net business saving. Measured in terms of current-period market prices, net business saving is necessarily equal to the sum of the sector's net increase in assets (measured in terms of current-period prices) minus the net increase in liabilities (also measured in terms of current-period prices) during the period.

Measured in terms of current market prices, the industry plans to acquire $p_{R1t} \cdot (R1^{T^*d}_{t+1} - R1^{T^*}_{t})$ in inventories of processed R1 during the current period. Let $B1_{R1t}$ represent the number of R1 industry bonds outstanding in Country One's bond market at the beginning of the current period. Let p_{B1} represent the current-period market price of bonds issued in Country One's bond market. Each bond outstanding presumably pays one unit of Country One's currency as interest income during the current period. Then the market value of the R1 industry's debt in Country One's bond market is represented by $p_{B1} \cdot B1_{R1t}$. In addition, let $B1^{s}_{R1(t+1)}$ denote the number of bonds the R1 industry plans to have outstanding by the end of the current period. Then the amount that the R1 industry plans to borrow in Country One's bond market during the current period is given by $p_{B1} \cdot (B1^{s}_{R1(t+1)} - B1_{R1t})$. The current level of planned market-based net business saving, S^{d}_{R1t}, by the R1 industry must be consistent with the market value of the sector's planned accumulation of inventories of processed R1 minus its planned current-period borrowing. Therefore, planned market-based net business saving amounts to

$$S^{d}_{R1t} \equiv p_{R1t} \cdot \left(R1^{T^*d}_{t+1} - R1^{T^*}_{t}\right) - p_{B1} \cdot \left(B1^{s}_{R1(t+1)} - B1_{R1t}\right) \tag{8.7}$$

The sector's planned dividends for the current period, Π^{d}_{R1t}, is given by

$$\begin{aligned}\Pi^{d}_{R1t} = p_{R1t} \cdot &\left\{\tau_{R1}(I1_t) \cdot T_{R1t}(h_{R1t} \cdot N1_{R1t}) - \left(R1^{T^*d}_{t+1} - R1^{T^*}_{t}\right)\right\} \\ &+ p^{G1}_{xt} \cdot \overline{R1}_t - W1_t \cdot h_{R1t} \cdot N1_{R1t} - B1_{R1t} - Tx_{G1R1} \\ &+ p_{B1} \cdot \left(B1^{s}_{R1(t+1)} - B1_{R1t}\right)\end{aligned} \tag{8.8}$$

where the planned accumulation of processed inventories is valued in terms of the current market price of R1, where $p^{G1}_{xt} \cdot \overline{R1}_t$ represents the subsidy that the G1 sector pays the R1 industry during the current period, and Tx_{G1R1} denotes the taxes the R1 industry pays the G1 sector.

At the beginning of the period, the R1 industry announces its product price, p_{R1t}. Let the following demand function represent the R1 industry's forecast of the current-period demand for its product:

$$R1H1^{de}_{t} = R1H1^{de}_{t}(p_{R1t}, \omega_{R1H1}) \cdot N1_t \tag{8.9}$$

where $R1H1_t^{de}(\bullet)$ denotes the R1 industry's forecast at the beginning of the current period of the current real per capita demand for R1 by the population of Country One and where $N1_t$ represents the population of Country One at time t. Assume that the derivative of $R1H1_t^{de}(\bullet)$ with respect to p_{R1t} is negative (the sign is verified under the specification of the economic behavior of the households in Country One); ω_{R1H1} denotes a vector of shift parameters that the R1 industry forecasts as also affecting the household sector's per capital demand for R1. Solving the inverse function for p_{R1t} yields

$$p_{R1t} = p_{R1t}\underset{-\qquad\quad +\qquad +}{\left(R1H1_t^{de}, \omega_{R1H1}, N1_t\right)} \tag{8.10}$$

where

$$\frac{\partial p_{R1t}}{\partial\left(R1H1_t^{de}\right)} \equiv \frac{1}{\left[\partial\left(R1H1_t^{de}\right)/\partial p_{R1t}\right]} < 0$$

$$\frac{\partial p_{R1t}}{\partial \omega_{R1H1}} \equiv \frac{-\left[\partial\left(R1H1_t^{de}\right)/\partial \omega_{R1H1}\right]}{\left[\partial\left(R1H1_t^{de}\right)/\partial p_{R1t}\right]} > 0$$

$$\text{and} \quad \frac{\partial p_{R1t}}{\partial N1_t} \equiv -\frac{\left[R1H1_t^{de}\right]}{\left[\partial\left(R1H1_t^{de}\right)/\partial p_{R1t}\right]} > 0 \tag{8.11}$$

An increase in ω_{H1} or $N1_t$ represents an outward shift in the R1 industry's forecast of the market demand for its product.

The price p_{R1t} given by (8.10) represents the maximum uniform price the R1 sector expects it can value each alternative quantity of R1 it transforms during the period. Based upon this function, the sector's forecasted current total revenue, TR_t^{R1e}, function is given by

$$\begin{aligned} TR_t^{R1e} &= p_{R1t} \cdot R1H1_t^{de} = p_{R1t}\left(R1H1_t^{de}, \omega_{R1H1}, N1_t\right) \cdot R1H1_t^{de} \\ &= TR_t^{R1e}\left(R1H1_t^{de},\ \omega_{R1H1},\ N1_t\right) \end{aligned} \tag{8.12}$$

Substituting the right-hand side of (8.6) for $R1H1_t^{de}$ in (8.12) yields

$$\begin{aligned} TR_t^{R1e} = TR_t^{R1e}\Big[&\tau_{R1}\left(I1_t\right) \cdot T_{R1t}\left(h_{R1t} \cdot N1_{R1t}\right) \\ &- \left(R1_{t+1}^{T^*d} - R1_t^{T^*}\right),\ \omega_{R1H1}, N1_t\Big] \end{aligned} \tag{8.13}$$

Substituting the right-hand side of (8.13) for the first term, $p_{R1t} \cdot \{\tau_{R1}(I1_t) \cdot T_{R1t} (h_{R1} \cdot N1_{R1t}) - (R1^{T^*d}_{t+1} - R1^{T^*}_t)\}$, on the right-hand side of (8.8) yields

$$\Pi^d_{R1t} = TR^{Rle}_t \left[\tau_{R1}(I1_t) \cdot T_{R1t}(h_{R1t} \cdot N1_{R1t}) - \left(R1^{T^*d}_{t+1} - R1^{T^*}_t\right),\right.$$
$$\left.\omega_{R1H1}, N1_t\right] - Tx_{G1R1} + p^{G1}_{xt} \cdot \overline{R1}_t - W1_t \cdot h_{R1t} \cdot N1_{R1t}$$
$$- B1_{R1t} + p_{B1} \cdot \left(B1^s_{R1(t+1)} - B1_{R1t}\right) \tag{8.14}$$

as the expression for the amount the R1 industry plans to distribute as dividends during the current period.

In a similar manner, the R1 industry must decide upon a preliminary forecast of next period's demand for its product, from which it obtains its anticipated revenue function associated with next period's demand:

$$TR^{Rle}_{t+1} = p^e_{R1(t+1)} \cdot R1H1^{de}_{t+1}$$
$$= p^e_{R1(t+1)}\left(R1H1^{de}_{t+1}, \omega^e_{R1H1}, N1^e_{t+1}\right) \cdot R1H1^{de}_{t+1}$$
$$= TR^{Rle}_{t+1}\left(R1H1^{de}_{t+1}, \omega^e_{R1H1}, N1^e_{t+1}\right) \tag{8.15}$$

where $R1H1^{de}_{t+1}$ denotes the number of units of R1 the R1 industry anticipates selling to its households next period and where $N1^e_{t+1}$ represents the R1 industry's forecast of Country One's population at the beginning of next period.

Assume that next period's planned production of transformed R1, $R1^{Te}_{t+1}$, is given by

$$R1^{Te}_{t+1} = \min\left[\left[1 + g^e_{R1}\left(B_{t+1}, P^*_{t+1}\right)\right] \cdot \left\{\left[1 + g_{R1}\left(B_t, P^*_t\right)\right] \cdot R1_t\right.\right.$$
$$\left.- \tau_{R1}(I1_t) \cdot T_{R1t}(h_{R1t} \cdot N1_{R1t})\right\} - \overline{R1}_{t+1}, \tau_{R1}(I1_t + \Delta I1)$$
$$\left.\cdot T^e_{R1(t+1)}\left(h^e_{R1} \cdot N1^e_{R1(t+1)}\right)\right] \tag{8.16}$$

In particular, next period's planned production of R1 is assumed to be constrained, first, by the amount of R1 the industry anticipates will be available for processing next period, $[1 + g^e_{R1}(B_{t+1}, P^*_{t+1})] \cdot R1^{d'}_{t+1} + g^e_{R1}(B_{t+1}, P^*_{t+1}) \cdot \overline{R1}_{t+1}$, and, second, by the level of transformation services provided by labor next period. The infrastructure expected to be in place at the beginning of next period is given by $I1_t + \Delta I1$. Assuming that the industry does not waste the raw renewable resource, next period's production may be represented by (8.17):

$$R1^{Te}_{t+1} = \left[1 + g^e_{R1}\left(B_{t+1}, P^*_{t+1}\right)\right] \cdot \left\{\left[1 + g_{R1}\left(B_t, P^*_t\right)\right] \cdot R1_t\right.$$
$$\left.- \tau_{R1}(I1_t) \cdot T_{R1t}(h_{R1t} \cdot N1_{R1t})\right\} - \overline{R1}_{t+1} \tag{8.17}$$

To avoid wasting either natural resources or transformation services, the industry plans to combine them in the following way:

$$\left[1 + g^e_{R1}\left(B_{t+1}, P^*_{t+1}\right)\right] \cdot \left\{\left[1 + g_{R1}\left(B_t, P^*_t\right)\right] \cdot R1_t - \tau_{R1}\left(I1_t\right) \cdot T_{R1t}\left(h_{R1t} \cdot N1_{R1t}\right)\right\} - \overline{R1}_{t+1} = \tau_{R1}\left(I1_t + \Delta I1\right) \cdot T^e_{R1(t+1)}\left(h^e_{R1} \cdot N1^e_{R1(t+1)}\right) \tag{8.18}$$

This restriction represents the combinations of R1 and transformation services along the expansion path associated with the processing of R1 next period. Therefore, the total labor hours the R1 industry plans to use next period can be expressed in terms of the stock of $R1_t$, the required inventory of R1 for the end of the period, and the number of hours the industry plans to use its current employees:

$$h^e_{R1} \cdot N1^e_{R1(t+1)} = h^e_{R1} \cdot N1^e_{R1(t+1)}\left(R1_t, \overline{R1}_{t+1}, h_{R1t} \cdot N1_{R1t}, B_t, P^*_t\right) \tag{8.19}$$

where

$$\frac{\partial\left(h^e_{R1} \cdot N1^e_{R1(t+1)}\right)}{\partial R1_t} = \frac{\left[1 + g^e_{R1}\left(B_{t+1}, P^*_{t+1}\right)\right] \cdot \left[1 + g_{R1}\left(B_t, P^*_t\right)\right]}{\tau_{R1}\left(I1_t + \Delta I1\right) \cdot \left[T^e_{R1(t+1)}\right]'} > 0$$

$$\frac{\partial\left(h^e_{R1} \cdot N1^e_{R1(t+1)}\right)}{\partial \overline{R1}_t} = -\frac{\left[1 + g^e_{R1}\left(B_{t+1}, P^*_{t+1}\right)\right]}{\tau_{R1}\left(I1_t + \Delta I1\right) \cdot \left[T^e_{R1(t+1)}\right]'} < 0 \tag{8.20}$$

$$\frac{\partial\left(h^e_{R1} \cdot N1^e_{R1(t+1)}\right)}{\partial\left(h_{R1t} \cdot N1_{R1t}\right)} = -\frac{\left\{\left[1 + g_{R1}\left(B_{t+1}, P^*_{t+1}\right)\right] \cdot \tau_{R1}\left(I1_t\right) \cdot \left[T_{R1t}\right]'\right\}}{\tau_{R1}\left(I1_t + \Delta I1_t\right)\left[T^e_{R1(t+1)}\right]'} < 0 \tag{8.21}$$

$$\frac{\partial\left(h^e_{R1} \cdot N1^e_{R1(t+1)}\right)}{\partial\left(B_t\right)} = \frac{\left(\partial g_{R1}/\partial B_t\right) \cdot R1_t}{\tau_{R1}\left(I1_t + \Delta I1_t\right) \cdot \left[T^e_{R1(t+1)}\right]'} > 0 \tag{8.22}$$

$$\frac{\partial\left(h^e_{R1} \cdot N1^e_{R1(t+1)}\right)}{\partial\left(P^*_t\right)} = \frac{\left(\partial g_{R1}/\partial P^*_t\right) \cdot R1_t}{\tau_{R1}\left(I1_t + \Delta I1_t\right) \cdot \left[T^e_{R1(t+1)}\right]'} < 0 \tag{8.23}$$

and where $\left[T^e_{R2(t+1)}\right]' = \left[dT^e_{R1(t+1)}/d\left(h^e_{R1} \cdot N1^e_{R1(t+1)}\right)\right]$ (8.24)

The industry's anticipated next-period dividends are given by

$$\begin{aligned}
\Pi^{d}_{R1(t+1)} &= p^{e}_{R1(t+1)} \cdot \Big(\big[1 + g^{e}_{R1}\left(B_{t+1}, P^{*}_{t+1}\right)\big] \cdot \big\{\big[1 + g_{R1}\left(B_{t}, P^{*}_{t}\right)\big] \cdot R1_{t} \\
&\quad - \tau_{R1}\left(I1_{t}\right) \cdot T_{R1t}\left(h_{R1t} \cdot N1_{R1t}\right)\big\} - \overline{R1}_{t+1} \Big) - Tx_{G1R1(t+1)} \\
&\quad + p^{G1}_{x(t+1)} \cdot \overline{R1}_{t+1} - W1_{t+1} \cdot h^{e}_{R1} \cdot N1^{e}_{R1(t+1)} - B1^{s}_{R1(t+1)} - S^{d}_{R1(t+1)} \\
&= p^{e}_{R1(t+1)} \cdot \Big[\big[1 + g^{e}_{R1}\left(B_{t+1}, P^{*}_{t+1}\right)\big] \cdot \big\{\big[1 + g_{R1}\left(B_{t}, P^{*}_{t}\right)\big] \\
&\quad \cdot R1_{t} - \tau_{R1}\left(I1_{t}\right) \cdot T_{R1t}\left(h_{R1t} \cdot N1_{R1t}\right)\big\} - \overline{R1}_{t+1} + R1^{T^{*}}_{t+1} \Big] \\
&\quad - Tx_{G1R1(t+1)} - W1_{t+1} \cdot h^{e}_{R1} \cdot N1^{e}_{R1(t+1)} \\
&\quad \left(R1_{t}, \overline{R1}_{t+1}, h_{R1} \cdot N1_{R1t}, B_{t}, P^{*}_{t}\right) \\
&\quad + p^{G1}_{x(t+1)} \cdot \overline{R1}_{t+1} - \left(1 + p_{B1}\right) \cdot B1^{s}_{R1(t+1)}
\end{aligned} \tag{8.25}$$

where $S^{d}_{R1(t+1)}$ denotes the industry's planned net business saving next period, which is necessarily the difference between its planned level of net wealth for the end of next period, assumed to equal zero, minus its planned level of net wealth for the beginning of next period, in terms of next period's anticipated market prices. At the beginning of the current period, the industry plans that by the beginning of next period it will hold a marketable inventory of processed R1, whose value in terms of next period's anticipated market prices will be $p^{e}_{R1(t+1)} \cdot R1^{T^{*}}_{t+1}$; it also plans that at the beginning of next period, its outstanding debt, in terms of next period's bond prices, which for simplicity we assume to equal the current-period bond price, will be equal to $p_{B1} \cdot B1^{s}_{R1(t+1)}$. Therefore, at the beginning of the current period, the industry's anticipated net wealth for the beginning of next period is given by $p^{e}_{R1(t+1)} \cdot R1^{T^{*}}_{t+1} - p_{B1} \cdot B1^{s}_{R1(t+1)}$ and next period's anticipated market-based net saving is represented by (8.26):

$$S^{d}_{R1(t+1)} = -\left(p^{e}_{R1(t+1)} \cdot R1^{T^{*}}_{t+1} - p_{B1} \cdot B1^{s}_{R1(t+1)}\right) \tag{8.26}$$

As it formulates its plans at the beginning of the current period, the R1 industry tentatively plans to announce a product price, $p_{R1(t+1)}$, at the beginning of next period. Let the following demand function represent the R1 industry's forecast of next period's demand for its product:

$$R1H1^{de}_{t+1} = R1H1^{de}_{t+1}\left(p_{R1(t+1)}, \omega^{e}_{R1H1}\right) \cdot N1^{e}_{t+1} \tag{8.27}$$

where $R1H1^{de}_{t+1}(\bullet)$ denotes the R1 industry's forecast at the beginning of the current period of the real per capita demand for R1 by the population of Country One next period and where $N1^{e}_{t+1}$ represents the Country One's anticipated population at the beginning of next period. It is assumed that the derivative of $R1H1^{de}_{t+1}(\bullet)$ with respect to $p_{R1(t+1)}$ is negative (the sign is verified with the formal specification of the economic behavior of the households in Country One); ω^{e}_{R1H1} denotes a vector of shift parameters that the R1 industry forecasts as also affecting the household sector's per capital demand for R1 next period. Solving the inverse function for $p_{R1(t+1)}$ yields

$$p_{R1(t+1)} = p_{R1(t+1)}\left(\underset{-}{R1H1^{de}_{t+1}}, \underset{+}{\omega_{R1H1}{}^{e}}, \underset{+}{N1^{e}_{t+1}}\right) \tag{8.28}$$

where

$$\frac{\partial p_{R1(t+1)}}{\partial\left(R1H1^{de}_{t+1}\right)} \equiv \frac{1}{\left[\partial\left(R1H1^{de}_{t+1}\right)/\partial p_{R1(t+1)}\right]} < 0 \tag{8.29}$$

$$\frac{\partial p_{R1(t+1)}}{\partial \omega^{e}_{R1H1}} \equiv -\frac{\left[\partial\left(R1H1^{de}_{t+1}\right)/\partial \omega^{e}_{R1H1}\right]}{\left[\partial\left(R1H1^{de}_{t+1}\right)/\partial p_{R1(t+1)}\right]} > 0 \tag{8.30}$$

and $$\frac{\partial p_{R1(t+1)}}{\partial N1^{e}_{t+1}} \equiv -\frac{\left[R1H1^{de}_{t+1}\right]}{\left[\partial\left(R1H1^{de}_{t+1}\right)/\partial p_{R1(t+1)}\right]} > 0 \tag{8.31}$$

An increase in ω^{e}_{R1H1} or $N1^{e}_{t+1}$ represents an outward shift in the R1 industry's forecast of next period's market demand for its product. The price $p_{R1(t+1)}$ given by (8.28) represents the maximum uniform price the R1 sector expects it can value each alternative quantity of R1 it sells next period. Based upon this function, the sector's forecasted next-period total revenue,TR^{R1e}_{t+1}, function is given by

$$\begin{aligned} TR^{Rle}_{t+1} &= p_{R1(t+1)} \cdot R1H1^{de}_{t+1} \\ &= p_{R1(t+1)}\left(R1H1^{de}_{t+1}, \omega^{e}_{R1H1}, N1^{e}_{t+1}\right) \cdot R1H1^{de}_{t+1} \\ &= TR^{Rle}_{t+1}\left(R1H1^{de}_{t+1}, \omega^{e}_{H1}, N1^{e}_{t+1}\right) \end{aligned} \tag{8.32}$$

Since the number of units of processed R1 that the R1 industry anticipates it will sell next period is equal to the amount of processed R1 it holds as inventory at the beginning of that period plus the amount of R1 it plans to process next period,

$$\begin{aligned} R1H1^{de}_{t+1} = {} & \left[1 + g^{e}_{R1}\left(B_{t+1}, P^{*}_{t+1}\right)\right] \cdot \left\{\left[1 + g_{R1}\left(B_t, P^{*}_{t}\right)\right] \cdot R1_t \right. \\ & \left. - \tau_{R1}\left(I1_t\right) \cdot T_{R1t}\left(h_{R1t}, N1_{R1t}\right)\right\} - \overline{R1}_{t+1} + R1^{T*}_{t+1} \end{aligned} \tag{8.33}$$

Substituting the right-hand side of (8.33) for $R1H1^{de}_{t+1}$ in (8.32) yields

$$\begin{aligned} TR^{Rle}_{t+1} = TR^{Rle}_{t+1} & \left[\left[1 + g^{e}_{R1}\left(B_{t+1}, P^{*}_{t+1}\right)\right] \cdot \left\{\left[1 + g_{R1}\left(B_t, P^{*}_{t}\right)\right] \cdot R1_t \right.\right. \\ & \left. - \tau_{R1}\left(I1_t\right) \cdot T_{R1t}\left(h_{R1t}, N1_{R1t}\right)\right\} \\ & \left. - \overline{R1}_{t+1} + R1^{T*}_{t+1}, \omega^{e}_{R1H1}, N1^{e}_{t+1}\right] \end{aligned} \tag{8.34}$$

Therefore the expression for the R1 industry's anticipated dividends next period is shown by (8.35):

$$\Pi^{d}_{R1(t+1)} = TR^{Rle}_{t+1}\Big[\big[1 + g^{e}_{R1}\left(B_{t+1}, P^{*}_{t+1}\right)\big] \cdot \big\{\big[1 + g_{R1}\left(B_{t}, P^{*}_{t}\right)\big] \cdot R1_{t}$$
$$-\tau_{R1}\left(I1_{t}\right) \cdot T_{R1t}\left(h_{R1t}, N1_{R1t}\right)\big\} - \overline{R1}_{t+1} + R1^{T^{*}}_{t+1}, \omega^{e}_{R1H1}, N1^{e}_{t+1}\Big]$$
$$- W1_{t+1} \cdot h^{e}_{R1} \cdot N1^{e}_{R1(t+1)}\left(R1_{t}, \overline{R1}_{t+1}, h_{R1} \cdot N1_{R1t}, B_{t}, P^{*}_{t}\right)$$
$$- Tx_{G1R1(t+1)} + p^{G1}_{x(t+1)} \cdot \overline{R1}_{t+1} - \left(1 + p_{B1}\right) \cdot B1^{s}_{R1(t+1)} \qquad (8.35)$$

Solving (8.35) for the industry's end-of-period supply of bonds, $B1^{s}_{R1(t+1)}$, yields

$$B1^{s}_{R1(t+1)} = \left[\frac{1}{\left(1 + p^{b1}_{t}\right)}\right] \cdot \Big\{-\Pi^{R1e}_{t+1} + TR^{R1e}_{t+1}\Big[\big[1 + g^{e}_{R1}\left(B_{t+1}, P^{*}_{t+1}\right)\big]$$
$$\cdot \big\{\big[1 + g_{R1}\left(Bt, P^{*}_{t}\right)\big] \cdot R1_{t} - \tau_{R1}\left(I1_{t}\right) \cdot T_{R1t}\left(h_{R1t} \cdot N1_{R1t}\right)\big\}$$
$$-R1_{t+1} + R1^{T^{*}}_{t+1}, \omega^{e}_{H1}, N1^{e}_{t+1}\Big] - Tx_{G1R1(t+1)} - W1_{t+1} \cdot h^{e}_{R1}$$
$$\cdot N1^{e}_{R1(t+1)}\left(R1_{t}, \overline{R1}_{t+1}, h_{R1t} \cdot N1_{R1t}, B_{t}, P^{*}_{t}\right)$$
$$+p^{G1}_{x(t+1)} \cdot \overline{R1}_{t+1}\Big\} \qquad (8.36)$$

Substituting the right-hand side of (8.36) for $B1^{s}_{R1(t+1)}$ in (8.14) yields the following expression for the present value of the industry's anticipated stream of dividends to its owners:

$$\Pi^{d}_{R1t} + \Pi^{d}_{R1(t+1)}/(1 + r_{1t})$$
$$= TR^{Rle}_{t}\Big[\tau_{R1}\left(I1_{t}\right) \cdot T_{R1t}\left(h_{R1t}, N1_{R1t}\right) - \left(R1^{T^{*}d}_{t+1} - R1^{T^{*}}_{t}\right), \omega_{R1H11}, N1_{t}\Big]$$
$$+ p^{G1}_{xt} \cdot \overline{R1}_{t} - W1_{t} \cdot h_{R1t} \cdot N1_{R1t} - \left(1 + p_{B1}\right) \cdot B1_{R1t} - Tx_{G1R1}$$
$$+\left[\frac{1}{(1 + r_{1t})}\right] \cdot \Big\{TR^{R1e}_{t+1}\Big[\big[1 + g^{e}_{R1}\left(B_{t+1}, P^{*}_{t+1}\right)\big] \cdot \big\{\big[1 + g_{R1}\left(B_{t}, P^{*}_{t}\right)\big] \cdot R1_{t}$$
$$-\tau_{R1}\left(I1_{t}\right) \cdot T_{R1t}\left(h_{R1t} \cdot N1_{R1t}\right)\big\} - \overline{R1}_{t+1} + R1^{T^{*}}_{t+1}, \omega^{e}_{R1H11}, N1^{e}_{t+1}\Big]$$
$$-Tx_{G1R1(t+1)} - W1_{t+1} \cdot h^{e}_{R1} \cdot N1^{e}_{R1(t+1)}\left(R1_{t}, \overline{R1}_{t+1}, h_{R1}\right.$$
$$\left.\cdot N1_{R1t}, B_{t}, P^{*}_{t}\right) + p^{G1}_{x(t+1)} \cdot \overline{R1}_{t+1}\Big\} \qquad (8.37)$$

where $1/\left(1 + r_{1}\right) = \left[p_{B1}/\left(1 + p_{B1}\right)\right]$.

Assume that at the beginning of the current period, the objective of the R1 industry is to maximize (8.37) with respect to $h_{R1} \cdot N1_{R1t}$ and $R1^{T*}_{t+1}$. The corresponding first-order conditions become

$$\frac{\partial[\Pi^d_{R1t} + \Pi^d_{R1(t+1)}/(1+r_1)]}{\partial(h_{R1} \cdot N1_{R1t})} \equiv \left[\frac{\partial(TR^{Rle}_t)}{\partial(R1H1^{de}_t)}\right] \cdot \tau_{R1}(I1_t) \cdot [\partial(h_{R1t} \cdot N1_{R1t})] - W1_t - \left[\frac{\partial(TR^{Rle}_{t+1})}{\partial(R1H1^{de}_{t+1})}\right] \cdot \tau_{R1}(I1_t) \cdot \frac{[\partial(T_{R1t})/\partial(h_{R1} \cdot N1_{R1t})]}{(1+r_{1t})} - \left[\frac{W1_{t+1}}{(1+r_{1t})}\right] \cdot \left[\frac{\partial\left(h^e_{R1} \cdot N1^e_{R1(t+1)}\right)}{\partial(h_{R1} \cdot N1_{R1t})}\right] = 0 \tag{8.38}$$

$$\frac{\partial\left[\Pi^d_{R1t} + \Pi^d_{R1(t+1)}/(1+r_1)\right]}{\partial(R1^{T*}_{t+1})} \equiv -\left[\frac{\partial(TR^{Rle}_t)}{\partial(R1H1^{de}_t)}\right] + \left[\frac{1}{(1+r_1)}\right] \cdot \left[\frac{\partial(T^{Rle}_{t+1})}{\partial(R1H1^{de}_{t+1})}\right] = 0 \tag{8.39}$$

From (8.39), condition (8.38) reduces to

$$-W1_t - \left[\frac{W1_{t+1}}{(1+r_1)}\right] \cdot \left[\frac{\partial\left(h^e_{R1} \cdot N1^e_{R1(t+1)}\right)}{\partial(h_{R1} \cdot N1_{R1t})}\right] = 0 \tag{8.40}$$

Totally differentiating (8.39) and (8.40) and then solving for the changes in $h_{R1} \cdot N1_{R1t}$ and $R1^{T*}_{t+1}$ yields the industry's demand function for current labor and its end-of-period demand for an inventory of the marketable renewable resource. To simplify the analysis, only the parameters entering the own first-order conditions are assumed to affect the individual demand functions.

Demand Function for $h_{R1t} \cdot N1_{R1t}$

From (8.40), the present value maximizing renewable resource industry in Country One uses labor during the current period up to the point at which the present value of the marginal cost of the labor time conserved next period from using more labor during the current period (because by using more labor during the current period, ceteris paribus, the industry has less renewable resource to harvest next period) is equal to the current wage rate. The greater the current money wage, $W1_t$, the greater the marginal cost of a unit of labor during the current period and the smaller the sector's demand for labor this period. The greater the money wage announced by the consumer goods industry for next period, the greater the present value of the labor time conserved next period by using more labor in the current period; a rise in $W1_{t+1}$ increases the renewable resource industry's demand for labor hours in the current period in Country One. An increase in the interest rate prevailing in Country One in the current period reduces the present value of the labor cost saved next period by harvesting (and storing) more renewable resource this period, thereby reducing the demand for labor hours in the current period. These factors result in the following demand function for labor hours in the current period:

$$(h_{R1t} \cdot N1_{R1t})^d = (h_{R1t} \cdot N1_{R1t})^d \, (\underset{-}{W1_t}, \underset{+}{W1_{t+1}}, \underset{-}{r_{1t}}) \tag{8.41}$$

Demand Function for $R1^{T^*}_{t+1}$

From (8.39), the sector will add to its end-of-period inventory of the transformed renewable resource to the point at which the present value of the marginal revenue from a unit of the transformed resource sold next period is equal to the opportunity cost, the marginal revenue forgone during the current period from the accumulation of an additional unit of inventory of the transformed product. The higher the current interest rate in Country One's bond market, $R1_t$, the lower will be the present value of the marginal revenue from selling a unit of the product next period by withholding it from the market this period:

$$R1^{T^*}_{t+1} = R1^{T^*}_{t+1} \, (\underset{-}{r_{1t}}) \tag{8.42}$$

Current Production of Transformed Renewable Resource, $R1^T_t$

From (8.2), the current-period production of the transformed renewable resource is given by

$$R1^T_t = \tau_{R1} (I1_t) \cdot T_{R1t}\left[(h_{R1t} \cdot N1_{R1t})^d \, (\underset{-}{W1_t}, \underset{+}{W1_{t+1}}, \underset{-}{r_{1t}})\right]$$

$$= R1^{T^*}_{t+1} \, (\underset{+}{I1_t}, \underset{-}{W1_t}, \underset{+}{W1_{t+1}}, \underset{-}{r_{1t}}) \tag{8.43}$$

Desired End-of-Period Inventory of Unprocessed Renewable Resource, $R1^{d'}_{t+1}$

From (8.4), the planned inventory of the unprocessed renewable resource for the end of the current period, in excess of the amount the G1 sector requires the industry to hold by the beginning of next period is given by

$$
\begin{aligned}
R1^{d'}_{t+1} &= \left[1 + g_{R1}\left(Bt, P^*_t\right)\right] \cdot R1_t - \tau_{R1}\left(I1_t\right) \cdot T_{R1t}\left(h_{R1t} \cdot N1_{R1t}\right) - \overline{R1}_{t+1} \\
&= \left[1 + g_{R1}\left(Bt, P^*_t\right)\right] \cdot R1_t - \tau_{R1}\left(I1_t\right) \\
&\quad \cdot T_{R1t}\left[\left(h_{R1t} \cdot N1_{R1t}\right)^d\left(W1_t, W1_{t+1}, r_{1t}\right)\right] - \overline{R1}_{t+1} \\
&= R1^{d'}_{t+1}\underset{+\quad -\quad +\quad +\quad -\quad +\quad -\quad -}{\left(B_t, P^*_t, R1_t, I1_t, W1_t, W1_{t+1}, r_{1t}, \overline{R1}_{t+1}\right)}
\end{aligned} \tag{8.44}
$$

Current-Period Price of R1

From (8.10), the current-period price that the renewable resource industry announces at the beginning of the current period is negatively related to the number of units of the resource the industry plans to sell during the current period, but positively related to the population of Country One's population and positively related to the parameters that shift its estimate of the demand function for its product outward:

$$
p_{R1t} = p_{R1t}\underset{-\quad +\quad +}{\left(R1H1^{de}_t, \omega_{R1H1}, N1_t\right)} \tag{8.10}
$$

From (8.6), the amount of the renewable resource the sector plans to sell during the current period is positively related to the number of hours it plans to use its current employees, positively related to its beginning inventory of the processed resource, but negatively related to its optimal end-of-period inventory of the resource:

$$
R1H1^{de}_t = \tau_{R1}\left(I1_t\right) \cdot T_{R1t}\left(h_{R1t} \cdot N1_{R1t}\right) - \left(R1^{T^*d}_{t+1} - R1^{T^*}_t\right) \tag{8.6}
$$

Substituting (8.41) and (8.42) respectively for $h_{R1t} \cdot N1_{R1t}$ and $R1^{T^*d}_{t+1}$ into (8.6) and then substituting the result into (8.10) yields the following pricing function:

$$
\begin{aligned}
p_{R1t} &= p_{R1t}\Big(\tau_{R1}\left(Il_t\right) \cdot T_{R1t}\left[\left(h_{R1t} \cdot N1_{R1t}\right)^d\left(W1_t, W1_{t+1}, r_1\right)\right] \\
&\quad - R1^{T^*d}_{t+1}\left(r_1\right) + R1^{T^*}_t, \omega_{H1}, N1_t\Big) \\
&= p_{R1t}\underset{-\quad +\quad -\quad +\quad -\quad +\quad +}{\left(I1t, W1_t, W1_{t+1}, r_1, R1^{T^*}_t, \omega_{R1H11}, N1_t\right)}
\end{aligned} \tag{8.45}
$$

where it is assumed that the interest rate effect upon the demand for labor dominates the interest rate effect upon the sector's desired end-of-period inventory.

Demand for $N1_{R1(t+1)}$

From (8.19), the renewable resource industry's demand for workers for next period in Country One is positively related to the amount of the renewable resource available at the beginning of the current period, negatively related to the minimum stock of the renewable resource the G1 sector sets for the beginning of next period, negatively related to the number of hours the industry uses its current workers, positively related to the size of the basic renewable resource, and negatively related to the amount of pollution at the beginning of the current period. Substituting (8.41) for $h_{R1t} \cdot N1_{R1t}$ in (8.19) yields the demand for workers for next period by the industry shown in (8.46):

$$\begin{aligned} h^e_{R1} \cdot N1^d_{R1(t+1)} &= h^e_{R1} \cdot N1^d_{R1(t+1)} \\ &\quad \left(R1_t, \overline{R1}_{t+1}, (h_{R1t} \cdot N1_{R1t})^d\,(W1_t, W1_{t+1}, r_{1t}), B_t, P^*_t\right) \\ &= h^e_{R1} \cdot N1^d_{R1(t+1)} \underset{+\qquad -\qquad +\qquad -\qquad +\quad +\quad -}{\left(R1_t, \overline{R1}_{t+1}, W1_t, W1_{t+1}, r_{1t}, B_t, P^*_t\right)} \end{aligned} \tag{8.46}$$

Supply of Bonds to B1 Market by the R1 Industry

Assuming that the R1 industry does not plan to engage in net business saving during the period, conditions (8.7) and (8.42) yield the following end-of-period supply of bonds to the B1 market by the R1 industry:

$$\begin{aligned} p_{B1} \cdot B1^{se}_{R1(t+1)} &= p_{R1t} \cdot \left(R1^{T^*d}_{t+1}(r_{1t}) - R1^{T^*}_t\right) + p_{B1} \cdot B1_{R1t} \\ &= p_{B1} \cdot B1^{se}_{R1(t+1)} \underset{-\qquad -\qquad +1}{\left(r_{1t}, R1^{T^*}_t, p^{b1}_t \cdot B1_{R1t}\right)} \end{aligned} \tag{8.47}$$

where the parametric effects upon the current price of the R1 resource are suppressed.

Dividends to Shareholders

From (8.8) and the assumption that current net business saving is equal to zero, the current dividends to shareholders are given by (8.48):

$$\begin{aligned} \Pi^d_{R1t} &= p_{R1t} \cdot \{\tau_{R1}(I1_t) \cdot T_{R1t}(h_{R1t} \cdot N1_{R1t})\} + p^{G1}_{xt} \cdot \overline{R1}_t \\ &\quad - W1_t \cdot h_{R1t} \cdot N1_{R1t} - B1_{R1t} - Tx_{G1R1} \end{aligned} \tag{8.48}$$

Country Two's Renewable Resource (R2) Industry

In a manner directly analogous to the derivation of the objective function for the R1 industry, the present value maximizing R2 industry's objective may be presented as

$$\begin{aligned}
&\Pi^{d}_{R2t} + \Pi^{d}_{R2(t+1)}/(1+r_{2t}) \\
&\quad = TR^{R2e}_{t}\left[\tau_{R2}(I2_t)\cdot T_{R2t}(h_{R2t}, N2_{R2t}) - \left(R2^{T^*d}_{t+1} - R2^{T^*}_{t}\right), \omega_{R2H2}, N2_t\right] \\
&\qquad + p^{G2}_{xt}\cdot \overline{R2}_t - W2_t\cdot h_{R2t}\cdot N2_{R2t} - (1+p_{B2})\cdot B2_{R2t} - Tx_{G2R2} \\
&\qquad + \left[\frac{1}{(1+r_{2t})}\right]\cdot\Big\{TR^{R2e}_{t+1}\left[\left[1+g^{e}_{R2}(B_{t+1}, P^{*}_{t+1})\right]\cdot\{\left[1+g_{R2}(B_t, P^{*}_{t})\right]\right. \\
&\qquad \left.\cdot R2_t - \tau_{R2}(I2_t)\cdot T_{R2t}(h_{R2t}, N2_{R2t})\} - \overline{R2}_{t+1} + R2^{T^*}_{t+1}, \omega^{e}_{R1H11}, N2^{e}_{t+1}\right] \\
&\qquad - Tx_{G2R2(t+1)} - W2_{t+1}\cdot h^{e}_{R2}\cdot N1^{e}_{R2(t+1)}\left(R2_t, \overline{R2}_{t+1}, h_{R2}\right. \\
&\qquad \left.\cdot N2_{R2t}, B_t, P^{*}_{t}\right) + p^{G2}_{x(t+1)}\cdot \overline{R2}_{t+1}\Big\} \qquad (8.49)
\end{aligned}$$

where $1/(1+r_{2t}) = \left[p_{B2}/\left(1+p_{B2}\right)\right]$.

Assume that at the beginning of the current period, the objective of the R2 industry is to maximize (8.49) with respect to $h_{R2}\cdot N2_{R2t}$ and $R2^{T^*}_{t+1}$. The corresponding first-order conditions become

$$\begin{aligned}
&\frac{\partial\left[\Pi^{d}_{R2t} + \Pi^{d}_{R2(t+1)}/(1+r_{2t})\right]}{\partial\left(h_{R2}\cdot N2_{R2t}\right)} \\
&\quad \equiv \left[\frac{\partial\left(TR^{R2e}_{t}\right)}{\partial\left(R2H2^{de}_{t}\right)}\right]\cdot\tau_{R2}(I2_t)\cdot\left[\frac{\partial\left(T_{R2t}\right)}{\partial\left(h_{R2t}\cdot N2_{R2t}\right)}\right] - W2_t \\
&\qquad - \left[\frac{\partial\left(TR^{R2e}_{t+1}\right)}{\partial\left(R2H2^{de}_{t+1}\right)}\right]\cdot\tau_{R2}(I2_t)\cdot\frac{\left[\partial\left(T_{R2t}\right)/\partial\left(h_{R2}\cdot N2_{R2t}\right)\right]}{(1+r_{2t})} \\
&\qquad - \left[\frac{W2_{t+1}}{(1+r_{2t})}\right]\cdot\left[\frac{\partial\left(h^{e}_{R2}\cdot N2^{e}_{R2(t+1)}\right)}{\partial\left(h_{R2}\cdot N2_{R2t}\right)}\right] = 0 \qquad (8.50)
\end{aligned}$$

$$\begin{aligned}
\frac{\partial\left[\Pi^{d}_{R2t} + \Pi^{d}_{R2(t+1)}/(1+r_{2t})\right]}{\partial\left(R2^{T^*}_{t+1}\right)} &\equiv -\left[\frac{\partial\left(TR^{R2e}_{t}\right)}{\partial\left(R2H2^{de}_{t}\right)}\right] \\
&\quad + \left[\frac{1}{(1+r_{2t})}\right]\cdot\left[\frac{\partial\left(TR^{R2e}_{t+1}\right)}{\partial\left(R2H2^{de}_{t+1}\right)}\right] = 0 \qquad (8.51)
\end{aligned}$$

From (8.51), condition (8.50) reduces to

$$-W2_t - \left[\frac{W2_{t+1}}{(1 + r_{2t})}\right] \cdot \left[\frac{\partial\left(h^e_{R2} \cdot N2^e_{R2(t+1)}\right)}{\partial\left(h_{R2} \cdot N2_{R2t}\right)}\right] = 0 \tag{8.52}$$

Totally differentiating (8.51) and (8.52) and then solving for the changes in $h_{R2} \cdot N2_{R2t}$ and $R2^{T^*}_{t+1}$ yields the industry's demand function for current labor and its end-of-period demand for an inventory of the marketable renewable resource. To simplify the analysis, only the parameters entering the own first-order conditions are assumed to affect the individual demand functions.

Demand Function for $h_{R2t} \cdot N2_{R2t}$

From (8.52), the present value maximizing renewable resource industry in Country Two uses labor during the current period up to the point at which the present value of the marginal cost of the labor time conserved next period from using more labor during the current period (because by using more labor during the current period, ceteris paribus, the industry has less renewable resource to harvest next period) is equal to the current wage rate. The greater the current money wage, $W2_t$, the greater the marginal cost of a unit of labor during the current period and the smaller the sector's demand for labor this period. The greater the money wage announced by the consumer goods industry for next period, the greater the present value of the labor time conserved next period by using more labor in the current period; a rise in $W2_{t+1}$ increases the renewable resource industry's demand for labor hours in the current period in Country Two. An increase in the interest rate prevailing in Country Two in the current period reduces the present value of the labor cost saved next period by harvesting (and storing) more renewable resource this period, thereby reducing the demand for labor hours in the current period. These factors result in the following demand function for labor hours in the current period:

$$(h_{R2t} \cdot N2_{R2t})^d = (h_{R2t} \cdot N2_{R2t})^d \underset{-}{(W2_t}, \underset{+}{W2_{t+1}}, \underset{-}{r_{2t})} \tag{8.53}$$

Demand Function for $R2^{T^*}_{t+1}$

From (8.51), the sector will add to its end-of-period inventory of the transformed renewable resource to the point at which the present value of the marginal revenue from a unit of the transformed resource sold next period is equal to the opportunity cost, the marginal revenue forgone during the current period from the accumulation of an additional unit of inventory of the transformed product. The higher the current interest rate in Country Two's bond market, $R2_t$, the lower will be the present value of the marginal revenue from selling a unit of the product next period by withholding it from the market this period:

$$R2^{T^*d}_{t+1} = R2^{T^*d}_{t+1}\underset{-}{(r_{2t})} \tag{8.54}$$

Current Production of Transformed Renewable Resource, $R2^T_t$

The current-period production of the transformed renewable resource is given by

$$R2^T_t = \tau_{R2}(I2_t) \cdot T_{R2t}\left[(h_{R2t} \cdot N2_{R2t})^d (\underset{-}{W2_t}, \underset{+}{W2_{t+1}}, \underset{-}{r_2})\right]$$

$$= R2^{T^*}_{t+1}(\underset{+}{I2_t}, \underset{-}{W2_t}, \underset{+}{W2_{t+1}}, \underset{-}{r_2}) \tag{8.55}$$

Desired End-of-Period Inventory of Unprocessed Renewable Resource, $R2^{d'}_{t+1}$

The planned inventory of the unprocessed renewable resource for the end of the current period, in excess of the amount the G2 sector requires the industry to hold by the beginning of next period is given by

$$\begin{aligned} R2^{d'}_{t+1} &= \left[1 + g_{R2}\left(Bt, P^*_t\right)\right] \cdot R2_t - \tau_{R2}(I2_t) \cdot T_{R2t}(h_{R2t} \cdot N2_{R2t}) - \overline{R2}_{t+1} \\ &= \left[1 + g_{R2}\left(Bt, P^*_t\right)\right] \cdot R2_t - \tau_{R2}(I2_t) \\ &\quad \cdot T_{R2t}\left[(h_{R2t} \cdot N2_{R1t})^d (W2_t, W2_{t+1}, r_{2t})\right] - \overline{R2}_{t+1} \\ &= R2^{d'}_{t+1}\left(\underset{+}{B_t}, \underset{-}{P^*_t}, \underset{+}{R2_t}, \underset{+}{I2_t}, \underset{-}{W2_t}, \underset{+}{W2_{t+1}}, \underset{-}{r_{2t}}, \underset{-}{\overline{R2}_{t+1}}\right) \end{aligned} \tag{8.56}$$

Current-Period Price of R2

The current-period price that the renewable resource industry announces at the beginning of the current period is negatively related to the number of units of the resource the industry plans to sell during the current period, but positively related to the population of Country Two and positively related to the parameters that shift its estimate of the demand function for its product outward:

$$p_{R2t} = p_{R2t}\left(\underset{-}{R2H2^{de}_t}, \underset{+}{\omega_{R2H2}}, \underset{+}{N2_t}\right) \tag{8.57}$$

The amount of the renewable resource the sector plans to sell during the current period is positively related to the number of hours it plans to use its current employees, positively related to its beginning inventory of the processed resource, but negatively related to its optimal end-of-period inventory of the resource:

$$R2H2_t^{de} = \tau_{R2}(I2_t) \cdot T_{R2t}(h_{R2t} \cdot N2_{R2t}) - \left(R2_{t+1}^{T^*d} - R2_t^{T^*}\right) \quad (8.58)$$

Substituting (8.53) and (8.54) respectively for $h_{R2t} \cdot N2_{R2t}$ and $R2_{t+1}^{T^*d}$ into (8.58) and then substituting the result into (8.57) yields the following pricing function:

$$\begin{aligned} p_{R2t} &= p_{R2t}\Big(\tau_{R2}(I2_t) \cdot T_{R2t}\big[(h_{R2t} \cdot N2_{R2t})^d (W2_t, W2_{t+1}, r_2)\big] \\ &\qquad -R2_{t+1}^{T^*d}(r_2) + R2_t^{T^*}, \omega_{R2H2}, N2_t\Big) \\ &= p_{R2t}\Big(\underset{-}{I2t}, \underset{+}{W2_t}, \underset{-}{W2_{t+1}}, \underset{+}{r_2}, \underset{-}{R2_t^{T^*}}, \underset{+}{\omega_{R2H2}}, \underset{+}{N2_t}\Big) \end{aligned} \quad (8.59)$$

where it is assumed that the interest rate effect upon the demand for labor dominates the interest rate effect upon the sector's desired end-of-period inventory.

Demand for $N2_{R2(t+1)}$

Just as in Country One, the renewable resource industry's demand for workers for next period in Country Two is positively related to the amount of the renewable resource available at the beginning of the current period, negatively related to the minimum stock of the renewable resource the G2 sector sets for the beginning of next period, negatively related to the number of hours the industry uses its current workers, positively related to the size of the basic renewable resource, and negatively related to the amount of pollution at the beginning of the current period. Therefore, the total labor hours the R2 industry plans to use next period can be expressed in terms of the stock of $R2_t$, the required inventory of R2 for the end of the period, and the number of hours the industry plans to use its current employees:

$$h_{R2}^e \cdot N2_{R2(t+1)}^e = h_{R2}^e \cdot N2_{R2(t+1)}^e\left(R2_t, \overline{R2}_{t+1}, h_{R2t} \cdot N2_{R2t}, B_t, P_t^*\right) \quad (8.60)$$

where

$$\frac{\partial\left(h_{R2}^e \cdot N2_{R2(t+1)}^e\right)}{\partial R2_t} = \frac{\left[1 + g_{R2}^e(B_{t+1}, P_{t+1}^*)\right] \cdot \left[1 + g_{R2}(B_t, P_t^*)\right]}{\tau_{R2}(I2_t + \Delta I2) \cdot \left[T_{R2(t+1)}^e\right]'} > 0$$

$$\frac{\partial\left(h_{R2}^e \cdot N2_{R2(t+1)}^e\right)}{\partial \overline{R2}_{t+1}} = -\frac{\left[1 + g_{R2}^e(B_{t+1}, P_{t+1}^*)\right]}{\tau_{R2}(I2_t + \Delta I2) \cdot \left[T_{R2(t+1)}^e\right]'} > 0$$

$$\frac{\partial\left(h^{e}_{R2}\cdot N2^{e}_{R2(t+1)}\right)}{\partial\left(h_{R2t}\cdot N2_{R2t}\right)}=-\frac{\left\{\left[1+g_{R2}\left(B_{t+1},P^{*}_{t+1}\right)\right]\cdot\tau_{R2}\left(I2_{t}\right)\left[T_{R2t}\right]'\right\}}{\tau_{R2}\left(I2_{t}+\Delta I2_{t}\right)\cdot\left[T^{e}_{R2(t+1)}\right]'}>0$$

$$\frac{\partial\left(h^{e}_{R2}\cdot N2^{e}_{R2(t+1)}\right)}{\partial\left(B_{t}\right)}=\frac{\left(\partial g_{R2}/\partial B_{t}\right)\cdot R2_{t}}{\tau_{R2}\left(I2_{t}+\Delta I2\right)\cdot\left[T^{e}_{R2(t+1)}\right]'}>0$$

$$\frac{\partial\left(h^{e}_{R2}\cdot N2^{e}_{R2(t+1)}\right)}{\partial\left(P^{*}_{t}\right)}=\frac{\left(\partial g_{R2}/\partial P^{*}_{t}\right)\cdot R2_{t}}{\tau_{R2}\left(I2_{t}+\Delta I2\right)\cdot\left[T^{e}_{R2(t+1)}\right]'}<0$$

and where $[T^{e}_{R2(t+1)}]' = [dT^{e}_{R2(t+1)}/d(h^{e}_{R2}\cdot N2^{e}_{R2(t+1)})]$.

Substituting (8.53) for $h_{R2t}\cdot N2_{R2t}$ in (8.60) yields the demand for workers for next period by the industry shown in (8.61):

$$\begin{aligned}
&h^{e}_{R2}\cdot N2^{d}_{R2(t+1)}\\
&\quad= h^{e}_{R2}\cdot N2^{e}_{R2(t+1)}\left(R2_{t},\overline{R2}_{t+1},\left(h_{R2t}\cdot N2_{R2t}\right)^{d}\left(W2_{t},W2_{t+1},r_{2t}\right),B_{t},P^{*}_{t}\right)\\
&\quad= h^{e}_{R2}\cdot N2^{d}_{R2(t+1)}\left(\underset{+}{R2_{t}},\underset{-}{\overline{R2}_{t+1}},\underset{+}{W2_{t}},\underset{-}{W2_{t+1}},\underset{+}{r_{2t}},\underset{+}{B_{t}},\underset{-}{P^{*}_{t}}\right)
\end{aligned}\tag{8.61}$$

Supply of Bonds to B2 Market by the R2 Industry

Assuming that the R2 industry does not plan to engage in net business saving during the period, the R2 industry's end-of-period supply of bonds to Country Two's bond market—before current interest rates and exchange rates are determined—is given by

$$\begin{aligned}
p_{B2}\cdot B2^{se}_{R2(t+1)} &= p_{R2t}\cdot\left(R2^{T^{*}d}_{t+1}\left(r_{2t}\right)-R2^{T^{*}}_{t}\right)+p_{B2}\cdot B2_{R2t}\\
&= p_{B2}\cdot B2^{se}_{R2(t+1)}\left(\underset{-}{r_{2t}},\underset{-}{R2^{T^{*}}_{t}},\underset{+}{p_{B2}\cdot B2_{R2t}}\right)
\end{aligned}\tag{8.62}$$

where the parametric effects upon the current price of the R2 resource are suppressed.

Dividends to Shareholders

The current dividends to shareholders are given by (8.63):

$$\begin{aligned}
\Pi^{d}_{R2t} &= p_{R2t}\cdot\left\{\tau_{R2}\left(I2_{t}\right)\cdot T_{R2t}\left(h_{R2t}\cdot N2_{R2t}\right)\right\}+p^{G2}_{xt}\cdot\overline{R2}_{t}\\
&\quad-W2_{t}\cdot h_{R2t}\cdot N2_{R2t}-B2_{R2t}-Tx_{G2R2}
\end{aligned}\tag{8.63}$$

Country Three's Renewable Resource (R3) Industry

In a manner analogous to the one used for the R1 industry, it is possible to obtain the following expression for the present value of the R3 industry's anticipated stream of dividends to its owners:

$$\begin{aligned}
&\Pi^{d}_{R3t} + \Pi^{d}_{R3(t+1)}/(1 + r_{3t}) \\
&\quad = TR^{R3e}_{t}\left[\tau_{R3}(I2_{t}) \cdot T_{R3t}(h_{R3t}, N3_{R3t}) - \left(R3^{T^{*}d}_{t+1} - R3^{T^{*}}_{t}\right), \omega_{R3H3}, N3_{t}\right] \\
&\qquad + p^{G3}_{xt} \cdot \overline{R3}_{t} - W3_{t} \cdot h_{R3t} \cdot N3_{R3t} - \left(1 + p_{B3}\right) \cdot B3_{R3t} - Tx_{G3R3} \\
&\qquad + \left[1/(1 + r_{3t})\right] \cdot \left\{TR^{R3e}_{t+1}\left[\left[1 + g^{e}_{R3}\left(B_{t+1}, P^{*}_{t+1}\right)\right] \cdot \left\{\left[1 + g_{R3}\left(B_{t}, P^{*}_{t}\right)\right]\right.\right.\right. \\
&\qquad \left.\left. \cdot R3_{t} - \tau_{R3}(I3_{t}) \cdot T_{R3t}(h_{R3t}, N3_{R3t})\right\} - \overline{R3}_{t+1} + R3^{T^{*}}_{t+1}, \omega^{e}_{R3H3}, N3^{e}_{t+1}\right] \\
&\qquad - Tx_{G3R3(t+1)} - W3_{t+1} \cdot h^{e}_{R3} \cdot N3^{e}_{R3(t+1)}\left(R3_{t}, \overline{R3}_{t+1}, h_{R3} \cdot N3_{R3t}, B_{t}, P^{*}_{t}\right) \\
&\qquad \left. + p^{G3}_{x(t+1)} \cdot \overline{R3}_{t+1}\right\} \qquad (8.64)
\end{aligned}$$

where $1/(1 + r_{3t}) = \left[p_{B3}/\left(1 + p_{B3}\right)\right]$.

Assume that at the beginning of the current period, the objective of the R3 industry is to maximize (8.64) with respect to $h_{R3} \cdot N3_{R3t}$ and$R3^{T^{*}}_{t+1}$. The corresponding first-order conditions become:

$$\begin{aligned}
&\frac{\partial\left[\Pi^{d}_{R3t} + \Pi^{d}_{R3(t+1)}/(1 + r_{3t})\right]}{\partial(h_{R3} \cdot N3_{R3t})} \\
&\quad \equiv \left[\frac{\partial(TR^{R3e}_{t})}{\partial\left(R3H3^{de}_{t}\right)}\right] \cdot \tau_{R3}(I3_{t}) \cdot \left[\frac{\partial(T_{R3t})}{\partial(h_{R2t} \cdot N3_{R3t})}\right] - W3_{t} \\
&\qquad - \left[\frac{\partial\left(TR^{R3e}_{t+1}\right)}{\partial\left(R3H3^{de}_{t+1}\right)}\right] \cdot \tau_{R3}(I3_{t}) \cdot \frac{\left[\partial(T_{R3t})/\partial(h_{R3} \cdot N3_{R3t})\right]}{(1 + r_{3t})} \\
&\qquad - \left[\frac{W3_{t+1}}{(1 + r_{3t})}\right] \cdot \left[\frac{\partial\left(h^{e}_{R3} \cdot N3^{e}_{R3(t+1)}\right)}{\partial(h_{R3} \cdot N3_{R3t})}\right] = 0 \qquad (8.65)
\end{aligned}$$

$$\begin{aligned}
&\frac{\partial\left[\Pi^{d}_{R3t} + \Pi^{d}_{R3(t+1)}/(1 + r_{3t})\right]}{\partial\left(R3^{T^{*}}_{t+1}\right)} \\
&\quad \equiv -\left[\frac{\partial(TR^{R3e}_{t})}{\partial\left(R3H3^{de}_{t}\right)}\right] + \left[\frac{1}{(1 + r_{3t})}\right] \cdot \left[\frac{\partial\left(T^{R3e}_{t+1}\right)}{\partial\left(R3H3^{de}_{t+1}\right)}\right] = 0 \qquad (8.66)
\end{aligned}$$

From (8.66), condition (8.65) reduces to

$$-W3_t - \left[\frac{W3_{t+1}}{(1+r_{3t})}\right] \cdot \left[\frac{\partial\left(h^e_{R3} \cdot N3^e_{R3(t+1)}\right)}{\partial\left(h_{R3} \cdot N3_{R3t}\right)}\right] = 0 \tag{8.67}$$

Totally differentiating (8.66) and (8.67) and then solving for the changes in $h_{R3} \cdot N3_{R3t}$ and $R3^{T^*}_{t+1}$ yields the industry's demand function for current labor and its end-of-period demand for an inventory of the marketable renewable resource. To simplify the analysis, only the parameters entering the own first-order conditions are assumed to affect the individual demand functions.

Demand Function for $h_{R3t} \cdot N3_{R3t}$

From (8.67), the present value maximizing renewable resource industry in Country Three uses labor during the current period up to the point at which the present value of the marginal cost of the labor time conserved next period from using more labor during the current period (because by using more labor during the current period, ceteris paribus, the industry has less renewable resource to harvest next period) is equal to the current wage rate. The greater the current money wage, $W3_t$, the greater the marginal cost of a unit of labor during the current period and the smaller the sector's demand for labor this period. The greater the money wage announced by the consumer goods industry for next period, the greater the present value of the labor time conserved next period by using more labor in the current period; a rise in $W3_{t+1}$ increases the renewable resource industry's demand for labor hours in the current period in Country Three. An increase in the interest rate prevailing in Country Three in the current period reduces the present value of the labor cost saved next period by harvesting (and storing) more renewable resource this period, thereby reducing the demand for labor hours in the current period. These factors result in the following demand function for labor hours in the current period:

$$(h_{R3t} \cdot N3_{R3t})^d = (h_{R3t} \cdot N3_{R32t})^d \underset{-\quad\;\; +\quad\;\; -}{(W3_t, W3_{t+1}, r_3)} \tag{8.68}$$

Demand Function for $R3^{T^*}_{t+1}$

From (8.66), the sector will add to its end-of-period inventory of the transformed renewable resource to the point at which the present value of the marginal revenue from a unit of the transformed resource sold next period is equal to the opportunity cost, the marginal revenue forgone during the current period from the accumulation of an additional unit of inventory of the transformed product. The higher the current interest rate in Country Three's bond market, $R3_t$, the lower will be the present value of the marginal revenue from selling a unit of the product next period by withholding it from the market this period:

$$R3^{T^*d}_{t+1} = R3^{T^*d}_{t+1}\underset{-}{(r_{3t})} \tag{8.69}$$

Current Production of Transformed Renewable Resource, $R3^T_t$

The current-period production of the transformed renewable resource is given by

$$\begin{aligned} R3^T_t &= \tau_{R3}(I3_t) \cdot T_{R3t}\left[(h_{R3t} \cdot N3_{R3t})^d \underset{-}{(W3_t}, \underset{+}{W3_{t+1}}, \underset{-}{r_{3t})}\right] \\ &= R3^{T^*}_{t+1}(\underset{+}{I3_t}, \underset{-}{W3_t}, \underset{+}{W3_{t+1}}, \underset{-}{r_{3t}}) \end{aligned} \tag{8.70}$$

Desired End-of-Period Inventory of Unprocessed Renewable Resource, $R3^{d'}_{t+1}$

The planned inventory of the unprocessed renewable resource for the end of the current period, in excess of the amount the G3 sector requires the industry to hold by the beginning of next period is given by

$$\begin{aligned} R3^{d'}_{t+1} &= \left[1 + g_{R3}\left(Bt, P^*_t\right)\right] \cdot R3_t - \tau_{R3}(I3_t) \cdot T_{R3t}(h_{R3t} \cdot N3_{R3t}) - \overline{R3}_{t+1} \\ &= \left[1 + g_{R3}\left(Bt, P^*_t\right)\right] \cdot R3_t - \tau_{R3}(I3_t) \\ &\quad \cdot T_{R3t}\left[(h_{R3t} \cdot N3_{R3t})^d (W3_t, W3_{t+1}, r_{3t})\right] - \overline{R3}_{t+1} \\ &= R3^{d'}_{t+1}\left(\underset{+}{B_t}, \underset{-}{P^*_t}, \underset{+}{R3_t}, \underset{+}{I3_t}, \underset{-}{W3_t}, \underset{+}{W3_{t+1}}, \underset{-}{r_{3t}}, \underset{-}{\overline{R3}_{t+1}}\right) \end{aligned} \tag{8.71}$$

Current-Period Price of R3

The current-period price that the renewable resource industry announces at the beginning of the current period is negatively related to the number of units of the resource the industry plans to sell during the current period, but positively related to the population of Country Three and positively related to the parameters that shift its estimate of the demand function for its product outward:

$$p_{R3t} = p_{R3t}\left(\underset{-}{R3H3^{de}_t}, \underset{+}{\omega_{R2H2}}, \underset{+}{N2_t}\right) \tag{8.72}$$

The amount of the renewable resource the sector plans to sell during the current period is positively related to the number of hours it plans to use its current employees, positively related to its beginning inventory of the processed resource, but negatively related to its optimal end-of-period inventory of the resource:

$$R3H3_t^{de} = \tau_{R3}(I3_t) \cdot T_{R3t}(h_{R3t} \cdot N3_{R3t}) - \left(R3_{t+1}^{T^*d} - R3_t^{T^*}\right) \tag{8.73}$$

Substituting (8.68) and (8.69) respectively for $h_{R3t} \cdot N3_{R3t}$ and $R3_{t+1}^{T^*d}$ into (8.73) and then substituting the result into (8.72) yields the following pricing function:

$$\begin{aligned} p_{R3t} &= p_{R3t}\left(\tau_{R3}(I3_t) \cdot T_{R3t}\left[(h_{R3t} \cdot N3_{R3t})^d (W3_t, W3_{t+1}, r_3)\right]\right. \\ &\quad \left. -R3_{t+1}^{T^*d}(r_3) + R3_t^{T^*}, \omega_{R3H3}, N3_t\right) \\ &= p_{R3t}\left(\underset{-}{I3t}, \underset{+}{W3_t}, \underset{-}{W3_{t+1}}, \underset{+}{r_3}, \underset{-}{R3_t^{T^*}}, \underset{+}{\omega_{R3H3}}, \underset{+}{N3_t}\right) \end{aligned} \tag{8.74}$$

where it is assumed that the interest rate effect upon the demand for labor dominates the interest rate effect upon the sector's desired end-of-period inventory.

Demand for $N3_{R3(t+1)}$

Just as in Country One, the renewable resource industry's demand for workers for next period in Country Three is positively related to the amount of the renewable resource available at the beginning of the current period, negatively related to the minimum stock of the renewable resource the G3 sector sets for the beginning of next period, negatively related to the number of hours the industry uses its current workers, positively related to the size of the basic renewable resource, and negatively related to the amount of pollution at the beginning of the current period. Therefore, the total labor hours the R3 industry plans to use next period can be expressed in terms of the stock of $R3_t$, the required inventory of R3 for the end of the period, and the number of hours the industry plans to use its current employees:

$$h_{R3}^e \cdot N3_{R3(t+1)}^e = h_{R3}^e \cdot N3_{R3(t+1)}^e \left(R3_t, \overline{R3}_{t+1}, h_{R3t} \cdot N3_{R3t}, B_t, P_t^*\right) \tag{8.75}$$

where

$$\frac{\partial\left(h_{R3}^e \cdot N3_{R3(t+1)}^e\right)}{\partial R3_t} = \frac{\left[1 + g_{R3}^e\left(B_{t+1}, P_{t+1}^*\right)\right] \cdot \left[1 + g_{R3}\left(B_t, P_t^*\right)\right]}{\tau_{R3}(I3_t + \Delta I3) \cdot \left[T_{R3(t+1)}^e\right]'} > 0$$

$$\frac{\partial\left(h_{R3}^e \cdot N3_{R3(t+1)}^e\right)}{\partial \overline{R3}_t} = -\frac{\left[1 + g_{R3}^e\left(B_{t+1}, P_{t+1}^*\right)\right]}{\tau_{R3}(I3_t + \Delta I3) \cdot \left[T_{R3(t+1)}^e\right]'} < 0$$

$$\frac{\partial\left(h^e_{R3}\cdot N3^e_{R3(t+1)}\right)}{\partial\left(h_{R3t}\cdot N3_{R3t}\right)} = -\frac{\left\{\left[1+g_{R3}\left(B_{t+1}, P^*_{t+1}\right)\right]\cdot\tau_{R3}\left(I3_t\right)\left[T_{R3t}\right]'\right\}}{\tau_{R3}\left(I3_t+\Delta I3_t\right)\cdot\left[T^e_{R3(t+1)}\right]'} < 0$$

$$\frac{\partial\left(h^e_{R3}\cdot N3^e_{R3(t+1)}\right)}{\partial\left(B_t\right)} = \frac{\left(\partial g_{R3}/\partial B_t\right)\cdot R3_t}{\tau_{R3}\left(I3_t+\Delta I3\right)\cdot\left[T^e_{R3(t+1)}\right]'} > 0$$

$$\frac{\partial\left(h^e_{R3}\cdot N3^e_{R3(t+1)}\right)}{\partial\left(P^*_t\right)} = \frac{\left(\partial g_{R3}/\partial P^*_t\right)\cdot R3_t}{\tau_{R3}\left(I3_t+\Delta I3\right)\cdot\left[T^e_{R3(t+1)}\right]'} < 0$$

and where $[T^e_{R3(t+1)}]' = [dT^e_{R3(t+1)}/d(h^e_{R3}\cdot N3^e_{R3(t+1)})]$.

Substituting (8.68) for $h_{R3t}\cdot N3_{R3t}$ in (8.75) yields the demand for workers for next period by the industry shown in (8.76):

$$\begin{aligned} h^e_{R3}\cdot N3^d_{R3(t+1)} &= h^e_{R3}\cdot N3^e_{R3(t+1)} \\ &\quad \left(R3_t, \overline{R3}_{t+1}, \left(h_{R3t}\cdot N3_{R3t}\right)^d\left(W3_t, W3_{t+1}, r_{3t}\right), B_t, P^*_t\right) \\ &= h^e_{R3}\cdot N3^d_{R3(t+1)}\left(\underset{+}{R3_t}, \underset{-}{\overline{R3}_{t+1}}, \underset{+}{W3_t}, \underset{-}{W3_{t+1}}, \underset{+}{r_{3t}}, \underset{+}{B_t}, \underset{-}{P^*_t}\right) \end{aligned} \tag{8.76}$$

Supply of Bonds to B3 Market by the R3 Industry

Assuming that the R3 industry does not plan to engage in net business saving during the current period, the R3 industry's end-of-period supply of bonds to Country Three's bond market—before current interest rates and exchange rates are determined—is given by

$$\begin{aligned} p_{B3}\cdot B3^{se}_{R3(t+1)} &= p_{R3t}\cdot\left(R3^{T^*d}_{t+1}\left(r_{3t}\right) - R3^{T^*}_t\right) + p_{B3}\cdot B3_{R3t} \\ &= p_{B3}\cdot B2^{se}_{R3(t+1)}\left(\underset{-}{r_{3t}}, \underset{-}{R3^{T^*}_t}, \underset{+}{p_{B3}\cdot B3_{R3t}}\right) \end{aligned} \tag{8.77}$$

where the parametric effects upon the current price of the R2 resource are suppressed.

Dividends to Shareholders

The current dividends to shareholders are given by (8.78):

$$\begin{aligned} \Pi^d_{R3t} &= p_{R3t}\cdot\left\{\tau_{R3}\left(I3_t\right)\cdot T_{R3t}\left(h_{R3t}\cdot N3_{R3t}\right)\right\} + p^{G3}_{xt}\cdot\overline{R3}_t \\ &\quad - W3_t\cdot h_{R3t}\cdot N3_{R3t} - B3_{R3t} - Tx_{G3R3} \end{aligned} \tag{8.78}$$

Chapter 9 contains a specification of the world's private and central banking sectors.

9

The Banking Sectors

Country One's Private Banking (PB1) Sector

Country One's private financial sector purchases and holds bonds issued in all three countries. The bonds it holds at the beginning of the current period generate income during the current period. The bonds it buys during the current period do not generate interest income until next period. To finance their purchases of interest-earning assets, Country One's private financial sector issues noninterest-earning checkable deposits denominated in its country's unit of account to its household customers. The sector incurs labor costs associated with servicing both its bond holdings and its checking account liabilities. Furthermore, because the checkable deposits are transferable into Country One's coin and currency on demand, the private banks in Country One hold excess reserves in the form of vault cash and/or deposits held at their central bank to reduce the transactions costs associated with servicing these accounts. The private financial sector is required to hold reserves equal to the required reserve ratio (set by its central bank) times the volume of its demand-deposit liabilities. For simplicity, the private financial sector's ability to borrow from the central bank is ignored here.

Let

$B1_{PB1t}$ = the number of Country One's bonds that Country One's private financial sector holds at the beginning of the current period.

$B2_{PB1t}$ = the number of Country Two's bonds that Country One's private financial sector holds at the beginning of the current period.

$B3_{PB1t}$ = the number of Country Three's bonds that Country One's private financial sector holds at the beginning of the current period.

$D1_{PB1t}$ = the volume of checkable deposits (valued in Country One's unit of account) that Country One's private financial sector has outstanding at the beginning of the current period (had outstanding at the end of last period).

ε = the current-period spot rate between the units of account of Country One and Country Two (value of Country Two's unit of account in terms of Country One's unit of account).

$\tilde{\varepsilon}$ = the current-period spot rate between the units of account of Country One and Country Three (value of Country Three's unit of account in terms of Country One's unit of account).

$h_{PB1t} \cdot N1_{PB1t}$ = the number of hours Country One's private financial sector uses its current employees.

NW_{PB1t} = the net wealth of Country One's private financial sector, measured in terms of Country One's unit of account.

p_{B1} = the current-period price (in Country One's unit of account) of Country One's bonds.

$p_{B2} \cdot \varepsilon$ = the current-period price (in Country One's unit of account) of Country Two's bonds.

$p_{B3} \cdot \tilde{\varepsilon}$ = the current-period price (in Country One's unit of account) of Country Three's bonds.

Π^d_{PB1t} = current-period dividends paid by Country One's private financial sector.

$\hat{r}_1$ = the required reserve ratio prevailing in Country One.

$X1_{PB1t}$ = the volume of excess reserves (valued in terms of Country One's unit of account) held by Country One's private financial sector at the beginning of the current period.

Consequently, the sector's net wealth at the beginning of the current period may be represented by

$$NW_{PB1t} = p_{B1} \cdot B1_{PB1t} + p_{B2} \cdot \varepsilon \cdot B2_{PB1t} + p_{B3} \cdot \tilde{\varepsilon} \cdot B3_{PB1t} + X1_{PB1t} - \left(1 - \hat{r}_1\right) \cdot D1_{PB1t} \tag{9.1}$$

The current-period dividends that Country One's private financial sector pays to its household sector are given by

$$\Pi^d_{PB1t} = B1_{PB1t} + \varepsilon \cdot B2_{PB1t} + \tilde{\varepsilon} \cdot B3_{PB1t} - W1_t \cdot h_{PB1t} \cdot N1_{PB1t} \tag{9.2}$$

The current wage expense of the private financial sector includes current labor costs associated with servicing its checkable deposits outstanding at the beginning of the period.

For simplicity, we assume that during the current period the number of transactions associated with the checkable-deposit liabilities held by Country One's households at the beginning of the current period is directly proportional to the real value of those deposits.

Let

T_{PB1t} = the number of transactions during the current period associated with Country One's private financial sector's checkable-deposit liabilities.

Then,

$$T_{PB1t} = \nu_{PB1} \cdot \left(\frac{D1_{PB1t}}{p_{R1t}} \right) \tag{9.3}$$

where ν_{PB1} is a positive constant and where p_{R1t} represents the current-period price of R1.

To complete the transactions during the current period dictated by the real volume of its checkable-deposit liabilities, Country One's private financial sector must employ real resources. For simplicity, it is assumed that labor is the only real input required and that it displays a positive, but diminishing, marginal product in completing these transactions. Excess reserves held by the private financial sector either as vault cash or as deposits held at Country One's central bank, however, conserve the amount of labor time required to carry out transactions, for, to the extent that the private financial sector holds excess reserves, a temporary "cash drain" can be met simply by drawing down those reserves, thereby obviating the need to sell another asset or to borrow temporarily for the purpose of meeting the cash drain. Therefore, excess reserves provide the same labor-saving function for the private financial sector that coin, currency, and checkable-deposit balances provide the household sector. Furthermore, since the number of transactions associated with servicing the sector's checkable-deposit liabilities is assumed to be proportional to the real value of these deposits, the real value of the sector's excess reserves will indicate their ability to conserve the sector's transactions time. Consequently, the following transformation function for completing the transactions associated with Country One's private financial sector's checkable-deposit liabilities is specified here:

$$T_{PB1t} = \zeta \left(h_{PB1t} \cdot N1_{PB1t}, \frac{X1_{PB1t}}{p_{R1t}} \right) \tag{9.4}$$

where $\zeta_1, \zeta_2 > 0$; $\zeta_{11}, \zeta_{22} < 0$; and $\zeta_{12} > 0$ and where $h_{PB1t} \cdot N1_{PB1t}$ represents the total number of hours Country One's private financial sector uses people to service its interest-bearing checkable-deposit liabilities during the current period.

According to (9.4), both labor and real excess reserves are productive in servicing the private financial sector's checkable-deposit liabilities during the current period; both have diminishing marginal products; and they are technical complements—the marginal product of each factor increases with a greater use of the other factor. Setting the right-hand side of (9.3) equal to the right-hand side of (9.4) yields the following implicit function:

$$\nu_{PB1} \cdot \left(\frac{D1_{PB1t}}{p_{R1t}} \right) = \zeta \left(h_{PB1t} \cdot N1_{PB1t}, \frac{X1_{PB1t}}{p_{R1t}} \right) \tag{9.5}$$

Solving (9.5) explicitly for the total labor hours necessary to service the sector's checkable-deposit liabilities yields the following:

$$h_{PB1t} \cdot N1_{PB1t} = \delta \left(\frac{D1_{PB1t}}{p_{R1t}}, \frac{X1_{PB1t}}{p_{R1t}} \right) \tag{9.6}$$

where

$$\delta(\bullet) > 0,\ \delta_1 = \frac{\nu_{PB1}}{\zeta_1} > 0,$$

$$\delta_2 = -\frac{\delta_2}{\zeta_1} < 0,$$

$$\delta_{11} = -\frac{\nu_{PB1} \cdot \zeta_{11}}{(\zeta_1)^2} > 0,$$

$$\delta_{22} = -\left(\frac{\zeta_{22}}{\zeta_1}\right) + \frac{\zeta_2 \cdot \zeta_{12}}{(\zeta_1)^2} < 0,$$

$$\delta_{12} = -\frac{\nu_{PB2} \cdot \zeta_{12}}{(\zeta_1)^2} > 0,$$

$$\delta_{21} = -\left(\frac{\zeta_{21}}{\zeta_1}\right) + \frac{\zeta_2 \cdot \zeta_{11}}{(\zeta_1)^2} < 0, \quad \text{and}$$

$$\delta_{11} \cdot \delta_{22} - \delta_{12} \cdot \delta_{21} = \frac{\nu_{PB2} \cdot [\delta_{11} \cdot \delta_{22} - \delta_{12} \cdot \delta_{21}]}{(\zeta_1)^3} > 0$$

The current labor requirement function associated with checkable deposits is drawn in figure 9.1.

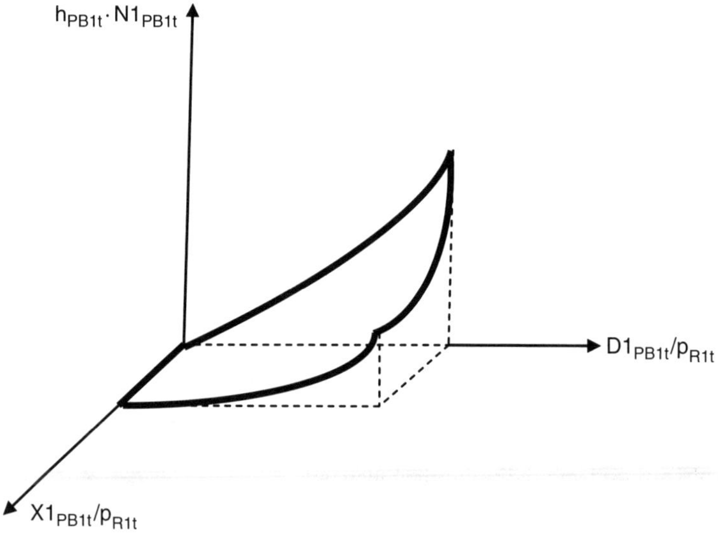

Figure 9.1 Current Labor Requirement for PB1

Let

$B1^d_{PB1(t+1)}$ = the number of Country One's bonds that Country One's private financial sector plans to hold by the end of the current period.

$B2^d_{PB1(t+1)}$ = the number of Country Two's bonds that Country One's private financial sector plans to hold by the end of the current period.

$B3^d_{PB1(t+1)}$ = the number of Country Three's bonds that Country One's private financial sector plans to hold by the end of the current period.

$D1^s_{PB1(t+1)}$ = the volume of checkable deposits outstanding at the end of the current period at Country One's private financial sector consistent with the plans of that sector (i.e., Country One's private financial sector's ex ante end-of-period supply of checkable deposits).

$N1^d_{PB1(t+1)}$ = Country One's private financial sector's end of current-period demand for employees to work next period.

$NW^d_{PB1(t+1)}$ = the net wealth Country One's private financial sector plans to hold by the end of the current period, expressed in terms of current-period prices (and Country One's unit of account).

$X1^d_{PB1(t+1)}$ = Country One's private financial sector's end-of-period demand for excess reserves (valued in terms of Country One's unit of account).

Then, in current-period prices, the net wealth attached to Country One's private financial sector's balance sheet planned for the end of the current period is given by

$$\begin{aligned} NW^d_{PB1(t+1)} = {} & p_{B1} \cdot B1^d_{PB1(t+1)} + p_{B2} \cdot \varepsilon \cdot B2^d_{PB1(t+1)} + p_{B3} \cdot \tilde{\varepsilon} \cdot B3^d_{PB1(t+1)} \\ & + X1^d_{PB1(t+1)} - \left(1 - \hat{r}_1\right) \cdot D1^s_{PB1(t+1)} \end{aligned} \tag{9.7}$$

Assume that the private financial sector distributes all of its current-period income to the household sector in Country One as dividends during the current period. Under this assumption, the planned net saving by Country One's private financial sector necessarily equals zero. Therefore, when both are measured in terms of current-period prices, Country One's private financial sector's net wealth planned for the end of the current period necessarily equals its beginning-of-period net wealth; the right-hand side of (9.1) necessarily equals the right-hand side of (9.7). Setting these two expressions equal to each other results in the following expression for Country One's private financial sector's end-of-period demand for bonds issued in Country One:

$$\begin{aligned} B1^d_{PB1(t+1)} = {} & \left(\frac{1}{p_{B1}}\right) \cdot \Big[p_{B1} \cdot B1_{PB1t} - p_{B2} \cdot \varepsilon \cdot \left(B2^d_{PB1(t+1)} - B2_{PB1t}\right)\Big] \\ & - p_{B3} \cdot \tilde{\varepsilon} \cdot \left(B3^d_{PB1(t+1)} - B3_{PB1t}\right) - \left(X1^d_{PB1(t+1)} - X1_{PB1t}\right) \\ & + \left(1 - \hat{r}_1\right) \cdot \left(D1^s_{PB1(t+1)} - D1_{PB1t}\right) \end{aligned} \tag{9.8}$$

According to (9.8), the value of the amount by which Country One's private financial sector plans to add to its holdings of Country One's bonds during the period, $p_{B1} \cdot (B1^d_{PB1(t+1)} - B1_{PB1t})$, must be equal to the amount it plans to add to its demand-deposit liabilities, net of additions to its required reserves, minus the sum of (1) the amount it plans to add to its holdings of bonds issued in Country Two and Country Three; and (2) the amount it plans to add to its holdings of excess reserves.

Let

$\Pi^d_{PB1(t+1)}$ = the amount Country One's private financial sector plans to distribute as dividends next period.

$W1_{t+1} \cdot h1^e_{t+1} \cdot N1^{de}_{PB1(t+1)}$ = the wage expense Country One's private financial sector expects this period to incur next period, where $W1_{t+1}$ represents the money wage that the nonrenewable resource industry announces at the beginning of the current period.

To close the model, it is assumed that at the beginning of the current period, the private financial sector plans to sell all assets and retire all outstanding liabilities by the end of next period. Therefore, as it formulates its plans this period, the sector plans to distribute to its owners next period all net income from its operations that period plus the value of its net wealth at the beginning of that period, all measured in terms of the prices the sector anticipates will prevail next period. Therefore, next period's anticipated dividends may be represented by the following expression:

$$\begin{aligned}\Pi^d_{PB1(t+1)} = {} & \left(1 + p_{B1}\right) \cdot B1^d_{PB1(t+1)} + \left(1 + p_{B2}\right) \cdot \varepsilon \cdot B2^d_{PB1(t+1)} \\ & + \left(1 + p_{B3}\right) \cdot \hat{\varepsilon} \cdot B3^d_{PB1(t+1)} + X1^d_{PB1(t+1)} - W1_{t+1} \\ & \cdot h1^e_{t+1} \cdot N1^{de}_{PB1(t+1)} - (1 - \widehat{r}_1) \cdot D1^s_{PB1(t+1)} \end{aligned} \tag{9.9}$$

Substituting the right-hand side of expression (9.8) for $B1^d_{PB1(t+1)}$ in (9.9) produces

$$\begin{aligned}\Pi^d_{PB1(t+1)} = {} & \left[\frac{(1 + p_{B1})}{p_{B1}}\right] \cdot \Big[p_{B1} \cdot B1_{PB1t} - p_{B2} \cdot \varepsilon \cdot \Big(B2^d_{PB1(t+1)} \\ & - B2_{PB1t}\Big)\Big] - p_{B3} \cdot \tilde{\varepsilon} \cdot \left(B3^d_{PB1(t+1)} - B3_{PB1t}\right) \\ & - \left(X1^d_{PB1(t+1)} - X1_{PB1t}\right) + \left(1 - \hat{r}_1\right) \cdot \left(D1^s_{PB1(t+1)} - D1_{PB1t}\right) \\ & + \left(1 + p_{B2}\right) \cdot \varepsilon \cdot B2^d_{PB1(t+1)} + \left(1 + p_{B3}\right) \cdot \tilde{\varepsilon} \cdot B3^d_{PB1(t+1)} \\ & + X1^d_{PB1(t+1)} - W1_{t+1} \cdot h1^e_{t+1} \cdot N1^{de}_{PB1(t+1)} \\ & - \left(1 - \hat{r}_1\right) \cdot D1^s_{PB1(t+1)} \end{aligned} \tag{9.10}$$

Next period's anticipated total labor hours devoted to servicing checkable deposits is assumed to be an increasing function of the real checkable deposits the sector plans to have outstanding by the beginning of that period and a decreasing function of the real value of the excess reserves it plans to hold by then. Let $N1^{d}_{PB1(t+1)}$ represent the number of people Country One's private financial sector plans to employ next period to service its checkable-deposit liabilities. Then, the total labor hours the sector plans to use next period to service its checkable-deposit liabilities may be given by

$$h1^{e}_{t+1} \cdot N1^{d}_{PB1(t+1)} = \phi\left(\frac{D1^{s}_{PB1(t+1)}}{p_{R1}{}^{e}}, \frac{X1^{d}_{PB1(t+1)}}{p_{R1}{}^{e}}\right) \tag{9.11}$$

where $\phi_1 > 0$, $\phi_2 < 0$, $\phi_{11}, \phi_{22} > 0$, $\phi_{12} < 0$, and $\phi_{11} \cdot \phi_{22} - (\phi_{12})^2 > 0$. The symbol $p_{R1}{}^{e}$ represents the price of R1 that the PB1 sector anticipates will prevail next period. The graph of the sector's demand for labor for servicing checkable deposits next period is analogous to the one drawn above in figure 9.1.

Assume that Country One's private financial sector attempts to maximize its present utility, that is, the level of utility it feels at time t. Present utility is assumed to be an increasing linear function of the present value of the sector's income stream, which is the amount that its owners (the home household sector) would have to place in its next best alternative at the beginning of the current period in order to duplicate, period by period, the real income to be generated by the private financial sector. Present utility is also enhanced by the value of Country One's bonds in its portfolio planned for the end of the current period and, to a greater or lesser extent, by the values of Country Two's and Country Three's bonds, respectively, in its portfolio planned for the end of the current period. Therefore, we view Country One's private financial sector as maximizing:

$$\begin{aligned}
Z \equiv\ & U1_{PB1}\left[p_{B1} \cdot B1^{d}_{PB1(t+1)}, p_{B2} \cdot \varepsilon \cdot B2^{d}_{PB1(t+1)}, p_{B3} \cdot \tilde{\varepsilon} \cdot B3^{d}_{PB1(t+1)}\right] \\
& + \Pi^{d}_{PB1t} + \frac{\Pi^{d}_{PB1(t+1)}}{(1 + r_1)} \\
\equiv\ & U1_{PB1}\Big[p_{B1} \cdot B1_{PB1t} - p_{B2} \cdot \varepsilon \cdot \left(B2^{d}_{PB1(t+1)} - B2_{PB1t}\right) \\
& - p_{B3} \cdot \tilde{\varepsilon} \cdot \left(B3^{d}_{PB1(t+1)} - B3_{PB1t}\right) - \left(X1^{d}_{PB1(t+1)} - X1_{PB1t}\right) \\
& + (1 + \hat{r}_1) \cdot \left(D1^{s}_{PB1(t+1)} - D1_{PB1t}\right), p_{B2} \cdot \varepsilon \cdot B2^{PB1d}_{t+1}, p_{B3} \cdot \tilde{\varepsilon} \cdot B3^{PB1d}_{t+1}\Big] \\
& \times B1_{PB1t} + \varepsilon \cdot B2_{PB1t} + \tilde{\varepsilon} \cdot B3_{PB1t} - W1_t \cdot \delta\left(\frac{D1_{PB1t}}{p_{R1t}}, \frac{X1_{PB1t}}{p_{R1t}}\right) \\
& + p_{B1} \cdot B1_{PB1t} - p_{B2} \cdot \varepsilon \cdot \left(B2^{d}_{PB1(t+1)} - B2_{PB1t}\right) \\
& - p_{B3} \cdot \tilde{\varepsilon} \cdot \left(B3^{d}_{PB1(t+1)} - B3_{PB1t}\right) - \left(X1^{d}_{PB1(t+1)} - X1_{PB1t}\right)
\end{aligned}$$

$$+ (1 + \hat{r}_1) \cdot \left(D1^s_{PB1(t+1)} - D1_{PB1t}\right)$$
$$+ \left[\frac{1}{(1 + r_1)}\right] \cdot [(1 + p_{B2})] \cdot \varepsilon \cdot B2^d_{PB1(t+1)} + (1 + p_{B3}) \cdot \tilde{\varepsilon} \cdot B3^d_{PB1(t+1)}$$
$$+ X1^d_{PB1(t+1)} - W1_{t+1} \cdot \phi\left(\frac{D1^s_{PB1(t+1)}}{p_{R1}{}^e}, \frac{X1^d_{PB1(t+1)}}{p_{R1}{}^e}\right)$$
$$- (1 - \hat{r}_1) \cdot D1^s_{PB1(t+1)} \tag{9.12}$$

where $1/(1 + r_1) = p_{B1}/(1 + p_{B1})$ and where the right-hand side of (9.6) has been substituted for $h_{PB1t} \cdot N1_{PB1t}$ and the right-hand side of (9.11) for $h1^e_{t+1} \cdot N1^d_{PB1(t+1)}$. The objective of the sector is to maximize Z with respect to $p_{B2} \cdot \varepsilon \cdot B2^d_{PB1(t+1)}$, $p_{B3} \cdot \tilde{\varepsilon} \cdot B3^d_{PB1(t+1)}$, $X1^d_{PB1(t+1)}$, and $D1^s_{PB1(t+1)}$. The solutions to these decision variables may then be substituted into expression (9.8) to obtain the sector's end-of-period demand for bonds issued by the borrowers in Country One.

The first-order conditions associated with the relevant choice variables are given by (9.13)–(9.16):

$$-\left[\frac{\partial U1_{PB1}}{\partial\left(p_{B1} \cdot B1^d_{PB1(t+1)}\right)}\right] + \left[\frac{\partial U1_{PB1}}{\partial\left(p_{B2} \cdot \tilde{\varepsilon} \cdot B2^d_{PB1(t+1)}\right)}\right] + \frac{(r_2 - r_1)}{(1 + r_1)} = 0 \tag{9.13}$$

According to (9.13), Country One's private banking sector will plan to add to its holdings of Country Two's bonds by the end of the current period up to the point at which the net marginal gain (loss) in utility by substituting a Country Two bond for a Country One bond is equal to the present value of the difference between the interest rates on the two bonds. If r_1 rises relative to r_2, the sector will reduce the value of its planned holdings of $p_{B2} \cdot \varepsilon \cdot B2^d_{PB1(t+1)}$, thereby raising $\partial U1_{PB1}/\partial(p_{B2} \cdot \varepsilon \cdot B2^d_{PB1(t+1)})$, and increase the value of its planned holdings of $p_{B1} \cdot B1^d_{PB1(t+1)}$, thereby reducing $\partial U1_{PB1}/\partial(p_{B1} \cdot B1^d_{PB1(t+1)})$. If r_2 rises relative to r_1, the sector will increase the value of its planned holdings of $p_{B2} \cdot \varepsilon \cdot B2^d_{PB1(t+1)}$, thereby reducing $\partial U1_{PB1}/\partial(p_{B2} \cdot \varepsilon \cdot B2^d_{PB1(t+1)})$, and decrease the value of its planned holdings of $p_{B1} \cdot B1^d_{PB1(t+1)}$, thereby raising $\partial U1_{PB1}/\partial(p_{B1} \cdot B1^d_{PB1(t+1)})$.

$$\left[\frac{\partial U1_{PB1}}{\partial\left(p_{B3} \cdot \tilde{\varepsilon} \cdot B3^d_{PB1(t+1)}\right)}\right] - \left(\frac{\partial U1_{PB1}}{\partial p_{B2} \cdot B1^d_{PB1(t+1)}}\right) + \frac{(r_3 - r_1)}{(1 + r_1)} = 0 \tag{9.14}$$

According to (9.14), Country One's private banking sector will plan to add to its holdings of Country Three's bonds by the end of the current period up to the point at which the net marginal gain (loss) in utility by substituting a Country Three bond for a Country One bond is equal to the present value of the difference between the interest rates on the two bonds. If r_1 rises relative to r_3, the sector will reduce the value of its planned holdings of $p_{B3} \cdot \tilde{\varepsilon} \cdot B3^d_{PB1(t+1)}$, thereby raising $\partial U1_{PB1}/\partial(p_{B3} \cdot \tilde{\varepsilon} \cdot B3^d_{PB1(t+1)})$, and increase the value of its planned holdings of $p_{B1} \cdot B1^d_{PB1(t+1)}$, thereby reducing $\partial U1_{PB1}/\partial(p_{B1} \cdot B1^d_{PB1(t+1)})$. If r_3 rises relative to r_1, the sector will increase the value of its planned holdings of $p_{B3} \cdot \tilde{\varepsilon} \cdot B3^d_{PB1(t+1)}$, thereby reducing $\partial U1_{PB1}/\partial(p_{B3} \cdot \tilde{\varepsilon} \cdot B3^d_{PB1(t+1)})$, and decrease the value of its planned holdings of $p_{B1} \cdot B1^d_{PB1(t+1)}$, thereby raising $\partial U1_{PB1}/\partial(p_{B3} \cdot \tilde{\varepsilon} \cdot B3^d_{PB1(t+1)})$:

$$-\frac{W1_{t+1} \cdot \phi_2}{p_{R1}} = r_1 + \left[\frac{\partial U1_{PB1}}{\partial\left(p_{B1} \cdot B1^d_{PB1(t+1)}\right)}\right] \cdot (1 + r_1) \tag{9.15}$$

Ceteris paribus, a one unit increase in the private banking sector's excess reserves planned for the end of the period in Country One will cost the sector a benefit of the amount $r_1 + [\partial U1_{PB1}/\partial(p_{B1} \cdot B1^d_{PB1(t+1)})] \cdot (1 + r_1)$ in interest and utility (as measured in terms of the alternative return on Country One's bonds). However, by adding a unit to excess reserves for the beginning of next period, the sector anticipates saving an amount $-W1_{t+1} \cdot \phi_2$ in wages that would otherwise be necessary to service the sector's checkable- deposit accounts next period. The higher the wage rate that the nonrenewable resource sector announces for next period, ceteris paribus, the greater will be the return to holding excess reserves by the beginning of that period. The higher the interest rate on Country One's bonds, the greater will be the opportunity cost of holding excess reserves by the beginning of next period:

$$\left\{r_1 + \left[\frac{\partial U1_{PB1}}{\partial\left(p_{B1} \cdot B1^d_{PB1(t+1)}\right)}\right] \cdot (1 + r_1)\right\} \cdot \left(1 - \hat{r}_1\right) = \frac{W1_{t+1} \cdot \phi_1}{p_{R1}} \tag{9.16}$$

Ceteris paribus, a one unit increase in the private banking sector's checkable-deposit liabilities by the end of the current period in Country One will earn a benefit in interest and marginal utility next period of the amount $\{r_1 + [\partial U1_{PB1}/\partial(p_{B1} \cdot B1^d_{PB1(t+1)})] \cdot (1 + r_1)\} \cdot (1 - \hat{r}_1)$ as the sector adds to its end of current period holdings of Country One's bonds.

Totally differentiating (9.13)–(9.16) and solving for the changes in $p_{B2} \cdot \varepsilon \cdot B2^d_{PB1(t+1)}$, $p_{B3} \cdot \tilde{\varepsilon} \cdot B3^d_{PB1(t+1)}$, $X1^{PB1d}_{t+1}$, and $D1^{PB1s}_{t+1}$ yields the sector's demand functions for bonds issued in Country Two and Country Three, its demand for excess reserves, and its supply of checkable deposits. To simplify the analysis, the parameters entering the own first-order conditions are assumed to dominate these respective decision variables.

Demand for Bonds Issued in Country Two

From the discussion of (9.13) presented above, the private banking sector's demand for bonds issued in Country Two may be given by

$$p_{B2} \cdot \varepsilon \cdot B2^{d}_{PB1(t+1)} = p_{B2} \cdot \varepsilon \cdot B2^{d}_{PB1(t+1)}\,(r_1, r_2) \tag{9.17}$$

Demand for Bonds Issued in Country Three

From the discussion of (9.14) presented above, the private banking sector's demand for bonds issued in Country Three may be given by

$$p_{B3} \cdot \tilde{\varepsilon} \cdot B3^{d}_{PB1(t+1)} = p_{B3} \cdot \tilde{\varepsilon} \cdot B3^{d}_{PB1(t+1)}\,(r_1, r_3) \tag{9.18}$$

Demand for Excess Reserves

From the discussion associated with condition (9.15), an increase in any of r_1 will induce the sector to reduce its end-of-period holdings of excess reserves, while an increase in the money wage announced by the nonrenewable resource industry for next period will cause the banking sector to increase its end-of-period demand for excess reserves. In addition, an increase in the current price level in Country One will increase the sector's nominal demand for excess reserves proportionally:

$$X1^{d}_{PB1(t+1)} = \left(\frac{X1^{d}_{PB1(t+1)}}{p^{e}_{R1}}\right)^{d}(\underset{-}{r_1}, \underset{+}{W1_{t+1}}) \cdot p^{e}_{R1} \tag{9.19}$$

Supply of Checkable Deposits

From (9.16), an increase in r_1 will increase the net return to the private banking sector from issuing an additional unit of checkable deposits by the end of the period, while an increase in the required reserve ratio, $\hat{r}_1$, will reduce the net return since only the excess reserves generated by an additional unit of checkable deposits may be used to add to the sector's bond holdings. An increase in the money wage increases the marginal cost of servicing an additional unit of checkable deposits, while an increase in the average price level reduces that cost, since it reduces the number of transactions on the average associated with a checkable deposit of a given nominal value:

$$D1^{S}_{PB1(t+1)} = \left(\frac{D1^{S}_{PB1(t+1)}}{p_{R1}{}^{e}}\right)^{S}(\underset{+}{r_1}, \underset{-}{\hat{r}_1}, \underset{-}{W1_{t+1}}) \cdot p_{R1}{}^{e} \tag{9.20}$$

Demand for Bonds Issued in Country One

Substituting the demand and supply functions obtained above into (9.8) yields the sector's demand for bonds issued in Country One's bond market:

$$\begin{aligned}
p_{B1}\cdot B1^{d}_{PB1(t+1)} &= p_{B1}\cdot B1_{PB1t} - p_{B2}\cdot\varepsilon\cdot\left(B2^{d}_{PB1(t+1)} - B2_{PB1t}\right)\\
&\quad - p_{B3}\cdot\tilde{\varepsilon}\cdot\left(B3^{d}_{PB1(t+1)} - B3_{PB1t}\right) - \left(X1^{d}_{PB1(t+1)} - X1_{PB1t}\right)\\
&\quad + \left(1-\hat{r}_1\right)\cdot\left(D1^{s}_{PB1(t+1)} - D1_{PB1t}\right)\\
&= -p_{B2}\cdot\varepsilon\cdot B2^{d}_{PB1(t+1)} - p_{B3}\cdot\tilde{\varepsilon}\cdot B3^{d}_{PB1(t+1)} - X1^{d}_{PB1(t+1)}\\
&\quad + \left(1-\hat{r}_1\right)\cdot D1^{s}_{PB1(t+1)} + NW_{PB1t}\\
&= -p_{B2}\cdot\varepsilon\cdot B2^{d}_{PB1(t+1)}\underset{-\ \ +}{(r_1,\ r_2)} - p_{B3}\cdot\tilde{\varepsilon}\cdot B3^{d}_{PB1(t+1)}\underset{-\ \ +}{(r_1,\ r_3)}\\
&\quad - \left(X1^{d}_{PB1(t+1)}/p^{e}_{R1}\right)^{d}\underset{-\ \ +}{(r_1,\ W1_{t+1})}\cdot p^{e}_{R1} + \left(1-\hat{r}_1\right)\\
&\quad \cdot\left(\frac{D1^{s}_{PB1(t+1)}}{p^{e}_{R1}}\right)^{S}\underset{+\ \ -\ \ -}{\left(r_1,\ \hat{r}_1,\ W1_{t+1}\right)}\cdot p^{e}_{R1} + NW_{PB1t}\\
&= p_{B1}\cdot B1^{d}_{PB1(t+1)}\underset{+\ \ -\ \ -\ \ -\ \ \ -\ \ \ \ \ \ +1}{\left(r_1,\ r_2,\ r_3,\ \hat{r}_1,\ W1_{t+1}, +NW_{PB1t}\right)} \qquad (9.21)
\end{aligned}$$

where $NW_{PB1t} = p_{B1}\cdot B1_{PB1t} + p_{B2}\cdot\varepsilon\cdot B2_{PB1t} + p_{B3}\cdot\tilde{\varepsilon}\cdot B3_{PB1t} + X1_{PB1t} - (1-\hat{r}_1)D1_{PB1t}$.

Demand for Current Labor Hours

The sector's demand for current labor hours is given by (9.6):

$$h_{PB1t}\cdot N1_{PB1t} = \delta\underset{+\qquad -}{\left(\frac{D1_{PB1t}}{p_{R1t}},\ \frac{X1_{PB1t}}{p_{R1t}}\right)} \qquad (9.6)$$

Demand for Workers for Next Period

The sector's demand for workers for next period is found by substituting (9.19) and (9.20) into (9.11):

$$h1^e_{t+1} \cdot N1^d_{PB1(t+1)} = \phi\left(\underset{+}{\frac{D1^S_{PB1(t+1)}}{p^e_{R1t}}}, \underset{-}{\frac{X1^d_{PB1(t+1)}}{p^e_{R1}}}\right)$$

$$= \phi\left[\left(\frac{D1^S_{PB1(t+1)}}{p^e_{R1t}}\right)^s (r_1, \hat{r}_1, W1_{t+1}), \left(\frac{X1^d_{PB1(t+1)}}{p^e_{R1t}}\right)^d \cdot (r_1, W1_{t+1})\right]$$

$$= h1^e_{t+1} \cdot N1^d_{PB1(t+1)}\left(\underset{+}{r_1}, \underset{-}{\hat{r}_1}, \underset{-}{W1_{t+1}}\right) \qquad (9.22)$$

Country One's Central Banking (CB1) Sector

The central banking sector in Country One holds bonds that have been issued by each of the three countries in the model.

Let

$p_{B1} \cdot B1_{CB1t}$ = the value of Country One's central bank's holdings of Country One's bonds at the beginning of the current period.

$p_{B2} \cdot \varepsilon \cdot B2_{CB1t}$ = the value of Country One's central bank's holdings of Country Two's bonds at the beginning of the current period in terms of Country One's unit of account.

$p_{B3} \cdot \tilde{\varepsilon} \cdot B3_{CB1t}$ = the value of Country One's central bank's holdings of Country Three's bonds at the beginning of the current period in terms of Country One's unit of account.

$MB1_t$ = the value of the monetary base outstanding at the beginning of the current period in Country One.

NW_{CB1t} = the net wealth of the central bank in Country One at the beginning of the current period.

The monetary base outstanding in Country One at the beginning of the current period, $MB1_t$, consists of the coin and currency outstanding at the beginning of the current period in Country One, $CU1_t$, plus the reserves held by the private banking sector in Country One at the beginning of the current period, R^*1_t, where reserves consist of the vault cash held by the private banks plus the deposits they hold at their central bank at the beginning of the current period. It is assumed that the private banks only hold vault cash and deposits at their central bank and that these are denominated exclusively in terms of Country One's unit of account.

From the above definitions, the net wealth of the central bank in Country One at the beginning of the current period is given by (9.23):

$$NW_{CB1t} = p_{B1} \cdot B1_{CB1t} + \varepsilon \cdot p_{B2} \cdot B2_{CB1t} + \tilde{\varepsilon} \cdot p_{B3} \cdot B3_{CB1t} - MB1_1 \quad (9.23)$$

During the current period, Country One's central bank earns interest income on all three types of bonds it holds at the beginning of the current period. It is assumed that this interest income is passed along to Country One's government sector during the period so that the net saving of the central bank during the current period is equal to zero.

$$S_{CB1t} = B1_{CB1t} + \varepsilon \cdot B2_{CB1t} + \tilde{\varepsilon} \cdot B3_{CB1t} - \Pi_{CB1t} = 0 \quad (9.24)$$

where

S_{CB1t} = net business saving by the central bank in Country One during the current period.
Π_{CB1t} = "dividends" paid by the CB1 sector during the current period to the G1 sector.

Let

$p_{B1} \cdot B1^d_{CB1(t+1)}$ = the value of Country One's central bank's planned holdings of Country One's bonds at the end of the current period (the CB1 sector's demand for Country One's bonds).
$\varepsilon \cdot p_{B2} \cdot B2^d_{CB1(t+1)}$ = the value of Country One's central bank's demand for Country Two's bonds for the end of the current period in terms of Country One's unit of account.
$\tilde{\varepsilon} \cdot p_{B3} \cdot B3^d_{CB1(t+1)}$ = the value of Country One's central bank's demand for Country Three's bonds for the end of the current period in terms of Country One's unit of account.
$MB1^s_{CB1(t+1)}$ = the value of the monetary base outstanding at the end of the current period in Country One consistent with the plans of Country One's central bank at the beginning of the current period.
$NW^d_{CB1(t+1)}$ = the net wealth of the central bank in Country One at the end of the current period in terms of current-period prices.

The planned net wealth of the central bank in Country One for the end of the current period is given by (9.25):

$$NW^d_{CB1(t+1)} = p_{B1} \cdot B1^d_{CB1(t+1)} + \varepsilon \cdot p_{B2} \cdot B2^d_{CB1(t+1)} + \tilde{\varepsilon} \cdot p_{B3} \cdot B3^d_{CB1(t+1)} - MB1^s_{CB1(t+1)} \quad (9.25)$$

Since the sector presumably does not engage in net saving during the current period, the net wealth in the balance sheet it plans for the end of the current period must equal the net wealth in its beginning-of-period balance sheet when both balance sheets are evaluated in the same set of prices, namely, the prices at which the various bonds trade during the current period. Therefore, from (9.25) and (9.23) it follows that (9.26) holds identically:

$$p_{B1}\cdot\left(B1^d_{CB1(t+1)} - B1_{CB1t}\right) + \varepsilon\cdot p_{B2}\cdot\left(B2^d_{CB1(t+1)} - B2_{CB1t}\right) + \tilde{\varepsilon}\cdot p_{B3}\cdot\left(B3^d_{CB1(t+1)} - B3_{CB1t}\right) \equiv MB1^s_{CB1(t+1)} - MB1_t \qquad (9.26)$$

According to the "cash flow restriction" or "budget constraint" specified in (9.26), the central bank in Country One may arbitrarily decide upon any three of $p_{B1}\cdot B1^d_{CB1(t+1)}$, $\varepsilon\cdot p_{B2}\cdot B2^d_{CB1(t+1)}$, $\tilde{\varepsilon}\cdot p_{B3}\cdot B3^d_{CB1(t+1)}$, and $MB1^s_{CB1(t+1)}$. Once it has chosen the values of any three of these variables, the value of the fourth variable is established by restriction (9.26).

Central Bank Open Market Operations

A decision by the central bank in Country One to increase its end-of-period holdings of Country One's bonds, holding constant its planned end-of-period holdings of bonds issued in both Country Two and Country Three, is referred to as an open market purchase of bonds by the central bank in Country One. The level of the monetary base at the end of the period consistent with this plan by the central bank, $MB1^s_{CB1(t+1)}$, necessarily increases by the same nominal value. An open market sale of bonds by the CB1 sector refers to a reduction in the sector's planned holdings of bonds at the end of the period, $p_{B1}\cdot B1^d_{CB1(t+1)}$, accompanied by an equivalent reduction in the nominal value of the country's monetary base consistent with the plans of the central banking sector, $MB1^s_{CB1(t+1)}$.

Central Bank Operations in Country Two's Bond Market

A decision by the central bank in Country One to increase its end-of-period holdings of Country Two's bonds, holding constant its planned end-of-period holdings of bonds issued in both Country One and Country Three, is referred to as a purchase of bonds denominated in Country Two's unit of account by the central bank in Country One. The CB1 sector increases $\varepsilon\cdot p_{B2}\cdot B2^d_{CB1(t+1)}$. The level of the monetary base at the end of the period consistent with this plan by the central bank, $MB1^s_{CB1(t+1)}$, necessarily increases by the same nominal value, measured in terms of Country One's unit of account. A sale of bonds denominated in Country Two's unit of account by the CB1 sector refers to a reduction in the sector's planned holdings of Country Two's bonds at the end of the period, $\varepsilon\cdot p_{B2}\cdot B2^d_{CB1(t+1)}$, accompanied by an equivalent reduction in the nominal value of the country's monetary base consistent with the plans of the central banking sector, $MB1^s_{CB1(t+1)}$.

A decision by the central bank in Country One to increase its end-of-period holdings of Country Two's bonds and to "sterilize" the transaction means that it increases $\varepsilon \cdot p_{B2} \cdot B2^{d}_{CB1(t+1)}$ and simultaneously reduces its end-of-period demand for its own country's bonds by the same amount; it reduces $p_{B1} \cdot B1^{d}_{CB1(t+1)}$. If it decides to sell Country Two's bonds and sterilize, it reduces $\varepsilon \cdot p_{B2} \cdot B2^{d}_{CB1(t+1)}$ and increases $p_{B1} \cdot B1^{d}_{CB1(t+1)}$ by the same amount to keep its own monetary base unchanged.

Central Bank Operations in Country Three's Bond Market

A decision by the central bank in Country One to increase its end-of-period holdings of Country Three's bonds, holding constant its planned end-of-period holdings of bonds issued in both Country One and Country Two, is referred to as a purchase of bonds denominated in Country Three's unit of account by the central bank in Country One. The CB1 sector increases $\tilde{\varepsilon} \cdot p_{B3} \cdot B3^{d}_{CB1(t+1)}$. The level of the monetary base at the end of the period consistent with this plan by the central bank, $MB1^{s}_{CB1(t+1)}$, necessarily increases by the same nominal value, measured in terms of Country One's unit of account.

A sale of bonds denominated in Country Three's unit of account by the CB1 sector refers to a reduction in the sector's planned holdings of Country Three's bonds at the end of the period, $\tilde{\varepsilon} \cdot p_{B3} \cdot B3^{d}_{CB1(t+1)}$, accompanied by an equivalent reduction in the nominal value of the country's monetary base consistent with the plans of the central banking sector, $MB1^{s}_{CB1(t+1)}$.

A decision by the central bank in Country One to increase its end-of-period holdings of Country Three's bonds and "sterilize" the transaction means that it increases $\tilde{\varepsilon} \cdot p_{B3} \cdot B3^{d}_{CB1(t+1)}$ and simultaneously reduces its end-of-period demand for its own country's bonds by the same amount to keep its monetary base unchanged; it reduces $p_{B1} \cdot B1^{d}_{CB1(t+1)}$. If it decides to sell foreign bonds and sterilize, it reduces $\tilde{\varepsilon} \cdot p_{B3} \cdot B3^{d}_{CB1(t+1)}$ and increases $p_{B1} \cdot B1^{d}_{CB1(t+1)}$ by the same amount to keep its own monetary base unchanged.

Country Two's Private Banking (PB2) Sector

In a manner directly analogous to the derivation of the private banking sector's demands in Country One, the following demand functions may be obtained for the private banks in Country Two.

Demand for Bonds Issued in Country One

The private banking sector's demand for bonds issued in Country One is given by

$$\left(\frac{p_{B1}}{\varepsilon}\right) \cdot B1^{d}_{PB2(t+1)} = \left(\frac{p_{B1}}{\varepsilon}\right) \cdot B1^{d}_{PB2(t+1)} \cdot B1^{PB2d}_{t+1}\underset{+\ \ -}{(r_1,\ r_2)} \qquad (9.27)$$

Demand for Bonds Issued in Country Three

The private banking sector's demand for bonds issued in Country Three is given by

$$\left[\frac{(p_{B3}/\tilde{\varepsilon})}{\varepsilon}\right] \cdot B3^{d}_{PB2(t+1)} = \left[\frac{(p_{B3}/\tilde{\varepsilon})}{\varepsilon}\right] \cdot B3^{d}_{PB2(t+1)}\underset{-\quad +}{(r_2,\ r_3)} \tag{9.28}$$

Demand for Excess Reserves

An increase in r_2 will induce the sector to reduce its end-of-period holdings of excess reserves, while an increase in the money wage announced by the capital goods industry for next period will cause the banking sector to increase its end-of-period demand for excess reserves. In addition, an increase in the current price level in Country One will increase the sector's nominal demand for excess reserves proportionally:

$$X2^{d}_{PB2(t+1)} = \left(\frac{X2^{d}_{PB2(t+1)}}{p^{e}_{R2}}\right)^{d} \underset{-\quad +}{(r_2,\ W2_{t+1})} \cdot p_{R2}{}^{e} \tag{9.29}$$

Supply of Checkable Deposits

An increase in r_1 will increase the net return to the private banking sector from issuing an additional unit of checkable deposits by the end of the period, while an increase in the required reserve ratio, $\hat{r}_2$, will reduce the net return, since only the excess reserves generated by an additional unit of checkable deposits may be used to add to the sector's bond holdings. An increase in the money wage increases the marginal cost of servicing an additional unit of checkable deposits, while an increase in the average price level reduces that cost, since it reduces the number of transactions on the average associated with a checkable deposit of a given nominal value:

$$D2^{s}_{PB2(t+1)} = \left(\frac{D2^{s}_{PB2(t+1)}}{p^{e}_{R2}}\right)^{s} \underset{+\quad -\quad -}{\left(r_2,\ \hat{r}_2,\ W2_{t+1}\right)} \cdot p^{e}_{R2} \tag{9.30}$$

Demand for Bonds Issued in Country Two

The sector's demand for bonds issued in Country Two's bond market is given by

$$p_{B2} \cdot B2^{d}_{PB2(t+1)} = -\left(\frac{p_{B2}}{\varepsilon}\right) \cdot B1^{d}_{PB2(t+1)} - \left[\frac{(p_{B3} \cdot \tilde{\varepsilon})}{\varepsilon}\right] \cdot B3^{d}_{PB2(t+1)}$$
$$- X2^{d}_{PB2(t+1)} + \left(1 - \hat{r}_2\right) \cdot D2^{s}_{PB2(t+1)} + NW_{PB2t}$$

$$= NW_{PB2t} - \left(\frac{p_{B1}}{\varepsilon}\right) \cdot B1^{d}_{PB2(t+1)}\,(\underset{+}{r_1}, \underset{-}{r_2}) - \left[\frac{p_{B3} \cdot \tilde{\varepsilon}}{\varepsilon}\right] \cdot B3^{d}_{PB2(t+1)}\,(\underset{-}{r_2}, \underset{+}{r_3})$$

$$- \left(\frac{X2^{d}_{PB2(t+1)}}{p_{R2}{}^{e}}\right)^{d} (\underset{-}{r_2}, \underset{+}{W2_{t+1}}) \cdot p_{R2}{}^{e} + \left(1 - \hat{r}_2\right)$$

$$\cdot \left(\frac{D2^{2}_{PB2(t+1)}}{p_{R2}{}^{e}}\right)^{s} \left(\underset{+}{r_2}, \underset{-}{\hat{r}_2}, \underset{-}{W2_{t+1}}\right) \cdot p_{R2}{}^{e}$$

$$= p_{B2} \cdot B2^{d}_{PB2(t+1)}\left(\underset{-}{r_1}, \underset{+}{r_2}, \underset{-}{r_3}, \underset{-}{\hat{r}_2}, \underset{-}{W2_{t+1}}, \underset{+1}{NW_{PB2t}}\right) \tag{9.31}$$

where $NW_{PB2t} = (p_{B1}/\varepsilon) \cdot B1_{PB2t} + p_{B2} \cdot B2_{PB2t} + [(p_{B3} \cdot \tilde{\varepsilon})/\varepsilon] \cdot B3_{PB2t} + X2_{PB2t} - (1 - \hat{r}_2) \cdot D2_{PB2t}$.

Demand for Current Labor Hours

The sector's demand for current labor hours is given by

$$h_{PB2t} \cdot N2_{PB2t} = \tilde{\delta}\left(\underset{+}{\frac{D2_{PB2t}}{p_{R2t}}}, \underset{-}{\frac{X2_{PB2t}}{p_{R2t}}}\right) \tag{9.32}$$

Demand for Workers for Next Period

The sector's demand for workers for next period is given by

$$h2^{e}_{t+1} \cdot N2^{d}_{PB2(t+1)} = \tilde{\phi}\left(\underset{+}{\frac{D2^{s}_{PB2(t+1)}}{p_{R2}{}^{e}}}, \underset{-}{\frac{X2^{d}_{PB2(t+1)}}{p_{R2}{}^{e}}}\right)$$

$$= \tilde{\phi}\left(\left(\frac{D2^{s}_{PB2(t+1)}}{p_{R2}{}^{e}}\right)^{s}\left(r_2, \hat{r}_2, W2_{t+1}\right), \left(\frac{X2^{d}_{PB2(t+1)}}{p_{R2}{}^{e}}\right)^{d}(r_2, W2_{t+1})\right)$$

$$= h2^{e}_{t+1} \cdot N2^{d}_{PB2(t+1)}\left(\underset{+}{r_2}, \underset{-}{\hat{r}_2}, \underset{-}{W2_{t+1}}\right) \tag{9.33}$$

Central Banking (CB2) Sector

The central banking sector in Country Two holds bonds that have been issued by each of the three countries in the model.

Let

$(p_{B1}/\varepsilon) \cdot B1_{CB2t}$ = the value of Country Two's central bank's holdings of Country One's bonds at the beginning of the current period in terms of Country Two's unit of account.

$p_{B2} \cdot B2_{CB2t}$ = the value of Country Two's central bank's holdings of Country Two's bonds at the beginning of the current period in terms of Country Two's unit of account.

$[(p_{B3}/\tilde{\varepsilon})/\varepsilon] \cdot B3_{CB2t}$ = the value of Country Two's central bank's holdings of Country Three's bonds at the beginning of the current period in terms of Country Two's unit of account.

$MB2_t$ = the value of the monetary base outstanding at the beginning of the current period in Country Two.

NW_{CB2t} = the net wealth of the central bank in Country Two at the beginning of the current period.

The monetary base outstanding in Country Two at the beginning of the current period, $MB2_t$, consists of the coin and currency outstanding at the beginning of the current period in Country Two, $CU2_t$, plus the reserves held by the private banking sector in Country Two at the beginning of the current period, R^*2_t, where reserves consist of the vault cash held by the private banks plus the deposits they hold at their central bank at the beginning of the current period. It is assumed that the private banks only hold vault cash and deposits at their central bank and that these are denominated exclusively in terms of Country Two's unit of account.

From the above definitions, the net wealth of the central bank in Country Two at the beginning of the current period is given by

$$NW_{CB2t} = \left(\frac{p_{B1}}{\varepsilon}\right) \cdot B1_{CB2t} + p_{B2} \cdot B2_{CB2t} + \left[\frac{(p_{B3} \cdot \tilde{\varepsilon})}{\varepsilon}\right] \cdot B3_{CB2t} - MB2_t \tag{9.34}$$

During the current period, Country Two's central bank earns interest income on all three types of bonds it holds at the beginning of the current period. It is assumed that this interest income is passed along to Country Two's government sector during the period so that the net saving of the central bank during the current period is equal to zero.

$$S_{CB2t} = \left(\frac{1}{\varepsilon}\right) \cdot B1_{CB2t} + B2_{CB2t} + \left(\frac{\tilde{\varepsilon}}{\varepsilon}\right) \cdot B3_{CB2t} - \Pi_{CB2t} = 0 \tag{9.35}$$

where

S_{CB2t} = net business saving by the central bank in Country Two during the current period.

Π_{CB2t} = "dividends" paid by the CB2 sector during the current period to the G2 sector.

Let

$(p_{B1}/\varepsilon) \cdot B1^d_{CB2(t+1)}$ = the value of Country Two's central bank's planned holdings of Country One's bonds at the end of the current period (the CB2 sector's demand for Country One's bonds) in terms of Country Two's unit of account.

$p_{B2} \cdot B2^d_{CB2(t+1)}$ = the value of Country Two's central bank's demand for Country Two's bonds for the end of the current period in terms of Country Two's unit of account.

$[(p_{B3} \cdot \tilde{\varepsilon})/\varepsilon] \cdot B3^d_{CB2(t+1)}$ = the value of Country Two's central bank's demand for Country Three's bonds for the end of the current period in terms of Country Two's unit of account.

$MB2^s_{CB2(t+1)}$ = the value of the monetary base outstanding at the end of the current period in Country Two consistent with the plans of Country Two's central bank at the beginning of the current period.

$NW^d_{CB2(t+1)}$ = the net wealth of the central bank in Country Two at the end of the current period in terms of current-period prices.

The planned net wealth of the central bank in Country Two for the end of the current period is given by

$$NW^d_{CB2t} = \left(\frac{p_{B1}}{\varepsilon}\right) \cdot B1^d_{CB2(t+1)} + p_{B2} \cdot B2^d_{CB2t} + \left[\frac{(p_{B3} \cdot \tilde{\varepsilon})}{\varepsilon}\right] \cdot B3^d_{CB2t} - MB2^s_{CB2(t+1)} \tag{9.36}$$

Since the sector presumably does not engage in net saving during the current period, the net wealth in the balance sheet it plans for the end of the current period must equal the net wealth in its beginning-of-period balance sheet when both balance sheets are evaluated in the same set of prices, namely, the prices at which the various bonds trade during the current period. Therefore, it follows that (9.37) holds identically:

$$\left(\frac{p_{B1}}{\varepsilon}\right) \cdot \left(B1^d_{CB2(t+1)} - B1_{CB2t}\right) + p_{B2} \cdot \left(B2^d_{CB2(t+1)} - B2_{CB2t}\right) + \left[\frac{(p_{B3} \cdot \tilde{\varepsilon})}{\varepsilon}\right] \cdot \left(B3^d_{CB2(t+1)} - B3_{CB2t}\right) = \left(MB2^s_{CB2(t+1)} - MB2_t\right) \tag{9.37}$$

According to the "cash flow restriction" or "budget constraint" specified in (9.37), the central bank in Country Two may arbitrarily decide upon any three of $(p_{B1}/\varepsilon) \cdot B1^d_{CB2(t+1)}$, $p_{B2} \cdot B2^d_{CB2(t+1)}$, $[(p_{B3} \cdot \tilde{\varepsilon})/\varepsilon] \cdot B3^d_{CB2(t+1)}$, and $MB2^s_{CB2(t+1)}$. Once it has chosen the values of any three of these variables, the value of the fourth variable is established by restriction (9.37).

Central Bank Open Market Operations

A decision by the central bank in Country Two to increase its end-of-period holdings of Country Two's bonds, holding constant its planned end-of-period holdings of bonds issued in both Country One and Country Three, is referred to as an open market purchase of bonds by the central bank in Country Two. The level of the monetary base at the end of the period consistent with this plan by the central bank, $MB2^s_{CB2(t+1)}$, necessarily increases by the same nominal value. An open market sale of bonds by the CB2 sector refers to a reduction in the sector's planned holdings of bonds at the end of the period, $p_{B2} \cdot B2^d_{CB2(t+1)}$, accompanied by an equivalent reduction in the nominal value of the country's monetary base consistent with the plans of the central banking sector, $MB2^s_{CB2(t+1)}$.

Central Bank Operations in Country One's Bond Market

A decision by the central bank in Country Two to increase its end-of-period holdings of Country One's bonds, holding constant its planned end-of-period holdings of bonds issued in both Country Two and Country Three, is referred to as a purchase of bonds denominated in Country One's unit of account by the central bank in Country Two. The CB2 sector increases $(p_{B1}/\varepsilon) \cdot B1^d_{CB2(t+1)}$. The level of the monetary base at the end of the period consistent with this plan by the central bank, $MB2^s_{CB2(t+1)}$, necessarily increases by the same nominal value, measured in terms of Country Two's unit of account. A sale of bonds denominated in Country One's unit of account by the CB2 sector refers to a reduction in the sector's planned holdings of Country One's bonds at the end of the period, $(p_{B1}/\varepsilon) \cdot B1^d_{CB2(t+1)}$, accompanied by an equivalent reduction in the nominal value of Country Two's monetary base consistent with the plans of the central banking sector, $MB2^s_{CB2(t+1)}$.

A decision by the central bank in Country Two to increase its end-of-period holdings of Country One's bonds and "sterilize" the transaction means that it increases $(p_{B1}/\varepsilon) \cdot B1^d_{CB2(t+1)}$ and simultaneously reduces its end-of-period demand for its own country's bonds by the same amount; it reduces $p_{B1} \cdot B2^d_{CB2(t+1)}$. If it decides to sell Country One's bonds and sterilize, it reduces $(p_{B1}/\varepsilon) \cdot B1^d_{CB2(t+1)}$ and increases $p_{B2} \cdot B2^d_{CB2(t+1)}$ by the same amount to keep its own monetary base unchanged.

Central Bank Operations in Country Three's Bond Market

A decision by the central bank in Country Two to increase its end-of-period holdings of Country Three's bonds, holding constant its planned end-of-period holdings of bonds issued in both Country One and Country Two, is referred to as a purchase of bonds denominated in Country Three's unit of account by the central bank in Country Two. The CB2 sector increases $[(p_{B3} \cdot \tilde{\varepsilon})/\varepsilon] \cdot B3^d_{CB2(t+1)}$. The level of the monetary base at the end of the period consistent with this plan by the central bank, $MB2^s_{CB2(t+1)}$, necessarily increases by the same nominal value, measured in terms of Country Two's unit of account. A sale of bonds denominated in Country Three's unit of account by the CB2 sector refers to a reduction in the sector's planned holdings of Country Three's bonds at the end of the period, $[(p_{B3} \cdot \tilde{\varepsilon})/\varepsilon] \cdot B3^d_{CB2(t+1)}$, accompanied by an equivalent reduction in the nominal value of the country's monetary base consistent with the plans of the central banking sector, $MB2^s_{CB2(t+1)}$.

A decision by the central bank in Country Two to increase its end-of-period holdings of Country Three's bonds and "sterilize" the transaction means that it increases $[(p_{B3} \cdot \tilde{\varepsilon})/\varepsilon] \cdot B3^d_{CB2(t+1)}$ and simultaneously reduces its end-of-period demand for its own country's bonds by the same amount to keep its monetary base unchanged; it reduces $p_{B2} \cdot B2^d_{CB2(t+1)}$. If it decides to sell foreign bonds and sterilize, it reduces $[(p_{B3} \cdot \tilde{\varepsilon})/\varepsilon] \cdot B3^d_{CB2(t+1)}$ and increases $p_{B2} \cdot B2^d_{CB2(t+1)}$ by the same amount to keep its own monetary base unchanged.

Country Three's Private Banking (PB3) Sector

Demand for Bonds Issued in Country One

The private banking sector's demand for bonds issued in Country One is given by

$$\left(\frac{p_{B1}}{\tilde{\varepsilon}}\right) \cdot B1^d_{PB3(t+1)} = \left(\frac{p_{B1}}{\tilde{\varepsilon}}\right) \cdot B1^d_{PB3(t+1)}\underset{+\ \ -}{(r_1,\ r_3)} \qquad (9.38)$$

Demand for Bonds Issued in Country Two

The private banking sector's demand for bonds issued in Country Two is given by

$$\left[\frac{(p_{B1} \cdot \varepsilon)}{\tilde{\varepsilon}}\right] \cdot B2^d_{PB3(t+1)} = \left[\frac{(p_{B1} \cdot \varepsilon)}{\tilde{\varepsilon}}\right] \cdot B2^d_{PB3(t+1)}\underset{+\ \ -}{(r_2,\ r_3)} \qquad (9.39)$$

Demand for Excess Reserves

An increase in r_3 will induce the sector to reduce its end-of-period holdings of excess reserves, while an increase in the money wage announced by the consumer goods industry for next period will cause the banking sector to increase its end-of-period demand for excess reserves:

$$X3^d_{PB3(t+1)} = X3^d_{PB3(t+1)}\underset{-\ \ \ \ +}{(r_3,\ W3_{t+1})} \qquad (9.40)$$

Supply of Checkable Deposits

An increase in r_3 will increase the net return to the private banking sector from issuing an additional unit of checkable deposits by the end of the period, while an increase in the required reserve ratio, $\hat{r}_3$, will reduce the net return since only the excess reserves generated by an additional unit of checkable deposits may be used to add to the sector's bond holdings. An increase in the money wage increases the marginal cost of servicing an additional unit of checkable deposits:

$$D3^s_{PB3(t+1)} = D3^s_{PB3(t+1)}\left(\underset{+}{r_3}, \underset{-}{\hat{r}_3}, \underset{-}{W3_{t+1}}\right) \tag{9.41}$$

Demand for Bonds Issued in Country Three

The sector's demand for bonds issued in Country Three's bond market is given by

$$\begin{aligned} p_{B3} \cdot B3^d_{PB3(t+1)} &= -\left(\frac{p_{B1}}{\tilde{\varepsilon}}\right) \cdot B1^d_{PB3(t+1)}\left(\underset{+}{r_1}, \underset{-}{r_3}\right) \\ &\quad - \left[\frac{(p_{B2} \cdot \varepsilon)}{\tilde{\varepsilon}}\right] \cdot B2^d_{PB3(t+1)}\left(\underset{+}{r_2}, \underset{-}{r_3}\right) \\ &\quad - X3^d_{PB3(t+1)}\left(\underset{-}{r_3}, \underset{+}{W3_{t+1}}\right) + (1 - \hat{r}_3) \\ &\quad \cdot D3^s_{PB3(t+1)}\left(\underset{+}{r_3}, \underset{-}{\hat{r}_3}, \underset{-}{W3_{t+1}}\right) + NW_{PB3t} \\ &= p_{B3} \cdot B3^d_{PB3(t+1)}\left(\underset{-}{r_1}, \underset{-}{r_2}, \underset{+}{r_3}, \underset{-}{\hat{r}_3}, \underset{-}{W3_{t+1}}, \underset{+1}{NW_{PB3t}}\right) \end{aligned} \tag{9.42}$$

where $NW_{PB3t} = (p_{B1}/\tilde{\varepsilon}) \cdot B1_{PB3t} + [(p_{B2} \cdot \varepsilon)/\tilde{\varepsilon}] \cdot B2_{PB3t} + p_{B3} \cdot B3_{PB2t} + X3_{PB3t} - (1 - \hat{r}_3) \cdot D3_{PB3t}$.

Demand for Current Labor Hours

The sector's demand for current labor hours is given by

$$h_{PB3t} \cdot N3_{PB3t} = \hat{\delta}\left(\underset{+}{\frac{D3_{PB3t}}{p_{R3t}}}, \underset{-}{\frac{X3_{PB3t}}{p_{R3t}}}\right) \tag{9.43}$$

Demand for Workers for Next Period

The sector's demand for workers for next period is given by

$$h3^e_{t+1} \cdot N3^d_{PB3(t+1)}$$

$$= \hat{\phi}\left(\underset{+}{\frac{D3^s_{PB3(t+1)}}{p^e_{R3}}}, \underset{-}{\frac{X3^d_{PB3(t+1)}}{p^e_{R3}}}\right)$$

$$= \hat{\phi}\left(D3^s_{PB3(t+1)}\left(\underset{+}{r3}, \underset{-}{\hat{r}3}, \underset{-}{W3_{t+1}}\right)/p^e_{R3}, X3^d_{PB3(t+1)}\left(\underset{-}{r3}, \underset{+}{W3_{t+1}}\right)/p^e_{R3}\right)$$

$$= h3^e_{t+1} \cdot N3^{PB3}_{t+1}\left(\underset{+}{r3}, \underset{-}{\hat{r}3}, \underset{-}{W3_{t+1}}\right) \quad (9.44)$$

Central Banking (CB3) Sector

The central banking sector in Country Three holds bonds that have been issued by each of the three countries in the model.

Let

$(p_{B1}/\tilde{\varepsilon}) \cdot B1_{CB3t}$ = the value of Country Three's central bank's holdings of Country One's bonds at the beginning of the current period in terms of Country Three's unit of account.

$[(p_{B2} \cdot \varepsilon)/\tilde{\varepsilon}] \cdot B2_{CB3t}$ = the value of Country Three's central bank's holdings of Country Two's bonds at the beginning of the current period in terms of Country Three's unit of account.

$p_{B3} \cdot B3_{CB3t}$ = the value of Country Three's central bank's holdings of Country Three's bonds at the beginning of the current period in terms of Country Three's unit of account.

$MB3_t$ = the value of the monetary base outstanding at the beginning of the current period in Country Three.

NW_{CB3t} = the net wealth of the central bank in Country Three at the beginning of the current period.

The monetary base outstanding in Country Three at the beginning of the current period, $MB3_t$, consists of the coin and currency outstanding at the beginning of the current period in Country Three, $CU3_t$, plus the reserves held by the private banking sector in Country Three at the beginning of the current period, R^*3_t, where reserves consist of the vault cash held by the private banks plus the deposits they hold at their central bank at the beginning of the current period. It is assumed that the private banks only hold vault cash and deposits at their central bank and that these are denominated exclusively in terms of Country Three's unit of account.

From the above definitions, the net wealth of the central bank in Country Three at the beginning of the current period is given by

$$NW_{CB3t} = \left(\frac{p_{B1}}{\tilde{\varepsilon}}\right) \cdot B1_{CB3t} + \left[\frac{(p_{B2} \cdot \varepsilon)}{\tilde{\varepsilon}}\right] \cdot B2_{CB3t} + p_{B3} \cdot B3_{CB3t} - MB3_t \quad (9.45)$$

During the current period, Country Three's central bank earns interest income on all three types of bonds it holds at the beginning of the current period. It is assumed that this interest income is passed along to Country Three's government sector during the period so that the net saving of the central bank during the current period is equal to zero.

$$S_{CB3t} = \left(\frac{1}{\tilde{\varepsilon}}\right) \cdot B1_{CB3t} + \left(\frac{\varepsilon}{\tilde{\varepsilon}}\right) \cdot B2_{CB3t} + B3_{CB3t} - \Pi_{CB3t} = 0 \quad (9.46)$$

where

S_{CB3t} = net business saving by the central bank in Country Three during the current period.
Π_{CB3t} = "dividends" paid by the CB3 sector during the current period to the G3 sector.

Let

$(p_{B1}/\tilde{\varepsilon}) \cdot B1^d_{CB3(t+1)}$ = the value of Country Three's central bank's planned holdings of Country One's bonds at the end of the current period (the CB3 sector's demand for Country One's bonds).
$[(p_{B2} \cdot \varepsilon)/\tilde{\varepsilon}] \cdot B2^d_{CB3(t+1)}$ = the value of Country Three's central bank's demand for Country Two's bonds for the end of the current period in terms of Country Three's unit of account.
$p_{B3} \cdot B3^d_{CB3(t+1)}$ = the value of Country Three's central bank's demand for Country Three's bonds for the end of the current period in terms of Country Three's unit of account.
$MB3^s_{CB3(t+1)}$ = the value of the monetary base outstanding at the end of the current period in Country Three consistent with the plans of Country Three's central bank at the beginning of the current period.
$NW^d_{CB3(t+1)}$ = the net wealth of the central bank in Country Three at the end of the current period in terms of current-period prices.

The planned net wealth of the central bank in Country Three for the end of the current period is given by (9.47):

$$NW^d_{CB3(t+1)} = \left(\frac{p_{B1}}{\tilde{\varepsilon}}\right) \cdot B1^d_{CB3(t+1)} + \left[\frac{(p_{B2} \cdot \varepsilon)}{\tilde{\varepsilon}}\right] \cdot B2^d_{CB3(t+1)} + p_{B3} \cdot B3^d_{CB3(t+1)} - MB3^s_{CB3(t+1)} \quad (9.47)$$

Since the sector presumably does not engage in net saving during the current period, the net wealth in the balance sheet it plans for the end of the current period must equal the net wealth in its beginning-of-period balance sheet when both balance sheets are evaluated in the same set of prices, namely, the prices at which the various bonds trade during the current period. Therefore, (9.48) holds identically:

$$(p_{B1}/\tilde{\varepsilon}) \cdot \left(B1^{d}_{CB3(t+1)} - B1_{CB3t}\right) + \left[\frac{(p_{B2} \cdot \varepsilon)}{\tilde{\varepsilon}}\right] \cdot \left(B2^{d}_{CB3(t+1)} - B2_{CB3t}\right)$$
$$+ p_{B3} \cdot \left(B3^{d}_{CB3(t+1)} - B3_{CB3t}\right) \equiv MB3^{s}_{CB3(t+1)} - MB3_{t} \qquad (9.48)$$

According to the "cash flow restriction" or "budget constraint" specified in (9.48), the central bank in Country Three may arbitrarily decide upon any three of $(p_{B1}/\tilde{\varepsilon}) \cdot B1^{d}_{CB3(t+1)}$, $[(p_{B2} \cdot \varepsilon)/\tilde{\varepsilon}] \cdot B2^{d}_{CB3(t+1)}$, $p_{B3} \cdot B3^{d}_{CB3(t+1)}$, and $MB3^{s}_{CB3(t+1)}$. Once it has chosen the values of any three of these variables, the value of the fourth variable is established by restriction (9.48).

Central Bank Open Market Operations

A decision by the central bank in Country Three to increase its end-of-period holdings of Country Three's bonds, holding constant its planned end-of-period holdings of bonds issued in both Country One and Country Two, is referred to as an open market purchase of bonds by the central bank in Country Three. The level of the monetary base at the end of the period consistent with this plan by the central bank, $MB3^{s}_{CB3(t+1)}$, necessarily increases by the same nominal value, $p_{B3} \cdot B3^{d}_{CB3(t+1)}$. An open market sale of bonds by the CB3 sector refers to a reduction in the sector's planned holdings of bonds at the end of the period, $p_{B3} \cdot B3^{d}_{CB3(t+1)}$, accompanied by an equivalent reduction in the nominal value of the country's monetary base consistent with the plans of the central banking sector, $MB3^{s}_{CB3(t+1)}$.

Central Bank Operations in Country One's Bond Market

A decision by the central bank in Country Three to increase its end-of-period holdings of Country One's bonds, holding constant its planned end-of-period holdings of bonds issued in both Country Two and Country Three, is referred to as a purchase of bonds denominated in Country One's unit of account by the central bank in Country Three. The CB3 sector increases $(p_{B1}/\tilde{\varepsilon}) \cdot B1^{d}_{CB3(t+1)}$. The level of the monetary base at the end of the period consistent with this plan by the central bank, $MB3^{s}_{CB3(t+1)}$, necessarily increases by the same nominal value, measured in terms of Country Three's unit of account. A sale of bonds denominated in Country One's unit of account by the CB3 sector refers to a reduction in the sector's planned holdings of Country One's bonds at the end of the period, $(p_{B1}/\tilde{\varepsilon}) \cdot B1^{d}_{CB3(t+1)}$, accompanied by an equivalent reduction in the nominal value of the country's monetary base consistent with the plans of the central banking sector, $MB3^{s}_{CB3(t+1)}$.

A decision by the central bank in Country Three to increase its end-of-period holdings of Country One's bonds and "sterilize" the transaction means that it increases $(p_{B1}/\tilde{\varepsilon}) \cdot B1^{d}_{CB3(t+1)}$ and simultaneously reduces its end-of-period demand for its own country's bonds by the same amount; it reduces $p_{B3} \cdot B3^{d}_{CB3(t+1)}$. If it decides to sell Country One's bonds and sterilize, it reduces $(p_{B1}/\tilde{\varepsilon}) \cdot B1^{d}_{CB3(t+1)}$ and increases $p_{B3} \cdot B3^{d}_{CB3(t+1)}$ by the same amount to keep its own monetary base unchanged.

Central Bank Operations in Country Two's Bond Market

A decision by the central bank in Country Three to increase its end-of-period holdings of Country Two's bonds, holding constant its planned end-of-period holdings of bonds issued in both Country One and Country Three, is referred to as a purchase of bonds denominated in Country Two's unit of account by the central bank in Country Three. The CB3 sector increases $[(p_{B2} \cdot \varepsilon)/\tilde{\varepsilon}] \cdot B2^{d}_{CB3(t+1)}$. The level of the monetary base at the end of the period consistent with this plan by the central bank, $MB3^{s}_{CB3(t+1)}$, necessarily increases by the same nominal value, measured in terms of Country Three's unit of account. A sale of bonds denominated in Country Three's unit of account by the CB3 sector refers to a reduction in the sector's planned holdings of Country Two's bonds at the end of the period, $[(p_{B2} \cdot \varepsilon)/\tilde{\varepsilon}] \cdot B2^{d}_{CB3(t+1)}$, accompanied by an equivalent reduction in the nominal value of the country's monetary base consistent with the plans of the central banking sector, $MB3^{s}_{CB3(t+1)}$.

A decision by the central bank in Country Three to increase its end-of-period holdings of Country Two's bonds and "sterilize" the transaction means that it increases $[(p_{B2} \cdot \varepsilon)/\tilde{\varepsilon}] \cdot B2^{d}_{CB3(t+1)}$ and simultaneously reduces its end-of-period demand for its own country's bonds by the same amount; it reduces $p_{B3} \cdot B3^{d}_{CB3(t+1)}$. If it decides to sell Country Two's bonds and sterilize, it reduces $[(p_{B2} \cdot \varepsilon)/\tilde{\varepsilon}] \cdot B2^{d}_{CB3(t+1)}$ and increases $p_{B3} \cdot B3^{d}_{CB3(t+1)}$ by the same amount to keep its own monetary base unchanged.

Chapter 10 contains a summary of the wages and prices that are announced by the various manufacturing sectors as well as their production and employment decisions for the current period.

10

Summary of Production, Employment, Wages, and Prices

Market Price of Pollution Allowances

In this section, the excess demands for pollution allowances are specified as a function of the market price of pollution allowances and the parameters (predetermined variables) that the various producers take as given at the beginning of the period. The price of pollution allowances is assumed to be determined at the same time that the individual industries set product prices and wages but before interest rates and exchange rates are established. The excess demands for pollution allowances by the nonrenewable resource industry, the capital goods industry, and the consumption goods industry are added and solved for the market price of pollution allowances that yields a zero aggregate excess demand for allowance. The resulting market price for pollution allowances is then substituted into the production functions and the factor demand functions of the various sectors.

$$\begin{aligned}\Omega^d_{NR} - \Omega_{NRt} &= W^*NR_t(\underset{+}{\varphi}, \underset{+}{I1_t}, \underset{+}{r_1}, \underset{-}{p_w}, \underset{-}{W1_t}, \underset{+}{K_{NRt}}) \\ &\quad - RW^*NR(\underset{-}{r_1}, \underset{+}{p_w}, \underset{-}{\varphi}, \underset{-}{W1_t}) - \Omega_{NRt}\end{aligned}$$

$$\Omega^d_{NR} - \Omega_{NRt} = \Omega^d_{NR}(\underset{+}{\varphi}, \underset{+}{I1_t}, \underset{+}{r_1}, \underset{-}{p_w}, \underset{?}{W1_t}, \underset{+}{K_{NRt}}) \tag{5.51}$$

$$\Omega^d_K - \Omega_{Kt} = W^*K_t\left(\underset{+}{\varphi_K}, \underset{+}{I2_t}, \underset{-}{p^K_{NRt}}, \underset{-}{p_w}, \underset{+}{\kappa}, \underset{+}{\delta}, \underset{+}{K_{Kt}}, \underset{+}{\varepsilon^K}, \underset{-}{W2_t}\right)$$

$$- SW^*K(p_w, \varphi_K, \varepsilon^K, W2_t) - \Omega K_t$$

$$+ \quad + \quad - \quad -$$

$$\Omega_K^d - \Omega_{Kt} = \Omega_K^d \left(\varphi_K, I2_t, p_{NRt}^K, p_w, \kappa, \delta, K_{Kt}, \varepsilon^K, W2_t\right) - \Omega_{Kt} \tag{6.54}$$

$$+ \quad + \quad - \quad\quad - \quad + \quad + \quad + \quad + \quad -$$

$$\Omega_{Ct}^d - \Omega_{Ct} = W^*C_t \left(\varphi_C, I3_t, p_{NRt}^C, p_w, \gamma, \tilde{\varepsilon}^C, W3_t, K_{Ct}, \kappa, \delta\right)$$

$$+ \quad + \quad - \quad\quad - \quad - \quad + \quad - \quad + \quad + \quad +$$

$$- SW^*C_t \left(p_w, \tilde{\varepsilon}^C, W3_t\right)$$

$$+ \quad + \quad -$$

$$= \Omega_{Ct}^d \left(\varphi_{Ct}, I3_t, p_{NRt}^C, p_w, \gamma, \tilde{\varepsilon}^C, W3_t, K_{Ct}, \kappa, \delta\right) - \Omega_{Ct} \tag{7.53}$$

$$+ \quad + \quad - \quad\quad - \quad - \quad + \quad - \quad + \quad + \quad +$$

The market price of pollution allowances (in terms of Country One's unit of account), p_w, is the price at which the market demand for pollution allowances is equal to the total number of pollution allowances issued in the three countries.

$$\Omega_{NR}^d(\varphi, I1_t, r_1, p_w, W1_t, K_{NRt}) + \Omega_K^d \left(\varphi_K, I2_t, p_{NRt}^K, pW, \kappa, \delta, K_{Kt}, \varepsilon^K, W2_t\right)$$

$$+ \; + \; + \; - \quad ? \quad ? \qquad\qquad + \quad + \quad - \quad\quad - \quad + \; + \; + \; + \quad -$$

$$\Omega_{Ct}^d \left(\varphi C, I3_t, p_{NRt}^C, p_w, \gamma, \tilde{\varepsilon}^C, W3_t, K_{Ct}, K, \delta\right) = \Omega_{NRt} + \Omega_{Kt} + \Omega_{Ct} \tag{10.1}$$

$$+ \quad + \quad - \quad\quad - \quad - \quad + \quad - \quad\quad + \quad + \quad +$$

At this juncture in the analysis, the exchange rates between countries and the countries' interest rates have not yet been established for the current period. Therefore, the market demand for pollution allowances depends upon the anticipated values of these variables that each respective industry forms at the beginning of the period.

Summary of Hours Worked, Production, Product Prices, and Wage Rates

This section contains a brief summary of the hours that each employer uses its current employees, the level of production in each industry, the product price announced by each industry, and the wage rate announced by the wage setter (nonrenewable resource, capital goods, and consumption goods industry) in the respective countries. The end-of-period demands for real and financial assets and the end-of-period supplies of financial assets are not determined until after production and pricing decisions are made because they will be influenced by the excess demands/supplies and inventory changes in the markets for the various goods.

Current Labor Hours

The current labor hours used by the government, nonfinancial business, and banking sectors in each country are summarized below.

Country One

The G1 sector's demands for labor hours for waste recycling and treatment, general public services, and infrastructure augmentation during the current period are summarized by (3.2), (3.5), and (3.21):

$$h_{G1t}^{W^*H1} \cdot N1_{G1t} = h_{G1t}^{W^*H1} \cdot N1_{G1t}(\underset{+}{W^*H1}, \underset{-}{\beta_1}) \tag{3.2}$$

$$h_{G1t}^{GH1} \cdot N1_{G1t} = h_{G1t}^{GH1} \cdot N1_{G1t}(\underset{+}{g_{1H1t}}, \underset{-}{K_{G1t}}) \tag{3.5}$$

$$h_{G1t}^{\Delta I} \cdot N1_{G1t} = h_{G1t}^{\Delta I} \cdot N1_{G1t}(\underset{+}{\Delta I1_t}) \tag{3.21}$$

The NR industry's demands for labor hours for transforming natural NR into marketable form and for recycling waste are summarized by (5.42) and (5.43):

$$h_{NR}^{d} = h_{NR}^{d}(\underset{+}{r_1}, \underset{-}{p_w}, \underset{-}{\varphi}, \underset{-}{W1_t}, \underset{+}{I1_t}) \tag{5.42}$$

$$h_{NR}^{w} = h_{NR}^{w}(\underset{-}{r_1}, \underset{+}{p_w}, \underset{-}{\varphi}, \underset{-}{W1_t}) \tag{5.43}$$

The R1 industry's demand for labor hours for transforming natural R1 into marketable form is summarized in (8.41):

$$(h_{R1t} \cdot N1_{R1t})^{d} = (h_{R1t} \cdot N1_{R1t})^{d}(\underset{-}{W1_t}, \underset{+}{W1_{t+1}}, \underset{-}{r_{1t}}) \tag{8.41}$$

The PB1 sector's demand for labor hours during the current period is summarized by (9.6):

$$h_{PB1t} \cdot N1_{PB1t} = \delta\left(\underset{+}{\frac{D1_{PB1t}}{p_{R1t}}}, \underset{-}{\frac{X1_{PB1t}}{p_{R1t}}}\right) \tag{9.6}$$

Country Two

The G2 sector's demands for labor for waste recycling and treatment, general public services, and infrastructure augmentation are summarized by (3.23), (3.25), and (3.28):

$$h_{G2t}^{W^*H2} \cdot N2_{G2t} = h_{G2t}^{W^*H2} \cdot N2_{G2t}(\underset{+}{W^*H2}, \underset{-}{\beta_2}) \tag{3.23}$$

$$h_{G2t}^{GH2} \cdot N2_{G2t} = h_{G2t}^{GH2} \cdot N2_{G2t}(\underset{+}{g_{2H2t}}, \underset{-}{K_{G2t}}) \tag{3.25}$$

$$h_{G2t}^{\Delta I} \cdot N2_{G2t} = h_{G2t}^{\Delta I} \cdot N2_{G2t}(\underset{+}{\Delta I2_t}) \tag{3.28}$$

The K industry's demands for labor hours for transforming NR^T into capital goods and for treating and storing waste are summarized by (6.42) and (6.43):

$$h_{Kt} = h_{Kt}\left(\underset{-}{p_{NRt}^K}, \underset{-}{p_w}, \underset{-}{\kappa}, \underset{-}{\varphi_K}, \underset{+}{\varepsilon^K}, \underset{-}{W2_t}, \underset{+}{I2_t}\right) \tag{6.42}$$

$$h_{Kt}^S = h_{Kt}^S\left(\underset{+}{p_w}, \underset{+}{\varphi_K}, \underset{-}{\varepsilon^K}, \underset{-}{W2_t}\right) \tag{6.43}$$

$$(h_{R2t} \cdot N2_{R2t})^d = (h_{R2t} \cdot N2_{R2t})^d(\underset{-}{W2_t}, \underset{+}{W2_{t+1}}, \underset{-}{r_{2t}}) \tag{8.53}$$

The PB2 sector's demand for labor hours during the current period is summarized by (9.32):

$$h_{PB2t} \cdot N2_{PB2t} = \tilde{\delta}\left(\underset{+}{\frac{D2_{PB2t}}{p_{R2t}}}, \underset{-}{\frac{X2_{PB2T}}{p_{R2t}}}\right) \tag{9.32}$$

Country Three

The G3 sector's demands for labor for waste recycling and treatment, general public services, and infrastructure augmentation are summarized by (3.31), (3.33), and (3.36):

$$h_{G3t}^{W^*H3} \cdot N3_{G3t} = h_{G3t}^{W^*H3} \cdot N3_{G3t}\underset{+}{W^*H3}, \underset{-}{\beta_3}) \tag{3.31}$$

$$h_{G3t}^{GH3} \cdot N3_{G3t} = h_{G3t}^{GH3} \cdot N3_{G3t}(\underset{+}{g_{3H3t}}, \underset{-}{K_{G3t}}) \tag{3.33}$$

$$h_{G3t}^{\Delta I} \cdot N3_{G3t} = h_{G3t}^{\Delta I} \cdot N3_{G3t}(\underset{+}{\Delta I3_t}) \tag{3.36}$$

The C industry's demands for labor hours for transforming NR^T into consumption goods and for treating and storing waste are summarized by (7.41) and (7.42):

$$h_{Ct} = h_{Ct}\left(p^C_{NRt}, p_w, \varphi_C, \gamma, \tilde{\varepsilon}^C, W3_t, I3_t\right) \tag{7.41}$$
$$\qquad - \quad - \quad - \quad - \quad + \quad - \quad -$$

$$h^S_{Ct} = h^S_{Ct}(p_w, \tilde{\varepsilon}^C, W3_t) \tag{7.42}$$
$$\qquad + \quad - \quad -$$

The R3 industry's demand for labor hours for transforming natural R3 into marketable form is summarized in (8.68):

$$(h_{R3t} \cdot N3_{R3t})^d = (h_{R3t} \cdot N3_{R32t})^d(W3_t, W3_{t+1}, r_3) \tag{8.68}$$
$$\qquad - \quad + \quad -$$

The PB3 sector's demand for labor hours during the current period is summarized by (9.43):

$$h_{PB3t} \cdot N3_{PB3t} = \hat{\delta}\left(\frac{D3_{PB3t}}{p_{R3t}}, \frac{X3_{PB3t}}{p_{R3t}}\right) \tag{9.43}$$
$$\qquad + \quad -$$

Production and Waste Generation

The goods and services produced in each country, including recycling and waste treatment and storage, and the wastes generated in each country, including depreciation, are summarized below.

Country One

The value of the G1 sector's contribution to waste disposal and treatment, general public services, and infrastructure augmentation, VA_{G1t}, is given by the sum of the wages paid by the G1 sector and the value of the transformed NR purchased during the current period.

$$\begin{aligned} VA_{G1t} = {} & W1_t \cdot h^{W^*H1}_{G1t} \cdot N1_{G1t} + W1_t \cdot h^{GH1}_{G1t} \cdot N1_{G1t} \\ & + W1_t \cdot h^{\Delta I}_{G1t} \cdot N1_{G1t}(\Delta I1_t) + p_{NRt} \cdot NRG1^T \end{aligned} \tag{10.2}$$

During the current period, the G1 sector generates waste equal to the physical depreciation of its physical capital, $\varepsilon^{G1} \cdot p_{Kt} \cdot \delta \cdot K_{G1t}$, in market value.

The gross production (in terms of mass) of the NR industry during the period is summarized by (5.46):

$$NR^{Ts}_t = \tau_{NR}(I1_t) \cdot T_{NRt}\left[h^d_{NR}(r_1, p_w, \varphi, W1_t, I1_t) \cdot N1_{NRt}, K_{NRt}\right]$$

$$= NR_t^{Ts}(r_1, p_w, \varphi, W1_t, I1_t, K_{NRt}) \qquad (5.46)$$
$$\qquad + \quad - \quad - \quad - \quad + \quad +$$

The waste (in terms of mass), including depreciation, generated by the NR industry is summarized by (5.49):

$$W^*NR_t = \varphi \cdot \tau_{NR}(I1_t) \cdot T_{NRt}\left[h_{NR}^{d}(r_1, p_w, \varphi, W1_t, I1_t), K_{NRt}\right]$$
$$\qquad + \quad - \quad - \quad - \quad + \quad +$$
$$+ \kappa \cdot \delta \cdot K_{NRt} = W^*NR_t(\varphi, I1_t, r_1, p_w, W1_t, K_{NRt}, \kappa, \delta) \qquad (5.49)$$
$$\qquad + \quad + \quad + \quad - \quad - \quad + \quad + \quad +$$

The waste recycled (in mass) by the NR industry is summarized by (5.50):

$$RW^*NR = T_{NRt}^{W}\left[h_{NR}^{W}(r_1, p_w, \varphi, W1_t)\right]$$
$$\qquad - \quad + \quad - \quad -$$
$$= RW^*NR(r_1, p_w, \varphi, W1_t) \qquad (5.50)$$
$$\qquad - \quad + \quad - \quad -$$

Production of the transformed renewable resource (in mass) by the R1 industry during the period is summarized by (8.43):

$$R1_t^T = \tau_{R1}(I1_t)T_{R1t}\left[(h_{R1t} \cdot N1_{R1t})^d(W1_t, W1_{t+1}, r_{1t})\right]$$
$$\qquad - \quad + \quad -$$
$$= R1_{t+1}^{T^*}(I1_t, W1_t, W1_{t+1}, r_{1t}) \qquad (8.43)$$
$$\qquad + \quad - \quad + \quad -$$

The value of the intermediate services provided by the PB1 sector is given by

$$B1_{PB1t} + \varepsilon \cdot B2_{PB1t} + \tilde{\varepsilon} \cdot B3_{PB1t} \qquad (10.3)$$

The value of the intermediate services provided by the CB1 sector is given by

$$B1_{CB1t} + \varepsilon \cdot B2_{CB1t} + \tilde{\varepsilon} \cdot B3_{CB1t} \qquad (10.4)$$

The implicit market value of the mass wasted by the household sector (and either recycled or treated and stored by G1) is summarized by

$$W1_t \cdot h_{G1t}^{W^*H1} \cdot N1_{G1t} \qquad (10.5)$$

Country Two

The value of the G2 sector's contribution to waste disposal and treatment, general public services, and infrastructure augmentation, VA_{G2t}, is given by

$$VA_{G2t} = W2_t \cdot h_{G2t}^{W*H2} \cdot N2_{G2t} + W2_t \cdot h_{G2t}^{GH2} \cdot N2_{G2t} + W2_t \cdot h_{G2t}^{\Delta I} \cdot N2_{G2t}(\Delta I2_t) + \left(\frac{p_{NRt}}{\varepsilon}\right) \cdot NRG2^T \quad (10.6)$$

During the current period, the G2 sector generates waste equal to the physical depreciation of its physical capital, $p_{K_t}^{\cdot}\delta \cdot K_{G1t}$, in market value.

The gross production of the capital goods industry (in units of capital) during the current period is summarized by (6.47):

$$\begin{aligned} K_t^T &= \tau_K(I2_t) \cdot T_{Kt}(h_K \cdot N2_{Kt}, K_{Kt}) \\ &= K_t^T\left(\underset{+}{K_{Kt}}, \underset{+}{I2_t}, \underset{-}{p_t^{NR}}, \underset{-}{p_w}, \underset{-}{\kappa}, \underset{-}{\varphi_K}, \underset{+}{\varepsilon^K}, \underset{-}{W2_t}\right) \end{aligned} \quad (6.47)$$

The waste generated by the sector (in terms of mass) is summarized by (6.52):

$$\begin{aligned} W^*K_t &= \varphi_K \cdot \tau_K(I2_t) \cdot T_{Kt}\left(h_{Kt}\left(\underset{-}{p_t^{NR}}, \underset{-}{p_w}, \underset{-}{\kappa}, \underset{-}{\varphi_K}, \underset{+}{\varepsilon^K}, \underset{-}{W2_t}, \underset{+}{I2_t}\right) \cdot N2_{Kt}, K_{Kt}\right) \\ &\quad + \kappa \cdot \delta \cdot K_{Kt} = W^*K_t\left(\underset{+}{\varphi_K}, \underset{+}{I2_t}, \underset{-}{p_{NRt}^K}, \underset{-}{p_w}, \underset{+}{\kappa}, \underset{+}{\delta}, \underset{+}{K_{Kt}}, \underset{+}{\varepsilon^K}, W2_t\right) \end{aligned} \quad (6.52)$$

The amount of waste treated and stored by the capital goods industry during the current period is given by (6.53):

$$\begin{aligned} SW^*K_t &= T_{Kt}^S\left[h_{Kt}^S\left(\underset{+}{p_w}, \underset{+}{\varphi_K}, \underset{-}{\varepsilon^K}, \underset{-}{W2_t}\right) \cdot N2_{Kt}\right] \\ &= SW^*K\left(\underset{+}{p_w}, \underset{+}{\varphi_K}, \underset{-}{\varepsilon^K}, \underset{-}{W2_t}\right) \end{aligned} \quad (6.53)$$

Production of the transformed renewable resource (in mass) by the R2 industry during the current period is summarized by (8.55):

$$\begin{aligned} R2_t^T &= \tau_{R2}(I2_t) \cdot T_{R2t}\left[(h_{R2t} \cdot N2_{R2t})^d(\underset{-}{W2_t}, \underset{+}{W2_{t+1}}, \underset{-}{r_2})\right] \\ &= R2_{t+1}^{T*}(\underset{+}{I2_t}, \underset{-}{W2t}, \underset{+}{W2_{t+1}}, \underset{-}{r_2}) \end{aligned} \quad (8.55)$$

The value of the intermediate services provided by the PB2 sector is given by

$$\left(\frac{1}{\varepsilon}\right) \cdot B1_{PB2t} + B2_{PB2t} + \left(\frac{\tilde{\varepsilon}}{\varepsilon}\right) \cdot B3_{PB2t} \quad (10.7)$$

The value of the intermediate services provided by the CB2 sector is given by

$$\left(\frac{1}{\varepsilon}\right) \cdot B1_{CB2t} + B2_{CB2t} + \left(\frac{\tilde{\varepsilon}}{\varepsilon}\right) \cdot B3_{CB2t} \tag{10.8}$$

The implicit market value of the mass wasted by the household sector (and either recycled or treated and stored by G2) is summarized by

$$W2_t \cdot h_{G2t}^{W^*H2} \cdot N2_{G2t} \tag{10.9}$$

Country Three

The value of the G3 sector's contribution to waste disposal and treatment, general public services, and infrastructure augmentation, VA_{G3t}, is given by

$$\begin{aligned} VA_{G3t} &= W3_t \cdot h_{G3t}^{W^*H3} \cdot N3_{G3t} + W3_t \cdot h_{G3t}^{GH3} \cdot N3_{G3t} \\ &\quad + W3_t \cdot h_{G3t}^{\Delta I} \cdot N3_{G3t}(\Delta I3_t) + \left(\frac{p_{NRt}}{\tilde{\varepsilon}}\right) \cdot NRG3^T \end{aligned} \tag{10.10}$$

During the current period, the G3 sector generates waste equal to the physical depreciation of its physical capital, $p_{Kt}(\varepsilon/\tilde{\varepsilon}) \cdot \delta \cdot K_{G1t}$, in market value.

The gross production of the consumption goods industry (in units of consumption goods) during the period is summarized by (7.46):

$$\begin{aligned} C_t^T &= \tau(I3_t) \cdot T_{Ct}(h_{Ct} \cdot N3_{Ct}, K_{Ct}) \\ &= C_t^T \left(p_{NRt}^C, p_w, \varphi_C, \gamma, \tilde{\varepsilon}^C, W3_t, I3_t, K_{Ct}\right) \\ &\qquad - \quad - \quad - \quad - + \quad - \quad + \quad + \end{aligned} \tag{7.46}$$

The waste generated by the sector (in terms of mass) is summarized by (7.51):

$$\begin{aligned} W^*C_t &= \varphi_C \cdot \tau(I3_t) \cdot T_{Ct}(h_{Ct} \cdot N3_{Ct}, K_{Ct}) + \kappa \cdot \delta \cdot K_{Ct} \\ &= \varphi_C \cdot \tau(I3_t) \cdot T_{Ct}\left[h_{Ct}\left(p_{NRt}^C, p_w, \varphi_C, \gamma, \tilde{\varepsilon}^C, W3_t, I3_t\right), K_{Ct}\right] \\ &\qquad\qquad - \quad - \quad - - + \quad - \quad + \\ &\quad + \kappa \cdot \delta \cdot K_{Ct} = W^*C_t\left(\varphi_C, I3_t, p_{NRt}^C, p_w, \gamma, \tilde{\varepsilon}^C, W3_t, K_{Ct}, \kappa, \delta\right) \\ &\qquad\qquad + \quad + \quad - \quad - - + \quad - \quad + \quad + + \end{aligned} \tag{7.51}$$

The amount of waste treated and stored by the capital goods industry during the period is given by (7.52):

$$\begin{aligned} SW^*K_t &= T_{Kt}^S\left(h_{Kt}^S\left(p_w, \varphi_K, \varepsilon^K, W2_t\right) \cdot N2_{Kt}\right) \\ &\qquad\qquad + \quad + \quad - \quad - \\ &= SW^*K(p_w, \varphi_K, \varepsilon^K, W2_t) \end{aligned} \tag{6.53}$$

$$+ \quad + \quad - \quad -$$

Production of the transformed renewable resource (in mass) by the R3 industry during the period is summarized by (8.70):

$$\begin{aligned} R3_t^T &= \tau_{R3}(I3_t) \cdot T_{R3t}\left[(h_{R3t} \cdot N3_{R3t})^d(W3_t, W3_{t+1}, r_{3t})\right] \\ &\qquad\qquad\qquad\qquad\qquad - \quad + \quad - \\ &= R3_{t+1}^{T^*}(I3_t, W3t, W3_{t+1}, r_{3t}) \qquad (8.70) \\ &\qquad + \quad - \quad + \quad - \end{aligned}$$

The value of the intermediate services provided by the PB3 sector is given by

$$\left(\frac{1}{\tilde{\varepsilon}}\right) \cdot B1_{PB3t} + \left(\frac{\varepsilon}{\tilde{\varepsilon}}\right) \cdot B2_{PB3t} + B3_{PB3t} \qquad (10.11)$$

The value of the intermediate services provided by the CB3 sector is given by

$$\left(\frac{1}{\tilde{\varepsilon}}\right) \cdot B1_{CB3t} + \left(\frac{\varepsilon}{\tilde{\varepsilon}}\right) \cdot B2_{CB3t} + B3_{CB3t} \qquad (10.12)$$

The implicit market value of the mass wasted by the household sector (and either recycled or treated and stored by G3) is summarized by

$$W3_t \cdot h_{G3t}^{W^*H3} \cdot N3_{G3t} \qquad (10.13)$$

Product Prices

Country One

At the beginning of the current period, the NR industry sets the following price for transformed NR:

$$\begin{aligned} p_{NRt} &= p_{NRt}\Big(\tau_{NR}(I1t) \cdot T_{NRt}\left[h_{NR}^d(r_1, p_w, \varphi, W_t, I1_t) \cdot N1_{NRt}, K_{NRt}\right] \\ &\qquad + NR_t^{T^*}, \omega_{NR,K}, \omega_{NR,C}, NRG1_t^{Tde} + NRG2_t^{Tde} + NRG3_t^{Tde}\Big) \\ &= p_{NRt}\Big(r_1, p_w, \varphi, W_t, I1_t, K_{NRt}, NR_t^{T^*}, \omega_{NR,K}, \omega_{NR,C}, NRG1_t^{Tde} \\ &\qquad - \quad + \; + \quad + \quad - \quad - \quad - \quad + \quad + \\ &\qquad + NRG2_t^{Tde} + NRG3_t^{Tde}\Big) \qquad (5.47) \\ &\qquad + \end{aligned}$$

At the beginning of the current period, the R1 industry sets the following price for its product:

$$p_{R1t} = p_{R1t}\Big(\tau_{R1}(I1_t) \cdot T_{R1t}\left[(h_{R1t} \cdot N1_{R1t})^d(W1_t, W1_{t+1}, r_1)\right]$$

$$-R1^{T^*d}_{t+1}(r_1) + R1^{T^*}_t, \omega_{H1}, N1_t\Big)$$

$$= p_{R1t}\Big(I1_t, W1_t, W1_{t+1}, r_1, R1^{T^*}_t, \omega_{R1H11}, N1_t\Big) \tag{8.45}$$

$$\quad - \quad + \quad - \quad + \quad - \quad + \quad +$$

Country Two

At the beginning of the current period, the capital goods industry sets the following price for its product:

$$p_{Kt} = p_{Kt}\Big(K^{de}_t, \omega_{KNR}, \omega_{KC}, KG1^{de}_t + KG2^{de}_t + KG3^{de}_t\Big)$$

$$\quad - \quad + \quad + \quad +$$

$$= p_{Kt}\Big(K_{Kt}, I2_t, p^K_{NRt}, p_w, \kappa, \varphi_K, \varepsilon^K, W2_t, r_2, \delta, \omega_{KNR}, \omega_{KC}, KG1^{de}_t$$

$$\quad - \quad - \quad + \quad + \; + \; + \quad - \quad + \quad - \; + \quad + \quad +$$

$$+KG2^{de}_t + KG3^{de}_t\Big) \tag{6.50}$$

$$+$$

The renewable resource industry in Country Two sets the following price for its product:

$$p_{R2t} = p_{R2t}\Big(\tau_{R2}(I2_t) \cdot T_{R2t}\Big[(h_{R2t} \cdot N2_{R2t})^d(W2_t, W2_{t+1}, r_2)\Big]$$

$$-R2^{T^*d}_{t+1}(r_2) + R2^{T^*}_t, \omega_{R2H2}, N2_t\Big)$$

$$= p_{R2t}\Big(I2_t, W2_t, W2_{t+1}, r_2, R2^{T^*}_t, \omega_{R2H2}, N2_t\Big) \tag{8.59}$$

$$\quad - \quad + \quad - \quad + \quad - \quad + \quad +$$

Country Three

At the beginning of the current period, the consumption goods industry sets the following price for its product:

$$p_{Ct} = p_{Ct}\Big(C^{de}_t, \omega_{CH1}, \omega_{CH2}, \omega_{CH3}\Big)$$

$$\quad - \quad + \quad + \quad +$$

$$= p_{Ct}\Big(p^C_{NRt}, p_w, \varphi_C, \gamma, \tilde{\varepsilon}^C, W3_t, I3_t, K_{Ct}, C_{Ct}, \omega_{CH1}, \omega_{CH2}, \omega_{CH3}\Big)$$

$$\quad + \quad + \quad + \; + \; - \quad + \quad - \quad - \quad - \quad + \quad + \quad +$$

The renewable resource industry in Country Three sets the following price for its product at the beginning of the current period:

$$\begin{aligned} p_{R3t} &= p_{R3t}\left(\tau_{R3}(I3_t)\cdot T_{R3t}\left[(h_{R3t}\cdot N3_{R3t})^{d}(W3_t, W3_{t+1}, r_3)\right]\right.\\ &\quad \left. - R3^{T^{*}d}_{t+1}(r_3) + R3^{T^{*}}_{t}, \omega_{R3H3}, N3_t\right)\\ &= p_{R3t}\left(\underset{-}{I3_t}, \underset{+}{W3_t}, \underset{-}{W3_{t+1}}, \underset{+}{r_3}, \underset{-}{R3^{T^{*}}_{t}}, \underset{+}{\omega_{R3H3}}, \underset{+}{N3_t}\right) \end{aligned} \tag{8.74}$$

Wage Rates

Country One

At the beginning of the current period, the nonrenewable resource industry sets the wage rate to be paid in Country One next period:

$$W1_{t+1} = W1\left(\underset{-}{p_w}, \underset{-}{\gamma_{NR}}, \underset{?}{\varphi}, \underset{?}{r_1}, \underset{+}{p^{NR}_{Kt}\cdot \varepsilon^{e}_{NR}}, \underset{+}{K_{NRt}}, \underset{-}{I1_t}, \underset{-}{\Delta I1_t}\right) \tag{5.48}$$

Country Two

At the beginning of the current period, the capital goods industry sets the wage rate to be paid in Country Two next period:

$$\begin{aligned} W2_{t+1} &= W2\left\{N2^{Te}_{K(t+1)}\left(\underset{-}{p_w}, \underset{-}{\kappa}, \underset{-}{\varphi_K}, \underset{+}{\varepsilon^{K}}\right) + N2^{Se}_{K(t+1)}\left(\underset{+}{p_w}, \underset{-}{\varepsilon^{K}}\right), \gamma_2\right\}\\ &= W2\left(\underset{-}{p_w}, \underset{-}{\gamma}, \underset{-}{\varphi_K}, \underset{+}{\varepsilon^{K}}, \underset{+}{\gamma_2}\right) \end{aligned} \tag{6.51}$$

Country Three

At the beginning of the current period, the consumption goods industry sets the wage rate to be paid in Country Three next period:

$$\begin{aligned} W3_{t+1} &= W3\left(\underset{+}{N3^{Se}_{t+1}}, \underset{+}{\gamma_3}\right)\\ &= W3\left[N3^{Te}_{C(t+1)}\left(\underset{-}{p_w}, \underset{+}{\tilde{\varepsilon}^{C}}, \underset{-}{\varphi_C}, \underset{-}{\gamma}\right) + N3^{Se}_{C(t+1)}\left(\underset{+}{p_w}, \underset{-}{\tilde{\varepsilon}^{C}}\right), \gamma_3\right] \end{aligned}$$

$$= W3\left(\underset{-}{p_W}, \underset{+}{\tilde{\varepsilon}^C}, \underset{-}{\varphi_C}, \underset{-}{\gamma}, \underset{+}{\gamma_3}\right) \tag{7.50}$$

Chapter 11 contains a specification of the conventional and green measures of national and world income and product for the present model.

11

Conventional and Green Measures of Income and Product

Value Added by Sector (in Terms of Market Transactions), VA-M

The value added by a sector in terms of market transactions is measured on the "product-originating" side by the value of the sector's production of marketable goods minus the sector's purchases of intermediate goods and services from other sectors. The value of the sector's production of marketable goods includes its sales to other sectors plus the changes in its inventories of marketable intermediate and final goods. VA-M is measured on the "income-originating" side by the factor and nonfactor costs of producing its marketable product. Income originating in the sector includes the wages, interest, depreciation, and profits generated by the sector's production of marketable goods.

In the present model, the household sectors do not produce value added in terms of market transactions. (In fact, as will be shown, these sectors produce negative *net* value added.) The government sectors do produce value added in terms of the sanitation services they provide their households, the infrastructure services they provide their agricultural and manufacturing sectors, and the general public services they provide their households. All business sectors (including the private banks and the central bank) also produce value added in this model.

Net business saving associated with market transactions is defined as a business sector's profits minus depreciation and minus its dividends paid, that is, as the sector's undistributed corporate profits. In the present framework, a sector's net business saving associated with market transactions must be allocated to a net change in its capital goods plus changes in its inventories of intermediate and final goods net of the change in the sector's liabilities (table 11.1).

Table 11.1 Value Added—Market—by Business Sectors

Wages	Sales
Interest paid to households	Change in inventory of market goods
Pollution allowances Purchased (net)	Subsidies received from government
	– Purchases of intermediate goods (includes interest paid to other countries)
Depreciation of K	
Dividends	– Business taxes
Market Income Originating (IO-M)	Market Product Originating (VA-M)

Table 11.2 Value Added—Market—by Government Sectors

Wages	Business taxes
Interest paid to household	Sanitation taxes
Depreciation of K	Taxes for general public services
	– Subsidies to Renewable resource industries
	– Government saving
	– Purchases of NR
Market Income Originating in Government Sector (IO-M-G)	Market Product Originating in Government Sector (VA-M-G)

The government sectors do not pay dividends. Consequently, government saving (net) corresponds to a government sector's revenue minus its current expenses (including depreciation). Government saving also necessarily equals the net change in the sector's capital goods minus the net change in its liabilities between the beginning and the end of the period (measured in terms of current-period prices) (table 11.2).

Country One

R1 Sector

The product originating in the R1 sector associated with market transactions, VA-M-R1, is equal to its sales of transformed R1 plus the subsidies it receives from the G1 sector plus the change in its inventories of transformed R1 minus the interest it pays to other sectors for intermediate services (i.e., other than to the H1 sector) minus taxes it pays to the G1 sector for services of infrastructure. The income originating in the R1 sector associated with market transactions, IO-M-R1, is equal to the wages the sector pays plus interest it pays to the H1 sector plus the dividends it pays to the H1 sector plus its net business saving. Income originating, IO-M-R1, is equal to product originating, VA-M-R1.

If it is assumed that net business saving by the R1 sector is equal to zero, then the change in physical capital held by the R1 sector (after depreciation) plus the changes in its inventories of intermediate goods and final goods (transformed R1) must equal the market value of the change in its outstanding bonds between the beginning and the end of the period.

NR Sector

The product originating in the NR sector associated with market transactions, VA-M-NR, is equal to sales of transformed NR plus the change in the inventory of transformed NR minus the interest paid to sectors other than H1 for intermediate services minus taxes paid to the G1 sector for services of infrastructure.

The income originating in the NR sector, IO-M-NR, is equal to the wages paid by the sector plus the interest it pays to the H1 sector plus its dividends to the H1 sector plus depreciation plus its net business saving. Income originating in the NR sector is equal to product originating in that sector. If it is assumed that net business saving is equal to zero, then the changes in inventories of physical capital and processed NR will be equal to the market value of the change in the sector's outstanding debt between the beginning and the end of the period.

G1 Sector

The product originating in the G1 sector associated with market transactions, VA-M-G1, is equal to the tax revenue it receives from R1 and NR for the services of infrastructure plus the taxes it receives from the H1 sector for sanitation and general public services minus the subsidy it pays to the R1 sector for maintaining a minimum stock of unharvested R1 minus the purchases of transformed NR by the G1 sector and minus the interest G1 pays to sectors other than H1, but plus the dividends it receives from the CB1 sector.

The income originating in the G1 sector associated with market transactions is equal to the wages paid by the sector plus the interest paid to the H1 sector plus government saving. Government saving by G1 is equal to the net increase in physical capital held by the government sector minus additional government borrowing. Income originating in the G1 sector, IO-M-G1, is equal to the product originating, VA-M-G1, in that sector.

PB1 Sector

The product originating in the PB1 sector, VA-M-PB1, is equal to the interest the sector receives from all other sectors. The income originating in the PB1 sector, IO-M-PB1, consists of the wages it pays its employees plus the dividends it pays the H1 sector plus its net business saving. If it is assumed that net business saving is equal to zero, then the market value of the PB1 sector's holdings of bonds issued in all three countries plus the change in its reserves during the period is equal to the change in its deposit liabilities during the period.

CB1 Sector

The product originating in the CB1 sector, VA-M-CB1, is defined by the interest it receives from all other sectors. The income originating in the CB1 sector, IO-M-CB1, is equal to the dividends paid to the G1 sector. Income originating in the CB1 sector is equal to the product originating in that sector. If net business saving by the CB1 sector is equal to zero, then the change in the monetary base—consisting of the change in reserves plus the change in coin and currency outstanding—is equal to the market value of the changes in the CB1 sector's holdings of bonds issued in all three countries.

Country Two

R2 Sector

The product originating in the R2 sector associated with market transactions, VA-M-R2, is equal to its sales of transformed R2 plus the subsidies it receives from the G2 sector plus the change in its inventories of transformed R2 minus the interest it pays to other sectors for intermediate services (i.e., other than to the H2 sector) minus taxes it pays to the G2 sector for services of infrastructure.

The income originating in the R2 sector associated with market transactions, IO-M-R2, is equal to the wages the sector pays plus interest it pays to the H2 sector plus the dividends it pays to the H2 sector plus its net business saving. Income originating, IO-M-R2, is equal to product originating, VA-M-R2.

If it is assumed that net business saving by the R2 sector is equal to zero, then the change in physical capital held by the R2 sector (after depreciation) plus the changes in its inventories of intermediate goods and final goods (transformed R2) must equal the market value of the change in its outstanding bonds between the beginning and the end of the period.

K Sector

The product originating in the K sector in association with market transactions, VA-M-K, is equal to the sales of physical capital by that sector plus the change in its inventories of physical capital minus interest paid to sectors (other than the H2) for intermediate services minus taxes paid to the G2 sector for services of infrastructure. The corresponding income originating in the K sector, IO-M-K, is equal to wages plus interest plus dividends plus depreciation plus its net business saving. If it is assumed that net business saving is equal to zero, then the changes in the sector's holdings of capital goods during the period is equal to the market value of the change in its debt outstanding during the period.

G2 Sector

The product originating in the G2 sector associated with market transactions, VA-M-G2, is equal to the tax revenue it receives from R2 and K for the services of infrastructure plus the taxes it receives from the H2 sector for sanitation and general public services minus the subsidy it pays to the R2 sector for maintaining a minimum stock of unharvested R2 minus the purchases of transformed NR by the G2 sector and minus the interest G2 pays to sectors other than H2, but plus the dividends it receives from the CB2 sector.

The income originating in the G2 sector associated with market transactions is equal to the wages paid by the sector plus the interest paid to the H2 sector plus government saving. Government saving by G2 is equal to the net increase in physical capital held by the government sector minus additional government borrowing. Income originating in the G2 sector, IO-M-G2, is equal to the product originating, VA-M-G2, in that sector.

PB2 Sector

The product originating in the PB2 sector, VA-M-PB2, is equal to the interest the sector receives from all other sectors. The income originating in the PB2 sector, IO-M-PB2, consists of the wages it pays its employees plus the dividends it pays the H2 sector plus its net business saving. If it is assumed that net business saving is equal to zero, then the market value of the PB2 sector's holdings of bonds issued in all three countries plus the change in its reserves during the period is equal to the change in its deposit liabilities during the period.

CB2 Sector

The product originating in the CB2 sector, VA-M-CB2, is defined by the interest it receives from all other sectors. The income originating in the CB2 sector, IO-M-CB2, is equal to the dividends paid to the G2 sector. Income originating in the CB2 sector is equal to the product originating in that sector. If net business saving by the CB2 sector is equal to zero, then the change in the monetary base—consisting of the change in reserves plus the change in coin and currency outstanding—is equal to the market value of the changes in the CB2 sector's holdings of bonds issued in all three countries.

Country Three

R3 Sector

The product originating in the R3 sector associated with market transactions, VA-M-R3, is equal to its sales of transformed R3 plus the subsidies it receives from the G3 sector plus the change in its inventories of transformed R3 minus the interest it pays to other sectors for intermediate services (i.e., other than to the H3 sector) minus taxes it pays to the G3 sector for services of infrastructure.

The income originating in the R3 sector associated with market transactions, IO-M-R3, is equal to the wages the sector pays plus interest it pays to the H3 sector plus the dividends it pays to the H3 sector plus its net business saving. Income originating, IO-M-R3, is equal to product originating, VA-M-R3.

If it is assumed that net business saving by the R3 sector is equal to zero, then the change in physical capital held by the R3 sector (after depreciation) plus the changes in its inventories of intermediate goods and final goods (transformed R3) must equal the market value of the change in its outstanding bonds between the beginning and the end of the period.

C Sector

The product originating in the C sector associated with market transactions, VA-M-C, is equal to its sales of consumption goods during the period plus the change in its inventory of C goods minus interest paid to sectors other than H1 for intermediate services minus taxes paid to G3 for the services of infrastructure. The income originating in the C sector associated with market transactions, IO-M-C, is equal to the wages it pays plus the interest it pays the H3 sector plus the dividends it pays plus depreciation plus its net business saving. If it is assumed that net business saving is equal to zero, then the market value of the change in the sector's inventory of consumption goods plus the change in its holdings of physical capital is equal to the change in its debt outstanding during the period.

G3 Sector

The product originating in the G3 sector associated with market transactions, VA-M-G3, is equal to the tax revenue it receives from R3 and C industries for the services of infrastructure plus the taxes it receives from the H3 sector for sanitation and general public services minus the subsidy it pays to the R3 sector for maintaining a minimum stock of unharvested R3 minus the purchases of transformed NR by the G3 sector and minus the interest G3 pays to sectors other than H3, but plus the dividends it receives from the CB3 sector.

The income originating in the G3 sector associated with market transactions is equal to the wages paid by the sector plus the interest paid to the H3 sector plus government saving. Government saving by G3 is equal to the net increase in physical capital held by the government sector minus additional government borrowing. Income originating in the G3 sector, IO-M-G3, is equal to the product originating, VA-M-G3, in that sector.

PB3 Sector

The product originating in the PB3 sector, VA-M-PB3, is equal to the interest the sector receives from all other sectors. The income originating in the PB3 sector, IO-M-PB3, consists of the wages it pays its employees plus the dividends it pays the H3 sector plus its net business saving. If it is assumed that net business saving is equal to zero, then the market value of the PB3 sector's holdings of bonds issued in all three countries plus the change in its reserves during the period is equal to the change in its deposit liabilities during the period.

CB3 Sector

The product originating in the CB3 sector, VA-M-CB3, is defined by the interest it receives from all other sectors. The income originating in the CB3 sector, IO-M-CB3, is equal to the dividends paid to the G3 sector. Income originating in the CB3 sector is equal to the product originating in that sector. If net business saving by the CB3 sector is equal to zero, then the change in the monetary base—consisting of the change in reserves plus the change in coin and currency outstanding—is equal to the market value of the changes in the CB3 sector's holdings of bonds issued in all three countries.

Conventional Net National Product and National Income by Country

The conventional measure of net national product, NNP, corresponds to the sum of VA-M for each sector in the present study minus the sum of depreciation of capital goods for each sector. The conventional measure of national income, NI, corresponds to the sum of IO-M for each sector in the present study minus the sum of depreciation of capital goods for each sector. In this study, personal income corresponds to national income minus government saving (net business saving is assumed to equal zero). Disposable income corresponds to personal income minus personal taxes for both sanitation and general public services (table 11.3).

Conventional Net World Product and World Income

Net world product arbitrarily measured in terms of Country One's unit of account is defined as the sum of the net national products of all three countries, measured in that unit of account:

$$\mathrm{NWP} = \mathrm{NNP}_1 + \varepsilon \cdot \mathrm{NNP}_2 + \tilde{\varepsilon}\mathrm{NNP}_3$$

World income, arbitrarily measured in terms of Country One's unit of account, is defined as the sum of the national incomes of all three countries, measured in that unit of account:

$$\mathrm{WI} = \mathrm{NI}_1 + \varepsilon \cdot \mathrm{NI}_2 + \tilde{\varepsilon} \cdot \mathrm{NI}_3$$

Table 11.3 Net National Product—Market—and National Income

Wages	Sales to domestic households, sales of capital goods, sales to the domestic government sector, and sales to foreigners (other than capital goods)
Interest paid to households	minus Imports(includes net interest paid)
Dividends	minus Depreciation of K
	plus Change in inventory (NR, K, C)
	plus Personal taxes (for sanitation and other public services)
	minus Government purchases of NR
National income = IO-M minus depreciation of K	Net National Product—Market = VA-M (conventional) minus depreciation of K

Values Added and Incomes Originating: Imputed and Net (by Sector)

As discussed above, the value added by a sector is equal to the value of the goods/services produced by that sector minus the value of the intermediate goods and services it purchases from other sectors. As defined here, *net* value added by a sector, NVA, consists of both a market and a nonmarket component. Net value added by a sector in terms of market transactions, NVA-M, is equal to its value added minus the value of the waste generated (including depreciation) by that sector net of the waste recycled or treated and stored by that sector. To the extent that a sector recycles, it adds value by reclaiming/restoring a resource; to the extent that a sector treats and stores waste, it adds value by reducing the toxicity of waste that would otherwise emerge as pollution and would thereby reduce the ability of the basic fungible resource to provide nutrients to the renewable resources. Imputed net value added, NVA-I, represents the nonmarket component of net value added. It consists of the imputed value of the nonmarket production of renewable resources by a sector net of the imputed value of the sector's consumption of renewable and nonrenewable resources. NVA for a sector is equal to the sum of its NVA-M and NVA-I.

The net values added by the households are negative (assuming the R1, R2, and R3 are explicit industries separate from the household sector), since the households produce waste without adding value to goods and services within the sector. The net values added by the government sectors are equal to the value of the waste they recycle and treat and store plus the value of the other health and human services they provide plus the value of the augmentation in the countries' infrastructures during the period. The tax and nontax revenue they receive minus current government saving serves as a means of imputing the value of these goods and services. In the factor income account, the government pays wages and interest and also pays a subsidy to its renewable resource industry for maintaining a minimum stock of that resource. The net values added by the central banks correspond to their values added and are imputed by the interest income they receive. The factor incomes they generate consist of the dividends they pay to their respective government sectors. The net values added by private banks also correspond to their values added. Both measures are equal to the interest incomes the sectors receive with their factor payments consisting of wages and dividends. The net values added by the nonfinancial business sectors are equal to the value of production minus (1) the value of intermediate goods they purchase from other firms; (2) the value of waste they generate (including depreciation) net of waste they recycle or treat and store (with the imputed value of the net amount of waste generated given by the value of the pollution allowances purchased); and (3) the sector's consumption of nonmarketable renewable and nonrenewable resources. The income payments associated with their net values added, defined here as net income originating, NIO, are equal to wages, interest, taxes, and dividends plus the imputed value of nonmarket production minus pollution allowances purchased and minus the imputed value of nonmarket consumption.

In this section the "net values added" (NVA) by the various governmental, household, financial, and nonfinancial business sectors are specified together with the corresponding "net incomes originating" (NIO) in those sectors.

NVA for a given sector is defined here as the sum of "net value added in terms of marketed goods and services, NVA-M," for that sector and its "imputed net value added in terms of nonmarketed goods and services, NVA-I."

NVA-M is defined here as the "value added in terms of market transactions, VA-M"—defined in the section entitled "Value Added by Sector (in Terms of Market Transactions), VA-M" above—minus the market value of waste generated (which includes depreciation of capital goods) net of waste recycled, or treated and stored by that sector. Therefore, NVA-M corresponds to VA-M minus the value of pollution allowances purchased (or plus the value of pollution allowances sold) by the sector.

NVA-I is defined here as the imputed value of the sector's nonmarket production minus the imputed value of its nonmarket consumption.

NIO is defined here as the net income earned by the factors of production in producing NVA. It consists of the "income-originating in terms of market transactions, IO-M," as defined above in the section entitled "Value Added by Sector (in Terms of Market Transactions), VA-M" minus the value of pollution allowances purchased (which includes depreciation of capital goods held by the sector) plus the "imputed net income from nonmarket activities."

For the business sectors, net income associated with market transactions corresponds to NVA-M on the product side and consists of the sum of profits, wages, interest paid to households minus the pollution credits purchased (net). Imputed net income associated with nonmarket activities corresponds to the imputed value added from nonmarket activities on the production side (or imputed net investment in terms of nonmarket activities), NVA-I. For households, imputed net income associated with nonmarket activity is negative and equal to the waste generated by the household sector. The imputed value of this waste is equal to the expenditure by the government in that country upon sanitation services (tables 11.4, 11.5, 11.6, and 11.7).

Table 11.4 Net Value Added—Market—and Net Income Originating

NIO-M = IO-M minus pollution allowances purchased (net)	NVA-M = VA-M minus value of waste generated net of waste recycled or treated and stored

Table 11.5 Net Value Added—Imputed—Business Sectors

Change in R industries' stock of unharvested R minus Imputed value of NR sector's consumption of NR	Change in R industries' stock of unharvested R minus Imputed value of NR sector's consumption of NR
Imputed net income originating in business sector	Imputed net value added in business sector

Table 11.6 Net Value Added—Imputed—Household Sectors

Waste generated in household sector (imputed value = cost to G sector of recycling or treating and storing this waste = sanitation taxes)	Waste generated in household sector (imputed value = cost to G sector of recycling or treating and storing this waste = sanitation taxes)
Imputed net income originating In household sector	Imputed net value added In household sector

Table 11.7 Net Value Added and Net Income Originating

NIO = NIO-M plus imputed value of nonmarket production minus imputed value of nonmarket consumption	NVA = NVA-M plus NVA-I = NVA-M plus imputed value of non-market production minus imputed value of nonmarket consumption

Net Values Added and Net Incomes Originating for Country One

Household Sector in Country One

NVA by Household Sector in Country One The NVA of household sector in Country One is negative and is equal to the imputed value of the pollution generated by the sector, that is, the estimated charge of the amount that would need to be spent (by the government sector) to recycle, treat, and/or store the waste generated by the households. At the beginning of the current period, this also corresponds to the taxes the government sector levies during the period to pay for the recycling, treatment, and storage of human waste.

$$NVA_{H1} = -Tx_{W^{*}G1t}$$

Net Income Originating in H1

$$NIO_{H1} = -W1_t \cdot h_t^{W^{*}G1} \cdot N1_t \text{ or } -Tx_{W^{*}G1t}.$$

Government Sector in Country One

NVA by Government Sector in Country One The NVA of the government sector in Country One is equal to the imputed value of the waste recycled, treated, and stored by the sector; the imputed value of the other health and human services provided by that sector; and the imputed value of the additions to the country's infrastructure by that sector. The interest paid by a government, to the extent that it is paid to other businesses, represents the value of intermediate services purchased by the government. The subsidy that the government pays the renewable resource industry also represents intermediate services purchased by the government from the

R1 industry, an intermediate service. The tax revenue the government receives minus current interest and subsidies serves as a means of imputing the value of the goods and services it provides. The deficit incurred by the government during the period also represents value added because the expenses by the government for the services it provides exceeds the taxes it receives.

$$\begin{aligned}NVA_{G1} &= Tx_{G1t} - \left(B1_{G1t}\text{minus interest paid to H1}\right)\\ &\quad + \text{deficit} - p^{G1}_{xt} \cdot \overline{R1}_t + \Pi_{CB1t}\end{aligned}$$

where

$Tx_{G1t} = Tx_{W*G1t} + Tx_{G1H1t} + Tx_{G1I1t}$.
Tx_{W*G1t} = taxes the G1 sector levies on the H1 sector to recycle, treat, and store human waste.
Tx_{G1H1t} = the (predetermined) tax revenue the G1 sector collects during the current period associated with health and human services the H1 sector elected last period to receive during the current period.
Tx_{G1H1t} = the level of corporate taxes the G1 sector announces at the beginning of the current period = $Tx_{NRG1} + Tx_{R1G1}$.

Net Income Originating in G1 On the factor income account, the government pays wages and interest to the households. To the extent that the government receives dividends from the central bank, it is able to pay workers more than the value of the services provided by the government. To the extent that the government saves (runs a deficit), it pays its employees less than (more than) the value of the services provided by the government:

$$NIO_{G1} = W1_t \cdot h_t^{W^*G1} \cdot N1_{G1t} + W1_t \cdot h_t^{g1H1} \cdot N1_{G1t} + W1_t \cdot h_t^{G1I1} \cdot N1_{G1t}$$

Nonrenewable Resource Industry

NVA by Nonrenewable Resource Industry The NVA by the nonrenewable resource industry consists of the net value of the marketable nonrenewable resource it produces minus the imputed value (opportunity cost) of the "raw" nonrenewable resource it extracts/mines and minus the value of the waste the industry generates (including depreciation of capital) net of the waste the industry recycles. The net value of production of the nonrenewable resource industry is equal to the value of the marketable resource produced, $p_{NRt} \bullet NR_t^{Ts}$, minus the value of the intermediate services the sector buys. In this model, the NR sector buys the intermediate services of the country's infrastructure by paying taxes to the government sector. In addition it buys intermediate services from other business sectors equal to the amount of interest it pays to other sectors minus the interest it pays the H1 sector. Therefore, the net value ot the marketable nonrenewable resource it produces is given by

$p_{NRt} \bullet NR_t^{Ts} - Tx_{NRG1}$ – ($B1_{NRt}$ minus interest paid to H1). The imputed value of the nonrenewable resource extracted is a more complicated expression.

The first-order condition for current labor hours devoted to the mining and extraction of the nonrenewable resource and its transformation into a marketable product is given by (5.38):

$$\begin{aligned}
\frac{\partial\left[\dfrac{\Pi^{d}_{NR(t+1)}}{(1+r_{1t})}+\Pi^{d}_{NRt}\right]}{\partial h_{NR}} &\equiv \left[\frac{1}{(1+r_{1t})}\right]\cdot\left[\frac{\partial TR^{NRe}_{t+1}}{\partial T^{Te}_{NR(t+1)}}\right]\cdot\Bigg\{-(1+\varphi)\cdot\tau_{NR}(I1_t)\\
&\quad\cdot\left[\frac{\partial T_{NRt}}{\partial(h_{NR}\cdot N1_{NRt})}\right]\Bigg\}\cdot N1_{NRt}\\
&\quad+\left[\frac{1}{(1+r_{1t})}\right]\cdot p_w\cdot\varphi\cdot\tau_{NR}(I1_t)\cdot\left[\frac{\partial T_{NRt}}{\partial(h_{NR}\cdot N1_{NRt})}\right]\cdot N1_{NRt}\\
&\quad-\left[\frac{1}{(1+r_{1t})}\right]\cdot\left[\frac{\partial\bar{C}}{\partial N1^{Te}_{NR(t+1)}}\right]\cdot\left[\frac{\partial N1^{Te}_{NR(t+1)}}{\partial(h_{NR}\cdot N1_{NRt})}\right]\cdot N1_{NRt}\\
&\quad+\left[\frac{\partial TR^{NRe}_{t}}{\partial T_{NRt}}\right]\cdot\tau_{NR}(I1_t)\cdot\left[\frac{\partial T_{NRt}}{\partial(h_{NR}\cdot N1_{NRt})}\right]\cdot N1_{NRt}\\
&\quad-p_w\cdot\varphi\cdot\tau_{NR}(I1_t)\cdot\left[\frac{\partial T_{NRt}}{\partial(h_{NR}\cdot N1_{NRt})}\right]\cdot N1_{NRt}-W1_t\cdot N1_{NRt}=0
\end{aligned} \tag{5.38}$$

According to (5.38), the nonrenewable resource industry will plan to add labor hours for the purpose of producing marketable NR during the period up to the point at which the present value of the marginal reduction in next period's net income is equal to the marginal increase in the current period's net income associated with adding an hour of labor to NR production this period. According to the first term on the right-hand side of the identity symbol in (5.38), as the industry adds a unit of labor to mine and extract a unit of NR this period, it reduces next period's anticipated revenue since the industry will have less NR available to market next period. A portion of the loss in next period's revenue is due to the extra waste generated during the current period associated with the mining and extraction of the resource. The second term on the right-hand side of (5.38) takes into account the fact that by having less NR available to extract/mine next period, the sector's cost of pollution allowances will fall, which reduces the cost next period of using more labor this period and therefore increases the present value of the sector's anticipated income stream to its owners. The third term on the right-hand side of (5.38) is also positive, indicating that if the sector has less available to produce next period, it will cut back on the number of employees it requires next period to mine and extract NR, thereby conserving next period's wage expense. Assuming that the sum of the first three terms is negative, the NR industry expects that next period's net income and therefore the present value of that income will decrease as the sector adds more labor hours in the current period. The fourth term on the right-hand side of (5.38) represents the current-period marginal revenue product from adding an extra unit of labor to the mining and extraction of NR this period. The fifth term represents the increase in the cost of obtaining pollution allowances for the extra waste generated in the process of producing more NR this period. The last term represents the extra wage expense this period of using an extra hour of labor. The value of the nonrenewable resource extracted/mined (consumed) during the current period is the opportunity cost of consuming that resource during the current period, namely, the present value of the net income the currently consumed resource could instead earn in the future if it were left unconsumed during the current period. From (5.38), the present value maximizing nonrenewable resource industry extracts the resource up to the point at which the net income from the extraction of the last unit of that resource during the current period is equal to the present value of the forgone future net income. Therefore, the marginal imputed value of a unit of the nonrenewable resource consumed during the current period may be taken to be $[\partial TR_t^{NRe}/\partial T_{NRt}] - pw \cdot \varphi - W1_t/\tau_{NR}(I1_t) \cdot [\partial T_{NRt}/\partial(h_{NR} \cdot N1_{NRt})]$, since this difference represents the current marginal net income from the consumption of a unit of the nonrenewable resource during the current period, with the marginal revenue of the current consumption given by $[\partial TR_t^{NRe}/\partial T_{NRt}]$, the marginal pollution allowance expense (associated with the extra waste produced by extracting a unit of the nonrenewable resource) given by $p_w \bullet \phi$, and the marginal labor expense associated with extracting the marginal unit of the resource given by $W1_t/\tau_{NR}(I1_t) \cdot [\partial T_{NRt}/\partial(h_{NR} \cdot N1_{NRt})]$. Therefore, the imputed value of the nonrenewable resource extracted during the current period is given by $[[\partial TR_t^{NRe}/\partial T_{NRt}] - pw \cdot \eta - W1_t/\{\tau_{NR}(I1_t) \cdot [\partial T_{NRt}/\partial(h_{NR} \cdot N1_{NRt})]\}] \cdot (NR_t - NR_{t+1})$. The value of the waste the industry generates net of the waste it recycles constitutes the third factor that must be considered in calculating the net value added by the nonrenewable resource industry. The value of the waste the industry generates net of the waste it recycles corresponds to the value of the pollution allowances the industry buys during the current period: $p_w \cdot [\Omega_{NR}^d(\varphi, I1_t, r_1, p_w, W1_t, K_{NRt}) - \Omega_{NRt}]$.

Therefore, the net value added by the nonrenewable resource industry, NVA_{NR}, is given by

$$NVA_{NR} = p_{NRt} \cdot NR_t^{Ts} - Tx_{NRG1} - \left(B1_{NRt} \text{ minus interest paid to H1}\right) - \left[\left[\frac{\partial TR_t^{NRe}}{\partial T_{NRt}}\right] - p_w \cdot \frac{\varphi - W1_t}{\left\{\tau_{NR}(I1_t) \cdot \left[\frac{\partial T_{NRt}}{\partial(h_{NR} \cdot N1_{NRt})}\right]\right\}}\right] \cdot (NR_t - NR_{t+1}) - p_w\left[\Omega_{NR}^d\left(\varphi, I1_t, r_1, p_w, W1_t, K_{NRt}\right) - \Omega_{NRt}\right] \tag{11.1}$$

Note that if the sector sells pollution allowances during the period, the value of the sales of these allowances represents an increase in the sector's net value added during the period.

Net Income Originating in NR Sector

$$NIO_{NR} = \Pi^{d}_{NRt} + W1_t \cdot (hNR + h^{w}_{NR}) \cdot N1_{NRt} + \text{interest paid by NR to H1}$$

$$- \left[\left[\frac{\partial TR^{NRe}_t}{\partial T_{NRt}} \right] - p_w \cdot \frac{\varphi - W1_t}{\left\{ \tau_{NR}(I1_t) \cdot \left[\frac{\partial T_{NRt}}{\partial (h_{NR} \cdot N1_{NRt})} \right] \right\}} \right] \cdot (NR_t - NR_{t+1}) \tag{11.2}$$

The sum of wages, dividends, and interest paid to the H1 sector overstates the net income originating in the NR sector by the imputed (implicit) dissaving associated with drawing down the sector's inventory of unprocessed nonrenewable resources during the period.

Renewable Resource Industry in Country One

NVA by Renewable Resource Industry in Country One The NVA by the renewable resource industry consists of the value of the marketable renewable resource it produces plus the value of the services it provides by maintaining the inventory of the renewable resource at or above the minimum level stipulated by the government (as measured by the subsidy it receives from the government for providing this service) minus the services it receives from other sectors as evidenced by the taxes and interest it pays plus the imputed value of the nonmarketed raw renewable resource it grows minus the imputed value (opportunity cost) of the "raw" renewable resource it harvests.

The value added of the marketable renewable resource produced net of the intermediate services the sector purchases is given by $p_{R1t} \bullet R1H1^{de}_t - Tx_{G1R1} - (B1^R 1_t$ net of interest paid to H1). The value of the service it provides by maintaining the raw renewable resource at or above the level stipulated by the government sector is given by $p^{G1}_X \bullet \overline{R1}_t$. The imputed value of the marketable renewable resource that the industry grows net of the amount it harvests is given by (11.3):

$$\left\{ \frac{\partial (TR^{R1e}_t)}{\partial (R1H1^{de}_t)} - \frac{W1_t}{\left[\tau_{R1}(I1_t) \cdot \left[\frac{\partial (T_{R1t})}{\partial (h_{R1t} \cdot N1_{R1t})} \right] \right]} \right\}$$

$$\cdot \left[g_{R1}(B_t, P^*_t) \cdot R1_t - R1_t - R1H1^{de}_t \right] \tag{11.3}$$

where $g_{R1}(B_t, P^*_t) \cdot R1_t - R1H1^{de}_t = (\overline{R1}_{t+1} + R1^{d'}_{t+1} - R1_t)$ and is equal to the addition to the stock of the raw renewable resource between the beginning and the end of the period. The amount in (11.3) is found from first-order condition (8.38), repeated below:

$$\partial \frac{\left[\Pi^{d}_{R1t} + \frac{\Pi^{d}_{R1(t+1)}}{(1+r_{1t})}\right]}{\partial\left(h_{R1} \cdot N1_{R1t}\right)} \equiv \left[\frac{\partial\left(TR^{R1e}_{t}\right)}{\partial\left(R1H1^{de}_{t}\right)}\right] \cdot \tau_{R1(I1_{t})} \cdot \left[\partial\left(h_{R1} \cdot N1_{R1t}\right)\right] - W1_{t}$$

$$- \frac{\left[\frac{\partial(TR^{R1e}_{t+1})}{\partial\left(R1H1^{de}_{t+1}\right)}\right] \cdot \tau_{R1}(I1_{t}) \cdot \left[\frac{\partial(T_{R1t})}{\partial(h_{R1} \cdot N1_{R1t})}\right]}{(1+r_{1t})}$$

$$- \left[\frac{W1_{t+1}}{(1+r_{1t})}\right] \cdot \left[\frac{\partial\left(h^{e}_{R1} \cdot N1^{e}_{R1(t+1)}\right)}{\partial(h_{R1} \cdot N1_{R1t})}\right] = 0 \tag{8.38}$$

The sum of the first two terms on the right-hand side of (8.38) divided by the marginal product of labor represents the imputed value of the opportunity cost lost next period due to an extra unit of production this period.

Therefore the net value added by the R1 sector is given by

$$\begin{aligned} NVA_{R1}d = {} & p_{R1t} \cdot R1H1^{de}_{t} + p^{x}G1_{t} \\ & - \left(B1^{R1}_{t} \text{minus interest paid to H1}\right) - Tx_{G1R1} \\ & + \left[\frac{\partial\left(TR^{R1e}_{t}\right)}{\partial\left(R1H1^{de}_{t}\right)} - \frac{W1_{t}}{\left\{\tau_{R1}(I1_{t})\left[\frac{\partial(T_{R1t})}{\partial(h_{R1t} \cdot N1_{R1t})}\right]\right\}}\right] \\ & \cdot \left[g_{R1}\left(B_{t}, P^{*}_{t}\right) \cdot R1_{t} - R1H1^{de}_{t}\right] \end{aligned}$$

Net Income Originating in the Renewable Resource Industry in Country One The net income originating for the renewable resource sector is equal to the value of the wages, interest, and dividends it pays its household sector plus the imputed saving associated with growing the raw renewable resource net of the amount it harvests during the current period:

$$\begin{aligned} NIO_{R1} = {} & \Pi^{d}_{R1t} + W1_{t} \cdot h_{R1t} \cdot N1_{R1t} + \text{interest paid by R1 to H1} \\ & + \left[\frac{\partial\left(TR^{R1e}_{t}\right)}{\partial\left(R1H1^{de}_{t}\right)} - \frac{W1_{t}}{\left\{\tau_{R1}(I1_{t}) \cdot \left[\frac{\partial(T_{R1t})}{\partial\left(h_{R1t} \cdot N1_{R1t}\right)}\right]\right\}}\right] \\ & \cdot \left[g_{R1}\left(B_{t}, P^{*}_{t}\right) \cdot R1_{t} - R1H1^{de}_{t}\right] \end{aligned} \tag{11.4}$$

Private Banking Sector in Country One

NVA by Private Banking Sector in Country One The net value added by the private banking sector in Country One is equal to the interest income it receives during the current period:

$$NVA_{PB1} = B1_{PB1t} + \varepsilon \cdot B2_{PB1t} + \tilde{\varepsilon} \cdot B3_{PB1t}$$

The net income generated by the sector consists of wages and dividends is given by

$$NIO_{PB1} = \Pi_{PB1t} + W1_t \cdot h_t^{PB1} \cdot N1_{PB1t} \tag{11.5}$$

Central Bank in Country One

NVA by Central Bank in Country One The net value added by the central banking sector in Country One is equal to the interest income it receives during the current period:

$$NVA_{CB1} = B1_{CB1t} + \varepsilon \cdot B2_{CB1t} + \tilde{\varepsilon} \cdot B3_{CB1t}$$

Net Income Originating in CB1 The net income originating in the central banking sector is equal to its profit from its operations:

$$NIO_{CB1} = \Pi_{CB1t}$$

Net Values Added and Net Incomes Originating for Country Two

Household Sector in Country Two

NVA by Household Sector in Country Two

$$NVA_{H2} = -Tx_{W*G2t}$$

Net Income Originating in H2

$$NIO_{H2} = W2_t \cdot h_t^{W*G2} \cdot N2_t \text{or} - Tx_{W*G2t}$$

The G2 Sector

NVA by Government Sector in Country Two

$$NVA_{G2} = Tx_{G2t} - \left(B2_{G2t} \text{ minus interest paid to H2}\right) - p_{xt}^{G2} \cdot \overline{R2}_t$$

where

$Tx_{G2t} = Tx_{W*G2t} + Tx_{G2H2t} + Tx_{g2I2t}$.

Tx_{W*G2t} = taxes the G2 sector levies on the H2 sector to recycle, treat, and store human waste.

Tx_{G2H2t} = the (predetermined) tax revenue the G2 sector collects during the current period associated with general public services the H2 sector elected last period to receive during the current period.

Tx_{G2I2t} = the level of corporate taxes the G2 sector announces at the beginning of the current period = $Tx_{KG1} + Tx_{R2G2}$.

NIO by Government Sector in Country Two

$$NIO_{G2} = W2_t \cdot h_t^{W^*G2} \cdot N2_{G2t} + W2_t \cdot h_t^{g2H2} \cdot N2_{G2t} + W2_t \cdot h_t^{g2I2} \cdot N2_{G2t} - IT_{CB2t} + S_{G2t} + \text{interest paid by G2 to H2}$$

Capital Goods Industry

NVA by Capital Goods Industry The NVA by the capital goods industry consists of the value of the capital goods it produces minus the intermediate services (public and private) it buys and minus the value of the waste the industry generates (including depreciation) net of the waste it recycles.

The value of production of capital goods minus the value of the intermediate services it buys is given by $p_{Kt} \cdot K_t^T - Tx_{KG2} - (B2_{Kt}$ minus interest paid to H2). The value of the waste the capital goods sector generates net of the waste it recycles is given by $(p_w/\varepsilon)[\Omega_K^d - \Omega_{Kt}]$. Therefore the net value added by the capital goods industry is given by $NVA_K = p_{Kt} \cdot K_t^T - Tx_{KG2} - (B2_{Kt}$ minus interest paid to H2) $- (p_w/\varepsilon) \cdot [\Omega_K^d - \Omega_{Kt}]$.

Note that if the sector sells pollution allowances during the period, the value of the sales of these allowances represents an increase in the sector's net value added during the period.

Net Income Originating in Capital Goods Sector

$$NIO_K = \Pi_{Kt}^d + W2_t \cdot \left(h_K + h_K^w\right) \cdot N2_{Kt} + \text{interest paid by K to H2}$$

The net income originating in the capital goods sector is equal to the sum of wages and dividends it pays plus the interest it pays to its household sector.

Renewable Resource Industry in Country Two

NVA by Renewable Resource Industry in Country Two The NVA by the renewable resource industry consists of the value of the marketable renewable resource it produces plus the value of the services it provides by maintaining the inventory of the renewable resource at or above the minimum level stipulated by the government (as measured by the subsidy it receives from the government for providing this service) minus the services it receives from other sectors as evidenced by the taxes and interest it pays (to the nonhousehold sector) plus the imputed value of the nonmarketed raw renewable resource it grows minus the imputed value (opportunity cost) of the "raw" renewable resource it harvests.

The value of the marketable renewable resource produced is given by $p_{R2t} \bullet R2H2_t^{de}$. The value of the intermediate services purchased by the R2 industry is represented by $Tx_{G2R2} + (B2_{R2t}$ minus interest paid to H2).

From (8.50), the imputed value of the marketable renewable resource that the R2 industry grows net of the amount it harvests is given by the sum of the first and second terms on the right side of that expression.

$$\frac{\partial\left[\Pi^{d}_{R2t}+\Pi^{d}_{R2(t+1)}/(1+r_{2t})\right]}{\partial(h_{R2}\cdot N2_{R2t})}\equiv\left[\frac{\partial(TR^{R2e}_{t})}{\partial(R2H2^{de}_{t})}\right]\cdot\tau_{R2}(I2_{t})\cdot\left[\frac{\partial(T_{R2t})}{\partial(h_{R2t}\cdot N2_{R2t})}\right]-W$$
$$-\left[\frac{\partial(TR^{R2e}_{t+1})}{\partial(R2H2^{de}_{t+1})}\right]\cdot\tau_{R2}(I2_{t})\cdot\frac{\left[\frac{\partial(T_{R2})}{\partial(h_{R2t}\cdot N2_{R2t})}\right]}{(1+r_{2t})}$$
$$-\left[\frac{W2_{t+1}}{(1+r_{2t})}\right]\cdot\left[\frac{\partial\left(h^{e}_{R2}\cdot N2^{e}_{R2(t+1)}\right)}{\partial(h_{R2}\cdot N2_{R2t})}\right]=0 \quad (8.50)$$

The sum of the first two terms on the right-hand side of (8.50) divided by the marginal product of labor represents the imputed value of the opportunity cost next period due to an extra unit of production this period:

$$\left\{\left[\frac{\partial(TR^{R2e}_{t})}{\partial(R2H2^{de}_{t})}\right]-\frac{W2_{t}}{\left[\tau_{R2}(I2_{t})\cdot\left[\frac{\partial(T_{R2t})}{\partial(h_{R2t}\cdot N2_{R2t})}\right]\right]}\cdot\left[g_{R2}(B_{t},P^{*}_{t})\cdot R2_{t}-R2H2^{de}_{t}\right]\right\}$$

where $[g_{R2}(B_{t},P^{*}_{t})\cdot R2_{t}-R2H2^{de}_{t}]=(\overline{R2}_{t+1}+R2^{d'}_{t+1}-R2_{t})$, which represents the addition to the stock of raw renewable resource between the beginning and the end of the period. Therefore, the net value added by the R2 industry is given by

$$NVA_{R2}=p_{R2t}\cdot R2H2^{de}_{t}+p^{G2}_{xt}\cdot\overline{R2}_{t}-\left(B2_{R2t}-\text{interest paid to H2}\right)$$
$$-Tx_{G2R2}+\left\{\left[\frac{\partial(TR^{R2e}_{t})}{\partial(R2H2^{de}_{t})}\right]-\frac{W2_{t}}{\left[\tau_{R2}(I2_{t})\cdot\left[\partial(h_{R2t}\cdot N2_{R2t})\right]\right]}\right\}$$
$$\cdot\left[g_{R2}\left(B_{t},P^{*}_{t}\right)\cdot R2_{t}-R2H2^{de}_{t}\right]$$

Net Income Originating in R2 Sector The net income originating for the renewable resource sector is equal to the value of the wages, interest and dividends it pays to its household sector plus the imputed saving associated with growing the raw renewable resource net of the amount it harvests during the current period.

$$NIO_{R2} = \Pi^{d}_{R2t} + W2_t \cdot h_{R2t} \cdot N2_{R1t} + \text{interest paid by R2 to H2}$$
$$+ \left\{ \left[\frac{\partial \left(TR^{R2e}_t\right)}{\partial \left(R2H2^{de}_t\right)} \right] - \frac{W2_t}{\left[\tau_{R2}\left(I2_t\right) \cdot \left[\frac{\partial(T_{R2t})}{\partial(h_{R2t} \cdot N2_{R2t})}\right]\right]} \right\}$$
$$\cdot \left[g_{R2}\left(B_t, P^*_t\right) \cdot R2_t - R2H2^{de}_t \right]$$

Private Banking Sector in Country Two

NVA by Private Banking Sector in Country Two The net value added by the private banking sector in Country Two is equal to the interest income it receives during the current period:

$$NVA_{PB2} = \left(\frac{1}{\varepsilon}\right) \cdot B1_{PB2t} + B2_{PB2t} + \left(\frac{\tilde{\varepsilon}}{\varepsilon}\right) \cdot B3_{PB2t}$$

Net Income Originating in PB2 Sector The net income generated by the sector consists of wages and dividends

$$NIO_{PB2} = \Pi_{PB2t} + W2_t \cdot h^{PB2}_t \cdot N2_{PB2t}$$

The Central Bank in Country Two

NVA by Central Bank in Country Two The net value added by the central banking sector in Country Two is equal to the interest income it receives during the current period.

$$NVA_{CB2} = \left(\frac{1}{\varepsilon}\right) \cdot B1_{CB2t} + B2_{CB2t} + \left(\frac{\tilde{\varepsilon}}{\varepsilon}\right) \cdot B3_{CB2t}$$

Net Income Originating in CB2 Sector The net income originating in the central banking sector

$$NIO_{CB2} = \Pi_{CB2t}$$

Net Values Added and Net Incomes Originating for Country Three

The H3 Sector

NVA by Household Sector in Country Three

$$NVA_{H3} = -Tx_{W*G3t}$$

Net Income Originating in H3

$$NIO_{H3} = -W3_t \cdot h^{W*G3}{}_t \cdot N3_t \text{ or } -Tx_{W*G3t}$$

The G3 Sector

NVA by Government Sector in Country Three

$$NVA_{G3} = Tx_{G3t} - (B3_{G3t} \text{ minus interest paid to H3}) - p^{G3}_{xt} \cdot R3_t$$

where

$Tx_{G3t} = Tx_{W*G3t} + Tx_{G3H3t} + Tx_{G3I3t}$.
Tx_{W*G3t} = taxes the G3 sector levies on the H3 sector to recycle/treat/store human waste
Tx_{G3H3t} = the (predetermined) tax revenue the G3 sector collects during the current period associated with general public services the H3 sector elected last period to receive during the current period.
Tx_{G3H3t} = the level of corporate taxes the G3 sector announces at the beginning of the current period = $Tx_{CG3} + Tx_{R3G3}$.

NIO in Government Sector in Country Three

$$NIO_{G3} = W3_t \cdot h_t^{W*G3} \cdot N3_{G3t} + W3_t \cdot h_t^{g3H3} \cdot N3_{G3t} + W3_t \cdot h_t^{g3I3} \cdot N3_{G3t} - \Pi_{CB3t} + S_{G3t} + \text{interest paid by G3 to H3}$$

Consumption Goods Industry

NVA by the Consumption Goods Industry The NVA by the consumption goods industry consists of the value of the consumption goods it produces minus the intermediate services (public and private) it buys and minus the value of the waste the industry generates (including depreciation) net of the waste it recycles.

The value of the sector's production of consumption goods minus the value of the intermediate services it buys is given by $p_{Ct} \cdot C_t^T - Tx_{CG3} - (B3_{Ct}$ minus interest paid to H3). The value of the waste it generates net of the waste it recycles is given by $-(p_w/\tilde{\varepsilon}) \cdot [\Omega_C^d - \Omega_{Ct}]$.

Therefore the net value added by the consumption goods industry may be expressed as $NVA_{KC} = p_{Ct} \cdot C_t^T - Tx_{CG3} - (B3_{Ct} \text{ minus interest paid to H3}) - (p_w/\tilde{\varepsilon}) \cdot [\Omega_C^d - \Omega_{Ct}]$.

Note that if the sector sells pollution allowances during the period, the value of the sales of these allowances represents an increase in the sector's net value added during the period.

Net Income Originating in C Sector $NIO_C = \Pi_t^{Cd} + W3_t \cdot (h_C + h_C^w) \cdot N3_{Ct}$ plus interest paid by C to H3. The net income originating in the consumption goods sector is equal to the sum of wages and dividends it pays plus the interest it pays to its household sector.

Renewable Resource Industry in Country Three

NVA by Renewable Resource Industry in Country Three The NVA by the renewable resource industry consists of the value of the marketable renewable resource it produces plus the value of the services it provides by maintaining the inventory of the renewable resource at or above the minimum level stipulated by the government (as measured by the subsidy it receives from the government for providing this service) minus the services it receives from other sectors as evidenced by the taxes and interest it pays (to the nonhousehold sector) plus the imputed value of the nonmarketed raw renewable resource it grows minus the imputed value (opportunity cost) of the "raw" renewable resource it harvests. The value of the marketable renewable resource produced is given by: $p_{R3t} \cdot R3H3_t^{de}$. The value of the intermediate services purchased by the R3 industry is represented by $Tx_{G3R3} + (B3_{R3t}$ minus interest paid to H3).

From (8.65), the imputed value of the marketable renewable resource that the R3 industry grows net of the amount it harvests is obtained from the first two terms on the right side of that expression

$$\frac{\partial\left[\Pi^d_{R3t} + \Pi^d_{R3(t+1)}/(1+r_{3t})\right]}{\partial(h_{R3}\cdot N3_{R3t})} \equiv \left[\frac{\partial(TR_t^{R3e})}{\partial(R3H3_t^{de})}\right]\cdot \tau_{R3}(I3_t)\cdot\left[\frac{\partial(T_{R3t})}{\partial(h_{R3t}\cdot N3_{R3t})}\right]$$

$$-W3_t - \left[\frac{\partial(TR_{t+1}^{R3e})}{\partial(R3H3_{t+1}^{de})}\right]\cdot \tau_{R3}(I3_t)\cdot \frac{\left[\dfrac{\partial(T_{R3t})}{\partial(h_{R3}\cdot N3_{R3t})}\right]}{(1+r_{3t})}$$

$$-\left[\frac{W3_{t+1}}{(1+r_{3t})}\right]\cdot\left[\frac{\partial\left(h^e_{R3}\cdot N3^e_{R3(t+1)}\right)}{\partial(h_{R3}\cdot N3_{R3t})}\right] = 0 \qquad (8.65)$$

The sum of the first two terms on the right-hand side of (8.65) divided by the marginal product of labor represents the imputed value of the opportunity cost next period due to an extra unit of production this period.

$$\left\{\left[\frac{\partial(TR_t^{R3e})}{\partial\left(R3H3_t^{de}\right)}\right] - \frac{W3_t}{\left[\tau_{R3}(I3_t)\cdot\left[\dfrac{\partial(T_{R3t})}{\partial(h_{R3t}\cdot N3_{R3t})}\right]\right]}\right.$$

$$\left.\cdot\left[g_{R3}\left(B_t, P_t^*\right)\cdot R3_t - R3H3_t^{de}\right]\right\}$$

where $[g_{R3}(B_t, P_t^*)\cdot R3_t - R3H3_t^{de}] = (\overline{R3}_{t+1} + R3^{d'}_{t+1} - R3_t)$, which is also the addition to the stock of the raw renewable resource between the beginning and the end of the period.

Therefore the net value added by the R3 industry during the current period is given by

$$NVA_{R3} = p_{R3t} \cdot R3H3_t^{de} + p_{xt}^{G3} \cdot \overline{R3}_t - (B3_{R3t} \text{ minus interest paid to H3})$$
$$- Tx_{G3R3} + \left\{ \left[\frac{\partial (TR_t^{R3e})}{\partial (R3H3_t^{de})} \right] - \frac{W3_t}{\left[\tau_{R3}(I3_t) \cdot \left[\frac{\partial (TR_{3t})}{\partial (h_{R3t} \cdot N2_{R3t})} \right] \right]} \right\}$$
$$\cdot \left[g_{R3} (B_t, P_t^*) \cdot R3_t - R3H3_t^{de} \right]$$

Net Income Originating in R3 Sector The net income originating for the renewable resource sector is equal to the value of the wages, interest and dividends it pays its household sector plus the imputed saving associated with growing the raw renewable resource net of the amount it harvests during the current period.

$$NIO_{R3} = \Pi_{R3t}^{d} + W3_t \cdot h_{R3t} \cdot N3_{R3t} + \text{interest paid by R3 to H3}$$
$$+ \left\{ \left[\frac{\partial (TR_t^{R3e})}{\partial (R3H3_t^{de})} \right] - \frac{W3_t}{\left[\tau_{R3} (I3_t) \cdot \left[\frac{\partial (T_{R3t})}{\partial (h_{R3t} \cdot N3_{R3t})} \right] \right]} \right\}$$
$$\cdot \left[g_{R3} (B_t, P_t^*) \cdot R3_t - R3H3_t^{de} \right]$$

The Private Banking Sector in Country Three

NVA by Private Banking Sector in Country Three The net value added by the private banking sector in Country Three is equal to the interest income it receives during the current period:

$$NVA_{PB3} = \left(\frac{1}{\tilde{\varepsilon}} \right) \cdot B1_{PB3t} + \left(\frac{\varepsilon}{\tilde{\varepsilon}} \right) \cdot B2_{PB3t} + B3_{PB3t}$$

Net Income Originating in PB3 Sector The net income generated by the sector consists of wages and dividends

$$NIO_{PB3} = \Pi_{PB3t} + W3_t \cdot h_t^{PB3} \cdot N3_{PB3t}$$

The Central Bank in Country Three

NVA by Central Bank in Country Three The net value added by the central banking sector in Country Three is equal to the interest income it receives during the current period:

$$NVA_{CB3} = \left(\frac{1}{\tilde{\varepsilon}} \right) \cdot B1_{CB3t} + \left(\frac{\varepsilon}{\tilde{\varepsilon}} \right) \cdot B2_{CB3t} + B3_{CB3t}$$

Net Income Originating in CB3 Sector The net income originating in the central banking sector:

$$NIO_{CB3} = \Pi_{CB3t}$$

Green Net National Product and Green National Income (by Country)

Green Net National Product is defined here for a country as the sum of the net values added, NVA = NVA − M + NVA − I, for each of its sectors. Green National Income for a country is defined here as the sum of the net incomes originating in each of its sectors.

Green Net National Product (GNNP) for Country One

$$\begin{aligned}
GNNP_1 &= NVA_{H1} + NVA_{G1} + NVA_{NR} + NVA_{R1} + NVA_{PB1} + NVA_{CB1} \\
&= -Tx_{W*G1t} + Tx_{G1t} - B_t^{g1} - p^x G1_t \cdot \overline{R1}_t \\
&\quad + p_{NRt} \cdot NR_t^{Ts} - Tx_{NRG1} - B1_{NRt} + B1_{H1t} \\
&\quad - \left[\left[\frac{\partial TR_t^{NRe}}{\partial T_{NRt}} \right] - p_w \cdot \varphi - \frac{W1_t}{\left\{ \tau_{NR}(I1_t) \cdot \left[\frac{\partial T_{NRt}}{\partial (h_{NR} \cdot N1_{NRt})} \right] \right\}} \right] \\
&\qquad \cdot (NR_t - NR_{t+1}) \\
&\quad - p_w \cdot \left[\Omega_{NR}^d \left(\varphi, I1_t, r1, p_w, W1_t, K_{NRt} \right) - \Omega_{NRt} \right] \\
&\quad + p_{R1t} \cdot R1H1_t^{de} + p_{xt}^{G1} \cdot \overline{R1}_t - B1_{R1t} - Tx_{G1R1} \\
&\quad + \left[\frac{\partial \left(TR_t^{R1e} \right)}{\partial \left(R1H1_t^{de} \right)} - \frac{W1_t}{\left\{ \tau_{R1}(I1_t) \cdot \left[\frac{\partial T_{R1t}}{\partial (h_{R1t} \cdot N1_{R1t})} \right] \right\}} \right] \\
&\qquad \cdot \left[g_{R1}\left(B_t, P_t^* \right) \cdot R1_t - R1H1_t^{de} \right] + B1_{PB1t} + \varepsilon \cdot B2_{PB1t} \\
&\quad + \tilde{\varepsilon} \cdot B3_{PB1t} + B1_{CB1t} + \varepsilon \cdot B2_{CB1t} + \tilde{\varepsilon} \cdot B3_{CB1t}
\end{aligned}$$

The value of intermediate services provided by firms is equal to $B1_{G1t} + B1_{NRt} + B1_{R1t}$ minus the interest paid to the households. In other words:

$GNNP_1$ = taxes H1 pays for health and human services provided by G1
+ value of marketable NR produced + value of marketable R1 produced
− value of pollution allowances purchased by NR industry − imputed value of

nonmarketable NR consumed + imputed value of nonmarketable R1 grown harvest + net interest received from abroad.

Green National Income (GNI) for Country One

$$
\begin{aligned}
GNI_1 &= NIO_{H1} + NIO_{G1} + NIO_{NR} + NIO_{R1} + NIO_{PB1} + NIO_{CB1} \\
&= -W1_t \cdot h_t^{W^*G1} \cdot N1_{G1t} + W1_t \cdot h_t^{W^*G1} \cdot N1_{G1t} + W1_t \cdot h_t^{G1H1} \\
&\quad \cdot N1_{G1t} + W1_t \cdot h_t^{G1I1} \cdot N1_{G1t} - \Pi_{CB1t} + SG1_t + \Pi^d_{NRt} + W1_t \\
&\quad \cdot \left(h_{NR} + h^w_{NR}\right) \cdot N1_{NRt} + \Pi^d_{R1t} + W1_t \cdot h_{R1t} \cdot N1_{R1t} \\
&\quad - \left[\left[\frac{\partial TR_t^{NRe}}{\partial T_{NRt}}\right] - p_w \cdot \eta - \frac{W1_t}{\left\{\tau_{NR}\left(I1_t\right) \cdot \left[\partial\left(h_{NR} \cdot N1_{NRt}\right)\right]\right\}}\right] \\
&\quad \cdot (NR_t - NR_{t+1}) + \Pi_{PB1t} + W1_t \cdot h_t^{PB1} \cdot N1_{PB1t} + \Pi_{CB1t} + B1_{H1t} \\
&\quad + \left[\frac{\partial\left(TR_t^{Rle}\right)}{\partial\left(R1H1_t^{de}\right)} - \frac{W1_t}{\left\{\tau_{R1}\left(I1_t\right) \cdot \left[\frac{\partial(T_{R1t})}{\partial(h_{R1t} \cdot N1_{R1t})}\right]\right\}}\right] \\
&\quad \cdot \left[g_{R1}\left(B_t, P_t^*\right) \cdot R1_t - R1H1_t^{de}\right] = W1_t \cdot h_t^{G1H1} \cdot N1_{G1t} + W1_t \\
&\quad \cdot h_t^{G1I1} \cdot N1_{G1t} + W1_t \cdot \left(h_{NR} + h^w_{NR}\right) \cdot N1_{NRt} + W1_t \cdot h_{R1t} \cdot N1_{R1t} \\
&\quad + \Pi^d_{NRt} + \Pi^d_{R1t} + S_{G1t} + B1_{H1t} - \left[\left[\frac{\partial TR_t^{NRe}}{\partial T_{NRt}}\right] - p_w \cdot \varphi\right. \\
&\quad \left. - \frac{W1_t}{\left\{\tau_{NR}\left(I1_t\right) \cdot \left[\frac{\partial T_{NRt}}{\partial(h_{NR} \cdot N1_{NRt})}\right]\right\}}\right] \cdot (NR_t - NR_{t+1}) \\
&\quad + \frac{\left[\frac{\partial\left(TR_t^{R1e}\right)}{\partial\left(R1H1_t^{de}\right) - W1_t}\right]}{\left\{\tau_{R1}\left(I1_t\right) \cdot \left[\frac{\partial T_{R1t}}{\partial(h_{R1t} \cdot N1_{R1t})}\right]\right\}} \cdot \left[g_{R1}\left(B_t, P_t^*\right) \cdot R1_t - R1H1_t^{de}\right]
\end{aligned}
$$

Green Net National Product (GNNP) for Country Two

$$
\begin{aligned}
GNNP_2 &= NVA_{H2} + NVA_{G2} + NVA_{G2} + NVA_{K} + NV_{R2} \\
&\quad + NVA_{PB2} + NVA_{CB2} \\
&= -Tx_{W^*G2t} + Tx_{G2t} - (B2_{G2t} \text{ minus interest paid to H2})
\end{aligned}
$$

$$- p_{xt}^{G2} \cdot \overline{R2}_t + p_{Kt} \cdot K_t^T - Tx_{KG2} - (B2_{G2t} \text{ minus interest paid to H2})$$
$$- \left(\frac{p_w}{\varepsilon}\right) \cdot \left[\Omega_K^d - \Omega_{Kt}\right]$$
$$+ p_{R2t} \cdot R2H2_t^{de} + p_{xt}^{G2} \cdot \overline{R2}_t - (B2_{R2t} \text{ minus interest paid to H2})$$
$$- Tx_{G2R2} + \left\{ \left[\frac{\partial \left(TR_t^{R2e}\right)}{\partial \left(R2H2_t^{de}\right)}\right] - \frac{W2_t}{\left[\tau_{R2}\left(I2_t\right) \cdot \left[\frac{\partial (T_{R2t})}{\partial (h_{R2t} \cdot N2_{R2t})}\right]\right]} \right\}$$
$$\cdot \left[g_{R2}\left(B_t, P_t^*\right) \cdot R2_t - R2H2_t^{de}\right]$$
$$+ \left(\frac{1}{\varepsilon}\right) \cdot B1_{PB2t} + B2_{PB2t} + \left(\frac{\tilde{\varepsilon}}{\varepsilon}\right) \cdot B3_{PB2t} + \left(\frac{1}{\varepsilon}\right) \cdot B1_{CB2t}$$
$$+ B2_{CB2t} + \left(\frac{\tilde{\varepsilon}}{\varepsilon}\right) \cdot B3_{CB2t}$$

The value of intermediate services provided by firms $= B2_{G2t} + B2_{Kt} + B2_{R2t}$ minus the interest paid to the households (H2).

$$\begin{aligned} GNNP_2 = {} & \text{taxes H2 pays for health and human services provided by G2} \\ & + \text{value of marketable K produced} + \text{value of marketable R2 produced} \\ & - \text{value of pollution allowances purchased by the K sector} \\ & + \text{imputed value of nonmarketable R2 grown net of harvest} \\ & + \text{net interest received from abroad.} \end{aligned}$$

Green National Income (GNI) for Country Two

$$GNI_2 = NIO_{H2} + NIO_{G2} + NIO_K + NIO_{R2} + NIO_{PB2} + NIO_{CB2}$$
$$= -W2_t \cdot h_t^{W*G2} \cdot N2_{G2t}(\text{or } - Tx_{W*G2t}) + W2_t \cdot h_t^{W*G2} \cdot N2_{G2t}$$
$$+ W2_t \cdot h_t^{G2H2} \cdot N2_{G2t} + W2_t \cdot h_t^{G2I2} \cdot N2_{G2t} - \Pi_{CB2t}$$
$$+ S_{G2t} + \text{interest paid by G2 to H2}$$
$$+ \Pi_{Kt}^d + W2_t \cdot \left(h_K + h_K^w\right) \cdot N2_{Kt} + \text{interest paid by K to H2}$$
$$+ \Pi_{R2t}^d + W2_t \cdot h_{R2t} \cdot N2_{R2t} + \text{interest paid by R2 to H2}$$
$$+ \left\{ \left[\frac{\partial \left(TR_t^{R2e}\right)}{\partial \left(R2H2_t^{de}\right)}\right] - \frac{W2_t}{\left[\tau_{R2}(I2_t) \cdot \left[\partial \left(h_{R2t} \cdot N2_{R2t}\right)\right]\right]} \right\}$$
$$\cdot \left[g_{R2}\left(B_t, P_t^*\right) \cdot R2_t - R2H2_t^{de}\right]$$
$$+ \Pi_{PB2t} + W2_t \cdot h_t^{PB2} \cdot N2_{PB2t} + \Pi_{CB2t} = W2_t \cdot h_t^{G2H2} \cdot N2_{G2t}$$
$$+ W2_t \cdot h_t^{G2I2} \cdot N2_{G2t} + S_{G2t} + B2_{H2t} + \Pi_{Kt}^d$$

$$+ W2_t \cdot (h_K + h_K^w) \cdot N2_{Kt} + \Pi^d_{R2t} + W2_t \cdot h_{R2t} \cdot N2_{G2t}$$

$$+ \left\{ \left[\frac{\partial (TR_t^{R2e})}{\partial (R2H2_t^{de})} \right] - \frac{W2_t}{\left[\tau_{R2}(I2_t) \cdot \left[\frac{\partial (T_{R2t})}{\partial (h_{R2t} \cdot N2_{R2t})} \right] \right]} \right\}$$

$$\cdot \left[g_{R2}(B_t, P_t^*) \cdot R2_t - R2H2_t^{de} \right] + \Pi_{PB2t} + W2_t \cdot h_t^{PB2} \cdot N2_{PB2t}$$

Green Net National Product (GNNP) for Country Three

$$\begin{aligned} GNNP_3 &= NVA_{H3} + NVA_{G3} + NVA_C + NVA_{R3} + NV_{PB3} + NVA_{CB3} \\ &= -Tx_{W^*G3t} + Tx_{G3t} - (B3_{G3t} \text{ minus interest paid to H3}) \\ &\quad - p_{xt}^{G3} \cdot \overline{R3}_t + p_{Ct} \cdot K_t^T - Tx_{CG3} - (B3_{Ct} \text{ minus interest paid to H3}) \\ &\quad - \left(\frac{p_w}{\tilde{\varepsilon}} \right) \cdot \left[\Omega_C^d - \Omega_{Ct} \right] + p_{R3t} \cdot R3H3_t^{de} + p_{xt}^{G3} \cdot \overline{R3}_t \\ &\quad - (B3_{R3t} \text{ minus interest paid to H3}) - Tx_{G3R3} \\ &\quad + \left\{ \left[\frac{\partial (TR_t^{R3e})}{\partial (R3H3_t^{de})} \right] - \frac{W3_t}{\left[\tau_{R3}(I3_t) \cdot \left[\frac{\partial (T_{R3t})}{\partial (h_{R3t} \cdot N2_{R3t})} \right] \right]} \right\} \\ &\quad \cdot \left[g_{R3}(B_t, P_t^*) \cdot R3_t - R3H3_t^{de} \right] + \left(\frac{1}{\tilde{\varepsilon}} \right) \cdot B1_{PB3t} + \left(\frac{\varepsilon}{\tilde{\varepsilon}} \right) \cdot B2_{PB3t} \\ &\quad + B3_{PB3t} + \left(\frac{1}{\tilde{\varepsilon}} \right) \cdot B1_{CB3t} + \left(\frac{\varepsilon}{\tilde{\varepsilon}} \right) \cdot B2_{CB3t} + B3_{CB3t} \end{aligned}$$

The value of intermediate services provided by firms = $B3_{G3t} + B3_{Ct} + B3_{R3t}$ minus the interest paid to the households (H3).

$GNNP_3$ = taxes H3 pays for health and human services provided by G3
+ value of marketable C produced + value of marketable R3 produced
− value of pollution allowances purchased by the C sector
+ imputed value of nonmarketable R3 grown net of harvest
+ net interest received from abroad.

Green National Income (GNI) for Country Three

$$\begin{aligned} GNI_3 &= NIO_{H3} + NIO_{G3} + NIO_C + NIO_{R3} + NIO_{PB3} + NIO_{CB3} \\ &= -W3_t \cdot h_t^{W^*G3} \cdot N3_{G3t} \ (\text{or } - Tx_{W^*G3t}) + W3_t \cdot h_t^{W^*G3} \cdot N3_{G3t} \end{aligned}$$

$$+ W3_t \cdot h_t^{W^*G3} \cdot N3_{G3t} + W3_t \cdot h_t^{G3I3} \cdot N3_{G3t} - \Pi_{CB3t}$$
$$+ S_{G3t} + \text{interest paid by G3 to H3} + \Pi_{Ct}^d$$
$$+ W3_t \cdot \left(h_C + h_C^w\right) \cdot N3_{Ct} + \text{interest paid by C to H3}$$
$$+ \Pi_{R3t}^d + W3_t \cdot h_{R3t} \cdot N3_{R3t} + \text{interest paid by R3 to H3}$$
$$+ \left\{ \left[\frac{\partial \left(TR_t^{R3e}\right)}{\partial \left(R3H3_t^{de}\right)} \right] - \frac{W3_t}{\left[\tau_{R3}(I3_t) \cdot \left[\frac{\partial (T_{R3t})}{\partial (h_{R3t} \cdot N3_{R3t})} \right] \right]} \right\}$$
$$\cdot \left[g_{R3}\left(B_t, P_t^*\right) \cdot R3_t - R3H3_t^{de} \right] + \Pi_{PB3t} + W3_t \cdot h_t^{PB3} \cdot N3_{PB3t}$$
$$+ \Pi_{CB3t} = W3_t \cdot h_t^{G3H3} \cdot N3_{G3t} + W3_t \cdot h_t^{G3I3} \cdot N3_{G3t} + S_{G3t}$$
$$+ B3_{H3t} + \Pi_{Ct}^d + W3_t \cdot \left(h_C + h_C^w\right) \cdot N3_{Ct} + \Pi_{R3t}^d + W3_t \cdot h_{R3t}$$
$$\cdot N3_{R3t} + \left\{ \left[\frac{\partial (TR_t^{R3e})}{\partial \left(R3H3_t^{de}\right)} \right] - \frac{W3_t}{\left[\tau_{R3}(I3_t) \cdot \left[\frac{\partial (T_{R3t})}{\partial \left(h_{R3t} \cdot N3_{R3t}\right)} \right] \right]} \right\}$$
$$\cdot \left[g_{R3}\left(B_t, P_t^*\right) \cdot R3_t - R3H3_t^{de} \right] + \Pi_{PB3t} + W2_t \cdot h_t^{PB3} \cdot N2_{PB3t}$$

Green Net World Product and Green World Income (in terms of Country One's currency)

$$GWP = GNNP_1 + \varepsilon \cdot GNNP_2 + \tilde{\varepsilon} \cdot NNP_3$$
$$GWI = GNI_1 + \varepsilon \cdot GNI_2 + \tilde{\varepsilon} \cdot GNI_3$$

In chapter 12, the nonbank sectors respond to the production, employment, and wage-setting and price-setting decisions made prior to the determination of interest rates and exchange rates.

12

Nonbank Sectors Revisited

Introduction

Once the nonbank business and government sectors have decided current period production levels, labor hours, product prices, and the wage rates to be paid next period, their objective functions must be revised and their new constrained optimization problems solved for their effective end-of-period demands for workers for next period and their effective end-of-period demands and supplies of real and financial assets and liabilities. The reason is that the nonbank businesses decided upon their production levels, prices, and wage rates before current interest rates and the actual product demands are established. Consequently, the nonbank business sectors must react to any unanticipated changes in inventories by the end of the period and to market interest rates and exchange rates established during the period. In addition, the government and household sectors formulated plans for current sanitation services and the level of general public services for next period before current prices and wages were announced and before the households learned their current disposable incomes. Now that this new information is available, the governments are free to vary the mix of employees and physical capital with which they will begin next period. The household sectors must now decide their effective current spending on renewable resources and consumption goods and their current saving as well as their asset portfolios for the end of the period.

Assuming that they have accurately forecast the wastes to be generated by their households, the G1, G2, and G3 sectors have already decided current labor hours for the purpose of providing current sanitation services and for the purpose of developing their infrastructures. Through their representatives in government, the household sector in each country has also informed its government as to the level of general public services it desires to receive next period (and agreed to the corresponding level of taxes necessary to finance these services). Given the level of public services decided by its households, the government sector must decide the optimal combination of employees and physical capital to have in place by the beginning of next period in order to provide these general public services.

Country One

The G1 Sector

Once the H1 sector has chosen $g_{1H1(t+1)}$, the G1 sector knows the minimum amount of the renewable resource, $\overline{R1}_{t+1}$, that will be necessary to support these services next period, given its estimate of the country's population at the end of the current period. Also, once the G1 sector has decided the current addition to its infrastructure, it has also decided the amount of the NR^T it will purchase this period, the amount of labor it will use in providing that addition to infrastructure, and the corresponding necessary level of corporate taxes. However, the government may need to alter its debt outstanding at the end of the period in light of the prices, interest rates, and exchange rates that have been revealed during the period.

At this point in the process, the G1 sector decides the optimal end-of-period levels of physical capital and employees as it attempts to minimize next period's outlays, given next period's production of general public services and anticipated revenue from the central bank:

$$\begin{aligned} Tx_{G1H1(t+1)} = {} & W1^{G1}_{t+1} \cdot h1 \cdot N1^{de}_{G1H1(t+1)} + \left(1 + p^{G1}_{B1t}\right) \cdot B1^{se}_{G1(t+1)} \\ & - (1-\delta) \cdot \varepsilon^{G1} \cdot p^{G1}_{K(t+1)} \cdot K^{de}_{G1(t+1)} \\ & - \Pi^{CB1G1}_{t+1} + p^{G1}_{x(t+1)} \cdot \overline{R1}_{t+1} \end{aligned} \tag{3.9}$$

$$\begin{aligned} \text{Min } O_{G1(t+1)} = {} & W1_{t+1} \cdot h_1 \cdot N1^{d}_{G1H1(t+1)} + (1 + p_{B1}) \cdot B1^{G1s}_{t+1} \\ & - (1-\delta) \cdot \varepsilon \cdot p^{G1}_{K(t+1)} \cdot K^{d}_{G1(t+1)} \\ & - \Pi^{CB1G1}_{t+1} + p^{G1}_{x(t+1)} \cdot \overline{R1}_{t+1} - Tx_{G1H1(t+1)} \end{aligned} \tag{12.1}$$

$$\text{w.r.t. } N1^{d}_{G1H1(t+1)} \text{ and } K^{d}_{G1(t+1)}$$

subject to

$$g_{1H1(t+1)} = \min\left[g1H1\left(h1 \cdot N1^{de}_{G1H1(t+1)}, K^{de}_{G1(t+1)}\right), \frac{\overline{R1}_{t+1}}{\left(\xi_{G1} \cdot N1^{e}_{t+1}\right)} \right] \tag{12.2}$$

with $g_{1H1i} > 0$, $g_{1H1ii} = 0$ for $i \neq j$, and subject to the G1 sector's combined current-period budget constraint for general public services, sanitation services, and infrastructure augmentation once current-period prices and exchange rates are known is given by

$$\begin{aligned}
B1^{s}_{G1(t+1)} = \left(\frac{1}{p_{B1}}\right) \cdot \Big\{ & W1_t \cdot h^{GH1}_{G1t} \cdot N1_{G1t} \\
& + \varepsilon \cdot p_{Kt} \cdot \left[K^{d}_{G1(t+1)} - (1-\delta) \cdot K_{G1t}\right] \\
& - \Pi^{CB1G1}_{t} + (1 + p_{B1}) \cdot B1_{G1t} + p_{xt} \cdot \overline{R1}_t - Tx_{G1H1t} \\
& + W1_t \cdot h^{W^*H1}_{G1t} \cdot N1_{G1t} - Tx_{W^*G1t} \\
& + W1_t \cdot h^{\Delta I}_{G1t} \cdot N1_{G1t}(\Delta I1_t) + p^{G1e}_{NRt} \cdot NRG1^{T} - Tx_{NRt} - Tx_{R1t} \Big\}
\end{aligned} \tag{12.3}$$

or

$$\begin{aligned}
\text{Min } O_{G1(t+1)} = \; & W1_{t+1} \cdot h1 \cdot N1^{d}_{G1H1(t+1)} \\
& - \varepsilon \cdot p^{G1}_{K(t+1)} \cdot (1-\delta) \cdot K^{d}_{G1(t+1)} - \Pi^{CB1G1}_{t+1} \\
& + p^{G1}_{K(t+1)} \cdot \overline{R1}_{t+1} - Tx_{g1H1(t+1)} \\
& + \left[\frac{(1+p_{B1})}{p_{B1}}\right] \cdot \Big\{ W1_t \cdot h^{GH1}_{G1t} \cdot N1_{G1t} \\
& + \varepsilon \cdot p_{Kt} \cdot \left[K^{d}_{G1(t+1)} - (1-\delta) \cdot K_{G1t}\right] \\
& - \Pi^{CB1G1}_{t} + (1 + p_{B1}) \cdot B1_{G1t} + p_{xt} \cdot \overline{R1}_t - Tx_{G1H1t} \\
& + W1_t \cdot h^{W^*H1}_{G1t} \cdot N1_{G1t} - Tx_{W^*G1t} + W1_t \cdot h^{\Delta I}_{G1t} \\
& \cdot N1_{G1t}(\Delta I1_t) + p^{G1e}_{NRt} \cdot NRG1^{T} - Tx_{NRt} - Tx_{R1t} \Big\} \\
& + \lambda \left[g_{1H1(t+1)} - g_{1H1}\left(h1 \cdot N1^{d}_{G1H1(t+1)}, K^{d}_{G1(t+1)}\right)\right]
\end{aligned} \tag{12.4}$$

The resulting first-order necessary conditions become

$$W1_{t+1} \cdot h1 - \lambda \cdot \left[\frac{\partial g_{1H1}}{\partial (h1)}\right] \cdot h1 = 0 \tag{12.5}$$

and

$$\left[\frac{(1+p_{B1})}{p_{B1}}\right] \cdot \varepsilon \cdot p_{Kt} - \varepsilon \cdot p^{G1}_{K(t+1)} \cdot (1-\delta) + \lambda \cdot \left[\frac{\partial g_{1H1}}{\partial \left(K^{d}_{G1(t+1)}\right)}\right] = 0 \tag{12.6}$$

According to these first-order conditions, the G1 sector will substitute employees for physical capital on the margin at the beginning of next period as the interest rate in Country One's bond market, r_1, or the price of physical capital, p_{Kt}, rises.

It will substitute physical capital for employees for next period on the margin the higher the wage rate announced this period by the nonrenewable resource industry. These considerations yield demand functions for workers by G1 for next period, $N1^d_{G1H1(t+1)}$, and for physical capital by G1 for the beginning of next period, $K^d_{G1(t+1)}$:

$$N1^d_{G1H1(t+1)} = N1^d_{G1H1(t+1)}(\underset{-}{W1_{t+1}}, \underset{+}{r_{1t}}, \underset{+}{p_{Kt}}, \underset{+}{\varepsilon}, \underset{+}{g_{1H1(t+1)}}) \tag{12.7}$$

$$K^d_{G1(t+1)} = K^d_{G1(t+1)}(\underset{+}{W1_{t+1}}, \underset{-}{r_{1t}}, \underset{-}{p_{Kt}}, \underset{-}{\varepsilon}, \underset{-}{\delta}, \underset{+}{g_{1H1(t+1)}}) \tag{12.8}$$

Once it has solved for its end-of-period demands for workers and capital, the G1 sector's end-of-period supply of bonds is given by

$$\begin{aligned} p_{B1} \cdot B1^s_{G1(t+1)} = {} & W1_t \cdot h^{GH1}_{G1t} \cdot N1_{G1t} + \varepsilon \cdot p_{Kt} \\ & \cdot \Big[K^d_{G1(t+1)}\left(W1_{(t+1)}, r_{1t}, p_{Kt}, \varepsilon, \delta, g_{1H1(t+1)}\right) \\ & -(1-\delta) \cdot K_{G1t}\Big] - \Pi^{CB1G1}_t + (1 + p_{B1}) \cdot B1_{G1t} \\ & + p^{G1}_{xt} \cdot \overline{R1}_t - Tx_{G1H1t} + W1_t \cdot h^{W^*H1}_{G1t} \cdot N1_{G1t} \\ & - Tx_{W^*G1t} + W1_t \cdot h^{\Delta I}_{G1t} \cdot N1_{G1t}(\Delta I1_t) \\ & + p_{NRt} \cdot NRG1^{Td}_t - Tx_{NRt} - Tx_{R1t} \end{aligned} \tag{12.9}$$

The R1 Industry

Now that the R1 industry has decided current production, the current price of its product, and the number of hours it will use its current employees, it has also decided the inventory of unprocessed R1 it wants to hold by the beginning of next period. In addition, it has also decided the number of people it plans to employ next period, $N1_{R1(t+1)}$, to process that inventory as well as next period's anticipated increase above the minimum end-of-period stock required by its government sector. The end-of-period stock of its processed inventory is established by current production and current sales, but this inventory does not affect next period's production. However, the end-of-period stock of the processed inventory will affect the price the sector sets for its product next period. It also affects the amount that the sector borrows during the current period.

The sector's end-of-period inventory of processed R1 is given by (8.5), repeated here as (12.10):

$$R1^{T^*}_{t+1} = R1^{T^*}_t + \tau_{R1}(I1_t) \cdot T_{R1t}(h_{R1t} \cdot N1_{R1t}) - R1H1_t \geq 0 \tag{12.10}$$

The sector's end-of-period supply of bonds is then established by the sector's unintended accumulation of the processed R1 during the period:

$$p_t^{b1} \cdot B1_{t+1}^{R1s} = p_{R1t} \cdot \left(R1_{t+1}^{T^*} - R1_t^{T^*}\right) + p_{B1} \cdot B1_t^{R1}$$
$$= p_{R1t} \cdot \left[\tau_{R1}(I1_t) \cdot T_{R1t}(h_{R1t} \cdot N1_{R1t}) - R1H1_t\right] + P_{B1} \cdot B1_t^{R1} \tag{12.11}$$

If the sector produces more than it sells during the current period, it issues more bonds during the period. If it sells more than it produces, it buys back some bonds, or even lends in the bond market. $R1H1 \leq R1_{t+1}^{T^*} + \tau_{R1}(I1_t) \cdot T_{R1t}(h_{R1t} \cdot N1_{R1t})$. If $R1H1 = R1_t^{T^*} + \tau_{R1}(I1_t) \cdot T_{R1t}(h_{R1t} \cdot N1_{R1t})$, then $p_t^{b1} \cdot B1_{t+1}^{R1s} = p_{R1t} \cdot (-R1_t^{T^*}) + p_t^{b1} \cdot B1_t^{R1}$. Therefore, while the current interest rate the sector anticipates will prevail during the current period affects its desired ending period inventory of processed R1 as it decides current production and product price, the actual amount of this inventory is established by current production and current sales. In the final analysis, the end-of-period supply of bonds to Country One's bond market by the renewable resource industry in Country One is independent of the current interest rate (although the sector's forecast of the current interest rate was important to its production and pricing decisions).

The NR Industry

Given that the nonrenewable resource industry has already decided the number of hours to use its current employees, the level of current production of processed NR, the current price of its product, and the wage rate it will pay its employees next period, its original objective function, (5.37), must be modified and solved for the sector's effective demand for workers for next period and physical capital for the beginning of next period:

$$\frac{\Pi_{NR(t+1)}^{d}}{(1+r_{1t})} + \Pi_{NRt}^{d}$$
$$= \left[\frac{1}{(1+r_{1t})}\right] \cdot \Big\{TR_{t+1}^{NRe}\big[\{NR_t - (1-\varphi) \cdot \tau_{NR}(I1_t) \cdot T_{NRt}$$
$$(h_{NR} \cdot N1_{NRt}, K_{NRt}) + T_{NRt}^{w}\left(h_{NR}^{w} \cdot N1_{NRt}\right)\Big\} / (1+\varphi),$$
$$\omega_{NR,K}^{e}, \omega_{NR,C}^{e}, NRG1_{t+1}^{Tde} + NRG2_{t+1}^{Tde} + NRG3_{t+1}^{Tde}\big]$$
$$+ (1-\delta) \cdot p_{K(t+1)}^{NR} \cdot \varepsilon \cdot K_{NR(t+1)}^{d} - Tx_{NRG1(t+1)}$$
$$- p_w \cdot \left[\left[\frac{\varphi}{(1+\varphi)}\right] \cdot \{NR_t - (1+\varphi) \cdot \tau_{NR}(I1_t) \cdot T_{NRt}(h_{NR} \cdot N1_{NRt}, K_{NRt})\right.$$
$$+ T_{NRt}^{w}\left(h_{NR}^{w} \cdot N1_{NRt}\right)\} - T_{NR(t+1)}^{S}\left(h_{NR}^{e} \cdot N1_{NR(t+1)}^{Se}\right) - \omega_{NR(t+1)}^{e}$$

$$- W1_{t+1} \cdot \left\{ N1^{Sd}_{NR(t+1)} + N1^{T}_{NR(t+1)} \left[\frac{NR_t}{(1+\varphi)}, h_{NR} \cdot N1_{NRt}, K_{NRt}, I1_t, \right. \right.$$

$$\left. \left. h^{w}_{NR} \cdot N1_{NRt}, K^{d}_{NR(t+1)} \right], \gamma_{NR} \right\} \cdot h^{e}_{NR} \Big\}$$

$$+ TR^{NRe}_{t} \left[\tau_{NR}(I1_t) \cdot T_{NRt}(h_{NR} \cdot N1_{NRt}, K_{NRt}) + NR^{T^*}_{t}, \right.$$

$$\left. \omega_{NRK}, \omega_{NRC}, NRG1^{Tde}_{t} + NRG2^{Tde}_{t} + NRG3^{Tde}_{t} \right]$$

$$- \delta \cdot p_{Kt} \cdot \varepsilon \cdot K_{NRt} - Tx_{NRG1t}$$

$$- p_w \cdot \left[\varphi \cdot \tau_{NR}(I1_t) \cdot T_{NRt}(h_{NR} \cdot N1_{NRt}, K_{NRt}) - T^{w}_{NRt}\left(h^{w}_{NR} \cdot N1_{NRt}\right) \right]$$

$$- W1_t \cdot \left(h_{NR} + h^{w}_{NR}\right) \cdot N1_{NRt} - (1 + p_{B1}) \cdot B1_{NRt}$$

$$- p_{Kt} \cdot \varepsilon \cdot \left(K^{d}_{NR(t+1)} - K_{NRt}\right) \tag{12.12}$$

where $(1+p_{B1})/p_{B1}$ becomes $(1+r_{1t})$ where $r_{1t} = 1/p_{B1}$. Because the sector decided when it set current production and product price how much marketable (transformed) NR to produce next period, the decision facing the sector at this point is the optimal combination of workers and capital with which to begin next period for producing NR^{T}_{t+1}. From (5.21), the sector has already chosen the isoquant for NR^{T}_{t+1}; it merely needs now to select the optimal combination of labor $N1^{Td}_{NR(t+1)}$ and $K^{d}_{NR(t+1)}$. Let this isoquant be given by (12.13). Clearly, once the sector has decided upon $K^{d}_{NR(t+1)}$, the amount of $N1^{Td}_{NR(t+1)}$ it will employ is also determined:

$$\overline{\overline{T}}^{Te}_{t+1} = \tau_{NR}(I1_t + \Delta I1_t) \cdot \overline{\overline{T}}^{Te}_{t+1}\left(h^{e}_{NR} \cdot N1^{Td}_{NR(t+1)}, K^{d}_{NR(t+1)}\right) \tag{12.13}$$

The demand for $N1^{Td}_{NR(t+1)}$, as a function of $K^{d}_{NR(t+1)}$, $\overline{\overline{T}}^{Te}_{t+1}$, and $\tau_{NR}(I1_t + \Delta I1_t)$ is given by

$$N1^{Td}_{NR(t+1)} = N1^{Td}_{NR(t+1)}\big(\underset{-}{K^{d}_{NR(t+1)}}, \underset{+}{\overline{\overline{T}}^{Te}_{t+1}}, \underset{-}{\tau_{NR}(I1_t + \Delta I1_t)}\big) \tag{12.14}$$

where the signs of the partials are found by totally differentiating (12.11) and solving for the change in $N1^{Td}_{NR(t+1)}$ in terms of the other variables.

Maximize (12.12) with respect to $K^{d}_{NR(t+1)}$ and $N1^{Td}_{NR(t+1)}$, with the right-hand side of (12.14) substituted for $N1^{Td}_{NR(t+1)}$. This yields the first-order necessary conditions (12.15) and (12.17):

$$\frac{\partial \left[\Pi^{NRd}_{t} + \dfrac{\Pi^{NRd}_{t+1}}{(1 + r_{1t})} \right]}{\partial K^{d}_{NR(t+1)}} \equiv -W1_{t+1} \cdot \left[\frac{\partial N1^{Td}_{NR(t+1)}}{\partial \left(K^{d}_{NR(t+1)}\right)} \right]$$

$$= (1 + r_{1t}) \cdot p_{Kt} \cdot \varepsilon + (1 - \delta) \cdot p^{NR}_{K(t+1)} \cdot \varepsilon \tag{12.15}$$

According to (12.15), the present value maximizing NR now purchases capital goods during the current period up to the point at which the anticipated marginal revenue product of physical capital held at the beginning of next period is equal to the user cost of capital, shown by the sum on the (far) right-hand side of (12.15). In this case, however, the marginal revenue product of capital refers to the cost saving to the sector from substituting a unit of capital for labor along the isoquant associated with next period's production of processed NR. From (12.15), the sector's effective end-of-period demand for physical capital is positively related to the wage rate the sector announced at the beginning of the period but negatively related to the current interest rate in Country One's bond market, the rate of physical depreciation, the current price of physical capital in terms of Country Two's unit of account, and the current value of Country Two's unit of account in terms of Country One's unit of account.

$$K^{d}_{NR(t+1)} = K^{d}_{NR(t+1)}(\underset{+}{W1_{t+1}}, \underset{-}{r_{1t}}, \underset{-}{\delta}, \underset{-}{p_{Kt}}, \underset{-}{\varepsilon}) \tag{12.16}$$

$$\frac{\partial\left[\Pi^{NRd}_{t} + \dfrac{\Pi^{NRd}_{t+1}}{(1+r_{1t})}\right]}{\partial N1^{Se}_{NR(t+1)}} \equiv p_{w} \cdot \left[\frac{\varphi}{(1+\varphi)}\right] \cdot \left[\frac{\partial T^{S}_{NR(t+1)}}{\partial\left(h^{e}_{NR} \cdot N1^{Se}_{NR(t+1)}\right)}\right] \cdot h^{e}_{NR} = W1_{t+1} \cdot h^{e}_{NR} \tag{12.17}$$

Condition (12.17) stipulates that the NR industry add to its stock of employees for the purpose of treating and storing waste next period up to the point at which the saving due to the reduction in pollution allowance purchases is equal to the marginal labor cost of hiring an additional worker next period. Since the wage rate has already been set, the marginal labor cost of an extra worker is $W1_{t+1} \cdot h^{e}_{NR}$. Consequently, the demand function for workers for next period to treat and store waste is given by

$$T^{Sd}_{NR(t+1)} = T^{Sd}_{NR(t+1)}(\underset{+}{p_{w}}, \underset{+}{\varphi}, \underset{-}{W1_{t+1}}) \tag{12.18}$$

NR Sector's Supply of Bonds

Given that the amount of processed nonrenewable resource that the sector sells during the period may not equal its planned sales, and assuming that the nonrenewable resource industry does not plan to engage in net saving during the period (i.e., it plans to distribute all net income during the current period as dividends), then, from (5.5) and (5.11), the sector's borrowing in Country One's bond market by the end of the current period corresponds to the sum of its planned and unplanned investment during the period. Its end-of-period supply of bonds to Country One's bond market is now given by

$$
\begin{aligned}
p_{B1}\cdot B1^{s}_{NR(t+1)} &= p_{B1}\cdot B1_{NRt} + p_{NRt}\cdot\left(NR^{T^*}_{t+1} - NR^{T^*}_{t}\right)\\
&\quad + p_{Kt}\cdot\varepsilon\cdot\left[K^{d}_{NR(t+1)}(r_1,\delta,p_{Kt}\cdot\varepsilon) - K_{NRt}\right]\\
&= p_{B1}\cdot B1_{NRt} + p_{NRt}\cdot\left[\tau_{NR}(I1_t)\cdot T_{NRt}(h_{NR}\cdot N1_{NRt},K_{NRt})\right.\\
&\quad \left.-NRK^{T}_{t} - NRC^{T}_{t} - NRG1^{T}_{t} - NRG2^{T}_{t} - NRG3^{T}_{t}\right]\\
&\quad + p_{Kt}\cdot\varepsilon\cdot\left[K^{d}_{NR(t+1)}(r_1,\delta,p_{Kt}\cdot\varepsilon) - K_{NRt}\right]\\
&= p_{B1}\cdot B1^{s}_{NR(t+1)}\big(\underset{+1}{p_{B1}\cdot B1_{NRt} - p_{NRt}\cdot NR^{T^*}_{t}},\underset{-}{r_1},\underset{-}{\delta},\underset{-}{p_{Kt}},\underset{-}{\varepsilon},\\
&\quad \underset{-}{K_{NRt}},\underset{-}{NRK^{T}_{t}},\underset{-}{NRC^{T}_{t}},\underset{-}{NRG1^{T}_{t}},\underset{-}{NRG2^{T}_{t}},\underset{-}{NRG3^{T}_{t}}\big)
\end{aligned}
\tag{12.19}
$$

where it is assumed the NR sector's demand for capital is elastic with respect to its price and where NRK^{T}_{t} corresponds to the actual amount of NR^{T} purchased by the capital goods industry in Country Two during the current period, NRC^{T}_{t} corresponds to the actual amount of NR^{T} purchased by the consumer goods industry in Country Three during the current period, $NRG1^{T}_{t}$ represents the amount of transformed NR purchased by the government sector in Country One, $NRG2^{T}_{t}$ represents the amount of transformed NR purchased by the government sector in Country Two, $NRG3^{T}_{t}$ denotes the amount of transformed NR purchased by the government sector in Country Three, $NR^{T^*}_{t}$ represents the initial inventory of transformed NR at the beginning of the period, and $NR^{T^*}_{t+1}$ denotes the end-of-current-period inventory of transformed NR.

Earlier the capital goods industry's demand for the nonrenewable resource was given by

$$
\begin{aligned}
NRK^{Td}_{t} &= (\kappa + \varphi_K)\cdot\tau_K(I2_t)\cdot T_{Kt}(h_K\cdot N2_{Kt},K_{Kt})\\
&= NRK^{Td}_{t}\big(\underset{+}{K_{Kt}},\underset{+}{I2_t},\underset{-}{p^{K}_{NRt}},\underset{-}{p_w},\underset{+}{\kappa},\underset{+}{\varphi_K},\underset{+}{\varepsilon^{K}},\underset{-}{W2_t}\big)
\end{aligned}
\tag{6.48}
$$

The consumption goods industry's demand for the nonrenewable resource was found to be

$$
\begin{aligned}
NRC^{Td}_{t} &= (\gamma + \varphi_C)\cdot\tau(I3_t)\cdot TC_t(h_{Ct}\cdot N3_{Ct},K_{Ct})\\
&= NRC^{Td}_{t}\big(\underset{-}{p^{C}_{NRt}},\underset{-}{p_w},\underset{+}{\varphi_C},\underset{+}{\gamma},\underset{+}{\tilde{\varepsilon}^{C}},\underset{-}{W3_t},\underset{+}{I3_t},\underset{+}{K_{Ct}}\big)
\end{aligned}
\tag{7.47}
$$

The G1 sector's demand for NR was given by

$$
NRG1^{Td}_{t} = \iota\cdot\Delta I1_t \tag{3.20}
$$

The amount of the nonrenewable resource the G2 sector uses in the transformation process is given by

$$NRG2_t^{Td} = \iota \cdot \Delta I2_t \tag{3.29}$$

The amount of the nonrenewable resource the G3 sector uses in the transformation process is given by

$$NRG3_t^{Td} = \iota \cdot \Delta I3_t \tag{3.37}$$

The H1 Sector

The first set of effective decisions facing the H1 sector at the beginning of the period encompassed the level of general public services the H1 sector instructs the G1 sector to provide next period, $g_{1H1(t+1)}$, together with the associated level of taxes necessary to receive them, $Tx_{G1H1(t+1)}$, and the number of births in the H1 sector during the current period, $\eta 1$. Since these decisions have already been made by the time the sector is ready to make its other decisions in light of information provided by the production, pricing, and employment decisions by the nonfinancial businesses and the government sectors, these decisions are ignored in setting up the sector's revised utility function. In this second step, the H1 sector decides its current and future (notional) consumption of consumer goods C, namely CH1, and the renewable resource R1, R1H1, its supply of workers to the labor market (for employment next period) and its end-of-period demands for Country One's money and bonds. As will be shown during a discussion of the financial markets, the H1 sector's effective current consumption demands, ex ante saving, its end-of-period labor supply, and its end-of-period demands for financial assets become mutually determined with current interest rates and exchange rates.

Given the current and future levels of sanitation and general public services the households anticipate and given current childbirths, the objective of the household sector at this juncture is to again maximize present utility, that is, the felicity the household sector experiences at the beginning of the current period in light of its plans for current and future consumption of both R1 and C and leisure. For simplicity, the H1 sector's present utility is assumed to be represented by additive positive increasing functions of the H1 sector's planned consumption per capita of R1 and C in both the current and next period and current and future leisure per capita. The analysis now also incorporates the productivity of money balances held by the H1 sector and allows the H1 sector to plan its saving during the current period in terms of both money and bond accumulations.

Productivity of Money

For simplicity, the amount of time the H1 sector spends undertaking transactions during a given period is assumed to be directly related only to the number of renewable resource goods, $R1_t$, that sector purchases that period but negatively related to the real amounts of money it holds at the beginning of that period; we ignore transactions time devoted to purchasing consumption goods imported from Country

Three and the corresponding productivity of holding foreign currency. Therefore, for the current period the following transactions-time function faced by the home country's household sector is assumed to be given by

$$\bar{\tau}_t^{H1} = \bar{\tau}_t^{H1}\left(\frac{R1H1_t, M1_t}{p_{R1t}}\right),$$
$$\text{where } \frac{\partial \bar{\tau}_t^{H1}}{\partial (R1H1_t)} > 0, \quad \frac{\partial \bar{\tau}_t^{H1}}{\partial \left(\frac{M1_t}{p_{R1t}}\right)} < 0 \tag{12.20}$$

where $\bar{\tau}_t^{H1}$ represents current-period transactions time for the H1 sector. In the interest of simplifying the analysis, current-period transactions time is ignored from this point forward because it does not affect the sector's end-of-period demand for money.

However, the H1 sector's transactions time next period presumably does depend upon the amount of real money balances the sector plans to hold by the beginning of that period. The fact that noninterest-bearing money conserves transactions time is the fundamental incentive for holding it at the beginning of the period. Let $\bar{\tau}_{t+1}^{H1}$ denote the amount of transactions time the H1 sector plans to incur next period with $R1H1_{t+1}^{de}$ representing the H1 sector's notional demand for R1 next period, $M1_{t+1}^{d}$ representing the H1 sector's (and the market) end-of-period demand for money denominated in terms of Country One's unit of account, and $p_{R1(t+1)}^{H1}$ denoting the H1 sector's anticipated price of R1 next period.

$$\bar{\tau}_{t+1}^{H1} = \bar{\tau}_{t+1}^{H1}\left[R1H1_{t+1}^{de}, \left(\frac{M1_{t+1}^{d}}{p_{R1(t+1)}^{H1}}\right)\right]$$

where

$$\frac{\partial \bar{\tau}_{t+1}^{H1}}{\partial \left(R1H1_{t+1}^{de}\right)} > 0, \quad \frac{\partial \bar{\tau}_{t+1}^{H1}}{\partial \left(\frac{M1_{t+1}^{d}}{p_{R1(t+1)}^{H1}}\right)} < 0$$
$$\frac{\partial^2 \bar{\tau}_{t+1}^{H1}}{\partial \left(R1H1_{t+1}^{de}\right)^2} = 0, \quad \frac{\partial^2 \bar{\tau}_{t+1}^{H1}}{\partial \left(R1H1_{t+1}^{de}\right) \partial \left(\frac{M1_{t+1}^{d}}{p_{R1(t+1)}^{H1}}\right)} < 0 \tag{12.21}$$
$$\frac{\partial^2 \bar{\tau}_{t+1}^{H1}}{\partial \left(\frac{M1_{t+1}^{d}}{p_{R1(t+1)}^{H1}}\right)^2} > 0$$

According to expression (12.21), ceteris paribus, an increase in the amount of R1 the sector anticipates buying next period increases next period's anticipated transactions time at a constant rate. But this rate is reduced to the extent that the sector plans to hold (real) money balances by the beginning of that period. In addition, ceteris paribus, the ability of an extra unit of real money balances to reduce transactions

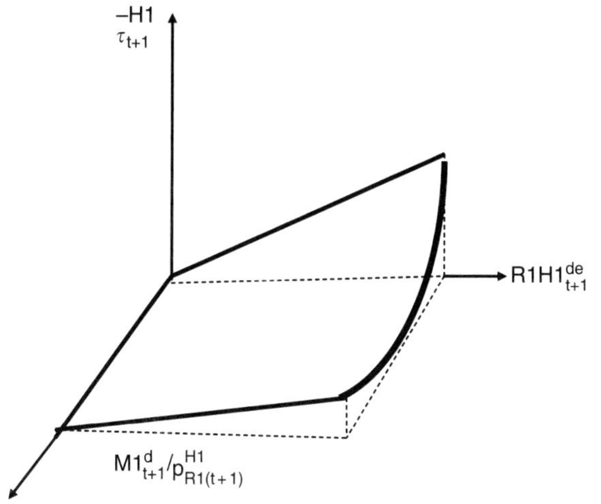

Figure 12.1 Next Period's Anticipated Transactions Time

time diminishes the larger the size of those balances (diminishing marginal product of money). See figure 12.1.

In this section, the analysis of the H1 sector changes to account for the fact that by this time the sector has already selected both the level of general public services to be provided by its government next period (as well as the corresponding level of next period's taxes it will pay) and the number of current-period childbirths. In addition, by this time the nonfinancial business sectors have also already announced the current-period prices of their products and the current wage rates (which actually will not be paid until next period). The H1 sector also knows by this point the wage income it will receive this period as well as the remainder of its current disposable income.

With the current wage rate already announced, the current economic behavior of the H1 sector depends upon whether it expects that the country's three employers (the R1, NR, and G1 sectors) will want to hire more or fewer people to work next period than the H1 sector wishes to supply. In this model, no one knows before the end of the current period how many people will actually become employed next period, because the nonfinancial business sectors' demands for labor for the end of the current period become jointly determined during the current period with current interest rates and exchange rates. Therefore, two alternative cases exist with respect to the formulation of the H1 sector's plans at this stage. In the "full-employment" case, the households anticipate that their ex ante end-of-period supply of labor will be no larger than the country's combined end-of-period market demand for labor. In this case, the households formulate their plans as if they are unconstrained with respect to their end-of-period supply of labor. In the "unemployment" case, the households anticipate that their ex ante end-of-period supply of labor may exceed the amount of labor their potential employers will want to employ by the end of the period. In this case, the households take their forecast of the end-of-period market demand for labor as a constraining parameter.

Utility Maximization for the Notional "Full-Employment" Case

At this point, the household sector attempts to maximize present utility with respect to its current consumption of R1 and C, its future consumption of R1 and C, its end-of-period portfolio, and the number of people that it will be employed by the end of the current period. This optimization problem closely corresponds to the one presented in chapter 4 except that the sector now knows the current values for current product prices and wages and also knows the levels of $g_{1H1(t+1)}$ and $T1_{t+1}$, equal to $Tx_{W^*G1t} + Tx_{G1H1t}$.

In this second step, the H1 sector contemplates allocating the total hours available to its adults next period, $h1^{T}_{t+1} \cdot N1_{t+1}$, between employment and leisure, where $h1^{T}_{t+1}$ represents the total number of hours available next period. The amount of time spent undertaking transactions is now incorporated into the analysis as a nuisance. (Transactions time differs from shopping time, which the households may not necessarily view as a nuisance.) Current transactions time is assumed to be positively related to current purchases of R1 and negatively related to the sector's predetermined real money balances held at the beginning of the current period. The H1 sector attempts to reduce next period's transactions time somewhat by planning to hold some real money balances for the beginning of that period. However, transactions time is assumed to be too small to affect the H1 sector's employment decision for next period.

Let

$N1_t$ = the population of Country One at the beginning of the current period.
$R1H1_t/N1_t$ = per capita consumption of R1 by H1 during the current period.
$CH1_t/N1_t$ = per capita consumption of C by H1 during the current period.
$h1^{T}_{t}$ = the total number of "hours" during the current period (after accounting for average hours spent childrearing).
$h1^{T}_{t} \cdot N1_t$ = the total number of hours available to the H1 sector during the current period.
$h1^{W}_{t}$ = the average number of hours the H1 adult population, $N1_t$, works during the current period.
$R1H1_{t+1}/N1_{t+1}$ = anticipated per capita consumption of R1 by H1 next period.
$CH1_{t+1}/N1_{t+1}$ = anticipated per capita consumption of C by H1 next period.
$h1^{T}_{t+1} \cdot N1_{t+1}$ = the total number of hours available to the H1 sector next period.
$h1^{s}$ = the standard number of working hours in Country One next period.
$N1^{s}_{t+1}$ = the number of people in H1 that plan to work next period.

The utility function of the H1 sector is associated with the second set of decisions with respect to present and future consumption of R1 and C per capita, future leisure per capita (time not spent working), and future transactions time per capita. Therefore, the following maximization problem faces Country One's household sector

in the present stage of decision making:
Maximize:

$$U1 = U1_{R1t}\left(\frac{R1H1_t}{N1_t}\right) + U1_{CH1t}\left(\frac{CH1_t}{N1_t}\right)$$

$$+ U1_{\tau t}\left\{\frac{\left[\bar{\tau}_t^{H1}\left(\frac{R1H1_t, M1_t}{p_{R1t}}\right)\right]}{N1_t}\right\}$$

$$+ U1_{R1(t+1)}\left[\frac{R1H1_{t+1}}{N1_{t+1}}\right] + U1_{CH1(t+1)}\left(\frac{CH1_{t+1}}{N1_{t+1}}\right)$$

$$+ U1_{\tau(t+1)}\left\{\frac{\bar{\tau}_{t+1}^{H1}\left[R1H1_{t+1}^{de}, \left(\frac{M1_{t+1}^{d}}{p_{t+1}^{Rle}}\right)\right]}{N1_{t+1}}\right\}$$

$$+ U1_{l(t+1)}\frac{\left[\left(h1_{t+1}^{T}\cdot N1_{t+1} - h1^{s}\cdot N1_{t+1}^{s}\right)\right]}{N1_{t+1}} \qquad (12.22)$$

All terms in (12.22) are positive except $U1_{\tau(t+1)}[\bullet]$, since next period's transactions time presumably yields negative utility at an increasing rate:

$$U1_{\tau(t+1)}[\bullet] < 0, \quad U1'_{\tau(t+1)}[\bullet] < 0, \quad U1''_{\tau(t+1)}[\bullet] < 0.$$

The household sector attempts to maximize present utility subject to its budget constraint. This constraint stipulates that total household spending on both privately produced products, C and R1, sanitation, $W^{*}G1$, and general public services, g_{1H1}, each period equals their current disposable income minus personal saving.

It is assumed that the households take their current wage and nonwage incomes as given but decide how many people they want to have employed next period. In terms of the abstract unit of account of Country One, the budget constraint facing the household sector during the current period is given by

$$\Pi1_t - Tx1_t + W1_t\cdot h1_t^{W}\cdot N1_t^{w} + B1_{H1t}$$
$$= p_{R1t}\cdot\left(\frac{R1H1_t}{N1_t}\right)\cdot N1_t + p_{Ct}\cdot\tilde{\varepsilon}\cdot\left(\frac{CH1_t}{N1_t}\right)\cdot N1_t + \left(M1_{t+1}^{d} - M1_t\right)$$
$$+ p_{B1}\cdot\left(B1_{H1(t+1)}^{d} - B1_{H1t}\right) \qquad (12.23)$$

where

$\Pi1_t$ = the dividends received from the R1, NR, and PB1 sectors this period.

And where

$Tx1_t = Tx_{W*G2t} + Tx_{G1H1t}$ = current-period taxes for sanitation and general public services.
$W1_t$ = the money wage that was announced last period by the NR sector and is paid by every employer in Country One during the current period.
$B1_{H1t}$ = the number of domestic bonds held by the H1 sector at the beginning of the current period. Each bond pays one unit of domestic money as interest during the current period. Therefore, this amount also represents the H1 sector's interest income during the period.
p_{R1H1t} = the price of R1 that prevails during the current period.
p_{CH1t} = the price of C that prevails during the current period (in terms of Country Two's unit of account).
$\tilde{\varepsilon}$ = the value of Country Three's unit of account in terms of Country One's unit of account.
$M1^d_{t+1}$ = the H1 sector's nominal demand for domestic money by the end of the current period.
$M1_{t+1}$ = the nominal amount of money held by the H1 sector at the beginning of the current period.
p_{B1} = the current-period price of Country One's bonds.
$B1^d_{H1(t+1)}$ = the number of domestic bonds the H1 sector plans to hold by the end of the current period.
$M1_{t+1}$ = the H1 sector's holdings at the beginning of the period of money issued in Country One.

The budget constraint the H1 sector anticipates facing next period is given by

$$\begin{aligned} &\Pi 1^e_{t+1} - Tx_{G1H1(t+1)}(g_{1H1(t+1)}) - Tx_{W*G1(t+1)} \\ &\quad + W1_{t+1} \cdot h1^s \cdot N1^s_{t+1} + (1 + p_{B1}) \cdot B1^d_{H1(t+1)} + M1^d_{t+1} \\ &\quad = p^{H1}_{R1(t+1)} \cdot \left(\frac{R1H1_{t+1}}{N1_{t+1}} \right) \cdot N1_{t+1} + p^{H1}_{C(t+1)} \end{aligned} \tag{12.24}$$

where

$\Pi 1^e_{t+1}$ = the total dividends the H1 sector anticipates receiving from the R1, NR, and PB1 sectors.
$p^{H1}_{R1(t+1)}$ = the price of R1 that the H1 sector anticipates will prevail next period.
$R1H1_{t+1}$ =the number of units of R1 the H1 sector anticipates buying next period.
$p^{H1}_{C(t+1)}$ = the price of C that the H1 sector anticipates will prevail next period (in terms of Country Three's unit of account).
$CH1_{t+1}$ = the number of units of C the H1 sector anticipates buying next period.
$M1^d_{t+1}$ = the H1 sector's demand for money for the end of the current period.

Solving (12.21) for $B1^{d}_{H1(t+1)}$,

$$B1^{d}_{H1(t+1)} = \Bigg[p^{H1e}_{R1(t+1)} \cdot \left(\frac{R1H1_{t+1}}{N1_t}\right) \cdot N1_t + p^{H1}_{C(t+1)} \cdot \tilde{\varepsilon} \cdot \left(\frac{CH1_{t+1}}{N1_t}\right) \cdot N1_t - M1^{d}_{t+1} - \Pi^{e}_{t+1} + Tx_{G1H1(t+1)}\left(g_{1H1(t+1)}\right) + Tx_{W^*G1(t+1)} - W1_{t+1} \cdot h1^{s} \cdot N1^{s}_{t+1}\Bigg] \Big/ (1 + p_{B1}) \quad (12.25)$$

Substituting the right-hand side of (12.25) for $B1^{H1d}_{t+1}$ into (12.23) yields

$$\Pi_t - Txl_t + W1_t \cdot h1^{W}_{t} \cdot N1^{w}_{t} + (1 + p_{B1}) \cdot B1_{H1t} + M1_t - M1^{d}_{t+1} + \left[\frac{1}{(1 + r_1)}\right] \cdot \left[\Pi^{e}_{t+1} - Tx_{G1H1(t+1)}\left(g_{1H1(t+1)}\right) + Tx_{W^*G1(t+1)} + W1_{t+1} \cdot h1^{s} \cdot N1^{s}_{t+1} + M1^{d}_{t+1}\right]$$
$$= p_{R1t} \cdot \left(\frac{R1H1_t}{N1_t}\right) \cdot N1_t + p_{Ct} \cdot \tilde{\varepsilon} \cdot \left(\frac{CH1_t}{N1_t}\right) \cdot N1_t + \left[\frac{1}{(1 + r_1)}\right] \cdot \left[p^{H1}_{R1(t+1)} \cdot \left(\frac{R1H1_{t+1}}{N1_{t+1}}\right) \cdot N1_{t+1} + p^{H1}_{C(t+1)} \cdot \tilde{\varepsilon} \cdot \left(\frac{CH1_{t+1}}{N1_{t+1}}\right) \cdot N1_{t+1}\right] \quad (12.26)$$

where $1/(1 + r_1) = p_{B1}/(1 + p_{B1})$ since $r_1 = 1/p_{B1}$. According to (12.26), the H1 sector's constraint states that the present value of current and future consumption must equal the present value of the sector's present and future disposable income and additions to (financial) wealth.

At this point in the analysis, the objective of the household sector in Country One is to maximize (12.22) subject to (12.26). Therefore the objective is to maximize

$$U1 = U1_{R1t}\left(\frac{R1H1_t}{N1_t}\right) + U1_{CH1t}\left(\frac{CH1_t}{N1_t}\right) + U1_{\tau t}\left\{\frac{\left[\bar{\tau}^{H1}_{t}\left(R1H1_t, M1_t/p_{R1t}\right)\right]}{N1_t}\right\} + U1_{R1(t+1)}\left[\frac{R1H1_{t+1}}{N1_{t+1}}\right] + U1_{CH1(t+1)}\left(\frac{CH1_{t+1}}{N1_{t+1}}\right) + U1_{\tau(t+1)}\left\{\bar{\tau}^{H1}_{t}\frac{\left[R1H1^{de}_{t+1}, \left(M1^{d}_{t+1}/p^{Rle}_{t+1}\right)\right]}{N1_{t+1}}\right\} + U1_{l(t+1)}\frac{\left[\left(h1^{T}_{t+1} \cdot N1_{t+1} - h1^{s} \cdot N1^{s}_{t+1}\right)\right]}{N1_{t+1}} + \lambda\Big\{\Pi1_t - Tx1_t + W1_t \cdot h1^{w}_{t} \cdot N1^{w}_{t} + (1+p_{B1}) \cdot B1_{H1t} + M1_t - M1^{d}_{t+1}$$

$$+\left[\frac{1}{(1+r_1)}\right]\cdot\left[\Pi^{e}_{t+1}-Tx_{G1H1(t+1)}\left(g_{1H1(t+1)}\right)+Tx_{W*G1(t+1)}\right.$$

$$\left.+W1_{t+1}\cdot h1^{s}\cdot N1^{s}_{t+1}+M1^{d}_{t+1}\right]$$

$$-\,p_{R1t}\cdot\left(\frac{R1H1_t}{N1_t}\right)\cdot N1_t-p_{Ct}\cdot\tilde{\varepsilon}\cdot\left(\frac{CH1_t}{N1_t}\right)\cdot N1_t$$

$$-\left[\frac{1}{(1+r_1)}\right]\cdot\left[p^{H1}_{R1(t+1)}\cdot\left(\frac{R1H1_{t+1}}{N1_{t+1}}\right)\cdot N1_{t+1}+p^{H1}_{C(t+1)}\cdot\tilde{\varepsilon}\right.$$

$$\left.\left.\cdot\left(\frac{CH1_{t+1}}{N1_{t+1}}\right)\cdot N1_{t+1}\right]\right\} \qquad (12.27)$$

First-Order Necessary Conditions (FONCs)

At this stage, the first-order necessary conditions for utility maximization with respect to current and future consumption of R1 and C per capita, end-of-period money balances, the end-of-period supply of labor, and the Lagrange multiplier are given by (12.28)–(12.34):

$$\left\{U1'_{R1t}+U1'_{\tau t}\cdot\left[\frac{\partial\overline{\tau}^{H1}_{t}}{\partial\left(R1H1_t/N1_t\right)}\right]\right\}-\lambda\cdot p_{R1t}\cdot N1_t=0 \qquad (12.28)$$

The sum inside braces in (12.28) denotes the net marginal present utility from an extra unit of current consumption of R1. As the sector increases current per capita consumption by one unit, present utility is affected in two ways. First, the increase in current consumption directly raises present utility, since $U'_{R1t}>0$. Second, the increase in current consumption increases current transactions time, $\overline{\tau}_1>0$, which decreases present utility, since $U'_{\tau(t+1)}<0$. Since λ and p_{R1t} are positive, (12.28) stipulates that if the home household sector decides to consume R1 during the current period, the net marginal present utility of that consumption must be positive.

Similarly, (12.29) stipulates that the H1 sector plans to consume R1 per capita next period up to the point at which the net marginal present utility from that consumption, shown by the sum inside braces in that equation, is equal to the present value of next period's anticipated marginal expenditure on R1 per capita:

$$\left\{U1'_{R1(t+1)}+U1'_{\tau(t+1)}\cdot\left[\frac{\partial\overline{\tau}^{H1}_{t+1}}{\partial\left(R1H1_{t+1}/N1_{t+1}\right)}\right]\right\}$$

$$-\,\lambda\cdot\left[\frac{1}{(1+r_1)}\right]\cdot p^{H1}_{R1(t+1)}\cdot N1_{t+1}=0 \qquad (12.29)$$

Analogous conditions, (12.30) and (12.31), hold for the H1 sector's current and anticipated future consumption per capita of consumption goods, except that, for simplicity, transactions time associated with purchasing consumption goods is ignored in these latter two conditions. This assumption simplifies the H1 sector's demand for money for the end of the period, allowing that demand to remain independent of the exchange rate between Country One and Country Three's units of account. The solution for current interest rates and exchange rates is simplified dramatically as a result.

$$U1'_{CH1t} - \lambda \cdot p_{Ct} \cdot \tilde{\varepsilon} \cdot N1_t = 0 \tag{12.30}$$

$$U1'_{CH1(t+1)} - \lambda \cdot \left[\frac{1}{(1+r_1)}\right] \cdot p^{H1}_{C(t+1)} \cdot \tilde{\varepsilon} \cdot N1_{t+1} = 0 \tag{12.31}$$

According to condition (12.32), the H1 sector will demand money balances for the end of the period up to the point at which the marginal utility (reduction in disutility associated with transactions time next period) of the anticipated marginal transactions time saved next period is equal to the present value of the marginal cost of adding to this period's end-of-period money, namely, the present value of the interest the sector forgoes next period because it accumulates noninterest-bearing money rather than Country One's bonds during the period on the margin:

$$\frac{U1'_{\tau(t+1)} \cdot \left[\frac{\partial \bar{\tau}^{H1}_{t+1}}{\partial\left(M1^d_{t+1}/p^{H1}_{R1(t+1)}\right)}\right]}{N1_{t+1} - \lambda \cdot p^{H1}_{R1(t+1)} \cdot \left[\frac{r_1}{(1+r_1)}\right]} = 0 \tag{12.32}$$

Finally, condition (12.33) stipulates that the H1 sector increases its supply of workers to the labor market up to the point at which the present marginal disutility of the reduction in future leisure is equal to the present value of the extra labor income to be received from the marginal employee:

$$-\frac{\left(U1'_{l(t+1)} \cdot h1^s\right)}{N1_{t+1} + \lambda \cdot \left[\frac{1}{(1+r_1)}\right] \cdot W1_{t+1} \cdot h1^s} = 0 \tag{12.33}$$

Condition (12.34) restates the budget constraint relevant to the H1 sector's decision making at this point:

$$\begin{aligned}
&\Pi1_t - Tx1_t + W1_t \cdot h1^w_t \cdot N1^w_t + \left(1 + p_{B1}\right) \cdot B1_{H1t} + M1_t - M1^d_{t+1} \\
&\quad + \left[\frac{1}{(1+r_1)}\right] \cdot [\Pi1^e_{t+1} - Tx_{G1H1(t+1)}\left(g_{1H1(t+1)}\right) - Tx_{W*G1(t+1)} \\
&\quad + W1_{t+1} \cdot h1^s \cdot N1^s_{t+1} + M1^d_{t+1}] \\
&= p_{R1t} \cdot \left(\frac{R1H1_t}{N1_t}\right) \cdot N1_t + p_{Ct} \cdot \tilde{\varepsilon} \cdot \left(\frac{CH1_t}{N1_t}\right) \cdot N1_t \\
&\quad + \left[\frac{1}{(1+r_1)}\right] \cdot \left[p^{H1}_{R1(t+1)} \cdot \left(\frac{R1H1_{t+1}}{N1_{t+1}}\right) \cdot N1_{t+1}\right. \\
&\quad \left. + p^{H1}_{C(t+1)} \cdot \tilde{\varepsilon} \cdot \left(\frac{CH1_{t+1}}{N1_{t+1}}\right) \cdot N1_{t+1}\right]
\end{aligned} \tag{12.34}$$

Subjective versus Market Rates of Substitution

The first-order conditions presented above provide the basis for a comparison of the various subjective and market rates of substitution that motivate the economic behavior of the H1 sector in deciding its current and (notional) future consumption of C and R1, its supply of workers to the labor market for next period, and its end-of-period demands for money and bonds. These choices are made with next period's public goods, next period's taxes, current disposable income, current product prices, and current wage rates already known to the H1 sector. A few of these rates of substitution are presented below.

Subjective versus Market Rates of Substitution between Current Consumption of C and R1

Rearranging terms and then dividing (12.28) by (12.30) yields

$$\frac{\{U1'_{R1t} + U1'_{\tau t} \cdot [\partial \bar{\tau}_t^{H1}/\partial\,(R1H1_t/N1_t)] \cdot N1t\}}{U1'_{CH1t}} = \frac{p_{R1t}}{\tilde{\varepsilon} \cdot p_{Ct}} \tag{12.35}$$

The left-hand side of (12.35) represents the H1 sector's subjective rate of substitution of current consumption of R1 for current consumption of C, that is, the amount of C it is willing to sacrifice in order to increase its consumption of R1 by one unit. The right-hand side denotes the corresponding market rate of substitution, that is, the amount of C the market requires the sector to give up in deciding to consume an additional unit of R1. According to this condition, the sector will consume C and R1 up to the point at which the subjective rate is equal to the market rate. An increase in the price of C, an increase in the value of Country Three's unit of account in terms of Country One's currency, or a decrease in the price of R1 causes the H1 sector, ceteris paribus, to increase its consumption of R1 and reduce its demand for C.

Subjective versus Market Rates of Substitution between Current Consumption of R1 and End-of-Period Money Balances

Rearranging terms and then dividing (12.28) by (12.32) yields

$$\frac{\left\{U1'_{R1t} + U1'_{\tau t}\left[\frac{\partial \bar{\tau}_t^{H1}}{\partial (R1H1_t/N1_t)}\right] \cdot N1t\right\}}{\left\{U1'_{\tau(t+1)} \cdot \left[\frac{\partial \bar{\tau}_{t+1}^{H1}}{\partial\left(M1_{t+1}^{d}/p_{t+1}^{R1e}\right)}\right]\right\}} = \frac{p_{R1t}}{\left\{p_{R1(t+1)}^{H1} \cdot [r_1/(1+r_1)]\right\}} \tag{12.36}$$

The left-hand side of (12.36) denotes the subjective rate of substitution of current consumption of a unit of R1 per capita for money balances held at the end of the current period. If the H1 sector decides to consume an extra unit of R1 per capita during the current period, its utility increases. The subjective rate of substitution indicates the maximum amount the sector is willing to decrease its end-of-period real money balances and incur the extra disutility of greater transactions time next period in order to maintain constant present utility in response to a unit increase in its current consumption of R1. The market rate of substitution of R1 for real money balances appears on the right-hand side of (12.36). A unit increase in R1 costs p_{R1t}. If the sector simultaneously reduces its end-of-period real money holdings, ceteris paribus, the present value of the opportunity cost to the sector of holding money balances at the end of the period falls by $p^{H1}_{R1(t+1)} \cdot [r_1/(1 + r_1)]$ where $p^{H1}_{R1(t+1)} \cdot r_1$ represents the anticipated increase in spending next period from the reduction in a unit of real money balances at the end of the current period. An increase in the current interest rate reduces the market rate of substitution of current consumption of R1 for real money balances held at the end of the current period. Therefore a rise in r_{1t} induces the sector to increase its demand for R1, ceteris paribus, and reduce its demand for real money balances for the end of the period.

Subjective versus Market Rates of Substitution between Current Consumption of R1 and Future Labor

Rearranging terms and then dividing (12.28) by (12.33) yields

$$\frac{-\left\{U1'_{R1_t} + U1'_{\tau t} \cdot \left[\frac{\partial \overline{\tau}^{H1}_t}{\partial (R1H1_t/N1_t)}\right] \cdot N1t\right\}}{\left(U1'_{l(t+1)} \cdot h1^s\right)} = \frac{-p_{R1t}}{\{[1/(1+r_1)] \cdot W1_{t+1} \cdot h1^s\}} \qquad (12.37)$$

Both the subjective and market rates of substitution in this case are negative. Ceteris paribus, an increase in labor next period decreases present utility. Therefore, if the household sector decides to add to its labor next period, it must also decide to increase current consumption, ceteris paribus, if it intends to keep present utility constant. By the same token, if the sector decides to add to its labor next period, it will be able to purchase $p_{R1t}/\{[1/(1 + r_1)] \cdot (W1_{t+1} \cdot h1^s)\}$ more R1 during the current period without jeopardizing its purchasing power over R1 next period. Ceteris paribus, the higher current product prices, the smaller will be the H1 sector's demand for current consumption and the smaller will be its supply of labor for next period as well. On the other hand, the higher the current wage rate, the greater its current consumption spending and the greater its supply of workers for next period.

Subjective versus Market Rates of Substitution between Current Consumption of R1 and Future Consumption of R1

Rearranging terms and then dividing (12.28) by (12.29) yields

$$\frac{\{U1'_{R1_t} + U1'_{\tau t}\,[\partial \overline{\tau}^{H1}_t / \partial\,(R1H1_t/N1_t)] \cdot N1t\}}{\left\{U1'_{R1(t+1)} + U1'_{\tau(t+1)} \cdot [\partial \overline{\tau}^{H1}_{t+1} / \partial\,(R1H1_{t+1}/N1_{t+1})]\right\}} = \frac{p_{R1t}}{[1/(1+r_1)] \cdot p^{H1e}_{R1(t+1)}} \qquad (12.38)$$

According to (12.38), holding constant the H1 sector's anticipated future price of R1, the sector will decrease current consumption of R1 and increase planned future consumption of R1 as the current interest rate rises. In an analogous fashion, the sector will also decrease current consumption of C as the rate of interest rises in Country One.

Country One's Household Sector's Demand and Supply Functions

The H1 sector's demand functions for R1, C, and end-of-period money balances together with its supply of labor function for next period emerge from the discussion to this point.

Let

$$\overline{Y}1 = \text{ current disposable income plus initial wealth } =$$

$$\Pi 1_t - Tx1_t + W1_t \cdot h1_t^w \cdot N1_t^w + (1 + p_{B1}) \cdot B1_t^{H1} + M1_t.$$

$$R1H1_t^d = R1H1_t^d \left(\underset{-}{p_{R1t}}, \underset{+}{\tilde{\varepsilon} \cdot p_{CH1t}}, \underset{+}{N1_t}, \underset{-}{r_{1t}}, \underset{+}{\overline{Y}1}, \underset{+}{W1_{t+1}} \right) \tag{12.39}$$

$$CH1_t^d = CH1_t^d \left(\underset{+}{p_{R1t}}, \underset{-}{\tilde{\varepsilon} \cdot p_{CH1t}}, \underset{+}{N1_t}, \underset{-}{r_{1t}}, \underset{+}{\overline{Y}1}, \underset{+}{W1_{t+1}} \right) \tag{12.40}$$

$$M1_{t+1}^d = M1_{t+1}^d \left(\underset{-}{r_{1t}}, \underset{+}{\overline{Y}1}, \underset{+}{W1_{t+1}} \right) \tag{12.41}$$

$$N1_{t+1}^s = N1_{t+1}^s \left(\underset{-}{r_{1t}}, \underset{-}{\overline{Y}1}, \underset{+}{W1_{t+1}} \right) \tag{12.42}$$

Then from (12.23), the H1 sector's end-of-period demand for Country One's bonds is given by

$$p_{B1} \cdot B1_{H1(t+1)}^d = \overline{Y}1 - p_{R1t} \cdot \left(\frac{R1H1_t}{N1_t} \right) \cdot N1_t - p_{Ct} \cdot \tilde{\varepsilon} \cdot \left(\frac{CH1_t}{N1_t} \right) \cdot N1_t$$

$$- \left(M1_{t+1}^d - M1_t \right)$$

$$p_{B1} \cdot B1_{H1(t+1)}^d = \overline{Y}1 - p_{R1t} \cdot R1H1_t^d - \tilde{\varepsilon} \cdot p_{Ct} \cdot CH1_t^d - M1_{t+1}^d$$

$$= p_{B1} \cdot B1_{H1(t+1)}^d \left(\underset{+}{\overline{Y}1}, \underset{+}{r_{1t}}, \underset{-}{W1_{t+1}}, \underset{+}{N1_t} \right) \tag{12.43}$$

The current budget constraint imposes the following restrictions:

$$p_{R1t} \cdot \left[\frac{\partial \left(R1H1_t^d \right)}{\partial \overline{Y}1} \right] + \left(\tilde{\varepsilon} \cdot p_{R1t} \right) \cdot \left[\frac{\partial CH1_t^d}{\partial \overline{Y}1} \right] + \frac{\partial M1_{t+1}^d}{\partial \overline{Y}1} \tag{12.44}$$

$$+\frac{\partial\left(p_{B1}\cdot B1^{d}_{H1(t+1)}\right)}{\partial\overline{Y}1}\equiv 1$$

$$p_{R1t}\cdot\left[\frac{\partial\left(R1H1^{d}_{t}\right)}{\partial\overline{Y}1}\right]+\left(\tilde{\varepsilon}\cdot p_{Ct}\right)\cdot\left[\frac{\partial CH1^{d}_{t}}{\partial\overline{Y}1}\right]+\frac{\partial M1^{d}_{t+1}}{\partial\overline{Y}1}$$

$$+\frac{\partial\left(p_{B1}\cdot B1^{d}_{H1(t+1)}\right)}{\partial\overline{Y}1}\equiv 1 \quad (12.45)$$

$$\left[\frac{\partial\left(p_{R1t}\cdot R1H1^{d}_{t}\right)}{\partial p_{R1t}}\right]+\left(\tilde{\varepsilon}\cdot p_{Ct}\right)\cdot\left[\frac{\partial CH1^{d}_{t}}{\partial p_{R1t}}\right]\equiv 0 \quad (12.46)$$

$$p_{R1t}\cdot\left[\frac{\partial R1H1^{d}_{t}}{\partial\left(\tilde{\varepsilon}\cdot p_{Ct}\right)}\right]+\left[\frac{\partial\left[\left(\tilde{\varepsilon}\cdot p_{Ct}\right)\cdot CH1^{d}_{t}\right]}{\partial\left(\tilde{\varepsilon}\cdot p_{Ct}\right)}\right]\equiv 0 \quad (12.47)$$

$$p_{R1t}\cdot\left[\frac{\partial\left(R1H1^{d}_{t}\right)}{\partial W1_{t+1}}\right]+\left(\tilde{\varepsilon}\cdot p_{Ct}\right)\cdot\left[\frac{\partial CH1^{d}_{t}}{\partial W1_{t+1}}\right]+\frac{\partial M1^{d}_{t+1}}{\partial W1_{t+1}}$$

$$+\frac{\partial\left(p_{B1}\cdot B1^{d}_{H1(t+1)}\right)}{\partial W1_{t+1}}\equiv 0 \quad (12.48)$$

Involuntary Unemployment Case

If the home household sector feels that the home employers' market demand for workers for next period constitutes an effective constraint upon the home households, then labor supply function (12.42) is no longer relevant. In this case also, the amount of labor the home households anticipate their employers will demand for next period now enters as a parameter in demand functions (12.39)–(12.41) and (12.43) and affects these demands in a manner similar to a change in $W1_{t+1}$ in those expressions.

Country Two

The G2 Sector

Once the H2 sector has chosen $g_{2H2(t+1)}$, the G2 sector knows $\overline{R2}_{t+1}$, given its estimate of the population in that country by the end of the current period. Also, once the G2 sector has decided the current addition to its infrastructure, it has also decided the amount of the NR it will purchase this period, the amount of labor it will use in providing that addition to infrastructure, and the corresponding necessary level of corporate taxes.

At this point in the process, the G2 sector decides the optimal end-of-period levels of physical capital and workers as it attempts to minimize next period's outlays, given next period's production of general public services and anticipated revenue from the central bank. In a manner analogous to the G2 sector's decision making at this step, the following decision functions emerge:

$$N2^{d}_{G2H2(t+1)} = N2^{d}_{G2H2(t+1)}\left(\underset{-}{W2_{t+1}}, \underset{+}{r_{2t}}, \underset{+}{p_{Kt}}, \underset{+}{g_{2H2(t+1)}}\right) \tag{12.49}$$

$$K^{d}_{G2(t+1)} = K^{d}_{G2(t+1)}\left(\underset{+}{W2_{t+1}}, \underset{-}{r_{2t}}, \underset{-}{p_{Kt}}, \underset{-}{\delta}, \underset{+}{g_{2H2(t+1)}}\right) \tag{12.50}$$

Once it has solved for its end-of-period demands for workers and capital, the G2 sector's end-of-period supply of bonds is given by

$$\begin{aligned} p_{B2} \cdot B2^{s}_{G2(t+1)} = {} & W2_t \cdot h^{GH2}_{G2t} \cdot N2_{G2t} + p_{Kt} \cdot \Big[K^{d}_{G2(t+1)} \\ & \left(W2_{t+1}, r_{2t}, p_{Kt}, \delta, g_{2H2(t+1)}\right) - (1-\delta) \cdot K_{G2t}\Big] \\ & - \Pi^{CB2G2}_{t} + \left(1 + p_{B2}\right) \cdot B2_{G2t} + p^{G2}_{xt} \cdot \overline{R2}_t - Tx_{G2H2t} \\ & + W2_t \cdot h^{W^*H2}_{G2t} \cdot N2_{G2t} - Tx_{W^*G2t} \\ & + W2_t \cdot h^{\Delta I}_{G2t} \cdot N2_{G2t}\,(\Delta I2_t) \\ & + (1/\varepsilon) \cdot p_{NRt} \cdot NRG2^{Td}_{t} - Tx_{Kt} - Tx_{R2t} \end{aligned} \tag{12.51}$$

The R2 Industry

Now that the R2 industry has decided current production, the current price of its product, and the number of hours it will use its current employees, it has also decided the inventory of unprocessed R2 it wants to hold by the beginning of next period. In addition, it has also decided the number of people it plans to employ next period, $N2_{R2(t+1)}$, to process that inventory as well as next period's anticipated increase above the minimum end-of-period stock required by its government sector. The end-of-period stock of its processed inventory is established by current production and current sales, but this inventory does not affect next period's production. However, the end-of-period stock of the processed inventory will affect the price the sector sets for its product next period. It also affects the amount that the sector borrows during the current period.

The sector's end-of-period inventory of processed R2 is analogous to (8.5) for the R1 industry; it is specified here as (12.52):

$$R2^{T^*}_{t+1} = R2^{T^*}_{t} + \tau_{R2}\,(I2_t) \cdot T_{R2t}\,(h_{R2t} \cdot N2_{R2t}) - R2H2_t \geq 0 \tag{12.52}$$

The sector's end-of-period supply of bonds is then established by the sector's unintended accumulation of the processed R2 during the period:

$$p_{B2} \cdot B1^{s}_{R2(t+1)} = p_{R2t} \cdot \left(R2^{T^*}_{t+1} - R2^{T^*}_{t}\right) + p_{B2} \cdot B2_{R2t}$$
$$= p_{R2t} \cdot (\tau_{R2}(I2_t) \cdot T_{R2t}(h_{R2t} \cdot N2_{R2t}) - R2H2_t) + P_{B2} \cdot B2_{R2t} \quad (12.53)$$

If the sector produces more than it sells during the current period, it issues more bonds during the period. If it sells more than it produces, it buys back some bonds, or even lends in the bond market. $R2H2 \leq R2^{T^*}_{t} + \tau_{R1}(I2_t) \cdot T_{R2t}(h_{R2t} \cdot N2_{R2t})$. If $R2H2 = R2^{T^*}_{t} + \tau_{R2}(I2_t) \cdot T_{R2t}(h_{R2t} \cdot N2_{R2t})$, then $p_{B2} \cdot B2^{s}_{R2(t+1)} = p_{R2t} \cdot (-R2^{T^*}_{t}) + p_{B2} \cdot B2_{R2t}$. Therefore, while the current interest rate the sector anticipates will prevail during the current period affects its desired ending-period inventory of processed R2 as it decides current production and product price, the actual amount of this inventory is established by current production and current sales. In the final analysis, the end-of-period supply of bonds to Country Two's bond market by the renewable resource industry in Country Two is independent of the current interest rate (although the sector's forecast of the current interest rate was important to its production and pricing decisions).

Capital Goods Industry

Given that the capital goods industry has already decided the number of hours to use its current employees, the level of current production, the current price of its product, and the wage rate it will pay its employees next period, its original objective function, (6.36), must be modified and solved for the sector's effective demand for workers for next period and physical capital for the beginning of next period. Now the objective is to maximize the sector's present value with respect to $K^{d}_{K(t+1)}$, $N2^{Te}_{K(t+1)}$, and $N2^{Se}_{K(t+1)}$ given the values for p_{Kt}, h_K, h^{S}_{K}, $W2_{t+1}$, and given the current market demand for its product:

$$\Pi^{d}_{Kt} + \frac{\Pi^{d}_{K(t+1)}}{(1+r_2)} = p_{Kt}\left\{KG1^{d}_{t} + KG2^{d}_{t} + KG3^{d}_{t} + KC^{d}_{t} - \left[K^{d}_{K(t+1)} - (1-\delta) \cdot K_{Kt}\right]\right\}$$
$$- \left(\frac{p^{NR}_{t}}{\varepsilon}\right) \cdot (\kappa + \varphi_K) \cdot \tau_K(I2_t) \cdot T_{Kt}(h_K \cdot N2_{Kt}, K_{Kt})$$
$$- Tx_{KG2t} - \left(\frac{p_w}{\varepsilon}\right) \cdot \left[\varphi_K \cdot \tau_K(I2_t) \cdot T_{Kt}(h_K \cdot N2_{Kt}, K_{Kt})\right.$$
$$\left. + \kappa \cdot \delta \cdot K_{Kt} - T^{S}_{Kt}\left(h^{S}_{K} \cdot N2_{Kt}\right)\right] - W2_t \cdot \left(h_K + h^{S}_{K}\right) \cdot N2_{Kt}$$
$$- (1 + p_{B2}) \cdot B2_{Kt} + \left[\frac{1}{(1+r_2)}\right] \cdot \left\{TR^{Ke}_{t+1}\left\{\tau_K(I2_t + \Delta I2)\right.\right.$$
$$\cdot T^{Te}_{K(t+1)}\left(h^{e}_{K} \cdot N2^{Te}_{K(t+1)}, K^{d}_{K(t+1)}\right)$$

$$- \left[K^{de}_{K(t+2)} - (1-\delta) \cdot K^{de}_{K(t+1)} \right], \omega^{*}_{KNR}, \omega^{*}_{KC}, KG1^{de}_{t+1}$$

$$+KG2^{de}_{t+1} + KG3^{de}_{t+1} \Big\} - \left(\frac{p_w}{\varepsilon}\right) \cdot \Big\{ \varphi_K \cdot \tau_K \left(I2_t + \Delta I2\right)$$

$$\cdot T^{Te}_{K(t+1)} \left(h^{e}_{K} \cdot N2^{Te}_{K(t+1)}, K^{d}_{K(t+1)} \right) - T^{S}_{K(t+1)} \left(h^{e}_{K} \cdot N2^{Se}_{K(t+1)} \right) \Big\}$$

$$- W2_{t+1} \cdot \left(N2^{Te}_{K(t+1)} + N2^{Se}_{K(t+1)} \right) - Tx_{KG2(t+1)}$$

$$- \left(\frac{p^{K}_{NR(t+1)}}{\varepsilon} \right) \cdot (\theta_K + \varphi_K) \cdot \tau_K \left(I2_t + \Delta I2\right)$$

$$\cdot T^{Te}_{K(t+1)} \left(h^{e}_{K} \cdot N2^{Te}_{K(t+1)}, K^{d}_{K(t+1)} \right) \Big\} \qquad (12.54)$$

First-Order Necessary Conditions

The corresponding first-order necessary conditions become

$$\frac{\partial \left[\Pi^{d}_{Kt} + \Pi^{d}_{K(t+1)}/(1+r_2) \right]}{\partial K^{d}_{K(t+1)}} \equiv -p_{Kt} + \left[\frac{1}{(1+r_2)} \right]$$

$$\cdot \left[\left\{ \left[\frac{\partial TR^{Ke}_{t+1}}{\partial K^{d}_{t+1}} \right] - \left\{ \left[\frac{(p_w \cdot \varphi_K)}{\varepsilon} \right] \right. \right. \right.$$

$$\left. + \frac{p^{K}_{NR(t+1)} \cdot (\theta_K + \varphi_K)}{\varepsilon} \right\} \cdot \tau_K \left(I2_t + \Delta I2\right)$$

$$\left. \left. \cdot \left[\frac{\partial T^{Te}_{K(t+1)}}{\partial K^{d}_{K(t+1)}} \right] \right\} + \left[\frac{\partial TR^{Ke}_{t+1}}{\partial K^{de}_{t+1}} \right] (1-\delta) \right] = 0 \qquad (12.55)$$

$$\frac{\partial \left[\Pi^{d}_{Kt} + \Pi^{d}_{K(t+1)}/(1+r_2) \right]}{\partial N2^{Te}_{K(t+1)}} \equiv \left[\frac{1}{(1+r_2)} \right] \cdot \left[\left[\frac{\partial TR^{K2e}_{t+1}}{\partial N2^{Te}_{K(t+1)}} \right] \cdot \tau_K \left(I2_t + \Delta I2\right) \right.$$

$$\cdot \left[\frac{\partial T^{Te}_{K(t+1)}}{\partial N2^{Te}_{K(t+1)}} \right] \cdot h^{e}_{K2} - \left[\frac{(p_w \cdot \varphi_K)}{\varepsilon} \right]$$

$$\cdot \tau_K \left(I2_t + \Delta I2\right) \cdot \left[\frac{\partial T^{K2e}_{t+1}}{\partial N2^{Te}_{K(t+1)}} \right] \cdot h^{e}_{K2}$$

$$
-\left[\frac{p^{K}_{NR(t+1)} \cdot (\kappa + \varphi_K)}{\varepsilon}\right] \cdot \tau_K \left(I2_t + \Delta I2\right)
$$

$$
\cdot \left[\left[\frac{\partial T^{Te}_{K(t+1)}}{\partial N2^{Te}_{K(t+1)}}\right] \cdot h^{e}_{K2} - W2_{t+1}\right] = 0 \tag{12.56}
$$

$$
\frac{\partial\left[\Pi^{d}_{Kt} + \Pi^{d}_{K(t+1)}/(1 + r_2)\right]}{\partial N2^{Se}_{K(t+1)}} \equiv + \left[\frac{1}{(1 + r_2)}\right]
$$

$$
\cdot \left[\left(\frac{p_w}{\varepsilon}\right) \cdot \left[\frac{\partial T^{S}_{K(t+1)}}{\partial N2^{Se}_{K(t+1)}}\right] \cdot h^{e}_{K} - W2_{t+1}\right] = 0 \tag{12.57}
$$

Demand Function for $K^{d}_{K(t+1)}$

According to (12.55), an increase in the rate of interest in Country Two's bond market, r_2, reduces the present value of the anticipated net revenue from an extra unit of physical capital held by the beginning of next period, thereby reducing the capital goods sector's demand for physical capital. An increase in the rate of depreciation, δ, reduces the sector's end-of-period demand for capital because it reduces the revenue the industry anticipates receiving next period by selling that portion of the extra capital that has not physically deteriorated by the end of next period. An increase in the price of pollution allowances, p_w, an increase in the amount of the nonrenewable resource contained in a unit of physical capital produced next period, κ, or an increase in the waste generated per unit of physical capital produced next period, φ_K, increases the sector's marginal cost of producing capital goods next period, causing the sector to reduce its demand for physical capital for the beginning of that period. An increase in the value of Country Two's unit of account in terms of Country One's unit of account, ε, produces the opposite result. Therefore, the following demand function for physical capital for the end of the current period by the capital goods industry is specified by (12.58):

$$
K^{d}_{K(t+1)} = K^{d}_{K(t+1)} \underset{-\quad - \quad - \quad - \quad - \quad - \quad +}{\left(p_{Kt}, r_2, \delta, p_w, \kappa, \varphi_K, \varepsilon\right)} \tag{12.58}
$$

Demand Function for $N2^{Te}_{K(t+1)}$

From (12.5), an increase in p_w, θ_K, or φ_K also increases the marginal cost next period of adding another worker for the purpose of producing capital goods. An increase in ε produces the opposite result. Therefore, the following demand function for workers to build capital goods next period is given by

$$N2^{Te}_{K(t+1)} = N2^{Te}_{K(t+1)}\left(\underset{-}{p_w}, \underset{-}{\kappa}, \underset{-}{\varphi_K}, \underset{+}{\varepsilon}, \underset{-}{W2_{t+1}}\right) \tag{12.59}$$

Demand Function for $N2^{Se}_{K(t+1)}$

From (12.5), an increase in p_w increases the value of the marginal revenue next period of adding another worker for the purpose of treating and storing waste. An increase in ε produces the opposite result. Therefore, the following demand function for workers to treat and store waste next period is given by

$$N2^{Se}_{K(t+1)} = N2^{Se}_{K(t+1)}\left(\underset{+}{p_w}, \underset{-}{\varepsilon}, \underset{-}{W2_{t+1}}\right) \tag{12.60}$$

Capital Goods Industry's Supply of Bonds

The amount of physical capital that is not sold during the current period and that does not physically depreciate is assumed to be added to the industry's inventory of K:

$$K_{K(t+1)} = (1-\delta)\cdot K_{Kt} + \tau_K(I2_t)\cdot T_{Kt}(h_K\cdot N2_{Kt}, K_{Kt}) - KG1^d_t - KG2^d_t - KG3^d_t - KGR^d_t - KC^d_t \geq 0 \tag{12.61}$$

where KNR^d_t corresponds to the actual amount of physical capital purchased by the nonrenewable resource industry in Country One during the current period, KC^d_t corresponds to the actual amount of physical capital purchased by the consumer goods industry in Country Three during the current period, $KG1^d_t$ denotes the amount of physical capital purchased by the G1 sector during the current period, $KG2^d_t$ represents the amount of physical capital purchased by the G2 sector during the current period, $KG3^d_t$ represents the amount of physical capital purchased by the G3 sector during the current period, δ represents the rate of depreciation of physical capital, and $K_{K(t+1)}$ denotes the end-of-current-period inventory of K held by the K industry.

Assuming that the capital goods industry does not plan to engage in net saving during the period (i.e., it plans to distribute all net income during the current period as dividends), then, from (6.10), the sector's end-of-period supply of bonds to Country Two's bond market is given by (6.55) where p_{Kt} is given by (6.50). The effects of parametric changes that affect the pricing decision are suppressed in (6.54), for simplicity.

$$p_{B2}\cdot B2^s_{K(t+1)} = p_{B2}\cdot B2_{Kt} + p_{Kt}\cdot\Big[\delta\cdot K_{Kt} + \tau_K(I2_t)\cdot T_{Kt}(h_K\cdot N2_{Kt}, K_{Kt}) - KG1^d_t - KG2^d_t - KG3^d_t - KNR^d_t - KC^d_t\Big] \tag{12.62}$$

H2 Sector

In a manner directly analogous to the earlier discussion of the H1 sector, the H2 sector's demand functions for R2, C, and end-of-period money balances together with its supply of labor function for next period emerge.

Let $\overline{Y}2$ = current disposable income plus initial wealth $= \Pi 2_t - Tx2_t + W2_t \cdot h2_t^w \cdot N2_t^w + (1 + p_{B2}) \cdot B2_{H2t} + M2_t$

$$R2H2_t^d = R2H2_t^d \left(\underset{-}{p_{R2t}}, \underset{+}{\left(\frac{\tilde{\varepsilon}}{\varepsilon}\right)} \cdot p_{Ct}, \underset{+}{N2_t}, \underset{-}{r_{2t}}, \underset{+}{\overline{Y}2}, \underset{+}{W2_{t+1}} \right) \tag{12.63}$$

$$CH2_t^d = CH2_t^d \left(\underset{+}{p_{R2t}}, \underset{-}{\left(\frac{\tilde{\varepsilon}}{\varepsilon}\right)} \cdot p_{Ct}, \underset{+}{N2_t}, \underset{-}{r_{2t}}, \underset{+}{\overline{Y}2}, \underset{+}{W2_{t+1}} \right) \tag{12.64}$$

$$M2_{t+1}^d = M2_{t+1}^d \left(\underset{-}{r_{2t}}, \underset{+}{\overline{Y}2}, \underset{+}{W2_{t+1}} \right) \tag{12.65}$$

$$N2_{t+1}^s = N2_{t+1}^s \left(\underset{-}{r_{2t}}, \underset{-}{\overline{Y}2}, \underset{+}{W2_{t+1}} \right) \tag{12.66}$$

Then analogous to (12.43), the H2 sector's end-of-period demand for Country Two's bonds is given by

$$\begin{aligned} p_{B2} \cdot B2_{H2(t+1)}^d &= \overline{Y}2 - p_{R2t} \cdot R2H2_t^d - \left(\frac{\tilde{\varepsilon}}{\varepsilon}\right) \cdot p_{Ct} \cdot CH2_t^d - M2_{t+1}^d \\ &= p_{B2} \cdot B2_{H2(t+1)}^d \left(\underset{+}{\overline{Y}2}, \underset{+}{r_{2t}}, \underset{-}{W2_{t+1}}, \underset{+}{N2_t} \right) \end{aligned} \tag{12.67}$$

The following restrictions hold by virtue of the current-period budget constraint:

$$p_{R2t} \cdot \left[\frac{\partial \left(R2H2_t^d\right)}{\partial \overline{Y}2} \right] + \left[\left(\frac{\tilde{\varepsilon}}{\varepsilon}\right) \cdot p_{Ct} \right] \cdot \left[\frac{\partial CH2_t^d}{\partial \overline{Y}2} \right] + \frac{\partial M2_{t+1}^d}{\partial \overline{Y}2} + \frac{\partial \left(p_{B2} \cdot B2_{H2(t+1)}^d\right)}{\partial \overline{Y}2} \equiv 1 \tag{12.68}$$

$$p_{R2t} \cdot \left[\frac{\partial \left(R2H2_t^d\right)}{\partial r_{2t}} \right] + \left[\left(\frac{\tilde{\varepsilon}}{\varepsilon}\right) \cdot p_{Ct} \right] \cdot \left[\frac{\partial CH2_t^d}{\partial r_{2t}} \right] + \frac{\partial M2_{t+1}^d}{\partial r_{2t}} + \frac{\partial \left(p_{B2} \cdot B2_{H2(t+1)}^d\right)}{\partial r_{2t}} \equiv 0 \tag{12.69}$$

$$\left[\frac{\partial\left(p_{R2t}\cdot R2H2_t^d\right)}{\partial p_{R2t}}\right]+\left[\left(\frac{\tilde{\varepsilon}}{\varepsilon}\right)\cdot p_{Ct}\right]\cdot\left[\frac{\partial CH2_t^d}{\partial p_{R2t}}\right]\equiv 0 \qquad (12.70)$$

$$p_{R2t}\cdot\left\{\frac{\partial\left(R2H2_t^d\right)}{\partial\left[(\tilde{\varepsilon}/\varepsilon)\cdot p_{Ct}\right]}\right\}+\left\{\frac{\partial\left\{\left[(\tilde{\varepsilon}/\varepsilon)\cdot p_{Ct}\right]\cdot CH2_t^d\right\}}{\partial\left[(\tilde{\varepsilon}/\varepsilon)\cdot p_{Ct}\right]}\right\}\equiv 0 \qquad (12.71)$$

$$p_{R2t}\cdot\left[\frac{\partial\left(R2H2_t^d\right)}{\partial W2_{t+1}}\right]+\left[\left(\frac{\tilde{\varepsilon}}{\varepsilon}\right)\cdot p_{Ct}\right]\cdot\left[\frac{\partial CH2_t^d}{\partial W2_{t+1}}\right]+\frac{\partial M2_{t+1}^d}{\partial W2_{t+1}}$$
$$+\frac{\partial\left(p_{B2}\cdot B2_{H2(t+1)}^d\right)}{\partial W2_{t+1}}\equiv 0 \qquad (12.72)$$

Involuntary Unemployment Case

If the home household sector feels that the home employers' market demand for workers for next period constitutes an effective constraint upon the home households, then labor supply function (12.66) is no longer relevant. In this case also, the amount of labor the home households anticipate their employers will demand for next period now enters as a parameter in demand functions (12.64)–(12.65) and (12.67) and affects these demands in a manner similar to a change in $W1_{t+1}$ in those expressions.

Country Three

The G3 Sector

Once the H3 sector has chosen $g_{3H3(t+1)}$, the G3 sector knows $\bar{R}\bar{3}_{t+1}$, given its estimate of the population in that country by the end of the current period. Also, once the G3 sector has decided the current addition to its infrastructure, it has also decided the amount of the NR it will purchase this period, the amount of labor it will use in providing that addition to infrastructure, and the corresponding necessary level of corporate taxes.

At this point in the process, the G3 sector decides the optimal end-of-period levels of physical capital and workers as it attempts to minimize next period's outlays, given next period's production of general public services and anticipated revenue from the central bank. In a manner analogous to the G3 sector's decision making at this step, the following decision functions emerge:

$$N3_{G3H3(t+1)}^d = N2_{G3H3(t+1)}^d\left(\underset{-}{W3_{t+1}}, \underset{+}{r_{3t}}, \underset{+}{p_{Kt}}, \underset{+}{g_{3H3(t+1)}}\right) \qquad (12.73)$$

$$K^{d}_{G3(t+1)} = K^{d}_{G3(t+1)}\left(W3_{t+1}, r_{3t}, p_{Kt}, \delta, \frac{\tilde{\varepsilon}}{\varepsilon}, g_{3H3(t+1)}\right) \tag{12.74}$$
$$\qquad\qquad + \quad - \; - \; - \; + \quad +$$

Once it has solved for its end-of-period demands for workers and capital, the G3 sector's end-of-period supply of bonds is given by

$$\begin{aligned} p_{B3} \cdot B3^{s}_{G3(t+1)} = {} & W3_t \cdot h^{GH3}_{G3t} \cdot N3_{G3t} + \left(\frac{\varepsilon}{\tilde{\varepsilon}}\right) \cdot p_{Kt} \\ & \cdot \left[K^{d}_{G3(t+1)}\left(W3_{t+1}, r_{3t}, p_{Kt}, \delta, g_{3H3(t+1)}\right) - (1-\delta) \cdot K_{G3t}\right] \\ & - \Pi^{CB3G3}_{t} + \left(1 + p_{B3}\right) \cdot B3_{G3t} + p^{G3}_{xt} \cdot \overline{R3}_t - Tx_{G3H3t} \\ & + W3_t \cdot h^{W^*H3}_{G3t} \cdot N3_{G3t} - Tx_{W^*G3t} \\ & + W3_t \cdot h^{\Delta I}_{G3t} \cdot N_{G3t}\left(\Delta I3_t\right) + \left(\frac{1}{\tilde{\varepsilon}}\right) \cdot p_{NRt} \cdot NRG3^{Td}_{t} \\ & - Tx_{Ct} - Tx_{R3t} \end{aligned} \tag{12.75}$$

The R3 Industry

Now that the R3 industry has decided current production, the current price of its product, and the number of hours it will use its current employees, it has also decided the inventory of unprocessed R3 it wants to hold by the beginning of next period. In addition, it has also decided the number of people it plans to employ next period, $N3_{R3(t+1)}$, to process that inventory as well as next period's anticipated increase above the minimum end-of-period stock required by its government sector. The end-of-period stock of its processed inventory is established by current production and current sales, but this inventory does not affect next period's production. However, the end-of-period stock of the processed inventory will affect the price the sector sets for its product next period. It also affects the amount that the sector borrows during the current period.

The sector's end-of-period inventory of processed R3 is analogous to (8.5) for the R1 industry and is represented here as (12.76):

$$R3^{T^*}_{t+1} = R3^{T^*}_{t} + \tau_{R3}\left(I3_t\right) \cdot T_{R3t}\left(h_{R3t} \cdot N3_{R3t}\right) - R3H3_t \geq 0 \tag{12.76}$$

The sector's end-of-period supply of bonds is then established by the sector's unintended accumulation of the processed R3 during the period:

$$\begin{aligned} p_{B3} \cdot B3^{s}_{R3(t+1)} &= p_{R3t} \cdot \left(R3^{T^*}_{t+1} - R3^{T^*}_{t}\right) + p_{B3} \cdot B3_{R3t} \\ &= p_{R3t} \cdot \left(\tau_{R3}\left(I3_t\right) \cdot T_{R3t}\left(h_{R3t} \cdot N3_{R3t}\right) - R3H3_t\right) + p_{B3} \cdot B3_{R3t} \end{aligned} \tag{12.77}$$

If the sector produces more than it sells during the current period, it issues more bonds during the period. If it sells more than it produces, it buys back some bonds, or even lends in the bond market. $R3H3 \leq R3_t^{T^*} + \tau_{R3}(I3_t) \cdot T_{R3t}(h_{R3t} \cdot N3_{R3t})$. If $R3H3 = R3_t^{T^*} + \tau_{R3}(I3_t) \cdot T_{R3t}(h_{R3t} \cdot N3_{R3t})$, then $p_{B3} \cdot B3^s_{R3(t+1)} = p_{R3t} \cdot (-R3_t^{T^*}) + p_{B3} \cdot B3_{R3t}$. Therefore, while the current interest rate the sector anticipates will prevail during the current period affects its desired ending-period inventory of processed R3 as it decides current production and product price, the actual amount of this inventory is established by current production and current sales. In the final analysis, the end-of-period supply of bonds to Country Three's bond market by the renewable resource industry in Country Three is independent of the current interest rate (although the sector's forecast of the current interest rate was important to its production and pricing decisions).

The Consumption Goods Industry

Given that the consumption goods industry has already decided the number of hours to use its current employees, the level of current production, the current price of its product, and the wage rate it will pay its employees next period, its original objective function must be modified and solved for the sector's effective demand for workers for next period and physical capital for the beginning of next period.

$$
\begin{aligned}
\Pi^d_{Ct} + \frac{\Pi^d_{C(t+1)}}{(1+r_{3t})} &= p_{Ct}\{CH1_t + CH2_t + CH3_t\} \\
&- \left[\frac{(p_{Kt}\cdot\varepsilon)}{\tilde{\varepsilon}}\right]\cdot\left[K^d_{C(t+1)} - (1-\delta)\cdot K_{Ct}\right] - Tx_{CG3t} \\
&- \left(\frac{p_{NRt}}{\tilde{\varepsilon}}\right)\cdot(\gamma+\varphi_C)\cdot\tau(I3_t)\cdot T_{Ct}(h_{Ct}\cdot N3_{Ct}, K_{Ct}) \\
&- \left(\frac{p_w}{\tilde{\varepsilon}}\right)\cdot\left[\varphi_C\cdot\tau(I3_t)\cdot T_{Ct}(h_{Ct}\cdot N3_{Ct}, K_{Ct})\right. \\
&\left. + \kappa\cdot\delta\cdot K_{Ct} - T^S_{Ct}\left(h^S_{Ct}\cdot N3_{Ct}\right)\right] - W3_t\cdot\left(h_{Ct}+h^S_{Ct}\right) \\
&\cdot N3_{Ct} - \left(1-p_{B3}\right)\cdot B3_{Ct} + \left[\frac{1}{(1+r_{3t})}\right] \\
&\cdot\left[TR^{Ce}_{t+1}\left\{\tau_C(I3_t+\Delta I3)\cdot T^{Te}_{C(t+1)}\left(h^e_C\cdot N3^{Te}_{C(t+1)}, K^d_{C(t+1)}\right),\right.\right. \\
&\qquad \left.\omega^*_{CH1}, \omega^*_{CH2}, \omega^*_{CH3}\right\} \\
&- \left[\frac{\left(p^C_{K(t+1)}\cdot\varepsilon\right)}{\tilde{\varepsilon}}\right]\cdot\left[K^{de}_{C(t+2)} - (1-\delta)\cdot K^{de}_{C(t+1)}\right] - \left(\frac{p_w}{\tilde{\varepsilon}}\right) \\
&\cdot\left\{\varphi_C\cdot\tau_C(I3_t+\Delta I3)\cdot T^{Te}_{C(t+1)}\left(h^e_C\cdot N3^{Te}_{C(t+1)}, K^d_{C(t+1)}\right)\right. \\
&\left. + \kappa\cdot\delta\cdot K^d_{C(t+1)} - T^S_{C(t+1)}\left(h^e_C\cdot N3^{Se}_{C(t+1)}\right)\right\}
\end{aligned}
$$

$$- W3_{t+1} \cdot \left(N3^{Te}_{C(t+1)} + N3^{Se}_{C(t+1)} \right) - Tx_{CG3(t+1)}$$

$$- \left(\frac{p^{C}_{NR(t+1)}}{\tilde{\varepsilon}} \right) \cdot (\gamma + \varphi_C) \cdot \tau_C \left(I3_t + \Delta I3 \right)$$

$$\cdot T^{Te}_{C(t+1)} \left(h^{e}_{C} \cdot N3^{Te}_{C(t+1)}, K^{d}_{C(t+1)} \right) \Big] \qquad (12.78)$$

where $1/(1 + r_3) = p_{B3}/(1 + p_{B3})$. The consumption goods industry's objective at the beginning of the current period is to maximize the right-hand side of (12.78) with respect to $K^{de}_{C(t+1)}$, $N3^{Te}_{C(t+1)}$, and $N3^{Se}_{C(t+1)}$. Doing so yields the first-order necessary conditions (12.79)–(12.81):

$$\frac{\partial \left[\Pi^{d}_{Ct} + \Pi^{d}_{C(t+1)} / \left(1 + r_{3t}\right) \right]}{\partial K^{de}_{C(t+1)}} = + \left[\frac{1}{(1 + r_{3t})} \right] \cdot \left[\left[\frac{\partial TR^{Ce}_{t+1}}{\partial C^{de}_{t+1}} \right] \cdot \tau_C \left(I3_t + \Delta I3 \right) \right.$$
$$\cdot \left[\frac{\partial T^{Te}_{C(t+1)}}{\partial K^{d}_{C(t+1)}} \right] + \left(\frac{p^{C}_{K(t+1)} \cdot \varepsilon}{\tilde{\varepsilon}} \right) \cdot (1 - \delta)$$
$$- \left(\frac{p_w}{\tilde{\varepsilon}} \right) \cdot \left\{ \varphi_C \cdot \tau_C \left(I3_t + \Delta I3 \right) \cdot \left[\frac{\partial T^{Te}_{C(t+1)}}{\partial K^{d}_{C(t+1)}} \right] \right.$$
$$\left. + \kappa \cdot \delta \right\} - \left(\frac{p^{C}_{K(t+1)}}{\tilde{\varepsilon}} \right) \cdot (\gamma \cdot \varphi_C) \cdot \tau_C \left(I3_t + \Delta I3 \right)$$
$$\left. \cdot \left[\frac{\partial T^{Te}_{C(t+1)}}{\partial K^{d}_{C(t+1)}} \right] \right] - \frac{\left(p_{Kt} \cdot \varepsilon \right)}{\tilde{\varepsilon}} = 0 \qquad (12.79)$$

$$\frac{\partial \left[\Pi^{d}_{Ct} + \Pi^{d}_{C(t+1)} / \left(1 + r_{3t}\right) \right]}{\partial N3^{Te}_{C(t+1)}} = \left[\frac{1}{(1 + r_{3t})} \right] \cdot \left[\left\{ \left(\frac{\partial TR^{Ce}_{t+1}}{\partial C^{de}_{t+1}} \right) - \left(\frac{p_w}{\tilde{\varepsilon}} \right) \cdot \varphi_C \right. \right.$$
$$\left. - \left(\frac{p^{C}_{NR(t+1)}}{\tilde{\varepsilon}} \right) \cdot (\gamma + \varphi_C) \right\} \cdot \tau_C \left(I3_t + \Delta I3 \right)$$
$$\cdot \left[\frac{\partial T^{Te}_{C(t+1)}}{\partial \left(h^{e}_{C} \cdot N3^{Te}_{C(t+1)} \right)} \right] \cdot h^{e}_{C}$$
$$\left. - W3_{t+1}\, h^{e}_{C} \right] = 0 \qquad (12.80)$$

$$\frac{\partial\left[\Pi^{d}_{Ct} + \Pi^{d}_{C(t+1)}/(1+r_{3t})\right]}{\partial N3^{Te}_{C(t+1)}} = \left[\frac{1}{(1+r_{3t})}\right] \cdot \left[\left(\frac{p_w}{\tilde{\varepsilon}}\right)\cdot\left(\frac{\partial T^{S}_{C3(t+1)}}{\partial N3^{Se}_{C(t+1)}}\right)\cdot h^{e}_{C} - W3_{t+1}\cdot h^{e}_{C}\right] = 0 \tag{12.81}$$

Totally differentiating conditions (12.79)–(12.81) and solving for the changes in $K^{de}_{C(t+1)}$, $N3^{Te}_{C(t+1)}$, and $N3^{Se}_{C(t+1)}$ yields the industry's effective end-of-period demand functions for physical capital and its demands for workers for next period.

Demand Function for $K^{de}_{C(t+1)}$

$$K^{de}_{C(t+1)} = K^{de}_{C(t+1)}\left(\underset{-}{r_{3t}}, \underset{-}{p_{Kt}}, \underset{-}{p_{NRt}}, \underset{-}{p_w}, \underset{-}{\varphi_C}, \underset{-}{\gamma}, \underset{-}{\kappa}, \underset{-}{\delta}, \underset{-}{\varepsilon}, \underset{+}{\tilde{\varepsilon}}, \underset{-}{W3_{t+1}}\right) \tag{12.82}$$

Demand Function for $N3^{Te}_{C(t+1)}$

$$N3^{Te}_{C(t+1)} = N3^{Te}_{C(t+1)}\left(\underset{-}{p_w}, \underset{+}{\tilde{\varepsilon}}, \underset{-}{\varphi_C}, \underset{-}{\gamma}, \underset{-}{W3_{t+1}}\right) \tag{12.83}$$

Demand Function for $N3^{Se}_{C(t+1)}$

$$N3^{Se}_{C(t+1)} = N3^{Se}_{C(t+1)}\left(\underset{+}{p_w}, \underset{-}{\tilde{\varepsilon}}, \underset{-}{W3_{t+1}}\right) \tag{12.84}$$

Consumer Goods Industry's Market Supply of Bonds

Assuming that the consumer goods industry does not plan to engage in net saving during the period, electing instead to distribute to its owners as dividends all the after tax net income it earns during the current period, then from (7.10), the sector's end-of-period supply of bonds to Country Three's bond market is given by (7.54), where p_{Ct} is given by (7.49) and $K^{d}_{C(t+1)}$ is given by (7.43). The effects of parametric changes that affect pricing decisions are assumed to be minor relative to those that affect the sector's end-of-period demand for physical capital.

$$\begin{aligned}
&p_{B3} \cdot B3^{s}_{C(t+1)} \\
&\quad = p_{B3} \cdot B3_{Ct} + p_{Ct} \cdot \left[\tau\left(I3_t\right) \cdot T_{Ct}\left(h_{Ct} \cdot N3_{Ct}, K_{Ct}\right) - CH1_t - CH2_t - CH3_t\right] \\
&\qquad + p_{Kt} \cdot \left(\frac{\varepsilon}{\tilde{\varepsilon}}\right) \cdot K^{d}_{C(t+1)}\left(\underset{-}{r_{3t}}, \underset{-}{p_{Kt}}, \underset{-}{p_{NRt}}, \underset{-}{p_w}, \underset{-}{\varphi_C}, \underset{-}{\gamma}, \underset{-}{\kappa}, \underset{-}{\delta}, \underset{-}{\varepsilon}, \underset{+}{\tilde{\varepsilon}}\right) \\
&\qquad - p_{Kt} \cdot \left(\frac{\varepsilon}{\tilde{\varepsilon}}\right) \cdot (1-\delta) \cdot K_{Ct} + p_{B3} \cdot B3_{Ct} \\
&\quad = p_{B3} \cdot K3^{s}_{C(t+1)}\left(\underset{-}{r_{3t}}, \underset{-}{p_{Kt}}, \underset{-}{p_{NRt}}, \underset{-}{p_w}, \underset{-}{\varphi_C}, \underset{-}{\gamma}, \underset{-}{\kappa}, \underset{-}{\delta}, \underset{-}{\varepsilon}, \underset{+}{\tilde{\varepsilon}}, \underset{-}{CH1_t + CH2_t + CH3_t}, \underset{+1}{p_{B3} \cdot B3_{Ct}}\right)
\end{aligned} \tag{12.85}$$

The number of consumption goods not sold during the current period is assumed to be added to the industry's inventory of consumption goods by the end of the period:

$$\begin{aligned}
C_{C(t+1)} &= C_{Ct} + \tau\left(I3_t\right) \cdot T_{Ct}\left(h_{Ct} \cdot N3_{Ct}, K_{Ct}\right) \\
&\quad - CH1_t - CH2_t - CH3_t \geq 0
\end{aligned} \tag{12.86}$$

where C_{Ct} represents the industry's initial inventory of consumer goods, $CH1_t$ corresponds to the actual number of consumer goods purchased by the households in Country One during the current period, $CH2_t$ corresponds to the actual number of consumer goods purchased by the households in Country Two during the current period, $CH3_t$ represents the actual number of consumer goods purchased by the households in Country Three during the current period, and $C_{C(t+1)}$ denotes the end-of-current-period inventory of consumer goods held by the consumer goods industry.

The H3 Sector

In a manner directly analogous to the earlier discussion of the H1 sector, the H3 sector's demand functions for R3, C, and end-of-period money balances together with its supply of labor function for next period emerge:

Let $\overline{Y}3$ = current disposable income plus initial wealth $= \Pi 3_t - Tx3_t + W3_t \cdot h3^{W}_t \cdot N3^{w}_t + (1 + p_{B3}) \cdot B3_{H3t} + M3_t$

$$R3H3^{d}_t = R3H3^{d}_t\left(\underset{-}{p_{R3t}}, \underset{+}{p_{Ct}}, \underset{+}{N3_t}, \underset{-}{r_{3t}}, \underset{+}{\overline{Y}3}, \underset{+}{W3_{t+1}}\right) \tag{12.87}$$

$$CH3^{d}_t = CH3^{d}_t\left(\underset{+}{p_{R3t}}, \underset{-}{p_{Ct}}, \underset{+}{N3_t}, \underset{-}{r_{3t}}, \underset{+}{\overline{Y}3}, \underset{+}{W3_{t+1}}\right) \tag{12.88}$$

$$M3^{d}_{t+1} = M3^{d}_{t+1}\left(\underset{-}{r_{3t}}, \underset{+}{\overline{Y}3}, \underset{+}{W3_{t+1}}\right) \tag{12.89}$$

$$N3^{s}_{t+1} = N3^{s}_{t+1}\left(\underset{-}{r_{3t}}, \underset{-}{\overline{Y}3}, \underset{+}{W3_{t+1}}\right) \tag{12.90}$$

The H3 sector's end-of-period demand for Country Three's bonds is given by

$$\begin{aligned} p_{B3} \cdot B3^{d}_{H3(t+1)} &= \overline{Y}3 - p_{R3t} \cdot R3H3^{d}_{t} - p_{Ct} \cdot CH3^{d}_{t} - M3^{d}_{t+1} \\ &= p_{B3} \cdot B3^{d}_{H3(t+1)}\left(\underset{+}{\overline{Y}3}, \underset{+}{r_{3t}}, \underset{-}{W3_{t+1}}, \underset{+}{N3_{t}}\right) \end{aligned} \tag{12.91}$$

The following restrictions hold by virtue of the current-period budget constraint:

$$p_{R32t} \cdot \left[\frac{\partial\left(R3H3^{d}_{t}\right)}{\partial \overline{Y}3}\right] + p_{Ct} \cdot \left[\frac{\partial CH3^{d}_{t}}{\partial \overline{Y}3}\right] + \frac{\partial M3^{d}_{t+1}}{\partial \overline{Y}3} + \frac{\partial\left(p_{B3} \cdot B3^{d}_{H3(t+1)}\right)}{\partial \overline{Y}3} \equiv 1 \tag{12.92}$$

$$p_{R3t} \cdot \left[\frac{\partial\left(R3H3^{d}_{t}\right)}{\partial r_{3t}}\right] + p_{Ct} \cdot \left[\frac{\partial CH3^{d}_{t}}{\partial r_{3t}}\right] + \frac{\partial M3^{d}_{t+1}}{\partial r_{3t}} + \frac{\partial\left(p_{B3} \cdot B3^{d}_{H3(t+1)}\right)}{\partial r_{3t}} \equiv 0 \tag{12.93}$$

$$\left[\frac{\partial\left(p_{R3t} \cdot R3H3^{d}_{t}\right)}{\partial p r_{3t}}\right] + p_{Ct} \cdot \left[\frac{\partial CH3^{d}_{t}}{\partial p_{R3t}}\right] \equiv 0 \tag{12.94}$$

$$p_{R3t} \cdot \left\{\frac{\partial\left(R3H3^{d}_{t}\right)}{\partial p_{Ct}}\right\} + \left[\frac{\partial\left\{p_{Ct} \cdot CH3^{d}_{t}\right\}}{\partial p_{Ct}}\right] \equiv 0 \tag{12.95}$$

$$p_{R3t} \cdot \left[\frac{\partial\left(R3H3^{d}_{t}\right)}{\partial W3_{t+1}}\right] + p_{Ct} \cdot \left[\frac{\partial CH3^{d}_{t}}{\partial W3_{t+1}}\right] + \frac{\partial M3^{d}_{t+1}}{\partial W3_{t+1}} + \frac{\partial\left(p_{B3} \cdot B3^{d}_{H3(t+1)}\right)}{\partial W3_{t+1}} \equiv 0 \tag{12.96}$$

Involuntary Unemployment Case

If the home household sector feels that the home employers' market demand for workers for next period constitutes an effective constraint upon the home households, then labor supply function (12.90) is no longer relevant. In this case also, the amount of labor the home households anticipate their employers will demand for next period now enters as a parameter in demand functions (12.87)–(12.89) and (12.91) and affects these demands in a manner similar to a change in $W1_{t+1}$ in those expressions.

In chapter 13, attention turns to the financial markets for the purpose of determining world interest rates and exchange rates.

13

World's Financial Markets

This model contains a total of six financial markets—three money markets and three bond markets. The three interest rates and the three exchange rates (once any two exchange rates are established, so is the third) are either established in these markets or maintained by policy measures carried out in these markets. At most five of these six markets are independent.

The manner in which interest rates and exchange rates are established depends upon whether the world's central banks manage interest rates or allow them to vary and whether they fix their exchange rates or allow them to float. Each central bank could engage in open market operations to control its country's monetary base or it could instead decide to stand ready to adjust its holdings of domestic bonds in order to manage their country's interest rate. Each country's central bank also could engage in sterilized or "monetized" (nonsterilized) periodic adjustments to its holdings of bonds issued in another country under a system of flexible exchange rates or it could instead attempt to stand ready continually to adjust its holdings of another country's bonds in order to maintain an arbitrary exchange rate between its country's unit of account and the unit of account of that country.

In this model, under flexible exchange rates and managed monetary bases (variable interest rates), the world's money markets (the market demands and ex ante supplies of money) are independent of the various exchange rates; in this case, the three interest rates are established simultaneously in the three money markets. Given these interest rates, two of the three bond markets (only two will be independent) may then be viewed as establishing the three exchange rates (only two of which are independent). Interest rates and exchange rates are established recursively in this case.

On the other hand, if each central bank decides to manage its country's interest rate, then each central bank stands ready to adjust its holdings of its country's bonds to maintain equilibrium in its bond market at the arbitrary interest rate. Since exchange rate variations affect the market supply of bonds in every bond market in this model (because exchange rates affect planned spending and therefore unplanned inventory investment that must be financed by producers), a change in exchange rates affects the amount by which each central bank must adjust its holdings of bonds to keep its interest rate fixed. As a result, holding constant the central bank's holdings of foreign assets, the country's monetary base will also adjust necessarily to changes in exchange rates. If all three central banks manage their own interest rate, the three money markets (only two of which are now independent) will establish two of the exchange rates, and, therefore, the third exchange rate as well.

Before an analysis of the implications of alternative central bank policies may proceed, it is necessary, first, to show that at most five of the six financial markets are independent. It should be recalled that because product prices and production levels are decided before spending takes place in this model, the producers may end the period with smaller or larger inventories than they intended when they set prices and production levels. Therefore, while the decision to produce determines total actual spending, subsequently the interest rates and exchange rates help to establish the composition of that spending between planned spending and unplanned changes to ending inventories. In each country, the bond market reflects not only the financing of planned investment and planned saving in the form of that country's bonds, but it also reflects the corresponding financing of unplanned changes in inventories by producers. The standard "IS curve" showing the level of income and actual spending consistent with total planned spending is both unnecessary and irrelevant within the present context in terms of establishing interest rates and exchange rates.

The World's Money Markets

This section contains a specification of the equilibrium conditions for each of the three money markets under the assumption of variable interest rates and flexible exchange rates. The demand for money in each country consists of the end-of-period demand by that country's household sector. The supply of money consists of the amount of checkable deposits and the amount of coin and currency that would be outstanding at the end of the period if the plans of the private banks and the central bank in that country were to materialize. The amount of checkable deposits at the end of the period consistent with the plans of the private banks in a country is given by $Di^{s}_{t+1}(\bullet)$ where $i = 1, 2$, or 3. The amount of coin and currency outstanding at the end of the period consistent with the plans of the central bank and the private banks is given by the difference between the end-of-period monetary base implied by the central bank's plans for the end of the period and the total amount of reserves at the end of the period consistent with the plans of the private banks. In the present model, the monetary base consistent with the central bank's plans for the end of the period is equal to the sum of its planned holdings of domestic and foreign bonds for the end of the period (ignoring the net wealth of the central bank). The total amount of reserves planned by the private banks is equal to the required reserves implied by their ex ante end-of-period supply of checkable deposits, $Di^{s}_{t+1}(\bullet)$, plus their planned holdings of excess reserves for the end of the period. The private banks' ex ante supply of checkable deposits for the end of the period (ignoring the net wealth of the private banks) is equal to the sum of the sector's end-of-period demands for reserves and domestic and foreign bonds.

Country One

The demand for money in Country One is given by the household sector's demand for M1 for the end of the period:

$$M1^d_{t+1} = \underset{-\ \ +}{M1^d(r_1, Y1)} \tag{13.1}$$

where Y1 denotes current-period disposable income of the H1 sector, but not its initial holdings of financial wealth.

Let $Cu1^s_{t+1}$ denote the coin and currency outstanding at the end of the period consistent with the plans of the private banks and the central bank in Country One:

$$Cu1^s_{t+1} = MB1^s_{t+1} - \hat{r}_1 \cdot \underset{+\,+\,+}{D1^s_{t+1}(r_1, r_2, r_3)} - \underset{-\ -\ -}{X1^d_{t+1}(r_1, r_2, r_3)} \tag{13.2}$$

Then the ex ante end-of-period supply of money, that is, the amount that would be outstanding at the end of the period consistent with the plans of the central bank and the private banking sector in Country One is given by

$$\begin{aligned} M1^s_{t+1} &= D1^s_{t+1}(r_1, r_2, r_3) + Cul^s_{t+1} \\ &= MB1^s_{t+1} + (1 - \hat{r}_1) \cdot \underset{+\ +\ +}{D1^s_{t+1}(r_1, r_2, r_3)} - \underset{-\ -\ -}{X1^d_{t+1}(r_1, r_2, r_3)} \\ &= M1^s_{t+1}\underset{+1\ \ -\ +\ +\ +}{\left(MB1^s_{t+1}, \hat{r}_1, r_1, r_2, r_3\right)} \end{aligned} \tag{13.3}$$

Equilibrium in Country One's money market is then given by

$$\underset{-\ \ +}{M1^d(r_1, Y1)} = M1^s_{t+1}\underset{+1\ \ -\ +\ +\ +}{\left(MB1^s_{t+1}, \hat{r}_1, r_1, r_2, r_3\right)} \tag{13.4}$$

Totally differentiating the expression in (13.4) yields

$$\begin{aligned} \left(\frac{\partial M1^d}{\partial r_1}\right) + \left(\frac{\partial M1^d}{\partial Y1}\right) dY1 = {} & d\left(MB1^s_{t+1}\right) - D1^s_{t+1} \cdot d\hat{r}_1 \\ & + (1 - \hat{r}_1) \cdot \left(\frac{\partial D1^s_{t+1}}{\partial r_1}\right) dr_1 \\ & + (1 - \hat{r}_1) \cdot \left(\frac{\partial D1^s_{t+1}}{\partial r_2}\right) dr_2 \\ & + (1 - \hat{r}_1) \cdot \left(\frac{\partial D1^s_{t+1}}{\partial r_3}\right) dr_3 \end{aligned} \tag{13.5}$$

This expression yields the following relationships between the interest rate that clears the money market in Country One, r_1, and the other variables that influence the excess demand in that market.

$$\frac{dr_1}{dY1} = -\frac{(\partial M1^d/\partial Y1)}{[(\partial M1^d/\partial r_1) - (1-\hat{r}_1)\cdot(\partial D1^s_{t+1}/\partial r_1)]} = -/- = +$$

$$\frac{dr_1}{dMB1^s} = \frac{1}{[(\partial M1^d/\partial r_1) - (1-\hat{r}_1)\cdot(\partial D1^s_{t+1}/\partial r_1)]} = 1/- = -$$

$$\frac{dr_2}{dr_1} = \left[\left(\frac{\partial M1^d}{\partial r_1}\right) - (1-\hat{r}_1)\cdot\frac{(\partial D1^s_{t+1}/\partial r_1)}{(1-\hat{r}_1)}\cdot\left(\frac{\partial D1^s_{t+1}}{\partial r_2}\right)\right] = -/+ = -$$

$$\frac{dr_3}{dr_1} = \left[\left(\frac{\partial M1^d}{\partial r_1}\right) - (1-\hat{r}_1)\cdot\frac{(\partial D1^s_{t+1}/\partial r_1)}{(1-\hat{r}_1)}\cdot\left(\frac{\partial D1^s_{t+1}}{\partial r_3}\right)\right] = -/+ = -$$

$$\frac{dr_3}{dr_2} = (1-\hat{r}_1)\cdot\frac{(\partial D1^s_{t+1}/\partial r_2)}{(1-\hat{r}_1)}\cdot\left(\frac{\partial D1^s_{t+1}}{\partial r_3}\right) = -/+ = -$$

In figure 13.1, the intercept of the M1 plane along the r_1 axis is a smaller value than its intercepts along the r_2 and r_3 axes. Ceteris paribus, an increase in Y1 causes the intercept on the r_1 axis to rise, while an increase in $MB1^s_{t+1}$ causes that intercept to move inward toward the origin.

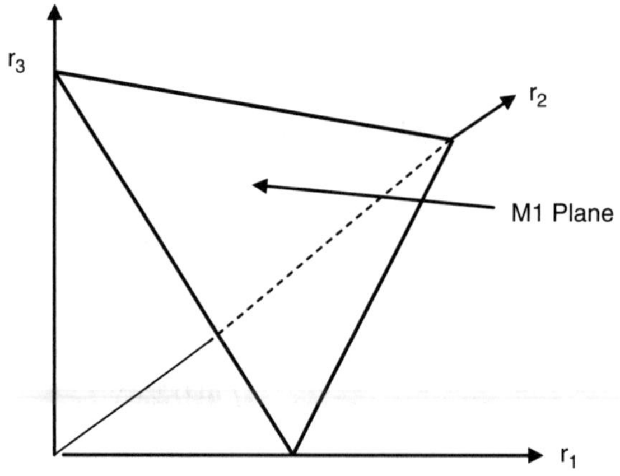

Figure 13.1 The M1 Plane

Country Two

The demand for money in Country Two is given by the household sector's demand for M2 for the end of the period:

$$M2^{d}_{t+1} = \underset{-\ \ +}{M2^{d}(r_2, Y2)} \tag{13.6}$$

where Y2 denotes current-period disposable income of the H2 sector, but not its initial holdings of financial wealth.

Let $Cu2^{s}_{t+1}$ denote the coin and currency outstanding at the end of the period consistent with the plans of the private banks and the central bank in Country Two:

$$Cu2^{s}_{t+1} = MB2^{s}_{t+1} - \hat{r}_2 \cdot \underset{+\ +\ +}{D2^{s}_{t+1}(r_1, r_2, r_3)} - \underset{-\ -\ -}{X2^{d}_{t+1}(r_1, r_2, r_3)} \tag{13.7}$$

Then the ex ante end-of-period supply of money, that is, the amount that would be outstanding at the end of the period consistent with the plans of the central bank and the private banking sector in Country Two is given by

$$\begin{aligned} M2^{s}_{t+1} &= D2^{s}_{t+1}(r_1, r_2, r_3) + Cu2^{s}_{t+1} \\ &= MB2^{s}_{t+1} + \left(1 - \hat{r}_2\right) \cdot \underset{+\ +\ +}{D2^{s}_{t+1}(r_1, r_2, r_3)} - \underset{-\ -\ -}{X2^{d}_{t+1}(r_1, r_2, r_3)} \\ &= M2^{s}_{t+1} \cdot \underset{+1\quad -\ +\ +\ +}{\left(MB2^{s}_{t+1}, \hat{r}_2, r_1, r_2, r_3\right)} \end{aligned} \tag{13.8}$$

Equilibrium in Country Two's money market is then given by

$$\underset{-\ \ +}{M2^{d}(r_2, Y2)} = M2^{s}_{t+1} \underset{+1\quad -\ +\ +\ +}{\left(MB2^{s}_{t+1}, \hat{r}_2, r_1, r_2, r_3\right)} \tag{13.9}$$

Totally differentiating the expression in (13.9) yields

$$\begin{aligned} \left(\frac{\partial M2^{d}}{\partial r_2}\right) dr_2 + \left(\frac{\partial M2^{d}}{\partial Y2}\right) dY2 = dMB2^{s} - D2^{S}_{t+1} \cdot d \\ + \left(1 - \hat{r}_2\right) \cdot \left(\frac{\partial D2^{s}_{t+1}}{\partial r_1}\right) dr_1 \\ + \left(1 - \hat{r}_2\right) \cdot \left(\frac{\partial D2^{s}_{t+1}}{\partial r_2}\right) dr_2 \\ + \left(1 - \hat{r}_2\right) \cdot \left(\frac{\partial D2^{s}_{t+1}}{\partial r_3}\right) dr_3 \end{aligned} \tag{13.10}$$

This expression yields the following relationships between the interest rate that clears the money market in Country Two, r2, and the other variables that influence the excess demand in that market:

$$\frac{dr_2}{dY2} = -\frac{(\partial M2^d/\partial Y2)}{[(\partial M2^d/\partial r_2) - (1-\hat{r}_2)\cdot(\partial D2^s_{t+1}/\partial r_2)]} = -/- = +$$

$$\frac{dr_2}{dMB2^s} = \frac{1}{[(\partial M2^d/\partial r_2) - (1-\hat{r}_2)\cdot(\partial D2^s_{t+1}/\partial r_2)]} = 1/- = -$$

$$\frac{dr_2}{dr_1} = (1-\hat{r}_2)\cdot\frac{(\partial D2^s_{t+1}/\partial r_1)}{[(\partial M2^d/\partial r_2) - (1-\hat{r}_2)\cdot(\partial D2^s_{t+1}/\partial r_2)]} = +/- = -$$

$$\frac{dr_3}{dr_2} = \frac{[(\partial M2^d/\partial r_2) - (1-\hat{r}_2)\cdot(\partial D2^s_{t+1}/\partial r_2)]}{(1-\hat{r}_2)\cdot(\partial D2^s_{t+1}/\partial r_3)} = -/+ = -$$

$$\frac{dr_3}{dr_1} = -(1-\hat{r}_2)\cdot\frac{(\partial D2^s_{t+1}/\partial r_1)}{(1-\hat{r}_2)}\cdot\left(\frac{\partial D2^s_{t+1}}{\partial r_3}\right) = -/+ = -$$

In figure 13.2, the intercept of the M2 plane along the r_2 axis is a smaller value than its intercepts along the r_1 and r_3 axes. Ceteris paribus, an increase in Y2 causes the intercept on the r_2 axis to rise, while an increase in $MB2^s_{t+1}$ causes the intercept on the r_2 axis to move inward toward the origin.

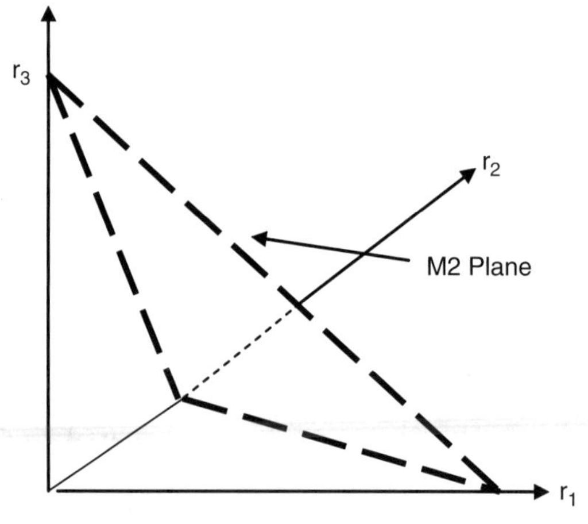

Figure 13.2 The M2 Plane

Country Three

The demand for money in Country Three is given by the household sector's demand for M3 for the end of the period:

$$M3^d = \underset{-\ \ +}{M3^d (r_3, Y3)} \tag{13.11}$$

where Y3 denotes current-period disposable income of the H3 sector, but not its initial holdings of financial wealth.

Let $Cu3^s_{t+1}$ denote the coin and currency outstanding at the end of the period consistent with the plans of the private banks and the central bank in Country Three:

$$Cu3^s_{t+1} = MB3^s_{t+1} - \hat{r}_3 \cdot \underset{+\ +\ +}{D3^s_{t+1} (r_1, r_2, r_3)} - \underset{-\ -\ -}{X3^d_{t+1} (r_1, r_2, r_3)} \tag{13.12}$$

Then the ex ante end-of-period supply of money, that is, the amount that would be outstanding at the end of the period consistent with the plans of the central bank and the private banking sector in Country Three is given by

$$\begin{aligned} M3^s_{t+1} &= MB3^s + (1 - \hat{r}_3) \cdot \underset{+\ +\ +}{D3^s_{t+1} (r_1, r_2, r_3)} - \underset{-\ -\ -}{X3^d_{t+1} (r_1, r_2, r_3)} \\ &= M3^s_{t+1} \left(\underset{+1}{MB3^s_{t+1}}, \underset{-}{\hat{r}_3}, \underset{+}{r_1}, \underset{+}{r_2}, \underset{+}{r_3} \right) \end{aligned} \tag{13.13}$$

Equilibrium in Country Two's money market is then given by

$$\underset{-\ \ +}{M3^d (r_3, Y3)} = M3^s_{t+1} \left(\underset{+1}{MB3^s_{t+1}}, \underset{-}{\hat{r}_3}, \underset{+}{r_1}, \underset{+}{r_2}, \underset{+}{r_3} \right) \tag{13.14}$$

Totally differentiating the expression in (13.14) yields

$$\begin{aligned} \left(\frac{\partial M3^d}{\partial r_3} \right) dr_3 + \left(\frac{\partial M3^d}{\partial Y3} \right) dY3 = dMB3^s &+ (1 - \hat{r}_3) \cdot \left(\frac{\partial D3^s_{t+1}}{\partial r_1} \right) dr_1 \\ &- D3^s_{t+1} \cdot d\hat{r}_3 \\ &+ (1 - \hat{r}_3) \cdot \left(\frac{\partial D3^s_{t+1}}{\partial r_2} \right) dr_2 \\ &+ (1 - \hat{r}_3) \cdot \left(\frac{\partial D3^s_{t+1}}{\partial r_3} \right) dr_3 \end{aligned} \tag{13.15}$$

This expression yields the following relationships between the interest rate that clears the money market in Country Three, r_3, and the other variables that influence the excess demand in that market:

$$\frac{dr_3}{dY3} = -\frac{(\partial M3^d/\partial Y3)}{[(\partial M3^d/\partial r_3) - (1-\hat{r}_3)\cdot(\partial D3^s_{t+1}/\partial r_3)]} = -/- = +$$

$$\frac{dr_3}{dMB3^s} = \frac{1}{[(\partial M3^d/\partial r_3) - (1-\hat{r}_3)\cdot(\partial D3^s_{t+1}/\partial r_3)]} = 1/- = -$$

$$\frac{dr_3}{dr_1} = (1-\hat{r}_3)\cdot\frac{(\partial D3^s_{t+1}/\partial r_1)}{[(\partial M3^d/\partial r_3) - (1-\hat{r}_3)\cdot(\partial D3^s_{t+1}/\partial r_3)]} = +/- = -$$

$$\frac{dr_3}{dr_2} = (1-\hat{r}_3)\cdot\frac{(\partial D3^s_{t+1}/\partial r_2)}{[(\partial M3^d/\partial r_3) - (1-\hat{r}_3)\cdot(\partial D3^s_{t+1}/\partial r_3)]} = +/- = -$$

$$\frac{dr_2}{dr_1} = -(1-\hat{r}_3)\cdot\frac{(\partial D3^s_{t+1}/\partial r_1)}{(1-\hat{r}_3)}\cdot\left(\frac{\partial D3^s_{t+1}}{\partial r_2}\right) = -/+ = -$$

In figure 13.3, The intercept of the M3 plane along the r3 axis is a smaller value than its intercepts along the r1 and r2 axes. Ceteris paribus, an increase in Y3 causes the intercept on the r3 axis to rise, while an increase in $MB3^s_{t+1}$ causes the intercept on the r3 axis to move inward toward the origin.

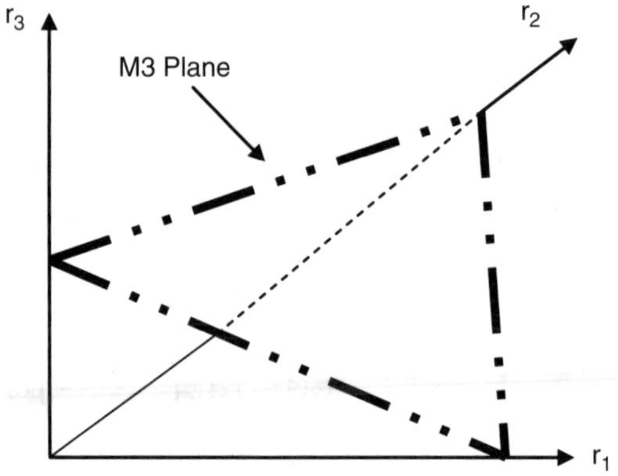

Figure 13.3 The M3 Plane

General Equilibrium Solution for r_1, r_2, and r_3

Linearizing the three equilibrium conditions for the world's money markets for r_1, r_2, and r_3 yields the following system:

$$\underset{-}{a11} \cdot dr1 + \underset{-}{a12} \cdot dr2 + \underset{-}{a13} \cdot dr3 = \underset{+}{dMB1} + \underset{-}{b11} \cdot dY1 + \underset{-}{b12} \cdot d\hat{r}_1 \quad (13.16)$$

$$\underset{-}{a21} \cdot dr1 + \underset{-}{a22} \cdot dr2 + \underset{-}{a23} \cdot dr3 = \underset{+}{dMB2} + \underset{-}{b21} \cdot dY2 + \underset{-}{b22} \cdot d\hat{r}_2 \quad (13.17)$$

$$\underset{-}{a31} \cdot dr1 + \underset{-}{a32} \cdot dr2 + \underset{-}{a33} \cdot dr3 = \underset{+}{dMB3} + \underset{-}{b31} \cdot dY3 + \underset{-}{b32} \cdot d\hat{r}_3 \quad (13.18)$$

The simultaneous solution for changes in r_1, r_2, and r_3 is given by

$$\begin{aligned} dr1 = \left(\frac{1}{detA}\right) \cdot \big[& \left(dMB1 + b11 \cdot dY1 + b12 \cdot d\hat{r}_1\right) \cdot (a22a33 - a32a23) \\ & - \left(dMB2 + b21 \cdot dY2 + b22 \cdot d\hat{r}_2\right) \cdot (a12a33 - a32a13) \\ & + \left(dMB3 + b31 \cdot dY3 + b32 \cdot d\hat{r}_3\right) \cdot (a12a23 - a22a13)\big] \end{aligned} \quad (13.19)$$

$$\begin{aligned} dr2 = \left(\frac{1}{detA}\right) \cdot \big[& - \left(dMB1 + b11 \cdot dY1 + b12 \cdot d\hat{r}_1\right) \cdot (a21a33 - a31a23) \\ & + \left(dMB2 + b21 \cdot dY2 + b22 \cdot d\hat{r}_2\right) \cdot (a11a33 - a31a13) \\ & - \left(dMB3 + b31 \cdot dY3 + b32 \cdot d\hat{r}_3\right) \cdot (a11a23 - a21a13)\big] \end{aligned} \quad (13.20)$$

$$\begin{aligned} dr3 = \left(\frac{1}{detA}\right) \cdot \big[& \left(dMB1 + b11 \cdot dY1 + b12 \cdot d\hat{r}_1\right) \cdot (a21a32 - a31a22) \\ & - \left(dMB2 + b21 \cdot dY2 + b22 \cdot d\hat{r}_2\right) \cdot (a11a32 - a31a12) \\ & + \left(dMB3 + b31 \cdot dY3 + b32 \cdot d\hat{r}_3\right) \cdot (a11a22 - a21a12)\big] \end{aligned} \quad (13.21)$$

where $detA < 0$; $(a22a33 - a32a23) > 0$, $(a11a33 - a31a13) > 0$, $(a11a22 - a21a12) > 0$.

It is also assumed that $(a12a33-a32a13) > 0$, $(a12a23-a22a13) < 0$, $(a21a33-a31a23) > 0$, $(a11a23 - a21a13) > 0$, $(a21a32 - a31a22) < 0$, and $(a11a32 - a31a12) > 0$ since the diagonal elements dominate the remaining ones. An increase in a country's ex ante monetary base, ceteris paribus, results in a lower interest rate in that country and a higher interest rate in the other two countries consistent with equilibrium in all three money markets. This result assumes that the central banks in all three countries allow their interest rates to vary and their exchange rates to fluctuate. Any change in MB1, MB2, or MB3 represents an arbitrary "one-shot" change associated with a corresponding "one-shot" change in the corresponding central bank's holdings of their own country's bonds or their holdings of bonds issued in another country.

If on the other hand the central bank in a country were to attempt to fix the interest rate in its own bond market, its end-of-period market demand for its bonds would need to change in the opposite direction whenever another sector altered its demand or supply of this country's bonds. In this case, holding constant the central bank's demands for bonds issued in other countries, its monetary base would change necessarily (in the opposite direction) whenever there were a change in another sector's demand or supply of this country's bonds. In this case, the monetary base changes with any changes that occur in the world's exchange rates. The reason is that a change in one or more exchange rates will affect the market demand or supply for a country's bonds, forcing the central bank to take counter measures if it is to keep its interest rate unchanged. If the central banks in all three countries simultaneously stand ready to keep their own country's interest rate fixed, then two of the three money market equilibrium conditions become independent in terms of whichever two exchange rates are viewed as independent.

Also, if a central bank were to attempt to fix the exchange rate between its unit of account and the unit of account of another country, its end-of-period market demand for the bonds issued in the other country will necessarily respond to any changes in the excess demand for items denominated in its unit of account relative to items denominated in the unit of account of the other country. Holding constant the central bank's demand for its own bonds, its planned end-of-period monetary base would necessarily change with the change in its end-of-period holdings of foreign bonds. In this case, the central bank's planned end-of-period monetary base changes endogenously.

The World's Bond Markets

The market demand function for bonds issued in a given country includes the demand for that country's bonds by the household sector in that country plus the demands for that country's bonds by all three private banking sectors and by all three central banks. The household sector's demand for its country's bonds is positively related to the rate of interest on those bonds. The demands for the country's bonds by the three private banking sectors is positively related to the interest rate on those bonds, but negatively related to the interest rates on the bonds issued in the other two countries. The nominal demand for domestic bonds by the central bank in a given country (measured in terms of that country's unit of account) is taken to be a policy variable. The nominal demand for bonds issued in another country by the central bank in a given country (measured in terms of the central bank's unit of account) is assumed to be given. This means that the nominal value of that demand in terms of the unit of account of the country in which the bond is issued will change if the exchange rate between the two countries changes.

The end-of-period ex ante market supplies of bonds in each country are more complicated. The following points become relevant to the derivation of the market demand and supplies for bonds in the three countries:

1. As ε rises, Country Two's goods become more expensive for Country One. Therefore, the demand for K falls by NR and G1. Also, Country One's goods become cheaper for Country Two. Therefore, the demand for NR increases for K and G2.
2. As $\tilde{\varepsilon}$ rises, Country Three's goods become more expensive for Country One. Therefore, the demand for C by H1 falls. Also, Country One's goods become cheaper for Country Three. Therefore, the demand for NR rises by G3 and C.
3. As $\tilde{\varepsilon}/\varepsilon$ rises, Country Three's goods become more expensive for Country Two. Therefore, the demand for C by H2 falls. Also, Country Two's goods become cheaper for Country Three. Therefore, the demand for K rises by G3 and C.
4. As ε rises, $B2^s$ rises by the K industry and by G2, $B1^s$ falls by the NR and G1 sectors. As $\tilde{\varepsilon}$ rises, $B3^s$ rises by the C industry and by G3, $B1^s$ falls for NR. As $\tilde{\varepsilon}/\varepsilon$ rises, $B3^s$ rises by the C industry and by G3, $B2^s$ by K industry falls. Therefore, $B1^s$ is negatively related to both ε and $\tilde{\varepsilon}$. $B1^s$ is also negatively related to r_1. $B2^s$ is positively related to ε but negatively related to $\tilde{\varepsilon}$. $B2^s$ is also negatively related to r_2. $B3^s$ is negatively related to ε but positively related to $\tilde{\varepsilon}$. $B3^s$ is also negatively related to r_3.

Country One's Bond Market

PB1 and CB1 fix their demands for B1 in terms of Country One's unit of account. Therefore, if either ε or $\tilde{\varepsilon}$ were to rise, these sectors' nominal demands for B1 would remain unchanged. PB2 and CB2 fix their demands for B1 in terms of Country Two's unit of account. Therefore, if ε were to increase these sectors would increase their nominal demands for B1 in terms of Country One's unit of account (holding constant unobservable expectations as to future exchange rates). PB3 and CB3 fix their demands for B1 in terms of Country Three's unit of account. Therefore, if $\tilde{\varepsilon}$ were to increase these sectors would increase their nominal demands for B1 in terms of Country One's unit of account (holding constant unobservable expectations as to future exchange rates). Consequently, the nominal market demand for B1 is an increasing function of both ε and $\tilde{\varepsilon}$ as well as r_1. The nominal demand is also negatively related to r_2 and r_3.

As ε rises, the cost of K to the G1 and NR industries rises so that G1 and NR borrow less in Country One's bond market to finance purchases of K. Therefore, the supply of bonds to Country One's bond market is negatively related to ε.

Country One's bond market consists of three borrowers (NR, R1, and G1) and seven lenders (H1, PB1, PB2, PB3, CB1, CB2, and CB3):

Market demand for B1:

H1 Sector's demand for B1:

$$p_{B1} \cdot B1^{d}_{H1(t+1)} = \overline{Y}1 - p_{R1t} \cdot \left(\frac{R1H1_t}{N1_t}\right) \cdot N1_t - p_{Ct} \cdot \tilde{\varepsilon} \cdot \left(\frac{CH1_t}{N1_t}\right) \cdot N1_t - \left(M1^{d}_{t+1} - M1_t\right)$$

$$p_{B1} \cdot B1^{d}_{H1(t+1)} = \overline{Y}1 - p_{R1t} \cdot R1H1^{d}_{t} - \tilde{\varepsilon} \cdot p_{Ct} \cdot CH1^{d}_{t} - M1^{d}_{t+1}$$
$$= p_{B1} \cdot B1^{d}_{H1(t+1)} \left(\overline{Y}1, r_{1t}, W1_{t+1}, N1_{t}\right) \qquad (12.43)$$
$$+ \quad + \quad - \quad +$$

Country One's private banking sector's demand for B1:

$$p_{B1} \cdot B1^{d}_{PB1(t+1)} = p_{B1} \cdot B1_{PB1t} - p_{B2} \cdot \varepsilon \cdot \left(B2^{d}_{PB1(t+1)} - B2_{PB1t}\right)$$
$$- p_{B3} \cdot \tilde{\varepsilon} \cdot \left(B3^{d}_{PB1(t+1)} - B3_{PB1t}\right) - \left(X1^{d}_{PB1(t+1)}\right.$$
$$\left. - X1_{PB1t}\right) + \left(1 - \hat{r}_1\right) \cdot \left(D1^{s}_{PB1(t+1)} - D1_{PB1t}\right)$$
$$= - p_{B2} \cdot \varepsilon \cdot B2^{d}_{PB1(t+1)} - p_{B3} \cdot \tilde{\varepsilon} \cdot B3^{d}_{PB1(t+1)} - X1^{d}_{PB1(t+1)}$$
$$+ \left(1 - \hat{r}_1\right) \cdot D1^{s}_{PB1(t+1)} + NW_{PB1t}$$
$$= - p_{B2} \cdot \varepsilon \cdot B2^{d}_{PB1(t+1)} \left(r_1, r_2\right) - p_{B3} \cdot \tilde{\varepsilon} \cdot B3^{d}_{PB1(t+1)} \left(r_1, r_3\right)$$
$$- \; + \qquad\qquad - \; +$$
$$- \left(\frac{X1^{d}_{PB1(t+1)}}{p^{e}_{R1}}\right)^{d} \left(r_1, W1_{t+1}\right) \cdot p^{e}_{R1} + \left(1 - \hat{r}_1\right)$$
$$- \quad +$$
$$\cdot \left(\frac{D1^{s}_{PB1(t+1)}}{p^{e}_{R1}}\right)^{S} \left(r_1, \hat{r}_1, W1_{t+1}\right) \cdot p^{e}_{R1} + NW_{PB1t}$$
$$+ \quad - \quad -$$
$$= p_{B1} \cdot B1^{d}_{PB1(t+1)} \left(r_1, r_2, r_3, \hat{r}_1, W1_{t+1}, +NW_{PB1t}\right) \qquad (9.21)$$
$$+ \quad - \; - \; - \quad - \qquad +1$$

where $NW_{PB1t} = p_{B1} \cdot B1_{PB1} + p_{B2} \cdot \varepsilon \cdot B2_{PB1t} + p_{B3} \cdot \tilde{\varepsilon} \cdot B3_{PB1t} + X1_{PB1t} - (1 - \hat{r}_1) \cdot D1_{PB1t}$.

Country Two's private banking sector's demand for B1:

$$\left(\frac{p_{B1}}{\varepsilon}\right) \cdot B1^{d}_{PB2(t+1)} = \left(\frac{p_{B1}}{\varepsilon}\right) \cdot B1^{d}_{PB2(t+1)} \cdot B1^{PB2d}_{t+1} \left(r_1, r_2\right) \qquad (9.27)$$
$$+ \quad -$$

Country Three's private banking sector's demand for B1:

$$\left(\frac{p_{B1}}{\tilde{\varepsilon}}\right) \cdot B1^{d}_{PB3(t+1)} = \left(\frac{p_{B1}}{\tilde{\varepsilon}}\right) \cdot B1^{d}_{PB3(t+1)} \left(r_1, r_3\right) \qquad (9.38)$$
$$+ \quad -$$

Country One's central bank's demand for B1: $p_{B1} \cdot B1^{d}_{CB1(t+1)}$
Country Two's central bank's demand for B1: $(p_{B1}/\varepsilon) \cdot B1^{d}_{CB2(t+1)}$
Country Three's central bank's demand for B1: $(p_{B1}/\tilde{\varepsilon}) \cdot B1^{d}_{CB3(t+1)}$
Market supply of Country One's bonds:
NR industry's supply of B1:

$$\begin{aligned} p_{B1} \cdot B1^{s}_{NR(t+1)} &= p_{B1} \cdot B1_{NRt} + p_{NRt} \cdot \left(NR^{T^*}_{t+1} - NR^{T^*}_{t}\right) + p_{Kt} \\ &\quad \cdot \varepsilon \cdot \left[K^{d}_{NR(t+1)}\left(r_1, \delta, p_{Kt} \cdot \varepsilon\right) - K_{NRt}\right] \\ &= p_{B1} \cdot B1_{NRt} + p_{NRt} \cdot \left[\tau_{NR}(I1_t) \cdot T_{NRt}\right. \\ &\quad (h_{NR} \cdot N1_{NRt}, K_{NRt}) - NRK^{T}_{t} - NRC^{T}_{t} - NRG1^{T}_{t} - NRG2^{T}_{t} \\ &\quad \left. - NRG3^{T}_{t}\right] + p_{Kt} \cdot \varepsilon \cdot \left[K^{d}_{NR(t+1)}\left(r_1, \delta, p_{Kt} \cdot \varepsilon\right) - K_{NRt}\right] \\ &= p_{B1} \cdot B1^{s}_{NR(t+1)} \Big(\underset{+1}{p_{B1} \cdot B1_{NRt}} - p_{NRt} \cdot NR^{T^*}_{t}, \underset{-}{r_1}, \underset{-}{\delta}, \underset{-}{p_{Kt}}, \\ &\quad \underset{-}{\varepsilon}, \underset{-}{K_{NRt}}, \underset{-}{NRK^{T}_{t}}, \underset{-}{NRC^{T}_{t}}, \underset{-}{NRG1^{T}_{t}}, \underset{-}{NRG2^{T}_{t}}, \underset{-}{NRG3^{T}_{t}}\Big) \end{aligned} \tag{12.19}$$

R1 industry's supply of B1:

$$\begin{aligned} p^{b1}_{t} \cdot B1^{R1s}_{t+1} &= p_{R1t} \cdot \left(R1^{T^*}_{t+1} - R1^{T^*}_{t}\right) + p_{B1} \cdot B1^{R1}_{t} \\ &= p_{R1t} \cdot \left[\tau_{R1}(I1_t) \cdot T_{R1t}(h_{R1t} \cdot N1_{R1t}) - R1H1_t\right] \\ &\quad + p_{B1} \cdot B1^{R1}_{t} \end{aligned} \tag{12.11}$$

G1 sector's supply of B1:

$$\begin{aligned} p_{B1} \cdot B1^{s}_{G1(t+1)} &= W1_t \cdot h^{GH1}_{G1t} \cdot N1_{G1t} + \varepsilon \cdot p_{Kt} \\ &\quad \cdot \left[K^{d}_{G1(t+1)}\left(W1_{(t+1)}, r_{1t}, p_{Kt}, \varepsilon, \delta, g_{1H1(t+1)}\right) - (1-\delta) \cdot K_{G1t}\right] \\ &\quad - \Pi^{CB1G1}_{t} + (1 + p_{B1}) \cdot B1_{G1t} + p^{G1}_{xt} \cdot \overline{R1}_t - Tx_{G1H1t} \\ &\quad + W1_t \cdot h^{W^*H1}_{G1t} \cdot N1_{G1t} - Tx_{W^*G1t} \\ &\quad + W1_t \cdot h^{\Delta I}_{G1t} \cdot N1_{G1t}(\Delta I1_t) + p_{NRt} \cdot NRG1^{Td}_{t} - Tx_{NRt} - Tx_{R1t} \end{aligned} \tag{12.9}$$

Market demand for B1:

$$p_{B1} \cdot B1^{d}_{t+1} = p_{B1} \cdot B1^{d}_{t+1}\Big(\underset{+}{r_1}, \underset{-}{r_2}, \underset{-}{r_3}, \underset{+1}{p_{B1} \cdot B1^{d}_{CB1(t+1)}}, p_{B1}$$
$$\underset{+1}{\cdot B1^{d}_{CB2(t+1)}}, \underset{+1}{p_{B1} \cdot B1^{d}_{CB3(t+1)}}\Big) \tag{13.22}$$

Market supply of B1:

$$p_{B1} \cdot B1^{s}_{t+1} = p_{B1} \cdot B1^{s}_{t+1}(\underset{-}{r_1}, \underset{-}{\varepsilon}, \underset{-}{\tilde{\varepsilon}}, \ldots) \tag{13.23}$$

Setting the demand for B1 equal to the supply of B1 and differentiating yields

$$\underset{+}{\left(\frac{\partial ED_{B1}}{\partial r_1}\right)} dr_1 + \underset{-}{\left(\frac{\partial ED_{B1}}{\partial r_2}\right)} dr_2 + \underset{-}{\left(\frac{\partial ED_{B1}}{\partial r_3}\right)} dr_3$$
$$+ \underset{+}{\left(\frac{\partial ED_{B1}}{\partial \varepsilon}\right)} d\varepsilon + \underset{+}{\left(\frac{\partial ED_{B1}}{\partial \tilde{\varepsilon}}\right)} d\tilde{\varepsilon} = 0 \tag{13.24}$$

where ED_{B1} denotes the excess demand for B1. This yields the following relationships:

$$\frac{d\varepsilon}{d\tilde{\varepsilon}} = -\frac{(\partial ED_{B1}/\partial \tilde{\varepsilon})}{(\partial ED_{B1}/\partial \varepsilon)} < 0.$$
$$\frac{d\varepsilon}{dr_1} = -\frac{(\partial ED_{B1}/\partial r_1)}{(\partial ED_{B1}/\partial \varepsilon)} < 0.$$
$$\frac{d\varepsilon}{dr_2} = -\frac{(\partial ED_{B1}/\partial r_2)}{(\partial ED_{B1}/\partial \varepsilon)} > 0.$$
$$\frac{d\varepsilon}{dr_3} = -\frac{(\partial ED_{B1}/\partial r_3)}{(\partial ED_{B1}/\partial \varepsilon)} > 0.$$

Figure 13.4 shows the combinations of ε and $\tilde{\varepsilon}$ consistent with equilibrium in the B1 market, given the interest rates in the three countries and the central banks' demands for B1 (holding the respective supplies of their monetary bases constant).

Country Two's Bond Market

The PB1 and CB1 sectors fix their demands for B2 in terms of Country One's unit of account. Therefore, if ε were to rise, these sectors' nominal demands for B2 would fall in terms of Country Two's unit of account (holding constant unobservable expectations as to future exchange rates). The PB2 and CB2 sectors fix their demands for B2 in terms of Country Two's unit of account. Therefore, if ε or $\tilde{\varepsilon}$ were to increase

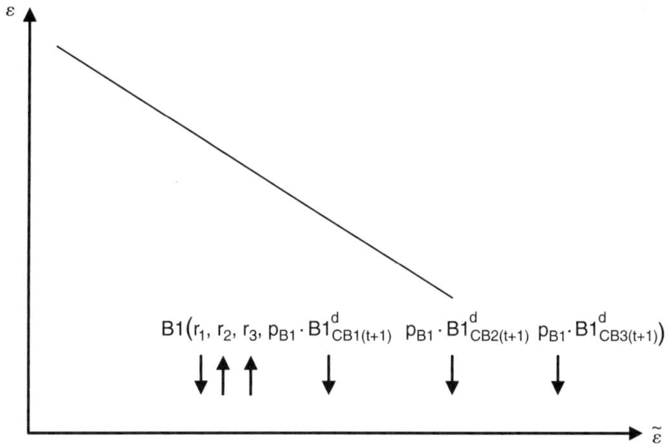

Figure 13.4 The B1 Locus

these sectors would not alter their nominal demands for B2 in terms of Country Two's unit of account, ceteris paribus. The PB3 and CB3 sectors fix their demands for B2 in terms of Country Three's unit of account. Therefore, if $\tilde{\varepsilon}/\varepsilon$ were to increase these sectors would increase their nominal demands for B2 in terms of Country Two's unit of account (holding constant unobservable expectations as to future exchange rates). Consequently, the nominal market demand for B2 is an increasing function of $\tilde{\varepsilon}$, but a decreasing function of ε.

As ε rises, since both the G1 and NR sectors buy less K, the K industry finds that its unplanned investment is rising so that it must borrow more in Country Two's bond market.

H2 sector's demand for B2:

$$p_{B2} \cdot B2^d_{H2(t+1)} = \overline{Y}2 - p_{R2t} \cdot R2H2^d_t - \left(\frac{\tilde{\varepsilon}}{\varepsilon}\right) \cdot p_{Ct} \cdot CH2^d_t - M2^d_{t+1}$$

$$= p_{B2} \cdot B2^d_{H2(t+1)} \underset{+\quad +\quad\ -\quad\ +}{\left(\overline{Y}2, r_{2t}, W2_{t+1}, N2_t\right)} \tag{12.67}$$

Country One's private banking sector's demand for B2:

$$p_{B2} \cdot \varepsilon \cdot B2^d_{PB1(t+1)} = p_{B2} \cdot \varepsilon \cdot B2^d_{PB1(t+1)} \cdot \underset{-\ \ +}{(r_1, r_2)} \tag{9.17}$$

Country Two's private banking sector's demand for B2:

$$p_{B2} \cdot B2^d_{PB2(t+1)} = -\left(\frac{p_{B2}}{\varepsilon}\right) \cdot B1^d_{PB2(t+1)} - \left[\frac{(p_{B3} \cdot \tilde{\varepsilon})}{\varepsilon}\right] \cdot B3^d_{PB2(t+1)}$$

$$- X2^d_{PB2(t+1)} + (1 - \hat{r}_2) \cdot D2^s_{PB2(t+1)} + NW_{PB2t}$$

$$= \mathrm{NW}_{\mathrm{PB2t}} - \left(\frac{p_{B1}}{\varepsilon}\right) \cdot B1^{d}_{PB2(t+1)}\underset{+\ -}{(r_1, r_2)} - \left[\frac{p_{B3}\cdot\tilde{\varepsilon}}{\varepsilon}\right] \cdot B3^{d}_{PB2(t+1)}\underset{-\ +}{(r_2, r_3)}$$

$$- \left(\frac{X2^{d}_{PB2(t+1)}}{p^{e}_{R2}}\right)^{d} \underset{-\quad +}{(r_2, W2_{t+1})} \cdot p^{e}_{R2} + \left(1 - \hat{r}_2\right) \cdot \left(\frac{D2^{2}_{PB2(t+1)}}{p^{e}_{R2}}\right)^{s}$$

$$\cdot \underset{+\ -\quad -}{\left(r_2, \hat{r}_2, W2_{t+1}\right)} \cdot p^{e}_{R2}$$

$$= p_{B2} \cdot B2^{d}_{PB2(t+1)}\underset{-\ +\ -\ -\quad -\qquad +1}{\left(r1, r2, r3, \hat{r}_2, W2_{t+1}, NW_{PB2t}\right)} \tag{9.31}$$

where $NW_{PB2t} = (p_{B1}/\varepsilon) \cdot B1_{PB2t} + p_{B2} \cdot B2_{PB2t} + \left[\left(p_{B3} \cdot \tilde{\varepsilon}_t\right)/\varepsilon_t\right] \cdot B3_{PB2t} + X2_{PB2t} - (1 - \hat{r}_2) \cdot D2_{PB2t}$.

Country Three's private banking sector's demand for B2:

$$\left[\frac{(p_{B1} \cdot \varepsilon)}{\tilde{\varepsilon}}\right] \cdot B2^{d}_{PB3(t+1)} = \left[\frac{(p_{B1} \cdot \varepsilon)}{\tilde{\varepsilon}}\right] \cdot B2^{d}_{PB3(t+1)}\underset{+\ -}{(r_2, r_3)} \tag{9.39}$$

Country One's central bank's demand for B2: $\varepsilon \cdot p_{B2} \cdot B2^{d}_{CB1(t+1)}$.

Country Two's central bank's demand for B2: $p_{B2} \cdot B2^{d}_{CB2(t+1)}$.

Country Three's central bank's demand for B2: $\left[\left(p_{B2} \cdot \varepsilon\right)/\tilde{\varepsilon}\right] \cdot B2^{d}_{CB3(t+1)}$.

K industry's supply of B2:

$$p_{B2} \cdot B2^{s}_{K(t+1)} = p_{B2} \cdot B2_{Kt} + p_{Kt} \cdot \left[\delta \cdot K_{Kt} + \tau_K(I2_t) \cdot T_{Kt}(h_K \cdot N2_{Kt}, K_{Kt}) - KG1^{d}_{t} - KG2^{d}_{t} - KG3^{d}_{t} - KNR1^{d}_{t} - KC^{d}_{t}\right] \tag{12.62}$$

R2 industry's supply of B2:

$$p_{B2} \cdot B1^{s}_{R2(t+1)} = p_{R2t} \cdot \left(R2^{T^*}_{t+1} - R2^{T^*}_{t}\right) + p_{B2} \cdot B2_{R2t} = p_{R2t} \cdot (\tau_{R2}(I2_t) \cdot T_{R2t}(h_{R2t} \cdot N2_{R2t}) - R2H2_t) + p_{B2} \cdot B2_{R2t} \tag{12.53}$$

G2 sector's supply of B2:

$$p_{B2} \cdot B2^{s}_{G2(t+1)} = W2_t \cdot h^{GH2}_{G2t} \cdot N2_{G2t} + p_{Kt} \cdot \left[K^{d}_{G2(t+1)}\left(W2_{t+1}, r_{2t}, p_{Kt}, \delta, g_{2H2(t+1)}\right) - (1-\delta) \cdot K_{G2t}\right] - \Pi^{CB2G2}_{t} + (1 + p_{B2}) \cdot B2_{G2t} + p^{G2}_{xt} \cdot \overline{R2}_t - Tx_{G2H2t} + W2_t \cdot h^{W^*H2}_{G2t} \cdot N2_{G2t} - Tx_{W^*G2t} + W2_t \cdot h^{\Delta I}_{G2t} \cdot N2_{G2t}(\Delta I2_t) + \left(\frac{1}{\varepsilon}\right) \cdot p_{NRt} \cdot NRG2^{Td}_{t} - Tx_{Kt} - Tx_{R2t} \quad (12.51)$$

Market demand for B2:

$$p_{B2} \cdot B2^{d}_{t+1} = p_{B2} \cdot B2^{d}_{t+1}\Big(\underset{-}{r_1}, \underset{+}{r_2}, \underset{-}{r_3}, \underset{+1}{p_{B2} \cdot B2^{d}_{CB1(t+1)}}, \underset{+1}{p_{B2} \cdot B2^{d}_{CB2(t+1)}}, \underset{+1}{p_{B2} \cdot B2^{d}_{CB3(t+1)}}\Big) \quad (13.25)$$

Market supply of B2:

$$p_{B2} \cdot B2^{s}_{t+1} = p_{B2} \cdot B2^{s}_{t+1}(\underset{-}{r_2}, \underset{+}{\varepsilon}, \underset{-}{\tilde{\varepsilon}}, \ldots) \quad (13.26)$$

Setting the demand for B2 equal to the supply of B2 and differentiating yields

$$\underset{-}{\left(\frac{\partial ED_{B2}}{\partial r_1}\right)} dr_1 + \underset{+}{\left(\frac{\partial ED_{B2}}{\partial r_2}\right)} dr_2 + \underset{-}{\left(\frac{\partial ED_{B2}}{\partial r_3}\right)} dr_3 + \underset{-}{\left(\frac{\partial ED_{B2}}{\partial \varepsilon}\right)} d\varepsilon + \underset{+}{\left(\frac{\partial ED_{B2}}{\partial \tilde{\varepsilon}}\right)} d\tilde{\varepsilon} = 0 \quad (13.27)$$

where ED_{B2} denotes the excess demand for B2. This yields the following relationships:

$$\frac{d\varepsilon}{d\tilde{\varepsilon}} = -\frac{(\partial ED_{B2}/\partial \tilde{\varepsilon})}{(\partial ED_{B2}/\partial \varepsilon)} > 0.$$

$$\frac{d\varepsilon}{dr_1} = -\frac{(\partial ED_{B2}/\partial r_1)}{(\partial ED_{B2}/\partial \varepsilon)} < 0.$$

$$\frac{d\varepsilon}{dr_2} = -\frac{(\partial ED_{B2}/\partial r_2)}{(\partial ED_{B2}/\partial \varepsilon)} > 0.$$

$$\frac{d\varepsilon}{dr_3} = -\frac{(\partial ED_{B1}/\partial r_3)}{(\partial ED_{B2}/\partial \varepsilon)} < 0.$$

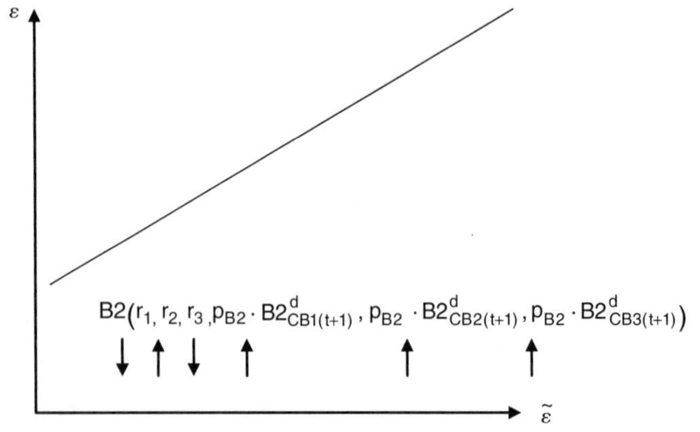

Figure 13.5 The B2 Locus

Figure 13.5 shows the combinations of ε and $\tilde{\varepsilon}$ consistent with equilibrium in the B2 market, given the interest rates in the three countries and the central banks' demands for B2 (holding their respective supplies of their monetary bases constant).

Country Three's Bond Market

The PB1 and CB1 sectors decide their demands for B3 in terms of Country One's unit of account. Therefore, if $\tilde{\varepsilon}$ were to rise, these sectors' nominal demands for B3 would fall in terms of Country Three's unit of account (holding constant unobservable expectations as to future exchange rates). The PB2 and CB2 sectors fix their demands for B3 in terms of Country Two's unit of account. Therefore, if $\tilde{\varepsilon}/\varepsilon$ were to increase these sectors would decrease their nominal demands for B3 in terms of Country Three's unit of account (holding constant unobservable expectations as to future exchange rates). The PB3 and CB3 sectors fix their demands for B3 in terms of Country Three's unit of account. Therefore, if either ε or $\tilde{\varepsilon}$ were to rise, these sectors' nominal demands for B3 would remain unchanged. Consequently, the nominal market demand for B3 is an increasing function of ε, but a decreasing function of $\tilde{\varepsilon}$.

As $\tilde{\varepsilon}$ rises, the H1 sector's demand for C falls and the H2 sector's demand for C also falls. Therefore, the C sector's supply of bonds in Country Three's bond market rises to finance the unplanned investment by the C industry. As ε rises, the value of Country Three's unit of account falls relative to Country Two's unit of account so that the H2 sector's demand for C rises. This causes the C industry's supply of bonds to Country Three's bond market to fall. Therefore, the market supply of bonds to Country Three's bond market is negatively related to ε.

The PB1 and CB1 sectors decide their demands for B1, B2, and B3 in terms of Country One's unit of account. Therefore, if either ε or $\tilde{\varepsilon}$ were to rise, these sectors' nominal demands for B1 would remain unchanged, but their demands for B2 would fall in terms of Country Two's unit of account should ε rise and their demands for B3 would fall in terms of Country Three's unit of account should $\tilde{\varepsilon}$ increase.

H3 sector's demand for B3:

$$p_{B3} \cdot B3^{d}_{H3(t+1)} = \overline{Y}3 - p_{R3t} \cdot R3H3^{d}_{t} - p_{Ct} \cdot CH3^{d}_{t} - M3^{d}_{t+1}$$
$$= p_{B3} \cdot B3^{d}_{H3(t+1)}\left(\underset{+}{\overline{Y}3}, \underset{+}{r_{3t}}, \underset{-}{W3_{t+1}}, \underset{+}{N3_{t}}\right) \quad (12.91)$$

Country One's private banking sector's demand for B3:

$$p_{B3} \cdot \tilde{\varepsilon} \cdot B3^{d}_{PB1(t+1)} = p_{B3} \cdot \tilde{\varepsilon} \cdot B3^{d}_{PB1(t+1)}\left(\underset{-}{r_1}, \underset{+}{r_3}\right) \quad (9.18)$$

Country Two's private banking sector's demand for B3:

$$\left[\frac{(p_{B3} \cdot \tilde{\varepsilon})}{\varepsilon}\right] \cdot B3^{d}_{PB2(t+1)} = \left[\frac{(p_{B1} \cdot \tilde{\varepsilon})}{\varepsilon}\right] \cdot B3^{d}_{PB2(t+1)}\left(\underset{-}{r_2}, \underset{+}{r_3}\right) \quad (9.28)$$

Country Three's private banking sector's demand for B3:

$$p_{B3} \cdot B3^{d}_{PB3(t+1)} = -\left(\frac{p_{B1}}{\tilde{\varepsilon}}\right) \cdot B1^{d}_{PB3(t+1)}\left(\underset{+}{r_1}, \underset{-}{r_3}\right) - \left[\frac{(p_{B3} \cdot \varepsilon)}{\tilde{\varepsilon}}\right] \cdot B2^{d}_{PB3(t+1)}\left(\underset{+}{r_2}, \underset{-}{r_3}\right)$$
$$- X3^{d}_{PB3(t+1)}\left(\underset{-}{r_1}, \underset{+}{W3_{t+1}}\right) + (1 - \hat{r}_3)$$
$$\cdot D3^{s}_{PB3(t+1)}\left(\underset{+}{r_1}, \underset{-}{\hat{r}_3}, \underset{-}{W3_{t+1}}\right) + NW_{PB3t}$$
$$= p_{B3} \cdot B3^{d}_{PB3(t+1)}\left(\underset{-}{r_1}, \underset{-}{r_2}, \underset{+}{r_3}, \underset{-}{\hat{r}_3}, \underset{-}{W3_{t+1}}, \underset{+1}{NW_{PB3t}}\right) \quad (9.42)$$

where $NW_{PB3t} = (p_{B1}/\tilde{\varepsilon}) \cdot B1_{PB3t} + [(p_{B2} \cdot \varepsilon)/\tilde{\varepsilon}] \cdot B2_{PB3t} + p_{B3} \cdot B3_{PB3t} + X3_{PB3t} - (1 - \hat{r}_3) \cdot D3^{s}_{PB3t}$.

Country One's central bank's demand for B3: $\tilde{\varepsilon} \cdot p_{B3} \cdot B3^{d}_{CB1(t+1)}$.

Country Two's central Bank's demand for B3: $[(p_{B3} \cdot \varepsilon_t)/\varepsilon_t] \cdot B3^{d}_{CB2(t+1)}$.

Country Three's central Bank's demand for B3: $p_{B3} \cdot B3^{d}_{CB3(t+1)}$.

C industry's supply of B3:

$$\begin{aligned}
p_{B3} \cdot B3^{s}_{C(t+1)} &= p_{B3} \cdot B3_{Ct} + p_{Ct} \cdot [\tau_{NR}(I3_t) \cdot T_{Ct}(h_{Ct} \cdot N3_{Ct}, K_{Ct}) \\
&\quad - CH1_t - CH2_t - CH3_t] \\
&\quad + p_{Kt} \cdot \left(\frac{\varepsilon}{\tilde{\varepsilon}}\right) \cdot K^{d}_{NR(t+1)}\left(\underset{-}{r_{3t}}, \underset{-}{p_{Kt}}, \underset{-}{p_{NRt}}, \underset{-}{p_{w}}, \underset{-}{\varphi_C}, \underset{-}{\theta_C}, \underset{-}{\kappa}, \underset{-}{\delta}, \underset{-}{\varepsilon}, \underset{+}{\tilde{\varepsilon}}\right) \\
&\quad - p_{Kt} \cdot \left(\frac{\varepsilon}{\tilde{\varepsilon}}\right) \cdot (1-\delta) \cdot K_{Ct} + B3_{Ct} \\
&= p_{B3} \cdot K3^{s}_{C(t+1)}\left(\underset{-}{r_{3t}}, \underset{-}{p_{Kt}}, \underset{-}{p_{NRt}}, \underset{-}{p_{w}}, \underset{-}{\varphi_C}, \underset{-}{\theta_C}, \underset{-}{\kappa}, \underset{-}{\delta}, \underset{-}{\varepsilon}, \underset{+}{\tilde{\varepsilon}}, CH1_t\right. \\
&\quad \left.\underset{-}{+ CH2_t + CH3_t}, \underset{+1}{p_{B3} \cdot B3_{Ct}}\right)
\end{aligned} \tag{13.28}$$

R3 industry's supply of B3:

$$\begin{aligned}
p_{B3} \cdot B3^{s}_{R3(t+1)} &= p_{R3t} \cdot \left(R3^{T^*}_{t+1} - R3^{T^*}_{t}\right) + p_{B3} \cdot B3_{R3t} \\
&= p_{R3t} \cdot (\tau_{R3}(I3_t) \cdot T_{R3t}(h_{R3t} \cdot N3_{R3t}) - R3H3_t) + p_{B3} \cdot B3_{R3t}
\end{aligned} \tag{12.77}$$

G3 sector's supply of B3:

$$\begin{aligned}
p_{B3} \cdot B3^{s}_{G3(t+1)} &= W3_t \cdot h^{GH3}_{G3t} \cdot N3_{G3t} + \left(\frac{\varepsilon}{\tilde{\varepsilon}}\right) \cdot p_{Kt} \\
&\quad \cdot \left[K^{d}_{G3(t+1)}\left(W3_{t+1}, r_{3t}, p_{Kt}, \delta, g_{3H3(t+1)}\right) - (1-\delta) \cdot K_{G3t}\right] \\
&\quad - \Pi^{CB3G3}_{t} + (1 + p_{B3}) \cdot B3_{G3t} + p^{G3}_{xt} \cdot \overline{R3}_t - Tx_{G3H3t} \\
&\quad + W3_t \cdot h^{W^*H3}_{G3t} \cdot N3_{G3t} - Tx_{W^*G3t} \\
&\quad + W3_t \cdot h^{\Delta I}_{G3t} \cdot N_{G3t}(\Delta I3_t) + \left(\frac{1}{\tilde{\varepsilon}}\right) \cdot p_{NRt} \cdot NRG3^{Td}_{t} \\
&\quad - Tx_{Ct} - Tx_{R3t}
\end{aligned} \tag{12.75}$$

Market demand for B3:

$$\begin{aligned}
p_{B3} \cdot B3^{d}_{t+1} &= p_{B3} \cdot B3^{d}_{t+1}\left(\underset{-}{r_1}, \underset{-}{r_2}, \underset{+}{r_3}, \underset{+1}{p_{B3} \cdot B3^{d}_{CB1(t+1)}}, \underset{+1}{p_{B3} \cdot B3^{d}_{CB2(t+1)}}, \underset{+1}{p_{B3} \cdot B3^{d}_{CB3(t+1)}}\right)
\end{aligned} \tag{13.29}$$

Market supply of B3:

$$p_{B3} \cdot B3^{s}_{t+1} = p_{B3} \cdot B3^{s}_{t+1}(\underset{-}{r_3}, \underset{+}{\varepsilon}, \underset{-}{\tilde{\varepsilon}}, \ldots) \tag{13.30}$$

Setting the demand for B3 equal to the supply of B3 and differentiating yields

$$\underset{-}{\left(\frac{\partial ED_{B3}}{\partial r_1}\right)} dr_1 + \underset{-}{\left(\frac{\partial ED_{B3}}{\partial r_2}\right)} dr_2 + \underset{+}{\left(\frac{\partial ED_{B3}}{\partial r_3}\right)} dr_3 + \underset{-}{\left(\frac{\partial ED_{B3}}{\partial \varepsilon}\right)} d\varepsilon + \underset{+}{\left(\frac{\partial ED_{B3}}{\partial \tilde{\varepsilon}}\right)} d\tilde{\varepsilon} = 0 \tag{13.31}$$

where ED_{B2} denotes the excess demand for B2. This yields the following relationships:

$$\frac{d\varepsilon}{d\tilde{\varepsilon}} = -\frac{(\partial ED_{B3}/\partial \tilde{\varepsilon})}{(\partial ED_{B3}/\partial \varepsilon)} > 0.$$

$$\frac{d\varepsilon}{dr_1} = -\frac{(\partial ED_{B3}/\partial r_1)}{(\partial ED_{B3}/\partial \varepsilon)} < 0.$$

$$\frac{d\varepsilon}{dr_2} = -\frac{(\partial ED_{B3}/\partial r_2)}{(\partial ED_{B3}/\partial \varepsilon)} < 0.$$

$$\frac{d\varepsilon}{dr_3} = -\frac{(\partial ED_{B3}/\partial r_3)}{(\partial ED_{B3}/\partial \varepsilon)} > 0.$$

Figure 13.6 shows the combinations of ε and $\tilde{\varepsilon}$ consistent with equilibrium in the B3 market, given the interest rates in the three countries and the central banks' demands for B3 (holding their respective supplies of their monetary bases constant).

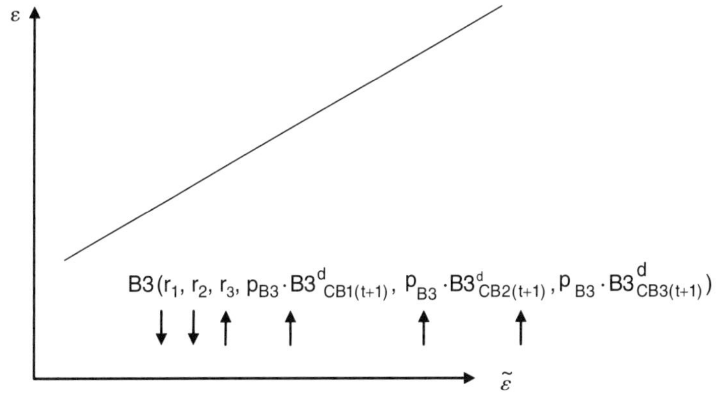

Figure 13.6 The B3 Locus

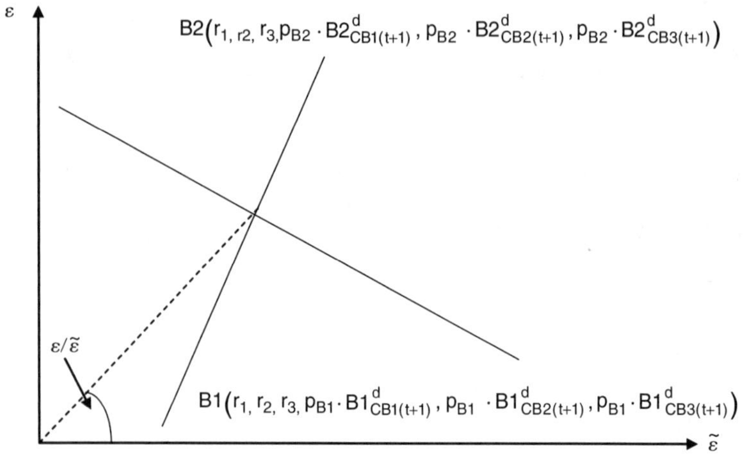

Figure 13.7 Joint Determination of World Exchange Rates

Figure 13.7 shows the joint determination of the world's exchange rates using the equilibrium conditions associated with equilibrium in the bond markets in Country One and Country Two.

In chapter 14, the cash flow restrictions facing the respective individual sectors are specified. These restrictions are then aggregated to find a restriction across markets for each of the three countries. The aggregation of the restrictions facing each country yields a worldwide restriction upon the financial markets.

14

Implications of the World's Cash Flow Constraints

Every sector in every country faces a cash flow (budget) constraint. The cash flow constraints facing the individual sectors in a country, when aggregated across that country's sectors, yield a community or countrywide cash flow constraint. The terms in this constraint may then be arranged to produce an equation that may be interpreted as a form of Walras's Law. In general, Walras's Law states that in a model containing n markets, the sum of the excess demands across the n markets must be equal to zero identically. In particular, if n-1 markets happen to be in equilibrium (characterized by excess demands equal to zero in those markets), then the nth market must also be in equilibrium. In the present context, it states that the excess demand for the money issued in that country plus the excess demand for bonds issued in that country plus that country's ex ante balance of payments deficits with each of the other two countries must be equal to zero identically. Importantly, the excess demands in the product markets do not appear explicitly in the community's budget constraint and therefore do not appear in the corresponding statement of Walras's Law for that country. The reason is that since the imperfectly competitive firms decide production and announce product price before product demand is revealed, they may experience unplanned changes in inventories by the end of the period. Since the firms do not engage in net business saving in this model, they absorb the excess supply or demand for their product by financing (or reducing their end-of-period debt) in their own bond market the unplanned investment or disinvestment. Consequently, any excess demand in a product market automatically becomes incorporated in that country's bond market.

As the countrywide budget constraints are aggregated (using a common unit of account) across all countries, a worldwide budget constraint emerges. The terms in this constraint may then be arranged to yield another version of Walras's Law, stating that the sum of the excess demands for money across all three countries plus the excess demands for bonds across all three countries must be equal to zero identically. This result was applied in chapter 13 to recursively solve first for the world's interest rates and then for the world's exchange rates. In that chapter, it was shown that under variable interest rates and flexible exchange rates the equilibrium conditions in the three money markets may be used to solve for the world's three interest rates and then given these interest rates, the equilibrium conditions in two of the bond markets may be employed to solve for any two of the exchange rates (only two of the three exchange rates are independent); the third bond market is not required to obtain a solution for the world's interest rates and exchange rates. The purpose of the present chapter is to show the validity of this approach.

Country One

The objective in this section is to derive the appropriate version of Walras's Law for Country One. The relevant budget constraints for the nonbank sectors were presented in chapter 12. The relevant budget constraints facing the banking sectors were given in chapter 9. These constraints provide the basis for the present derivation.

The H3 sector's disposable income is given by

$$DI_{H1} \equiv \Pi_{NRt} + \Pi_{R1t} + \Pi_{PB1t} + W1t\Big(h^{T}_{NRt} \cdot N1_{NRt} + h^{R}_{NRt} \cdot N1_{Rt} + h^{T}_{R1t} \cdot N1_{R1t} + h_{PB1t} \cdot N1_{PB1} + h_{W*G1} \cdot N_{G1} + h_{G1H1} \cdot N_{G1} + h_{G1I1} \cdot N_{G1}\Big) + B1_{H1t} - Tx1_{t} \tag{14.1}$$

where

$$\Pi_{NRt} \equiv p_{NRt} \cdot NR^{T} - p_{Kt} \cdot \varepsilon \cdot \delta \cdot K_{NRt} - Tx_{NRG1} - p_{w} \cdot \left(\Omega^{d}_{NRt} - \Omega_{NRt}\right) - B1_{NRt} - W1_{t} \cdot h^{T}_{NRt} \cdot N1_{NRt} - W1_{t} \cdot h^{R}_{NRt} \cdot N1_{NRt} \tag{14.2}$$

$$\Pi_{R1t} \equiv p^{G1}_{xt} \cdot \overline{R1}_{t} + p_{R1t} \cdot R1^{T} - Tx_{R1G1t} - B1_{R1t} - W1_{t} \cdot h^{T}_{R1t} \cdot N1_{R1t} \tag{14.3}$$

$$\Pi_{PB1t} \equiv B1_{PB1t} + \varepsilon \cdot B2_{PB1t} + \tilde{\varepsilon} \cdot B3_{PB1t} - W1_{t} \cdot h_{PB1t} \cdot N1_{PB1} \tag{14.4}$$

Therefore, the H1 sector's current disposable income may be written as

$$DI_{H1} \equiv p_{NRt} \cdot NR^{T} - p_{Kt} \cdot \varepsilon \cdot \delta \cdot K_{NRt} - Tx_{NRG1} - p_{W} \cdot \left(\Omega^{d}_{NRt} - \Omega_{NRt}\right) - B1_{NRt} + p^{G1}_{xt} \cdot \overline{R1}_{t} + p_{R1t} \cdot R1^{T} - Tx_{R1G1t} - B1_{R1t} + B1_{PB1t} + \varepsilon \cdot B2_{PB1t} + \tilde{\varepsilon} \cdot B3_{PB1t} - W1_{t}(h_{W*G1} \cdot N_{G1} + h_{G1H1} \cdot N_{G1} + h_{G1I1} \cdot N_{G1}) + B1_{H1t} - Tx1_{t} \tag{14.5}$$

H1 Budget Constraint

The H1 sector's budget constraint stipulates that its current disposable income is equal to the sum of the sector's planned consumption during the period plus its planned accumulation of (domestic) bonds plus its planned accumulation of (domestic) money balances during the period:

$$
\begin{aligned}
&p_{NRt} \cdot NR^{T} - p_{Kt} \cdot \varepsilon \cdot \delta \cdot K_{NRt} - Tx_{NRG1} - p_{w} \cdot \left(\Omega^{d}_{NRt} - \Omega_{NRt}\right) - B1_{NRt} \\
&\quad + p^{G1}_{xt} \cdot \overline{R1}_{t} + p_{R1t} \cdot R1^{T} - Tx_{R1G1t} - B1_{R1t} + B1_{PB1t} \\
&\quad + \varepsilon \cdot B2_{PB1t} + \tilde{\varepsilon} \cdot B3_{PB1t} + W1_{t}\,(h_{W^{*}G1} \cdot N_{G1} + h_{G1H1} \cdot N_{G1} \\
&\quad + h_{G1I1} \cdot N_{G1}) + B1_{H1t} - Tx_{G1H1t} - Tx_{W^{*}G1t} \\
&\equiv p_{R1t} \cdot (R1H1^{d}) + \tilde{\varepsilon} \cdot p_{Ct} \cdot (CH1^{d}) + \left(M1^{d}_{t+1} - M1_{t}\right) \\
&\quad + p_{B1} \cdot \left(B1^{d}_{H1(t+1)} - B1_{H1t}\right) \qquad (14.6)
\end{aligned}
$$

G1 Budget Constraint

The G1 sector's current-period budget constraint may be written as

$$
\begin{aligned}
P_{B1} \cdot B1^{s}_{G1(t+1)} = {} & W1_{t} \cdot \left(h^{GH1}_{G1t} + h^{W^{*}H1}_{G1t} + h^{\delta I}_{G1t}\right) \cdot N1_{G1t} - B1_{CB1t} \\
& - \varepsilon \cdot B2_{CB1t} - \tilde{\varepsilon} \cdot B3_{CB1t} + \varepsilon \cdot p_{Kt} \cdot \Big[K^{d}_{G1(t+1)} \\
& -(1-\delta) \cdot K_{G1t}\Big] + (1 + p_{B1}) \cdot B1_{G1t} + p^{G1}_{xt} \cdot \overline{R1}_{t} \\
& - Tx_{G1H1t} - Tx_{W^{*}G1t} + p_{NRt} \cdot NRG1^{Td}_{t} - Tx_{NRt} - Tx_{R1t} \qquad (14.7)
\end{aligned}
$$

where $\Pi^{CB1G1}_{t} = B1_{CB1t} + \varepsilon \cdot B2_{CB1t} + \tilde{\varepsilon} \cdot B3_{CB1t}$.

R1 Budget Constraint

The R1 industry's budget constraint is given by

$$
p_{B1} \cdot \left(B1^{s}_{R1(t+1)} - B1_{R1t}\right) = p_{R1t} \cdot (\tau_{R1}(I1_{t}) \cdot T_{R1t}(h_{R1t} \cdot N1_{R1t}) - R1H1_{t}) \qquad (14.8)
$$

NR Budget Constraint

The budget constraint for the NR industry is given by

$$
\begin{aligned}
p_{B1t} \cdot \left(B1^{s}_{NR1(t+1)} - B1_{NRt}\right) = {} & p_{NRt} \cdot \big[\tau_{NR}(I1_{t}) \cdot T_{NRt}(h_{NR} \cdot N1_{NRt}, K_{NRt}) \\
& - NRK_{t} - NRC_{t} - NRG1_{t} - NRG2_{t} - NRG2_{t} \\
& - NRG3_{t}\big] + p_{Kt} \cdot \varepsilon \cdot \left[K^{d}_{NR(t+1)} - K_{NRt}\right] \qquad (14.9)
\end{aligned}
$$

PB1 Budget Constraint

The budget constrain facing the PB1 sector is given by

$$(1-\hat{r}_1)\cdot\left(D1^{s}_{PB1(t+1)}-D1_{PB1t}\right)-\left(X1^{d}_{PB1(t+1)}-X1_{PB1t}\right)$$
$$=p_{B1}\cdot\left(B1^{d}_{PB1(t+1)}-B1_{PB1t}\right)+\varepsilon\cdot p_{B2}\cdot\left(B2^{d}_{PB1(t+1)}-B2_{PB1t}\right)$$
$$+\tilde{\varepsilon}\cdot p_{B3}\cdot\left(B3^{d}_{PB1(t+1)}-B3_{PB1t}\right) \quad (14.10)$$

CB1 Budget Constraint

Finally, the budget constraint for the CB1 sector is given by

$$\left(MB1^{d}_{CB1(t+1)}-MB1_{CB1t}\right)=p_{B1}\cdot\left(B1^{d}_{CB1(t+1)}-B1_{CB1t}\right)$$
$$+\varepsilon\cdot p_{B2}\cdot\left(B2^{d}_{CB1(t+1)}-B2_{CB1t}\right)$$
$$+\tilde{\varepsilon}\cdot p_{B3}\cdot\left(B3^{d}_{CB1(t+1)}-B3_{CB1t}\right) \quad (14.11)$$

Sum of Country One's Budget Constraints

The sum of the six constraints relevant to the sectors in Country One, namely, (14.6)–(14.11), is given by (14.12):

$$p_{NRt}\cdot NR^{T}-p_{Kt}\cdot\varepsilon\cdot\delta\cdot K_{NRt}-Tx_{NRG1}-p_{w}\cdot\left(\Omega^{d}_{NRt}-\Omega_{NRt}\right)+p^{G1}_{xt}\cdot\overline{R1}_{t}$$
$$+p_{R1t}\cdot R1^{T}-Tx_{R1G1t}-B1_{R1t}+B1_{PB1t}+\varepsilon\cdot B2_{PB1t}+\tilde{\varepsilon}\cdot B3_{PB1t}$$
$$+W1_{t}(h_{W^{*}G1}\cdot N_{G1}+h_{G1H1}\cdot N_{G1}+h_{G1I1}\cdot N_{G1}+h_{G1I1}\cdot N_{G1})$$
$$+B1_{H1t}-Tx_{G1H1t}-Tx_{W^{*}G1t}+p_{B1}\cdot\left(B1^{s}_{G1(t+1)}-B1_{G1t}\right)$$
$$+p_{B1}\cdot\left(B1^{s}_{R1(t+1)}-B1_{R1t}\right)+p_{B1}\cdot\left(B1^{s}_{NR(t+1)}-B1_{NRt}\right)$$
$$+(1-\hat{r}_1)\cdot\left(D1^{s}_{PB1(t+1)}-D1_{PB1t}\right)-\left(X1^{d}_{PB1(t+1)}-X1_{PB1t}\right)$$
$$+\left(MB1^{d}_{CB1(t+1)}-MB1_{CB1t}\right)$$
$$\equiv p_{R1t}\cdot\left(R1H1^{d})+\tilde{\varepsilon}\cdot p_{Ct}\cdot(CH1^{d}\right)$$
$$+\left(M1^{d}_{t+1}-M1_{t}\right)+p_{B1}\cdot\left(B1^{d}_{H1(t+1)}-B1_{H1t}\right)$$
$$+W1_{t}(h_{W^{*}G1}\cdot N_{G1}+h_{G1H1}\cdot N_{G1}+h_{G1I1}\cdot N_{G1})+B1_{G1t}-B1_{CB1t}$$

$$
\begin{aligned}
&- \varepsilon \cdot B2_{CB1t} - \tilde{\varepsilon} \cdot B3_{CB1t} + \varepsilon \cdot p_{Kt} \cdot \left[K^{d}_{G1(t+1)} - (1-\delta) \cdot K_{G1t}\right] \\
&+ p^{G1}_{xt} \cdot \overline{R1}_t - Tx_{G1H1t} - Tx_{W^*G1t} + p_{NRt} \cdot NRG1_t - Tx_{NRt} - Tx_{R1t} \\
&+ p_{R1t}\left[\tau_{R1}(I1_t) \cdot T_{R1t}(h_{R1t} \cdot N1_{R1t}) - R1H1_t\right] \\
&+ p_{NRt}\left[\tau_{NR}(I1_t) \cdot T_{NRt}(h_{NR} \cdot N1_{NRt}, K_{NRt}) - NRK_t - NRC_t - NRG1_t\right. \\
&\left. - NRG2_t - NRG3_t\right] + p_{Kt} \cdot \varepsilon \cdot \left[K^{d}_{NR(t+1)} - K_{NR_t}\right] \\
&+ p_{B1} \cdot \left(B1^{d}_{PB1(t+1)} - B1_{PB1t}\right) + \varepsilon \cdot p_{B2} \cdot \left(B2^{d}_{PB1(t+1)} - B1_{PB1t}\right) \\
&+ \tilde{\varepsilon} \cdot p_{B3} \cdot \left(B3^{d}_{PB1(t+1)} - B3_{PB1t}\right) + p_{B1} \cdot \left(B1^{d}_{CB1(t+1)} - B1_{CB1t}\right) \\
&+ \varepsilon \cdot p_{B2} \cdot \left(B2^{d}_{CB1(t+1)} - B1_{CB1t}\right) + \tilde{\varepsilon} \cdot p_{B3} \cdot \left(B3^{d}_{CB1(t+1)} - B3_{CB1t}\right)
\end{aligned}
\tag{14.12}
$$

Equation (14.12) reduces to (14.13):

$$
\begin{aligned}
&- p_{w} \cdot \left(\Omega^{d}_{NRt} - \Omega_{NRt}\right) - B1_{NRt} - B1_{R1t} + B1_{PB1t} + \varepsilon \cdot B2_{PB1t} + \tilde{\varepsilon} \cdot B3_{PB1t} \\
&\quad + B1_{H1t} + p_{B1} \cdot \left(B1^{s}_{G1(t+1)} - B1_{G1t}\right) + p_{B1} \cdot \left(B1^{s}_{R1(t+1)} - B1_{R1t}\right) \\
&\quad + p_{B1} \cdot \left(B1^{s}_{NR(t+1)} - B1_{NR1t}\right) + (1 - \hat{r}_1) \cdot \left(D1^{s}_{PB1(t+1)} - D1_{PB1t}\right) \\
&\quad - \left(X1^{d}_{PB1(t+1)} - X1_{PB1t}\right) + \left(MB1^{d}_{CB1(t+1)} - MB1_{CB1t}\right) \\
&\equiv p_{R1t} \cdot (R1H1^{d}) \\
&\quad + \tilde{\varepsilon} \cdot p_{Ct} \cdot (CH1^{d}) + \left(M1^{d}_{t+1} - M1_t\right) + p_{B1} \cdot \left(B1^{d}_{H1(t+1)} - B1_{H1t}\right) \\
&\quad + B1_{G1t} - B1_{CB1t} - \varepsilon \cdot B2_{CB1t} + \tilde{\varepsilon} \cdot B3_{CB1t} + \varepsilon \cdot p_{Kt} \cdot \left[K^{d}_{G1(t+1)}\right. \\
&\quad \left. -(1-\delta) \cdot K_{G1t}\right] + p_{NRt} \cdot NRG1_t - p_{R1t} \cdot (R1H1_t) + p_{NRt} \cdot [-NRK_t \\
&\quad - NRC_t - NRG1_t - NRG2_t - NRG3_t] + p_{Kt} \cdot \varepsilon \cdot \left[K^{d}_{NR(t+1)}\right. \\
&\quad \left. -(1-\delta) \cdot K_{NRt}\right] + p_{B1} \cdot \left(B1^{d}_{PB1(t+1)} - B1_{PB1t}\right) + \varepsilon \cdot p_{B2} \cdot \left(B2^{d}_{PB1(t+1)}\right. \\
&\quad \left. -B1_{PB1t}\right) + \tilde{\varepsilon} \cdot p_{B3t} \cdot \left(B3^{d}_{PB1(t+1)} - B3_{PB1t}\right) + p_{B1} \cdot \left(B1^{d}_{CB1(t+1)} - B1_{CB1t}\right) \\
&\quad + \varepsilon \cdot p_{B2} \cdot \left(B2^{d}_{CB1(t+1)} - B1_{CB1t}\right) + \tilde{\varepsilon} \cdot p_{B3} \cdot \left(B3^{s}_{CB1(t+1)} - B3_{CB1t}\right)
\end{aligned}
\tag{14.13}
$$

where $B1_{NRt} + B1_{R1t} + B1_{G1t} \equiv B1_{H1t} + B1_{PB1t} + B1_{CB1t} + B1_{PB2t} + B1_{CB2t} + B1_{PB3t} + B1_{CB3t}$.

Define the ex ante overall balance-of-payments surplus in Country One with Country Two, in terms of Country One's unit of account, by the following:

$$\begin{aligned}
BP12 = {} & p_{NR}(NRK + NRG2) + p_{B1}(B1^{PB2d} - B1^{PB2}) \\
& + p_{B1}\left(B1^{CB2d} - B1^{CB2}\right) + \varepsilon \cdot B2_{PB1t} + \varepsilon \cdot B2_{CB1t} \\
& - p_{Kt} \cdot \varepsilon \cdot \left[K^{d}_{NR(t+1)} - (1-\delta) \cdot K_{NRt}\right] - \varepsilon \cdot p_{Kt} \cdot \left[K^{d}_{G1(t+1)}\right. \\
& \left. -(1-\delta) \cdot K_{G1t}\right] - \varepsilon \cdot p_{B2} \cdot \left(B2^{d}_{PB1(t+1)} - B2_{PB1t}\right) \\
& + \varepsilon \cdot p_{B2} \cdot \left(B2^{d}_{CB1(t+1)} - B1_{CB1t}\right) + B1_{PB2t} + B1_{CB2t} \qquad (14.14)
\end{aligned}$$

In addition, define the ex ante overall balance-of-payments surplus in Country One with Country Three, in terms of Country One's unit of account, by the following:

$$\begin{aligned}
BP13 = {} & p_{NR}(NRC + NRG3) + p_{B1}(B1^{PB3d} - B1^{PB3}) \\
& + p_{B1}(B1^{CB3d} - B1^{CB3}) + \tilde{\varepsilon} \cdot B3_{PB1t} + \tilde{\varepsilon} \cdot B3_{CB1t} - \tilde{\varepsilon} \cdot p_{Ct} \cdot (CH1^{d}) \\
& - \tilde{\varepsilon} \cdot p_{B3t} \cdot \left(B3^{d}_{PB1(t+1)} - B3_{PB1t}\right) - \tilde{\varepsilon} \cdot p_{B3t} \cdot \left(B3^{d}_{CB1(t+1)}\right. \\
& \left. -B3_{CB1t}\right) - B1_{PB3t} - B1_{CB3t} \qquad (14.15)
\end{aligned}$$

Then, (14.13) reduces to the following statement of Walras's Law for Country One:

$$\begin{aligned}
& (M1^{s} - M1^{d}) + p_{B1} \cdot (B1^{s} - B1^{d}) + BP12 + BP13 \\
& - p_{w} \cdot \left(\Omega^{d}_{NRt} - \Omega_{NRt}\right) \equiv 0 \qquad (14.16)
\end{aligned}$$

where $p_w \cdot (\Omega^{d}_{NRt} - \Omega_{NRt})$ represents the NR sector's excess demand for pollution allowances.

Country Two

Walras's Law for Country Two may be obtained following steps similar to those used to find (14.16). Summing across the budget constraints of the sectors in Country Two yields the following result:

$$\begin{aligned}
& p_{R2t} \cdot \{\tau_{R2}(I2_t) \cdot T_{R2t}(h_{R2t} \cdot N2_{R2t})\} + p^{xG2}_{t} \cdot \overline{R2}_{t} - B2_{R2t} - Tx_{G2R2} \\
& + p_{Kt}\{\tau_{K}(I2_t) \cdot T_{Kt}(h_{k} \cdot N2_{Kt}, K_{Kt}) - \delta_{K} \cdot K_{Kt}\} - \left(\frac{p^{NR}_{t}}{\varepsilon}\right) \cdot NRK - Tx_{K_{G2t}} \\
& - \left(\frac{p_w}{\varepsilon}\right) \cdot \left(\Omega^{d}_{Kt} - \Omega_{Kt}\right) - B2^{K}_{t} + \left(\frac{1}{\varepsilon}\right) \cdot B1_{PB2} + B2_{PB2t} + \left(\frac{\tilde{\varepsilon}}{\varepsilon}\right) \cdot B3_{PB2t}
\end{aligned}$$

$$
\begin{aligned}
&- W2_t\,(h_{W^*G2}\cdot N2_{G2} + h_{G2H2}\cdot N2_G + h_{G2I2}\cdot N2_{G1}) + B2_{H2t} - Tx2_t\\
&+ p_{B2t}\cdot\left(B2^{G2s}_{t+1} - B2_{G2t}\right) + p_{B2t}\cdot\left(B2^{R2s}_{t+1} - B2^{R2}_t\right) + p_{B2t}\cdot\left(B2^{Ks}_{t+1} - B2^{K}_t\right)\\
&+ (1-\hat{r}_2)\cdot\left(D2^{s}_{PB2(t+1)} - D2_{PB2t}\right) - \left(X2^{d}_{PB2(t+1)} - X2_{PB2t}\right)\\
&+ \left(MB2^{d}_{CB2(t+1)} - MB2_{CB2t}\right)\\
\equiv\ & p_{R2t}\cdot(R2H2^{d}) + \left(\frac{\tilde{\varepsilon}}{\varepsilon}\right)\cdot p_{Ct}\cdot(CH2^{d})\\
&+ \left(M2^{d}_{t+1} - M2_t\right) + p_{B2}\cdot\left(B2^{d}_{H2(t+1)} - B2_{H2t}\right) + W2_t\cdot h^{g2H2}_t\cdot N2_{G2t}\\
&+ p_{Kt}\cdot\left[K^{d}_{G2(t+1)} - (1-\delta)\cdot K_{G2t}\right] - \left(\frac{1}{\varepsilon}\right)\cdot B1_{CB2t} - B2_{CB2t}\\
&- \left(\frac{\tilde{\varepsilon}}{\varepsilon}\right)\cdot B3_{CB2t} + B2_{G2t} + p^{G2}_{xt}\cdot\overline{R}2_t - Tx_{G2H2t} + W2_t\cdot h^{W^*G2}_t\cdot N2_{G2t}\\
&- Tx_{W^*G2t} + W2_t\cdot h^{g2I2}_t\cdot N_{G2t}(\delta I2_t) + \left(\frac{1}{\varepsilon}\right)\cdot p_{NRt}\cdot NRG2_t\\
&- Tx_{Kt} - Tx_{R2t} + p_{R2t}\cdot(\tau_{R2}(I2_t)\cdot T_{R2t}(h_{R2t}\cdot N2_{R2t}) - R2H2_t)\\
&+ p_{Kt}\cdot\left[\tau_K(I2_t)\cdot T_{Kt}(h_K\cdot N2q_{Kt}, K_{Kt}) - \delta_K\cdot K_{Kt} - KNR_t\right.\\
&\left.-KC_t - KG1_t - KG2_t - KG3_t\right] + \left(\frac{1}{\varepsilon}\right)\cdot p_{B1t}\cdot\left(B1^{d}_{PB2(t+1)} - B1_{PB2t}\right)\\
&+ p_{B2t}\cdot\left(B2^{d}_{PB2(t+1)} - B2_{PB2t}\right) + \left(\frac{\tilde{\varepsilon}}{\varepsilon}\right)\cdot p_{B3t}\cdot\left(B3^{d}_{PB2(t+1)} - B3_{PB2t}\right)\\
&+ \left(\frac{1}{\varepsilon}\right)\cdot p_{B1t}\cdot\left(B1^{d}_{CB2(t+1)} - B1_{CB2t}\right) + p_{B2t}\cdot\left(B2^{d}_{CB1(t+1)} - B2_{CB2t}\right)\\
&+ \left(\frac{\tilde{\varepsilon}}{\varepsilon}\right)\cdot p_{B3t}\cdot\left(B3^{d}_{CB2(t+1)} - B3_{CB2t}\right) \qquad (14.17)
\end{aligned}
$$

Expression (14.17) reduces to (14.18):

$$
\begin{aligned}
&- B2_{R2t} - \left(\frac{p_{NRt}}{\varepsilon}\right)\cdot NRK - \left(\frac{p_w}{\varepsilon}\right)\cdot\left(\Omega^{d}_{Kt} - \Omega_{Kt}\right) - B2^{k}_t + B2_{PB2t}\\
&+ \left(\frac{\tilde{\varepsilon}}{\varepsilon}\right)\cdot B3_{PB2t} + B2_{H2t} + p_{B2t}\cdot\left(B2^{G2s}_{t+1} - B2_{G2t}\right) + p_{B2t}\cdot\left(B2^{R2s}_{t+1} - B2^{R2}_t\right)\\
&+ p_{B2t}\cdot\left(B2^{Ks}_{t+1} - B2^{K}_t\right) + \left(\frac{1}{\varepsilon}\right)\cdot B1_{PB2t} + (1-\hat{r}_2)\cdot\left(D2^{s}_{PB2(t+1)} - D2_{PB2t}\right)\\
&- \left(X2^{d}_{PB2(t+1)} - X2_{PB2t}\right) + \left(MB2^{d}_{CB2(t+1)} - MB2_{CB2t}\right)
\end{aligned}
$$

$$
\begin{aligned}
&\equiv \left(\frac{\tilde{\varepsilon}}{\varepsilon}\right) \cdot p_{Ct} \cdot (CH2^{d}) + \left(M2^{d}_{t+1} - M2_{t}\right) + p_{B2t} \cdot \left(B2^{d}_{H2(t+1)} - B2_{H2t}\right) \\
&\quad + p_{Kt} \cdot \left[K^{d}_{G2(t+1)} - (1-\delta) \cdot K_{G2t}\right] - \left(\frac{1}{\varepsilon}\right) \cdot B1_{CB2t} - B2_{CB2t} \\
&\quad - \left(\frac{\tilde{\varepsilon}}{\varepsilon}\right) \cdot B3_{CB2t} + B2_{G2t} + \left(\frac{1}{\varepsilon}\right) \cdot p_{NRt} \cdot NRG2_{t} \\
&\quad + p_{Kt} \cdot [-KNR_{t} - KC_{t} - KG1_{t} - KG2_{t} - KG3_{t}] \\
&\quad + \left(\frac{1}{\varepsilon}\right) \cdot p_{B1t} \cdot \left(B1^{d}_{PB2(t+1)} - B1_{PB2t}\right) + p_{B2t} \cdot \left(B2^{d}_{PB2(t+1)} - B2_{PB2t}\right) \\
&\quad + \left(\frac{\tilde{\varepsilon}}{\varepsilon}\right) \cdot p_{B3t} \cdot \left(B3^{d}_{PB2(t+1)} - B3_{PB2t}\right) + \left(\frac{1}{\varepsilon}\right) \cdot p_{B1t} \cdot \left(B1^{d}_{CB2(t+1)} - B1_{CB2t}\right) \\
&\quad + p_{B2t} \cdot \left(B2^{d}_{CB1(t+1)} - B2_{CB2t}\right) + \left(\frac{\tilde{\varepsilon}}{\varepsilon}\right) \cdot p_{B3t} \cdot \left(B3^{d}_{CB2(t+1)} - B3_{CB2t}\right)
\end{aligned}
\tag{14.18}
$$

Following steps similar to those above, the ex ante overall balance-of-payments surplus of Country Two with Country Three in terms of Country Two's unit of account, BP23, is defined as

$$
\begin{aligned}
BP23 = {} & p_{Kt} \cdot [KC_{t} + KG3_{t}] + p_{B2} \left(B2^{d}_{PB3(t+1)} - B2_{PB3t}\right) \\
& + p_{B2} \left(B2^{d}_{CB3(t+1)} - B2_{PB3t}\right) + \left(\frac{\tilde{\varepsilon}}{\varepsilon}\right) \cdot B3_{PB2t} + \left(\frac{\tilde{\varepsilon}}{\varepsilon}\right) \cdot B3_{CB2t} \\
& - \left(\frac{\tilde{\varepsilon}}{\varepsilon}\right) \cdot p_{B3} \cdot \left(B3^{d}_{PB2(t+1)} - B3_{PB2t}\right) \\
& - \left(\frac{\tilde{\varepsilon}}{\varepsilon}\right) \cdot p_{B3t} \cdot \left(B3^{d}_{CB2(t+1)} - B3_{CB2t}\right) - B2_{PB3t} - B2_{CB3t}
\end{aligned}
\tag{14.19}
$$

Then, Walras's Law for Country Two, in that country's unit of account becomes

$$
\begin{aligned}
& (M2^{s} - M2^{d}) + p_{B2} \cdot (B2^{s} - B2^{d}) - \left(\frac{1}{\varepsilon}\right) \cdot BP12 + BP23 \\
& - \left(\frac{p_{W}}{\varepsilon}\right) \cdot \left(\Omega^{d}_{Kt} - \Omega_{Kt}\right) \equiv 0
\end{aligned}
\tag{14.20}
$$

where $(p_{W}/\varepsilon) \cdot (\Omega^{d}_{Kt} - \Omega_{Kt})$ represents the K sector's excess demand for pollution allowances in terms of Country Two's unit of account and where $B2_{Kt} + B2_{R2t} + B2_{G2t} \equiv B2_{H2t} + B2_{PB2t} + B2_{CB2t} + B2_{PB1t} + B2_{CB1t} + B2_{PB3t} + B2_{CB3t}$.

Country Three

Summing across the budget constraints of the sectors in Country Three yields the following result:

$$
\begin{aligned}
& p_t^C \cdot \tau(I3_t) \cdot (h_{Ct} \cdot N3_{Ct}, K_{Ct}) - \left[\frac{(p_t^{Ke} \cdot \varepsilon)}{\tilde{\varepsilon}} \right] \cdot \delta \cdot K_{Ct} - Tx_{CG3} \\
& - \left(\frac{p_t^{NRe}}{\tilde{\varepsilon}} \right) \cdot NRC_t - \left(\frac{p_w}{\tilde{\varepsilon}} \right) \cdot \left[\Omega_{Ct}^d - \Omega_{Ct} \right] - B3_t^C \\
& + p_{R3t} \cdot \{ \tau_{R3}(I3_t) \cdot T_{R3t}(h_{R3t} \cdot N3_{R3t}) \} + p_t^{xG3} \cdot \overline{R3}_t - B3_t^{R3} - Tx_{G3R3} \\
& + (1 + \tilde{\varepsilon}) \cdot B1_{PB3t} + \left(\frac{\varepsilon}{\tilde{\varepsilon}} \right) \cdot B2_{PB3t} + B3_{PB3t} + W3_t \cdot (h_{W*G3} \cdot N3_{G3} \\
& + h_{G3H3} \cdot N3_{G3} + h_{G3I3} \cdot N3_{G3}) + B3_{H3t} - Tx3_t + p_{B3t} \\
& \cdot \left(B3_{t+1}^{G3s} - B3_{G3t} \right) + p_{B3t} \cdot \left(B3_{t+1}^{R3s} - B3_t^{R3} \right) + p_{B3t} \cdot \left(B3_{t+1}^{Gs} - B3_t^C \right) \\
& + (1 - \hat{r}_3) \cdot \left(D3_{PB3(t+1)}^s - D3_{PB3t} \right) - \left(X3_{PB3(t+1)}^d - X3_{PB3t} \right) \\
& + \left(MB3_{CB3(t+1)}^d - MB3_{CB3t} \right) \\
\equiv\ & p_{R3t} \cdot (R3H3^d) + p_{Ct} \cdot (CH3^d) \\
& + \left(M3_{t+1}^d - M3_t \right) + p_{B3} \cdot \left(B3_{H3(t+1)}^d - B3_{H3t} \right) + W3_t \cdot h_t^{G3H3} \cdot N3_{G3t} \\
& + \left(\frac{\varepsilon}{\tilde{\varepsilon}} \right) \cdot p_{Kt} \cdot \left[K_{G3(t+1)}^d - (1 - \delta) \cdot K_{G3t} \right] - \left(\frac{1}{\tilde{\varepsilon}} \right) \cdot B1_{CB3t} - \left(\frac{\varepsilon}{\tilde{\varepsilon}} \right) \cdot B2_{CB3t} \\
& - B3_{CB3t} + B3_{C3t} + p_{xt}^{G3} \cdot \overline{R3}_t - Tx_{G3H3t} + W3_t \cdot h_t^{W*G3} \cdot N3_{G3t} \\
& - Tx_{W*G3t} + W3 \cdot h_t^{g3I3} \cdot N_{G3t}(\delta I3_t) + \left(\frac{1}{\tilde{\varepsilon}} \right) \cdot p_{NRt} \cdot NRG3_t \\
& - Tx_{Ct} - Tx_{R3t} + p_{R3t} \cdot (\tau_{R3}(I3_t) \cdot T_{R3t}(h_{R3t} \cdot N3_{R3t}) - R3H3_t) \\
& + p_t^{Ke} \cdot \left(\frac{\varepsilon}{\tilde{\varepsilon}} \right) \cdot \left[K_{C(t+1)}^d - K_{Ct} \right] + p_{Ct}[\tau(I3_t) \cdot T_{Ct}(h_{Ct} \cdot N3_{Ct}, K_{Ct}) \\
& - CH1_t - CH2_t - CH3_t] + \left(\frac{1}{\tilde{\varepsilon}} \right) \cdot p_{B1t} \cdot \left(B1_{PB3(t+1)}^d - B1_{PB3t} \right) \\
& + \left(\frac{\varepsilon}{\tilde{\varepsilon}} \right) \cdot p_{B2t} \cdot \left(B2_{PB3(t+1)}^d - B2_{PB3t} \right) + p_{B3t} \cdot \left(B3_{PB3(t+1)}^d - B3_{PB3t} \right) \\
& + \left(\frac{1}{\tilde{\varepsilon}} \right) \cdot p_{B1t} \cdot \left(B1_{CB3(t+1)}^d - B1_{CB3t} \right) + \left(\frac{\varepsilon}{\tilde{\varepsilon}} \right) \cdot p_{B2t} \cdot \left(B2_{CB3(t+1)}^d \right. \\
& \left. - B2_{CB3t} \right) + p_{B3t} \cdot \left(B3_{CB3(t+1)}^d - B3_{CB3t} \right) \qquad (14.21)
\end{aligned}
$$

Expression (14.21) reduces to (14.22):

$$
\begin{aligned}
&-\left[\frac{(p_t^{Ke}\cdot \varepsilon)}{\tilde{\varepsilon}}\right]\cdot \delta \cdot K_{Ct} - \left(\frac{p_t^{NRe}}{\tilde{\varepsilon}}\right)\cdot NRC_t - \left(\frac{p_W}{\tilde{\varepsilon}}\right)\cdot \left[\Omega_{Ct}^{d} - \Omega_{Ct}\right] \\
&- B3_t^{C} - B3_t^{R3} + \left(\frac{1}{\tilde{\varepsilon}}\right)\cdot B1_{PB3t} + \left(\frac{\varepsilon}{\tilde{\varepsilon}}\right)\cdot B2_{PB3t} + B3_{PB3t} + B3_{H3t} \\
&+ p_{B3t}\cdot\left(B3_{t+1}^{G3s} - B3_{G3t}\right) + p_{B3t}\cdot\left(B3_{t+1}^{R3s} - B3_t^{R3}\right) + p_{B3t}\cdot\left(B3_{t+1}^{Cs} - B3_t^{C}\right) \\
&+ (1-\hat{r}_3)\cdot\left(D3_{PB3(t+1)}^{s} - D3_{PB3t}\right) - \left(X3_{PB3(t+1)}^{d} - X3_{PB3t}\right) \\
&+ \left(MB3_{CB3(t+1)}^{d} - MB3_{CB3t}\right) \\
\equiv\ & p_{R3t}\cdot(R3H3^{d}) + p_{Ct}\cdot(CH3^{d}) \\
&+ \left(M3_{t+1}^{d} - M3_t\right) + p_{B3}\cdot\left(B3_{H3(t+1)}^{d} - B3_{H3t}\right) \\
&+ \left(\frac{\varepsilon}{\tilde{\varepsilon}}\right)\cdot p_{Kt}\cdot\left[K_{G3(t+1)}^{d} - (1-\delta)\cdot K_{G3t}\right] - \left(\frac{1}{\tilde{\varepsilon}}\right)\cdot B1_{CB2t} \\
&- \left(\frac{\varepsilon}{\tilde{\varepsilon}}\right)\cdot B2_{CB2t} - B3_{CB2t} + B3_{G3t} + \left(\frac{1}{\tilde{\varepsilon}}\right)\cdot p_{NRt}\cdot NRG3_t \\
&+ p_{R3t}(-R3H3_t) + p_{Kt}\cdot\left(\frac{\varepsilon}{\tilde{\varepsilon}}\right)\cdot\left[K_{C(t+1)}^{d} - K_{Ct}\right] \\
&+ p_{Ct}\left[-CH1_t - CH2_t - CH3_t\right] + \left(\frac{1}{\tilde{\varepsilon}}\right)\cdot p_{B1}\cdot\left(B1_{PB3(t+1)}^{d} - B3_{PB3t}\right) \\
&+ \left(\frac{\varepsilon}{\tilde{\varepsilon}}\right)\cdot p_{B2}\cdot\left(B2_{PB3(t+1)}^{d} - B2_{PB3t}\right) + p_{B3}\cdot\left(B3_{PB3(t+1)}^{d} - B3_{PB3t}\right) \\
&+ \left(\frac{1}{\tilde{\varepsilon}}\right)\cdot p_{B1t}\cdot(B1_{CB3(t+1)}^{d} - B1_{CB3t}) + \left(\frac{\varepsilon}{\tilde{\varepsilon}}\right)\cdot p_{B2t}\cdot\left(B2_{CB3(t+1)}^{d} - B2_{CB3t}\right) \\
&+ p_{B3t}\cdot\left(B3_{CB3(t+1)}^{d} - B3_{CB3t}\right) \qquad (14.22)
\end{aligned}
$$

Following steps similar to those outlined above, Walras's Law for Country Three in terms of that country's unit of account is given by

$$
\begin{aligned}
&(M3^{s} - M3^{d}) + p_{B3}\cdot(B3^{s} - B3^{d}) - \left(\frac{1}{\tilde{\varepsilon}}\right)\cdot BP13 - \left(\frac{\varepsilon}{\tilde{\varepsilon}}\right)\cdot BP23 \\
&\quad - \left(\frac{p_W}{\tilde{\varepsilon}}\right)\cdot(\Omega_{Ct}^{d} - \Omega_{Ct}) \equiv 0 \qquad (14.23)
\end{aligned}
$$

where $(p_W/\tilde{\varepsilon})\cdot(\Omega_{Ct}^{d} - \Omega_{Ct})$ represents the C sector's excess demand for pollution allowances in terms of Country Three's unit of account and where $B3_{Ct} + B3_{R3t} + B3_{G3t} \equiv B3_{H3t} + B3_{PB3t} + B3_{CB3t} + B3_{PBt1} + B3_{CB1t} + B3_{PBt2} + B3_{CB2t}$.

Walras's Law for the World's Financial Markets

Expressing (14.16), (14.20), and (14.23) in terms of Country One's unit of account and summing across these three identities yields the following:

$$(M1^s - M1^d) + p_{B1} \cdot (B1^s - B1^d) + BP12 + BP13 - p_w \cdot \left(\Omega^d_{NRt} - \Omega_{NRt}\right)$$
$$+ \varepsilon \cdot (M2^s - M2^d) + \varepsilon \cdot p_{B2} \cdot (B2^s - B2^d) - BP12 + \varepsilon \cdot BP23$$
$$- p_w \cdot \left(\Omega^d_{Kt} - \Omega_{Kt}\right) + \tilde{\varepsilon} \cdot (M3^s - M3^d) + \tilde{\varepsilon} \cdot p_{B3} \cdot (B3^s - B3^d)$$
$$- BP13 - \varepsilon \cdot BP23 - p_w \cdot \left(\Omega^d_{Kt} - \Omega_{Kt}\right) \equiv 0 \qquad (14.24)$$

Since the market price for pollution allowances cleared prior to the setting of market prices, production, and wages and before the determination of interest rates and exchange rates, the sum of the market excess demands for pollution allowances in terms of Country One's unit of account, $p_w \cdot (\Omega^d_{NRt} - \Omega_{NRt}) + p_w \cdot (\Omega^d_{Kt} - \Omega_{Kt}) + p_w \cdot (\Omega^d_{Ct} - \Omega_{Ct})$, may be taken at this point to equal zero, with any differences between the actual expenditure on pollution allowances after exchange rates are established and the planned expenditures on pollution allowances ex ante assumed to be minor. Then Walras's Law for the world economy becomes

$$(M1^s - M1^d) + \varepsilon \cdot (M2^s - M2^d) + \tilde{\varepsilon} \cdot (M3^s - M3^d) + p_{B1} \cdot (B1^s - B1^d)$$
$$+ \varepsilon \cdot p_{B2} \cdot (B2^s - B2^d) + \tilde{\varepsilon} \cdot p_{B3} \cdot (B3^s - B3^d) \equiv 0 \qquad (14.25)$$

Chapter 15 contains a specification of the end-of-period stocks of natural resources, manufactured goods, financial assets, and human populations as a result of current economic activity.

15

End-of-Period Stocks

Introduction

The end-of-period stocks of natural resources consist of the fungible basic resource, B_{t+1}; the stock of the unextracted/unmined nonrenewable resource, NR_{t+1}; and the unharvested stocks of the renewable resources in the three countries, $R1_{t+1}$, $R2_{t+1}$, and $R3_{t+1}$. The stocks of manufactured goods at the end of the period consist of the stock of the transformed nonrenewable resource, NR^*_{t+1}; the stocks of the transformed natural resources, $R1^*_{t+1}$, $R2^*_{t+1}$, and $R3^*_{t+1}$; the stock of capital goods, K_{t+1}; the stock of consumption goods, C_{t+1}; and the three infrastructures $I1_{t+1}$, $I2_{t+1}$, and $I3_{t+1}$. The human populations (in terms of mass) at the end of the period are represented by the amounts $H1_{t+1}$, $H2_{t+1}$, and $H3_{t+1}$, while their populations in terms of numbers are given by $N1_{t+1}$, $N2_{t+1}$, and $N3_{t+1}$. The end-of-period stocks of treated and stored waste are given by $WS1_{t+1}$, $WS2_{t+1}$, and $WS3_{t+1}$, and the end-of-period stock of pollution (untreated waste) is denoted by P^*.

The end-of-current-period stock of the basic slowly renewable resource, B_{t+1}, is assumed to be predetermined by the beginning-of-period stocks of B_t, $R1_t$, $R2_t$, $R3_t$, and P^*_t.

$$\begin{aligned} B_{t+1} = B_t + A\left(B_t, R1_t, R2_t, R3_t, P^{\cdot}_t\right) - g_1\left(R1_t, B_t, P^{\cdot}_t\right) \\ - g_2\left(R2_t, B_t, P^{\cdot}_t\right) - g_3\left(R3_t, B_t, P^{\cdot}_t\right) \end{aligned} \tag{15.1}$$

However, the global stock of this fungible basic resource at the end of next period, B_{t+2}, does depend upon current-period activity:

$$\begin{aligned} B_{t+2} = B_{t+1} + A\left(B_{t+1}, R1_{t+1}, R2_{t+1}, R3_{t+1}, P^*_{t+1}\right) - g_1\left(R1_{t+1}, B_{t+1}, P^*_{t+1}\right) \\ - g_2\left(R2_{t+1}, B_{t+1}, P^*_{t+1}\right) - g_3\left(R3_{t+1}, B_{t+1}, P^*_{t+1}\right) \end{aligned} \tag{15.2}$$

The level of pollution at the end of the current period, P^*_{t+1}, is assumed to correspond to the maximum allowable amount of pollution the three countries have agreed upon through international treaty. Presumably, the countries issue during the current period a corresponding amount of pollution allowances to prevent the level of pollution exceeding this level.

The stocks of country-specific unharvested renewable resources, $R1_{t+1}$, $R2_{t+1}$, and $R3_{t+1}$, at the end of the period are given by their respective stocks at the beginning of the period plus their respective natural growths during the period minus the respective amounts of these resources transformed into marketable product during the period but plus the amount of organic human waste recycled by the respective government sectors in their countries:

$$R1_{t+1} = R1_t + g_1\left(R1_t, B_t, P_t^*\right) - R1^T - \alpha_1 \cdot OW^*H1 \tag{15.3}$$

$$R2_{t+1} = R2_t + g_2\left(R2_t, B_t, P_t^*\right) - R2^T - \alpha_2 \cdot OW^*H2 \tag{15.4}$$

$$R3_{t+1} = R3_t + g_3\left(R3_t, B_t, P_t^*\right) - R3^T - \alpha_3 \cdot OW^*H3 \tag{15.5}$$

where, for instance, OW^*H1 represents the total household organic waste generated in Country One and where $\alpha 1$ represents the fraction of total household organic waste recycled as R1 by the G1 sector. The amount of the natural R1 transformed during the period, R1T, for instance, is determined by the R1 industry and is equal to $\tau_{R1}(I1t) \cdot T_{R1t}(h_{R1t} \cdot N1_{R1t})$, which in turn depends upon the infrastructure in place at the beginning of the period, I1t, and the number of labor hours used by the industry during the period. The end-of-period inventories of the unharvested natural resources must be at least as great as the amounts required by their respective government sectors.

The stocks of transformed/processed R1, R2, and R3 at the end of the period, $R1^{T^*}_{t+1}$, $R1^{T^*}_{t+1}$, and $R1^{T^*}_{t+1}$ are given respectively by

$$R1^{T^*}_{t+1} = R1^{T^*}_t + \tau_{R1}(I1_t) \cdot T_{R1t}(h_{R1t} \cdot N1_{R1t}) - R1H1_t \geq 0 \tag{15.6}$$

$$R2^{T^*}_{t+1} = R2^{T^*}_t + \tau_{R2}(I2_t) \cdot T_{R2t}\,(h_{R2t} \cdot N2_{R2t}) - R2H2_t \geq 0 \tag{15.7}$$

$$R3^{T^*}_{t+1} = R3^{T^*}_t + \tau_{R3}(I3_t) \cdot T_{R3t}(h_{R3t} \cdot N3_{R3t}) - R3H3_t \geq 0 \tag{15.8}$$

where, for instance, $R1H1_t$ corresponds to the actual amount of transformed R1 purchased by the households in Country One during the current period, $R1^{T^*}_t$ represents the initial inventory of transformed R1 at the beginning of the period, and $R1^{T^*}_{t+1}$ denotes the end-of-current-period inventory of transformed R1. The labor hours that the renewable resource industries use during the period are negatively related to the wage rates, $W1_t$, $W2_t$, and $W3_t$, paid in their respective countries during the period. The amounts of the transformed renewable resources purchased by the household sectors in each country, $R1H1_t$, $R2H2_t$, and $R3H3_t$, are given, respectively, by

$$R1H1^d_t = R1H1^d_t\left(\underset{-}{p_{R1t}}, \underset{+}{\tilde{\varepsilon} \cdot p_{Ct}}, \underset{+}{N1_t}, \underset{-}{r_{1t}}, \underset{+}{\overline{Y}1}, \underset{+}{W1_{t+1}}\right) \tag{15.9}$$

$$R2H2^d_t = R2H2^d_t\left(\underset{-}{p_{R2t}}, \underset{+}{(\tilde{\varepsilon}/\varepsilon) \cdot p_{Ct}}, \underset{+}{N2_t}, \underset{-}{r_{2t}}, \underset{+}{\overline{Y}2}, \underset{+}{W2_{t+1}}\right) \tag{15.10}$$

$$R3H3_t^d = R3H3_t^d \underset{-}{(p_{R3t}}, \underset{+}{p_{Ct}}, \underset{+}{N3_t}, \underset{-}{r_{3t}}, \underset{+}{\overline{Y}3}, \underset{+}{W3_{t+1})} \quad (15.11)$$

From the above, ceteris paribus, the stock of the transformed renewable resource in a given country at the end of the period will be negatively related to the wage rate paid in that country during the current period, the level of disposable income in that country during the period, the country's population at the beginning of the period, the wage rate announced for next period in that country, the price of consumption goods, and the value of Country Three's unit of account relative to the units of account in Country One and Country Two. Ceteris paribus, the end-of-period stock of the transformed renewable resource in a given country will increase as the price of that transformed resource increases and as the interest rate in that country rises.

Ceteris paribus, central bank policies that reduce interest rates or increase the value of Country Three's unit of account relative to the others cause the demands for the renewable resources to rise and their end-of-period inventories to fall. Ceteris paribus, a public policy undertaken in the past that enhances a country's beginning-of-period infrastructure will cause current production of the transformed renewable resource in that country to increase, thereby increasing the country's end-of-period stock of the transformed resource but reducing its end-of-period stock of the unharvested resource. A public policy that increases the fraction of human organic waste recycled during the period in a given country causes the end-of-period inventory of the unharvested resource to grow. A public policy that raises the minimum required end-of-period inventory of that resource, ceteris paribus, potentially causes the end-of-period inventory to rise.

The total mass of the unextracted/unprocessed nonrenewable resource at the end of the period, NR_{t+1}, is equal to its mass at the beginning of the period, NR_t, minus the amount of the nonrenewable resource extracted/processed/transported during the period, NR^T, minus the waste generated by the NR industry in extracting and converting NR into a marketable product, W*NR, but plus the amount of NR recycled by the NR industry during the period, RW*NR. (For simplicity, it is assumed that neither the capital goods nor the consumption goods industry recycles its waste into NR.)

$$NR_{t+1} = NR_t - NR^T - W^*NR + RW^*NR \quad (15.12)$$

where

$$NR_t^T = \tau_{NR}(I1_t) \cdot T_{NRt}(h_{NR} \cdot N1_{NRt}, K_{NRt}) \quad (15.13)$$

$$W^*NR = \varphi \cdot \tau_{NR}(I1_t) \cdot T_{NRt}(h_{NR} \cdot N1_{NRt}, K_{NRt}) + \kappa \cdot \delta \cdot K_{NRt} \quad (15.14)$$

$$RW^*NR_t = T_{NRt}^w (h_{NR}^w \cdot N1_{NRt}) \quad (15.15)$$

$$h_{NR}^d = h_{NR}^d(\underset{+}{r_1}, \underset{-}{p_w}, \underset{-}{\varphi}, \underset{-}{W1_t}, \underset{+}{I1_t}) \quad (15.16)$$

and

$$h^{w}_{NR} = h^{w}_{NR}\left(r_1, p_w, \varphi, W1_t\right) \qquad (15.17)$$
$$\qquad\qquad - \quad + \quad - \quad -$$

Since the NR industry decides how many hours to use its current employees before it learns current interest rates, the relevant observable variables affecting the NR sector's labor hours decisions in the current period pertain to the market price of pollution allowances, the wage rate paid during the current period, the portion of NR wasted per unit of NR extracted/mined this period, and the available infrastructure at the beginning of the period. Ceteris paribus, the higher the wage rate paid during the current period, the smaller the amounts of NR extracted, wasted, and recycled during the period, with the net effect being to increase the end-of-period stock of the unmined resource. An earlier technical advance that reduces the amount of wasted NR per unit of NR extracted during the current period, φ, will cause the end-of-period stock of unmined NR to rise, assuming that the effect operating through (15.14) dominates.

An earlier public policy that improves the beginning-of-period infrastructure in Country One will increase the amount of the natural NR extracted/mined during the period as well as the waste generated by the industry.

The total mass of the extracted/processed/transported nonrenewable resource at the end of the period, $NR^{T^*}_{t+1}$, is equal to its mass at the beginning of the period, $NR^{T^*}_{t}$, plus the amount of the natural nonrenewable resource transformed during the period minus the amount of the processed NR purchased by the capital goods industry, NRK, the consumption goods industry, NRC, and the three government sectors, NRG1, NRG2, and NRG3:

$$\begin{aligned} NR^{T^*}_{t+1} &= NR^{T^*}_{t} + NR^{T} - NRK^{T} \\ &\quad - NRC^{T} - NRG1^{T} - NRG2^{T} - NRG3^{T} \geq 0 \end{aligned} \qquad (15.18)$$

where

$$\begin{aligned} NRK^{Td}_{t} &= (\theta_K + \varphi_K)\cdot \tau_K(I2_t)\cdot T_{Kt}(h_K \cdot N2_{Kt}, K_{Kt}) \\ &= NRK^{Td}_{t}\left(K_{Kt}, I2_t, p^{K}_{NRt}, p_w, \theta_K, \varphi_K, \varepsilon^{K}, W2_t\right) \\ &\qquad\quad + \quad + \quad - \quad - \quad + \quad + \quad + \quad - \end{aligned} \qquad (15.19)$$

$$\begin{aligned} NRC^{Td}_{t} &= (\theta_C + \varphi_C)\cdot \tau(I3t)\cdot T_{Ct}(h_{Ct}\cdot N3_{Ct}, K_{Ct}) \\ &= NRC^{Td}_{t}\left(p^{C}_{NRt}, p_w, \varphi_C, \theta_C, \tilde{\varepsilon}^{C}, W3_t, I3_t, K_{Ct}\right) \\ &\qquad\quad - \quad - \quad + \quad + \quad + \quad - \quad + \quad + \end{aligned} \qquad (15.20)$$

$$NRG1^{Td}_{t} = \iota \cdot \delta I1_t \qquad (15.21)$$

$$NRG2^{Td}_{t} = \iota \cdot \delta I2_t \qquad (15.22)$$

and

$$NRG3_t^{Td} = \iota \cdot \delta I3_t \tag{15.23}$$

From the above, the K and C industries' demands for NR during the current period are negatively related to the wage rates paid in their respective countries. Their demands are also negatively related to the market price of pollution allowances but positively related to the amount of NR embodied in a unit of K or C and the amount of NR wasted in producing a unit of K or C. Therefore, ceteris paribus, a reduction in the maximum number of pollution allowances issued by the world's government sectors causes the price of pollution allowances to rise, reducing the K and C industries' demands for mined/extracted NR, and increases the inventory of that resource at the end of the period. An earlier technical advance that decreases either the amount of NR embodied in a unit of K or C or the amount of NR necessarily wasted in producing a unit of K or C, ceteris paribus, reduces the current-period demand for transformed NR and increases its end-of-period stock. The larger the infrastructure in Country Two at the beginning of the period, the greater is the demand for transformed NR by the K industry; the larger the infrastructure in Country Three at the beginning of the period, the greater is the demand for transformed NR by the C industry during the period. In both instances, the end-of-period stock of transformed NR decreases. A decision by any of the government sectors to expand the infrastructure in that country causes the end-of-period stock of transformed NR to fall.

The stock of capital held by the K industry at the end of the period is equal to its initial stock, K_{Kt}, minus depreciation, $\delta \cdot K_{Kt}$, plus its current production of capital goods, K_t^T, minus the amount of physical capital purchased by the three government sectors, the NR industry, and the C industry during the period:

$$\begin{aligned} K_{K(t+1)} = (1-\delta) \cdot K_{Kt} + K_t^T - KG1_t^d - KG2_t^d - KG3_t^d \\ - KNR_t^d - KC_t^d \geq 0 \end{aligned} \tag{15.24}$$

where

$$\begin{aligned} K_t^T &= \tau_K(I2_t) \cdot T_{Kt}(h_K \cdot N2_{Kt}, K_{Kt}) \\ &= K_t^T \left(\underset{+}{K_{Kt}}, \underset{+}{I2_t}, \underset{-}{p_{NRt}}, \underset{-}{p_w}, \underset{-}{\theta_K}, \underset{-}{\varphi_K}, \underset{+}{\varepsilon^K}, \underset{-}{W2_t} \right) \end{aligned} \tag{15.25}$$

$$K^d_{G1(t+1)} = K^d_{G1(t+1)}\left(\underset{+}{W1_{t+1}}, \underset{-}{r_{1t}}, \underset{-}{p_{Kt}}, \underset{-}{\varepsilon}, \underset{-}{\delta}, \underset{+}{g_{1H1(t+1)}}\right) \tag{15.26}$$

$$K^d_{G2(t+1)} = K^d_{G2(t+1)}\left(\underset{+}{W2_{t+1}}, \underset{-}{r_{2t}}, \underset{-}{p_{Kt}}, \underset{-}{\delta}, \underset{+}{g_{2H2(t+1)}}\right) \tag{15.27}$$

$$K^d_{G3(t+1)} = K^d_{G3(t+1)}\left(\underset{+}{W3_{t+1}}, \underset{-}{r_{3t}}, \underset{-}{p_{Kt}}, \underset{-}{\delta}, \underset{+}{\tilde{\varepsilon}/\varepsilon}, \underset{+}{g_{3H3(t+1)}}\right) \tag{15.28}$$

$$K^{d}_{NR(t+1)} = K^{d}_{NR(t+1)}\left(\underset{+}{W1_{t+1}}, \underset{-}{r_{1t}}, \underset{-}{\delta}, \underset{-}{p_{Kt}}, \underset{-}{\varepsilon}\right) \tag{15.29}$$

and

$$K^{de}_{C(t+1)} = K^{de}_{C(t+1)}\left(\underset{-}{r_{3t}}, \underset{-}{p_{Kt}}, \underset{-}{p_{NRt}}, \underset{-}{p_{w}}, \underset{-}{\varphi_{C}}, \underset{-}{\theta_{C}}, \underset{-}{\theta_{K}}, \underset{-}{\delta}, \underset{-}{\varepsilon}, \underset{+}{\tilde{\varepsilon}}, \underset{+}{W3_{t+1}}\right) \tag{15.30}$$

From the above, the end-of-period demands for capital by the government sectors and the NR and C industries are positively related to the wage rates announced at the beginning of the period in their respective countries but negatively related to the price of physical capital. Labor and the services of capital are substitutes in most of the production functions. The C industry's demand is also negatively related to the price of the nonrenewable resource because the nonrenewable resource and transformation services provided by physical capital are technical complements. The greater the general public services a household sector in a given country elects for next period, the greater is the corresponding government sector's end-of-current-period demand for physical capital to generate those services. All the demands for capital are negatively related to the common rate of physical depreciation of capital.

Each sector's demand for physical capital is also negatively related to the interest rate in its country, since each sector borrows the funds in its own country to finance its real investment. An increase in ε, ceteris paribus, makes physical capital more expensive for sectors outside Country Two and reduces their demands for capital. An increase in $\tilde{\varepsilon}$, ceteris paribus, makes physical capital less expensive for the C industry and for the G3 sector, inducing them to buy more capital by the end of the period.

Given its earlier decision as to the amount of K to produce during the period, the end-of-period stock of physical capital held by the K industry moves in the opposite direction of the above responses in each case.

The stock of consumption goods held by the C industry at the end of the period is equal to its initial stock, C_{Ct}, plus its current production of those goods, $\tau(I3_t) \cdot T_{Ct}(h_{Ct} \cdot N3_{Ct}, K_{Ct})$, minus the consumption goods purchased by the three household sectors:

$$\begin{aligned} C_{C(t+1)} = {} & C_{Ct} + \tau(I3_t) \cdot T_{Ct}(h_{Ct} \cdot N3_{Ct}, K_{Ct}) \\ & - CH1_t - CH2_t - CH3_t \geq 0 \end{aligned} \tag{15.31}$$

where

$$h_{Ct} = h_{Ct}\left(\underset{-}{p^{C}_{NRt}}, \underset{-}{p_{w}}, \underset{-}{\varphi_{C}}, \underset{-}{\theta_{C}}, \underset{+}{\tilde{\varepsilon}^{C}}, \underset{-}{W3_t}, \underset{+}{I3_t}\right) \tag{15.32}$$

$$CH1^{d}_{t} = CH1^{d}_{t}\left(\underset{+}{p_{R1t}}, \underset{-}{\tilde{\varepsilon} \cdot p_{CH1t}}, \underset{+}{N1_t}, \underset{-}{r_{1t}}, \underset{+}{\overline{Y}1}, \underset{+}{W1_{t+1}}\right) \tag{15.33}$$

$$CH2^{d}_{t} = CH2^{d}_{t}\left(\underset{+}{p_{R2t}}, \underset{-}{(\tilde{\varepsilon}/\varepsilon) \cdot p_{Ct}}, \underset{+}{N2_t}, \underset{-}{r_{2t}}, \underset{+}{\overline{Y}2}, \underset{+}{W2_{t+1}}\right) \tag{15.34}$$

and

$$CH3^d_t = CH3^d_t \left(\underset{+}{p_{R3t}}, \underset{-}{p_{Ct}}, \underset{+}{N3_t}, \underset{-}{r_{3t}}, \underset{+}{\overline{Y}3}, \underset{+}{W3_{t+1}} \right) \tag{15.35}$$

The household sectors' demands for consumption goods are negatively related to the price of consumption goods but positively related to the price of the (untraded) renewable resource in its own country. Consumption goods are treated as normal goods in all three countries. Ceteris paribus, an increase in ε reduces the price of consumption goods for households in Country Two because a rise in ε strengthens the unit of account in Country Two relative to Country Three. An increase in $\tilde{\varepsilon}$ reduces the value of the units of account in both Country One and Country Two relative to Country Three and therefore tends to reduce the demands for consumption goods by the households in Country One and Country Two. Given its earlier decision as to how many units of consumption goods to produce, the C industry's ending inventory of consumption goods moves in the opposite direction of these responses in each case.

The stock of treated and stored waste at the end of the period, S_{t+1}, is equal to the stock of stored waste at the beginning of the period, S_t, plus the waste treated and stored by the three government sectors, $(1-\alpha_1)\cdot W^*G1$, $(1-\alpha_2)\cdot W^*G2$, and $(1-\alpha_3)\cdot W^*G3$; by the capital goods industry, SW^*K; and by the consumption goods industry, SW^*C, during the period. The total human waste generated by the H1 sector, W^*G1, consists of the organic waste, OW^*H1, and the inorganic waste it generates, which corresponds to the mass of C consumed by the H1 sector, $\gamma \cdot CH1$. Analogously, total human waste generated by the H2 and H3 sectors, respectively, and either recycled or treated and stored, W^*G2 and W^*G3, is equal to the sums of OW^*H2 and $\gamma \cdot CH2$ and of OW^*H3 and $\gamma \cdot CH3$, respectively:

$$\begin{aligned} S_{t+1} = S_t &+ (1-\alpha_1)\cdot W^*G1 + (1-\alpha_2)\cdot W^*G2 \\ &+ (1-\alpha_3)\cdot W^*G3 + SW^*K + SW^*C \end{aligned} \tag{15.36}$$

where

$$W^*G1 = OW^*H1 + \gamma \cdot CH1^d_t \tag{15.37}$$

$$W^*G2 = OW^*H2 + \gamma \cdot CH2^d_t \tag{15.38}$$

$$W^*G3 = OW^*H3 + \gamma \cdot CH3^d_t \tag{15.39}$$

$$\begin{aligned} SW^*K_t = \min \big[&\varphi_K \cdot \tau_K (I2_t) \cdot T_{Kt} (h_K \cdot N2_{Kt}, K_{Kt}) \\ &+ \kappa \cdot \delta \cdot K_{Kt} - \Omega^d_{Kt}, T^S_{Kt} \left(h^S_K \cdot N2_{Kt} \right) \big] \end{aligned} \tag{15.40}$$

and where SW^*K_t represents the amount of waste (in terms of mass) treated and stored during the current period, Ω^d_{Kt} represents the industry's desired holdings of pollution allowances, and $T^S_{Kt}(\bullet)$ represents the transformation function for treating and storing waste during the current period. For simplicity, we assume that labor is the only resource necessary to provide this service.

$$SW^*C_t = \min\left[\varphi_C \cdot \tau(I3_t) \cdot T_{Ct}\left(h_{Ct} \cdot N3_{Ct}, K_{Ct}\right) + \kappa \cdot \delta \cdot K_{Ct} - \Omega^d_{Ct},\right.$$
$$\left.T^S_{Ct}\left(h^S_{Ct} \cdot N3_{Ct}\right)\right] \geq 0 \qquad (15.41)$$

where SW^*C_t represents the amount of waste (in terms of mass) treat and stored during the current period, Ω^d_{Ct} represents the consumer goods industry's of pollution allowances, and $T^S_{Ct}(\bullet)$ represents transformation function for treating and storing waste during the current period. For simplicity, we assume that labor is the only resource necessary to provide this service.

The amount of pollution (untreated waste) at the end of the period, P^*_{t+1}, is equal to the amount of pollution at the beginning of the period, P^*_t, plus the waste generated by the NR, K, and C sectors and by the H1, H2, and H3 sectors, minus the waste recycled by the NR industry, the waste treated and stored by the K industry, the waste treated and stored by the C industry, the waste either recycled or treated and stored by the G1, G2, and G3 sectors and the waste assimilated by the basic fungible renewable resource:

$$P^*_{t+1} = P^*_t + \left(W^*NR - RW^*NR\right) + \left(W^*K - SW^*K\right)$$
$$+ \left(W^*C - SW^*C\right) - A\left(B_t, R1_t, R2_t, P^*_t\right) \qquad (15.42)$$

where $(W^*NR - RW^*NR)$ represents the pollution generated by the NR industry, $(W^*K - SW^*K)$ represents the pollution generated by the K industry, and $(W^*C - SW^*C)$ represents the pollution generated by the C industry. Since the government sectors either recycle or treat and store all waste generated by their respective households in this model, household activity does not result in a net increase in the level of pollution.

The total mass of each of the human populations at the end of the period ($H1_{t+1}$, $H2_{t+1}$, and $H3_{t+1}$) is equal to the population's mass at the beginning of the period ($H1_t$, $H2_t$, and $H3_t$, respectively) plus the amount of the renewable resource the corresponding household sector consumes during the period minus the organic waste generated by these households—including that resulting from death—(OW^*H1, OW^*H2, and OW^*H3):

$$H1_{t+1} = H1_t + R1H1 - OW^*H1 \qquad (15.43)$$

$$H2_{t+1} = H2_t + R2H2 - OW^*H2 \qquad (15.44)$$

$$H3_{t+1} = H3_t + R3H3 - OW^*H3 \qquad (15.45)$$

The human population in each country at the end of the period exceeds its population at the beginning of the period by the excess of births over deaths:

$$N1_{t+1} = N1_t + \eta_1 \cdot N1_t - \mu^*_{N1}\left[P^*_t, g_{H1t}, (w_{1t} - w_{I1t})^2\right] \cdot N1_t \qquad (15.46)$$

$$N2_{t+1} = N2_t + \eta_2 \cdot N2_t - \mu^*_{N2}\left[P^*_t, g_{H2t}, (w_{2t} - w_{I2t})^2\right] \cdot N2_t \qquad (15.47)$$

$$N3_{t+1} = N3_t + \eta_3 \cdot N3_t - \mu^*_{N3}\left[P^*_t, g_{H3t}, (w_{3t} - w_{I3t})^2\right] \cdot N3_t \qquad (15.48)$$

where, for instance, $w_{1t}(= H1_t/N1_t)$ represents the average weight per person in Country One at beginning of the current period and where w_{I1t} denotes the "ideal" weight per person in that country. The total organic mass generated by the households during the period, OW*H1, OW*H2, and OW*H3, minus the mass of organic human waste generated by the households as humans die in Country One, Country Two, and Country Three during the period, $w_{1t} \cdot \mu^*_{N1}[P^*_t, g_{H1t}, (w_{1t} - w_{I1t})^2] \cdot N1_t \cdot w_{2t} \cdot \mu^*_{N2}[P^*_t, g_{H2t}, (w_{1t} - w_{I2t})^2] \cdot N2_t$, and $w_{3t} \cdot \mu^*_{N3}[P^*_t, g_{H3t}, (w_{3t} - w_{I3t})^2] \cdot N3_t$, represents the organic waste generated by the household sectors during the period unrelated to death.

Finally, the number of people employed in a given country by the end of the current period (for the purpose of working next period) is equal to the minimum of the households supply of workers and the market demand for workers by the renewable resource industry, the mining/manufacturing industry, the private banking industry, and the government sector located in that country. Let $N1^e_{t+1}$, for instance, represent the number of people employed by the end of the current period to work next period in Country One.

The number of people employed in Country One by the end of the period is given by

$$N1^e_{t+1} = \min\left(N1^s_{t+1}, N1^d_{G1H1(t+1)} + N1^d_{R1(t+1)} + N1^{Td}_{NR(t+1)} + N1^d_{PB1(t+1)}\right) \tag{15.49}$$

where

$$N1^s_{t+1} = N1^s_{t+1}\left(\underset{-}{r_{1t}}, \underset{-}{\overline{Y}1}, \underset{+}{W1_{t+1}}\right) \tag{15.50}$$

$$N1^d_{G1H1(t+1)} = N1^d_{G1H1(t+1)}\left(\underset{-}{W1_{t+1}}, \underset{+}{r_{1t}}, \underset{+}{p_{Kt}}, \underset{+}{\varepsilon}, \underset{+}{g_{1H1(t+1)}}\right) \tag{15.51}$$

$$N1^d_{R1(t+1)} = N1^d_{R1(t+1)}\left(\underset{+}{R1_t}, \underset{-}{\overline{R1}_t}, \underset{+}{W1_t}, \underset{-}{W1_{t+1}}, \underset{+}{r_{1t}}, \underset{+}{B_t}, \underset{-}{P^*_t}\right) \tag{15.52}$$

$$N1^{Td}_{NR(t+1)} = N1^{Td}_{NR(t+1)}\left(\underset{-}{W1_{t+1}}, \underset{+}{r_{1t}}, \underset{+}{\delta}, \underset{+}{p_{Kt}}, \underset{+}{\varepsilon}\right) \tag{15.53}$$

and

$$N1^d_{PB1(t+1)} = N1^d_{PB1(t+1)}\left(\underset{+}{r_1}, \underset{-}{\hat{r}_1}, \underset{-}{W1_{t+1}}\right) \tag{15.54}$$

The number of people employed in Country Two by the end of the period is given by

$$N2^{e}_{t+1} = \min\left(N2^{s}_{t+1}, N2^{d}_{G2H2(t+1)} + N2^{d}_{R2(t+1)} + N2^{Te}_{K(t+1)} + N2^{d}_{PB2(t+1)}\right) \quad (15.55)$$

where

$$N2^{s}_{t+1} = N2^{s}_{t+1}\left(\underset{-}{r_{2t}}, \underset{-}{\overline{Y}2}, \underset{+}{W2_{t+1}}\right) \quad (15.56)$$

$$N2^{d}_{G2H2(t+1)} = N2^{d}_{G2H2(t+1)}\left(\underset{-}{W2_{t+1}}, \underset{+}{r_{2t}}, \underset{+}{p_{Kt}}, \underset{+}{g_{2H2(t+1)}}\right) \quad (15.57)$$

$$N2^{d}_{R2(t+1)} = N2^{d}_{R2(t+1)}\left(\underset{+}{R2_{t}}, \underset{-}{\overline{R2}_{t+1}}, \underset{+}{W2_{t}}, \underset{-}{W2_{t+1}}, \underset{+}{r_{2t}}, \underset{+}{B_{t}}, \underset{-}{P^{*}_{t}}\right) \quad (15.58)$$

$$N2^{Te}_{K(t+1)} = N2^{Te}_{K(t+1)}\left(\underset{-}{p_{w}}, \underset{-}{\theta_{K}}, \underset{-}{\varphi_{K}}, \underset{+}{\varepsilon}, \underset{-}{W2_{t+1}}\right) \quad (15.59)$$

and

$$N2^{d}_{PB2(t+1)} = N2^{d}_{PB2(t+1)}\left(\underset{+}{r_{2}}, \underset{-}{\hat{r}_{2}}, \underset{-}{W2_{t+1}}\right) \quad (15.60)$$

The number of people employed in Country Three by the end of the period is given by

$$N3^{e}_{t+1} = \min\left(N3^{s}_{t+1}, N3^{d}_{G3H3(t+1)} + N3^{d}_{R3(t+1)} + N3^{Te}_{C(t+1)} + N3^{PB3}_{t+1}\right) \quad (15.61)$$

where

$$N3^{s}_{t+1} = N3^{s}_{t+1}\left(\underset{-}{r_{3t}}, \underset{-}{\overline{Y}3}, \underset{+}{W3_{t+1}}\right) \quad (15.62)$$

$$N3^{d}_{G3H3(t+1)} = N3^{d}_{G3H3(t+1)}\left(\underset{-}{W3_{t+1}}, \underset{+}{r_{3t}}, \underset{+}{p_{Kt}}, \underset{+}{g_{3H3(t+1)}}\right) \quad (15.63)$$

$$N3^{d}_{R3(t+1)} = N3^{d}_{R3(t+1)}\left(\underset{+}{R3_{t}}, \underset{-}{\overline{R3}_{t+1}}, \underset{+}{W3_{t}}, \underset{-}{W3_{t+1}}, \underset{+}{r_{3t}}, \underset{+}{B_{t}}, \underset{-}{P^{*}_{t}}\right) \quad (15.64)$$

$$N3^{Te}_{C(t+1)} = N3^{Te}_{C(t+1)}\left(\underset{-}{p_w}, \underset{+}{\tilde{\varepsilon}}, \underset{-}{\varphi_C}, \underset{-}{\theta_C}, \underset{-}{W3_{t+1}}\right) \tag{15.65}$$

and

$$N3^{PB3}_{t+1} = N3^{PB3}_{t+1}\left(\underset{+}{r_3}, \underset{-}{\hat{r}_3}, \underset{-}{W3_{t+1}}\right) \tag{15.66}$$

Once all of these end-of-period stocks are determined, new rounds of decision making occur for next period similar to the ones presented in this study for the current period. The equations summarized in chapter 10 with respect to current production, employment, wages, and prices together with the financial market equations specified in chapters 15 and 16 and the end-of-period stocks listed in the present chapter together constitute a complete global model of integrated economic and ecological activity.

In this model, net business saving has been set equal to zero for all firms and banks. This was done partly for simplicity but also partly as a prescriptive measure. The ability of firms to engage in net business saving allows them to ignore the opportunity cost to their shareholders of retaining earnings rather than distributing them to the firms' owners and allowing them to earn the market return in their own bond markets. In the present model, every firm distributes all earnings to their shareholders and then borrows the funds back from their owners if they anticipate they can earn higher than the market return on their own projects with these borrowed funds.

16

Alternative Central Bank Policies

A central bank may allow the interest rate in its country to vary, managing instead its monetary base through occasional open market operations, or it may allow its monetary base to vary, managing instead the country's interest rate through continual adjustments in its holdings of domestic bonds. In addition, a central bank may allow the value of another country's unit of account to fluctuate relative to its own unit of account, by adjusting its holdings of foreign bonds arbitrarily and occasionally without trying to maintain a particular exchange rate; or it may decide to manage the exchange rate between its unit of account and that of another country by continually buying and selling foreign bonds. Whether the central bank occasionally or continually trades foreign bonds, it may finance those trades either by allowing its monetary base to change or by sterilizing potential effects upon its monetary base by altering as well its holdings of domestic bonds in the direction opposite to its change in foreign bond holdings.

The basic ingredients to a discussion of central bank policy include the specifications of the three money and bond market equilibrium conditions, the budget constraint facing the central bank under discussion, and the general overall version of Walras's Law. However, if a central bank fixes its exchange rate relative to another country's, then the version of Walras's Law specific to that country also becomes relevant.

Case 1: All Interest Rates Variable and All Exchange Rates Flexible

In this case, the three money markets establish the three interest rates prevailing in the world economy, while any two of the three bond markets may be viewed as establishing the world's three exchange rates (any two of which are independent).

This result follows from the overall version of Walras's Law developed in chapter 14:

$$(M1^s - M1^d) + \varepsilon \cdot p_{B2} \cdot (M2^s - M2^d) + \tilde{\varepsilon} \cdot (M3^s - M3^d) + p_{B1} \cdot (B1^s - B1^d) + \varepsilon \cdot p_{B2} \cdot (B2^s - B2^d) + \tilde{\varepsilon} \cdot p_{B3} \cdot (B3^s - B3^d) \equiv 0 \quad (14.25)$$

In chapter 13, the equilibrium conditions for the three money markets were found to be given by

$$\underset{-\ +}{M1^d(r_1, Y1)} = M1^s_{t+1}\big(\underset{+1}{MB1^s_{CB1(t+1)}}, \underset{-\ +\ +\ +}{\hat{r}_1, r_1, r_2, r_3}\big) \quad (16.1)$$

$$\varepsilon \cdot \underset{-\ +}{M2^d(r_2, Y2)} = \varepsilon \cdot M2^s_{t+1}\big(\underset{+1}{M2^s_{CB2(t+1)}}, \underset{-\ +\ +\ +}{\hat{r}_2, r_1, r_2, r_3}\big) \quad (16.2)$$

$$\tilde{\varepsilon} \cdot \underset{-\ +}{M3^d(r_3, Y3)} = \tilde{\varepsilon} \cdot M3^s_{t+1}\big(\underset{+1}{MB3^s_{CB3(t+1)}}, \underset{-\ +\ +\ +}{\hat{r}_3, r_1, r_2, r_3}\big) \quad (16.3)$$

Open Market Purchase by CB1

Suppose the central bank in Country One engages in a onetime purchase of domestic bonds equal to $d\big(p_{B1} \cdot B1^d_{CB1(t+1)}\big) > 0$, with its end-of-period holdings of both foreign bonds remaining unchanged. Then from CB1's budget constraint,

$$p_{B1} \cdot \big(B1^d_{CB1(t+1)} - B1_{CB1t}\big) + \varepsilon \cdot p_{B2} \cdot \big(B2^d_{CB1(t+1)} - B2_{CB1t}\big) + \tilde{\varepsilon} \cdot p_{B3} \cdot \big(B3^d_{CB1(t+1)} - B3_{CB1t}\big) \equiv MB1^s_{CB1(t+1)} - MB1_t \quad (16.4)$$

The central bank's planned value for the monetary base in Country One changes by

$$d\big(MB1^s_{CB1(t+1)}\big) = d\big(p_{B1} \cdot B1^d_{CB1(t+1)}\big) > 0 \quad (16.5)$$

The result is that in Country One's money market the market supply of M1 for the end of the period increases by the same amount, thereby affecting the joint solution for the world's three interest rates. From (13.19)–(13.21), the increase in $MB1^s_{CB1(t+1)}$ causes the following changes in world interest rates:

$$\frac{dr_1}{d\big(MB1^s_{CB1(t+1)}\big)} = \frac{(a22a33 - a32a23)}{(\det A)} < 0 \quad (16.6)$$

$$\frac{dr_2}{d\big(MB1^s_{CB1(t+1)}\big)} = \frac{-(a21a33 - a31a23)}{(\det A)} > 0 \quad (16.7)$$

$$\frac{dr_3}{d\big(MB1^s_{CB1(t+1)}\big)} = \frac{-(a21a32 - a31a22)}{(\det A)} > 0 \quad (16.8)$$

where det A < 0; $(a22a33 - a32a23) > 0$; $(a11a33 - a31a13) > 0$; $(a11a22 - a21a12) > 0$.

It is also assumed that $(a12a33 - a32a13) > 0$, $(a12a23 - a22a13) > 0$, $(a21a33 - a31a23) > 0$, $(a11a23 - a21a13) > 0$, $(a21a32 - a31a22) > 0$, and $(a11a32 - a31a12) > 0$ since the diagonal elements dominate the off-diagonal elements.

An open market purchase of domestic bonds by the CB1 sector, resulting in an increase in $MB1^s_{CB1(t+1)}$, causes the current-period interest rate in Country One to fall and the interest rates to rise in the other two countries. As $MB1^s_{CB1(t+1)}$ increases, the money supply in Country One increases; ceteris paribus, r_1 must fall for the demand for money to increase and restore equilibrium in the money market in Country One. However, as r_1 falls, the private banks in Country Two and Country Three reduce their demands for the bonds issued by Country One. The volume of checkable deposits they plan to have outstanding by the end of the period also falls in both countries. The reductions in the money supplies in Country One and Country Two induced by the fall in r_1 mean that for equilibrium to be restored in the money markets in these two countries, the interest rate must rise in each country in order that the demand for money in each country will fall as well. The fall in r_1 induces the NR and G1 sectors to borrow more in their bond markets in order to finance additional spending on physical capital it demands from the K industry. The rise in r_2 induces the K industry and the G2 sector to reduce their planned investment in physical capital during the period. The rise in r_3 induces the C industry and the G3 sector to do the same. Consequently, an increase in $MB1^s_{CB1(t+1)}$ may expand real investment in Country One, but it will reduce real planned investment in Country Two and Country Three. If the reduction in real investment by the G2, G3, and K sectors were to exceed the increase in physical capital purchased by the NR and G1 sectors, then the K industry will end the current period, ceteris paribus, with a greater ending inventory of capital goods than it originally planned. Ceteris paribus, the expansion of $MB1^s_{CB1(t+1)}$ may—but not necessarily—lead to a lower production of capital goods in Country Two next period.

To find the effects upon the world's exchange rates resulting form CB1's open market purchase, the increase in the CB1 sector's demand for domestic bonds and the changes in the equilibrium world interest rates must be incorporated into the world's bond markets.

The equilibrium conditions for the bond markets in Country One and Country Two, written in terms of the changes in ε and $\tilde{\varepsilon}$ resulting from the changes in $p_{B1} \cdot B1^d_{CB1(t+1)}$ and the equilibrium values of r_1, r_2, and r_3, are given by

$$\underset{+}{\left(\frac{\partial ED_{B1}}{\partial r_1}\right)} dr_1 + \underset{-}{\left(\frac{\partial ED_{B1}}{\partial r_2}\right)} dr_2 + \underset{-}{\left(\frac{\partial ED_{B1}}{\partial r_3}\right)} dr_3 + \underset{+}{\left(\frac{\partial ED_{B1}}{\partial \varepsilon}\right)} d\varepsilon + \left(\frac{\partial ED_{B1}}{\partial \tilde{\varepsilon}}\right) d\tilde{\varepsilon} + \left(p_{B1} \cdot B1^d_{CB1(t+1)}\right) = 0 \qquad (13.24)$$

or

$$\left(\frac{\partial ED_{B1}}{\partial \varepsilon}\right) d\varepsilon + \left(\frac{\partial ED_{B1}}{\partial \tilde{\varepsilon}}\right) d\tilde{\varepsilon}$$

$$= \underset{+}{-d\left(p_{B1} \cdot B1^{d}_{CB1(t+1)}\right)} - \underset{+}{\left(\frac{\partial ED_{B1}}{\partial r_1}\right)} dr_1 - \underset{-}{\left(\frac{\partial ED_{B1}}{\partial r_2}\right)} dr_2 - \underset{-}{\left(\frac{\partial ED_{B1}}{\partial r_3}\right)} dr_3$$

$$\underset{-}{\left(\frac{\partial ED_{B2}}{\partial r_1}\right)} dr_1 + \underset{+}{\left(\frac{\partial ED_{B2}}{\partial r_2}\right)} dr_2 + \underset{-}{\left(\frac{\partial ED_{B2}}{\partial r_3}\right)} dr_3 + \underset{-}{\left(\frac{\partial ED_{B2}}{\partial \varepsilon}\right)} d\varepsilon$$

$$+ \underset{+}{\left(\frac{\partial ED_{B2}}{\partial \tilde{\varepsilon}}\right)} d\tilde{\varepsilon} = 0 \tag{13.27}$$

or

$$\underset{-}{\left(\frac{\partial ED_{B2}}{\partial \varepsilon}\right)} d\varepsilon + \underset{+}{\left(\frac{\partial ED_{B2}}{\partial \tilde{\varepsilon}}\right)} d\tilde{\varepsilon}$$

$$= -\left(\frac{\partial ED_{B2}}{\partial r_1}\right) dr_1 - \left(\frac{\partial ED_{B2}}{\partial r_2}\right) dr_2 - \left(\frac{\partial ED_{B2}}{\partial r_3}\right) dr_3$$

The joint solution to $d\varepsilon$ and $d\tilde{\varepsilon}$ is given by (16.9) and (16.10):

$$\frac{\begin{bmatrix} \{[-d(p_{B1} \cdot B1^{d}_{CB1(t+1)}) - (\partial ED_{B1}/\partial r_1)dr_1 - (\partial ED_{B1}/\partial r_2)dr_2 \\ -(\partial ED_{B1}/\partial r_3)dr_3] \cdot (\partial ED_{B2}/\partial \tilde{\varepsilon})\} \\ -\{[-(\partial ED_{B2}/\partial r_2)dr_2 - (\partial ED_{B2}/\partial r_3)dr_3] \cdot (\partial ED_{B1}/\partial \tilde{\varepsilon})\} \end{bmatrix}}{\{(\partial ED_{B1}/\partial \varepsilon) \cdot (\partial ED_{B2}/\partial \tilde{\varepsilon}) - (\partial ED_{B2}/\partial \varepsilon) \cdot (\partial ED_{B1}/\partial \tilde{\varepsilon})\}} \tag{16.9}$$

The direct effect upon ε of the open market purchase in Country One, $d\left(p_{B1} \cdot B1^{d}_{CB1(t+1)}\right)$, is negative, but the indirect effects upon ε operating through r_1, r_2, and r_3 are mixed. The negative direct effect exists because as CB1 increases its end-of-period demand for bonds issued in Country One, ceteris paribus, ε must fall to restore equilibrium in the B1 market. As ε falls, it becomes cheaper for the NR industry and the G1 sector to purchase capital goods from the K industry in Country Two. As a result, the NR and G1 sectors tend to borrow more in the B1 market as ε falls. Without further information, the net effect upon ε due to an open market purchase by CB1 is indeterminate.

$$d\tilde{\varepsilon} = \frac{\begin{bmatrix} \{[-(\partial ED_{B2}/\partial r_1)dr_1 - (\partial ED_{B2}/\partial r_2)dr_2 - (\partial ED_{B2}/\partial r_3)dr_3] \cdot (\partial ED_{B2}/\partial r_1)\} \\ -\{[-d(p_{B1} \cdot B1^{d}_{CB1(t+1)}) - (\partial ED_{B1}/\partial r_1)dr_1 - (\partial ED_{B1}/\partial r_2)dr_2 \\ -(\partial ED_{B1}/\partial r_3)dr_3] \cdot (\partial ED_{B2}/\partial \varepsilon)\} \end{bmatrix}}{\{[(\partial ED_{B1}/\partial \varepsilon) \cdot (\partial ED_{B2}/\partial \tilde{\varepsilon}) - (\partial ED_{B2}/\partial \tilde{\varepsilon}) \cdot (\partial ED_{B1}/\partial \tilde{\varepsilon})]\}} \tag{16.10}$$

The direct effect of the open market purchase by CB1 upon $\tilde{\varepsilon}$ is negative; the indirect effects operating through changes in r_1, r_2, and r_3 are mixed. The negative direct effect upon $\tilde{\varepsilon}$ results exists because as CB1 buys bonds on the open market, ceteris paribus, $\tilde{\varepsilon}$ must fall to restore equilibrium in the B1 market so that the market supply of B1 will increase to meet the rise in demand for B1. As $\tilde{\varepsilon}$ falls, it becomes more expensive for the C industry and the G3 sector to buy the transformed nonrenewable resource from the NR industry. As a result the demands for NR by the C and G3 sectors decrease, ceteris paribus, causing unplanned inventory investment by the NR industry and causing that sector to borrow more in the B1 market. Without further information, the net effect upon $\tilde{\varepsilon}$ due to an open market purchase by CB1 is indeterminate. The effect upon the exchange rate $\tilde{\varepsilon}/\varepsilon$ due to an open market purchase by CB1 is also indeterminate in this model.

Sterilized Purchase of Country Two's Bonds by CB1

If CB1 buys Country Two's bonds but sterilizes the purchase by selling bonds in its own bond market (reduces its end-of-period demand for its own bonds) equal to the value of the bonds it buys, then from CB1's budget constraint,

$$d\left(p_{B1} \cdot B1^{d}_{CB1(t+1)}\right) = -d\left(\varepsilon \cdot p_{B2} \cdot B2^{d}_{CB1(t+1)}\right) < 0 \tag{16.11}$$

This transaction does not affect the money market in any country, and therefore leaves all interest rates unchanged. However, the excess demand for the bonds issued in Country One and Country Two are directly affected. Since any two of the three bond market equilibrium conditions may be used to solve for the resulting changes in ε and $\tilde{\varepsilon}$, it is simpler to use either the equilibrium conditions for B1 and B3 or for B2 and B3 than to use the combination of conditions for equilibrium in the B1 and B2 markets. The equilibrium conditions for B1 and B3 are used here:

$$\underset{+}{\left(\frac{\partial ED_{B1}}{\partial \varepsilon}\right)} d\varepsilon + \underset{+}{\left(\frac{\partial ED_{B1}}{\partial \tilde{\varepsilon}}\right)} d\tilde{\varepsilon} + \underset{-}{d\left(p_{B1} \cdot B1^{d}_{CB1(t+1)}\right)} = 0 \tag{16.12}$$

$$\underset{-}{\left(\frac{\partial ED_{B3}}{\partial \varepsilon}\right)} + \underset{+}{\left(\frac{\partial ED_{B3}}{\partial \tilde{\varepsilon}}\right)} d\tilde{\varepsilon} = 0 \tag{16.13}$$

The joint solution to $d\varepsilon$ and $d\tilde{\varepsilon}$ is given by (16.14) and (16.15):

$$d\varepsilon = \frac{\left\{\left[-d(p_{B1} \cdot B1^{d}_{CB1(t+1)})\right] \cdot \left(\partial ED_{B3}/\partial \tilde{\varepsilon}\right)\right\}}{\{(\partial ED_{B1}/\partial \varepsilon) \cdot (\partial ED_{B3}/\partial \tilde{\varepsilon}) - (\partial ED_{B3}/\partial \varepsilon) \cdot (\partial ED_{B1}/\partial \tilde{\varepsilon})\}} > 0 \tag{16.14}$$

$$d\tilde{\varepsilon} = \frac{\left[(\partial ED_{B3}/\partial \varepsilon) \cdot d(p_{B1} \cdot B1^{d}_{CB1(t+1)})\right]}{\left\{(\partial ED_{B1}/\partial \varepsilon) \cdot (\partial ED_{B3}/\partial \tilde{\varepsilon}) - (\partial ED_{B3}/\partial \varepsilon) \cdot (\partial ED_{B1}/\partial \tilde{\varepsilon})\right\}} > 0 \tag{16.15}$$

Country One's unit of account depreciates relative to the units of account in Country Two and Country Three. In this case, since the world's interest rates remain unaffected, the changes in the exchange rates are due exclusively to the direct effect associated with the CB1's reduced end-of-period demand for B1. Ceteris paribus, the reduction in the CB1's end-of-period demand for B1 must be accompanied by a drop in the market supply of B1, and the changes in ε and $\tilde{\varepsilon}$ must be consistent with that reduction in market supply. The direct effects are the opposite of those discussed above for an open market purchase by CB1. A similar result to these direct effects upon ε and $\tilde{\varepsilon}$ occurs for a sterilized purchase of Country Three's bonds by CB1, which can be verified using the equilibrium conditions for the B1 and B2 markets.

Nonsterilized Purchase of Country Two's Bonds by CB1

If CB1 purchases a certain amount of Country Two's bonds by allowing its own monetary base to increase, then the effects upon the world's interest rates are qualitatively the same as those associated with an open market purchase of bonds by Country One. The interest rate in Country One falls, while the interest rates in Country Two and Country Three increase:

$$\underset{+}{\left(\frac{\partial ED_{B1}}{\partial r_1}\right)} dr_1 + \underset{-}{\left(\frac{\partial ED_{B1}}{\partial r_2}\right)} dr_2 + \underset{-}{\left(\frac{\partial ED_{B1}}{\partial r_3}\right)} dr_3 + \underset{-}{\left(\frac{\partial ED_{B1}}{\partial \varepsilon}\right)} d\varepsilon + \underset{+}{\left(\frac{\partial ED_{B1}}{\partial \tilde{\varepsilon}}\right)} d\tilde{\varepsilon} = 0 \tag{16.16}$$

or

$$\underset{+}{\left(\frac{\partial ED_{B1}}{\partial \varepsilon}\right)} d\varepsilon + \underset{+}{\left(\frac{\partial ED_{B1}}{\partial \tilde{\varepsilon}}\right)} d\tilde{\varepsilon} = -\underset{+}{\left(\frac{\partial ED_{B1}}{\partial r_1}\right)} dr_1 - \underset{-}{\left(\frac{\partial ED_{B1}}{\partial r_2}\right)} dr_2 - \underset{-}{\left(\frac{\partial ED_{B1}}{\partial r_3}\right)} dr_3 - \underset{-}{\left(\frac{\partial ED_{B2}}{\partial r_1}\right)} dr_1 + \underset{+}{\left(\frac{\partial ED_{B2}}{\partial r_2}\right)} dr_2 + \underset{-}{\left(\frac{\partial ED_{B2}}{\partial r_3}\right)} dr_3 + \underset{-}{\left(\frac{\partial ED_{B2}}{\partial \varepsilon}\right)} d\varepsilon + \underset{+}{\left(\frac{\partial ED_{B2}}{\partial \tilde{\varepsilon}}\right)} d\tilde{\varepsilon} + d\left[\left(\frac{1}{\varepsilon}\right) \cdot (p_{B2} \cdot B2_{CB1(t+1)^d})\right] = 0 \tag{16.17}$$

or

$$\underset{-}{\left[\left(\frac{\partial ED_{B2}}{\partial \varepsilon}\right) - \left(\frac{1}{\varepsilon}\right)^2 \cdot \left(p_{B2} \cdot B2^d_{CB1(t+1)}\right)\right]} d\varepsilon + \underset{+}{\left(\frac{\partial ED_{B2}}{\partial \tilde{\varepsilon}}\right)} d\tilde{\varepsilon} = -\left(\frac{\partial ED_{B2}}{\partial r_1}\right) dr_1 - \left(\frac{\partial ED_{B2}}{\partial r_2}\right) dr_2 - \left(\frac{\partial ED_{B2}}{\partial r_3}\right) dr_3 - \left(\frac{1}{\varepsilon}\right) \cdot d\left[\left(p_{B2} \cdot B2^d_{CB1(t+1)}\right)\right]$$

The direct effects of the purchase of Country Two's bonds by CB1 upon the exchange rates are to increase ε and to decrease $\tilde{\varepsilon}$. But, as in the case in which CB1 buys its own bonds, the net effects upon the exchange rates are indeterminate because the indirect effects operating through the interest rate changes are indeterminate.

Purchase of Country Two's Bonds and Sale of Country Three's Bonds by CB2

A possibility provided by a three-country model consists of CB1, for instance, buying some bonds issued in, say, Country Two and selling some of its Country Three bond holdings. Since no change takes place in the monetary base of any country, the equilibrium conditions in the world's money markets remain unaffected; the world's interest rates do not change. Using the equilibrium conditions for the bond markets in Country One and Country Two, the purchase of Country Two's bonds produces the same direct effects upon the exchange rates as those associated with a nonsterilized purchase of those bonds. Consequently, ε increases and $\tilde{\varepsilon}$ decreases.

Case 2: CB1 Manages the Interest Rate in Country One under Flexible Exchange Rates

In this case, the end-of-period demand for domestic bonds by the central bank in Country One is endogenously determined with the central bank adjusting its demand to maintain the interest rate r_1, say, $\bar{r}_1$, at the arbitrary level chosen by CB1:

$$\begin{aligned} p_{B1} \cdot B1^d_{CB1(t+1)} \equiv\ & p_{B1} \cdot B1^s_{t+1}(\bar{r}_1, \varepsilon, \tilde{\varepsilon}, \ldots) - p_{B1} \cdot B1^d_{PB1(t+1)}(\bar{r}_1, r_2, r_3) \\ & - p_{B1} \cdot B1^d_{CB2(t+1)} - p_{B1} \cdot B1^d_{PB2(t+1)}(\bar{r}_1, r_2, r_3) \\ & - p_{B1} \cdot B1^d_{CB3(t+1)} - p_{B1} \cdot B1^d_{PB3(t+1)}(\bar{r}_1, r_2, r_3) \\ \equiv\ & p_{B1} \cdot B1^d_{CB1(t+1)}(\underset{-}{\bar{r}_1}, \underset{+}{r_2}, \underset{+}{r_3}, \underset{-}{\varepsilon}, \underset{-}{\tilde{\varepsilon}}, \ldots) \end{aligned} \tag{16.18}$$

From CB1's budget constraint, only two of the remaining three policy variables, $p_{B2} \cdot B2^d_{CB1(t+1)}$, $p_{B3} \cdot B3^d_{CB1(t+1)}$, and $MB1^s_{CB1(t+1)}$, may be chosen arbitrarily; the remaining policy variable must maintain CB1's budget constraint. It is assumed here that CB1 allows its monetary base to change with its holdings of $p_{B1} \cdot B1^d_{CB1(t+1)}$. Therefore, the new expression for $MB1^s_{CB1(t+1)}$ is given by

$$\begin{aligned} MB1^s_{CB1(t+1)} \equiv\ & p_{B1} \cdot B1^d_{CB1(t+1)}(\underset{-}{\bar{r}_1}, \underset{+}{r_2}, \underset{+}{r_3}, \underset{-}{\varepsilon}, \underset{-}{\tilde{\varepsilon}}, \ldots) \\ & + p_{B2} \cdot B2^d_{CB1(t+1)} + p_{B3} \cdot B3^d_{CB1(t+1)} \end{aligned} \tag{16.19}$$

Substituting (16.19) into (16.1) produces the following three money-market equilibrium conditions:

$$\underset{-\;+}{M1^d(\bar{r}_1, Y1)} = M1^s_{t+1}\big[p_{B1} \cdot \underset{+1}{B1^d_{CB1(t+1)}}(\bar{r}_1, r_2, r_3, \varepsilon, \tilde{\varepsilon}, \ldots) + p_{B2} \cdot B2^d_{CB1(t+1)}$$
$$+ p_{B3} \cdot B3^d_{CB1(t+1)}, \underset{-\;+\;+\;+}{\hat{r}_1, \bar{r}_1, r_2, r_3}\big] \qquad (16.20)$$

$$\varepsilon \cdot \underset{-\;+}{M2^d(r_2, Y2)} = \varepsilon \cdot \underset{+1}{M2^s_{t+1}}\big(MB2^s_{CB2(t+1)}, \underset{-\;+\;+\;+}{\hat{r}_2, \bar{r}_1, r_2, r_3}\big) \qquad (16.21)$$

$$\tilde{\varepsilon} \cdot \underset{-\;+}{M3^d(r_3, Y3)} = \tilde{\varepsilon} \cdot \underset{+1}{M3^s_{t+1}} \cdot \big(MB3^s_{CB3(t+1)}, \underset{-\;+\;+\;+}{\hat{r}_3, \bar{r}_1, r_2, r_3}\big) \qquad (16.22)$$

Conditions (16.20)–(16.22) contain the four unknowns: r_2, r_3, ε, and $\tilde{\varepsilon}$. Adding the equilibrium condition for the bond market in Country Two or the bond market in Country Three yields a system of four independent equations in these unknowns. In fact, this new system may be solve recursively, using (16.21) and (16.22) to solve for r_2 and r_3 and then using (16.20) and, say, the equilibrium condition for the bond market in Country Two to solve for ε and $\tilde{\varepsilon}$.

CB1 Purchase of B2

If CB1 buys some bonds issued in Country Two, but continues to leave its own interest rate unchanged, the results are somewhat different from those obtained earlier for a nonsterilized purchase of Country Two's bonds. In the present case, none of the three interest rates change; r_1 is held constant by CB1 arbitrarily (taking "defensive" measures if necessary in Country One's bond market) while r_2 and r_3 remain unchanged because no change takes place in the money markets in Country Two or Country Three. The money market equilibrium condition for Country One together with, say, the bond market equilibrium condition for Country Three can be used to find the changes in ε and $\tilde{\varepsilon}$ due to the purchase of B2 by CB1. From (16.20), the money market in Country One remains in equilibrium for the following changes in ε and $\tilde{\varepsilon}$ due to a nonsterilized change in $p_{B2} \cdot B2^d_{CB1(t+1)}$:

$$\underset{-}{\left[\frac{\partial\big(p_{B1} \cdot B2^d_{CB1(t+1)}\big)}{\partial\varepsilon}\right]} \cdot d\varepsilon + \underset{-}{\left[\frac{\partial\big(p_{B1} \cdot B1^d_{CB1(t+1)}\big)}{\partial\tilde{\varepsilon}}\right]} d\tilde{\varepsilon} = -d\big(p_{B2} \cdot B2^d_{CB1(t+1)}\big) \qquad (16.23)$$

From the equilibrium condition for the bond market in Country Three, the following changes in ε and $\tilde{\varepsilon}$ are consistent with maintaining equilibrium in that market due to a nonsterilized change in $p_{B2} \cdot B2^{d}_{CB1(t+1)}$:

$$\underset{+}{\left[\frac{\partial\left(p_{B3} \cdot B3^{s}_{t+1}\right)}{\partial \varepsilon}\right]} \cdot d\varepsilon + \underset{-}{\left[\frac{\partial\left(p_{B3} \cdot B3^{s}_{t+1}\right)}{\partial \tilde{\varepsilon}}\right]} d\tilde{\varepsilon} = 0 \tag{16.24}$$

Solving (16.23) and (16.24) jointly for the qualitative changes in ε and $\tilde{\varepsilon}$ reveals that both exchange rates increase as a result of a nonsterilized purchase of B2 by CB1.

A Managed Increase in the Interest Rate r_1

Holding constant CB1's end-of-period demands for bonds issued in Country Two and Country Three, if CB1 arbitrarily decides to raise $\bar{r}_1$, it must decrease its end-of-period demand for bonds in that market and stand ready to enter the bond market in Country One to maintain the new rate. The M2 and M3 markets can be solved for the changes in r_2 and r_3 resulting from the change in $\bar{r}_1$. Then the changes in $\bar{r}_1$, r_2, and r_3 may be inserted into the expressions for the B2 and B3 equilibrium conditions to solve for changes in the exchange rates:

$$\underset{-}{\left[\frac{\partial(ED_{M2})}{\partial r_2}\right]} \cdot dr_2 + \underset{-}{\left[\frac{\partial(ED_{M2})}{\partial r_3}\right]} \cdot dr_3 = -\underset{-}{\left[\frac{\partial(ED_{M2})}{\partial \bar{r}_1}\right]} \cdot d\bar{r}_1 \tag{16.25}$$

$$\underset{-}{\left[\frac{\partial(ED_{M3})}{\partial r_2}\right]} \cdot dr_2 + \underset{-}{\left[\frac{\partial(ED_{M3})}{\partial r_3}\right]} \cdot dr_3 = -\underset{-}{\left[\frac{\partial(ED_{M3})}{\partial \bar{r}_1}\right]} \cdot d\bar{r}_1 \tag{16.26}$$

Assuming that the diagonal elements in the coefficient matrix on the left-hand sides of (16.25) and (16.26) dominate, a rise in $\bar{r}_1$ will produce a fall in both r_2 and r_3. These results are similar to those for an open market purchase by CB1 discussed at the beginning of this chapter:

$$r_2 = r_2(\underset{-}{\bar{r}_1}) \tag{16.27}$$

$$r_3 = r_3(\underset{-}{\bar{r}_1}) \tag{16.28}$$

Solve the following two equations for the changes in ε and $\tilde{\varepsilon}$:

$$\underset{-}{\left(\frac{\partial ED_{B2}}{\partial \varepsilon}\right)} d\varepsilon + \underset{+}{\left(\frac{\partial ED_{B2}}{\partial \tilde{\varepsilon}}\right)} d\tilde{\varepsilon}$$

$$= -\underset{-}{\left(\frac{\partial ED_{B2}}{\partial r_1}\right)} d\bar{r}_1 - \underset{-}{\left(\frac{\partial ED_{B2}}{\partial r_2}\right)} dr_2 - \underset{-}{\left(\frac{\partial ED_{B2}}{\partial r_3}\right)} dr_3 \tag{16.29}$$

$$\left(\frac{\partial ED_{B3}}{\partial \varepsilon}\right) d\varepsilon + \left(\frac{\partial ED_{B3}}{\partial \tilde{\varepsilon}}\right) d\tilde{\varepsilon}$$

$$\quad + \qquad\qquad -$$

$$= -\left(\frac{\partial ED_{B3}}{\partial r_1}\right) d\bar{r}_1 - \left(\frac{\partial ED_{B3}}{\partial r_2}\right) dr_2 - \left(\frac{\partial ED_{B3}}{\partial r_3}\right) dr_3 \qquad (16.30)$$

$$- \qquad\qquad - \qquad\qquad +$$

An increase in $\bar{r}_1$ produces indeterminate qualitative effects upon ε and $\tilde{\varepsilon}$.

A Managed Increase in r_1 by CB1 with CB2 and CB3 also Managing Their Respective Interest Rates

If CB1 decides to raise its interest rate, with the central banks in Country Two and Country Three holding their interest rates constant, then two of the three money market equilibrium conditions are independent and may be used in principle to solve for the qualitative changes in ε and $\tilde{\varepsilon}$. For instance, in terms of changes in ε and $\tilde{\varepsilon}$ the equilibrium conditions in the M1 and M2 markets may be expressed by (16.31) and (16.32):

$$\left[\left(\frac{\partial ED_{M1}}{\partial \varepsilon}\right)\right] \cdot d\varepsilon + \left[\frac{\partial (ED_{M1})}{\partial \tilde{\varepsilon}}\right] \cdot d\tilde{\varepsilon} = -\left[\frac{\partial (ED_{M1})}{\partial \bar{r}_1}\right] \cdot d\bar{r}_1 \qquad (16.31)$$

$$+ \qquad\qquad +$$

$$\left[\frac{\partial (ED_{M2})}{\partial \varepsilon}\right] \cdot d\varepsilon + \left[\frac{\partial (ED_{M2})}{\partial \tilde{\varepsilon}}\right] \cdot d\tilde{\varepsilon} = -\left[\frac{\partial (ED_{M2})}{\partial \bar{r}_1}\right] \cdot d\bar{r}_1 \qquad (16.32)$$

$$- \qquad\qquad +$$

Once again, the qualitative effects upon ε and $\tilde{\varepsilon}$ remain indeterminate without making further assumptions about the relative effects of changes in $\bar{r}_1$, ε, and $\tilde{\varepsilon}$ upon the excess demand functions in Country One and Country Two.

Case 3: CB1 Fixes ε but Allows $\tilde{\varepsilon}$ to Fluctuate with All Interest Rates Variable

In this section, the central bank in Country One buys or sells some of its holdings of Country Two's bonds to maintain a given exchange rate, $\bar{\varepsilon}$, between the units of account in the two countries. Consequently, the expression for the balance of payments of Country One with Country Two becomes relevant, as does the version of Walras's law applicable to Country One:

$$BP12 = p_{NR}(NRK + NRG2) + p_{B1}(B1^{PB2d} - B1^{PB2}) + p_{B1}(B1^{CB2d} - B1^{CB2})$$
$$+ \varepsilon \cdot B2_{PB1t} + \varepsilon \cdot B2_{CB1t} - p_{Kt} \cdot \varepsilon \cdot \left[K^{d}_{NR(t+1)} - (1 - \delta) \cdot K_{NRt}\right]$$

$$- \varepsilon \cdot p_{Kt} \cdot \left[K^{d}_{G1(t+1)} - (1-\delta) \cdot K_{G1t}\right] - \varepsilon \cdot p_{B2} \cdot \left(B2^{d}_{PB1(t+1)} - B2_{PB1t}\right)$$
$$- \varepsilon \cdot p_{B2} \cdot \left(B2^{d}_{CB1(t+1)} - B1_{CB1t}\right) - B1_{PB2t} - B1_{CB2t} \qquad (16.33)$$

$$(M1^{s} - M1^{d}) + p_{B1} \cdot (B1^{s} - B1^{d}) + BP12 + BP13 \equiv 0 \qquad (16.34)$$

where the purchases or sales of pollution allowances are assumed to be small relative to the other items in (16.34).

From (16.33), CB1 maintains $\bar{\varepsilon}$ by endogenously setting its purchases of Country Two's bonds to keep the overall ex ante balance of payments, BP12, equal to zero. Consequently, the CB1 sector's endogenously determined demand for Country Two's bonds during the period becomes

$$\bar{\varepsilon} \cdot p_{B2} \cdot \left(B2^{d}_{CB1(t+1)} - B2_{CB1t}\right)$$
$$= p_{NR}(NRK + NRG2) + p_{B1}\left(B1^{d}_{PB2(t+1)} - B1_{PB2t}\right)$$
$$+ p_{B1}\left(B1^{d}_{CB2(t+1)} - B1_{CB2t}\right) + \bar{\varepsilon} \cdot B2_{PB1t} + \bar{\varepsilon} \cdot B2_{CB1t}$$
$$- p_{Kt} \cdot \bar{\varepsilon} \cdot \left[K^{d}_{NR(t+1)} - (1-\delta) \cdot K_{NRt}\right] - \bar{\varepsilon} \cdot p_{Kt} \cdot \left[K^{d}_{G1(t+1)}\right.$$
$$\left. - (1-\delta) \cdot K_{G1t}\right] - \bar{\varepsilon} \cdot p_{B2}\left(B2^{d}_{PB1(t+1)} - B2_{PB1t}\right) - B1_{PB2t} - B1_{CB2t} \qquad (16.35)$$

From (16.35), Walras's law for Country One is given by (16.36):

$$(M1^{s} - M1^{d}) + p_{B1} \cdot (B1^{s} - B1^{d}) + BP13 \equiv 0 \qquad (16.36)$$

Also, the budget constraint for the CB1 sector becomes

$$p_{B1} \cdot \left(B1^{d}_{CB1(t+1)} - B1_{CB1t}\right) + \tilde{\varepsilon} \cdot p_{B3} \cdot \left(B3^{d}_{CB1(t+1)} - B3_{CB1t}\right)$$
$$+ p_{NR}\left(NRK + NRG2\right) + p_{B1}\left(B1^{d}_{PB2(t+1)} - B1_{PB2t}\right)$$
$$+ p_{B1}\left(B1^{d}_{CB2(t+1)} - B1_{CB2t}\right) + \bar{\varepsilon} \cdot B2_{PB1t} + \bar{\varepsilon} \cdot B2_{CB1t}$$
$$- p_{Kt} \cdot \bar{\varepsilon} \cdot \left[K^{d}_{NR(t+1)} - (1-\delta) \cdot K_{NRt}\right] - \bar{\varepsilon} \cdot p_{Kt} \cdot \left[K^{d}_{G1(t+1)} - (1-\delta) \cdot K_{G1t}\right]$$
$$- \bar{\varepsilon} \cdot p_{B2} \cdot \left(B2^{d}_{PB1(t+1)} - B2_{PB1t}\right) - B1_{PB2t} - B1_{CB2t} \equiv MB1^{s}_{CB1(t+1)} - MB1_{t} \qquad (16.37)$$

Now only two of the three policy variables under the control of the CB1 sector are independently established. Once the CB1 sector decides any two of the amounts $MB1^{s}_{CB1(t+1)}$, $p_{B1} \cdot B1^{d}_{CB1(t+1)}$, or $\tilde{\varepsilon} \cdot p_{B3} \cdot B3^{d}_{CB1(t+1)}$, it has automatically decided that the third variable will adjust to maintain (16.37).

Since the central bank in Country One fixes the exchange rate between its country and Country Two, the relevant version of Walras's law for Country Two becomes

$$(M2^{s} - M2^{d}) + p_{B2} \cdot (B2^{s} - B2^{d}) + BP23 \equiv 0 \qquad (16.38)$$

The relevant version of Walras's law for Country Three remains

$$(M3^{s} - M3^{d}) + p_{B3} \cdot (B3^{s} - B3^{d}) - BP23 \equiv 0 \qquad (16.39)$$

Two cases will be considered here.

Nonsterilized Purchase/Sale of Country Two's Bonds by CB1 to Fix ε

In the first case, CB1 decides to not sterilize any purchases/sales of Country Two's bonds it must make to keep ε fixed at $\bar{\varepsilon}$. In this case, $MB1^s_{CB1(t+1)}$ becomes an endogenous variable given by

$$\begin{aligned} MB1^s_{CB1(t+1)} \equiv\ & MB1_t + p_{B1} \cdot \left(B1^d_{CB1(t+1)} - B1_{CB1t}\right) + \tilde{\varepsilon} \cdot p_{B3} \cdot \left(B3^d_{CB1(t+1)}\right. \\ & \left. - B3_{CB1t}\right) + p_{NR}(NRK + NRG2) + p_{B1}\left(B1^d_{PB2(t+1)} - B1_{PB2t}\right) \\ & + p_{B1}\left(B1^d_{CB2(t+1)} - B1_{CB2t}\right) + \bar{\varepsilon} \cdot B2_{PB1t} + \bar{\varepsilon} \cdot B2_{CB1t} \\ & - p_{Kt} \cdot \varepsilon \cdot \left[K^d_{NR(t+1)} - (1-\delta) \cdot K_{NRt}\right] \\ & - \bar{\varepsilon} \cdot p_{Kt} \cdot \left[K^d_{G1(t+1)} - (1-\delta) \cdot K_{G1t}\right] \\ & - \bar{\varepsilon} \cdot p_{B2} \cdot \left(B2^d_{PB1(t+1)} - B2_{PB1t}\right) - B1_{PB2t} - B1_{CB2t} \end{aligned} \quad (16.40)$$

Substituting the right-hand side of (16.40) for $MB1^s_{CB1(t+1)}$ in the expression for equilibrium in Country One's money market yields the following equation in the four unknowns, r_1, r_2, r_3, and $\tilde{\varepsilon}$:

$$\begin{aligned} & \left[\frac{\partial(ED_{M1})}{\partial r_1}\right] \cdot dr_1 + \left[\frac{\partial(ED_{M1})}{\partial r_2}\right] \cdot dr_2 + \left[\frac{\partial(ED_{M1})}{\partial r_3}\right] \cdot dr_3 \\ & = d\left\{MB1_t + p_{B1} \cdot \left(B1^d_{CB1(t+1)} - B1_{CB1t}\right) + \tilde{\varepsilon} \cdot p_{B3} \cdot \left(B3^d_{CB1(t+1)} - B3_{CB1t}\right)\right. \\ & + p_{NR}(NRK + NRG2) + p_{B1}\left(B1^d_{PB2(t+1)} - B1_{PB2t}\right) \\ & + p_{B1}(B1^d_{CB2(t+1)} - B1_{CB2t}) + \bar{\varepsilon} \cdot B2_{PB1t} + \bar{\varepsilon} \cdot B2_{CB1t} \\ & - p_{Kt} \cdot \bar{\varepsilon} \cdot \left[K^d_{NR(t+1)} - (1-\delta) \cdot K_{NRt}\right] \\ & - \bar{\varepsilon} \cdot p_{Kt} \cdot \left[K^d_{G1(t+1)} - (1-\delta) \cdot K_{G1t}\right] \\ & \left. -\bar{\varepsilon} \cdot p_{B2}\left(B2^d_{PB1(t+1)} - B2_{PB1t}\right) - B1_{PB2t} - B1_{CB2t}\right\} \end{aligned} \quad (16.41)$$

The linearized approximations to the equilibrium conditions for the money markets in Country Two and Country Three may still be written as

$$\left[\frac{\partial(ED_{M2})}{\partial r_1}\right] \cdot dr_1 + \left[\frac{\partial(ED_{M2})}{\partial r_2}\right] \cdot dr_2 + \left[\frac{\partial(ED_{M2})}{\partial r_3}\right] \cdot dr_3 = d\left(MB2^s_{CB2(t+1)}\right) \quad (16.42)$$

$$\left[\frac{\partial(ED_{M3})}{\partial r_1}\right] \cdot dr_1 + \left[\frac{\partial(ED_{M3})}{\partial r_2}\right] \cdot dr_2 + \left[\frac{\partial(ED_{M3})}{\partial r_3}\right] \cdot dr_3 = d\left(MB3^s_{CB3(t+1)}\right) \quad (16.43)$$

The addition of the equilibrium condition for the bond market in Country One, Country Two, or Country Three completes the system of independent equations and, in principle, produces a solution to the system. However, the solution depends upon which of these three equilibrium conditions is chosen. If the equilibrium condition for the bond market in Country One is selected, then, from (16.36), the solution reflects the combination of the three interest rates and the exchange rate $\tilde{\varepsilon}$ that is consistent with overall ex ante balance of payments equilibrium between Country One and Country Three. In this case, the overall ex ante balance of payments between Country Two and Country Three may not be equal to zero; if it happens to be nonzero, then the excess demand for bonds issued in Country Two will be equal to the excess supply of bonds issued in Country Three, or vice versa, when measured in terms of a common unit of account.

On the other hand, if the equilibrium condition for the bond market in Country Two is selected as the fourth equation in the system used to solve for the three interest rates and $\tilde{\varepsilon}$, then the solution is consistent with a zero overall ex ante balance of payments between Country Two and Country Three. In this case, the overall balance of payments of Country One with Country Three may not be equal to zero. If it happens to be nonzero, then the excess demand for bonds issued in Country One will be equal to the excess supply of bonds issued in Country Three, or vice versa, when measured in terms of a common unit of account.

Finally, if the equilibrium condition for the bond market in Country Three is selected as the fourth equation in the system used to solve for the three interest rates and $\tilde{\varepsilon}$, then, from (16.39), the solution is consistent with a zero overall balance of payments between Country Three and the rest of the world, that is, between Country Three and the consolidated balance with Country One and Country Two combined; corresponding to this solution, BP13 plus BP23 is equal to zero when they are measured in terms of a common unit of account. In this case, the overall balance of payments of Country One with Country Three may be nonzero, in which case the overall balance of payments of Country Two with Country Three will also be nonzero and opposite in sign and amount when measured in terms of a common unit of account. Simultaneously, from (16.36) and (16.38), the excess demand for bonds issued in Country One will equal the excess supply of bonds issued in Country Two, or vice versa, when both are measured in terms of the same unit of account.

The three alternative bond market equilibrium conditions—written in terms of changes in the three interest rates and the exchange rate $\tilde{\varepsilon}$—are given by (16.46), (16.49), and (16.52):

Market demand for B1 is given by

$$p_{B1} \cdot B1^{d}_{t+1} = p_{B1} \cdot B1^{d}_{t+1} \cdot (\underset{+}{r_1}, \underset{-}{r_2}, \underset{-}{r_3}, \underset{+1}{p_{B1} \cdot B1^{d}_{CB1(t+1)}}, \underset{+1}{p_{B1} \cdot B1^{d}_{CB2(t+1)}}, \underset{+1}{p_{B1} \cdot B1^{d}_{CB3(t+1)}}) \tag{16.44}$$

Market supply of B1 is given by

$$p_{B1} \cdot B1^{s}_{t+1} = p_{B1} \cdot B1^{s}_{t+1} \cdot (\underset{-}{r_1}, \underset{-}{\varepsilon}, \underset{-}{\tilde{\varepsilon}}) \tag{16.45}$$

Setting the demand for B1 equal to the supply of B1 and differentiating yields

$$\underset{+}{\left(\frac{\partial ED_{B1}}{\partial r_1}\right)} dr_1 + \underset{-}{\left(\frac{\partial ED_{B1}}{\partial r_2}\right)} dr_2 + \underset{-}{\left(\frac{\partial ED_{B1}}{\partial r_3}\right)} dr_3 + \underset{+}{\left(\frac{\partial ED_{B1}}{\partial \tilde{\varepsilon}}\right)} d\tilde{\varepsilon} = 0 \tag{16.46}$$

The coefficients of the four variables carry the same signs as they would under the case of a flexible ε.

However, the equilibrium condition in Country Two's bond market changes because the market demand for Country Two's bonds by CB1 is now endogenously determined.

Market demand for B2 is given by

$$\begin{aligned} p_{B2} \cdot B2^{d}_{t+1} &= p_{B2} \cdot B2^{d}_{t+1} \cdot \Big(\underset{+}{r_1}, \underset{+}{r_2}, \underset{-}{r_3}, \underset{+1}{p_{B2} \cdot B2^{d}_{CB1(t+1)}}, \underset{+1}{p_{B2} \cdot B2^{d}_{CB2(t+1)}}, \underset{+1}{p_{B2} \cdot B2^{d}_{CB3(t+1)}}\Big) \\ &+ p_{NR}(NRK + NRG2) + p_{B1}\left(B1^{d}_{PB2(t+1)} - B1_{PB2t}\right) \\ &+ p_{B1}\left(B1^{d}_{CB2(t+1)} - B1_{CB2t}\right) + \bar{\varepsilon} \cdot B2_{PB1t} + \bar{\varepsilon} \cdot B2_{CB1t} \\ &- p_{Kt} \cdot \bar{\varepsilon} \cdot \left[K^{d}_{NR(t+1)} - (1-\delta) \cdot K_{NRt}\right] \\ &- \bar{\varepsilon} \cdot p_{Kt} \cdot \left[K^{d}_{G1(t+1)} - (1-\delta) \cdot K_{G1t}\right] \\ &- \bar{\varepsilon} \cdot p_{B2}\left(B2^{d}_{PB1(t+1)} - B2_{PB1t}\right) - B1_{PB2t} - B1_{CB2t} \end{aligned} \tag{16.47}$$

Market supply of B2 is given by

$$p_{B2} \cdot B2^{s}_{t+1} = p_{B2} \cdot B2^{s}_{t+1} \cdot (\underset{-}{r_2}, \underset{+}{\bar{\varepsilon}}, \underset{-}{\tilde{\varepsilon}}) \tag{16.48}$$

Setting the demand for B2 equal to the supply of B2 and differentiating yields

$$\underset{?}{\left(\frac{\partial ED_{B2}}{\partial r_1}\right)} dr_1 + \underset{?}{\left(\frac{\partial ED_{B2}}{\partial r_2}\right)} dr_2 + \underset{?}{\left(\frac{\partial ED_{B2}}{\partial r_3}\right)} dr_3 \underset{+}{\left(\frac{\partial ED_{B2}}{\partial \tilde{\varepsilon}}\right)} d\tilde{\varepsilon} = 0 \tag{16.49}$$

Now the demand for Country Two's bonds by the central bank in Country One becomes positively related to the PB2 sector's demand for Country One's bonds and negatively related to the PB1 sector's demand for Country Two's bonds. Strictly speaking, as a result, the effect of an increase in any interest rate upon the excess demand for Country Two's bonds is indeterminate. Consequently, the effect upon $\tilde{\varepsilon}$ is indeterminate.

The equilibrium condition in the bond market for Country Three remains unchanged from its earlier specification under a flexible ε.

Market demand for B3 is given by

$$p_{B3} \cdot B3^{d}_{t+1} = p_{B3} \cdot B3^{d}_{t+1} \cdot \Big(\underset{-}{r_1}, \underset{-}{r_2}, \underset{+}{r_3}, \underset{+1}{p_{B3} \cdot B3^{d}_{CB1(t+1)}}, \underset{+1}{p_{B3} \cdot B3^{d}_{CB3(t+1)}}, \underset{+1}{p_{B3} \cdot B3^{d}_{CB3(t+1)}}\Big) \tag{16.50}$$

Market supply of B3 is given by

$$p_{B3} \cdot B3^{s}_{t+1} = p_{B3} \cdot B3^{s}_{t+1} \cdot (\underset{-}{r_3}, \underset{-}{\bar{\varepsilon}}, \underset{+}{\tilde{\varepsilon}}, \ldots) \tag{16.51}$$

Setting the demand for B3 equal to the supply of B3 and differentiating yields

$$\underset{-}{\left(\frac{\partial ED_{B3}}{\partial r_1}\right)} dr_1 + \underset{-}{\left(\frac{\partial ED_{B3}}{\partial r_2}\right)} dr_2 + \underset{+}{\left(\frac{\partial ED_{B3}}{\partial r_3}\right)} dr_3 + \underset{+}{\left(\frac{\partial ED_{B3}}{\partial \varepsilon}\right)} d\varepsilon + \underset{-}{\left(\frac{\partial ED_{B3}}{\partial \tilde{\varepsilon}}\right)} d\tilde{\varepsilon} = 0 \tag{16.52}$$

Sterilized Purchase/Sale of Country Two's Bonds by CB1 to Fix ε

In the second case, the central bank in Country One decides to sterilize its endogenous transactions in Country Two's bond market so that its transactions in its own bond market become endogenously determined and become

$$\begin{aligned} p_{B1} \cdot \left(B1^{d}_{CB1(t+1)} - B1_{CB1t}\right) &\equiv -\tilde{\varepsilon} \cdot p_{B3} \cdot \left(B3^{d}_{CB1(t+1)} - B3_{CB1t}\right) + p_{NR}(NRK + NRG2) \\ &+ p_{B1}\left(B1^{d}_{PB2(t+1)} - B1_{PB2t}\right) - p_{B1}\left(B1^{d}_{CB2(t+1)} - B1_{CB2t}\right) \\ &+ \bar{\varepsilon} \cdot B2_{PB1t} + \bar{\varepsilon} \cdot B2_{CB1t} + p_{Kt} \cdot \bar{\varepsilon} \cdot \left[K^{d}_{NR(t+1)} - (1-\delta) \cdot K_{NRt}\right] \\ &+ \bar{\varepsilon} \cdot p_{Kt} \cdot \left[K^{d}_{G1(t+1)} - (1-\delta) \cdot K_{G1t}\right] + \bar{\varepsilon} \cdot p_{B2} \cdot \left(B2^{d}_{PB1(t+1)} \right. \\ &\left. - B2_{PB1t}\right) + B1_{PB2t} + B1_{CB2t} + MB1^{s}_{CB1(t+1)} - MB1_{t} \end{aligned} \tag{16.53}$$

Because the monetary base in Country One once again becomes an exogenously determined policy variable, expression (16.41) becomes

$$\left[\frac{\partial(ED_{M1})}{\partial r_1}\right]\cdot dr_1+\left[\frac{\partial(ED_{M1})}{\partial r_2}\right]\cdot dr_2+\left[\frac{\partial(ED_{M1})}{\partial r_3}\right]\cdot dr_3$$
$$= d\left(MB1^{s}_{CB1(t+1)}\right) \tag{16.54}$$

Expressions (16.42), (16.43), and (16.54) may again be used to solve for the three interest rates r_1, r_2, and r_3. The bond market in any one of the three countries may then be used to solve for $\tilde{\varepsilon}$. The value of $\tilde{\varepsilon}$ that emerges in the solution again depends upon which bond market equilibrium condition is chosen to combine with the three money market equilibrium conditions. The qualitative results in terms of which overall ex ante balance of payments is in equilibrium (besides, of course, the overall balance of payments between Country One and Country Two) are precisely the same as those discussed for a nonsterilized purchase/sale of Country Two's bonds by CB1 in order to maintain ε at $\bar{\varepsilon}$.

The three alternative bond market equilibrium conditions are now (16.57)–(16.59), shown below.

The market demand for B1 must be adjusted to account for CB1's endogenous demand for B1. As a result, the market demand for B1 becomes

$$p_{B1}\cdot B1^{d}_{t+1}=p_{B1}\cdot B1^{d}_{t+1}\cdot\left(\underset{+}{r_1},\underset{+}{r_2},\underset{-}{r_3},\underset{+1}{p_{B1}\cdot B1^{d}_{CB2(t+1)}},\underset{+1}{p_{B1}\cdot B1^{d}_{CB3(t+1)}}\right)$$
$$-\tilde{\varepsilon}\cdot p_{B3}\cdot\left(B3^{d}_{CB1(t+1)}-B3_{CB1t}\right)+p_{NR}(NRK+NRG2)$$
$$-p_{B1}\left(B1^{d}_{PB2(t+1)}-B1_{PB2t}\right)+p_{B1}\left(B1^{d}_{CB2(t+1)}-B1_{CB2t}\right)$$
$$-\bar{\varepsilon}\cdot B2_{PB1t}-\bar{\varepsilon}\cdot B2_{CB1t}+p_{Kt}\cdot\bar{\varepsilon}\cdot\left[K^{d}_{NR(t+1)}-(1-\delta)\cdot K_{NRt}\right]$$
$$+\bar{\varepsilon}\cdot p_{Kt}\cdot\left[K^{d}_{G1(t+1)}-(1-\delta)\cdot K_{G1t}\right]+\bar{\varepsilon}\cdot p_{B2}\left(B2^{d}_{PB1(t+1)}\right.$$
$$\left.-B2_{PB1t}\right)+B1_{PB2t}+B1_{CB2t}+MB1^{s}_{CB1(t+1)}-MB1_t \tag{16.55}$$

The market supply of B1 is given by (16.56):

$$p_{B1}\cdot B1^{d}_{t+1}=p_{B1}\cdot B1^{d}_{t+1}\cdot(\underset{-}{r_1},\underset{-}{\tilde{\varepsilon}},\underset{-}{\bar{\varepsilon}},\ldots) \tag{16.56}$$

Setting the demand for B1 equal to the supply of B1 and differentiating with respect to the interest rates and $\tilde{\varepsilon}$ yields

$$\underset{?}{\left(\frac{\partial ED_{B1}}{\partial r_1}\right)}dr_1+\underset{?}{\left(\frac{\partial ED_{B1}}{\partial r_2}\right)}dr_2+\underset{?}{\left(\frac{\partial ED_{B1}}{\partial r_3}\right)}dr_3+\underset{+}{\left(\frac{\partial ED_{B1}}{\partial\tilde{\varepsilon}}\right)}d\tilde{\varepsilon}=0 \tag{16.57}$$

Now the demand for Country One's bonds by the central bank in Country One becomes negatively related to the PB2 sector's demand for Country One's bonds and positively related to the PB1 sector's demand for Country Two's bonds. Strictly speaking, as a result, the effect of an increase in any interest rate upon the excess demand for Country Two's bonds is indeterminate. Consequently, the effect upon $\tilde{\varepsilon}$ is indeterminate.

The market demand for B2 is the same as that given in (16.47) and the equilibrium condition in the B2 market is the same as that given in (16.49). Again because the signs of the effects of the changes in the interest rates upon the excess demand for B2 are indeterminate, so is the effect upon $\tilde{\varepsilon}$ when the B2 market is chosen to solve for $\tilde{\varepsilon}$:

$$\underset{?}{\left(\frac{\partial ED_{B2}}{\partial r_1}\right)} dr_1 + \underset{?}{\left(\frac{\partial ED_{B2}}{\partial r_2}\right)} dr_2 + \underset{?}{\left(\frac{\partial ED_{B2}}{\partial r_3}\right)} dr_3 + \underset{+}{\left(\frac{\partial ED_{B2}}{\partial \tilde{\varepsilon}}\right)} d\tilde{\varepsilon} = 0 \tag{16.58}$$

The equilibrium condition in the bond market for Country Three remains basically unchanged from its earlier specification under a flexible ε:

$$\underset{-}{\left(\frac{\partial ED_{B3}}{\partial r_1}\right)} dr_1 + \underset{-}{\left(\frac{\partial ED_{B3}}{\partial r_2}\right)} dr_2 + \underset{+}{\left(\frac{\partial ED_{B3}}{\partial r_3}\right)} dr_3 + \underset{-}{\left(\frac{\partial ED_{B3}}{\partial \tilde{\varepsilon}}\right)} d\tilde{\varepsilon} = 0 \tag{16.59}$$

From the above analysis, the effects of central bank policies upon interest rates and exchange rates depend upon whether some interest rates are managed and whether some exchange rates are fixed. Furthermore, these effects depend upon whether a bank sterilizes its purchases of foreign bonds under flexible or fixed exchange rates. It is difficult to imagine that a central bank can foresee the effects of its policy actions upon its own economy even in the current period.

17

Technological Change and Public Policies

Technical change takes several forms in this model. First, technical change may reduce the unavoidable amount of mass wasted associated with the production of the transformed nonrenewable resource, or the production of capital goods, or the production of consumption goods. Second, technology may reduce the amount of mass necessarily contained within a unit of capital goods or consumption goods. Third, technology may reduce the rate of physical depreciation of capital goods or the amount of labor services necessary to convert a unit of waste into recycled product or treated and stored mass. Fourth, a technical improvement may reduce the mass necessary to add a unit to a country's infrastructure.

Effects of Technical Change

Technical change that reduces the unavoidable amount of waste associated with the production of transformed NR, φ. As shown in chapter 5, a reduction in φ either reduces the amount of waste that the nonrenewable resource industry must recycle during the period or the number of pollution allowances the sector must buy at the beginning of the period for each unit of the nonrenewable resource it transforms during the period. In either case, a fall in φ reduces the marginal cost of producing an extra unit of NR^T, inducing the sector to increase the number of labor hours involved in processing the raw nonrenewable resource, increase current production of NR^T, reduce the market price of the transformed resource, and increase current dividends paid to its shareholders during the current period.

The fall in the price of the transformed nonrenewable resource, ceteris paribus, increases the amount of that resource demanded by the capital and consumption goods industries because it reduces the marginal cost of producing a unit of physical capital or a unit of consumption goods. In addition, the fall in p_{NRt} reduces the cost to the three government sectors of purchasing the NR^T, which they use to add to their respective infrastructures during the period. Because it is assumed that the decisions as to how much to add to infrastructures during the current period is made before p_{NRt} is announced, the amount of NR^T purchased during the current period by the government sectors is not affected by the fall in price. However, the fall in price does diminish, ceteris paribus, the amount that the government sectors need to borrow during the current period, thereby tending to reduce the end-of-period market supplies of bonds in all three bond markets. This in turn reduces the amount of taxes each government will need to collect next period to provide a given amount of general public services next period. The menus that the government sectors present to their household sectors next period for the following period will involve both a lower marginal cost and a lower average cost of general public services if the lower price of the transformed nonrenewable resource were to persist. In general, a fall in the amount of waste produced in transforming a unit of the nonrenewable resource spreads throughout the world economy in the form of lower prices for all goods that use NR^T and lower interest rates in all three countries due to the fall in the government sectors' supplies of bonds to their respective bond markets.

Technical change that reduces the mass contained in a unit of physical capital, κ, reduces physical depreciation, δ, or reduces the wasted NR per unit of capital produced, φ_K. A technical advance that reduces the mass contained in a unit of physical capital, κ, reduces the marginal cost of producing an extra unit of capital goods. As a result, the capital goods sector increases the number of hours it uses its current employees, increases its current production of physical capital, reduces the price it announces for capital goods, and increases its end-of-period demand for physical capital to produce capital goods next period. In addition, the sector increases the amount of labor it demands for next period and raises the wage rate, $W2t + 1$, it announces this period in order to attract the additional employees for next period. Finally, a reduction in the mass contained in a unit of physical capital reduces the amount of the nonrenewable resource the capital goods industry requires to produce capital and therefore reduces its demand for the nonrenewable resource in the current period. The amount of waste generated by the capital goods industry through physical depreciation is also reduced causing the sector to demand fewer pollution allowances during the period. Ceteris paribus, this reduces the market price of pollution allowances.

A reduction in the amount of wasted NR in the production of a unit of capital goods, φ_K, produces essentially the same effects upon the decisions of the capital goods industry as does a reduction in the mass embodied in a unit of physical capital. A reduction in the rate of physical depreciation produces virtually the same effects upon the decision making of the capital goods industry as does a reduction in the mass embodied within a unit of capital. However, the effects of a reduction in physical depreciation extend to the government sectors in all three countries as well as to the NR and C industries. Because the rate of depreciation reduces the user cost of capital, all governments and all industries that use physical capital will tend to increase their end-of-period demands for that good.

Technical change that reduces the mass contained in a unit of consumption goods, γ. A technical advance that reduces the amount of the nonrenewable resource required to produce a unit of consumption goods, γ, reduces the marginal cost of producing consumption goods. This induces the consumption goods industry to increase the number of hours it uses its current employees, to increase current production of consumption goods, to reduce the price of consumption goods it announces at the beginning of the current period and increases its end-of-period demand for capital with which to produce consumption goods next period. In addition, the sector increases the amount of labor it demands for next period and raises the wage rate, $W3_{t+1}$, it announces this period in order to attract the additional employees for next period. The sector reduces its demand for the nonrenewable resource for the current period. However, because the sector's production of consumption goods increases, the amount of waste it generates rises, causing the sector's demand for pollution allowances to increase, which puts upward pressure upon the market price of pollution allowances. Because the sector's demand for physical capital increases, its end-of-period supply of bonds to the B3 market increases, putting upward pressure upon the rate of interest in that market, r_3.

Public Policies

The public policies discussed here fall into three general categories: tariffs, infrastructure enhancement, and changes in pollution allowances.

A Tariff upon Consumption Goods Levied by the G1 Sector

If the G1 sector levies a tariff upon the consumption goods purchased by its household sector, the tariff produces revenue to the G1 sector, which the sector may use to reduce the taxes it must collect next period either from the H1 sector to add a given amount to general public services or from the R1 and NR sectors this period to add a given amount to the country's infrastructure.

Because the imposition of the tariff also raises the price of consumption goods in Country One, the household sector in Country One will tend to substitute the transformed renewable resource produced in Country One, $R1^T$, for consumption goods on the margin. The reduction in the H1 sector's demand for consumption goods causes the consumption goods industry to reduce its production of consumption goods. As a result, the industry will also tend to reduce its end-of-period demand for physical capital and labor and to reduce its demand for the nonrenewable resource that it buys from Country One. The wage rates in Country One and Country Three tend to fall as does the price of the nonrenewable resource.

Infrastructure Enhancement by the G1 Sector

A decision by the G1 sector to add to Country One's infrastructure has the immediate effect of increasing the market demand for NR and raising the price of that resource. Current production of NR increases as does the number of hours the NR industry uses its current employees. However, the rising price of the nonrenewable resource increases the marginal cost to the government sectors in the other two countries of adding to their own infrastructures. It also increases the marginal cost of building capital goods and consumption goods. Next period, with the added infrastructure in place, the marginal cost to both the nonrenewable industry and the renewable resource industry will diminish. As a result, future employment will increase along with future production. The money wage will increase in Country One, and product prices will be lower for R1 and NR.

A Reduction in the Number of Pollution Allowances

An international agreement to reduce the number of pollution allowances issued worldwide affects all the business sectors that produce waste as a byproduct. As a result of the decrease in the number of pollution allowances issued, the price of pollution allowances rises. This causes the NR, K, and C sectors to reduce the number of hours they employ workers to manufacture goods from the raw and transformed nonrenewable resource. In addition, these sectors raise the prices of their products and increase the number of hours they use current labor to recycle or treat and store waste. The extraction/mining of the nonrenewable resource falls. To the extent that firms use more labor to produce their products than they do to recycle or treat and store waste, they also reduce the wage rates they announce for next period. Households in each country find that the price of consumption goods produced by the C industry has risen relative to the renewable resource in their country; on the margin, they substitute goods made from their country's renewable resource for consumption goods made from the nonrenewable resource.

18

Summary and Conclusions

The complete unified model of the world economy operating within the global ecosystem consists of the production, employment, pricing, and wage-setting functions summarized in chapter 10 plus the financial market equilibrium conditions specified in chapter 15, the restrictions on these conditions presented in chapter 16, and the end-of-period equations for the real resources, the manufactured goods, the human populations, and the stocks of financial assets. Once all of these end-of-period stocks are determined, new rounds of decision making occur for next period similar to the ones presented in this study for the current period. Together, these equations of motion propel the world economy and the global ecology through time. In principle, these functions could provide the basis for numerical simulations that would reveal the sensitivity of the system to alternative assumptions regarding mortality rates, the amount of mass wasted per unit of each capital or consumption good produced , the ability of the basic resource to assimilate waste, the growth rates of the renewable resources, the ability of labor and capital services to transform mass into capital or consumption goods, et cetera.

The objective of this study has been threefold. One purpose has been to specify a model that demonstrates how the world economy and the global ecology interact in a close but discernable way. A second purpose has been to highlight specifically some of the contributions that governments make to macroeconomic production and employment. A third purpose has been to show the importance of explicitly specifying the economic decisions involving the various bond markets.

Typically, macroeconomic models reflect the assumption is that labor and capital are the only important inputs in production. However, the conservation of mass stipulates that the mass embodied in a unit of output cannot exceed—and indeed typically falls short of—the mass applied to the production process. Labor and capital may be substitutes in terms of providing the transformation services that convert raw materials into finished product, but the level of these transformation services and the raw materials applied in the production process must be applied in fixed proportions if unnecessary waste is to be avoided. Capital may be a substitute for labor in transforming raw materials, but together the raw materials and the labor and capital that transform raw materials into other goods are complements in production.

Macroeconomic models tend to reflect the tacit assumption that the income that government spending generates for those who own the factors of production that are used in producing the goods the government is buying represents the only benefit of government spending. In the present study, on the other hand, markets do not incorporate all the costs or all the benefits derived from economic activity. Maintaining a minimum stock of a renewable resource in one country provides a benefit to all inhabitants not only by supporting the basic fungible resource but also by reducing the mortality rates and by improving the general public services across all countries. International agreements are necessary to force manufacturers everywhere to internalize the costs they impose upon the ecology/economy when they release pollution into the environment.

Simpler single-country models of open economies tend to be "perfect"; they assume perfect competition, perfect foresight (possibly with white noise), and perfect substitutability among goods and financial assets. These models produce neat unambiguous effects with respect to the effects of central bank policies upon interest rates and exchange rates. This study indicates that these straightforward results may not carry over to more complex models in which competition is imperfect, in which price setters and wage setters have genuine uncertainty as to the demands for their products or as to the supplies of labor, and in which both the world's various goods and its various financial assets are imperfect substitutes for one another. In the present model, neither open market operations nor sterilized or nonsterilized purchases of foreign assets by a central bank produce iron-clad qualitative responses in the world's financial markets. Much depends on what other central banks are doing in terms of whether interest rates are managed and whether exchange rates are held constant through central bank policies. The present model suggests that no central bank can possibly foresee the qualitative effects upon the world economy and the global ecology resulting from its actions.

Popular assertions that central banks can control spending and therefore avoid inflation and recessions by manipulating interest rates do not hold up in the present model. By manipulating interest rates, a central bank not only administers the relative price between labor and capital in its own country, but it also induces either increased or decreased use of the various raw materials used in production; some of the unintended effects may include adverse feedback effects upon the central bank's economy.

These results beg the question "What is the primary function of a central bank?" Stripped to its essentials, the primary purpose of a central bank is to provide for an elastic monetary base that can fluctuate "with the needs of trade." Although discounting has been discredited as a policy tool for controlling economic activity, it nevertheless provides a market-based way to inject new funds or to withdraw unwanted funds from the marketplace. A central bank that relies upon discounting to provide a fluid stock of base money will not produce the unintended effects upon the world economy or the global ecosystem necessarily associated with an active interventionist stance if it sets the discount rate at the bank's revenue or profit maximizing level without regard to other variables (Whitmore 1997).

Bibliography

Ayres, R. U., and A. V. Kneese "Production, Consumption and Externalities," *American Economic Review* 59 (1969): 282–297.

Folke, Carl, "Ecological Principles and Environmental Economic Analysis," 895–911, in *Handbook of Environmental and Resource Economics,* Jeroen C. J. M. van den Bergh (ed.). Northampton, MA: Edgar Elgar Publishing, 1999.

Heyes, A., "A Proposal for the Greening of the Textbook Macro: IS-LM-EE," *Ecological Economics* 32 (2000): 1–7.

Ierland, E. C. van, "Environment in Macroeconomic Modeling," chapter 41 in *Handbook of Environmental and Resource Economics,* Jeroen C. J. M. van den Bergh (ed.). Northampton, MA: Edgar Elgar Publishing, 1999.

Kneese, A. V., R. U. Ayres, and R. d'Arge, *Economics and the Environment: A Materials Balance Approach*. Washington, DC: Resources for the Future, 1970.

Lawn, P. A., "On Heyes' IS-LM-EE Proposal to Establish an Environmental Macroeconomics," *Environmental and Developmental Economics* 8 (2003): 31–56.

Miller, N. C., "The Structure of Open Economy Macro-Models," *Journal of International Money and Finance* 5, no. 1 (1986): 75–89.

Turner, R. Kerry, "Environmental and Ecological Economics Perspectives," 1001–1033 in *Handbook of Environmental and Resource Economics,* Jeroen C. J. M. van den Bergh (ed.). Northampton, MA: Edgar Elgar Publishing, 1999.

van den Bergh, Jeroen C. J. M., Chapter 6 in *Ecological Economics and Sustainable Development.* Northampton, MA: Edgar Elgar Publishing, 1996.

Whitmore, H. W., *Global Environmental Macroeconomics.* Armonk, NY: M. E. Sharpe, 1999.

———, et al., *Integration of an Economy under Imperfect Competition with a Twelve-Cell Ecological Model.* Washington, DC: United States Environmental Protection Agency, EPA/600/R-06/046, 2006.

———, *World Economy Macroeconomics.* Armonk, NY: M. E. Sharpe, 1997.

Index